*Handbook of*

# DATA CENTER
# MANAGEMENT

*Second Edition*

# Handbook of

# DATA CENTER

# MANAGEMENT

## *Second Edition*

Layne C. Bradley, Editor

CRC Press
Taylor & Francis Group
Boca Raton  London  New York

CRC Press is an imprint of the
Taylor & Francis Group, an **informa** business

First published 1994 by Auerbach Publications
Taylor & Francis Group
6000 Broken Sound Parkway NW, Suite 300
Boca Raton, FL 33487-2742

Reissued 2018 by CRC Press

© 1994 by Taylor & Francis
CRC Press is an imprint of Taylor & Francis Group, an Informa business

No claim to original U.S. Government works

A Library of Congress record exists under LC control number: 95120527

Publisher's Note
The publisher has gone to great lengths to ensure the quality of this reprint but points out that some imperfections in the original copies may be apparent.

Disclaimer
The publisher has made every effort to trace copyright holders and welcomes correspondence from those they have been unable to contact.

ISBN 13: 978-1-138-50574-2 (hbk)
ISBN 13: 978-1-138-55945-5 (pbk)
ISBN 13: 978-0-203-71272-6 (ebk)

Visit the Taylor & Francis Web site at http://www.taylorandfrancis.com and the CRC Press Web site at http://www.crcpress.com

# Contributors

**Layne C. Bradley**
Vice-President of Information Technology, GAINSCO, Fort Worth TX and Vice-President of Agents Processing Systems, Inc.

**Norman H. Carter**
President and CEO, Project Management Integration for Development Systems International, Inc., Studio City CA.

**Frank Collins**
Professor and Coopers & Lybrand Scholar, University of Miami's School of Business, Coral Gables FL.

**John L. Connor**
Director of Automation Products Marketing, Boole & Babbage, Inc., Dallas TX.

**Paul Cullen**
EDP Audit Specialist, Norwest Audit Services, Inc., Minneapolis MN.

**Ken Doughty**
Information Systems Auditor, Coles-Myer (Australia's largest retailer).

**Ronald G. Earles**
Senior EDP Audit Specialist, Enron Corp.

**Gordon C. Everest**
Associate Professor of MIS and Data Base Management Systems, Carlson School of Management, University of Minnesota.

**Carl Fink**
Senior Manager, Boston Consulting Office of Deloitte & Touche.

**Thomas Fleishman**
Vice-President and Director of Information Services, Kaiser Permanente Medical Care Program, Pasadena CA.

**Edward H. Freeman**
Attorney, West Hartford CT.

**Louis Fried**
Vice-President, IT Consulting, SRI International, Menlo Park CA.

**David Friend**
Chairperson, Pilot Software, Inc., Cambridge MA.

**Frederick Gallegos**
Manager of the Management Science Group, US General Accounting Office.

**John E. Gessford**
President, Modern Information Services, San Marino CA.

**Thomas R. Halsell**
Senior Auditor, Basic Four, Orange CA.

**Gilbert Held**
Director, 4-Degree Consulting, Macon GA.

**Ira Hertzhoff**
President, Datagram, a Division of Tholian (Holdings), Inc., Columbus OH.

**David D. Ittner**
Battery Service Manager, Liebert Customer Service and Support, Columbus OH.

**Gita Jayachandra**
Network Management Consultant, San Jose CA.

**Yemmanur Jayachandra**
Senior Consultant, Bank of America, San Francisco CA.

**Jerome Kanter**
Director, Center for Information Management Studies, Babson College, Babson Park MA.

**Marc C. Kelly**
Vice-President, Small Business and Select Markets Division, Massachusetts, Blue Cross and Blue Shield, Boston MA.

**Kenneth Kousky**
President, Wave Technologies Training, Inc., St. Louis MO.

**John Levis**
Former Manager, Deloitte & Touche, Toronto, Canada.

**Gary Mann**
Assistant Professor of Accounting, University of Texas, El Paso TX.

**Thornton A. May**
Director, Tenex Consulting, Burlington MA.

**Sally Meglathery**
Director of EDP Audit, New York Stock Exchange.

**Bob Moeller**
Senior Corporate EDP Audit Manager for Sears, Roebuck & Co, Chicago IL.

**Nathan J. Muller**
Independent Consultant, Oxford CT.

**John P. Murray**
Data Center Manager and Senior Management Consultant, Viking Insurance Co., Madison WI.

**Jeff Murrell**

Manager of Operations and Customer Support, Information Systems and Services Division, Texas Instruments, Inc., Plano TX.

**Randall A. Nagy**

Principal Software Development Engineer, Informix Software, Inc., Menlo Park CA.

**Stuart Nelson**

Principal, Minnesota Office of CSC Consulting, Computer Sciences Corp., Minnesota MN.

**Miles H. Overholt**

Certified Management Consultant and Principal, The Communication Link Co., Palmyra NJ.

**Raymond J. Posch**

Technical Staff of Covia, the Operator of the Apollo Automated Reservation System.

**Kenneth P. Prager**

Certified Management Consultant and Principal, The Communication Link Co., Palmyra NJ.

**Fay Donohue-Rolfe**

Vice-President, Plan Initiatives, Massachusetts Blue Cross and Blue Shield, Boston MA

**Richard Ross**

Director of the Decision Strategies Group, Greenwich CT.

**Hugh W. Ryan**

Partner, TSI-Worldwide Group, Anderson Consulting, Chicago IL.

**Hal Sanders**

CEO, Nusan Corp., Watsonville CA.

**Donald Saelens**

CIO, Minnesota Department of Revenue, St. Paul MN.

**Peter von Schilling**

Manager, Deloitte & Touche, Toronto, Canada.

**Daniel F. Schulte**

Systems Specialist in Information Services, Southwestern Bell Telephone Co, St. Louis MO.

**Roshan L. Sharma**

Principal, Telecom Network Science, Dallas TX.

**Kenneth A. Smith**

Director of Eastern Region Consulting Operations, Sungard Planning Solutions, Wayne PA.

## Contributors

**Stewart L. Stokes, Jr.**

Senior Vice-President, QED Information Sciences, Inc., Wellesley MA.

**Christine B. Tayntor**

Manager of Finance and Corporate Staff Applications, Allied Signal, Inc., Morristown NJ.

**Jon William Toigo**

Independent Writer and Consultant, Dunedin FL.

**Rob Walton**

President, Rob Walton Associates, Redmond WA.

**Madeline Weiss**

President, Weiss Associates, Inc., Bethesda MD.

**James C. Wetherbe**

Author, Expert on Use of IS to Improve Organizational Performance and Competitiveness.

**Mead Bond Wetherbe, Jr.**

Independent Consultant; Director, Executive Education Center, Loyola University, New Orleans LA.

**Roger B. White, Jr.**

Senior Analyst, Network Technical Services, Provo UT.

**Bryan Wilkinson**

Director of Information Systems Audit at Teledyne, Inc., Los Angeles CA.

**William A. Yarberry, Jr.**

Director of Operations Research, Enron Corp.

**George W. Zobrist**

Faculty of Computer Science, University of Missouri-Rolla.

# Contents

*Contents*

# Introduction

When the planning for this second edition of the *Handbook of Data Center Management* was begun, I reviewed the original edition and the three subsequent yearbooks that have been published. The theme that we developed the handbook around was change—or, more accurately, the management of change.

Well, this is the second edition of the handbook, and our purpose remains unchanged. As I write this, however, it seems the pace of change has increased to an almost uncontrollable level. As with many industries in the US, the information systems industry is undergoing a major transition. Most of the traditional concepts and management approaches are being scrutinized as never before and, in many cases, are being discarded entirely in favor of something new. The economic, organizational, and technology changes are occurring so rapidly, and in such volume, that it is easy to understand why many IS professionals view the current situation as one of major confusion.

So, too, the data center manager is seeing rapid change and confusion with regard to the data center and its operations. In general, "the walls of the data center are coming down." The continued proliferation of microcomputer networks and the introduction of client/server architecture has opened up the data center more than at any time in the past. Many companies seem to be making a mad dash to do away with the mainframe, and the data center, at all costs as a way to reduce expenses. To their dismay, however, companies have found after considerable time, effort, and financial expense, that microcomputer networks and client/server-type architectures are not always the solutions in themselves. Many are finding that the mainframe still has a vital role to play. As a result, the architecture that seems to be emerging combines the mainframe and various derivatives of microcomputer networks in such a way as to meet the company's overall computing needs. Thus, client/server architecture embraces the mainframe rather than negates it.

Even though the data center structure may be changing, its role, and that of the data center manager, may be growing rather than diminishing. The data center manager's very challenging role today is becoming one of managing an extremely complex environment consisting of mainframe, minicomputer, and LAN technologies. A major challenge, indeed, but one that offers excitement, new career opportunities, and a chance to continue to be a major change agent in today's corporations.

In this second edition of the handbook, we continue to offer a look at many of the changes affecting the data center manager and provide suggestions from fellow IS practitioners regarding ways to manage these changes.

## CLIENT/SERVER

This topic dominates the industry media today. It seems that every vendor of mainframe software is rapidly converting its current mainframe products, or developing new ones, to address this new concept. Of course, with all of the current hype regarding client/server architecture, it is often difficult to even understand what it is. Certainly, the concept of gaining more computing power at less cost appeals to corporate management today. As a result, often the IS organization is directed to move to client/server as quickly as possible, with the idea being to eliminate the mainframe environment and its associated costs. Although there certainly have been some successes implementing this new approach, they have not been without difficulty and there have been some not so successful projects. In this edition of the handbook, we take a look at client/server computing and provide information regarding what it is, when to use it, how to implement it, and its effect on the data center manager and the data center.

## STRATEGIC PLANNING

The notion of a strategic plan for the data center, given the state of confusion and change that exists in the industry today may seem out of place. In actuality, there has never been a more important time to develop a strategy for operating the data center. A strategic plan is critical to chaos to some kind of order. The data center cannot operate in isolation, either from the rest of the IS organization or the company. The data center today is no longer just a data factory churning out endless reports or providing online service to users. It is a mixture of old and the new technologies, a focus for the change that is taking place, a communications center, and a line of demarcation between the IS organization and the user community. Thus, having a plan for operating and going forward is not a luxury, it is an absolute necessity.

## HUMAN RESOURCES MANAGEMENT

The term *human resources* has been around for a long time. Today, its significance is greater than it has ever been. Human resources in the data center are becoming increasingly scarce. Given the current trend toward downsizing organizations, including the data center, the data center manager may find him- or herself in a critical situation with regard to available personnel to perform the mission of the data center. In fact, not only must fewer data center personnel perform all the functions they have in the past, they must take up the slack created by the loss of personnel as well as take on new challenges. Knowing how to get the maximum productivity out of personnel becomes a very demanding challenge for the data center manager.

## DATA CENTER MANAGEMENT

At one time, managing the data center was a relatively straightforward operation. It was a complex and demanding role. Nevertheless, there were some constants in the environment and some degree of predictability regarding what was expected of the data center and its manager. Today, however the data center manager deals with issues that weren't even relevant five years ago. Therefore, the rules have changed dramatically and the manager must be aware of what is required to ensure that the data center functions efficiently, cost-effectively, and, in some cases, profitably. There are new tools, procedures, and management techniques, and it is mandatory for the data center manager to be aware of these.

## NETWORKS

More than any other single factor, the rapid deployment and implementation of local area networks has affected the operation and role of the data center. These networks initially allowed the users to break away from the data center and develop their own computing environments. However, it has become apparent that often these networks by themselves are incapable of meeting all of the company's computing needs. Thus, these users are migrating back to the data center and being connected to the mainframe. This approach changes the nature of mainframe processing, the future role of the data center, and the mission of the data center manager. Thus, it is important that the data center manager thoroughly understand the nature of these types of networks and how they must be managed in the mainframe environment.

## HOW TO USE THIS HANDBOOK

As was stated in the first edition of the handbook, it was envisioned as a tool. A close-at-hand desk reference. That is still its purpose. It has been developed for and written by practitioners of data center management. The articles in it have been carefully selected to be current, relevant, hands-on, and representative of the issues that are facing today's data center manager. It is intended to give practical advice as well as stimulate your thinking regarding how to solve problems that you encounter on a day-to-day basis. Each section has an introductory discussion of the issues covered in that section and a short overview of each chapter so that you can quickly scan through it and find that information that you currently need.

I highly recommend that you keep this handbook close to you. Often, a few minutes of quick reading can point you in a direction you need to go with regard to resolving a problem or developing a new approach. There is information here that can expand your knowledge in areas you are unfamiliar with, update knowledge of subjects your are well acquainted with or provide good sources you can refer to when developing business plans or presentations that you must provide to upper management. It is, in effect, a working consultant for you. I encourage you to use it that way.

## ACKNOWLEDGMENTS

This handbook would not exist without the many fine data center managers who, though busy as they are, have taken time to share their ideas and experiences with the rest of us. I admire them greatly for their willingness to take on a very demanding job in today's information system industry, that of managing a data center, and for sharing their experience. I also encourage any of you who would like to consider writing about your experiences to contact Auerbach. There is always a need for good, current information.

I also want to thank Auerbach Publications for its continuing interest in this publication. I have been associated with Auerbach for several years now, and I have thoroughly enjoyed that association. There have been many fine editors who have worked with and assisted me over the years. In particular, I would like to thank Deb Rhoades. She has been the one constant through the original handbook, the three yearbooks, and now, this second edition of the handbook. She is a true professional in the field of publishing, and her assistance has been invaluable.

LAYNE C. BRADLEY
Arlington, Texas
March 1994

# Section I
# Strategic Planning

P lanning has always been a major responsibility of the data center manager. Knowing how to plan effectively, and finding the time to make it happen, has also always been the challenge. As a result, developing long-range or strategic plans has, unfortunately, been low on the data center manager's list of priorities.

Today, the role of planning has perhaps become more important to the data center manager than many of the daily operational aspects of running the data center. In fact, from a career perspective, planning may be the most important aspect of the data center manager's job.

The United States is moving rapidly toward an information-based economy. The impact of integrating technology into our society will create dramatic changes in the way we live and work. Thus, planning how to integrate technology into the business organization is critical.

However, for the data center manager, planning today involves much more than merely determining future hardware or software upgrades or developing the production schedules to meet user needs. Rather, it involves understanding the company's business, the company's strategic business goals, the elements of the business plan, and how systems, and the data center in particular, can help drive the company's goals and plans.

This section contains several articles that are designed to help the data center manager better understand the overall planning process, the changes taking place in the data center that must be taken into account, and tools and methods that can be used to develop effective strategic plans.

Chapter I-1, "Long-Range Information Systems Planning," and Chapter I-2, "Developing a Strategic Information Plan," provide an excellent framework for understanding what a strategic plan consists of and how to go about developing it.

Although IS organizations are employing fewer personnel as a result of the current corporate downsizing trend, the demand for services and systems by users continues to grow. One way to address this problem is through the use of outside systems integrators, who can offer total systems implementation services. Chapter I-3, "A Data Center Manager's Guide to Systems Integrators," provides guidance for using systems integrators and describes their role in the data center manager's strategic plans.

With the advent of end-user computing, it might be said that "the walls of the data center are coming down." The rapid deployment of LAN-based personal computer systems and the current interest in client-server architecture means greater pressure on the data center manager to provide more local processing power on the user's desks. Chapter I-4, "Defining End-User Computing's New Role in IS," provides a blueprint the data center manager can follow to successfully plan for effectively integrating end-user computing in the overall strategic plan.

# I-1
# Long-Range Information Systems Planning

*ROBERT R. MOELLER*

Virtually every organization has a long-range plan that describes how the organization will achieve its goals. Although these long-range plans often describe new product strategies, areas for market expansion, and other goals, they often do not describe the decision support structure that is needed to implement them. A key component of an organization's support structure is its IS function, which includes processing data, managing communications networks, and developing software systems. In some organizations, the IS function may require such personnel as data base administrators, an end-user computing support staff, and other specialists.

The IS function is an important component of most organizations. Although an organization may be involved in a variety of businesses, the IS function provides key support. To contribute to the overall success of the organization, the IS function also needs its own long-range plan, which should be consistent with the overall management plan and support the ongoing requirements and activities of IS operations.

In the past, long-range IS plans were relatively easy to construct. IS management reviewed its current activities, considered any new systems needs that resulted from senior management's long-range plan, and forecast future personnel and hardware needs. Forecasting hardware needs was often particularly easy because data center managers could ask their mainframe hardware vendors about the next logical upgrade to their computer equipment and therefore could plan to install that equipment at an appropriate time. There were also only minimal changes in such areas as data base technology, operating systems, and communications.

This process, however, is no longer that easy. IS management currently faces many alternatives with respect to its future direction and growth. The use of expert systems, CASE tools, and end-user computing (among other developments) has dramatically changed the way new systems are developed. In addition, information systems play an increasingly important role in supporting other organizational activities. The growth cf electronic data interchange (EDI)-based systems is one example of such systems support.

There has been a significant rise in the application of new technologies in recent years. Microcomputers have become powerful reduced instruction set computing (RISC)-based workstations. These machines have replaced many minicomputers. Programming, once done in third-generation languages (e.g., COBOL), is now done in fourth-generation, graphics interface-oriented, or object-oriented languages. Similarly, there have been significant developments in communications—for example, wireless systems for connecting terminals. Older technologies have not gone away, and many are still practical; however, the IS professional must decide on the most effective of them by weighing older, well-known approaches against newer, developing technologies.

Because so many options are available, a long-range IS plan is increasingly important to the IS function in today's typical organization. If such a plan does not already exist, it is critical that IS management draft a plan that is consistent with overall organization plans and that supports ongoing IS activities. Once developed and approved, the plan can serve as a tool to aid both the IS department and the entire organization in future growth strategies and directions.

This chapter can help data center managers and other IS professionals develop and draft an effective long-range plan. The chapter addresses the following tasks and considerations:

- Developing the plan at the appropriate level: strategic, functional, or operational.
- Understanding the various external and internal factors that may influence the planning process.
- Organizing a project to develop the plan, including establishing the planning team and defining plan goals.
- Developing the plan by gathering information about the organization, evaluating alternative technologies, and analyzing costs and benefits.
- Completing the plan and taking appropriate steps to secure management approval for it.
- Monitoring and updating the plan.

The completed long-range IS plan should help the overall organization better understand how the IS function can support future activities and growth. Every IS department, regardless of size, should develop such a plan.

## LEVELS OF IS PLANNING

Any IS plan must support a hierarchy of information systems needs. These include management's strategic plans and the decisions necessary to achieve overall goals, functional IS requirements to support the current growth of organizational units, and operational information needs. Long-range IS plans must support these strategic, functional, and operational levels of planning. Separate plans can be developed for each level of planning, or a single plan can incorporate all three levels. Managers should understand the purposes and functions of each planning level.

The plan must also support the entire organization. Because some units may need more advanced IS functions than others, it may be effective to divide the plan by business unit. For other organizations, a geographic division may be appropriate. Whether a single-plan or a divided-plan strategy is adopted, the overall long-range IS plan should include the strategic, functional, and operational levels.

## Strategic Plans

Managers use strategic plans to define the overall mission of an organization and to chart that organization's desired direction in future years. Some (usually large) organizations draft formal strategic plans outlining long-range goals and the strategies and general steps necessary to achieve them. Other (often smaller) organizations state their strategic plans in a relatively simple mission or goal statement that succinctly explains the organization's reason for existence. In a few organizations, strategic plans are not formally written but are a series of long-range goals that the organization's chief executive communicates to the organization's staff.

For example, an organization may state in its strategic plan that its long-range goal is to be the leading manufacturer of widgets with at least an $x\%$ market share within five years. The strategic plan should then outline steps to achieve that goal. This may include the organization's investing in new equipment to expand the capacity of plants, building new widget plants, or expanding through acquisition. The plan may also include marketing steps necessary to achieve that level of market share.

A long-range IS strategic plan is not too different from the organizational strategic plan. This plan should set some overall information systems objectives and should outline the steps necessary to achieve them. A long-range IS strategic plan might focus on how information systems could best support the overall long-range plans of the organization. It might also outline steps to advance IS technology irrespective of any other organizational plans.

To use the previous example, if the organization's overall strategic plan is to establish a major market share in the manufacture of widgets, the IS department's long-range strategic plan should outline the steps necessary to help achieve that overall objective. For example, if the organization plans to increase business by acquiring new equipment and increasing productivity, the IS plan's objective might be to support the organization in that increased level of manufacturing activity. The work steps in the IS plan might explain how manufacturing systems would be upgraded and improved to support this level of activity. It might also outline new systems or computer hardware requirements.

Alternatively, the IS department's long-range strategic plan might address only issues within the IS function. For example, the plan might include an objective to move from centralized to distributed computing. The plan steps would outline the necessary systems modifications, organizational changes, and hardware needs necessary to achieve the plan objectives.

The plan should also state, by describing a strategy's advantages and disadvantages, the reasons for selecting it. This discussion should give the readers of the planning report (usually senior management) enough information to allow them to agree to the plan's recommendations.

The long-range, strategic IS plan is the type most often found in business. These plans are frequently ineffective; broadly defined objectives and action steps come easy to IS managers, but the detailed procedures necessary to accomplish the plan are often left out. This type of plan is written with much flourish, presented to senior management, and then filed and all but forgotten. A proper, well-reasoned long-range IS plan should not just be filed away but should be an active element supporting management's overall plan. It must be achievable and must point the IS department in a proper direction.

Long-range, strategic IS plans are difficult to construct because they require considerable data and information gathering from sources within the organization. They also depend greatly on outside factors and influences (e.g., technological constraints, existing IS limitations, or overall management policy constraints).

A long-range, strategic IS plan probably cannot have a time horizon much broader than approximately five years because technology moves too fast to plan information systems much beyond this period. Nevertheless, a long-range IS plan that describes where information systems will be in four or five years and contains action steps to achieve that objective can be a valuable planning document for both the IS department and the entire organization.

The strategic plan states in broad terms the directions for the IS department. More detailed plans are needed to translate these broad goals into actual steps that will allow the IS department to implement or achieve the planned results. These are accomplished through more detailed functional plans or operational plans.

## Functional Plans

Functional plans affect the information systems support for major functional areas in the organization (e.g., manufacturing and product marketing). A long-range functional IS plan differs from a strategic IS plan in that it outlines the steps to improve IS support within a limited area. In addition, the functional plan often describes these steps within an existing area of the organization. For example, a strategic plan might describe how information systems might be developed to support a new manufacturing product line, but a functional plan would describe steps to improve IS operations within an existing plant.

A long-range, functional IS plan can be a subset of an overall strategic plan or can be totally separate. As a subset, the plan usually takes the form of work or action steps. A long-range strategic plan may, for example, call for the introduction of just-in-time ( JIT) manufacturing procurement operations. A subordinate functional plan might outline steps to add EDI interfaces to various applications and to convince vendors to modify their trading systems and participate in the EDI program.

## Operational Plans

Operational plans are directed at much shorter-range objectives than either functional or strategic IS plans. For example, an operational plan might cover the steps necessary to convert from an existing data base product to a new relational data base software product. Another example would be a plan to implement a logical security system that covers all applications. If an organization has a rudimentary system in place, the operational plan has to include establishing ownership of applications and standards for user IDs and passwords. The logical security software can then be implemented across all of the applications.

Long-range operational plans are often subsets of functional or strategic plans. Typically, these plans are also much more detailed than the other two plan types. To implement a strategic or functional IS plan, it is usually necessary to develop and follow a series of detailed, operational plans. The time period for operational plans is often no more than one or two years.

The operational plan has a much shorter life span than the strategic or functional plans, but a series of operational plans are usually constructed and implemented during the periods covered by the strategic and functional plans. Because the operational plan's detailed action steps follow the broad guidelines of the strategic plan, implementation details may require modification to carry out the broad strategic objectives. The strategic plan may call for a remote sales force to convert to hand-held radio frequency terminals. With this technology changing so quickly, operational details for achieving that plan may change. If the time frame for the operational plan is relatively short, IS management can modify implementation details when that is appropriate.

An IS manager responsible for developing a long-range plan should thoroughly understand how these three levels of IS planning differ and how they relate to one another. A long-range strategic IS plan is often of little value unless it is supported by functional and operational plans that cover shorter time periods and outline detailed work steps.

## FACTORS INFLUENCING LONG-RANGE IS PLANNING

The IS function in an organization should not operate in a vacuum. When the IS department develops a long-range plan, it must consider other factors that can influence IS in general as well as the details of the proposed IS plan.

## Management Policies and Strategies

Perhaps the most important factors influencing any long-range IS plan are the general strategies and policies of senior management. IS managers must be aware of how senior management wants to organize its overall activities, what resources senior management is willing to allocate to the IS function, and how senior management expects IS to assist the organization's future growth.

In their pursuit of maximizing technological goals, some IS professionals ignore these management policies when they conflict with technological goals. This can result in an inappropriate or unused long-range plan. (It can also limit a manager's career.)

During the early 1970s, many IS departments developed a technology-driven, mainframe-based strategy that centralized all computing. At the same time, the management of many organizations decentralized decision making. IS departments that attempted to centralize their operations when organizational decision making was being decentralized found themselves with problems. An example is when an IS department installs centralized computer applications that can be effective only if the department receives extensive input from the users. Strong controls are inherent with this type of centralized application, but may be irrelevant if users rely on their own computer systems to create reports, which they rely on instead of the output from the centralized application.

This situation was somewhat alleviated because some operational units worked to bypass centralized computing by taking advantage of end-user computing. Nevertheless, IS management can be faulted for ignoring or missing an overall management strategy.

It is quite easy for IS management to miss an overall management policy or strategy when developing IS plans—often because senior management does not see the strategic implications of technically oriented IS plans and approves them even though they are contrary to other, overall strategies. IS managers must be aware of this and explain their plans to senior management accordingly.

## External and Competitive Factors

IS managers are often faced with a variety of external factors (e.g., technological or competitive trends) that influence long-range planning. Although senior management may be generally aware of these factors, IS professionals must deal directly with such factors and their impact on planning decisions.

One influencing factor is the implementation of a highly successful strategic system by an organization's major competitor. For example, two competitors in a printing business may each sell large lots of their products to customers with multiple locations. One printing company may suddenly announce the installation of a new information system that allows customer access: customers can control their inventory levels and allocate products to their locations. This would be viewed as a major strategic information system for one competitor, and the other company would be forced to consider the impact of this development when developing its long-range IS plan.

EDI is another example of an external factor that can change the way organizations build their systems and how they conduct business. Although EDI-type systems have been in use for years in some industries (e.g., the airlines), their use has spread in recent years with the establishment of recognized data format interchange standards. An organization may have been conducting business for years using established, paper-based business transactions. A large customer, however, may suddenly inform the organization that if it wants to continue the trading relationship, the organization must convert its sales order, invoicing, and cash receipts systems to EDI. This will certainly require some modifications to information systems. Changes will also be required for various administrative and control procedures outside of the IS function.

Although IS managers must be aware of external developments and consider their potential impact, this is not always easy. They often find it difficult to obtain accurate information regarding such developments. In some situations, the general terms of a competitive development may be known but detailed information may be difficult for outsiders to obtain. Although some organizations broadly describe their new competitive tools in trade publications, a closer investigation may reveal that much of this published material is not true.

As much as possible, IS managers must closely monitor outside factors. Marketing, manufacturing, and other support personnel can often provide valuable information. Trade publications can often be another valuable source of information.

## Technological Factors

Changes in systems technology can greatly influence any long-range IS plan. These changes include both new products and practices designed to increase productivity as well as existing products that are currently installed but at the end of their life cycle. Because technology extends beyond computer hardware, IS managers must also consider the impact of new software tools and new approaches to operations and systems development.

Innovation is not always a result of new technologies. The actual technology may have been around for a long time. But new hardware or software will often make that technology practical. For example, expert system-based approaches have been tried since the earliest days of computing, when computer scientists wrote programs that would allow those early machines to play such games as chess. However, expert systems have only recently become a practical approach for IS management to consider, thanks to a combination of powerful software tools, better machines, and successful applications.

Digital image processing is another example. Rudimentary hardware has

9

been available for a long time. New hardware, however, makes this a cost-effective way to process, store, and distribute paper documents. An IS professional may learn of other organizations that have applied image processing successfully, and it then becomes an option to consider.

Through trade periodicals, other publications and vendor briefings, IS professionals should be able to keep up with ongoing technological changes. This information allows IS managers to plan future hardware and software with some assurance regarding the capabilities of these new technologies. Consequently, this information is usually a significant factor in any long-range IS plan.

Technological trends can influence IS plans in another way. In some situations, the data center or IS department may have no specific reason to change or upgrade a particular type of equipment or software tool, but a vendor may decide to stop supporting a product and therefore may influence an IS manager's plan for conversion from that older product.

### Existing Systems Constraints

The existing hardware and software environment can greatly influence and even constrain a long-range IS plan. Almost always, the IS department must maintain its existing information systems base even while moving in a new direction outlined in a long-range plan. New systems or hardware must be built with adequate interfaces or bridges to connect them to existing devices. This is often a difficult process that reduces the expected savings from the new system.

In addition, creative long-range planners can somewhat avoid the constraint of existing systems by building their own transition bridges from existing information systems to the proposed ones. This process, however, may extend the time required to implement an overall long-range plan. In any event, the status of current systems will significantly influence the long-range IS plan. Most organizations do not have the resources to build a new system in parallel and then turn off the old one.

## ORGANIZING THE IS PLANNING PROJECT

A long-range IS plan is a major effort requiring input from or participation of many key individuals in the organization. However, once the long-range plan has been developed and approved, it should serve as a guideline to direct IS activities for several years. Because a substantial amount of time and resources may be required to construct the plan, senior management must understand the planning process and the expected objectives of the completed plan.

### Establishing the Planning Team

A thorough and comprehensive long-range IS plan cannot, for the most part, be written by one individual. Instead, an effective plan requires input from various sources and disciplines and is best constructed by an IS planning team. In addition, such plans are often best developed iteratively.

An IS planning team is usually established under the guidance of the IS director or the chief information officer (CIO). When an organization supports multiple IS functions—including processing at different locations (e.g., at independent divisions of an organization), separate groups processing on different platforms, and extensive departmental computing within one facility—a higher-level management group is often more appropriate to authorize the establishment of an IS planning team. A project leader should be assigned to head the planning team. In some situations (e.g., if potential contention over the planning process is perceived), the organization should consider contracting with an outside consultant to head the planning team.

The planning team may also want to consider using an outside consultant or consulting firm, when a particular consulting firm has had significant experience in some newer technological area (e.g., digital image processing). Or a consultant may add major project planning experience to the long-range planning project team.

There are drawbacks to the use of outside consultants—for example, the consulting firm brings its expert to the initial sales presentation meetings and then assigns to the project its less experienced staff members. Credentials and project experience should be closely checked before contracting with any consultant. In addition, outside consultants can be expensive.

To be effective, the IS strategic planning team should consist of personnel who have a unique blend of professional management, operations, and systems analysis experience coupled with an in-depth knowledge of the organization and its mission. Although such a team often operates most effectively with no more than six members, the members should be those who know most about the organization. In addition to this core team, additional staff members with special expertise or skills may be used for limited periods of time.

Each team member should be responsible for one specific area of expertise that (ideally) corresponds to that person's experience or training. In addition, each team member should be assigned a backup area of responsibility to allow for some overall backup in the planning effort in the event another team member can no longer participate.

For example, in a distribution company with several facilities, a long-range IS planning team might consist of the following personnel:

- A long-range planning project manager.
- A distribution systems specialist.
- An inventory systems specialist.
- A computer hardware and operations specialist.
- A communications specialist.
- An office automation and end-user computing specialist.

Membership on the planning team should not be restricted to IS technical personnel. Depending on the types of new systems projects that are anticipated, key members of user organizations should also be included. They are best able to define their requirements, and they should also be able to discuss both competitive pressures and trends in the industry.

The particular makeup of the team would depend on the industry or business of the organization. It would also assume that certain actions may be taken as part of future planning activities. For example, in the distribution company described, senior management may have decided that the distribution locations should use EDI to communicate with one another and with outside suppliers and vendors. As a result, a telecommunications specialist was added to the planning team.

In addition, the planning team members in the example cited would probably rely on other technical specialists to provide planning input in selected areas. For example, the hardware and operations specialist team member might use the services of the organization's data base administrator to provide input on long-range data base planning. Similarly, the distribution systems specialist might rely on someone from the cost accounting department to provide advice on certain accounting practices.

## Defining the Goals and Objectives of the IS Plan

The IS planning team must first establish a set of broad goals for its planning effort. These goals should include such matters as the level of the final planning product—strategic, functional, operational, or multilevel. As part of the goal process, the IS planning team should have a clear idea of the time period that the plan should cover as well as the time period in which the IS planning team should complete its planning efforts. Senior management should be involved in this goal-setting process.

After the overall planning goals have been established, the IS planning team should define the organization's overall IS requirements. Senior management should also participate in this function by defining the organization's overall objectives. Because the definition of objectives is usually an iterative process, senior management involvement should continue as the plan develops and as its objectives are modified. This involvement may not solve all the difficulties because management's goals may be very general and lacking in detail. Careful definition of these objectives for the IS plan is the most important task of the planning team. If defined properly, these objectives can be used as a yardstick against which the success or failure of future plans can be measured. If the organization's objectives are defined poorly, the long-range plan could become an almost worthless document.

After the objectives have been defined and agreed on, the planning team must select an appropriate methodology for the plan's development. It is often effective for the planning team to use a planning horizon of four to five years and develop a scenario on the basis of the future impact of current trends and conditions. That scenario should then logically define the expected operating environment. To achieve this, the team must make some assumptions regarding the organization's mission in the future as well as the magnitude of change that the organization must sustain to remain operating in this projected environment. The team should also consider current and anticipated competition in the field.

This analysis of the impact of change is a useful tool for defining long-range planning objectives. The team members, working with senior management and selected line managers, should attempt to develop a consistent set of management and operating policies that define the levels of decision making likely to be operating in the projected environment. Determination of the information systems requirements necessary to support the decision levels is the next step in this process.

For example, a manufacturing organization has assembled an IS planning team and has given it a goal of constructing a five-year strategic IS plan. As a first step, the planning team might work with senior management to analyze current trends in its own manufacturing process as well as current external factors affecting the organization. The planning team would consider the impact of these current developments and would attempt to describe the organization's environment five years hence (i.e., the plan's time frame). These developments might be:

- Increasing automation in the manufacturing process should significantly reduce the labor content of the typical manufactured product.
- Increasing manufacturing automation may also make it necessary to eliminate some older plant facilities and move to newer plants in the future.
- The increasing use of just-in-time procurement may encourage an organization that supplies many of its manufactured products as subassemblies for other manufacturing firms to rethink its distribution channels.
- The increasing and, in some cases, mandatory requirement for EDI will eliminate many paper transactions and change automated procedures.
- An organization's concerns with product liability litigation (which management expects to increase) may create a need for detailed configuration and component data on its products to allow it to establish and prove an originating batch.

These are just a few examples of factors that an organization considers when analyzing the impact of potential change. The planning team should recognize that there may be an information systems-related concern or solution associated with each of these potential change factors. However, the planning team must first gather additional information regarding the accuracy of these assumptions.

The IS planning team should assemble a detailed set of scenarios of potential organizational change, similar to those described in the preceding examples. Although the team eventually will test these in greater detail and may discard some of them, these scenarios should help the team define its objectives. The long-range IS plan should provide the organization with information systems resources that support these probable scenarios.

## Anticipating Potential Conflicts and Problems

Although the IS planning team has been given a general set of goals by senior management for a long-range IS plan and the team has developed a set of objectives on the basis of probable scenarios, it may face some difficult problems and conflicts. If the team can anticipate these and modify its plans accordingly, it will provide the organization with a much more usable long-range IS plan.

A successful long-range plan may be most threatened by a planning team composed of members with biases that will improperly influence the planning product. For example, a planning team could be composed only of personnel with traditional mainframe backgrounds, which would be a problem if the organization were moving toward an end-user and networked workstation computing environment. The effect of the final long-range IS plan on the organization is predictable: senior management would probably ignore the mainframe-oriented plan and continue with its own end-user computing networking strategies.

This situation could occur if manufacturing or engineering personnel have developed successful workstation-based applications that are not part of the centralized computing environment. Over time, such users may sell management on the success of their localized approaches. The centralized IS function may therefore have difficulty in selling their more centralized approach.

Because the problem of a biased planning team will always be present, the members of IS or general management who are responsible for selecting team members should take care to choose personnel who do not appear to have particular biases. Management should evaluate the objectivity of these planning team members during periodic progress meetings. If a problem arises during the course of the plan development, management should first counsel the biased team member and, if unsuccessful, should replace that member.

There is often a fine line between the biased team members and the true planning visionary. The visionary may convince the team to make a significant jump from safe and accepted strategies to new ground, even though this type of counsel frequently entails some risk. Management and members of the planning team must weigh the choices between the visionary approach and the often more conservative team consensus strategy.

The planning team should be careful of the assumptions it makes about the business; mistakes can steer the plan in the wrong direction. For example, the team may assume—perhaps under the direction of a wishfully thinking manager—that the organization plans to open smaller plants that are closer to key customers, when market realities and other influences suggest otherwise. The planning team should state its objectives and assumptions when it presents its results to senior management and other personnel.

There is always the risk that the long-range recommendations will not be agreed to or accepted by senior management, so the team should hold periodic status meetings to inform senior management of its progress and potential recommendations. At these meetings, the team can describe its objectives and solicit the guidance and support of management.

It is difficult to overcome a highly politicized work environment. The planning team should be aware of such obstacles and take whatever steps it can to see that its work is taken seriously by senior management.

## DEVELOPING THE LONG-RANGE PLAN

The planning project must be structured around a task-by-task development plan, a well-defined set of checkpoints, and milestone review deadlines. The development plan should define:

- *The primary planning for work activities to be accomplished.* For example, which existing applications must be reviewed and which operational areas must be examined in detail.
- *When the work activities are to be accomplished.* A formal master schedule should be developed.
- *The measurable, reviewable, and tangible products to be produced from each work activity.* These should be defined to help the team measure the progress of its planning efforts.
- *The resource requirements needed to accomplish each work task.* For example, a detailed understanding of a current information system may be necessary to define future directions. Personnel and machine resources needed to gain this understanding should be estimated.

This preliminary work, which enables the planning team to start its information gathering and evaluation work, can be time-consuming. The result, however, should be a well-thought-out and effective long-range IS plan.

### Gathering Information

The task team must accumulate information by conducting structured interviews with management, professional, and staff personnel. These interviews should be planned; that is, the questions should be prepared in advance and given in written form to interviewees at least one week before any actual face-to-face meeting.

Interviewees should be given the choice of preparing their responses in writing or answering the questions during oral interviews. Even if written responses are prepared, the interviewers should attempt to meet all interviewees to clarify any ambiguities in their responses. In these interviews, the interviewers should be careful not to give false signals that will produce irrelevant responses. If the interviewer somehow implies (misleadingly) that an operation may be closed down, the persons being interviewed may give answers chosen to protect that operation.

The IS planning team should designate two team members to conduct and evaluate each interview. The interviewers should take notes on all interviewees' responses. The interviewers can then use this information in conjunction with the interviewees' written answers to develop summary interview notes.

For each interview, the interview team should develop a formal topic paper stating perceived needs in the user area surveyed. These topic papers should also include an analysis of the interview, which should be reviewed and commented on by the interviewees before including the papers in the planning documentation. These topic papers can be used for management briefings regarding the project's progress and should be part of the planning team's documentation.

In some organizations, the planning team may find that office politics prevents interviewees from speaking for the record. The IS planning team should attempt to cope with this unfortunate situation—for example, by summarizing the topic papers in such a manner that no individual is identified in the planning documentation.

This information gathering process should allow the planning team to evaluate whether the original objectives and the projected future scenarios are correct. Key individuals in the organization will have given their opinions on the following questions:

- How do you see your function or organization changing over the next five years?
- Are your current information systems adequate to support these planned changes?
- Do you agree with the projected future scenarios and objectives of this planning effort? If not, why?
- What type of information systems support would you like to see over the next five years?
- Do you have plans for additional information systems outside of the traditional IS department?
- What are the greatest strengths and weaknesses of the existing information systems supporting the organization?
- Are you aware of any innovations being made by the competition that appear to give them a competitive advantage?

This list can be expanded to suit different organizations. These questions, however, illustrate the type of information that should be gathered during this phase of long-range IS planning.

## Gathering Information from Other Sources

The team should attempt to gather information from other sources. A direct competitor will almost certainly not reveal its plans, but there may be other organizations, not direct competitors, that conduct tours and display their uses of technology. For example, an organization that is in the household-moving business may wish to see a competitor's digital image processing system for managing freight bills. A moving company competitor would not want to share this information, yet a company in an unrelated business (or an image processing vendor) might.

There are other sources of this kind of information. A member of the technical staff of an otherwise secretive competitor might be quite willing to discuss a new technique at an academic or professional conference. There may be other sources of information about new technologies and competitors. The organization that succeeds is probably one that does not worry so much about staying even with a competitor but instead attempts to develop the innovative idea that will move it ahead.

## Evaluating Existing Systems and Technologies

In addition to the interviews, a key task in the creation of any long-range IS plan is the evaluation of existing information systems. This entails an inventory and evaluation of automated and manual information systems used throughout the organization. In the early days of data processing, this was a relatively easy process. The IS planning team needed only to assess the central computer system. Today, this process is not nearly as easy. A typical organization may use the central computer for controlled systems, a mainframe-based information center for user-controlled systems, departmental computers for some local systems, a separate laboratory for developing expert systems, and numerous microcomputers.

This evaluation should be specifically directed at determining these systems' current and future value. Those elements of the current information system that are judged to be valuable in a long-range plan, coupled with the information needs that were determined from the structured interviews with management, constitute a preliminary inventory of the organization's information support needs.

The IS planning team should also consider information systems projects in progress. In particular, the team should consider any new hardware or software technologies that are being acquired. If the IS department has recently decided to acquire communications network equipment, long-range plans must take these purchases into consideration.

Each inventory item, either by itself or in conjunction with others, should be analyzed relative to the information produced, the system for producing and delivering the information, and the relative worth of that information. The planning team should attempt to conceptually evaluate these systems and areas for improvement. These conceptual designs for information system delivery should be reviewed for appropriateness and completeness by senior management.

The result of this phase of long-range planning should be a set of evaluations of all existing systems as well as conceptual designs of potential new information systems. The IS planning team may want to ask specialists (e.g., systems analysts) to help with this process. Consideration should also be given to evolving hardware and software technology. The IS planning team should consult with the organization's current technology vendors for an update on their future plans. Team members may also want to consider other sources of information (e.g., outside consultants, specialized seminars, and various professional publications).

## Establishing Management Review Checkpoints

To provide positive and direct management controls, a management committee should meet periodically to review the progress and accomplishments of the IS planning team. This management committee should be responsible for:

- Authorizing the framework of organizational policies and procedures within which the various planning tasks will be managed.
- Approving the planning team's findings, conclusions, and recommendations and authorizing actions to be taken during later planning steps.
- Approving and providing resources to advance the long-range planning project, as required.

This committee should be composed of members of senior management, who should monitor the team's progress and exert their influence on task developments. When appropriate, the planning team should introduce new technologies or hardware to the management committee through presentations by vendors or outside consultants.

To help the management committee properly review planning progress, the IS planning committee should prepare monthly progress reports. Such reports should formally define what has been accomplished during the reporting period, any problems encountered and solved or pending resolution, and what is to be accomplished during the next period. These reports should also document areas in which senior management intervention is required to resolve a problem. This reporting process also allows the team to highlight situations in which the scope of the overall planning project must be modified because a particular objective is either unachievable or impractical.

## Performing a Cost/Benefit Analysis

The IS planning team must help management define the costs and benefits for each element of the information systems plan. Basically, the production costs of each plan element must be defined in terms of personnel resources and equipment needs, and the expected benefits relative to the information systems enhancements defined by involved users must be specified.

The benefits and value of information elements can be developed in four primary categories: eliminating costs, avoiding costs, reducing risks, and improving the organization's competitive advantage. The first two categories can be quantified and costed fairly easily. However, some subjective judgment and reliance on soft numbers will always be a part of the development of this information. Therefore, when preparing these estimates, the planning team should try to define only actual costs.

The last two categories are the most important and the most difficult. They greatly depend on intuitive and subjective evaluations by the manager who will use the information. The planning team must work hard to quantify this area with the appropriate management. In some cases, only tentative estimates can be used. For example, a particular department in an organization may decide that an expert system would provide positive decision support benefits to its group. If the organization has no experience with expert systems, however, the development cost of such a system, as well as a benefits estimate, can be only tentative.

Despite the risk of using soft numbers in the cost/benefit analysis, the IS planning team should seriously attempt to match projected costs and benefits. The IS planning team should pay careful attention to documenting this process, including all of the assumptions and estimates made during planning. This data should be reviewed with and approved by senior management.

## THE LONG-RANGE IS PLAN

Much of the effort involved in the development of a long-range IS plan occurs during the organizing, information gathering, and evaluating tasks—that is, before the development of the actual planning document. The final product of this effort (the plan itself) is the document that should initiate management change and result in positive benefits to the organization in the long run. Therefore, it is important that this final product of the IS planning team's efforts be an effective long-range plan.

The final long-range IS plan should consist of three primary elements: a plan objective, a description of specific future projects, and a development schedule. First, the document should discuss the initial assumptions and objectives that were used to initiate the planning project. This section should also describe how the plan will serve specific organizational missions and goals.

The next section of the plan should discuss specific new hardware, communications, and systems development projects or subprojects. These may be new information systems, enhancements to existing systems, or other automation efforts. Each of these items should be defined in the context of:

- The source and availability of data elements that are required to produce desired information or support new systems.
- A definition of how the new system or data will reduce uncertainty involved in specific management or operational decisions.

- The frequency and rate of response required for the information.
- The cost of any new required equipment, software, and staffing costs, including the cost of development and implementation of new applications.
- The conceptual plan for development of the various information elements.

The final section of the plan should consist of a timed and phased development schedule outlining the required steps to implement each element of the plan. The following information should be included for each projected plan element in the schedule:

- Estimated resource requirements.
- Priority resource assignments.
- Implementation time frames.

## SELLING THE PLAN TO MANAGEMENT AND USERS

A properly constructed long-range IS plan involves considerable effort for an IS department and for the total organization. Because it should have been reviewed by senior management and users at various points during its development, it should yield no major surprises when completed. However, the completed plan may point to some major potential changes in information systems strategy within the organization; therefore, it must be actively accepted by senior management.

The planning team and IS management must often sell the completed plan to senior management, possibly by summarizing the costs and benefits again. The team may ask management to formally approve the plan's recommendations; such approval is critical because the plan typically requires the expenditure of resources and the adjustment of organizational practices.

Management often views technology-based plans with some suspicion. Therefore, although the plan may outline five or more years of activity, the planning team and IS management may ask senior management to approve and fund only the first year or two of actions outlined in the plan. This often provides a greater chance for success than a request for approval and funding for the entire plan.

If the long-range plan describes major changes in user departments, it is also necessary to sell the plan to those constituencies. Even when a plan has been approved by senior management, reluctant users can significantly impede plan progress.

The planning team should report on the long-range plan through presentations and summary reports to various involved user groups, especially if there are plans to significantly change computing practices. For example, if the long-range plan suggests that central IS will maintain only central data bases and certain key systems and that most applications will be moved to end user-controlled file servers and local area networks, users must be convinced of the advantages of this approach. This may require demonstrations, visits to other sites using this approach, and explanation of overall cost saving.

## UPDATING THE LONG-RANGE PLAN

The acceptance of a completed long-range IS plan is the beginning rather than the end of an effort. This is partly because a primary function of any long-range plan is to develop criteria for detailed, short-range planning. Short-range planning is often initiated as users in various departments develop action plans to implement their responsibilities within the long-range IS plan.

The long-range planning effort is also only a beginning because it should not serve as a frozen document for the duration of the planning period. In preparing the document, the planning team has made various assumptions and projections for a period of years into the future. However, numerous factors included in the plan can and will change, which may modify the plan over time. The long-range IS plan should be reviewed and updated at least annually.

A group comprising IS personnel and senior management should review the long-range plan quarterly or semiannually with the following questions in mind:

- To date, what actions have been taken in accordance with the long-range plan?
- Are the results of those actions yielding the benefits outlined in the plan?
- Have there been any significant changes in the mission of the overall organization that would alter the IS plan?
- Have there been any significant technological changes in IS hardware or software that would alter the plan?
- On the basis of plan accomplishments to date, should any changes be made to the future action steps outlined in the plan?

IS management may find it necessary to make adjustments to the document—for example, modification of implementation schedules or minor changes to objectives based on organization changes. The plan document should be revised to reflect these changes and should be reissued to all involved persons so that the plan continues to be an effective and relevant document in future years.

In some situations, major changes to the organization may cause the plan to quickly become out of date. When this occurs, the review team should initiate a new long-range planning effort to reflect those changes.

If there are no substantive changes, a long-range IS plan that has been well thought out and approved by senior management can be an effective document in guiding an organization and helping it to develop new and more effective information systems. The plan can also measure the progress of the organization in general and the IS department in particular for achieving future objectives.

## SUMMARY

Long-range information systems planning stems from management's need to know what is likely to happen in the near and distant future. It should be an effort dedicated to providing managers with insight regarding the logical and probable impact of current IS-related activities on future organizational operations. The team of IS professionals that produces such a long-range plan must understand and agree with the organization's overall management style. Moreover, all who participate in such planning should be made aware of the importance of their efforts in the future mission of the organization.

The long-range IS plan can be an important tool for both the IS department and senior management in an organization. Such a plan will help the IS department better understand how it can help support the overall mission of the organization. Although the development of such a plan can be time-consuming, the final product can be an effective aid for plotting future hardware, software, and information systems strategies.

# I-2
# Developing a Strategic Information Plan

*RAYMOND J. POSCH*

B usiness decisions may involve difficult choices affecting large-scale investments, strategic directions, and critical organizational goals (i.e., those in which the CEO or chief operations officer would be involved). Business decisions can also involve somewhat simpler choices regarding issues related to production, administration, or any other department (i.e., those decisions handled daily and hourly by line workers, clerks, supervisors, specialists, and managers).

The variety of these decisions demonstrates that businesses depend on information at all levels for both daily operations and longer-term strategies. When high-quality information is made easily accessible to the various decision makers at all levels throughout an organization, the decisions are more effective, and if these decisions are implemented properly in subsequent actions, the organization is better positioned to achieve its goals. The content and form of the information as well as the way it is communicated and managed are important factors to success. These are the basic, underlying premises of information strategy—that information is crucial to business success, that its importance must be recognized, and that the information resources must be managed as strategic assets.

Information does not exist entirely on its own. Most organizations have information systems comprising computer hardware, software, and networks to manage information and perform the intended processing as well as the facilities and people necessary to develop and support those systems.

Information resources can be grouped into three types:

- *Information services.* The computer applications for the processing, storage, retrieval, transmission, and presentation of information.
- *Information infrastructure.* The hardware, software, systems, staff, facilities, and other elements that support the delivery of information services.
- *The information itself.* The data that allows the organization to conduct business operations.

The more robust (in terms of functional capabilities) and flexible the infrastructure, the more easily applications can be developed and integrated. The more capable the infrastructure and the more rich the base of information, the more powerful the services that can be delivered.

Information resources are complex and require a great deal of attention, money, and work. The IS infrastructure in particular needs careful long-range planning, investment, development, and management. In addition, because business functions are increasingly becoming automated, information resources are becoming more vital to conducting business. They must be viewed globally and strategically not just operationally. An organization therefore must have a cohesive long-term strategy for information resource management at both the business and technical levels to effectively support its goals.

To develop such an information strategy, the following actions are recommended:

- Developing a strategic business plan.
- Conducting an information resource audit.
- Developing a strategic information systems plan.

The objective of these actions is to produce a written strategic information plan that can be clearly understood by senior management. The strategic information plan should consist of the following components:

- An information resource audit statement.
- An information strategy statement.
- An information systems architecture statement.
- A strategic IS organizational statement.
- An information strategy implementation plan.

This chapter discusses in detail the steps to be taken in each of the three phases of the plan and includes guidelines for writing the plan.

## DEVELOPING A STRATEGIC BUSINESS PLAN

The purpose of strategic business planning is to specify a few important business goals and a strategy for attaining them. The purpose of strategic information planning is to supplement the business plan by defining a strategy that supports the important business goals through appropriate information management activities. Strategic business planning must precede strategic information planning.

Information management plans that are not linked to strategic business goals, no matter how well thought out, lead to problems that are often prevalent in operations and systems departments. Such systems plans typically specify information technology (IT) strategies and IS plans that support the tactical requirements of the various user departments but do not address the critical business goals. The resulting misalignment between IS goals and business goals results in conflicting IS priorities among internal groups and the misallocation of IS resources.

If an organization does not have a strategic plan with well-defined business goals, the business strategy must handle whatever needs arise at any given time. This results in ever-changing priorities and numerous disputes as to the exact nature of the goals. In such environments, any systems plan is imperiled from the start.

Strategic planning is often confused with long-range planning. A strategy is a plan for achieving an objective by focusing on critical goals. Therefore, the objective of strategic planning is to identify the most important goals and determine the most important actions for attaining those goals. An organization can develop a long-range plan that is not strategic or can develop a strategic plan that need not be long range.

In reality, strategic planning may need to address multiple time frames—short range (i.e., one year or less), mid range (i.e., two to three years), and long range (i.e., four years or longer)—with different goals for each. Strategic plans focus primarily on goals. In contrast, tactical plans focus on actions that satisfy immediate requirements, including those that implement strategy, and operational plans explain in detail steps needed to make tactics fully operational.

## The Partnership Between Corporate and IS Management

The ideal situation is one in which information strategy development is viewed as an extension of the strategic business planning process. This requires that business managers recognize that information is critical to their success and perceive information management as a strategic business issue. Senior IS managers must often take the lead in educating senior corporate managers, especially in helping them view information strategy as an extension of business strategy. The strategic planning process provides an excellent opportunity for IS and corporate managers to build a partnership, in which they work closely together to plan and implement a business strategy that acknowledges information's vital role in the functioning of the organization.

## The Strategic Business Planning Process

Strategic business planning, when its focus is broadened to include information strategy development, typically involves the following six steps:

1. Identifying the planning time frames.
2. Identifying the main goals for the time frames.
3. Identifying the critical information required to support the goals.
4. Estimating the time and resource, including information resources, required to achieve the goals.
5. Evaluating the high-level trade-offs of expected benefits versus costs. If appropriate, goals should be redefined and steps 3, 4, and 5 repeated until satisfied.
6. Writing the strategic business plan to explain the main goals and the

strategies for accomplishing those goals in clear and concise language. The plan must then be communicated, at least in summary form, to the staff.

Strategic business planning begins by identifying the planning time frame (usually one to three years) and the main goals that the organization wants to achieve in that time frame. Goals are commonly stated in relation to such areas as products, markets, sales, positioning relative to competition, and profitability. Goals, however, should also be included in terms of strengths and capabilities (to be obtained from the organization's infrastructure). The main goals should be strategic in nature and critical to the success of the organization in the planned time frame.

One method of determining the main goals is to identify critical success factors and then translate them into specific goals. The number of goals should be limited—three to six goals for each business unit and, overall, three to six most-critical goals for the organization. In general, the fewer the goals, the more likely they will be met. Once the goals are determined, they should be ranked according to priority so that it is clear which are most and least important. An important step in incorporating information strategy into the business planning process is identification of the critical information needs. This is discussed in the following section.

### Identifying Critical Information Needs

For each main business goal, the business managers must identify the critical high-level information needed to support the goal. For example, the first-cut, high-level, critical information requirements for a marketing division in a highly competitive industry might be as follows:

- Detailed reporting on market penetration for the organization and prominent competitors worldwide.
- Graphic presentations of market shares and market trends.
- Quantitative and qualitative analyses of customer or buyer perceptions.

For the information needs to be well understood, however, these first-cut requirements must be expanded into more detailed descriptions. The first-cut requirements in the example have been expanded into more detail as follows:

- Monthly market penetration reports must be developed that provide estimated unit sales, percentage of total sales, and percentage of total estimated market, categorized by North America first, then Europe, Asia, and the rest of the world for the organization and its top 10 competitors.
- Charts must be developed showing the same information graphically with the addition of time-line trends.
- Online sales and performance figures must be updated at least weekly but preferably daily for the most recent day, week, month, year-to-date, or other specified time period. These figures must show unit sales, revenues,

sales expenses, operating expenses, and net profit organized according to product line, sales region, and sales team, and a comparison must be made to the corresponding figures of the previous year.

- Numeric and narrative analyses of surveys must be conducted at least annually, showing trends, satisfaction levels, and other important data regarding customers and, for comparative purposes, other buyers in the market who are not customers. The information should be organized according to product categories, regions, customer industries, and other pertinent factors.

This level of detail will be required for evaluating whether existing information resources can satisfy the marketing division's needs or, if they cannot, what changes will be necessary to help the existing resources meet those needs. In cases in which a significant degree of uncertainty exists about how well existing systems meet the strategic needs, an information resource audit (i.e., the next phase of the strategic information plan, which is described in detail in a subsequent section of this chapter) might be needed at this point to clarify the information management activities required.

### Preparing the Strategic Plan

After the critical information needs have been identified, the necessary information resource requirements (e.g., computers, networks, and data bases), along with other resource requirements (e.g., people and dollars), must then be estimated for each goal. Operations and systems managers are responsible for estimating information resource requirements; other business managers must estimate the requirements for resources from their business units. Certain resources can be used to serve multiple corporate goals; therefore, the planning process must reflect the plan as a whole, not just the individual goals independently. Resources for building and maintaining the infrastructure are especially important and should not be diverted to short-term needs. External as well as internal resources can be used (e.g., at least part of the needs of the marketing division described in the previous section could be met by using external resources). Specific high-level tactics, activities, and projects (e.g., development of new systems or enhancement of existing systems) must be roughly defined at this stage to gain some appreciation of what is needed to achieve the goals.

On the basis of those high-level tactics, time and resource requirements for the business goals must be estimated to evaluate the costs. Whenever possible, quantifiable benefits and returns on investment should also be estimated. Estimates do not need to be exact but should be reliable within an order of magnitude. Significant impacts and risks (which may or may not be quantified) should also be identified. In addition, because the plan may address multiple time periods, it must have a time line as well. Certain projects (e.g., those that develop the information infrastructure) may take multiple years to implement. Ultimately, it must be decided whether the expected benefits of the goals are worth the predicted costs and risks or whether a different set of goals should be specified.

Furthermore, strategic planning, like all types of planning, is an iterative process consisting of rounds of specifying and estimating, followed by evaluating the risks and trade-offs (i.e., costs versus benefits). When the iterations have finished it is helpful to rank the high-level tactics and projects for each business unit and for the organization as a whole within each planning time frame.

The final task of strategic business planning is to write a strategic business plan as a document (at least in summary form) for everyone in the organization, though the information must be treated as proprietary and confidential. It should explain, as clearly and concisely as possible, the most important business goals and the assumptions for both the overall organizational strategy and the high-level tactics of each business unit, including the IS division. Developed this way, the information strategy will be fully integrated into the business plan.

## CONDUCTING AN INFORMATION RESOURCE AUDIT

An information resource audit is an assessment of the assets and liabilities of existing information resources. The audit should cover the information systems (i.e., applications), hardware, software, networks, tools, IS department and staff, data bases, and metadata (i.e., data definitions) of the organization. It is useful to differentiate among the three main types of resources: infrastructure, applications, and information. The audit can be applied at multiple levels and for multiple purposes; for the strategic information plan, however, it is most useful at a high level. In other words, the assessment should avoid too much detail and must clearly define the greatest strengths and weaknesses of the information resources.

### Performing the Audit

The audit is best performed after the strategic business plan has been completed or at least after the critical information needs have been identified. The audit should focus on how well those critical information needs are presently being satisfied. Other critical high-level strengths and weaknesses should also be assessed. Any systems under development that are pertinent to major assets or liabilities must be included. The audit can be performed by IS managers (from a service provider's perspective) with a review conducted by corporate management, or the audit can be performed by non-IS business managers (from a client's perspective) with a review conducted by IS management.

### Writing and Reviewing the Assessment

The product of the audit is a clearly written statement disclosing the findings of the audit. On the liability side, the audit statement should describe what is needed to correct deficiencies (e.g., subject data bases or a centralized data dictionary or repository) and why, but it should not explain in fine detail how the changes are to be executed. Similarly, the assets should be briefly described in terms of what is needed and why.

The audit statement should relate directly to the strategic business plan and should be written for senior management. A review process of one or more iterations will be needed to ensure that the assessment is strategic in nature and indeed correctly identifies the significant assets and liabilities among corporate information resources.

## The Enterprise Information Atlas

The enterprise information atlas consists of information maps and is a useful but optional product of the audit. Exhibit I-2-1 presents one type of information map, which shows the sources and uses for information in one particular information services company.

The purpose of the information map is to help managers as well as others in the organization comprehend the organization's information resources and how they relate to the goals and functioning of the organization. Information maps are not only educational tools but reference sources and, perhaps from the IS perspective, marketing tools as well. Information maps depict the relationships of information resources at various functional levels in the organization and can be used to help answer such questions as, What systems (i.e., applications) or data bases are sources of information or services to the various business units or corporate functions? The maps should be as graphic as possible, showing, for example, how information relates organizationally, geographically, and operationally as well as how it relates to the planning and management process.

If automated, information maps can be stored in a data base or repository with online access and can depict the organization's information resources at several levels: high level (i.e., strategic), mid level (i.e., tactical), and detail level (i.e., operational). To support the strategic plan, different maps may be required for different time frames (e.g., in the current state, with a projection at the end of a short-range plan, or with the projection at the end of a mid-range plan). The maps would not contain the details of a full data dictionary or repository but might well include such organizational models as data models or entity-relationship models. If the information maps are not automated, they can be included in a document serving as a supplement to the audit statement (though they can also stand alone). The maps should be updated with each subsequent cycle of strategic planning and information resource auditing, if not more frequently.

Information maps can be most easily implemented at a high level and in document form and as such would probably derive the most benefits, especially in educating senior managers about the organization's information resources and the importance of information. If they are automated, however, information

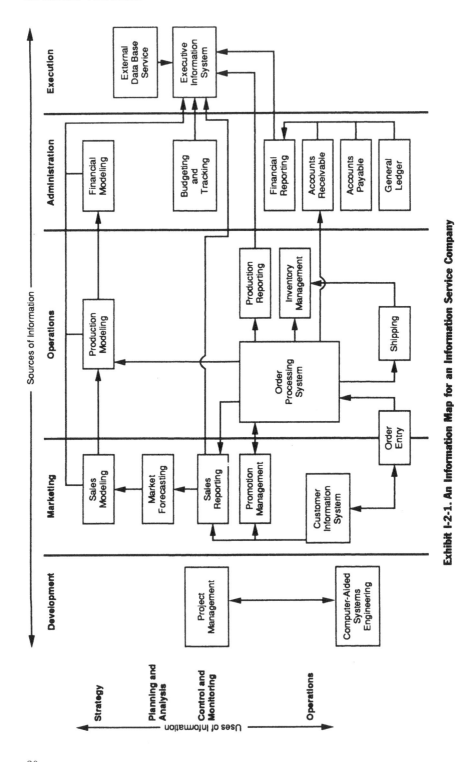

**Exhibit I-2-1. An Information Map for an Information Service Company**

maps would provide a useful resource for the organization as a whole and in particular for the data administration or data resource management group that would be responsible for their maintenance. CASE tools that are encyclopedia or repository based would probably offer the best technology for automating the information maps.

## DEVELOPING A STRATEGIC INFORMATION SYSTEMS PLAN

The first phase—strategic business planning—identified key business goals, critical information needs, and the information management strategy for meeting the business goals. The second phase—the information resource audit—identified the significant assets and liabilities among the corporate information resources, especially as they relate to the information requirements of the strategic plan. The purpose of the third phase—strategic information systems planning—is to complete the strategic information planning process and to develop the written strategic information plan.

Five steps are involved in strategic information systems planning. They are:

1. Developing or refining the IS architecture.
2. Developing or refining the strategic IS organizational plan.
3. Completing the business-level IS plan.
4. Completing the information strategy statement.
5. Preparing the information strategy implementation plan.

These steps are discussed in the following sections.

### Developing or Refining the IS Architecture

With the great number of new IS technologies and options and with the ever-increasing need for consistency and integration, it is important that the organization have an architecture that defines the preferred technologies, methods, and directions that the organization will use and follow for its business information systems. The purpose of an IS architecture is to clearly define how corporate systems are to be constructed and how they will appear or act. The purpose is to narrow the approach, set expectations for both users and IS staff, and specify standards and guidelines that support efficient, effective information systems.

Development of the IS architecture should begin with an architectural reference model. Most organizations are developing systems on the basis of a distributed model. Because of the critical issues related to systems integration, however, planners must not only evaluate information resources by their location but also clearly differentiate between infrastructure, applications (i.e., business and user service), and information. Therefore, a two-dimensional information resource model such as that illustrated in Exhibit I-2-2 is a more effective starting point. The infrastructure is the foundation and the public

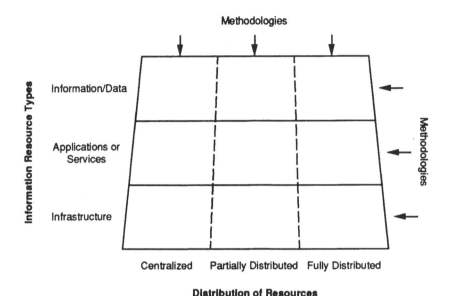

**Exhibit I-2-2. Information Resource Architectural Reference Model**

utility; it directs the information flow and provides facilities for information management. Applications deliver services to users; they are built on the basis of the infrastructure and are integrated and share information through it. Information is the asset that is stored, processed, moved, and managed by means of the applications and infrastructure.

Each of these three main information resource types can be distributed centrally, regionally, or departmentally (i.e., partially distributed), or they can be distributed to the user (fully distributed). Those information resources that provide the means of interconnection and integration of other distributed information resources (e.g., wide area networks, local area networks, phone systems, and integrative software layers and services) are some of the most critical elements of the information infrastructure.

IS architectures are quite complex. The reference model (such as the one in Exhibit I-2-2) decomposes the architecture into smaller architectural pieces, thereby making it easier to understand. On the basis of this model, the process of developing the architecture is probably best organized in the following sequence of architectural units:

- Information or data.
- Information applications, or high-level services.
- The information infrastructure, consisting of networking and communications, computing hardware, and software.
- Methodologies.

For each of these architectural units, the architecture should address the distribution of resources (i.e., whether resources are distributed centrally, departmentally, or to the user). Methodologies are also an important part of the architecture and can be thought of as applying to both dimensions (i.e., resource types as well as the distribution of the resources). Each architectural unit is described in further detail in the following sections.

**Information or Data.** The information should specify the following details:

- How information will support the business goals.
- What the objectives are for information access and information services for the users.
- What technologies will be used for information storage and presentation.
- What kinds of information are important.
- How the information will usually be managed.

This architectural unit must address such issues as data base technology and applications (including issues related to distinctions between nonrelational, relational, and object-oriented data bases and between distributed and centralized data bases, as well as determining which DBMSs are to be supported), data resource management (including issues of what repository should be used, distributed versus centralized ownership, and the balancing of priorities), and data administration (including issues of data dictionary maintenance, access control, and standards enforcement). In the future, it will become increasingly important that this architectural unit address information regarding all media types (e.g., data, voice, video, audio, graphics, or document images).

**Information Applications.** This architectural unit must define what the general approach will be to applications and user services. It should address such issues as which applications should run on which hardware and software platforms, development of applications versus purchase of packaged applications, levels of integration between applications, use of underlying services (i.e., hardware, software, and communications), and user interface standards.

**The Information Infrastructure.** The infrastructure architectural unit can be broken down into three primary areas: networking, hardware, and software. The networking portion should identify the strategies or target technologies for interconnecting computing equipment, both locally and across wide areas, and how, more generally, users will connect with departmental, regional, and central services. The networking architectural unit must define the voice (i.e., telephone), video conferencing, and data networking strategies as well as the degrees of integration of these networks. For long-range time frames, goals (e.g., gigabit bandwidths supporting multiple protocols) can be identified without specifying which technologies will be used. For short-range time frames, specific technologies (e.g., token-ring LAN's bridged across an SNA network with T1 trunks) might be selected as standards. The hardware architecture should specify which computer systems and user workstations will be used to perform the actual computing and information processing work. The software architecture should identify the preferred operating systems, data base management systems, programming languages, and software strategies to be used for consistency and integration (e.g., low-level software services).

**Methodologies.** Methodologies should be established governing stages of the information resource life cycles (e.g., planning, analysis, design, development, testing, deployment, maintenance, origination, update, archival, and management) and across both dimensions of the architectural model (see Exhibit I-2-2). It may be appropriate to have life cycle methodologies that are distinctly different among the main information resource types (i.e., information, applications, and infrastructure). The methodologies will also likely have differences among central, departmental, and user-level resources. Such techniques as systems engineering, CASE, joint and rapid application design, information engineering, and applications development environments (e.g., AD/Cycle) may provide useful methodologies and tools, though they may not address full information resource management as defined by the architectural model.

In addition, because IS architecture is primarily future oriented, the architecture should address different architectural goals at different points in time as well as the issues concerning the current base of systems (i.e., the applications and infrastructure) and how they will conform over time to a new architecture. One of the objectives of the architecture is to provide reasonable consistency over time while adapting to new requirements and new technologies.

**The Architecture Statement.** IS management should write the information systems architecture statement describing the overall architecture clearly and succinctly for senior management. The architecture statement should begin with an executive summary followed by supporting levels of architectural strategy. Depending on the magnitude (i.e., the size and diversity) of the organization and the scope (i.e., number and size) of its systems, the statement may need to be supplemented by multiple documents (perhaps elaborating on each of the architectural units described in the preceding paragraphs). The statement must be reviewed annually as part of the strategic planning cycle and, if appropriate, modified to reflect new business conditions, strategies, and technologies.

## Developing or Refining the Strategic IS Organizational Plan

Because the IS department is such a critical element in how the organization manages its information, the organization also must establish a plan for the IS department itself. Changing business structures, more distributed (i.e., lower-level) information technology deployment, and advances in computing and networking technologies are causing changes in the way operations and systems personnel are organized and managed. The IS department must effectively support the information strategy and the IS architecture. However, because of its importance, this issue should be addressed and documented in a separate strategic IS organizational statement.

IS management should develop the IS organizational strategy in close partnership with senior management. The current information processing environment is more highly distributed and therefore usually requires IS support that is likewise more distributed. For example, many businesses have hybrid-structure IS departments with decentralized IS development and support staff actually reporting to or being part of the business units and centralized IS staff for planning, maintenance, and enforcement of the architecture and for data administration. Whatever IS organizational structure is used, the strategy must be well defined in this statement, specifying a time line and developmental as well as service-level objectives. The IS organizational statement also must be reviewed and updated with the annual strategic planning cycle.

## Completing the Business-Level IS Plan

Strategic IS planning at a business level (i.e., with an integrated view of the organization) should be completed during the strategic business planning phase, when the information strategy was originally developed. Before proceeding with implementation planning, however, IS management should review the information needs, high-level tactics, identified projects, expected benefits, and associated resource requirements for their continuing validity in relation to architectural and organizational decisions or other new developments that may have subsequently occurred.

Planning is a process of iteration and refinement. IS management must ensure that the process does not become too detailed and drawn out. During this step, changes to the information strategy statement (usually with regard to the tactics and projects or the estimated resource requirements) may result. If the time or cost estimates change significantly, the impact on the original business plan must be evaluated.

## Completing the Information Strategy Statement

Most of the effort for the information strategy statement has already been completed in the first two phases. What remains at this point is to bring together and clarify the overall information strategy for the organization, explain the critical information needs and how they relate to the business goals, and describe the information management plans and resource assumptions in the strategic business plan. Architectural and organizational strategies should be reflected at a high level, with differentiation between the development of infrastructure and the development of applications (i.e., business services).

Strategic directions, important goals, and the orders of magnitude of project time and cost are more important than specific breakdowns of the projects and their costs.

The information strategy statement should explain how the goals, strategies, and high-level tactics are arranged according to priorities across business units. It should be clear, concise, and written for senior management (i.e., the CEO, chief operations officer, and business unit managers). IS management should write the information strategy statement, and the document should be reviewed and approved by senior management.

### Preparing the Information Strategy Implementation Plan

The final step in strategic information resource planning is to create a plan for implementing the information strategy. The implementation plan should be prepared by IS management and addressed at a high level (i.e., in less detail) to senior management, and it should consolidate the planned activities of the information strategy statement, the information systems architecture statement, and the strategic IS organizational statement into a single reference document. It should identify and explain critical assumptions, dependencies, resource issues, and events. The information strategy implementation plan, when completed, will become a primary reference for IS project planning, management, and control as well as status reviews.

### SUMMARY

Information strategy requires that business executives recognize information resources as critical corporate assets (and future information requirements) that must be taken into account in the business planning process. Once this is clearly understood and accepted, information management becomes a business issue in which senior management must play an active role. Information strategy is an important part of information management and is best communicated through a strategic information plan.

The strategic information planning process, however, can become a hindrance or a barrier if it is allowed to get mired in too much analysis and debate. To avoid this problem, the strategic information plan must be developed at a high level, with active participation by senior management, and in a reasonably short time (three to six weeks beyond the strategic business planning process). It is important that the strategic information plan be seen as strategic, be developed quickly, and become the focal point for an ongoing business partnership between senior and IS management.

The plan does not have to address every issue but must establish the overall strategic direction. (A more thorough strategic information plan, especially in the area of IS architecture, which requires in-depth knowledge of information technologies and the foresight to judge the best architecture for a particular organization, will actually take years to evolve.) When it is initially prepared, the strategic information plan should be considered a basic plan that will undoubtedly change as the process becomes better understood and as the architecture matures with time. More effort can be channeled into refining the strategic information plan later, but having an effective strategic information plan that will implement the business vision should be high priority for every business executive, CIO, and IS manager.

# I-3
# A Data Center Manager's Guide to Systems Integrators

*THORTON A. MAY*

Systems integration is becoming part of the collective computational experience of most major global corporations. According to some research, the general systems integration market is thought to be growing at a robust compound annual rate of more than 20%, with such specialized niches as the network integration sector growing at a more rapid 38%. The market is expected to reach the $35 billion range by 1995 (up from $6 billion in 1989).

The current business environment is one of the factors that has accelerated systems integration's rise to importance. Organizations are now required to generate differentiated products and services to preserve their competitive position. This environemnt no longer encourages or guarantees the survival of organizations unable or unwilling to do new things. Another factor is the increasingly expensive range of rapidly evolving technologies, which require specialized expertise; yet measurements, mind-sets, and stagnating sales growth have kept organizations from investing in programs designed to develop internal competences. The growing realization is that traditional structural and managerial modes are dysfunctional in the current environment.

The systems integration industry is singularly positioned to help organizations create unique products and services—with much of the differentiation being provided by the value-added assemblage of complex technology components that otherwise would not be available to organizations. In addition, as current technology investments come to the end of their useful economic lives, integrators are playing a major role in planning and delivering the next generation of hardware, software, and peripheral devices.

For example, integrators are playing the leading role in the migration to a client/server architecture. Integrators are also likely to assist organizations migrating from a one-dimensional text-based computing environment to one in which voice, video, and animation dominate. For these reasons, systems integration can be seen as the defining phenomenon of the information age today.

Tenex Consulting has done research into the workings of the systems integration marketplace. The research primarily studied the imaging market and focused on approximately 250 imaging applications that involved significant reengineering initiatives and the heavy use of systems integrators. The study examined the reasons organizations turn to systems integrators and the lessons learned from working with them. These lessons, described throughout the rest of this chapter, are intended to help the consumer of systems integration services evaluate the integrators' offerings and manage the relationship with service suppliers.

## STAFFING FOR THE CHANGING INFORMATION TECHNOLOGY INFRASTRUCTURE

The declining relevance and increased cost associated with maintaining the current technology infrastructure have contributed significantly to the systems integration market's growth. The move to distributed computing, the use of nontraditional computing devices (e.g., laptop, notebook, palmtop, and pen-based computers), and the complicated connectivity requirements of wireless, LAN, WAN, and FDDI technology have expanded the specialized skill sets required to conceptualize, design, prototype, develop, implement, and reap the benefits of a rapidly evolving technology. In a word, there is more to know.

In the current environment, most organizations simply do not have the specialized technical expertise they need to create and maintain differentiated product and service sets. In no organization studied was there a balanced division of labor between those possessing ascendant-technology skills (i.e., client-server and distributed computing) and those possessing less-relevant skill sets.

The lack of skilled staff in key emerging technology areas leaves many organizations exposed and vulnerable. For example, a major process manufacturer recently achieved a milestone. Despite the fact that it operates in a very diverse technological environment, it was able to achieve total connectivity among its knowledge workers by way of E-mail. Thus, independent of the technology platform, an engineer in a remote plant can swap messages with an accountant at headquarters.

The problem is that the system was built and understood by only one employee. People know when this employee goes on vacation because they experience a noticeable degradation in system performance. Although management moved some traditional COBOL programmers in to back up the E-mail expert, the less-skilled transplants never learned the technology. In fact, in some cases, they degraded the productivity of the one employee who knew what was going on. It is this type of situation in which organizations cannot meet the demands for new skills that the changing technology infrastructure places on them, that organizations typically call in systems integrators.

One of the areas in which systems integrators add value is in their possession of esoteric technology skills. One of the city of Chicago's evaluation criteria in awarding a $40-million, five-year parking violations contract to an outside systems integrator hinged on the need for that integrator to be expert in a wide range of technologies (e.g., imaging, geographical information systems, portable terminals, and handheld computers).

In reality, however, systems integrators are wrestling with the same human capital problems that businesses are. For the majority of systems integrators, 50% to 75% of their professional staff is proficient in technologies that are destined for extinction during the next five years. The systems integration marketplace represents one of the largest human retooling efforts ever conducted.

During the process of shopping for a systems integrator, all potential systems integrators should be ranked according to their investments in their professionl staffs. Arthur Andersen habitually plows 55% of its profits back into the business. The systems integration market is filled with competing claims regarding whose people are better trained and who spends more on continuing professional education. Such claims need to be evaluated the same way a college or graduate program would: by examining the curriculum, evaluating the faculty, and interviewing the alumni.

Very few systems integrators have skills covering all emerging technology areas, much less profound knowledge in all areas. For example, when a systems integrator asserts that its organization has extensive imaging and multimedia experience, it is probably not blatantly lying. When it claims that every member of the team is an expert in that area, the truth is usually being stretched a bit.

The best defense against the quite-prevalent practice of overstating credentials is to conduct periodic on-site audits, comparing the capabilities of the people promised in the proposal with the capabilities of the people who actually show up to do the work. There is no need to eliminate less-skilled integrators from project teams (to do so would preclude their ever becoming proficient), but the client should perhaps receive an economic royalty from all subsequent work junior staff members perform (in other words, the client should be compensated for providing a forum for experimental learning to take place).

Organizations often really do need systems integrators. Computer hardware vendors, communications equipment suppliers, and user organizations need help putting the various pieces of the technology puzzle together. The managerial acumen, to say nothing of the capital intensity required, usually prohibit an organization from doing it all by itself.

## SHOPPING FOR SOLUTIONS

The shift in the nature of competition is significant enough to warrant characterization as a new physics of competition. Time-honored strategies of product positioning (i.e., pricing and prestige) and features and functions are giving way to strategies highlighting internal service and support delivery capabilities.

When organizations go to the marketplace today, most are not looking for a specific product; they are looking for a technology-enhanced solution to a business problem. The major technology vendors have recognized this for a long time. However, transforming a product-based sales force into a consultative sales unit is a difficult undertaking. The solutions of earnest vendor-sponsored consultants always seem to feature enormous amounts of equipment yet have been largely unsuccessful. Systems integrators are positioned to conceptualize solutions and, more important, render them feasible, using a blend of technology components from multiple sources.

The abbreviated life cycle associated with most technology products coupled with the move to targeted micromarkets has reduced the amount of money a manufacturer can wrest from a given product. (Computer scientists at Carnegie Mellon University contend that a computer generation now lasts only three years.) Well-established positions in product segments are not guarantees of continuing profits. This reality has catalyzed many hardware vendors to enter the systems integration market aggressively.

## SERVICE AND PRICING STRATEGIES

Exhibit I-3-1 shows the many types of integrators operating in the market today. Hardware vendors, software vendors (e.g., Microsoft Corp., whose consulting group currently has more than 200 consultants working in seven countries with more than 150 engagements under their belt and more than 50% of their work tied directly to Microsoft product), phone companies, aerospace companies, accounting and financial services firms, strategic business consultants, and industry specialists are all trying to participate in the systems integration market. Each brings a particular management style, structure, and skill set to an integration project.

The diversity of participants in the systems integration market creates diverse behaviors and strategies. At the bottom of the hierarchy are mom-and-pop operations that specialize in installing basic applications on basic technology platforms. Their expertise tends to be vendor specific, and their billing structure precisely inflects their expertise base. When operating in a technology environment they are familiar with, they quote fixed-price fees. When they are working outside their field of expertise, they may insist on time-and-materials contracts. These market participants typically come from the technical support staffs of vendors. Periodic work force reductions in the vendor community have added significantly to the size of this segment of the integration market.

Some integrators prefer to compete on the basis of technological firepower. Historically, Electronic Data Systems Corp. (EDS), when confronted with a technology set it views as important but does not possess a great deal of in-house experience with, has been known to go out and buy or heavily invest in the leading supplier of that technology. Corporate management at EDS

**Aerospace**

The Boeing Co.
Grumman Corp.
McDonnell-Douglas
Martin Marietta Corp.

**Federal Government Suppliers**

American Management Sytems, Inc.
CACI International, Inc.

**Big Six**

Andersen Consulting
   (division of Arthur Andersen & Co.)
Coopers & Lybrand
KPMG Peat Marwick

**Business Consultants**

A.T. Kearney, Inc.
Booz, Allen & Hamilton, Inc.

**Chains**

Businessland, Inc.
Computerland Corp.

**Chip Vendors**

Motorola, Inc.
Texas Instruments, Inc.

**Emerging Markets**

Lotus Development Corp.
Microsoft Corp.
Oracle Corp.

**Facilities Managers**

Electronic Data Systems Corp.

**Industry Specialists**

Avid, Inc.
PRC, Inc.
General Electric Co.

**Phone Companies**

Ameritech
AT&T
Bell Atlantic
Cincinnati Bell
GTE Centel
NYNEX

**Software Houses**

Bolt Beranek and Newman, Inc.
Cap Gemini America
CSC Index, Inc.

**Technical Consultants**

Arthur D. Little

**Vendors**

Control Data Corp.
Digital Equipment Corp.
Hewlett-Packard Co.
IBM Corp.
Sun Microsystems, Inc.
Unisys Corp.

**Exhibit I-3-1. Partial List of Companies Providing Systems Integration**

makes no secret of the importance it places on the emerging multimedia market.

Most integrators have not moved aggressively in the laptop, notebook, and palmtop technology segments, citing the vicious price competition and limited possibilities for fee-based services. However, all major integrators are making substantial investments in getting their communications skills in order. Several integrators have used an acquisition strategy (e.g., Ernst & Young acquired Network Strategies, Inc.). Some have chosen to grow their own expertise. Others have forged alliances with networking vendors.

Virtually all the major integrators are aggressively positioning themselves for the demand for business process redesign or business reengineering. Most have spun off or created separate consutling entities to capitalize on this $2 billion marketplace. Some are using customized work-flow automation tools to differentiate themselves. For example:

- Andersen Consulting developed its Business Process Reengineering Tool.
- CACI International, Inc., launched SIMprocess.

- Coopers & Lybrand created Sparks.
- Digital Equipment Corp. introduced Team-Route.
- Reach Software Corp. released Work-Man, a mail-based object-oriented platform for building a wide range of work flow applications.

Some integrators, such as Integris (the integration wing of Bunn HN Information Systems, Inc.), operate along the entire spectrum of activity including LAN implementation; others, such as Ernst & Young, seek to focus themselves primarily in the network design and applications development segments. There are as many positioning strategies as there are integrators. Some focus on relationships, some on vertical-market expertise, some on the ability to muster capital, some on risk appetite, and some on contracting flexibility or guarantees.

Each organization and each project team can vary significantly in terms of scope and scale of projects they can manage effectively. Pricing varies greatly, as well, among the players in the market. There also exists a range of systems integration services for which there are segmented pricing levels. At the bottom of the pricing scale is a less creative and more standard form of systems development (reflecting the behavior set among junior programmers just out of school).

Many systems integrators make their margins by charging premium hourly rates for programmers with only basic skills. If a business needs C programmers, all it should pay for is their services, not extensive network advertising, not elaborate corporate office, and certainly not elevated salaries.

The systems integration market offers an array of unique examples of aggressive and innovative pricing programs. For example, to win the city of Chicago's $40-million, parking violations contract, EDS submitted a proposal that offered to take some portion of its fees on a pay-for-performance basis. More than 19 million parking tickets are reported to be outstanding in Chicago—with a face value in excess of $420 million. The contract specifies that EDS will receive 18% of all fines collected associated with tickets outstanding less than 12 months and 26% of those more than a year old.

Organizations should know that they can hire more than one systems integrator. In fact, some organizations select one systems integrator to help them shop for other systems integrators. The resulting team of diverse integrators may include some to help establish direction, some to provide input to advanced technology projects, and others to trudge through basic programming duties. The designated shopper plays four fundamental roles:

- Identifying the set of skills necessary.
- Identifying the members of the systems integrator community who possess those skills.
- Determining a pricing structure appropriate for the services provided.
- Sculpting a management process that keeps all the parties in the integration effort moving forward constructively.

Organizations working with systems integrators sometimes learn that legitimate factors frequently lead to a one-time emergency project turning into a sizable and long-lived service contract. This occurs because:

- The systems integrators have skills that are required but not possessed by the organization.
- The systems integrators provide external exposure (i.e., they know what competitors are doing and what is happening in other industries).
- They provide access to senior management.
- They have the ability to operate across the organization.

One of the negative aspects of systems integration in action is that the reward structure in many integration houses focuses on selling the next job. The wise user of systems integration services should establish rules up front about access to senior management. Huge amounts of professional time are lost when systems integrators attempt to cross-sell while at the client site. They should be reminded that they are being paid to deliver the technological components of a business solution, not to sell their next piece of work.

## Evaluating Performance

How can a consumer of systems integration services rate one integrator over another? A set of objective measures can help user organizations evaluate whether performance is lacking.

Systems integrators themselves are uncertain regarding the metrics that are most appropriate for driving the business. One major systems integrator's primary success criterion is whether the client sues it at the end of an engagement.

Systems integrators are only as good as the contract a business writes with them. The major contribution to the success of the collaboration that existed between American Express and its systems integrator during the design, development, and delivery of the widely discussed enhanced billing system was the specificity with which milestones were delineated and the fact that the integrator reaped substantive financial rewards for performance above contract specification. Conversely, stiff penalties were imposed for unacceptable performance.

The evolving process whereby new technology enters organizations is undergoing monumental change. Some organizations are beginning to refocus management attention on the critical question of what their organizations are capable of doing with a given technology. With the notable exception of some massive and poorly administered federal procurements based on technical superiority, a pattern of technology use is emerging that seeks to leverage human endeavor rather than eliminate it. During the latter part of the 1980s, academics came to focus their attention on the user-system interface. Management scholars have come to the conclusion that the quality of the tools is not as important as the quality of tool use.

## PREVAILING TECHNICAL ORIENTATION

Very few systems integrators have been able to evolve beyond their technical roots to focus on metatechnology issues (e.g., how to make money or improve service with a given technology). Usually, organizations turn to systems integrators for the following reasons:

- To obtain a unique skill set or expertise.
- To realize cost reduction.
- To achieve crisis management.
- To bolster (or replace) in-house capabilities.
- To enjoy labor flexibility.

The most frequently cited reason for engaging a systems integrator is the need to access specific technological skills. The systems integration market is a rapidly changing market; every day someone new enters the market and someone old leaves it. Systems integration houses are sold, bought, and merged with the regularity of commodity trades. General Motors is so bullish on systems integration services that it has two: the well-known EDS and the less well known Hughes Information Technology Co.

In 1990, systems integrators made recommendations influencing the placement of more than $15 billion worth of hardware and software. Their fees for doing so exceeded $10 billion. It is therefore safe to say that for every three dollars a business spends on the gear, it is going to spend two on the systems integrator. Research conducted at the Nolan Norton Institute in the imaging market revealed a ratio of three to one: for every three dollars spent on imaging hardware/software, the user organization paid one dollar to the systems integrator.

Organizations seeking to evaluate who's who and, more important, whether a given systems integrator is right for its needs, should look closely at the supplier's roots. The framework shown in Exhibit I-4-2 depicts the basic orientation of the systems integrator (ranging from business to technological) on the y-axis and the particular functional area of expertise for which an integrator is known (e.g., strategy, implementation or facilities management) along the x-axis. A systems integrator whose basic orientation is business would be most effective in helping a client develop or plan a business strategy. On the other hand, an integrator with roots in the technology side of the industry would be a better choice if systems management and maintenance are what the organization needs help with.

The changing nature of competition has refocused management attention on the critical question of what an organization is capable of doing. A corresponding recognition has emerged that because people work best in groups, a technology strategy that seeks to connect the various parties involved in the entire business process is not only feasible but critical to the success of the enterprise.

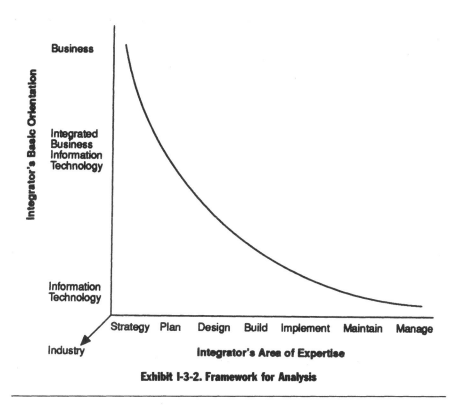

**Exhibit I-3-2. Framework for Analysis**

## SUMMARY

The evidence indicates that major resources and revenues are being allocated or generated by professional service organizations (systems integrators) seeking to provide clients with the technological component of a business solution. The industry is fragmented, with wild-eyed technologists on one side facing off against deep-thinking strategists and vertical-market specialists on the other. The market is immature and relatively unstable and still exhibits areas of inefficiency, including the use of dubious ethics, and suspicious business practices. Quality control and consistency of delivery are unsubstantiated by the activities of many systems integrators. For these reasons, it is imperative to determine how a systems integrator goes about establishing strategic direction, how it chooses and creates desired core competences, and how it allocates scarce capital to a seemingly endless array of deserving projects.

Systems integrators have become a major factor in the way organizations evaluate, fund, and implement technologies. Although they are probably one of the most important forces in the emerging information age, they are not the only force. If systems integrators are to become a constructive and valuable force, they must be driven by user organizations. Many organizations use the Greyhound school of systems integration and leave the driving to the integrators. This is perhaps the worst mistake an organization can make.

47

# I-4
# Defining End-User Computing's New Role in IS

*CHRISTINE B. TAYNTOR*

E nd-user computing departments are at a critical juncture. A decade ago they were the primary (if not the sole) sources of support for their clients' individual computing needs. With the advent of microcomputers and shrink-wrapped tools, those requirements can now be met by a host of outside consultants and vendors or sometimes even by the clients themselves. At the same time, because users have become computer literate, their needs are more sophisticated. User needs are also more demanding as corporate downsizing forces the professional staff to assume new responsibilities and increase productivity.

Technology, too, has evolved at a rate that is almost revolutionary. Small standalone microcomputers with their limited processing ability have been replaced by local area networks that can provide virtually limitless computing capacity. Clearly, the world in which end-user computing exists has changed significantly. The EUC department must adapt to the new environment and forge a new role for itself within the IS function and with clients. This chapter discusses the challenges facing the end-user computing department and suggests a blueprint for developing its expanded role.

## MASTERING NEW END-USER TECHNOLOGY

The need to harness computer technology and make it available to the organization's professional staff is the reason end-user computing departments exist. In many cases, EUC's responsibilities have evolved and expanded without any formal planning. The EUC department has the opportunity to define its functions and to reshape its role within the organization. The first step in any redefinition of technical roles is to understand the key technologies. For today's EUC department, the single most important technology is the local area network.

### The LAN Challenge

During the past few years, companies have slowly discovered and then increasingly embraced the benefits of local area network technology. The first LANs were used primarily so that individual microcomputers could share peripheral devices, especially laser printers and plotters. Because many microcomputer users also needed access to mainframes, the use of LANs soon expanded to include connectivity. Gateways provided fast, relatively inexpensive connections to the mainframe, eliminating the need for separate cabling and emulation cards.

Although LANs are valuable for these functions, their greatest benefits are derived from the exploitation of software, not the sharing of hardware. It is in this area that the EUC department can take a leadership role and promote the use of local area networks. When the EUC department understands the potential, it can educate its clients. There are three primary types of LAN software: standard microcomputer applications, groupware, and custom software.

**Standard Microcomputer Applications.** A corporation derives several benefits from the use of standard microcomputer applications on the LAN, including reduced costs. Many microcomputer applications, such as word processing, spreadsheets, and graphics, are available in LAN versions. In these installations, a single copy of the scftware is loaded on the file server, and individual microcomputers access the central copy. Out-of-pocket costs are reduced in two ways. First, individual workstation licenses, which include only documentation rather than software media, are less expensive than standalone copies. Second, because the software is loaded on the central file server rather than on the individual microcomputer's hard disks, workstations can have smaller disk drives, which represents another cost reduction.

For the EUC department, there is a third benefit: reduced support. Because the software is loaded on a single server rather than on a hundred microcomputers, the effort required for both the initial installation and subsequent upgrades is substantially reduced. Furthermore, troubleshooting is simplified because all users have the same version of the software, and there are no variations in the way it was configured. By promoting the use of LAN software loaded on the server, EUC is able to provide a consistent level of service to a larger client population without adding staff.

**Groupware.** With the growth of LANs, new types of software are being offered on the LAN platform. Although these programs go by a variety of names, collectively they can be considered groupware, because they enable teams, departments, or entire companies to work together electronically. Groupware includes electronic mail (E-mail) and calendaring software.

LAN-based groupware has gained popularity for several reasons. Cost reduction is the first. In many cases, most notably E-mail, LAN software has replaced systems previously running on a mainframe. Not only is the purchase price of this software substantially lower than a mainframe version, but the cost of running LAN applications is also less, because there are fewer overhead costs associated with LAN operations than with a typical mainframe computer room.

Cost is, however, only one reason for a company to replace its mainframe systems with LAN applications. Ease of use and greater functional capability are the others. Microcomputer software, especially applications developed for the LAN environment, has been written with the business user in mind. Graphical user interfaces, color coding of fields, online help, and simple commands make these programs much easier to use than the mainframe packages written a decade ago. From the view of EUC, the ease of use of new LAN-based systems translated into reduced effort for training and ongoing support.

**Custom Software.** As companies seek ways of reducing their systems development and support costs, many are turning into the third type of LAN software: custom software. These companies are downsizing mainframe applications and rewriting them for the LAN platform. Downsizing provides companies the opportunity to create new types of applications, using a variety of architectures. The most common are client-server applications (which place portions of the code on the individual workstation and others on the data base or file server) and distributed data bases (which store data in the locations where it is accessed most often, rather than in a centralized data base). Custom software, whether or not it is deployed on the LAN, would appear to be the sole responsibility of the applications development group, yet its creation and support raise the possibility of new roles for EUC (which are discussed in more detail later in this chapter).

## Regulating the LAN Environment

For EUC the immediate challenge of local area networks is to become their champion. There are two aspects to championship. The first is to promote the use of the new technology, instructing clients and other IS groups in the potential uses of LANs, including the implementation of the various types of software. The second, and arguably the more important, role EUC should play is to ensure that LANs are properly supported.

Connecting individual microcomputers to a LAN involves far more than the installation of a network card and some cabling. It is not just a physical change; it is a philosophical shift that mandates new roles and responsibilities. By connecting microcomputers and allowing them to share files as well as such peripherals as laser printers, LANs give individual users substantially more power. Not only can they access information that someone else created, but they can change it. Just as important, an event that occurs on one microcomputer, including the introduction of a virus, can affect every other microcomputer attached to the LAN. The microcomputer is no longer a machine for personal use alone. It has become part of the reality of corporate computing. Consequently, the microcomputer requires more support and control. This is a fundamental change, and one that EUC departments must address.

There is little controversy in ensuring that LANs receive the support they require. Most clients are glad to relinquish responsibility for such administrative tasks as backing up data and would prefer that an IS group provide system administration and performance monitoring. Recognizing that these functions are vital for the success of a LAN, the EUC department should play an active role in ensuring that they are performed regularly and professionally. In particular, backup and disaster recovery, including off-site storage of data and tests to demonstrate that the recovery procedures work, should be standardized. Although EUC may not actually perform all the support functions, at a minimum it should establish written procedures and ensure that they are followed.

Gaining acceptance for increased LAN support is relatively easy. Assuming control is not, although it is of equal importance. The challenge for EUC departments is to avoid the political pitfalls inherent in imposing control on a previously unregulated function.

Because one microcomputer can affect another in the LAN environment, it is essential to regulate all software loaded on individual workstations. This regulation includes scanning for viruses but can be extended to include determining that directory conventions are followed and that such key files as autoexec.bat and config.sys are not modified. There are three primary ways to achieve this goal.

**Attaching Diskless Workstations to the LAN.** The use of diskless workstations prevents the problem from occurring because there is no way to place software on local microcomputers. It does not, however, address the needs of corporations that have a large base of microcomputers with hard disks already attached to the LAN. For these organizations, it may not be economically feasible to replace functional microcomputers with diskless workstations.

The second disadvantage of this approach is that it ignores the issue of personal computing and assumes that all requirements can be met with a standard set of software. For many companies this is not a valid assumption. Although all departments can benefit from using a single word processor or spreadsheet, an individual department—or one person within that department—might require a unique piece of software.

**Loading Software Only on the File Server.** Although this policy requires careful monitoring, it can be effective. Its primary disadvantage is the same as for diskless workstations: the curtailment of personal computing. In addition, some software does not run effectively on network disk drives.

**Requiring Standard Software for the File Server with All Other Software Screened and Installed by EUC.** If followed, this policy resolves the need to protect the LAN from infected software and also permits individuals to use nongeneric tools. This approach also requires careful monitoring.

EUC faces a challenge when implementing any of these methods of controlling the workstations attached to the LAN. Because most companies have evolved to LANs from a collection of standalone microcomputers, professionals have often had autonomy in deciding what software they will use. It is to be expected that they will resist any organization's attempts to regulate their use of microcomputers. Before EUC institutes controls, it should gain key clients' acceptance of the policy. The EUC department must develop a business case for control, placing a monetary value on both the hardware and software and demonstrating the dangers of viruses. When client buy-in has been achieved, microcomputers should be surveyed and the software standardized. Relatively inexpensive software can be used to record the software loaded on individual workstations and to flag any unauthorized additions.

## The GUI Challenge

Another key technology for EUC to understand and exploit is the graphical user interface (GUI). Whereas LAN technology can be seen as providing the foundation for new types of software, the GUI is the framework laid on top of that foundation. For most people, GUIs are viewed as a combination of icons, mice, and windows. Others characterize GUIs as click-and-drag technology because many commands are executed in that manner.

The benefits of GUIs extend beyond imaginatively designed pictures and pointing devices. EUC should promote graphical rather than character-based applications for three basic reasons: consistency, intuitiveness, and multitasking. The first two reasons result in reduced training for subsequent graphical programs; the third can change the way clients work.

Consistency is one of the trademarks of graphical applications. Properly designed, they all work similarly. Menu bars are arranged in the same order with identical terminology, and the same mouse actions initiate identical functions. This design provides a distinct advantage over character-based software with its random use of function keys and its all too frequent use of arcane command structures. Once uses have learned that a file can be retrieved by clicking on the file option from the primary menu bar, then clicking on **open** from the pull-down menu that the first click produced, they are able to retrieve files from all graphic applications with no further training. The advantage to users is obvious.

GUIs also provide a level of intuitiveness not usually found in character-based applications. Menu keys are labeled with easily understood commands, and systems are invoked by the user's clicking on a clearly labeled icon rather than having to type a command. Combined with consistency, the intuitive nature of GUIs results in decreased training needs. After users have learned to maneuver their way through a graphical application, they are able to access other graphical programs without the need for training in the mechanics of the system. Only application-specific training is required. Because GUIs help users develop self-sufficiency, they lower users' ongoing support requirements. For the EUC department, the reduced training and support are primary benefits derived from promoting the use of graphical applications.

Multitasking, or the ability to run more than one application at the same time, is the third characteristic of GUIs that provides substantial benefits. The use of multitasking allows the client to switch from one application to another and to easily transfer data between them. This ability can change the way clients view computer systems. Instead of being tools that are used on an occasional albiet daily basis, GUI systems can become an integral part of the way clients work by permitting them to operate naturally. Because of the multitasking capability of a GUI, all applications can be open and running at the same time, eliminating the overhead of logging in and out. GUIs also simplify data exchange by allowing data to be moved between systems through a cut-and-paste process. Portions of a file can be moved far more simply than in a traditional file export-import process.

**The Value of a Standard GUI.** The challenge for EUC, then, is to understand the power of a GUI and to promote its use through client education and technical demonstrations. It is important to recognize the importance of using a single GUI and of its corollary: to ensure that all packaged software follows the interface's conventions. There are currently four popular GUIs: the Apple Macintosh, Microsoft Windows, IBM's OS/2 Presentation Manager, and UNIX X-Windows. Although there are many similarities among them, there are also differences. Because one of the primary goals of using a GUI is consistency, it is important to standardize around one interface.

A related issue that must also be considered is to evaluate all packaged software for compliance with the standard GUI. The reason once again is consistency. After a client has learned that radio buttons are round and function differently from square check boxes, it would be confusing to introduce a software product with square radio buttons; the value of the graphical interface would be reduced.

**When Not to Use GUIs.** In addition, it is important for the end-user computing department to know when not to recommend a GUI. Although the consistency of screen layouts and commands simplifies learning multiple graphical applications, there is still an initial learning curve to overcome. Moving to a graphical interface requires mastering new techniques, not the least of which is the use of a mouse. According to a study by Temple, Barker, Sloane (Lexington, MA), users require more time to learn their first graphical system than they would a comparable character-based application. For clients who will use only one package, a character-based version may be the better choice.

Similarly, if the client requires high throughput of transactions using a single application (e.g., a data entry function), a graphical interface may not be the correct choice. Even a skilled operator requires additional time to switch from the keyboard to a pointing device. In high-volume data entry, simple key-driven character-based applications have an advantage over graphical interfaces.

## MEETING CLIENT NEEDS

Clients' needs and expectations have changed throughout the years. Many companies have gone through a downsizing, reducing their clerical staff and middle-management ranks. This situation places increased pressure on the professional staff. Because the work load has not decreased, even though the number of personnel has, professionals are now expected to assume more responsibilities and to perform different types of work. More business users are keying documents rather than delegating that work to a support staff member, and they often prepare their own presentations, rather then having the graphics arts department design and produce slide presentations. Similarly, in-depth analyses that might once have been assigned to a junior analyst are frequently the responsibility of managers.

Clients' expectations have changed, too. Many clients have developed a high level of computer literacy and are aware of the latest product developments. Their children use microcomputers. They may themselves frequent software stores. In some cases, clients drive software acquisition decisions.

These changes have placed new demands on the EUC department. Technical and product knowledge remain essential. EUC must have an in-depth understanding of hardware and software products to be able to train clients and to resolve problems and questions. Increasingly, however, excellent analytical skills are needed when working with users. The successful EUC department must be able to identify its clients' true requirements and to distinguish what clients need from what they think they want.

To be fully effective, however, EUC should adopt formal analysis methods. These usually will be the same techniques that systems developers use, including such methodologies as information engineering and business requirements analysis that provide a structure for interviewing clients and outlining system requirements. The goal of these methodologies is to determine why and how functions are performed as well as what is being performed. This knowledge is essential for resolving underlying problems rather than simply addressing symptoms.

### Delivering Tools for the Business User

In addition, the EUC department must understand the difference between data and information, and it should implement tools to turn data into information. The end-user computing staff should offer clients tools with which to perform exception reporting and trend analysis and to link information from various sources. These sources include external services (e.g., market research and news services), as well as data bases created within the company.

The challenge becomes that of defining and implementing a suite of products to increase professional productivity. In the majority of cases, these tools will be LAN-based and use a GUI for integration.

The basic set of tools can be divided into three categories: reporting and analysis, communications, and personal management tools. Spreadsheets and query tools traditionally fall into the first category. Added to them is the growing class of LAN-based executive information systems (EISs). EIS software permits trend analysis, exception reporting, and drill-down capabilities to successively lower levels of detail—features that were previously available only on costly mainframe executive information systems. Reporting and analysis are classic EUC tools. What has changed is the sophistication and power of the products.

Users also require simple, reliable ways of communicating the results of that analysis. Word processing and presentation graphics have been standard microcomputer applications for almost a decade and have been the traditional method of communication. Although their importance will continue, EUC should seek products that permit the output of the reporting tools to be easily integrated without any rekeying or complex importing procedures. At the same time, other forms of communication should be added to the suite of microcomputer software. These include LAN-based electronic mail and group calendaring programs as well as fax cards and servers to allow the paperless transfer of documents.

The final category of shrink-wrapped software that should be part of the professional's portfolio is a personal management tool. Rudimentary project management systems are available to help professionals schedule and track the progress of their work. In addition, personal information managers include individual calendaring, basic data bases with flexible reporting, tools for expense reporting, and phone dialers.

After EUC has delivered a set of software to meet the user community's requirements, it can then address the specific needs of each user department. This effort demands that EUC stake a new role for itself.

## Forging New Roles With Developers and Users

If it is to remain a key contributor to the organization, the EUC department must become an integral part of the systems development process—a process that is itself undergoing change. Just as clients are placing new demands on the EUC department, they are also requiring more from the applications development staff.

Clients are demanding that new custom applications provide the same ease of use they find in shrink-wrapped software. They are, in short, asking for GUI applications. At the same time, the capabilities they demand from new systems differ from previous requirements. Static reporting and transaction processing are no longer sufficient. Clients must have systems that allow them to react quickly to changing business requirements. They must be able to combine data in constantly varying ways to perform ad hoc analyses almost instantly. This has forced the IS function to rethink the type of applications it delivers. To meet client needs and at the same time downsize applications and shift toward client-server systems, IS departments have recognized the necessity for finding new ways to develop systems. EUC can—and should—be part of this process.

CASE tools and methodologies meet some of the requirements of new systems, as does the emphasis on reusable code that allows applications to be deployed more quickly. One extension of the reusablecode concept is to incorporate shrink-wrapped software into custom applications. Instead of writing calculation routines, applications pass data to a spreadsheet. Similarly, a word processing system can be used to generate reports, with LAN-based electronic mail as the transport mechanism. When the concept of producing information rather than data is employed, only those portions of a report that are important to the user are delivered to that individual's mailbox. This approach to systems development has been pioneered in several companies and has proved to be effective in delivering accurate systems within a shortened cycle time.

Other companies have determined that the primary role of the applications developers is to create data bases, leaving actual reporting of that data to the clients. The key to the success of this approach is the selection and implementation of powerful, easy-to-use reporting and analysis tools.

Although developing applications has not been part of the traditional end-user computing department's responsibilities, EUC can play a valuable role in new systems development. Developing modern systems requires an in-depth knowledge of graphical user interfaces and shrink-wrapped software, both of which are areas of expertise for EUC rather than the applications development staff. Similarly, evaluating and implementing reporting tools has been EUC's responsibility.

The challenge for EUC is to define its role in relation to both developers and clients. In the past, clients had two IS contacts, one for office systems and personal computing, the other for custom applications. The implementation of integrated systems has blurred the line between the two groups, and sometimes clients are not certain whom to contact for a specific request. To ensure that it continues to provide a high level of service, the IS department should establish a single focal point for clients. In the attempt to choose between EUC and applications development, arguments can be made on behalf of each group. Depending on the choice, the EUC staff's role can be established in one of two ways.

**EUC as Systems Integrator.** Although this has not been EUC's traditional role, it can be postulated that new systems are nontraditional. For LAN-based applications that incorporate graphical shrink-wrapped software with custom work, EUC has the greater working knowledge of the software that the client actually uses. Assuming that this interface is of greater importance to clients than is internal processing, EUC is able to provide a level of support to the client higher than application development. If EUC serves as the primary contact, its role can be viewed as that of a systems integrator, conducting the analysis, selecting packaged software, contracting with the applications developers for the design, creation, and performance of the data base, then implementing the various pieces of the system.

**EUC as Consultant.** Holding to more traditional roles, it can be argued that the applications developers have greater design skills and a more detailed knowledge of the functions each department performs and are therefore more easily able to create systems that meet the unique needs of a user department. With the applications development group serving as the primary contact, EUC's role becomes that of a consultant, identifying shrink-wrapped packages that can be incorporated into the overall system and advising the developers on graphical systems design.

Either of these approaches can be successful, depending on the politics of the company and the strengths of the individual staff members. The key challenge for EUC is to ensure that it is an integral part of the team, whether as primary contact or as consultant. Certain basic organizational changes can speed up the integration process.

EUC should be stationed near the applications development group. Too often in the past, EUC has been viewed as a separate group with different problems and objectives. Physical proximity will help break down barriers and foster an information exchange. Similarly, occasional joint staff meetings with developers may help to underline the fact that both groups are part of IS and that they share a common goal: providing the best possible service to the client community.

## Building the Staff

To meet new client expectations, EUC must be a highly effective department with a focused set of skills. That skill set differs considerably from the one that produced successful EUC departments in the past. The future for end-user computing staff requires the development of new skills as well as a honing of existing ones. There are five types of skills that will become ever more important for EUC staff in the future.

**Hardware and Software Evaluation.** This has always been a key re-sponsibility of EUC, but there must be less emphasis on evaluating standalone products and more on integration capabilities. When evaluating software, it is important to consider how each system can be used in conjunction with the others in the portfolio. Hardware components are increasingly judged by how well they integrate into the local area network. This level of evaluation is more demanding than single-product testing because it requires a detailed understanding of all products as well as the ways they can be used together.

**Client Support and Problem Resolution.** This is another skill that has been a part of the traditional EUC staff and that continues to be important; however, problem resolution is made more complex by software products that are integrated. In addition, with the growing use of microcomputers for production systems, users have less tolerance for system outages. EUC may eventually be required to diagnose and correct problems almost instantaneously. Its problem-solving skills and ability to respond quickly must be nothing less than excellent.

**Training.** The third traditional EUC skill is training. With training, the focus has shifted from the use of character-based EUC tools to graphical systems. Two aspects of this changing focus are mechanical and functional changes. The mechanical change is from the keyboard to a mouse. When computers were introduced to managers, many of them were reluctant to learn keyboard skills. The issue nowadays is teaching them how to use another input device. EUC must be sensitive to its clients' fear of change.

Functional change is perhaps more critical. Training for the future is less concerned with the operational aspects of a system (e.g., which command to use) and instead focuses on how to use a product to resolve a business problem. Functional changes require EUC staff to have a high level of knowledge of both the software product and the client's business.

**High-Level Analysis.** If it is to play an active role in systems development, the EUC staff should develop this skill, which has not been part of its traditional skill set. The EUC staff should be given training in the techniques and tools needed to understand a function in its entirety, rather than focusing on its individual pieces. The difference is one of scope and formality.

**Formal Presentations.** This represents another new skill EUC staff must acquire if they are to be key players in future systems development. The EUC staff should develop and deliver oral and written presentations to convince clients of the need for new systems. It should also be able to assist in the development of the business case to justify those new systems. In the past, EUC has been highly effective in selling its ideas to clients through informal and one-on-one presentations. As it becomes part of the systems development team, EUC will need to change the focus of its presentation style and add formality.

## Training and Experience

After the skill set has been defined, all members of the EUC staff should be evaluated to determine how well they meet the new requirements and where they need training. An effective method of documenting the results of the evaluation is the use of a rating form similar to the one shown in Exhibit I-4-1. There are two portions of the form. Part one (Exhibit I-4-1a), which represents skills that can be quantified objectively, should be completed first by the employee then by the manager. Part two (Exhibit I-4-1b) is a subjective evaluation of an employee's skills and should be completed by the manager, then discussed with the employee.

The skills matrix that emerges becomes the input to the next step: the training and experience plan. The goal of this plan is to identify the training courses and developmental projects that are needed to close the gap between the EUC staff's current skill level and the level it will require in the future. Formal training should be coupled with specific experience in the form of developmental projects. These projects have greater value if they meet real business needs rather than being workbook or laboratory experiments.

Because EUC's role continues to evolve, building new skills should be seen as a continuing process. Needs should be evaluated periodically, and new training programs developed as part of the employee's annual review cycle. Only by ensuring that its staff remains current in key skills will EUC be effective in serving its clients.

## BLUEPRINT FOR SUCCESS

Successful EUC departments do not just happen. They are built through careful planning and the implementation of policies that are constantly refined as conditions change. In short, they are the result of successful management. This takes several forms, depending on whether EUC assumes an active role in the systems development.

### Making the Transition to Systems Developer

As EUC becomes an integral part of the systems development process, it is essential that IS management recognize potential stumbling blocks and work to eliminate them. Although a myriad of problems face EUC, there are three that require immediate action: the concerns of the applications developers, those of the clients, and most important, those of the EUC staff itself.

It is natural to expect resistance from the applications development staff as EUC products and skills become a more important part of the systems development process. This is a fundamental change that marks the first time another group has been a key player in systems development, and to the applications developers it represents a real threat. Taken to its extreme, the threat may appear to be that EUC is replacing the applications development group.

The EUC staff's concerns are just the opposite: they do not want to be seen as programmers. Their skills have traditionally centered on providing support and responding to ad hoc requests, rather than participating in a lengthy systems development process. The change from being task to project

Employee Name:_____

Title: _____

Date: _____

| Skill | Employee Rating | Manager Rating |
|---|---|---|
| Hardware and Software | | |
|   Microcomputer components (including peripherals) | | |
|   LAN components (including operating system) | | |
|   Standard software (WP, spreadsheets, etc.) | | |
|   Specialized software (department-specific) | | |
|   Other (please specify) | | |
| Training | | |
|   Formal training classes | | |
|   One-on-one training | | |
| Analysis | | |
|   Hardware and software evaluation | | |
|   Informal client needs analysis | | |
|   Formal requirements definition | | |
| Formal Presentations | | |
|   Oral presentations | | |
|   Written presentations | | |

**Notes:**

| Rating | Description |
|---|---|
| 1 | Attended course or one-year experience or less. |
| 2 | General experience using the skill—one to five years' experience. |
| 3 | Extensive experience. |
| 4 | Proficient enough to teach. |

### a. Quantifiable Skills

| Skill | Manager Rating |
|---|---|
| Client support and problem resolution | |
| Speed of resolution | |
| Accuracy of resolution | |
| Timely follow-up | |
| Clarity of communication | |
| Relationship with client department | |

**Notes:**

| Rating | Description |
|---|---|
| 1 | Unsatisfactory |
| 2 | Below expectations |
| 3 | Meets expectations |
| 4 | Exceeds expectations |
| 5 | Outstanding |

### b. Subjective Analysis

**Exhibit I-4-1. EUC Skills Rating Form**

driven is a basic one that may generate a high level of anxiety. Even though this transition takes place within IS, users are not immune to concerns. They are not certain their daily needs will be met because EUC's new responsibility may assume precedence over its other responsibilities.

## Delineating Roles

To help resolve those concerns and prevent them from becoming obstacles to the development of new systems, it is important to clearly delineate respective roles. EUC management should work with applications development managers to define the functions each group is to perform. This agreement should detail primary responsibility as well as the support roles for the two groups. Not only should this agreement be clearly communicated to both staffs, but is should be written and distributed to all staff members. Interdepartmental meetings and project teams that combine the two groups are also important steps in increasing communication and breaking down barriers.

Open communication is key with all groups, including clients. Some of their concerns can be addressed by developing a contract that establishes service levels for key functions. These would include the availability of the local area network, the response time for problems and questions, and the time required to install new software. By publishing such a contract—and adhering to it—EUC clearly demonstrates to its clients that it can continue to provide the same high level of support it has always provided, even though its role may be expanding to include nontraditional functions.

The transition to new roles and responsibilities should be viewed as an evolutionary process, but an orderly and planned one. To increase the probability of success, it should be managed like any other project. There should be a formal, written transition plan with tasks, assignments, and target dates, all of which should be monitored as carefully as any high-priority project would be. By using formal project management techniques, the change takes on a visibility and importance that informal projects lack. It also has a greater probability of success.

A high level of effective communications is essential for all EUC departments, whether or not they are assuming development responsibilities. From the view of EUC management, that communication is with four groups and takes slightly different forms with each.

**Communicating with Clients.** EUC should provide three primary types of information of its clients: specific work done for the individual department, general services EUC provides, and new product information.

All too often, clients have only a general knowledge of the services EUC has provided and therefore do not perceive the value of the work. It is important to keep clients informed of all projects the department has done for them as well as the number of help calls it has resolved. For this, periodic status reports and meetings with key clients can be useful. Although some companies issue status reports or conduct quarterly meetings, a monthly frequency may be more desirable.

An EUC newsletter can be useful in disseminating all three types of information. Success stories, highlighting specific departments' use of products, can augment status reports as well as encourage the use of those products. A newsletter is especially effective in describing the services EUC provides and can be a primary method of publicizing them. In addition, EUC frequently arranges new product demonstrations. These demos, which are usually performed by the vendor, are a key method of gaining client buy-in to new products and the latest versions of existing ones.

EUC staff must have feedback on its performance if it is to build on its strengths and correct its weaknesses. One way of obtaining this feedback is to survey clients, formally or informally, about the services EUC has provided. Some EUC departments include a report card similar to the one shown in Exhibit 1-4-2 with their status reports. Completing the forms is optional, but EUC encourages feedback (both positive and negative) from users by responding to each completed questionnaire.

**Communicating with Vendors.** Although communications with vendors are usually less formal than with clients, it is nonetheless important to keep them frequent and to ensure that they are bidirectional. EUC should apprise key vendors of its overall plans, especially as they relate to the purchase of products. In return, it should expect vendors to provide demos for clients and to brief EUC on new products as well as future product directions.

**Communicating with Applications Developers.** As roles evolve, it is increasingly important for EUC to communicate effectively with the applications development staff and to asist them in increasing their skills in working with the user community. One method of accomplishing this is to invite developers to new product demos and to include them in product evaluations. Like vendors, developers should be kept informed of overall plans. Ideally, they should be involved in developing those plans and should include EUC in formulating theirs because many of the technologies are interdependent.

**Communicating with Other EUC Staff.** The need for frequent, open communication among the EUC staff is essential when the group is faced with new challenges and a changing environment. One method of increasing communication is to institute daily briefings. These may be held at the beginning of the work day and used to recap any problems that occurred the previous day as well as to outline new plans. Although this effort can be viewed as status reporting that would benefit only the manager, the value is far greater. It provides all members of the staff with information about their department's projects, encourages team work and joint problem solving, and makes the manager easily accessible.

Like most aspects of the effective manager's job, communication demands

EUC encourages users to complete the following survey and give a frank assessment of EUC performance. Please indicate your satisfaction with EUC services by checking the appropriate box for each question.

**A. Problem Resolution**

1. Was the problem corrected the first time it was reported?
   _____Yes  _____No
   Comments:

2. If problem could not be corrected immediately, were you informed of progress?
   _____Yes  _____No
   Comments:

3. Was the consultant courteous?
   _____Yes  _____No
   Comments:

**B. Hardware and Software Installation**

1. Was all work completed on time?
   _____Yes  _____No
   Comments:

2. Was all work done correctly the first time?
   _____Yes  _____No
   Comments:

3. Was the consultant courteous?
   _____Yes  _____No
   Comments:

**C. Training**

1. Was training provided when requested?
   _____Yes  _____No
   Comments:

2. As a result of the training, can you use the system?
   _____Yes  _____No
   Comments:

3. Was the trainer courteous?
   _____Yes  _____No
   Comments:

**D. Other**

1. Did the quality of EUC's work meet your expectations?
   _____Yes  _____No
   Comments:

2. Did any member of the EUC staff perform exceptionally well?
   _____Yes  _____No
   Comments:

3. Were there any problems?
   _____Yes  _____No
   Comments:

**E. Overall Satisfaction**

Please circle the number which best represents the level of service EUC provided.

   5   Outstanding
   4   Exceeded requirements
   3   Met requirements
   2   Below requirements
   1   Unsatisfactory

**Exhibit I-4-2. Customer Satisfaction Survey**

a significant commitment of time and energy. The benefits outweigh the investment, however, because open communication is one of the prime building blocks of a successful organization.

## ACTION PLAN

Fundamental changes in the way business users view computing are inevitable as organizations make their way into the twenty-first century. The end-user computing department must take steps to address those changes. Five actions EUC departments should take are:

1. Surveying clients to determine what their future needs will be. As client departments undergo business function reengineering, it is likely that totally new systems will be required.
2. Evaluating the organization's current technology platform and determining what changes will be required to meet future needs.
3. Meeting with applications development managers to share the results of step two and to learn about their future plans.
4. Working with the applications development managers to develop the two groups' respective roles and responsibilities.
5. Providing the EUC staff with training to meet the new expectations.

# Section II
# Data Center Management

M anaging a data center has become a monumental task. Data center managers must grapple daily with issues that they did not even consider 10 years ago, and the pace continues to quicken.

At one time, the data center was considered by many corporate managers to be a sort of data factory. Requests for service were submitted and end products, usually in the form of hard-copy reports, were returned. This is no longer the case. The data center manager now faces a complex mixture of business and technical issues. Many data centers are expected to operate as profit centers. Given the diverse issues facing data center managers, this section addresses issues that are associated with the management of the data center from a business and management perspective, rather than a purely technical one.

Chapter II-1, "Cost-Effective Management Practices for the Data Center," addresses an area of increasing concern for the data center manager—keeping expenses down while meeting the growing demand of users for more services. This situation becomes a delicate balancing act for the data center manager, and one that requires a great deal of skill.

Although it is not receiving the media attention it once did, outsourcing continues to be very much a part of the data center management scene. Many data center managers find themselves in the midst of a move toward outsourcing or in the role of justifying why the data center should not be outsourced. Thus, the data center manager must be as informed as possible about the benefits and drawbacks of outsourcing. Chapter II-2, "The Outsourcing Alternative," provides an overview of the business considerations associated with outsourcing.

Senior management often is not interested in outright outsourcing of IS or data center functions, but looks to downsize the organization to reduce costs. This approach involves not only reducing personnel but changing the IS architecture from a mainframe environment to networks of file servers and microprocessors. Chapter II-3, "Downsizing Computer Resources: Planning, Implementation, and Management," provides practical guidelines for developing a downsizing plan.

As microprocessors have proliferated throughout the organization, user requests for assistance in using them and connecting them to the mainframe have soared. As a result, most IS organizations have established help desks to provide technical assistance for users. The help desk is often under the direct control of the data center manager. Although the help desk concept has been successful, maintaining its effectiveness requires a great deal of management expertise and attention. Chapter II-4, "Fine Tuning the Help Desk: Goals and Objectives," provides guidelines for ensuring that the help desk continues to be an effective and useful support tool.

During this period of rapid transition that the data center manager is facing with regard to changing technology, he or she must stay as current as possible. New definitions of technology continue to proliferate—and many of these definitions tend to blur and create confusion. In Chapter II-5, "Client/ Server vs. Cooperative Processing," the author provides a clear definition of these two emerging system approaches and some of their basic characteristics.

Although the concept of distributed computing has been around for many years now, it is perhaps being implemented on a wider scale today than ever before. Thus, it is important that the data center manager clearly understand how to manage such a computing environment. Chapter II-6, "Managing Distributed Computing," discusses ways the data center manager can establish and manage distributed architectures.

Outsourcing continues to be an area of major concern for the data center manager. Controlling costs is still a driving factor in the decision to outsource data center operations. However, there are many other considerations that must be taken into account. Chapter II-7, "Making the Decision to Outsource," discusses many of the risks, and benefits, associated with outsourcing in an effort to assist the data center manager in becoming as knowledgeable about this area as possible.

Another major area of corporate management concern today is quality. This is true not only of products that may be produced, but services that are provided as well. The data center certainly falls in the category of service provider. Thus, it is imperative that data center managers do all they can to provide consistent, first-class quality service to their customers. Chapter II-8, "Achieving Quality in Data Center Operations," provides a framework that the data center manager can use to plan and implement a quality service program.

Given the continued emphasis on increasing productivity, data center automation is still a topic of major interest to the data center manager. Many advances have been made during the past few years toward providing near-total data center automation. Chapter II-9, "Automating the Data Center" presents a nine-step plan for doing just that and can be used as a guide by the data center manager involved with or planning for a major data center automation project.

# II-1
# Cost-Effective Management Practices for the Data Center

*GILBERT HELD*

D ata center managers must maintain the highest possible level of economic efficiency in the data center. Toward this end, they must be aware of all methods for reducing data center costs. This chapter outlines the core activities and functions that together represent the major expenses in operating a data center. For each activity and function, methods to control costs are presented.

## MAJOR LINE ITEM EXPENSES

The major line item expenses associated with a typical data center are as follows:

- Staff:
  —Employees.
  —Contractor personnel.
- Hardware:
  —Capital expenses.
  —Noncapital and lease expenses.
- Software:
  —Purchases.
  —Leases.
- Maintenance.
- Utilities.
- Communications facilities.
- Supplies.

Although the expenditure for any particular line item and its percentage of total expenses varies among data centers, in aggregate these items represent between 90% and 95% of all data center expenditures.

## REDUCING STAFF COSTS

For most organizations, direct and indirect payroll expenses over time significantly exceed all other costs associated with data center operations. Thus, by using methods to limit staff costs, the manager can significantly control the cost of the center. Two of the more cost-effective methods managers should consider are a lights-out operation and downsizing.

### Lights-Out Operation

The term *lights-out* is used for an unattended data center. A lights-out operation implies an obvious reduction in staffing costs because the data center operates without personnel.

Most organizations that implement a lights-out data center restrict unattended operations to second and third shifts, when the need for manual intervention can be minimized through the use of such automation programs as job schedulers, task managers, and automated tape libraries. Even the few organizations that have implemented a third-shift lights-out data center must periodically run the data center with employees—drive heads must be cleaned, printed output has to be moved to the distribution center, and backup tapes must be transported to an off-site storage location. Nevertheless, utility programs can considerably reduce staffing needs, permitting a near lights-out operation to rapidly pay for itself through the avoidance of second- and third-shift premiums as well as through a reduction in the number of primary shift employees.

A wide selection of traditional mainframe automation software is available for purchase or leasing. Such products include applications for job scheduling, tape management, disk management, and multiple-console support utility programs.

**Job Schedulers.** A job scheduler is a utility program that allows data center personnel to define criteria, which the program then uses to queue jobs for execution. Some queues may be assigned a high priority to perform an immediate or near-immediate execution: placement in other queues may result in a deferred execution (e.g., in the evening). Job-scheduling software can perform a task previously performed by one or more data center employees.

**Tape Management Software.** This option provides a data center with a volume-tracking capability, enabling tape librarians to effectively manage hundreds, thousands, or tens of thousands of tapes and to locate and mount requested tapes rapidly.

**Disk Management Software.** This software enhances the data center's ability to allocate online storage to users and to back up data onto tapes or cartridges. In addition, some disk management storage utilities include a data compression feature, which compresses data during a tape backup operation.

For organizations with more than a few hundred tapes, disk management software is used to compress onto one tape data that would usually require the storage capacity of three or more tapes. This saving can offset the cost of the program—and probably provide even more payback.

**Multiple-Console Support.** A multiple-console support program provides large data centers with the ability to have personnel control computer operations outside the data center. Managers at an appropriate security level may be permitted to use their terminals or access the computer through a microcomputer, enabling them to assign priority to jobs and perform other functions.

**LAN Administration.** In addition to its applicability to data center operations, a lights-out operating philosophy is applicable to the corporate local area network (LAN). Third-party programs can automate many key LAN functions, such as initiating file backup operations of each server on the network at predefined times.

## Downsizing

The four major expenses associated with staffing a data center are:

- The number of employees and their pay rates.
- Contractor support.
- Overtime.
- Shift operations and differential pay.

For most organizations, the number of employees directly supporting data center operations and their pay rates and benefits represent the largest staff expense. Some organizations have outsourced all or a portion of data center operations either to reduce costs or to obtain an experienced pool of employees at locations where the hiring of data processing personnel is difficult. As an alternative to outsourcing, downsizing data center operations is a practical method of controlling or reducing staffing expenses.

With a downsizing strategy, a company encourages employees reaching retirement age to leave the company. A fraction of these employees are replaced by younger, lower-paid personnel. This method reduces considerably direct personnel expenses. However, the IS manager must consider that many of those employees urged to retire early represent a pillar of knowledge and experience: the manager may not find it practical to lose this resource. Thus, most managers may wish to take a close look at productivity tools, contractor support, overtime, and shift operations in the quest to control staffing expenses.

**Productivity Tools.** In addition to those automation tools previously mentioned to achieve a near lights-out operation, there are hundreds of programs for automating operations on platforms ranging from mainframes to LAN servers.

An automation tool replaces a repetitive process by automating its operation. As a result of the tool's use, employee productivity increases or fewer employees are needed to perform an activity. By comparison, a productivity tool allows an employee to perform a job more efficiently; it is not designed to replace a repetitive process.

For example, a remote control software program allows a LAN administrator to access and control networks at other corporate locations. One administrator can control multiple networks at different geographical locations as if the administrator's personal computer were locally attached to each network. The productivity tool is used to extend the span of control of employees and provide a mechanism to control more cost-effectively distributed networks. Similarly, remote control software products, such as Hewlett-Packard's series of distributed systems control programs, allow a central site operator to control the operation of minicomputers at distributed data centers, thereby reducing the need to hire additional operational staff. In both these examples, the operations are random processes and the productivity tool extends the operational capability of an employee, but it does not replace the process.

**Contractors.** For most organizations, contractor support provides a level of expertise not available from in-house employees. Because most contractor employees are billed at an annual salary level that is 30% to 50% higher than employee salary levels, eliminating or minimizing the use of this resource can result in significant savings. One way to eliminate or reduce the use of contractor personnel is to identify the skills they employ that are not available from current employees. The data center manager can review the records of employees to determine whether they are capable of learning the skills employed by contractor personnel. If so, the manager could contemplate having employees take the appropriate vendor courses and attend public seminars to acquire the previously contractor-supplied skills. Once employees obtain adequate skill levels, they can work with contractor employees for awhile to obtain on-the-job training, eventually phasing out contractor support.

**Overtime.** By controlling overtime and shift operations, the data center manager may also be able to maintain data center operations within budget. Overtime usually begins as a mechanism to perform a necessary operation, such as extending shift coverage to support the testing of new software or a similar function. Without appropriate controls, it becomes easy for employees to request and receive permission to use overtime to substitute for sick, vacationing, or otherwise absent workers. All too often, overtime use expands significantly and can become the proverbial budget buster. Such alternatives to overtime as compensatory time should be considered. These alternatives can eliminate or reduce the use of overtime.

**Shift Operations.** Shift operations not only require the use of additional employees but involve premium pay rates through shift differentials. Controlling shift operations can significantly contain personnel costs. Possible methods of reducing shift operations include:

- Obtaining additional processing and peripheral device capacity to finish jobs.
- Altering the job flow mixture to execute jobs that do not require operator intervention after the prime shift.
- Requiring nonprime shift jobs to be executed on specific days and at specific times.

## HARDWARE COSTS

Over the life cycle of a computer system, its hardware cost typically represents the second or third largest expenditure of funds. Controlling the cost of hardware is a means for the data center manager to maintain expenditures within budget.

### Capital and Noncapital Expenses

Most organizations subdivide hardware expenditures into capital and noncapital expenses. Capital expenses must be depreciated over a period of years even though they are paid on acquisition. Noncapital hardware expenses can be written off during the year the equipment is acquired; however, the current limit for this category of hardware is $10,000. Because most hardware expenditures exceed this limit, this chapter discusses hardware that is capitalized.

There are several practical methods for controlling the cost of capitalized equipment. These methods include:

- Obtaining plug-compatible peripherals to satisfy peripheral expansion requirements.
- Using a lease to minimize one-time expenditures of new equipment additions.
- Buying used equipment to satisfy some or all of the data center's processing and peripheral expansion requirements.
- Platform reduction.

The major risk in acquiring used equipment is the availability and cost of maintenance. If availability of maintenance is not a problem and cost is reasonable, employing used equipment can considerably reduce equipment costs.

**Platform Reduction.** Platform reduction refers to downsizing to client/server technology to replace conventional mainframe and minicomputer-based applications. The rationale for considering a platform reduction is economics. A 486-based server can operate at 30 millions of instructions per second (MIPS) for a fraction of the cost of an equivalent MIPS mainframe. Of course, previously developed applications must also be moved off the mainframe, which is not a trivial task. Organizations with extensive mainframe applications can require anywhere from 18 months to two or more years to move a series of mainframe applications to client/server technology. The additional expense of moving applications to a new platform includes a period in which many programmers are no longer available to enhance existing applications because their primary effort is focused on program conversion. The most successful platform reduction efforts involve an orderly migration of applications or the successful replacement of mainframe applications with client/server applications.

*Example.* An organization has an IBM 3090E supporting 300 employees using Lotus 1-2-3/M, WordPerfect, a CICS application, and PROFS for electronic mail. The mainframe versions of 1-2-3 and WordPerfect can be replaced by equivalent and more functional client/server products. PROFS can be replaced by one of 10 or more LAN E-mail programs. Thus, only the customized CICS application requires a conversion effort.

An orderly migration to client/server technology may entail installing the network, training employees to use the LAN, loading the ready-made client/server programs, and providing any additional user training. The conversion of the customized CICS applications to run on the client/server platform would be planned to coincide with the end of this transition effort. Such planning minimizes the time required to move to a new computing platform. In addition, such a plan would enable the organization to expediently cancel mainframe software licenses and maintenance service that for a 3090E can range between $10,000 and $25,000 a month. An expeditious and orderly migration to a new computing platform can have a considerable financial impact on the organization's bottom line.

## SOFTWARE COSTS

Line item expenses associated with software are generally subdivided into purchase and lease products. For example, a data center's computer operating system and utilities may be available only on a lease basis, whereas application programs may be available for purchase only.

### Leasing and Purchasing

The data center manager should be aware that many mainframe products are priced on a monthly lease basis. The expense of leasing for 30 months usually equals the cost of purchasing the product. Excluding the potential interest earned on the difference between the expense associated with an immediate purchase and the lease of software, the organization should generally purchase any software product that it anticipates using for more than 30 months. If it purchases such a product, the organization will begin to accrue savings on the software after using it for 30 months. The savings cumulatively increase each month the product is used after this break-even point.

## Multiple Processors

Another area in which data center managers can control software costs involves multiple-processor data centers. Because most computer manufacturers charge a monthly fee for each product use site, based on the number and types of computers the product operates on, reducing production installation to one or a few computers can provide savings.

For example, a data center with multiple IBM 3090 processors uses CICS and PROFS as well as other IBM software products. If multiple copies of each software product were licensed to run on each processor, the software licensing fee would significantly exceed the licensing fee charged for running CICS on one processor and PROFS on the second processor. In this case, it might be beneficial to establish a cross-domain network to enable users to access either processor from a common front-end processor channel attached to each 3090 computer system.

For client/server applications, the financial savings possible from obtaining LAN-compliant software rather than individual copies of a product can be considerable. For example, a data base program that is sold for $499 on an individual basis may be obtained as a network-compliant program capable of supporting 50 concurrent users for $1,995. The data center manager should examine the different types of PC software licenses and the cost of individual versus LAN licenses.

## MAINTENANCE

The data center manager can control hardware maintenance through:

- Third-party maintenance.
- Conversion of on-site to on-call support.
- Replacing old equipment with newer, more sophisticated products.

Although savings from the use of third-party maintenance and the conversion of on-site to on-call maintenance support are relatively self-explanatory, the topic of reducing expenditures by replacing old equipment with more sophisticated products requires some elaboration.

Most computer manufacturers guarantee the availability of spare parts for hardware for a specified time, such as five years from product introduction. After that time, spare parts may or may not be available from the original equipment manufacturer. If not, the organization may be forced to pay inflated prices for spare parts from third-party equipment vendors to prolong the life of aging hardware. In addition, monthly maintenance fees are usually based on the age of hardware, with maintenance costs rising as equipment life increases. At a certain point, it becomes more economical to purchase or lease newer equipment than to pay rising maintenance costs that can exceed the monthly lease and maintenance cost of the newer equipment.

As for software maintenance costs, most vendors price maintenance according to the numbers and types of computers on which their software product operates. The data center manager can control software maintenance cost by following the suggestion previously discussed for software—reducing the number of products used by dedicating specific processors to specific functions, instead of running copies of the same product on each processor.

## UTILITIES AND CONSERVATION PRACTICES

Conservation is a practical method for controlling the cost of data center operations. Two of the most practical utility costs over which a data center manager may have significant control are water and electricity.

If the data center processors use chilled water for cooling, the manager should stipulate that the water be recirculated. Not only does recirculation reduce the organization's water bill, it also reduces the electric bill and possibly even the sewage bill. After chilled water is used for processor cooling, the water temperature is usually below that of natural water. Therefore, a smaller amount of energy is required to recool the used water than to chill new water. Because many cities and counties bill sewage charges on the basis of the amount of water consumed, recirculating chilled water also reduces water consumption.

### Equipment Replacement

The cost of operating old equipment usually exceeds that of more sophisticated products designed to use very large scale integration (VLSI) circuitry. For data center configurations with front-end processors, disk drives, and mainframes that run 24 hours a day, seven days a week, the cost of electricity can be significant. By examining equipment for components that consume an inordinate amount of energy, performing an operational cost analysis, and replacing equipment when justified, the data center manager may realize considerable operational cost savings.

**Examples.** A data center is located in a large metropolitan area, such as New York City or Los Angeles, where the cost of electricity can easily exceed 10 cents per kilowatt-hour (kWh).

Some front-end processors manufactured in the mid-1980s consume 15,000 watts per hour, whereas more modern equipment using VLSI circuitry may require 3,500 watts per hour. Because most front-end processors run continuously except during upgrading or periodic maintenance, they consume power 24 hours a day, 350 days a year—or 8,400 hours a year. If a front-end processor consumes 15,000 watts of electricity per hour, it uses 126,000 kilowatts of power per year (15,000 watts × 8,400 hours/year). At a cost of 10 cents per kWh, the cost of providing power to the processor is $12,000 per year.

A newer front-end processor that consumes 3,500 watts of electricity per hour, costs $2,940 per year to run, or $9,600 less. Over the typical five-year life of most front-end processors, the extra cost of electrical consumption of the older processor would exceed $48,000. This cost by itself would probably not justify acquiring new equipment. However, considered in tandem with the excess maintenance costs associated with older equipment, this alternative could provide sufficient savings to justify the acquisition of new equipment.

As another example, such laser printer manufacturers as Hewlett-Packard, IBM, and others are developing a standard for a dual-mode laser printer. They recognize that laser printers usually are powered on throughout the day but actively print for only a short period. Energy-efficient laser printers have a standby mode of operation that can reduce power consumption considerably: these savings are especially meaningful in areas where the cost of electricity exceeds 10 cents per kWh.

## COMMUNICATIONS

If the data center provides computational support for remote locations, the data center manager should consider analyzing its expenditures for voice and data communications. Depending on the number of remote locations and traffic volumes between those sites and the data center, the manager may find several methods to control the organization's communications cost. Two of the more practical methods are the development of a T1 backbone network and negotiation of a Tariff 12 agreement.

### T1 Backbone Network

A T1 backbone network permits voice and data to share transmission on high-speed digital circuits. A T1 circuit provides the capacity of 24 voice-grade channels at a monthly cost of approximately 8 voice channels. If the organization's voice and data traffic requirements between two locations exceed 8 individual voice lines, T1 circuits can significantly reduce the cost of communications.

### Tariff 12 Negotiations

This tariff enables organizations with large communications requirements to negotiate special rates with AT&T and other communications carriers. According to vendors' information, discounts in excess of 50% have been obtained for multiyear contracts with a value of $5 million to $10 million per year. For organizations with communications requirements that do not justify Tariff 12 negotiations, savings may still be achieved with regard to each carrier providing service between the organization's remote locations and its data center. In addition to investigating AT&T, MCI Communications Corp., and US Sprint, the manager may wish to examine the cost of transmission facilites of such alternative local access carriers as Metropolitan Fiber Systems of Chicago, which provides local access to long-distance carriers in more than 50 cities throughout the US. The choice of this alternative may permit the manager to reduce the cost of the organization's local and long-distance communications.

## SUPPLIES

One of the most overlooked areas for controlling the cost of data center operations is consumable supplies. Most consumable supplies are purchased repeatedly throughout the year. The data center manager can reduce the cost of these supplies by grouping the requirements of several departments, consolidating expenditures on a monthly or quarterly basis to purchase larger quantities of needed supplies. This action typically results in a decrease in the unit cost per 100 disks, per cartons of 1,000 sheets of multipart paper, and similar supplies.

Another technique is forecasting supply requirements for longer periods. For example, purchasing multipart paper on a quarterly basis instead of each month may reduce both the per-carton cost of paper and shipping charges.

## SUMMARY

This chapter describes several practical actions data center managers can consider to control data center costs. Although only a subset of these actions may be applicable to a particular data center, by considering each action as a separate entity the manager can effectively consider the cost of many line items that cumulatively represent the major cost of operating a data center. This process is a helpful way to review current expenditures and serves as a guide to the various options for containing or reducing data center operations costs. In an era of budgetary constraints, such cost-control actions can only increase in importance to all managers.

# II-2
# The Outsourcing Alternative

*JOHN P. MURRAY*

M any organizations have begun to take an interest, ranging from mild to enthusiastic, in outsourcing. The need to reduce expenses, coupled with the opportunity to rid the organization of at least some aspects of the IS function, can be a powerful incentive to company executives to seriously consider outsourcing. The increased interest in the topic among clients and vendors ensures that data center managers can expect to spend more time dealing with the issue in some form in the future.

In some instances, outsourcing may improve the inadequate performance of certain IS functions, or it may offer opportunities to cut expenses. For example, the current marketing efforts of many of the leading outsourcing vendors are focused on the data center because the data center expense is a large and highly visible item. The data center is, however, by no means the only candidate for outsourcing. Systems development and integration work is outsourced by some organizations.

Correctly managed, outsourcing may improve IS operations, customer service, and credibility. However, the organization considering outsourcing should think about the potential long-term effects that can result from turning over control of the business's various IS functions—or even the entire function—to outside managers.

An organization's sudden interest in outsourcing may, in some cases, be indicative of a more basic problem or set of problems in the organization. Whatever the issues are that prompt management to look at the outsourcing alternative, an object analysis of the source of the problem is in order. Pinpointing the problem source may present opportunities to make improvements in the organization and, in the process, perhaps eliminate the need for outsourcing.

## THE LONG-TERM EFFECTS OF OUTSOURCING

A typical justification for outsourcing is that a particular IS function does not appear to be an integral part of the business. Management questions the efficacy of devoting scarce resources and management effort to a function that can be fulfilled more effectively and less expensively by an outside vendor.

Although this promise of more efficient service at reduced cost is appealing, outsourcing is more complex than is readily apparent. Organizations frequently enter outsourcing agreements without proper analysis and thought.

In some situations, outsourcing is at best a short-term solution to a long-term problem. If an organization begins to outsource for the wrong reasons, its mistake may not be realized for several years. Even if the mistake does become apparent relatively early, the customer probably has little recourse other than to abide by the outsourcing contract. The option of disputing the contract is likely to be an expensive proposition.

The long-term effects of any outsourcing agreement—no matter how appealing—must be carefully considered. The organization should examine the realistic business implications of removing the functions from its direct control. Again, these effects may not be immediately apparent and may not even surface for some time; however, the possible long-term implications of

---

**Pros**

- The organization is relieved of the responsibility for management of those IS functions that are taken over by the outsourcing vendor.
- The outsourcing agreement should reduce expenses for the organization, at least in the near future.
- If carried out selectively, the outsourcing arrangement allows the IS department to concentrate on the most critical issues in the organization. The sections requiring less high-level expertise (e.g., technical support and the data center) can be relegated to the outsourcing vendor, allowing the in-house IS staff to focus on applications development concerns.
- The outsourcing contract can generate some revenue for the organization indirectly, through the sale of data center assets (e.g., disk drives and the mainframe).
- The contract provides an opportunity to reduce the IS department head count.

**Cons**

- Outsourcing removes some control of the information processing function from the IS department, which could seriously affect that department's mission-critical functions.
- The short-term savings provided by the outsourcing contract could be negated in the future, should the organization decide to reintegrate the outsourced function.
- The outsourcing vendor may not feel obligated to keep the outsourced function up to date and may use outdated technology to save money.
- Outsourcing can create morale problems in the IS department, particularly if in-house employees begin to fear that their function will be outsourced as well.
- Any contingency not addressed in the original agreement must be renegotiated. Post-contract negotiations are likely to be troublesome and costly for the client.
- Vendor stability cannot be guaranteed.
- Predicting the future of an organization is at best difficult, and predicting the effects of a current outsourcing contract on the basis of unknown future changes is even more difficult.
- Hidden agendas can create a disadvantageous situation for the unwary client. The organization should exercise extreme caution when examining an outsourcing contract, paying special attention to possible ulterior motives on the part of the vendor.

**Exhibit II-2-1. Outsourcing Pros and Cons**

outsourcing, including all the disadvantages, must be acknowledged. Exhibit II-2-1 summarizes the pros and cons of outsourcing that must be fully explored before the contract is signed.

One pitfall for many organizations is that a smooth marketing effort aimed at the highest level of the organization can create a climate in which decisions are made without an understanding of their practical ramifications. To forge an effective and appropriate outsourcing arrangement or to find alternative solutions for organizational problems, the decision-making process must involve those directly affected by the outsourcing. Toward this end, the IS staff must contribute actively to the solution of the problem at hand, whether or not the final scheme involves outsourcing.

## THE MANAGEMENT ISSUES

Although outsourcing may seem the logical solution for cost-related problems, other measures to resolve problems can be taken before outsourcing becomes a necessity. For example, facing up to the issue of poor management in the data center (or any other IS function) and taking the appropriate action to strengthen management may be a much better solution in the long term than outsourcing. Outsourcing should not be undertaken as a reaction to poor management in the IS department.

Furthermore, sometimes the problems associated with the performance of the IS function have more to do with factors outside the department than within it. There may be a lack of interest in and attention to the function at the senior management level. The difficulty may stem from strong resistance to change on the part of the departments the IS function is attempting to serve. In short, the causes of dissatisfaction with information processing may be beyond the control of IS management. If that is the case, it is questionable that the introduction of outsourcing will bring about much in the way of improvement.

Under certain conditions, however, outsourcing may prove to be the most efficient solution to an organization's information processing needs. For example, an organization may find itself with a growing backlog of requests to make enhancements to existing production systems. If the level of both technical and business knowledge is so low within the IS department that little or no progress can be made without a dramatic increase in staff, the organization may discover that the most it can do is move to a set of packages that would eventually replace the existing systems.

Managing both a greatly accelerated maintenance effort and the movement to a portfolio of new packaged systems to run a large portion of the business would require additional talent. In this example, outsourcing the enhancement backlog may clear the way for movement to the new systems with the existing staff. Therefore, IS managers should realize that outsourcing is not inherently detrimental to the IS department.

## The Role of IS Management

Developing a knowledge of outsourcing issues sufficient to be able to present relevant issues to senior management in a businesslike manner is only part of the IS management team's responsibility. The team must also be able to formulate a plan to address those issues that an outsourcing contract proposes to solve. If IS management perceives that the improvements targeted by outsourcing can be addressed in-house the team must be prepared to provide workable alternatives to the outsourcing contract.

The vendor, who wishes to capture an organization's outsourcing business, will likely talk about the issues of service levels and problem and change control. The members of the IS management team must also be able to address these issues.

Because many organizations may not view IS as a mainstream business function, IS managers must be prepared to counteract this attitude from senior management. The IS function is indisputably critical to the business; relinquishing control of the function, no matter how attractive it might appear to the organization's business managers, must be approached with caution.

Senior management may see the role of IS management, in light of the outsourcing decision, as a purely defensive stance. Although this may not be the case, objections raised by IS managers can appear to be protectionist. To overcome this hurdle, the IS group must build the strongest and most realistic case possible, which it should present in an unemotional manner. If outsourcing does not make sound business sense, that case should be developed and presented; conversely, if aspects of outsourcing are appropriate and in the best interests of the organization, they should be recognized.

## Developing a Counterplan for Keeping IS In-House

When building a case against outsourcing, the marketing and business skills of IS managers will be tested to the extent that they find themselves dealing with experienced sales and marketing people who have probably negotiated contracts in the past. The IS department might, given the staff's relative inexperience, consider using an outside party to help present its case. A consultant to assist in the development of the case can bring a different perspective to the issues. In addition, someone with strong marketing skills could be particularly effective in convincing the organization's senior management to retain the work within the IS department.

It is in the best interest of IS management to develop a plan for those areas in which outsourcing seems inappropriate. Outsourcing may prove to be more beneficial in some sections of the department than in others, yet decisions about these areas should also be made by the installation's management, not by an outside party. This is particularly important the outside party has a vested interest in the outcome.

## Presenting the Alternatives to Outsourcing

A plan to improve efficiency by keeping IS work in-house should include a strategy to address the issues that have been identified. The scope of this effort must be stated in order to understand what needs to be accomplished on the part of senior management. Each component of the plan must be assigned a priority so that those pertaining to the business issues can be addressed immediately. Details must be provided about the required human resources and other expenses required to accomplish the plan's goals. A schedule that is based on the items identified and the priorities assigned in the plan should also be devised to lay out what is to be accomplished and when.

When this preliminary work has been completed, IS management should present its plan to senior management. The IS management team must assure senior management that it can deliver what is required and acknowledge that its performance is to be measured against what it has proposed in the plan. IS management must further commit to specific objectives developed as a result of the issues identified. Some examples of objectives might include:

- A reduction of information processing expense (e.g., of 3% of the existing budget) without a reduction in current processing service levels to be implemented within six months of approval of the plan.
- The establishment of a joint application development ( JAD) process to improve the manner in which applications systems are developed and implemented to take effect within four months of the plan's approval.
- The establishment of a set of well-defined customer service levels for the data center operation. This could include:
  —Network response time goals.
  —A reduction of total production jobs rerun in a month to a certain percentage of all production jobs.
  —Improved response time to all help desk calls and the resolution of 95% of all calls within five working days.
- The installation of a concise applications project management and reporting and control system to identify all approved projects, their completion dates, and current status.

If, after examining the conditions that have created the need for improvement, outsourcing is judged to be the most effective solution, specific decision points should be developed so that a series of tests can be concluded throughout the vendor selection process, both to define how specific items are to be addressed and to determine whether the answers provided by the vendors are adequate and realistic. The success of the outsourcing venture depends more on the management and negotiation skills of the customer than those of the vendor. Everything must be in writing, clearly spelled out and fully understood by all the parties to the agreement.

## OUTSOURCING TECHNICAL SUPPORT

In many instances, a reasonably strong case can be built to support outsourcing IS technical support. Although this function is important to the continuing operation of the business, its operations do not have to be performed entirely by the organization's employees or conducted wholly on site at the particular location. In addition, there is usually a limited business relationship to the function. The work is technical and is, with limited variation, the same in all organizations.

There are sound business reasons for considering outsourcing the technical support function. Technical support personnel, who are expensive, can be difficult to find and retain. Because of the common characteristics of the work within the structure of a particular operating system, the skills of the individuals are readily transferable. In addition, because much of the work can be accomplished from a remote location, having several people on site may be unnecessary.

Three factors that should be considered when an organization contemplates outsourcing technical support are training, service, and control.

### Training

Because effectively managing the technical support section is difficult for many organizations, transferring the function to an agency with the appropriate management skill and experience could prove to be a sound decision. Training is expensive and must be ongoing to remain current with the changing technology. Some organizations, unwilling to make the required training investment, allow the technical support function to lag behind; consequently, morale suffers because employees are not able to continually upgrade their skills.

### Improved Service

In addition to the more obvious benefits of reduced cost and simplification of the associated personnel issues, outsourcing can improve service levels. If the chosen outsourcing vendor has a competent and experienced staff, these staff members will introduce new techniques and approaches. Extensive experience with several organizations is a factor that should recommend a vendor to an organization.

### Assigning Control

If an organization decides to outsource its technical support function, it should consider the issue of ultimate control over the function's operations. Although technical support is not a mainstream business function, the decisions regarding the use of technology cannot be made outside the organization. The vendor should be encouraged to offer suggestions and present proposals, but final decision-making authority must remain with the IS staff. To meet this need, some members of the IS department must stay current with developments in the operating software world. As an alternative, an independent consultant could be engaged to periodically review the work plans of the technical support outsourcing vendor. Control, regardless of the function being outsourced, must be recognized as a prime consideration. Relinquishing control could pose serious problems for the organization.

If the vendor retains too much power, the consequences of the contract can be disastrous to the organization. Discovering that control resides in the inappropriate hands after an agreement has been reached will not help the organization much. If all power is held by the outsourcer, it may prove difficult and expensive to raise the levels of service provided by the vendor. Particularly in the context of data center outsourcing, which is discussed later in this chapter, the contract must be regarded as a long-term arrangement.

## UNDERSTANDING THE OUTSOURCING AGREEMENT

If an organization decides to further explore an outsourcing arrangement with an outside vendor, it should take every precaution to safeguard its operations against all possible contingencies. Although most vendors want to render high levels of service to their outsourcing customers, they may hesitate to raise issues that might jeopardize their chances of obtaining a contract. In addition, they are not likely to raise issues that will make management of the contract more difficult after it has been signed. The customer therefore must be attentive, careful, and knowledgeable. The burden to protect the organization rests with the organization, not with the vendor.

### Contract Negotiations

Members of the IS management team who may become involved in the negotiations with outsourcing vendors must perform the necessary detail work to develop the best contract. Nothing should be left to chance: anything that can affect the processes involved in the outsourcing contract must be analyzed, and the implications resulting from actions with regard to these processes must be clearly understood. After these areas have been identified, the contract should be written to preclude future problems. This can be an onerous task, but it is necessary.

Should a dispute arise, the vendor will rely on the language of the contract to settle the debate. IS managers cannot rely on a handshake or a verbal agreement to work out the details at a later date. Usually, after an agreement has been reached, the original vendor representatives are replaced by technical or operations managers. These managers have a different perspective and set of interests from those of the salesperson; as a result, the relationship between the organization and the vendor may change. During the negotiating stage, IS managers must consider all the details and ensure that all conditions are stated in writing.

All too often, organizations make decisions in response to strong sales pressure from vendors. There are many instances of sales made at some level above the IS department—these situations frequently become IS nightmares. Even sales made at the IS department level can ultimately deliver much less than the original agreement seemed to promise. Caution in these areas must be exercised by both business and IS management.

The organization should consider seeking assistance outside the managerial group when examining the outsourcing contract. Consulting legal counsel and seeking outside assistance from another organization are actions that can significantly help preclude contract problems.

**Legal Expertise.** To avoid disadvantageous situations caused by unclear wordings or legal loopholes, the organization's attorneys should carefully review the outsourcing contract before proceeding with the agreement. IS managers should not ignore the legal expertise provided by these attorneys, which is to their benefit to follow.

**Outside Assistance.** The organization should ensure that the contract is formulated so that the vendor can deliver the services promised in the agreement and earn a profit. If the vendor, whether through inexperience or some other reason, has agreed to conditions that do not allow it to cover necessary costs, the vendor may renege on the stated services in the future. Organizations would be well advised to consider consulting someone with experience in outsourcing contracts to avoid creating this situation. Although every contingency cannot be anticipated, taking this precaution is a prudent approach.

## OUTSOURCING THE DATA CENTER

When an organization seriously considers outsourcing its data center, one crucial aspect of the contract is the way in which service levels will be set and monitored. Another important point is determining what will occur in the event of a dramatic change in the work load or setup of the data center. The organization must also ensure that the contract addresses outsourcing fees. These and other considerations are discussed in the following sections.

### Setting and Monitoring Data Center Service Levels

The question of service levels to be rendered by the outsourcing contract has a decided impact on the efficacy of the data center. The organization should determine what penalties, if any, to charge if the outsourcing arrangement fails to meet the agreed-on service levels. An organization that has a set of service levels in place that it is working to strengthen may be managed well enough to determine its own service levels. By contrast, organizations without an adequate understanding of service levels may be at the mercy of the vendors in defining the data center's performance standards.

If an organization has not clearly defined its own service requirements, it may encounter difficulty in its dealings with the vendor. The vendor's presentations concerning service levels and the benefits the vendor can provide will likely sound appealing to senior-level executives of the business. When these promises of improvement are coupled with the ability to reduce data center expense, the interest of the business executives will be heightened. A vendor who presents a contract without defining service levels implies the absence of problem-tracking and change-control agreements. In this case, a business executive who is unfamiliar with data center operations may perceive such agreements as offering considerable savings in hardware maintenance charges. The organization should beware of such agreements, which are usually much more desirable in theory than in practice.

## Anticipating Changes in Data Center Work Load

The organization should define the effects of a change in the work load of the data center on the outsourcing fee. The organization must determine whether (and by how much) the outsourcing fee will be affected by an increase or a decrease in the load.

Similarly, the organization should ask who will define the work load and the criteria for determining the change in fees. In addition, it is important to ascertain whether the appropriate fees have been clearly addressed in a schedule or left for later consideration. These factors must be clearly understood and discussed before the contract is signed because they may make the difference between the organization's receiving a fair amount of services for the fees charged and paying too much. Senior management must recognize the inherent risk connected with a dramatic work load increase in the data center processing schedules. Although an increased work load will most likely be accommodated by the outsourcer, it is not advisable to allow the vendor to determine the increases in the charges, especially on an ad hoc basis.

For example, an insurance company with an outsourcing agreement in place decides to expand to three new states in the following year. This change is estimated to increase the online processing load by 30% and the batch processing load by 15%. If such a situation has not been anticipated and adequately addressed in the contract, a difficult condition may arise—although the new states may be accommodated, the organization may have no choice but to process the work generated by these states through the outsourcing vendor.

Given the scenario, in which the circumstance has not been thought out in advance and covered in the contract, the vendor controls the important decisions concerning the organization's information processing operations. Even if the outcome is of no particular consequence, the inherent risk is too great to leave to chance.

## Controlling Fee Increases

The organization should ensure that the contract contains a provision to cap annual increases in outsourcing fees. An organization cannot expect to retreat from any type of outsourcing agreement—and data center outsourcing in particular—without undertaking some expense. The vendor is going to take steps to protect itself against the effects of inflation; the organization must likewise guard against inordinate or inappropriate expenses that are left to the vendor's discretion.

## Provisions for Downsizing the Data Center

Radical equipment changes and downsizing efforts can wreak havoc in an organization when plans are not made before the contract is signed. Downsizing deserves considerable thought.

Many people working in mainframe environments have strong feelings against downsizing, a sentiment that is based largely on the fear of losing their jobs. That concern, though perhaps unjustified, is understandable. Downsizing is nonetheless becoming increasingly popular, particularly as an expense-reduction strategy, and should be recognized as a possible eventuality. The organization should ask questions regarding the possible need to move to a new hardware platform and who makes the decisions about the equipment. The organization should question whether it will have the option to downsize and, if so, at what cost. The vendor's experience in downsizing should be determined as well as any possible ulterior motives. The vendor may be unenthusiastic about downsizing if the move is not in the vendor's best interest.

For the outsourcer, a downsizing effort is likely to be attractive as a means to reduce outsourcing costs. However, if the organization does not want the outsourced function to be downsized and the outsourcing vendor disagrees with the decision, the organization may find itself at the mercy of the vendor.

Senior management must be made aware that moving to a different hardware platform, whether a different vendor or smaller hardware, is by no means a small or risk-free task. If the outsourcer decides arbitrarily to make such a move, the consequences to the organization could be unfortunate. Unless the contract is very clear in this area, the majority of the risk is going to rest with the customer, not with the outsourcer. For example, a contract may state only that the vendor will provide information processing hardware sufficient to accommodate the processing requirements of the customer. Further, the contract may contain a clause stating that the customer is liable for any expense incurred by the vendor's decision to convert to different equipment. It is the responsibility of each organization to safeguard against such incidents by thoroughly examining its situation and the outsourcing contract.

## Use of Old Technology

Should the vendor propose to use old equipment to cut costs, the client must be able to determine whether such a change will be advantageous to the organization. It can be argued that the outsourcer is seeking to fatten profits by continuing to use old technology well past its useful life. In such an event, the customer could end up having to depend on a collection of obsolete and inefficient equipment.

In addition, there are competitive considerations. The continued use of obsolete technology might preclude the organization from entering new business areas or being able to match competitors' new product or service offerings. The expense of upgrading the technology might turn out to be prohibitive, regardless of the benefits to be derived.

Another issue has to do with the particular vendor chosen for the process. Some hardware vendors who have entered the outsourcing business may require that clients use their products. Such a contract could require that any and all subsequent hardware (and software, if applicable) decisions about the course of growth or change be based on the vendor's products. This may or may not be acceptable to the organization; however, the ramifications must be carefully weighed.

## REINTEGRATING OUTSOURCED RESOURCES

In some instances, an organization may need to bring an outsourced function back into the organization. This contingency should be acknowledged and planned for during the initial contract considerations. Because outsourcing is a service in which the vendors usually have more experience than their customers, IS departments that outsource often fall into difficult situations caused—at least partially—by their incomplete understanding of the implications of entering a contract. For example, the vendor, in an attempt to obtain business, might underbid a contract, which it later finds itself unable to honor, or a vendor may after some time decide to withdraw from the outsourcing business because it no longer seems practical.

In addition, an organization's circumstances change. What effect will the old contract have on the newly changed organization? The majority of outsourcing contracts being written today require long-term commitments, and it is difficult to predict changes in an organization's configuration in five or six years—not to mention in a decade or more.

### A Lesson from the Past

Some years ago, several organizations found themselves facing unanticipated problems and loss when a large third-party vendor of mainframe hardware failed to support its product. In those instances, difficult as they may have been, the losses were limited to hardware expense and some legal fees. Prospective outsourcing clients should heed this example. Should a similar fate visit the customers of an outsourcing supplier, the resulting losses could be much more severe, depending on the extent of the particular arrangement. Rebuilding an entire data center function could be a monumental task, and rebuilding a large-scale IS function quickly enough to smoothly resume operations might be nearly impossible. Again, the short-term gains must be carefully weighed against the potential risk.

## Protective Measures

Although the costs of keeping a function in-house may seem to outweigh the risk of an outsourcing vendor's default, the possibility always exists that an outsourcing vendor may be unable to support a contract. Some important issues must be thought out to protect the organization should the vendor renege on its agreement. For example, if the organization finds it necessary to bring the outsourced function back in-house, it should determine how the transition back to in-house processing, or to another outsourcing vendor, will be handled.

Before the contract is signed, a series of potential situations, or business contingency plans, should be drawn up to highlight for the organization the negative impact of a vendor default. The customer must carefully consider the issues involved and then protect the interests of the business to the greatest possible extent.

**Necessary Expense.** In the event of a default, the customer is certain to encounter additional expense. The organization should ensure that the contract obligates the vendor to cover such expense. Should the vendor default, obtaining compensation at that time will probably be impossible; therefore, the organization should ensure that some sort of protective provision exists in the contract—for example, protection might be provided by an escrow account.

## SUMMARY

Outsourcing can be regarded as either an onus or a challenge. Although outsourcing may be an inappropriate plan of action in certain cases, simply investigating this option can be advantageous to an organization by causing the organization's employees to examine their own effectiveness and productivity.

An outsourcing investigation can encourage managers of the IS department to look carefully at the way the function is being managed. This investigation, in highlighting areas for improvement, can help improve the organization's operations without the need for outsourcing. The investigation can, for example, identify those areas of operation that are redundant, unnecessary, or wasteful.

The investigation can also indicate those organizational functions that are performing efficiently. Turning the outsourcing investigation into a positive challenge should be an incentive to IS managers to approach the process with an open mind. Whether or not an organization decides to outsource a particular IS function, a well-conducted analysis of all aspects of outsourcing as it relates to the organization can produce positive results.

# II-3
# Downsizing Computer Resources: Planning, Implementation, and Management

*NATHAN J. MULLER*

W ith regard to information systems, downsizing is the process of shifting appropriate processing resources from centralized mainframes to servers and microcomputers on a local area network (LAN). The primary objective of downsizing is twofold: to free mainframes from processing data that can be done by relatively inexpensive computers and to expedite users' access to the information and resources they need to do their jobs.

Downsizing, however, entails more than simply moving applications from a mainframe to servers and microcomputers. Many companies are discovering that downsizing constitutes a major modification in business philosophy, and in the way the organization uses the vast amount of information at its disposal.

Downsizing allows applications and information to be located closer to the departments and individuals using these resources. Within this type of distributed environment, the underlying architecture is designed to provide access to the required data, regardless of its location in the network or the technology required to retrieve it. Therefore, downsizing can offer companies several new productivity options, particularly in:

- Managing systems, support, and maintenance costs.
- Applications development.
- Managing new technology implementation.
- Optimizing data access throughout the organization

## BENEFITS OF DOWNSIZING

Downsizing applications from the centralized mainframe to local area networks holds many potential advantages, including the following:

- Downsized applications may run as fast or faster on microcomputers and workstations than on mainframes, at only a fraction of the cost. For instance, the cost of processing power in terms of MIPS (millions of instructions per second) is conservatively estimated at $100,000 on a mainframe and only $500 on a microcomputer.
- Even if downsizing does not improve response time, it can improve response time consistency.
- In a distributed environment, the organization is not locked into a particular vendor, as is typically the case in a minicomputer- or mainframe-based environment.
- In the process of rewriting applications to run in the downsized environment, there is the opportunity to realize greater functional capability and efficiency from the software.
- In the downsized environment, the heavier reliance on off-the-shelf applications programs reduces the number of programmers and analysts needed to support the organization. In addition, users play a greater role in systems development, which further reduces the number of staff members dedicated to IS support.
- In the distributed computing environment, information can be accessed instantly by those individuals who are the most capable of exploiting it. Consequently, the quality and timeliness of decision making can be improved, allowing a more effective corporate response in dynamic business environments.
- With business operations streamlined through downsizing, the lag time between applications and business processes can be substantially shortened or eliminated, enabling the corporation to realize significant competitive advantage.

## MAKING THE TRANSITION
### The Mainframe's Role

Although concentrating most data processing and information storage at the mainframe has become inefficient, eliminating the mainframe should not necessarily be an objective of downsizing. The mainframe can be retained to perform tedious tasks, such as number crunching, which can free users to perform other tasks. Upon completion of processing, the user can then simply retrieve the results from the mainframe. In fact, this is the idea behind another trend, known as client/server computing.

In some cases, it can even be counterproductive to shift all applications to the LAN. Putting this much load onto an existing network could overwhelm the backbone. Not only can this slow or deny access to the distributed computing resources, but it can force the company to spend even more money on new facility installation and expansion.

Another factor that must be entered into the cost/benefits equation is that all microcomputers and workstations are not necessarily built to do everything mainframes can. An application that requires the sorting of millions of items accumulated every hour or so can take several hours to execute on a microcomputer. Moreover, high-volume transaction processing applications can overwork disk drives to the point of wearing them out.

## The Distributed Processing Environment

The distributed processing environment can take many forms. There is no universal solution; what works for one organization may not work for another. Several commonly used computing architectures can be chosen from. Each is discussed in the following paragraphs.

**Dedicated File Servers.** These can be used on the local area network to control access to application software and to prevent users from modifying or deleting files that may be stored locally. Typically, several file servers are deployed throughout the network, each supporting a single application (e.g., electronic mail, facsimile, graphics, or specific types of data bases).

**Superservers.** With so many organizations looking to downsize applications from mainframes to local area networks, the superserver concept is becoming a key strategic tool. Superservers are high-end microcomputers specifically equipped to act as network servers. These systems typically come with multiple high-speed processors, offer data storage in the gigabyte range, and use mainframelike restoral and security techniques. Although a superserver may be used to support multiple applications, it is ideal for processing-intensive applications (e.g., CAD/CAM), relational data base applications, and applications based on expert systems or neural networking.

**Data Sharing.** Users can publish parts of their hard disks to let others access them. Although this approach is economical in that it does not rely on a dedicated file server, it has several disadvantages that can outweigh cost concerns. Unlike servers, this data sharing scheme does not have a central administration facility to enforce data base integrity, perform backups, or control access. In addition, the performance of each user's hard disk may degrade significantly when accessed by other users.

**Minicomputers as File Servers.** Using a minicomputer as a file server might entail using equipment like an IBM 400/AS, a DEC VAX, or an HP 9000 connected to an Ethernet. The drawbacks of this file-sharing solution are high cost, amount of setup time needed, limited expansion possibilities, and the need for continual administrative vigilance to keep the system working properly.

A variation of using the minicomputer as a server is using the existing mainframe as a server. This scenario requires that the mainframe back up, restore, and archive data from multiple LAN servers. This is an important role for the mainframe, considering that 90% of microcomputer-based LANs lack a strong backup capability. In fact, it is a popular view that the primary role of mainframes as network servers is to help users back up critical files on LAN servers.

The mainframe can also provide additional space for users with large storage requirements. The mainframe can even play a role as a data base server in large organizations whose users need access to corporatewide information, such as customer records or accounting data.

**Client/Server Approach.** Using this approach, an application program is divided into two parts on the network. The client portion of the program, or front end, which is run by individual users at their desks, performs such tasks as querying data bases, producing printed reports, and entering new records. These functions can be carried out through a common access language, which operates in conjunction with existing application programs. The front-end part of the program executes on the user's workstation, drawing on its random access memory (RAM) and CPU.

The server portion of the program, or back end, is resident on a computer that is configured to support multiple clients. This setup offers users shared access to numerous application programs as well as to printers, file storage, data base management, communications, and other capabilities. Consequently, the server is typically configured with more RAM and higher-speed CPUs (or multiple CPUs) than are the clients connected to it over the network.

## Transition Aids

Standardization of such entities as Structured Query Language (SQL) for data base access, operating systems, and graphical user interfaces (GUIs) can ease the transition from centralized to distributed computing. These tools allow companies to maintain a smooth information flow throughout the organization and realize a substantial reduction in end-user training requirements while reaping the economic and performance benefits of hardware diversity.

The X Windowing System, for example, permits the creation of a uniform presentation interface that prevents users from having to learn multiple ways of accessing data across different computing platforms. Under X Windows, there is a single GUI front end that allows users to access multiple mainframe or server sessions simultaneously. These sessions can be displayed in separate windows on the same screen. X Windows also allows users to cut and paste data among the applications displayed in different windows.

In situations in which downsizing is appropriate, the option of distributing the application load among the various computing devices on the network can be effective in managing the company's information technology investments while enabling the organization to achieve its business goals efficiently and economically. However, the extent to which distributed systems can be effectively implemented often depends on the expertise of the in-house staff. For use in a distributed environment, mainframe applications would have to be modified and methods developed for effectively managing data resources across multiple types of hardware. Many companies that lack the required expertise have turned to systems integrators.

## The Role of Systems Integrators

After obtaining and implementing hardware and software from diverse vendors, downsizing requires the proper integration of these components. Just because these components are less expensive than those for mainframe systems does not mean that integration is easy. Often, the reverse is true; these systems can be complex and require a high level of expertise to integrate. This is why many companies have sought the services of systems integrators. The use of such firms is often justified because systems integrators typically have the following qualifications:

- Specialized industry knowledge, awareness of technology trends, and experiences gained from a broad customer base.
- Knowledge of specific protocols, interfaces, and cabling.
- A reputation for doing quality work within a limited time frame.
- The ability to transfer knowledge to existing systems staff, which can then take over responsibility for ongoing management, administration, and control.
- The capability, as an outside party, to act as a catalyst in implementing change and to validate or fine-tune in-house plans.

Even with the help of a systems integrator, the skills and knowledge of in-house IS staff members may have to be upgraded. Depending on the skill level of the staff members, it may take years to fully downsize core business applications. One solution may be to adopt a two-tier approach to applications, which entails keeping existing applications on larger systems but implementing new applications on the LAN. Another solution may be to outsource the management of the data center, the LAN, or both.

## ORGANIZATIONAL ISSUES

The promised benefits of downsizing are often too compelling to ignore: improved productivity, increased flexibility, and cost saving. Without proper planning, however, these benefits can be offset by controversy engendered by ongoing internal problems and other organizational issues.

Such problems are often at least partially the fault of differences between two opposing mind-sets—mainframe and microcomputer—within the organization, which results in competition for control of critical resources. Consequently, downsizing in an atmosphere of enmity can quickly erupt into a high-stakes game, supercharged by heated bickering and political maneuvering. Managing such challenges is often more difficult than dealing with the technical issues.

The impetus for change is twofold. Senior management is continuously looking for ways to streamline operations to improve financial performance; and end users, who are becoming more technically proficient, resent paying exorbitant mainframe charges and want immediate access to data that they perceive as belonging to them. Downsizing is increasingly looked upon by both camps as the most feasible solution.

The ubiquitous microcomputer, which is providing increasingly more performance per dollar every year, is making downsizing very attractive. Some industry analysts have predicted that as much as 80% of corporate computing power will reside on microcomputer networks by the mid-1990s. Some of these desk-top machines already have the computing power of 76 MIPS, rivaling many of today's mainframes. The feasibility of downsizing, however, does not revolve around technical issues alone.

## The Mainframe Mind-Set

Mainframe managers are often forced to adopt a defensive posture during the downsizing effort because it usually means that they must give up something: resources (in the form of budget and staff), power and prestige, and control of mission-critical applications. In addition—and perhaps as important—they regard the downsizing as the sacrifice of an operating philosophy in which they have invested considerable time and effort throughout their careers. Suddenly abandoning this philosophy to pursue a move that may turn out to be just another management fad can be a bitter pill to swallow.

In the past, mainframe managers have frequently been insufficiently attuned to the needs of users. Whereas users originally wanted access to the host, mainframe managers often seem focused on other things, such as upgrading a particular software package, adding a certain controller, or waiting for a programmer to finish working on a specific piece of code. Mainframe managers clearly had their own agenda, which did not always include serving the needs of others. Unable to wait, users took matters into their own hands. Today, in large corporations, about one in four desktop systems is networked—by its user.

Users' rapid adoption of desktop computers did not occur because of the data center's failure to provide fast applications; rather, it occurred because the data center failed to provide applications quickly. By focusing on their own needs, IS personnel tended to lose sight of the real business issues.

## The Microcomputer Mind-Set

With microcomputers now well entrenched in corporate offices, individuals, work groups, and departments have become acutely aware of the benefits of controlling information resources and of the need for data coordination. In becoming informationally self-sufficient and being able to share resources through local-area networks, these groups of users can better control their own destinies. For instance, they can increase the quality and timeliness of their decision making, execute transactions faster, and become more responsive to internal and external constituencies.

In many cases, this arrangement has the potential of moving accountability to the lowest common point in the organization, where many end users think it properly belongs. This scenario also has the potential of peeling back layers of bureaucracy that have traditionally stood between users and centralized resources.

### Resolving Emotional and Political Issues

Change can be very threatening to those most affected by it. This is especially true of downsizing, because it essentially involves a redistribution of responsibilities and, consequently, of power and influence. Therefore, the issues of feelings and perceptions must be addressed first to ensure success with the issues that address technical requirements.

The best way to defuse emotional and political time bombs that can jeopardize the success of downsizing is to include all affected parties in the planning process. The planning process should be participative and should start with the articulation of the organizational goals targeted by the downsizing effort, outlining anticipated costs and benefits. This stage of the planning process should also address the most critical concern of the participants—how they will be affected. Once the organizational goals are known, these become the new parameters within which the participants can shape their futures.

## GUIDELINES FOR SUCCESS

The technologies involved in downsizing are neither simple nor straightforward. An organization cannot afford to have each individual department research, implement, and support various complex technologies. Instead, a single group (e.g., IS) must be responsible for this. This department, however, must be responsive to other departments' business needs and must be technically competent and capable of proving that it can perform these tasks for the good of the entire organization.

As with any corporatewide project, there are actions an organization should take when downsizing that, if followed, can increase the chances of yielding a successful outcome:

- Forming a committee of IS staff members, corporate management, departmental management, and representative end users to explore, propose, define, review, and monitor the progress of the project. This approach is usually effective for both short- and long-range planning.
- Identifying the applications that are appropriate for downsizing. The initial project should be of limited scope that is easy to define and control, and its success should be easy to determine. The urge to accomplish too

much too quickly should be resisted; instead, small successes should be encouraged and built upon.

- Identifying the work and information flows that are currently in place for the existing system and determining the effect the project will have on those processes.
- Determining which staff members will be the owners of the data and which will be responsible for maintaining that information.
- Identifying clearly the project's objectives and quantifying the benefits these objectives will provide the company.
- Obtaining the support and involvement of senior management from the start and securing their commitment to the project's objectives and benefits.
- Ensuring that the rationale for downsizing is based on strategic business goals rather than on political ambition or some other private agenda that could easily derail the project.
- Reviewing on a regular basis the progress of the project with the multidepartmental committee, modifying the plan as the committee deems appropriate.

A well-defined and well-implemented training program can also help ensure the success of a downsizing project. This includes preparing documentation and developing training courses designed to acquaint users with how to work in the distributed operating environment and the specific procedures governing such things as logging on, backups, restoral, and the use of the help desk.

This approach to downsizing, which involves all present and future users in shaping their own IS system, not only facilitates cooperation but has the effect of spreading ownership of the solution among all participants. Instead of a solution dictated by senior management, which often engenders resistance through emotional responses and political manuevering, the participative approach provides each party with a stake in the outcome of the project. With success comes the rewards associated with a stable work environment and shared vision of the future; with failure comes the liabilities associated with a chaotic work environment and uncertainty about the future. Although participative planning takes more time, its effects are often more immediate and long lasting than imposed solutions, which are frequently resisted and short-lived.

### Setting Objective Criteria

Downsizing is not the best solution for certain applications, such as those that span multiple divisions or departments. Therefore, the participative planning process can be helpful in reaching a consensus on which applications qualify for possible offloading from the mainframe to the desktop. This minimizes disputes and further removes emotion and politics from the downsizing effort. Issues that should be examined in the participatory planning process are discussed in the following sections.

**Mission Criticality.** There is currently some controversy about whether mission-critical applications should be moved from mainframes to local area networks. Any application that serves a large number of users across organizational boundaries, requires ongoing changes, and conveys great competitive advantage to the company can be deemed mission-critical. Of these, any application that helps users accomplish the mission of a department, is highly specialized, and requires few ongoing changes to be propagated through various corporatewide data bases is an ideal candidate for downsizing.

**Response-Time Requirements.** Sometimes information must be decentralized to ensure a quick response to competitive pressures. This decentralization permits multiple users to instantly apply their knowledge and expertise to the resolution of a given problem and to share information across microcomputer and LAN systems without having to wait for access to mainframe-resident data bases (assuming that these are available and up to date when a mainframe port is finally accessed).

A marketing department, for example, might want control of product pricing and availability information so that it can quickly reposition its offerings against its competitors'. Other candidates for decentralization are applications that are highly aligned with product and service development, such as CAD/CAM and CASE.

**Control.** From the perceived absence of LAN management tools stems the users' concern about their ability to exercise control in the LAN environment. On the mainframe, data reliability is virtually guaranteed, because there is only one place where all data resides. In addition to providing better control, this structure facilitates keeping the data organized, current, and more secure. However, new tools are emerging that provide managers with sophisticated control capabilities that go well beyond simple file transfer.

This higher level of control is provided by change management tools that allow managers to centrally control the distribution and installation of operating systems, application programs, and data files. Verification reports are provided on each transmission to confirm the contents' arrival at the proper destination, the success or failure of the installation, and the discovery of any errors. Changes to software and the addition of unauthorized software are reported automatically. Data compression and decompression can be performed on large files to prevent network throughput problems during heavy use. Data files can be collected for consolidation or backup.

**Security.** An ongoing concern of mainframe managers is security—the protection of sensitive information from unauthorized access as well as from accidental corruption and damage. In the centralized computing environment, an acceptable level of security is maintained by such methods as passwords, work space partitioning, and access levels. Data base maintenance and periodic back-ups, which ensure the integrity of the data, are easy to conduct. Although possible, it is much harder to implement such controls in the decentralized computing environment, in which individuals must be entrusted with such responsibilities.

Advocates of downsizing must be willing to shoulder the responsibilities for security, not just demand the applications be moved to the desktop for the sake of convenience. In fact, the feasibility of the downsizing request can sometimes be discerned quickly by determining whether users are serious about accepting responsibility for security and whether they are receptive to training in such areas as performing backups in accordance with IS guidelines.

Applications that require minimal security are obvious candidates for downsizing. Applications that require the use of highly sensitive information (e.g., corporate financial data) can remain on the mainframe, where access can be more effectively controlled.

**Interconnectivity.** Applications that involve a high degree of interconnectivity among users are best implemented in a decentralized environment of microcomputer and LAN systems. A publishing operation, for example, typically entails the movement of information among multiple users in a work group. At a higher level, text and graphics are gathered from multiple work groups for document assembly. The assembled document is then transmitted to a printing facility, where it is output in paper form. If attempted in a centralized environment, this kind of application would tie up mainframe resources, denying other users access to the limited number of ports, for example. Therefore, any specialized application that requires a high degree of interconnectivity with local or remote users is a prime candidate for downsizing.

**End-User Expertise.** The success of a proposed downsizing effort may hinge on how knowledgeable end users are about their equipment and applications. If users are not capable of determining whether a problem is hardware- or software-oriented, for example, they may still require a high degree of support from the IS department. This is an important concern, considering that the motivation behind many downsizing efforts is to eliminate IS staff.

Downsizing is not simply a matter of buying a desktop computer for each staff member, connecting these computers together, handing out applications packages, and hoping for the best. Instead of eliminating staff, downsizing may result only in the redeployment of current staff to supply extensive assistance to inexperienced users, provide training and technical support, set up and enforce security procedures, operate a help desk, evaluate equipment for acquisition, and deal with unexpected crises (e.g., limiting the corruption of data from computer viruses).

**Attitudes of IS Personnel.** A concern related to the users' expertise is the attitudes of IS staff. The crucial question to be answered is whether current IS staff members are willing and able to change with the times; specifically, do they have the skills necessary to deal effectively with end users in all of these areas? If key IS staff members have a strictly mainframe attitude, they may have to be replaced with personnel more attuned to end-user needs. This extreme scenario is probably unnecessary in most cases, however.

During the participative planning process, other department heads can become sensitive to the anxiety that IS staff are possibly experiencing. Other department managers can make the idea of downsizing more palatable to IS staff by pointing out that this endeavor is a formidable challenge that represents a vital, experience-building opportunity. In becoming a partner in the project's success, IS staff will have contributed immeasurably toward a revitalized organizational structure that is better equipped to respond to competitive pressures.

**Hidden Costs.** The primary motivation for downsizing has ostensibly been to cut costs. Organizations frequently think that the switch to cheap microcomputers connected over LANs from expensive mainframes will cut their budgets and help them realize productivity benefits in the bargain. This attitude ignores the hidden costs associated with downsizing.

In fact, many times, little or no money is saved immediately as a result of downsizing. Moving applications to microcomputers and LANs requires specialized management, technical staff, and testing equipment. The money saved by trimming IS staff is inevitably spent in maintaining a problem-free distributed computing environment.

As mentioned earlier in this chapter, downsizing frequently entails a redeployment of IS staff. One of the key roles of IS staff, once downsizing is approved, is to create the architecture on which dispersed systems will be built. IS staff may also be charged with controlling and managing the connectivity of the company's networks and setting guidelines and a methodology for using the network. Consequently, even though downsizing may have initially been motivated by the desire to trim IS staff and reduce costs, the head count may not change significantly—if at all.

## Assuming a Leadership Role

With users already taking the initiative to link local area networks to form truly enterprisewide networks, it is incumbent upon IS staff to assert a leadership role; after all, users are not network architects. Too often, IS managers are content with the role of spectator rather than of participant. When users encounter the technical complexity of such concepts as the fiber distributed data interface (FDDI), many IS managers prefer to take no action rather than attempt to explain the concept to users. Consequently, with desktop systems linked throughout the company, data center personnel may find themselves surrounded by competent users whom they never took seriously.

As more equipment is added into this environment in the form of bridges, routers, and multiplexers, new support capabilities must be added, usually in the form of specialized personnel. This too is an excellent opportunity for IS staff to assume a leadership role. The peripheral activities of operating networks provide ample justification for maintaining existing IS staff—and perhaps even augmenting staff. With more vendors to deal with, personnel are required to administer such things as contracts, responses to trouble calls, inventory, and invoice and payment reconciliation. Some companies are trying to rid themselves of such encumbrances by outsourcing these responsibilities to an outside firm.

Outsourcing is generally defined as contracting out the design, implementation, and management of information systems and networks. Even this arrangement provides opportunities for IS staff, because it often entails their transfer to the outsourcing vendor with comparable pay and benefits. They not only continue working at the same company but become exposed to other opportunities as well.

When it comes to the question of downsizing, it is incumbent upon the IS department to assume leadership for another reason: if downsizing is forced on the organization from senior management or is planned by another department, IS staff will face greater loss of credibility and influence and will have to accept any decisions imposed upon it. Leadership, however, enhances credibility and influence, which in turn leads to control.

### Middle Management Quandary

Throughout the 1980s and 1990s, IS managers have witnessed the growth of microcomputing on the desktop. This trend has empowered the individual and fueled the rise of knowledge workers, enabling them to manage more tasks, make more informed decisions, and become more creative. As desktop computers continue to become equipped with more processing power and the available software continues to take full advantage of it, desktop computers will empower the group, increasing productivity exponentially. As a result, employees will find the barriers between departments effectively dissolved, permitting companies to react quickly to changes and opportunities in the marketplace. In fact, the organization of the future will be based on resource sharing, with local and wide area networks facilitating this sharing.

Potentially, the ultimate expression of downsizing comes in the form of peer-to-peer communication, whereby any user can access information at any time and at any level from any other user. This capability further encourages top-heavy organizations to streamline the ranks of middle management. Indeed, today's groupware concept complements the trend toward downsizing. The term groupware refers to software that allows specialized individuals to engage in collaborative efforts, tapping the processing power of workstations and drawing on a set of shared resources to arrive at timely solutions.

As more applications and information technology are moved to the desktop, many department managers see themselves threatened with obsolescence. This need not be the case, however. Downsizing can actually be a liberating force that frees middle managers to perform long-neglected tasks, such as recruiting, staff development, training, work scheduling, performance evaluation, devising and administering incentive plans, and counseling. These tasks will grow in importance as organizations move more applications to the desktop, introduce new technologies into the workplace, and increase their reliance on less elaborate management structures to compete in the marketplace more effectively.

With the shortage of appropriately skilled knowledge workers expected to continue well into the next century, corporations will have to allocate more resources to training and continuing education. Middle management seems ideally positioned to shoulder these responsibilities as well as to administer advanced programs to continually upgrade the skills and expertise of more experienced workers.

Because competitive pressures are likely to intensify, the challenge for most companies becomes to develop the best structure to face this situation. Individual companies will respond differently to this challenge. Many will choose to decentralize information resources. Some will turn to external sources (i.e., outsourcing) to manage the flow of information and to maintain complex networks so that attention can be better focused on the core business. Others may even tighten central corporate control. A few may choose to experiment with fluid, ad hoc management structures.

Whatever the structure, the objectives must include minimizing operating costs and formulating a more appropriate deployment of staff. The traditional centralized IS function may not give way to decentralization or even disappear entirely: it will likely change dynamically as the needs of the organization dictate.

There is little likelihood that mainframes will disappear entirely. Mainframes offer many advantages over desktop computers, such as processing power and storage capacity. Their security and management features are still superior to microcomputer and LAN systems, though this situation is starting to change. Moreover, certain repetitive and tedious applications (e.g., transaction processing), which typically involve the manipulation of voluminous amounts of data and require many hours to complete, are better suited for the mainframe environment. These may never migrate to the desktop, even if they have the MIPS to handle them.

## SUMMARY

Claims that downsizing is the wave of the future and that the mainframe is dead are generalizations that have little relevance to the real world. Each organization must free itself from such generalizations when considering whether or not downsizing offers an economical solution to its particular problems of information access and resource sharing.

The results of downsizing, however, are potentially too compelling to ignore. Among these results is the wide range of benefits over the existing centralized mainframe environment, including lower processing costs, configuration flexibility, a more responsive applications development environment, and systems that are easier to use. In addition, networked, distributed processing systems may provide the most cost-effective way for users to access, transfer, and share corporate information.

The cost benefits of downsizing can be near-term, as in the reduction or redeployment of internal IS staff, or long-term, as in the investment in newer applications and technologies. Determining the benefits of downsizing, the extent to which it will be implemented, who will do it, and the justification of its up-front costs are highly subjective activities. The answers will not appear in the form of solutions borrowed from another company. In fact, the likelihood of success will be greatly improved if the downsizing effort is approached as a custom engineering project.

# II-4
# Fine Tuning the Help Desk: Goals and Objectives

*CHRISTINE B. TAYNTOR*

W hen help desks were first introduced, their mission was simple: help unsophisticated end users operate their personal computers and obtain a basic proficiency with the software installed on the personal computers. The challenges were straightforward. Not only were the personal computers standalone machines, but the software packages being used were usually limited to word processing and spreadsheets.

In retrospect, those were the halcyon days. Since then, the world of end-user computing has changed dramatically, with a new level of complexity being added in three key areas: hardware, software, and customer requirements.

In many cases, standalone computers have been replaced by personal computers linked into extensive local and wide area networks (LANs and WANs). This has increased both users' dependence on their machines and the possiblity that one person's error could affect an entire community. It has also complicated the help desk's responsibilities. To be successful, the help desk staff has had to expand its area of expertise to include at least the fundamentals of network operating systems.

Today's software makes that of the early 1980s appear primitive, as vendors incorporate an increasing variety of features into their products. Word processing packages now include many of the tools that were previously found only in high-end desktop publishing products, and spreadsheets boast integrated spell checkers and query tools. In addition, many users have migrated from DOS to Windows, adding complexity as they run multiple products simultaneously. For the help desk staff, problem diagnosis has become substantially more difficult. Not only have they had to develop expertise in the new, more complex applications, but they now need to understand the relationships between the applications.

If the changes in hardware and software have been dramatic, they have been overshadowed by the evolution of the help desk's customer base. Whereas a decade ago, users were relatively unsophisticated and content to perform only basic functions on their computers, today's customers have a far higher comfort level with personal computers. Many are highly computer literate and willing to experiment, stretching the envelope of packaged software. They are no longer content with simple directions on how to boot a computer or construct a basic spreadsheet. Instead, they want in-depth explanations of how to link a spreadsheet with a graphics package and tie them both into a word processing document, then send the results to a dozen people by electronic mail.

As customers' levels of expertise have grown, so too have their demands on the help desk staff. They expect nothing less than excellence and are frequently vocal if their expectations are not met. If the help desk is to be successful and to continue to be an important part of the corporation, it must change, adjusting its services and skills to meet the new requirements.

## THE ABCs OF FINE TUNING

After a company has recognized the need for change in its help desk operation, the question becomes one of how and where to start. Three basic steps can facilitate an orderly transition to the help desk of the future:

- *Defining the ultimate help desk.* This is the vision of excellence for the future. It will become the benchmark against which performance can be measured.
- *Establishing the baseline.* This invovles determining where the organization is now. Comparing current performance to the goals established in the first step can help identify the areas in which performance improvements are required.
- *Managing the evolution.* After the plan has been developed, basic management techniques are needed to ensure that the plan is implemented rather than becoming only an historical document.

The next section explores these steps and their tasks in more detail.

## CHARTING THE COURSE

Before a company initiates any organizational changes, it should have clearly established goals and a plan to achieve them. Without such a formal vision, change is unmanageable and may have unpredictable results. Three fundamental tasks are required to define the ultimate help desk: establishing a vision, identifying the services to be provided, and defining optimum service levels.

### Establishing a Vision

One of the key elements in defining the future is to clearly outline the functions that the help desk can and cannot perform. Before this level of detail can be reached, however, the organization needs an overall framework—a statement of who and what it is. In short, the help desk needs a mission statement.

In the simplest terms, a mission statement is a short written summary of a group's purpose and values. It explains what the group does and how those functions affect its customers, its own staff, and the company as a whole. An analysis of a sample mission statement for a help desk is included as Exhibit II-4-1.

## Identifying the Services to Be Provided

Although the mission statement addresses services in general terms, management should define them very specifically, because what the team is expected to do directly affects both the staffing level and the skills that are required. Specific questions should be answered at this point.

Is the help desk responsible for resolving the majority of all problems, or is its primary function to route questions to the appropriate expert? The answer to this question determines how large the staff must be, because solving a problem takes substantially longer than simply routing it to another person.

---

### Mission Statement

We, the members of the ABC Co. data center help desk, are dedicated to providing fast, accurate answers to customers' questions about personal computers and software. We are a team that shares knowledge and values mutual respect and support. By providing personalized attention and quality responses, we enable our customers to improve their personal productivity at the same time that we foster a positive image of the information systems department.

### Analysis

*What are the functions of the help desk?*

Two functions are clearly outlined: providing accurate answers to customers' questions about personal computers and software, and providing personalized attention and quality responses. By omission, the mission statement indicates that this help desk does not support mainframe-based systems, nor does it install hardware and software.

*What is the impact on customers?*

This is also explicit. The help desk serves as an enabler for improving personal productivity.

*What is the impact on the information systems department?*

Again, this is clearly stated. By its actions, the help desk staff fosters a positive image for the entire department.

*What is the impact on the company as a whole?*

Although not explicitly outlined, customers' improved personal productivity should have a positive impact on the company's bottom line.

*What are the help desk staff's values?*

These are clearly stated: teamwork, mutual respect, sharing of knowledge, and commitment to excellence.

**Exhibit II-4-1. Sample Mission Statement and Analysis**

Similarly, the more problems the help desk is expected to resolve, the greater the depth of product knowledge and training required.

Although additional staff and more extensive training may appear to have negative implications, positive effects can be realized if the help desk is made responsible for problem resolution. When responsibility is centralized, synergies can occur. The help desk staff is usually located together, allowing the members to share information and assist each other in solving problems. This is not always true of the individual experts to whom problems are forwarded. When knowledge is pooled, many problems can be resolved more quickly, thereby reducing costs and improving customer service.

Another benefit, and one whose value should not be underestimated, is the job enrichment that results from resolving problems rather than logging and forwarding them. For many organizations, the help desk is a group with high staff turnover and early burnout. Both of these problems can be minimized by giving the help desk more responsibility—changing its role from that of a conduit, forced to deal with irate customers but rarely being able to create customer satisfaction, to one of a problem solver, with the concomitant rewards.

Should the help desk provide services other than problem resolution? Some companies have expanded the role of the help desk beyond problem resolution to include such functions as installing and upgrading software, performing preventive maintenance on personal computers and servers, and providing product training to customers. This expansion of services can have both positive and negative effects on the organization. On the negative side, if the help desk is to assign additional responsibilities, increased staff and more training are required.

From the staff's view, the added responsibilities can be either positive or negative, depending on the personalities involved and the corporate culture. The new functions can be perceived as job enrichment and a way to learn more about the hardware and software the team supports. They may also be viewed as diluting the primary mission of the help desk: resolving problems.

## Defining Service Levels

After management has decided which services the team should provide, the next task is to determine performance levels. It is not sufficient to state that the help desk can respond quickly to customer inquiries, because quickly is a subjective term. Instead, the help desk should have specific, measurable performance targets. Examples include:

- Of all calls, 95% should be answered before the third ring.
- Of all problems, 93% should be resolved with no callback (i.e., customers receive their answer during their first call to the help desk).

Because help desk performance is measured against the target performance levels, those service levels must be achievable. One way to establish acceptable performance measures is to benchmark other companies, determining the levels that they have set and that they meet. Like all benchmark efforts, several caveats are characteristic of this one:

- The companies' environments should be similar. A help desk that supports dumb terminals attached to a mainframe running core transaction processing systems has different performance expectations from one that supports personal computers attached to LANs running personal productivity tools.
- The companies being benchmarked should be recognized as providing above-average or excellent service levels. Learning how a mediocre performer sets its goals does not facilitate developing a world class help desk.

Although it is important for service levels to be achievable, it is even more critical that they meet customer expectations. Too often management has developed targets in a vacuum without consulting the end user. Although some companies are reluctant to ask for customer input to the goal-setting process, this is an essential step toward improving satisfaction. One way to obtain and use requirements is with a customer survey. A sample survey section is included as Exhibit II-4-2.

## ESTABLISHING AND EVALUATING THE BASELINE

After the first step is complete, the organization knows what it considers to be a fully functional help desk and is typically anxious to proceed with the implementation of that ultimate vision. An essential intermediate step exists, however, that must not be ignored. The organization must measure its current performance and compare that to the goals established in the setting of the vision. Without this step, the organization is proceeding blindly, making changes without being certain of their impact or knowing whether those changes are treating symptoms rather than resolving underlying problems.

Before an effective implementation plan can be developed, the organization must complete three key tasks:

- Establishing a baseline of current performance.
- Determining how large a gap exists between the present help desk and the ideal that was identified.
- Performing a gap analysis (i.e., determining the underlying causes of the discrepancies).

For those companies that have implemented formal metrics programs for their help desk, measuring current performance presents no challenge. They already know how many calls they handle per day, how long the average caller waits for a response, and what level of satisfaction their customers have with the answers they are given. Many other companies, however, have few if any statistics about the help desk and must compile them.

### Customer Survey—Help Desk Services

Help, please! The help desk needs your feedback to know what services it should provide. We urge you to complete the attached questionnaire and return it to us by _____. Please answer only for yourself, not for your entire department.

*Hours of Operation*—Please indicate the hours when you would like someone from the help desk to be available to assist you.

Weekdays: from _____ to _____

Weekends and holidays (check one):

       _____ from _____ to _____

       _____ on call (able to reach the office within one hour)

       _____ in the office when arranged with _____ hours advance notice

*Call Answering*

1. When you call the help desk, your phone should be answered in:

       _____ 2 rings

       _____ 3–5 rings

       _____ 5–7 rings

       _____ 8–10 rings

       _____ more than 10 rings

2. The call should be answered by:

       _____ a person who can answer the question

       _____ someone who can transfer you to a person with the answer

       _____ a receptionist

       _____ voice mail

3. If you leave a message with voice mail or a receptionist, you should receive a follow-up within:

       _____ 5 minutes or less

       _____ 15 minutes or less

       _____ 30 minutes or less

       _____ 1 hour or less

       _____ 2 hours or less

       _____ 4 hours or less

       _____ the same working day

       _____ the next working day

*Problem Response*

1. The first help desk person you talk to:

       _____ should be able to help you immediately

       _____ should be able to help you after a short (less than one minute) hold

       _____ may call back with the answer

**Exhibit II-4-2. Sample Help Desk Customer Survey**

2. If it is necessary for someone to call you back, follow-up should be within:

_____ 5 minutes or less

_____ 15 minutes or less

_____ 30 minutes or less

_____ 1 hour or less

_____ 2 hours or less

_____ 4 hours or less

_____ the same working day

_____ the next working day

3. The time from when you first call the help desk until you get the correct answer should be:

_____ 5 minutes or less

_____ 15 minutes or less

_____ 30 minutes or less

_____ 1 hour or less

_____ 2 hours or less

_____ 4 hours or less

_____ the same working day

_____ the next working day

**Exhibit II-4-2. (continued)**

---

Although automated tools can simplify the collection of metrics and increase the accuracy of the data, statistics can also be gathered manually. At a minimum, each member of the help desk staff should record the number of calls he or she answers each day, how many are forwarded to someone else for resolution, and how many require follow-up. Although it is more difficult to compute manually, it is also helpful to calculate the minimum, average, and maximum length of time before a call is fully resolved. There are important metrics that are used to measure future performance.

Customer satisfaction, which is a key element of current performance, can be obtained either by interviews (e.g., in person or by telephone) or through a survey. One approach is to expand the customer requirements survey shown in Exhibit II-4-2 to include two columns, one to record the current situation and the other to indicate the customer's needs.

For organizations that have not yet implemented metrics programs, several caveats apply:

- *Be honest with the staff.* Measurement is frequently perceived as an attempt by management to identify and punish poor performance. Although it is impossible to completely allay these fears, management should explain that the statistics are used to measure improvements for the group as a whole, rather than for individuals, and that nothing is inherently good or bad about the baseline. It is simply a measurement of the current situation. Future performance and widening the gap between that and current performance are key.

- *Do not rush.* A meaningful baseline cannot be established in a day or a week. To ensure that seasonal swings in activity (e.g., the implementation of a new software release) do not skew the statistics, they should be gathered over a period of at least a calendar quarter.

Establishing a baseline is not easy, but it is essential to the success of the help desk fine-tuning program.

After the goals and the baseline have been established, it is relatively simple to determine the gap between them. The third task, determining the causes of these discrepancies, requires substantially more time and effort. The proper focus, however, can minimize the length of time needed.

Because of the type of work the help desk performs, only three key variables in performance exist: the staff, the automated tools they use, and their customers. Because the help desk cannot mandate changes in its customer base, the fine-tuning program should focus on the help desk and its tools. By analyzing each of these, the manager can identify areas for improvement.

Specific questions that can help pinpoint problems concerning the help desk staff include:

- *Has everyone been fully trained on all supported products?* Without adequate technical training, the staff requires more time to resolve problems or may be forced to refer calls to a second-level support person.
- *Does the staff have fully developed customer service skills?* Although most companies recognize the need for technical training, fewer provide basic customer service education to their help desk staff. If customer satisfaction is less than desired, one cause may be inadequate training. Commercially available courses (in both instructor-led and audio-video tape versions) demonstrate the correct way to answer the phone, to deal with unhappy callers, and to elicit the key information for problem resolution without annoying the caller.
- *Is the staff skilled at providing training?* In addition to resolving problems, the help desk staff is also expected to provide informal training in the use of both hardware and software products, yet they are frequently given no guidance in the best ways to help adults learn. Like all other skills, this one can be enhanced by formal instructions—in this case, train-the-trainer courses.
- *Is the staff large enough?* Although this is frequently the first staff-related question a manager asks, it should be the last, because the inability to respond quickly enough to calls can be caused by lack of training as well as a shortage of people. After the manager is convinced that the staff is fully trained and operating at peak efficiency, if response targets are not being met, the probable cause is too few people in the help desk group.

Specific questions that can help pinpoint problems with tools include:

- *Is the staff using automated tools for problem tracking and resolution?* A comprehensive system is a key element in establishing the help desk of the future. With the increased demands being placed on the help desk, manual methods of tracking problems and documenting their resolution are no longer sufficient. Although they can accomplish the basic goals of measurement, manual methods are labor-intensive, diverting the help desk from its primary objective: responding to customers.
- *Is the automated tool a complete one?* Simply tracking the number of calls and calculating the time required to resolve them is not enough. A comprehensive help desk system should:
  —Provide for and require documentation of all steps taken to resolve a problem, the person performing them, and the time required for each. This establishes accountability and allows the manager to identify potential areas for increased training by quantifying the length of time each individual needs to resolve a specific type of problem.
  —Facilitate the management of solutions-in-progress by providing automated reminders of open calls. This feature eliminates neglect of unresolved problems caused by the constant stream of new calls.
  —Escalate unresolved problems. In a comprehensive call tracking system, each problem is assigned a severity code, which determines the length of time it can remain unresolved without being escalated to the next level within the organization. This ensures that critical problems are given priority and alerts management before they become disasters. Customer satisfaction and confidence in the help desk typically increase when the system provides automated escalation.

---

Once a company has realized the need for fine tuning its help desk, several basic steps must be taken to facilitate an orderly transition. The following fundamental tasks can help define the ultimate help desk:

☐ Establishing a vision:
  • Functions the help desk can and cannot perform should be clearly outlined.
  • A mission statement is needed to provide an overall framework.

☐ Identifying the services to be provided:
  • The more problems the help desk is expected to resolve, the greater the depth of product knowledge and training for the staff is required.
  • Responsibilities, in addition to problem resolution, can have either positive or negative effects, depending on corporate culture.

☐ Defining optimum service levels:
  • The help desk must establish specific, measurable performance targets.
  • Service levels must be achievable.
  • Service levels must ultimately meet and satisfy customer expectations.

**Exhibit II-4-3. Action Checklist**

- *Is problem resolution aided by maintaining an easily accessed history of previous problems and their solutions?* The goal of such a system is to share expertise and expedite problem handling, thus increasing both the help desk's productivity and customer satisfaction.

## ACTION PLAN

The primary responsibility of any help desk is to efficiently and economically service the needs of the computer and communications users of an organization. Over time, however, the help desk must be fine tuned to keep pace with the ever-changing needs of those users. After the need to make changes in the present structure has been established, the processes of evaluation and refinement can begin. The Action Checklist in Exhibit II-4-3 can help guide this effort.

# II-5
# Client/Server vs. Cooperative Processing

*DAVID FRIEND*

B ecause the cooperative processing model offers more centralized control than the distributed client/server architecture, it is highly useful for widespread enterprise applications or applications in which data base replication is impractical. By keeping data and applications in one central repository, cooperative processing overcomes certain problems associated with application and data integrity, maintenance of enterprisewide applications, and data security—problems that are difficult to solve with distributed client/server products.

However, these advantages come at a certain price. The purpose of this chapter is to help data center managers compare the characteristics of cooperative processing with those of distributed client/server computing and to identify the applications and hardware environments that work best with these solutions. Each has its advantages and limitations.

Armed with this information, readers can take the self-test in Exhibit II-5-1. The test is designed to help readers determine whether cooperative processing is an appropriate technology for their organizations' applications.

## DEPARTMENTAL VERSUS ENTERPRISEWIDE APPLICATIONS

Client/server computing and its cooperative processing variant are the two most important technologies for realizing the potential benefits of downsizing and distributed computing. These distributed computing topologies can provide superior performance at a lower price than traditional host-based solutions.

Distributed client/server computing distributes the processing workload somewhat more efficiently than does cooperative processing. Because distributed client/server applications can be built and supported at the departmental level, they have proliferated work group by work group, often haphazardly.

Although mainframe performance has been surpassed by distributed client/server systems, no amount of speed or performance can overcome the lack of security inherent in such distributed systems, nor can they make such

This self-test helps data center managers determine when to use cooperative processing and when to use a client/server solution.

**1. Application is required to run standalone (e.g., on a notebook computer).**

Cooperative Processing                    Client/Server

5  4  3  2  1  0  1  2  3  4  5

Standalone operation almost always indicates a client/server application. It is inefficient to run a cooperative processing application where centralized control is of no value.

**2. Applications incorporate scanned images, voice annotation, or other large objects.**

Cooperative Processing                    Client/Server

5  4  3  2  1  0  1  2  3  4  5

Moving large data objects around requires the kind of bandwidth found only on a LAN. The use of such objects normally indicates a client/server solution.

**3. All users are on the same LAN and all run Windows.**

Cooperative Processing                    Client/Server

5  4  3  2  1  0  1  2  3  4  5

This sounds like a pure LAN-based application for which client/server is a natural.

**7. Data integrity or security is of paramount importance.**

Cooperative Processing                    Client/Server

5  4  3  2  1  0  1  2  3  4  5

Because of cooperative processing's centralized control of data and applications, data stays only in one place, where it can be kept secure. Every user sees the same version of the data. On the other hand, distributed data bases from several vendors are beginning to address these problems in the LAN environment.

**8. Data must be collected from multiple sources and made into a sensible form.**

Cooperative Processing                    Client/Server

5  4  3  2  1  0  1  2  3  4  5

Collecting data from multiple sources into a single data base implies the centralized data base typical of cooperative processing applications.

**9. Data is constantly changing, and users are spread out geographically.**

Cooperative Processing                    Client/Server

5  4  3  2  1  0  1  2  3  4  5

If users are spread out geographically, a LAN-based solution probably requires multiple LANs and replication of data across the various servers. If the data is changing frequently, the replication process becomes too inefficient and costly, and a cooperative processing approach, with its centralized data repository, becomes a far more efficient solution.

Exhibit II-5-1. The Cooperative Processing Versus Distributed Client/Server Self-Test

**4. Response time is of paramount importance.**

Cooperative Processing | | | | | | | | | | Client/Server
5 4 3 2 1 0 1 2 3 4 5

Because a client/server application executes solely on the microcomputer, it does not compete for resources with other server applications, and response time is as fast as that of the underlying data base. The response time of the server data base, however, can still cause problems when a server or network is overloaded.

**5. Data must be accessed live from many different sources.**

Cooperative Processing | | | | | | | | | | Client/Server
5 4 3 2 1 0 1 2 3 4 5

Whereas both client/server and cooperative processing can access a range of data bases, client/server's open architecture facilitates accessing many sources of data simultaneously.

**6. The application requires access to huge amounts of data.**

Cooperative Processing | | | | | | | | | | Client/Server
5 4 3 2 1 0 1 2 3 4 5

Very large data bases are typically associated with constant updating, a low percentage of data actually used, and a requirement for moving large amounts of data to the computation engine. Cooperative processing can be of value if network bandwidth is a problem or if the data is constantly changing, thereby making distributed data bases problematical.

**10. The application is enterprisewide and must be accessible anywhere across a wide range of communications, including phone lines, 3270 coaxial cable, and other low-bandwidth, non-LAN connections.**

Cooperative Processing | | | | | | | | | | Client/Server
5 4 3 2 1 0 1 2 3 4 5

Cooperative processing makes efficient use of communications bandwidth. Numerical computation all takes place at the server and only the data that is actually displayed on the screen must be downloaded to the microcomputer. Conversely, if all users are on a single LAN, client/server is the obvious solution.

**11. The system is a collection of both enterprisewide applications and locally supported applications. Users are on LANs with gateways to a host or other servers.**

Cooperative Processing | | | | | | | | | | Client/Server
5 4 3 2 1 0 1 2 3 4 5

Cooperative processing should be used for centrally supported applications, and client/server for the applications that are supported locally. Cooperative processing's file transfer capabilities can distribute client/server applications and data base updates to individual servers if needed.

**Exhibit II-5-1.** *(continued)*

117

systems a good fit for hierarchically organized businesses in which centralized control is important. The peer-to-peer topology of pure client/server solutions makes them ideal for local and departmental solutions. The more hierarchical topology of cooperative processing makes it more appropriate for enterprisewide applications in which users are geographically dispersed and data is constantly changing.

Some information systems have a greater need for centralized control and sophisticated security. By their nature, mainframe operating systems are designed for enterprisewide solutions, serving everyone in the organization from top to bottom. Cooperative processing takes advantage of the security and centralized control of a mainframe system while offloading as much processing as possible to the workstation. However, because this centralized control requires that more of the processing take place on the host than would be the case in distributed client/server computing, these advantages come at a price.

## A FURTHER COMPARISON

There are superficial similarities between cooperative processing and distributed client/server systems. In both cases, computing is distributed between microcomputers and back-end processors. In the case of cooperative processing, these are generally referred to as the workstation and host. In distributed client/server computing, they are referred to as the client and server. Physically, both systems comprise a microcomputer on the desktop hooked up to a larger processor that is shared by all application users. The network that connects the microcomputer and the host/server may be different, however, because as a general rule, distributed client/server applications require much greater bandwidth than cooperative processing applications (the bandwidth issue is discussed in more detail later in the chapter).

The most important difference between distributed client/server and cooperative processing is where control of the application resides. In the case of a distributed client/server application, control resides at the workstation. The application runs on the workstation, and the client application is in charge. The client application tells the server what to do, and the server, as its name implies, provides back-end services. In client/server application, the client is in charge and sends requests for data and computing services to the server.

Just the opposite is true with cooperative processing: the application resides on the host. The host is in charge and tells the workstation what to do, and the workstation provides various front-end services, such as laying out a screen or creating a graph. Not only does the data base reside on the host, so does the application. The workstation executes machine-intensive tasks under the command of the host-based application (see Exhibit II-5-2).

### Architectural Differences

In a distributed client/server application, there are really two completely separate pieces of software. The client software and server software are completely

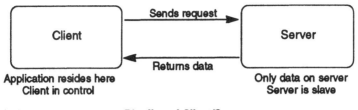

**a. Distributed Client/Server**

**b. Cooperative Processing**

**Exhibit II-5-2. Distributed Client/Server Versus Cooperative Processing Model**

independent, interconnected through an industry standard, open systems protocol. For example, the user might have a spreadsheet application running on the client machine, talking to a data base on the server. In fact, one client machine can talk to multiple servers and one server can talk to multiple clients by using an open protocol that all the different clients and servers understand.

In a cooperative processing application, the software running on the host and the software running on the microcomputer are two pieces of one integrated system. One cannot be used without the other. The data that flows over the network is encoded in a special proprietary language (see Exhibit II-5-3).

Even though the connection between the host and workstation is closed (i.e., the workstation can talk only to its associated host, and vice versa), the user can still attach other host products, such as SQL data bases, through an application program interface on the host. Similarly, the workstation portion of a cooperative processing application can talk to other workstation programs (e.g., spreadsheets) through a workstation interface such as Windows' Dynamic Data Exchange. Only the communication between the host and the workstation is closed.

The advantage of having a closed architecture between the host and the workstation is that the application has complete control of everything that goes across the network. It is this closed architecture and the intelligence built into the software at both ends of the wire that allow highly interactive programs such as Pilot's Command Center, the Sears/IBM's Prodigy system, or Compu-Serve to operate over low-bandwidth phone lines.

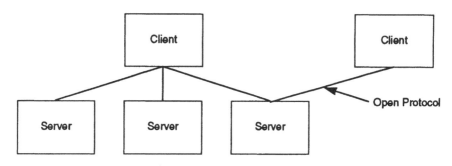

**a. Distributed Client/Server Model**

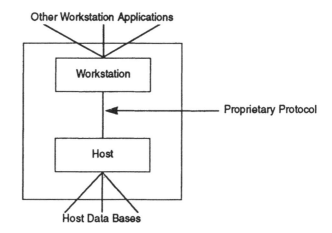

**b. Cooperative Processing Application**

**Exhibit II-5-3. Open Versus Proprietary Protocol**

## CENTRALIZED VERSUS DISTRIBUTED APPLICATIONS AND DATA

One of the advantages of distributed client/server computing is that applications can be developed by users without IS involvement. If the server with its data bases is maintained by IS support staff, users can still hook up whatever client software they want and build their own applications.

The server becomes, in effect, a library, and IS becomes the librarian, helping users find the data they need, though not necessarily helping them use it. Data and applications are distributed to the user's microcomputer or LAN server.

The advantages of openness can become a disadvantage when IS support staff are held accountable for the user's applications. If the applications developer cannot control the application running on the user's microcomputer, the developer cannot ensure that what the user sees on the screen is correct.

In addition, security cannot be enforced once the data is out of the control of IS staff. Data security and data integrity are two of the most vexing problems associated with distributed client/server applications.

Cooperative processing applications are more like traditional host-based applications, because both applications and data reside on the host where, presumably, they are under IS control. Users are guaranteed to see exactly the same data and applications at any time. IS staff can have total control regardless of whether users are local or around the world. The trade-off is that somewhat less processing is offloaded to the workstation and the interface between the host and workstation is closed, which makes it harder to snap in other pieces of software.

## WORKSTATION CACHING

Anyone who has used a cooperative processing system has probably noticed that the system seems to get faster the more it is used. A workstation caching scheme ensures that the user never has to send any screen templates or data to the workstation more than once.

A cooperative processing screen consists of a template, which is sent from the host to the microcomputer. The template includes predefined areas for data, text, pictures, icon, and hot spots. Once this template has been received by the workstation, it is cached—that is, saved on the workstation's disk, along with a unique version stamp. Anytime the template is needed for a data display, it is recalled from disk and merged with data coming from the host (see Exhibit II-5-4). The complete screen (template plus data) is cached temporarily in case it is needed again during the session. Anytime a cached template is used,

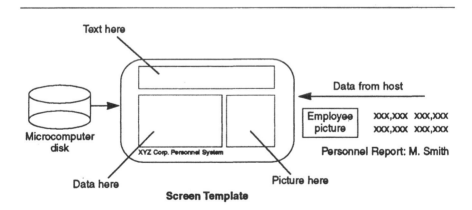

**Note:**
The template is retrieved from the microcomputer's cache and merged with data transmitted from the host.

**Exhibit II-5-4. A Cooperative Processing Screen Template**

the microcomputer checks with the host to make sure the version has not been updated on the host.

The two benefits of this caching scheme are speed and terse communications. Recalling a cached template from disk takes only a fraction of a second (compared with perhaps 5 to 10 seconds to transmit the template in the first place). After a while, most of the screens the user sees have been accessed previously and cached. Consequently, the system gets faster the more it is used. Furthermore, only the bare minimum of information needs to be transmitted across the network. This reduces network costs and, more important, further contributes to fast response time. The sample cooperative session, illustrated in Exhibit II-5-5, shows how the host and microcomputer interact and use caching to speed up response and minimize communications.

## COOPERATIVE PROCESSING AS A WAY TO SIMPLIFY DOWNSIZING

The centralized control and unique communications characteristics of cooperative processing can simplify downsizing. Cooperative processing combines the advantages of a high-quality graphical user interface (GUI), much of the cost efficiencies of distributed client/server computing, and most of the desirable security and integrity features of a mainframe application.

The biggest complaints about traditional host-based applications concern cost, speed, and quality of human interface. Microcomputer software has set the market's level of expectations for ease of use and attractiveness. Both these characteristics are made possible by the inexpensive processing power of a microcomputer. Graphical interfaces, such as Windows, require a lot of computing power if they are to run fast, however.

A traditional mainframe and dumb terminal cannot give the user the kind of graphical interface that exists on a basic microcomputer; there is no point-and-click mouse capability, no high-quality color graphics, and response times are unpredictable. The whole business is expensive because all the computing must be done on the host, where the MIPS are most expensive.

Downsizing typically involves rewriting applications to run in a distributed environment, as shown in Exhibit II-5-6. Instead of each remote location having a live connection to the mainframe, each location has its own LAN with its own server and local data bases. The LANs are linked together in a wide area network (WAN). It is important to remember that the bandwidth of a LAN is usually several orders of magnitude greater than the bandwidth of the WAN (which may be as simple as a 9,600-baud line). Although large amounts of data can be moved cheaply from server to workstation, moving data from one server to another is considerably slower and more costly. This means that distributed client/server applications (which typically depend on the high bandwidth of a LAN) do not operate effectively across different LANs. In other words, a client on the LAN in London cannot use the server in Chicago and

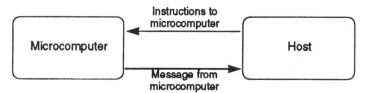

| Microcomputer | Host |
|---|---|
| • AUTOEXEC starts microcomputer software. Log-on script connects microcomputer to host. | • Host identifies user and looks up user's first screen. |
| | • Host asks microcomputer if it has screen on disk already. |
| • Microcomputer responds "yes" and sends version stamp. | • Host recognizes version as obsolete and sends latest version. |
| • Microcomputer displays screen and stores it for future use. | • Host awaits instructions from microcomputer. |
| • User clicks on icon for "Finance Report." Microcomputer sends notification to host. | • Host looks up what it is supposed to do when user clicks this icon. |
| | • Host tells microcomputer it needs screen template XYZ. |
| • Microcomputer responds "I have version xxx." | • Host says, "Display it." |
| | • Host accesses data base, does computations and ships data to fill in template. |
| • Microcomputer displays template and data, then saves it for reuse during session. | • Host awaits instructions from microcomputer. |
| • User clicks on a number on the screen in order to see trend bar graph. | • Host accesses historical data from data base and sends it to microcomputer with instructions to turn numbers into a bar chart. |
| • Microcomputer captures incoming numbers, creates bar chart. | • Host awaits instructions from microcomputer. |

**Exhibit II-5-5. Sample Cooperative Processing Session**

get reasonable response time because the bandwidth across the WAN is much lower than the bandwidth of one of the LANs.

Because it is usually not practical to run an application across the WAN, the application must be replicated on each LAN server to make it accessible to everyone in the organization. This creates another problem: centralized control over the application is lost. There is no longer just one copy of the data and application on a mainframe that everyone shares.

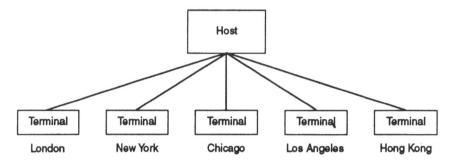

a. Central Host Links to Terminals by Phone Lines or Packet Switching Networks

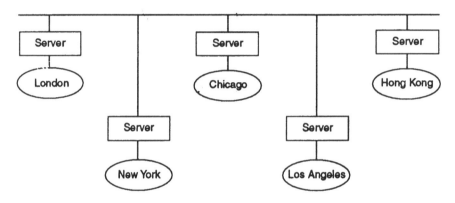

b. Remote Locations Have Live Connection to the Mainframe

**Exhibit II-5-6. Mainframe-Based Versus Distributed Application**

Organizations trying to downsize traditional host-based applications frequently discover this the hard way. They wind up with different versions of
data and applications on different servers and microcomputers, and there is
no easy way for IS staff to ensure the accuracy or integrity of what users see
on the screen. This is one of the reasons such applications are referred to as
fragile, and it is one of the reasons that distributed client/server applications
require significantly more manual labor to maintain than host-based applications. Because cooperative processing applications require much less bandwidth than distributed client/server applications, they can operate across a
WAN to a centralized host. At the same time, much of the processing is offloaded
to the users' workstations, thereby affording some of the economies inherent
in distributed client/server applications. In addition, because the workstations
can run popular GUIs, users get the same state-of-the-art interfaces offered
by distributed client/server applications.

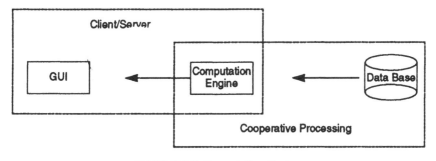

**Exhibit II-5-7. Computation Engine**

## COMPUTATION ENGINES

Why do distributed client/server applications require so much more network bandwidth? The answer lies partly in where on the network computation and data manipulation take place (see Exhibit II-5-7). In either a distributed client/ server or cooperative processing application, data gets to the screen in three steps: from the data base to the computation engine to the graphical user interface.

The amount of data that flows from the data base to the computation engine is much larger than the amount that flows from the computation to the GUI. For example, if there is a data base of daily sales of 1,000 products and the user wants to see total sales monthly for the year to date (and the user is roughly 3 months into the year), about 90,000 numbers would have to be retrieved from the data base and passed to the computation engine, where they would be added up into 3 monthly year-to-date figures. The resulting totals would then be passed to the GUI. In this case, there would be only 3 numbers passed from the computation engine to the GUI, whereas there are 90,000 numbers passed from the data base to the computation engine.

If the computation engine resides on the microcomputer, as is the case in most distributed client/server applications, a lot more bandwidth is needed to get all the data to the workstation quickly. If the computation engine is on the host, as it is in cooperative processing, very little bandwidth is needed because the user is sending only the summarized data. A well-designed coopera-tive processing application usually works acceptably even over phone lines, which would be far too slow for most distributed client/server applications.

## FIVE CARDINAL RULES OF COOPERATIVE PROCESSING

There are five important rules for designing any cooperative processing system; these rules are at work in any commercial cooperative processing product or development environment.

*Rule 1. Keep Total Host Processing to an Absolute Minimum.* The key is to make the microcomputer work as hard as possible. Only those operations that must architecturally remain on the host should execute on the host. Usually this means data bases, consolidating computation (to reduce network traffic), and application logic. The actual operations, such as formatting screens or creating graphs, should execute on the workstation.

*Rule 2. Provide the Fastest Possible Access to Information and Use Caching for Instantaneous Access to Repeat Data.* Low-band-width communications reduce information bandwidth to the logical minimum possible. Fast links should be provided between the computation engine and underlying data bases, especially fast access to relational data bases.

*Rule 3. Never Force the Data Base to Access the Same Data More Than Once.* It is important to cache anything at the workstation that might be needed again and to always use version stamps to make updating automatic.

*Rule 4. Keep Communications Between the Microcomputer and Mainframe to the Logical Minimum.* Terse codes should be used to instruct the workstation and compress data transmission wherever possible.

*Rule 5. Preserve All the Security and Integrity Features of the Host Operating System.* Because control resides on the host, there is no need to give up any of the security features usually found on the host.

## SUMMARY

Data center managers want to take best advantage of their options where downsizing and distributed computing is concerned. This chapter explains the characteristics, limitations, and advantages of two distributed topologies. The cooperative processing versus distributed client/server self-test (see Exhibit II-5-1) is a quick way to determine when to use cooperative processing and when to use a client/server solution for an organization's applications.

# II-6
# Managing Distributed Computing

*RICHARD ROSS*

M any concerns of data center managers relate directly to the issues of distributing information technology to end users. The explosive rate at which information technology has found its way into the front office, combined with the lack of control by the data center organization, has left many data center managers at a loss as to how they should best respond. The following issues are of special concern:

- Where should increasingly scarce people and monetary resources be invested?
- What skills will be required to implement and support the new environment?
- How fast should the transition from a centralized computing environment to a distributed computing environment occur?
- What will be the long-term impact of actions taken today to meet short-term needs?
- What will be the overall ability of the data center group to deliver to new standards of service created by changing user expectations in a distributed computing environment?

The inability to resolve these issues is causing a conflict in many organizations. Particularly in large companies during the past decade, the rule of thumb for technology investment has been that the opportunity cost to the business unit of not being able to respond to market needs will always outweigh the savings accruing from constraining technology deployment. This has resulted in a plethora of diverse and incompatible systems, often supported by independent organizations. In turn, these developments have brought to light another, even greater risk—that the opportunity cost to the corporation of not being able to act as a single entity will always outweigh the benefit of local flexibility.

The recent experiences of some businesses provide good examples of this conflict. One concerned a global retailer with sales and marketing organizations in many countries. To meet local market needs, each country had its own management structure with independent manufacturing, distribution, and systems organizations. The result was that the company's supply chain became clogged—raw materials sat in warehouses in one country while factories in another went idle; finished goods piled up in one country while store shelves were empty in others; costs rose as the number of basic patterns proliferated. Perhaps most important, the incompatibility of the systems prevented management from gaining an understanding of the problem and from being able to pull it all together at the points of maximum leverage while leaving the marketing and sales functions a degree of freedom.

Another example comes from a financial service firm. The rush to place technology into the hands of traders has resulted in a total inability to effectively manage risk across the firm or to perform single-point client service or multiproduct portfolio management.

## WANTED—A NEW FRAMEWORK FOR MANAGING

The problem for data center managers is that a distributed computing environment cannot be managed according to the lessons learned during the last 20 years of centralized computing. First and foremost, the distributed computing environment developed largely because the data center organization could not deliver appropriate levels of service to the business units. Arguments about the ever-declining cost of desktop technology are all well and good, but the fact of the matter is that managing and digesting technology is not the job function of users. If the data center organization could have met their needs, it is possible users would have been more inclined to forgo managing their own systems.

The inability of data centers to meet those needs while stubbornly trying to deliver centralized computing has caused users to go their own ways. It is not just the technology that is at fault. The centralized computing skills themselves are not fully applicable to a distributed computing environment. For example, the underlying factors governing risk, cost, and quality of service have changed. Data center managers need a new framework that helps them to balance the opportunity cost to the business unit against that to the company while optimizing overall service delivery.

## DEFINING THE PROBLEM: A MODEL FOR DCE SERVICE DELIVERY

To help data center managers get a grip on the problem, this chapter proposes a model of service delivery for the distributed computing environment (DCE). This model focuses on three factors that have the most important influence on service, as well as on the needs of the business units versus the corporation—risk, cost, and quality (see Exhibit II-6-1). Each factor is analyzed to understand its cause and then to determine how best to reduce it (in the case of risk and cost) or increase it (as in quality).

Risk in any systems architecture is due primarily to the number of independent elements in the architecture (see Exhibit II-6-2). Each element carries

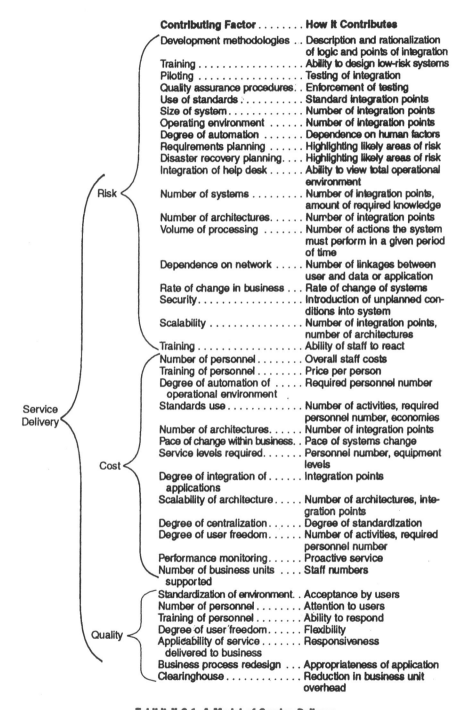

**Contributing Factor** . . . . . . . **How It Contributes**

**Risk**

Development methodologies . . Description and rationalization of logic and points of integration
Training . . . . . . . . . . . . . . . . . Ability to design low-risk systems
Piloting . . . . . . . . . . . . . . . . . Testing of integration
Quality assurance procedures . . Enforcement of testing
Use of standards . . . . . . . . . . Standard integration points
Size of system . . . . . . . . . . . . Number of integration points
Operating environment . . . . . Number of integration points
Degree of automation . . . . . . Dependence on human factors
Requirements planning . . . . . . Highlighting likely areas of risk
Disaster recovery planning. . . . Highlighting likely areas of risk
Integration of help desk . . . . . . Ability to view total operational environment
Number of systems . . . . . . . . Number of integration points, amount of required knowledge
Number of architectures. . . . . . Number of integration points
Volume of processing . . . . . . . Number of actions the system must perform in a given period of time
Dependence on network . . . . . Number of linkages between user and data or application
Rate of change in business . . . Rate of change of systems
Security. . . . . . . . . . . . . . . . . Introduction of unplanned conditions into system
Scalability . . . . . . . . . . . . . . . Number of integration points, number of architectures
Training . . . . . . . . . . . . . . . . . Ability of staff to react

**Cost**

Number of personnel . . . . . . . Overall staff costs
Training of personnel . . . . . . . Price per person
Degree of automation of . . . . . Required personnel number
  operational environment
Standards use . . . . . . . . . . . . Number of activities, required personnel number, economies
Number of architectures. . . . . . Number of integration points
Pace of change within business. . Pace of systems change
Service levels required. . . . . . . Personnel number, equipment levels
Degree of integration of . . . . . . Integration points
  applications
Scalability of architecture . . . . . Number of architectures, integration points
Degree of centralization. . . . . . Degree of standardization
Degree of user freedom. . . . . . Number of activities, required personnel number
Performance monitoring. . . . . . Proactive service
Number of business units . . . . Staff numbers
  supported

**Quality**

Standardization of environment. . Acceptance by users
Number of personnel . . . . . . . Attention to users
Training of personnel . . . . . . . Ability to respond
Degree of user freedom. . . . . . Flexibility
Applicability of service . . . . . . . Responsiveness
  delivered to business
Business process redesign . . . Appropriateness of application
Clearinghouse . . . . . . . . . . . . Reduction in business unit overhead

Service Delivery

**Exhibit II-6-1. A Model of Service Delivery**

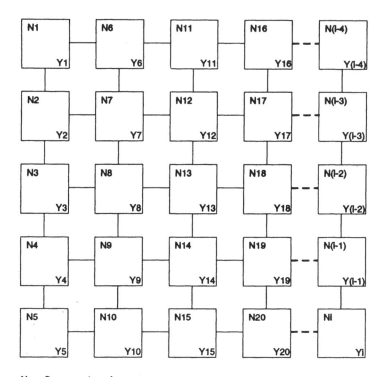

N = Component number

Y = Component risk

Given fully independent components, total network risk is equivalent to the sum of the individual component risks, 1 to I. Thus, the way to minimize risk is either to minimize I (i.e., to have a centralized computing environment) or to minimize Y for each component by standardizing on components with minimum risk profiles.

**Exhibit II-6-2. Optimization of Risk in a Network**

its own risk, say for failure, and this is compounded by the risk associated with the interface between each element.

This is the reason that a distributed computing environment has a greater operational risk than a centralized one—there are more independent elements in a DCE. However, because each element tends to be smaller and simpler to construct, a DCE tends to have a much lower project risk than a centralized environment. Thus, one point to consider in rightsizing should be how soon a system is needed. For example, a Wall Street system that is needed right away and has a useful competitive life of only a few years would be best built in a distributed computing environment to ensure that it gets online quickly. Conversely, a manufacturing system that is not needed right away but will remain in service for years is probably better suited for centralization.

One other difference between a distributed environment and a centralized environment is the impact of a particular risk. Even though a DCE is much more likely to have a system component failure, each component controls such a small portion of the overall system that the potential impact of any one failure is greatly reduced. This is important to take into account when performing disaster planning for the new environment.

Cost is largely a function of staff levels (see Exhibit II-6-3). As the need for service increases, the number of staff members invariably increases as well. People are flexible and can provide a level of service far beyond that of automation. Particularly in a dynamic environment, in which the needs for response are ill-defined and can change from moment to moment, people are the only solution.

Unfortunately, staff is usually viewed as a variable cost, to be cut when

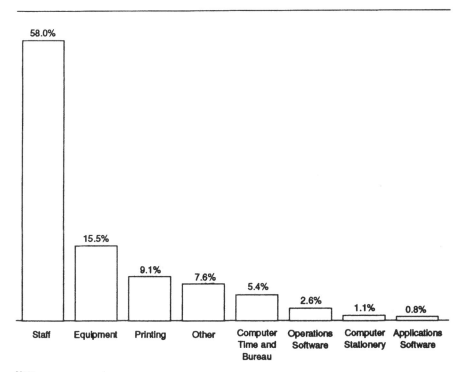

**Note:**

*Average of organizations studied; total IS costs

SOURCE: Decision Strategies Group

**Exhibit II-6-3. Cost Profile of the IS Function**

the need for budget reductions arises. This results in a decrease in service delivered that is often disproportionately larger than the savings incurred through staff reductions.

Finally, quality is a subjective judgment, impossible to quantify but the factor most directly reated to the user's perception of service where information technology is concerned. In essence, the perception of quality is proportional to the response to three questions:

- Can users accomplish their tasks?
- Can they try new things to get the job done?
- Are they being paid the attention they deserve?

It is interesting to note that except for the sheer ability to get the job done, the perception of quality is not necessarily a factor of how much technology a user is provided with. Instead, quality is largely a function of the degree of freedom users have to try new things and whether they are being listened to. This may mean that for many organizations, a simpler environment—one in which the user has fewer technological options but has ready access to human beings—is more satisfying.

This view is in direct contrast with the approach many companies have taken of delivering more capabilities to the users in an effort to increase their perception of service delivered. One of the most important factors in the perceived quality of service delivery is the ability of the support technology to work unnoticed. Because of the similarities between this need and the way in which the US telephone network operates (a customer picks up the phone and the service is invariably there), the term *dial tone* is used to describe such a background level of operation.

One problem with highly functional IS environments is that users must think about them to use them. This is not the case with the telephone system, which operates so dependably that its customers have integrated it into their routine working practices and use it without much conscious effort. The phone companies maintain this level of usefulness by clearly separating additional features from basic service and letting the customer add each new feature as the customer desires.

This can be contrasted with the typical business system that represents an attempt to deliver a package of functions on day one and to continually increase its delivered functionality. The impact on users is that they are forced to continually adapt to changes, are not allowed to merge the use of the system into the background, and must continually stop delivering on their jobs just to cope with the technology. This coping might be as simple as looking something up in a manual or changing a printer cartridge, or it may mean not working at all while the system is rebooted.

Does anyone ever call up AT&T and congratulate it for keeping the nation's phones working that day? Of course not. Yet IS organizations are continually disappointed when users do not seem to appreciate that they have delivered 99.99% availability and a 24-hour help desk.

## COMPLEXITY: THE BARRIER TO SERVICE DELIVERY

In general, the basic driver to each of the three service factors is complexity. Complexity augments risk by increasing the number of interfaces between system elements as well as the number of elements themselves. It raises cost by increasing the need for staff as the only way to deal with ill-defined environments. Finally, it affects quality by making it harder to provide those services that users base their perception of quality on (i.e., dial tone and personal attention), in response to which even more staff are added.

This, then, is the paradoxical environment in which data center managers operate. To improve the quality of service, they find themselves increasing the risk and cost of the operation. Improved application delivery cycles result in more systems to manage. End-user development tools and business unit-led development multiply the number of architectures and data formats. Enlarging access to corporate data through networks increases the number of interfaces. Conversely, trying to improve the risk and cost aspects, typically through standardization of the environment, usually results in decreased levels of service delivered because of the constraints placed on the user freedom. This paradox did not exist in the good old days of centralized computing, when the data center function dictated the service level.

## FIVE PIECES OF ADVICE FOR MANAGING DISTRIBUTED COMPUTING

The measure of success in a distributed computing environment is therefore the ability to deliver service through optimizing for the factors of risk, cost, and quality while meeting the needs of both the business units and the corporation. It sounds like a tall order, but it is not impossible. There are five key practices involved in corporate information processing:

- Manage tightly, but control loosely.
- Organize to provide service on three levels.
- Choose one standard—even a single bad one is better than none or many good ones.
- Integrate data at the front end—do not homogenize on the back end.
- Minimize the use of predetermined architectures.

## MANAGE TIGHTLY, BUT CONTROL LOOSELY

The situation for the Allied paratroopers at the Bulge was grim. Vastly outnumbered, outgunned, and in a logistically poor location, they faced a greater likelihood of total annihilation than of any sort of victory. Yet they managed to hold out for days, waiting for reinforcements and beating an orderly retreat when they finally came.

In Korea, the First Marine Division at Chosin Reservoir and the Second Infantry Division at Kunu-ri faced the Chinese backlash from the UN decision to cross the 38th parallel. The marines retreated in good order, bringing their dead and wounded and all their equipment with them and disabling between a quarter and a third of all Chinese troops along the way. The army in Korea, in contrast, suffered many casualties, lost most of its equipment, and escaped as a scattered bunch of desperate men.

What do these battle stories signify for the manager of a distributed computing environment? They highlight the need for flexible independence at the front lines, based on a solid foundation of rules and training and backed up with timely and appropriate levels of support. The marines in Korea and the army at the Battle of the Bulge reacted flexibly to the situation at hand; in addition, they were backed by rigorous training that reinforced standards of action as well as by a supply chain that made action possible. In contrast, the army in Korea suffered from a surfeit of central command, which clogged supply lines and rendered the frontline troops incapable of independent action.

In the distributed computing environment, the users are in the thick of battle, reacting with the best of their abilities to events moment by moment. The data center manager can support these troops in a way that allows them to react appropriately or makes them stop and call for a different type of service while customers get more and more frustrated.

## Two Tools

Two tools that are key to enabling distributed management are business process redesign (BPR) and metrics. BPR gets the business system working first, highlights the critical areas requiring support, builds consensus between the users and the data center organization as to the required level of support, and reduces the sheer number of variables that must be managed at any one time. In essence, playing BPR first allows a company to step back and get used to the new environment.

Without a good set of metrics, there is no way to tell how effective data center management has been or where effort needs to be applied moment to moment. The metrics required to manage a distributed computing environment are different from those data center management is used to. With central computing, management basically accepted that it would be unable to determine the actual support delivered to any one business. Because centralized computing environments are so large and take so long to implement, their costs and performance are spread over many functions. For this reason, indirect measurements were adopted when speaking of central systems, measures such as availability and throughput.

However, these indirect measurements do not tell the real story of how much benefit a business might derive from its investment in a system. With distributed computing, it is possible to allocate expenses and effort not only to a given business unit but to an individual business function as well. Data center managers must take advantage of this capability by moving away from the old measurements of computing performance and refocusing on business metrics, such as return on investment.

In essence, managing a distributed computing environment means balancing the need of the business units to operate independently while fiercely protecting corporate synergy. Metrics can help do this by providing a clear and honest basis for discussion. Appropriately applied standards can help, too. For example, studies show that in a large system, as much as 90% of the code can be reused. This means that a business unit could reduce its coding effort by some theoretical amount up to that 90%—a forceful incentive to comply with such standards as code libraries and object-oriented programming.

For those users who remain recalcitrant in the face of productivity gains, there remains the use of pricing to influence behavior. However, using pricing to justify the existence of an internal supplier is useless. Instead, pricing should be used as a tool to encourage users to indulge in behavior that supports the strategic direction of the company.

For example, an organization used to allow any word processing package that the users desired. It then reduced the number of packages it would support to two, but still allowed the use of any package. This resulted in an incurred cost due to help desk calls, training problems, and system hangs. The organization eventually settled on one package as a standard, gave it free to all users, and eliminated support for any other package. The acceptance of this standard package by users was high, reducing help calls and the need for human intervention. Moreover, the company was able to negotiate an 80% discount over the street price from the vendor, further reducing the cost.

This was clearly a benefit to everyone concerned, even if it did not add up from a transfer pricing point of view. That is, individual business units may have suffered from a constrained choice of word processor or may have had to pay more, even with the discount, but overall the corporation did better than it otherwise would have. In addition to achieving a significant cost savings, the company was able to drastically reduce the complexity of its office automation environment, thus allowing it to deliver better levels of service.

## ORGANIZE TO PROVIDE SERVICE ON THREE LEVELS

The historical data center exists as a single organization to provide service to all users. Very large or progressive companies have developed a two-dimensional delivery system: part of the organization delivers business-focused service (particularly applications development), and the rest acts as a generic utility. Distributed computing environments require a three-dimensional service delivery organization. In this emerging organization model, one dimension of service is for dial tone, overseeing the technology infrastructure. A second dimension is for business-focused or value-added services, ensuring that the available technology resources are delivered and used in a way that maximizes benefit to the business unit. The third dimension involves overseeing synergy, which means ensuring that there is maximum leverage between each business unit and the corporation.

Dial-tone computing services lend themselves to automation and outsourcing. They are too complex to be well managed or maintained by human activity alone. They must be stable, because this is the need of users of these services. In addition, they are nonstrategic to the business and lend themselves to economies of scale and hence are susceptible to outsourcing (see Exhibits II-6-4 and II-6-5).

Value-added services should occur at the operations as well as at the development level. For example, business unit managers are responsible for overseeing the development of applications and really understanding the business. This concept should be extended to operational areas, such as training, maintenance, and the help desk. When these resources are placed in the

| Common Operational Problem | Responsiveness to Automation |
|---|:---:|
| Equipment hangs | ● |
| Network contention | ◖ |
| Software upgrades | ● |
| Equipment upgrades | ○ |
| Disaster recovery | ● |
| Backups | ● |
| Quality assurance of new applications | ● |
| Equipment faults (e.g., print cartridge replacement, disk crash) | ○ |
| Operator error (e.g., forgotten password, kick out plug) | ○ |
| Operator error (e.g., not understanding how to work application) | ● |

Responsiveness
High      ●
Medium   ◖
Low        ○

SOURCE: Interviews and Decision Strategies Group analysis

**Exhibit II-6-4. Responsiveness of Operations to Automation**

| Dial Tone Function | Applicability |
|---|:---:|
| Equipment maintenance | ● |
| Trouble calls | ● |
| Help desk | ● |
| Installations | ● |
| Moves and changes | ● |
| Billing | ◑ |
| Accounting | ◑ |
| Service level contracting | ○ |
| Procurement | ○ |
| Management | ○ |

Applicability
High ●
Medium ◑
Low ○

SOURCE: Interviews and Decision Strategies Group analysis

**Exhibit II-6-5. Applicability of Outsourcing to Dial Tone**

business unit, they are better positioned to work with the users to support their business instead of making the users take time out to deal with the technology.

People do not learn in batch. They learn incrementally and retain information pertinent to the job at hand. This is the reason that users need someone to show them what they need to accomplish the job at hand. Help desks should be distributed to the business units so that the staff can interact with the users, solve problems proactively (before performance is compromised) and accumulate better information to feed back to the central operation.

The third level of service—providing maximum leverage between the business unit and the corporation—is perhaps the most difficult to maintain and represents the greatest change in the way data center managers do business today. Currently, staff members in charge of the activities that leverage across all business units are the most removed from those businesses. Functions such as strategic planning, test beds, low-level coding, and code library development tend to be staffed by technically excellent people with little or no business knowledge. This situation must be turned around; senior staff must be recruited with knowledge of the business functions, business process redesign, and corporate planning. These skills are needed to take the best of each business unit, combine it into a central core, and deliver it back to the businesses.

## CHOOSE ONE STANDARD

In the immortal words of the sneaker manufacturer, "Just do it." If the key to managing a distributed computing environment is to reduce complexity, then implementing a standard is the thing to do. Moreover, the benefits to be achieved from even a bad standard, if it helps to reduce complexity, outweigh the risks incurred from possibly picking the wrong standard. The message is clear: there is more to be gained from taking inappropriate action now than from waiting to take perfect action later.

It should be clear that IT is moving more and more toward commodity status. The differences between one platform and another will disappear over time. Even if management picks a truly bad standard, it will likely merge with the winner in the next few years, with little loss of investment. More important, the users are able to get on with their work. In addition, it is easier to move from one standard to the eventual winner than from many.

Even if management picks the winner, there is no guarantee that it will not suffer a discontinuity. IBM made its customers migrate from the 360 to 370 architecture. Microsoft is moving from DOS to Windows to Windows NT. UNIX is still trying to decide which version it wants to be. The only thing certain about information technology is the pace of change; there is little use in waiting for things to quiet down before making a move.

## INTEGRATE DATA AT THE FRONT END

At the very core of a company's survival is the ability to access data as needed. Companies have been trying for decades to find some way to create a single data model that standardizes the way it stores data and thus allows for access by any system.

The truth of the matter is that for any sufficiently large company (i.e., one with more than one product in one market), data standardization is unrealistic. Different market centers track the same data in different ways. Different systems require different data formats. New technologies require data to be stated in new ways. To try to standardize the storage of data means ignoring these facts of life to an unreasonable extent.

To try to produce a single model of all corporate data is impossible and meaningless. Models invariably grow to be so large that they cannot be implemented. They impose a degree of integration on the data that current systems technology cannot support, rendering the largest relational data base inoperative. And they are static, becoming obsolete shortly after implementation, necessitating constant reworking. Moreover, monolithic data models represent unacceptable project risk.

The standardization approach also ignores the fact that businesses have 20 to 30 years' worth of data already. Are they to go back and recreate all this to satisfy future needs? Probably not. Such a project would immobilize a business and the creation of future systems for years to come.

Systems designed to integrate and reconcile data from multiple sources, presenting a single image to the front end, intrinsically support the client/server model of distributed computing and build flexibility into future applications. They allow data to be stored in many forms, each optimized for the application at hand. More important, they allow a company to access its data on an as-needed basis. These integration systems are an important component to successfully managing future growth.

## LESS ARCHITECTURE IS MORE

To overdesign a systems architecture is to overly constrain the organization. Most architecture arises as a function of rightsizing of applications on the basis of where the data must be stored and used. Understanding this helps the data center manager size the network and associated support infrastructure.

The management of risk and impact also drives architecture by forcing redundancy of systems and, in some cases, mandating the placement of data repositories regardless of user preferences. Assessing project versus operational risk helps to determine whether a system is built for central or distributed use.

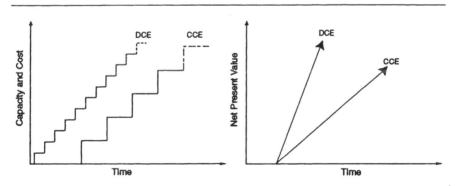

Distributed computing environment (DCE) has a higher net present value because its capacity can be used sooner relative to its marginal costs when compared with the centralized computing environment (CCE).

SOURCE: Decision Strategies Group

**Exhibit II-6-6. Net Present Value of Distributed Versus Centralized Computing**

This view is one in which the business needs drive the shape of the architecture. It results in a dynamic interconnection of systems that respond flexibly to business needs. Under a centralized computing environment, it was impractical to employ such an approach. It took so long and cost so much to implement a system that investment had to come before business need. This necessitated preplanning of an architecture as an investment guide.

The economics of distributed computing are different. Systems cost much less and can be quickly implemented. This means that their use can be responsive to business needs instead of anticipative. It also results in a greater net present value, for even though their operational costs might be higher, distributed computing environments are more immediately useful for a given level of investment (see Exhibit II-6-6).

## SUMMARY

There indeed exists a framework for managing the new computing environment, one that in fact more directly relates to the business than their old way of managing did. Data center managers who master it enhance their opportunities to become members of corporate business management teams instead of simply suppliers of computing services.

Success in a distributed computing environment requires a serious culture shift for data center managers. They must loosen up their management styles, learning to decentralize daily control of operations. They must provide direction to staff members so that they can recognize synergies among business units. Some jobs that were viewed as low-level support activities (e.g. value-added services such as help desk and printer maintenance) must be recognized as key to user productivity and distributed. Others, viewed as senior technical positions (e.g. dial-tone functions such as network management and installations) might best be outsourced, freeing scarce resources.

Most important, data center managers must understand the shift in power away from themselves and toward users. The data center organization is no longer the main provider of services; it now must find a role for itself as a manager of synergy, becoming a facilitator to business units as they learn to manage their own newfound capabilities.

# II-7
# Making the Decision to Outsource

*LAYNE C. BRADLEY*

The trend toward outsourcing has apparently not abated. More and more, organizations are considering outsourcing as a possible solution for controlling IS costs. It is estimated that as many as one out of three companies will choose outsourcing by the end of the 1990s. Regardless of the actual number of companies that do make that choice, it is apparent that outsourcing all or selected parts of an IS organization is becoming an often-used management strategy.

Despite its popularity, outsourcing requires careful planning and is complex to implement. Many organizations are experimenting with outsourcing applications development as well as data center operations. Often, these experiments result in exceptional successes; just as often, however, their outcome is far less successful than what was anticipated.

This chapter is designed to help management in deciding whether to outsource and in implementing an outsourcing program. It examines the benefits and risks involved in turning over certain IS operations to an outside vendor. This chapter also discusses how to interview and negotiate with outsourcing vendors and how to handle employees affected by outsourcing.

## TRENDS IN OUTSOURCING

In the past, data center operations has been a popular target for outsourcing. In comparison to applications development, data center operations has been considered as a low-level IS activity, because it tended to be more labor intensive and repetitive. Nevertheless, data center operations demanded a large investment in personnel and hardware. As corporations began looking for ways to cut IS costs, data center operations became a top candidate for outsourcing.

Corporate management usually believed data center operations were like manufacturing operations and basically could be performed by anyone. As a result, the idea of obtaining data center services from an outside vendor at a lower cost became tempting. Unfortunately, this idea was simplistic and did not take into account many pitfalls and risks, which eventually harmed some companies that outsourced the operations of their data centers.

One IS area that is becoming a popular candidate for outsourcing is applications development. Because applications development is such a complex process, the idea of outsourcing this particular area of IS is somewhat controversial. Applications development is usually considered to be central to a company's IS structure, and this viewpoint has been generally accurate. The applications development group builds the software systems needed to run the company's daily business, create a competitive edge, and control the company's internal data.

Unfortunately, as more demand is placed on the appplications development group for more systems, the applications backlog, which plagues many organizations, grows. New systems are delayed for longer periods of time, costs rise, technological competitive edges disappear, and finally, users and corporate management become highly frustrated. As a result, some companies are considering outsourcing applications development.

## RISKS AND BENEFITS OF OUTSOURCING

Some of the general risks involved in outsourcing that management should be aware of include:

- The financial stability of the vendor.
- The processing capacity of the vendor.
- Loss of key personnel before completing a contract.
- Failure of the vendor to perform as promised.

Cost is another relevant issue that management must consider. This includes costs associated with:

- Planning associated with outsourcing.
- Contract negotiations.
- Lost productivity as rumors begin to circulate.
- Bringing the operation back in-house should the vendor fail to perform.

Outsourcing is an option for many different areas in IS. The data center and applications development are the two areas that appear to be receiving the most consideration today. The operations of these two functions are considerably different, as are the risks associated with trying to outsource them.

The risks in outsourcing data center operations are:

- The inability of the vendor to maintain up-to-date hardware and software.
- The inability of the vendor to maintain sufficient processing power to ensure acceptable response times.
- Failure of the vendor to meet agreed-on service levels.
- Loss of key personnel who are knowledgeable about operations but do not wish to work for the outsourcing vendor.

Outsourcing applications development involves a different set of risks that include:

- Loss of control over strategic direction of development projects.
- Failure by the vendor to provide an effective development environment (e.g., a CASE-based environment).
- Loss of key development personnel who do not want to work for the outsourcing vendor.
- Failure to reduce costs or the applications backlog.

Despite the risks associated with outsourcing applications development, there are valid reasons for considering this option. Some of these reasons include:

- *Reduced costs.* Outsourcing vendors can provide services at a negotiated rate and reduce personnel costs.
- *Lack of internal expertise on particular technologies.* Often, an IS organization does not have or is unable to hire personnel who have expertise in particular technologies. An outsourcing vendor's primary business is to provide services, and to be competitive, it must constantly upgrade and improve the skill level of its personnel.
- *Difficulty recruiting and maintaining qualified personnel.* Because of geographic location, cost of living, lack of budget, or other reasons, an IS organization may have problems recruiting and keeping quality development personnel.
- *Poor quality personnel.* A development group may decide that it simply does not have the type and level of personnel needed to initiate a major new project.
- *Lack of sufficient personnel to meet user demands.* With the trend toward downsizing in many companies today, a development organization may simply not have sufficient personnel to meet the demands of users.

## DECIDING TO OUTSOURCE

It is important not to confuse outsourcing with contract programming. Many companies use contract programmers for specific projects. Usually, these are temporary assignments lasting from a few weeks to months and, occasionally, years. Outsourcing, however, involves turning over the entire applications development process to an outside vendor.

Under an outsourcing agreement, users define their needs and the vendor then becomes responsible for developing and maintaining the required systems. Corporate management can easily fall into a trap by not clearly defining its reason for outsourcing. If it is done primarily in reaction to frustration with the applications group's inability to complete the work load in a timely manner, outsourcing may merely transfer the problem from an in-house group to an outsourcing group.

Users usually become frustrated with IS because the development organization has an extensive backlog of user requests. The users claim that the development group is unresponsive to its needs. Thus, the demand for some action to be taken can cause management to consider outsourcing as a remedy to this problem.

The problem, however, may in fact involve such considerations as lack of sufficient personnel, poor procedures, lack of quality management, and lack of current technologies (e.g., CASE tools). Unless these issues are addressed, outsourcing may simply move the problem to another management team.

Although an outside vendor may be able to implement new methodologies and development tools, both vendor and users must understand that some time may pass before the backlog is significantly reduced. Failure of both parties to understand this point and to set clear and realistic expectations and objectives can quickly lead to frustration and disappointment.

When making the decision to outsource, management must ask itself the following questions:

- The development of application systems should effectively support business strategies—will the outsourcing vendor be able to effectively support these strategies?
- How knowledgeable is the outsourcing vendor about the organization's competitive environment, the organization's position in this environment, and the goals the organization is trying to reach?
- If, for any reason, the outsourcing agreement should not work out successfully, what alternatives exist? How quickly could the operation be brought back in-house? What would be the costs?
- What procedures are needed to coordinate actions between the organization and the outsourcing vendor to ensure that user needs are met?

## PLANNING TO OUTSOURCE

Once it has been decided that outsourcing is an option for meeting an organization's goals and objectives, a great deal of planning must take place before talks are held with potential vendors. Several factors must be considered; these are discussed in the following sections.

### Employee Issues

What should employees be told about management's decision to consider outsourcing? A typical first reaction is to tell them nothing and to keep the decision secret as long as possible. Although this approach may have benefits, it rarely works. Every organization has a formal and an informal structure, and the informal structure is usually better informed than the formal one. There is simply no way to keep a potential change of the size of this decision a secret from the informal structure. Once word has leaked, rumors distort the actual situation. If communication with employees is not handled properly, the organization could lose some highly qualified individuals.

How to handle communication in such a situation is a controversial issue. Some suggested guidelines are:

- Employees should be told that outsourcing is under consideration, emphasizing that no decisions have yet been made.
- Employees should be informed that potential vendors will be visiting to provide presentations. This is important; the sight of strangers going to closed-door meetings is potent fuel for rumors.
- Employees should be assured that they will be kept informed to the extent that this is practical.
- Any rumors that arise should be addressed immediately. The longer rumors are allowed to continue unanswered, the more damage they cause.

In most cases, the outsourcing vendor hires most, if not all, of the current employees. If that is going to be the case, the employees should know. Briefings should be held with employees and the vendor to discuss such issues as benefits, organizational structure, and new career opportunities. If not all employees will be hired and an outplacement program will be offered, the affected employees should know the details of this program.

It is important that the employees be treated as professionals. Applications development staff members are usually highly skilled, well-educated individuals, and they should be treated as such. They know what is currently happening in the industry and that outsourcing is a growing trend. Although employees may be unsettled by the fact that their organization is considering outsourcing, treating them in a professional manner, keeping them informed, and addressing their questions will help settle their worries.

## Retaining Control

Before awarding the outsourcing contract, a major issue that must be considered and planned for: control. A popular myth in corporate management is that outsourcing is equivalent to turning over the IS operation to a vendor, receiving a monthly invoice for services rendered, and ending involvement with that IS operation. Such an attitude toward outsourcing is a prescription for failure, particularly for outsourcing applications development.

Outsourcing the data center is a different proposition from outsourcing applications development. Data center operations are relatively well-defined and repetitive. Although applications development does follow a type of systematic methodology, the development process is characterized by activities that are difficult to define. These activities include personal interactions between development staff and users, technical reviews and progress meetings, prototype demonstrations, and production turnover meetings.

With an in-house applications development operation, these activities are under direct control of the IS group. Once applications development has been outsourced, the vendor is responsible for these activities. However, the control of these activities must remain with the organization. It must be determined how the control function will be implemented effectively. Specific items to be considered include:

- Type and schedule of regular meetings to be held with the vendor, users, and corporate management (e.g., project reviews, planning sessions, budget meetings, design and specification meetings, and production turnover meetings).
- Type and frequently of such required reports as status reports and statements of work.

## CONTACTING VENDORS

Most vendors have a predefined, generic contract, which covers outsourcing arrangements for typical operations. There are, however, few typical operations, and signing such a contract all but guarantees difficulties. The specific issues involved in outsourcing applications development discussed earlier in this chapter should be addressed in detail in the contract.

Many outsourcing agreements have been completed in recent years. Some of these have been covered so extensively in the media that no organization should be unprepared for contract negotiations. There are also reputable and experienced consultants who can provide valuable assistance.

Outsourcing applications development is a major strategic change that must be done carefully. Before entering into contract discussions, management should know:

- Why outsourcing has been taken as an option.
- What specific benefits are expected.
- How the outsourcing arrangement should be conducted on a daily basis.
- How to end the arrangement if it does not work out.
- If necessary, how to recover and restart the IS operation.

Management should think through these issues carefully and develop a written plan to address them before interviews are held with vendors. With such a plan, management is prepared for vendor interviews and negotiations, which will subsequently be directed by management's concerns and not the vendor's.

### Interviewing Vendors

Identifying a qualified vendor to handle applications development can be a difficult task. Several vendors who provide outsourcing services for data center operations, telecommunications, and network management, but those capable of effectively handling applications development are few.

As mentioned earlier in this chapter, there is a difference between contracting programmers for specific projects and outsourcing the entire applications development group. There are many companies who provide contract programmers, and these should not be taken for applications development outsourcing organizations.

When interviewing potential vendors, at least the following questions should be asked:

- How long has the company been in business?
- How stable is it? (The outsourcing company's audited financial statement can answer this question.)
- How many clients do they have and can references be provided?
- How many clients are similar?
- What type of development methodologies does the outsourcing vendor use?
- What is the history of the company? Was it established to do outsourcing? Did it evolve from a contract programming company?
- What types of training programs does the company offer its employees? Are staff kept up to date with current technologies?
- What is the company's management style? Is it a compatible style?

It is important to know whether a vendor has had any outsourcing arrangements fail and, if so, why. Reputable vendors are usually willing to share this information to the extent they can. They should also be willing to provide a reference list. Several of these references should be contacted to determine whether the vendor could meet requirements. Questions that should be posed to these references include:

- What types of development methodologies does the outsourcing vendor use?
- Is the vendor up to date with current technologies?
- What type of turnover rate does the vendor experience?
- How responsive is the vendor to user needs?
- Are projects completed on a timely basis?
- Does the vendor maintain high quality standards?

## SUMMARY

Outsourcing is receiving a great deal of attention today. However, it must not be considered as a quick fix for financial difficulties. The decision to outsource must be well thought out, and once the decision has been made, the entire process must be planned in detail.

Outsourcing applications development offers a different set of challenges than does outsourcing data center operations. Some of the challenges of outsourcing include:

- Maintaining effective control over development activities that have been outsourced.
- Ensuring that corporate objectives continue to be met.
- Ensuring that the outsourcing vendor meets user needs on a timely basis.
- Ensuring that projected cost savings are realized.

To meet these challenges, management must know why it wants to outsource and must spend considerable time and care in selecting the proper outsourcing vendor. Failure to do so could lead to disastrous consequences.

# II-8
# Achieving Quality in Data Center Operations

*JEFF MURRELL*

Improving quality has become an economic necessity, because customers increasingly demand improved value in the products and services they purchase. In addition, corporate profitability demands 100% productivity for every dollar the corporation spends. Improving quality is free because it reduces the costs of rework, service, and replacement. High quality can result in improved customer perception of value, which can also reduce costs.

Corporations need effective information services to compete, and data center management is feeling the brunt of today's competitive environment. Data center operations management is competing with outsourcers, who are winning over the data center function. Only through high-quality operations can the advances of the outsourcers be staved off.

Both internal and external data center customers are becoming increasingly computer-literate. As a result, they are increasing demands for availability, capability, cost-effectiveness, and quality. To satisfy these requirements, the data center and its customers must develop a partnership.

Individual data center staff members also feel the need to improve quality. In general, data center staff members need to feel a level of personal satisfaction from their work and the quality of service they provide to customers. They also know that their professional success and security depends in large part on the ability of their organization to remain competitive.

This chapter examines how these needs for improving the quality of data center operations can be met through the Malcolm Baldrige National Quality Award (MBNQA) framework. The award was established in 1987 to foster quality in US industry. Named after former Secretary of the Commerce Department Malcolm Baldridge, the award is administered by the National Institute of Standards and Technology and the American Society for Quality Control and is awarded by the president.

## THE MALCOLM BALDRIDGE QUALITY AWARD

The award was created to promote awareness and understanding of total quality, to foster improvement in performance, and to promote the sharing of

|  | Points |
|---|---|
| Leadership | 90 |
| Information and Analysis | 80 |
| Strategic Quality Planning | 60 |
| Human Resource Development and Management | 150 |
| Management of Process Quality | 140 |
| Quality and Operational Results | 180 |
| Customer Focus and Satisfaction | 300 |
|  | 1,000 |

**Exhibit II-8-1. Malcolm Baldridge Quality Award Evaluation Categories**

---

quality practices among businesses. Any company having more than 50% of its employees or assets in the US, or any division of such a company that makes more than 50% of its revenue from outside customers, can compete for the award. Every year, the award is given to at most two winners in each of the following categories:

- Manufacturing.
- Service.
- Small Business.

The award is won by companies that have exceeded a certain benchmark level of quality. The award committee examines not only how a contestant plans for quality. It also examines how the contestant implements a total quality plan and the plan's results. Contestants are evaluated in 89 areas addressed in the seven categories listed in Exhibit II-8-1. A contestant may be awarded as many as 1,000 points, and the largest share of points can be won in the customer focus and satisfaction category. This point system underscores that a satisfied customer is the proof of a contestant's commitment to total quality.

Winners of the award can use the award in their marketing strategy. In winning the award, however, they are required to share their techniques with others. This chapter examines how techniques used by previous winners for achieving total quality can be applied to data center operations. One technique that all winners have in common is that they continuously look for new areas for improvement. (The next time they apply for the award, they are expected to improve on their winning score.)

## THE ROLE OF THE DATA CENTER MANAGER

Data center management must set the overall climate for quality. One way to establish this climate is to promote the following:

- *Customer focus.* Everyone in the data center has a customer who, by defining the requirements to be met, defines total quality. The data center manager should promote customer awareness by actively encouraging data center personnel to interact with customers to understand their requirements and to communicate the results of quality improvement.

- *Continuous improvement.* Quality is not attained by being satisfied with the status quo. For example, 99% systems availability or two-second response time is no longer adequate. These may be acceptable milestones in a quality improvement program, but the ultimate goal must be 100% quality as defined by the customer.
- *Involving all staff members.* Management must ensure that all employees can express their suggestions and ideas for achieving quality.

The data center operations manager must look at quality as a discipline and keep current with changes in this discipline. This can be done by attending trade conferences, reading relevant literature, and networking with colleagues to share and learn quality practices.

The manager must also implement a program that defines metrics by which data center operations can be measured and reported. Once measurements are obtained, they can be compared to those of other companies to establish areas for special focus. This process is known as benchmarking and is discussed in a later section of this article.

Data center operations managers should also promote total quality outside the organization. The MBNQA committee examines how the top management of contestant companies promotes quality beyond their own organizations. Data center managers can be ambassadors of quality to their customers. It is equally important for data center managers to communicate the message of quality to senior management and let it know that achieving quality is a goal of the data center.

## ASSESSING QUALITY

Assessing quality is one step in the MBNQA framework. When assessing data center performance, data center managers must measure quality and not quantity. For example, a typical data center contains 500 MIPS of computing power and 2T bytes of direct access storage, processes a million transactions a day, and prints 10 million pages of laser output a month. These quantitative metrics gauge the size of the center's operations and could be used to select a comparison group for benchmarking. However, these metrics do not assess the quality of the operations.

Such metrics as percent availability, cycle time, and price do provide a qualitative view. It is important that data center operations managers use metrics that their customers can understand. It may be useful to measure systems availability, for instance, but it is more valuable to measure availability of an application to its end users. Such a metric might include not only systems availability but also the availability of the applications data base, of the network connection to the customer, and of the terminal used to access the application.

Price is also a valid qualitative metric if it is cost based and stated in terms the customer can understand. For example, cost per account-payable-invoice-processed relates more to business value than a cost in terms of inquiry task time and I/O.

After a set of metrics has been chosen and the quality of the center's operations has been measured, the measurements should be compared. A comparison to customer expectations will yield information that can be used to decide if the appropriate set of metrics has been chosen and if performance is approaching requirements. A formal customer survey may be conducted, or simple one-to-one interviews with key customer representatives can be used as a general guide.

Comparisons to other organizations often provide the impetus for improvement and indicate areas that should be improved. Comparison with peers and MBNQA winners is valuable but can be arduous in terms of arranging schedules and ensuring the same categories are being compared. Competitions held by publishers and other industry groups allow a unique opportunity for comparison. The most authoritative assessment, however, comes from a formal benchmarking effort.

### Assessment Tools

Several tools aid in presenting information in a clear and concise way and should be used in the quality assessment. These tools include:

- *Bar graphs.* These are often used to make comparisons. They can also be used effectively in dealing with suppliers to compare performance against the competition.
- *Pie charts.* These are useful in presenting a point-in-time analysis (e.g., an analysis of which applications are creating console message traffic or of the breakdown of tape-library activity).
- *Line graphs.* These are effective for showing results over a period of time.

| Help Desk Calls | | | Batch Abends | |
|---|---|---|---|---|
| **Subject** | **Percentage** | **Code** | **Reason** | **Percentage** |
| Security | 10 | SOFF | Dataset Missing | 5 |
| PWS Software | 9 | SOC7 | Data Exception | 5 |
| Datacom | 6 | SOFF | Unable to Allocate | 4 |
| LAN | 5 | U1500 | DB on/off Condition | 4 |
| EDI | 5 | U0888 | Tape/Disk Error | 4 |
| Voice | 4 | S04E | DB2 | 4 |
| Help Desk | 4 | S322 | Time-Out | 4 |
| Consulting | 3 | S004 | BDT, EDI | 4 |
| PWS Order | 3 | SB37 | Disk Space | 3 |
| Other | 20 | SD37 | File Full | 2 |

**Exhibit II-8-2. Sample Pareto Charts**

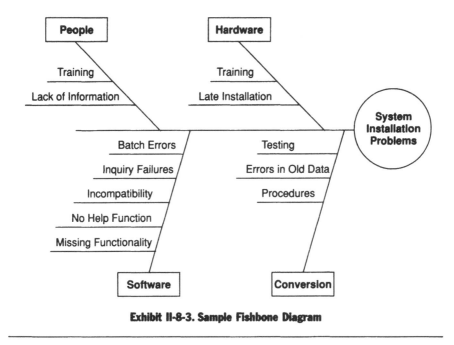

**Exhibit II-8-3. Sample Fishbone Diagram**

- *Pareto charts.* Named after their inventor Vilfredo Pareto, these charts are effective for showing the causes of a problem in descending order of their frequency. Pareto postulated that the top 20% of causes usually account for 80% of a problem. Exhibit II-8-2 presents a sample Pareto chart.
- *Fishbone diagrams.* These can be used by quality teams to understand and categorize causes of low quality to identify areas that require more focused attention. Exhibit II-8-3 shows a sample fishbone diagram.

## BENCHMARKING

Such companies as Real Decisions, Inc., Compass Corp., and Nolan Norton conduct benchmarking studies of data center operations and compare the results of the studies to those of other customers. If a data center participates in a formal benchmark study, the following guidelines should be followed:

- *Allocating sufficient time.* Gathering input for the study is a dedicated effort that may require days or weeks. It is important to spend quality time.
- *Working with the benchmarker.* Data center managers should work with those conducting the study to ensure that the data they provide for the study is the same type of data stored in the benchmark data base. For

example, when counting disk storage, one data center might include data sets allocated to disk and another might not.

- *Conducting benchmark studies frequently and regularly.* Maintaining quality demands continuous improvement, and a point-in-time assessment cannot meet the demands of quality. However, a frequency higher than once per year is probably not going to show demonstrable improvement.
- *Studying leaders.* After the benchmark results are known, data center managers should study the examples set by quality leaders.
- *Using the results for internal public relations.* The results of the benchmark study should be shown to customers and senior management to prove that the data center's operations are competitive and to highlight the areas targeted for improvement. Outsourcers remain in business by focusing on areas where they can be more efficient, but a data center manager can stave off outsourcers by focusing on areas that need improvement.

The following should be avoided when participating in a benchmark study:

- *Limiting the analysis solely to the company's industry.* Data center managers can learn much from data centers whose companies are involved in unrelated industries.
- *Accepting nebulous, generic results.* The benchmarker should provide explicit and detailed results and meaningfully interpret these results. The benchmarker should not be allowed to give observations and recommendations that anyone reading the trade press could give. Data center managers should be aware of form reports in which only the company name has been changed.
- *Rationalizing.* Data center managers should not rationalize a poor performance comparison. Instead, they should find out how the data centers that did well in certain categories achieved those results.

## PLANNING CONSIDERATIONS

In planning for a total quality environment, data center managers should ensure that all data center staff members understand that quality is part of their jobs and not the responsibility of a quality control department. It is very helpful to charter one individual with articulating and promoting the message of quality. This person can also be spokesperson to external parties interested in the data center's quality process. This individual can also arrange training programs, team meetings, and reviews that are part of an ongoing quality program.

Quality must be regarded as a journey and not a destination. Achieving quality is a multiyear investment—not the program of the year—and must be integrated with everyday operations. Aggressive goals must be set, and higher goals should be set once the original ones have been attained. Setting goals in terms of a percentage is recommended for the data center embarking on a quality program. Once the goal of 99% performance has been reached, however, goals should be set in terms of parts-per-million, which is more meaningful in this case. Such companies as Motorola, Inc., IBM Corp., and Texas Instruments, Inc. have as their quality standard six sigma, which equates to a failure rate of one in 3.4 million.

## INVOLVING STAFF

The data center staff is key in realizing quality. Data center management must provide an environment that facilitates the full participation of each staff member in realizing quality. A professional development infrastructure should become part of the data center's budget to ensure that training is available. At least 10 days of technical training per person per year should be budgeted. This amount should not be cut, because keeping the staff's technical skills current is crucial to quality performance. Career counseling should also be provided to ensure that the staff can realize their fullest potential. Employees should be given feedback on their performance, and good performance should be rewarded.

Not only are individual contributions important, but teams play an important part in realizing quality. Teams that cross functions and departments can often accomplish what one individual cannot. Although empowerment is currently a buzzword, giving personnel the feeling of empowerment can be advantageous if they feel empowered to act on behalf of the customer without having to check with their superiors. (Customers also appreciate this.)

## QUALITY ASSURANCE

Quality is ensured when customers are involved in designing the solution to their needs. The service-level agreement states their expectations for the service to be provided by the data center. By providing service at or above the agreement level, the data center's role is ensured in the customer's operations. The service-level agreement also allows actual performance to be compared to expected performance, which can be used to determine areas for improvement.

The data center manager can internally access processes to identify areas for improvement. For example, analysis of the contributors to cycle time in correcting a system outage or in addressing a help-desk call could cause the elimination of steps that add no value to the result. Supplier involvement is also key to quality success. Contracts should stipulate specific quality performance measures. Competitive assessments should include cost, quality issues, and total cost of ownership. Suppliers should be part of a partnership with the data center to provide quality.

## MEASURING RESULTS

Such metrics as IS cost as a percentage of corporate revenue, IS headcount as a percentage of the corporate total, and comparison to competitor's product price can demonstrate quality performance over time and continuous improvement. The data center's contributions to the organization's operations can be measured in terms of systems availability, on-time completion of production processing, and abend frequency for both online and batch processing.

Metrics about staff also indicate the quality of the organization. The rate of employee turnover, percentage of staff contributing suggestions for improvement, average number of training days, and favorable attitude survey scores are such personnel metrics. The current trend toward organizational flattening makes the contributor-to-supervisor ratio a measure of employee empowerment. This metric should be used with care, because some argue that there is a limit to the effectiveness with which a flat organization can operate. The ideal contributor-to-supervisor ratio is probably in the range of 10 : 1; however this ratio varies by function.

Measuring and reporting results of a quality improvement program is a powerful tool for promoting the effectiveness of data center operations to senior management. Goals can be set at the corporate level and progress toward these goals can be reported over time.

On the operational level, daily performance can be tracked using various logging mechanisms, and a sophisticated performance tracking system can automatically notify key personnel when performance boundaries are exceeded. Availability tracking systems can be fed by automated operations tools, so that an entry is made automatically when an application or CPU is out of service. The operator is prompted for descriptive information and is saved the tedium of logging time down, time up, and elapsed time.

An extremely sophisticated system for tracking quality can be used by individual business entities to set their performance goals. Actual performance data is automatically fed into a data base by various tracking systems. Executive reports can be generated using an executive information system interface.

## THE IMPORTANCE OF CUSTOMER SATISFACTION

Customer satisfaction is central to quality. Data center managers may think they understand what constitutes quality, but their customers are the ones who know what quality is. Using advisory boards, teams, or simple one-on-one meetings, data center managers can work with customers to establish the priorities for service-level achievement and the metrics by which quality is measured.

Every staff member in the data center must be aware that she or he has a customer. The console operator's customer may be a technical support staff member who needs a change installed, the tape library operator's customer is the owner of the batch job, and the help desk is a key customer contact area.

The help desk is often where the customer's opinion of the data center is formed. Therefore, the help desk is a prime area for focusing on quality. Tracking such metrics as call-abandon rate, average hold time, and percentage of immediate answers measures the performance of the help desk. However, a deeper understanding of this area's performance can be obtained by having customers rate its service and by measuring cycle time.

Complaint management is an interesting area for measuring customer satisfaction. Many organizations treat a complaint as a nuisance, but every complaint is an opportunity to improve quality if the cause of the complaint is found. For every person calling the help desk, there may be 10 other customers with the same problem, and correcting the problem for the caller does not help the other 10 who did not call. When the help desk receives a call from a customer with a complaint, the help desk should do more than find the solution to the problem. Follow-up calls should be made to ensure that customer is satisfied. To obtain a higher level of customer satisfaction, the customers can be rewarded with free service for reporting a quality problem.

When striving to maintain a high level of customer satisfaction, data center managers should be aware that customers always demand increasingly higher levels of satisfaction. What customers consider to be a high performance level today, they will eventually consider to be a standard level of performance.

## Use of Surveys

Surveys are an effective way to solicit customer feedback on satisfaction levels. When using surveys, data center management should:

- *Carefully select the survey population.* Different groups of customers exist and their interests are different. For example, system developers may expect subsecond response time, but end users might be satisfied with a slower response.
- *Ensure relevant sample size.* Data center managers must ensure that the survey does not sample less than a statistically significant part of the customer population.
- *Conduct the survey regularly.* To ensure that performance is improving, the survey should be conducted regularly.
- *Share survey results with the customer.* If customers are informed about the results and what the data center will do to improve performance, they will be more inclined to fill out the next survey.

When using surveys to measure customer satisfaction, center managers should avoid:

- *Leading survey participants.* A survey should not contain questions that lead the customer to a given answer. For example, when asked if they would like better response time, most customers will answer yes.
- *Asking obvious questions.* One such question is asking customers if they would be willing to pay for better response time.
- *Asking irrelevant questions.* The survey should contain only questions that contribute to understanding the customer satisfaction.

- *Using a scale for giving responses.* If survey participants are asked to give their answers according to a scale from 1 to 5, the overall answer will always be between 3.5 and 4.0, which tells nothing.
- *Rationalizing results.* Data center managers should not rationalize survey results. An example of such rationalizing is to think that a result is attributable to the customers' inability to understand the question.

## SUMMARY

Customer satisfaction is key to providing quality, and every data center staff member has a customer who determines requirements and defines what constitutes quality. To implement a successful quality improvement program for data center operations, the following steps, as outlined in the MBNQA framework, should be followed:

- Performance should be assessed using metrics that can measure quality.
- Results of the assessment should be compared with those of other data centers.
- The data center's operations should be benchmarked.
- A quality improvement plan should be developed, based on the benchmark study.
- All staff members must be involved in the pursuit of quality.
- Customer satisfaction should be used as the basis of any quality improvement program.

When embarking on a quality improvement program, data center managers must also remember that the pursuit of quality is an ongoing process and not the attainment of a fixed set of goals; quality is a journey and not a destination.

# II-9
# Automating the Data Center

*JOHN L. CONNOR*

Data center automation packages are designed to help data center personnel manage their center's operations. These systems handle such ordinary operations as operator messages, system start-up and shutdown, and simple time-initiated processing. Many have additional features.

Packages that solve the most complex problems are also generally the most difficult to use. However, if they have been properly selected and implemented, such automation products are still reasonably easy to use.

Exhibit II-9-1 lists the advantages of automating as many operations as possible. Manual tasks that have been automated are performed with increased speed and accuracy. Consequently, automating the manual tasks required to run a company's data center hardware increases the availability, speed, and accuracy of the applications that run on it.

## PLANNING FOR AUTOMATION

Many organizations make the mistake of selecting an automation tool and then trying to make their automation needs fit this product. This process is backward; the objectives and other key requirements of the data center should be defined first. Then, the data center manager should select a product that can accomplish the required objectives in the appropriate time frame. By following the nine-step plan described in this chapter, data center managers can ensure that they select the correct product and implement it properly.

The amount of time they take to complete each step in the plan depends on several factors, including how many people can work on the step, the coding requirements of any automated procedures involved in the step, and the automation product selected. The data center manager need not complete all nine steps without pause. Rather, the manager may consider steps one through four as one phase and go on to subsequent steps at a later time.

### The Importance of a Champion

A critical component of the success of an automation project is the project manager who implements it. This person must inform and persuade the company's decision makers that automated operations will greatly benefit the

| Manual Data Processing System | Automated System |
|---|---|
| Provides inconsistent results. | Provides predictable results. |
| Is reliant on human communication. | Is reliant on minimum human communication. |
| Takes seconds to respond. | Takes microseconds to respond. |
| Depends on human emotions and health. | Is nonemotional and does not get sick. |
| Is limited by the speed of human thought. | Reasons at machine speeds and has imbedded expertise. |
| Is affected by the availability of human resources. | Involves a reduced reliance on the expertise and availability of humans. |
| Is limited by the human attention span. | Does not get distracted. |
| Is reactive. | Is proactive. |

**Exhibit II-9-1. A Comparison of Manual and Automated Systems**

---

company. Who should this champion be? Ideally, it should be someone in management, but anyone can initiate interest in automated operations.

The project manager must clearly explain all the possible problems involved with the automation project. The manager must try to ensure that everyone who will be involved in the project looks forward to its challenges and the opportunity to work together it presents for management, applications, operations, and systems personnel at all the company's information processing locations.

## STEP ONE: CREATING THE IMPLEMENTATION PLAN

The first step of introducing advanced automation is the development of an automation plan. This plan should be created and reviewed by all who will participate in the automation project. Because the project will demand human and capital resources from many areas of the company, both management and technical personnel should contribute the plan. However, the plan should be managed by only one person.

Because an automation project is not completed overnight, the key groups involved in it must communicate regularly to stay abreast of the project's progress. The main reason automation projects fail is usually that plan participants have failed to communicate such matters as:

- What each phase of the project is trying to accomplish.
- Why the tasks in each phase are being performed.
- How the plan's progress will be measured.
- What task comes next.
- What the benefits of the automation project are to a particular department or organization or to the entire company.

## Plan Contents

The automation plan must include the items discussed in the following paragraphs.

**A Mission Statement.** The mission statement is a broad statement by senior management that reflects the intent of the automation project. This statement sets the general aims of the project and demonstrates that the project has the commitment of senior management, which is fundamental to its success. The following is a sample mission statement:

> To remain competitive in the industry, the company must maintain online service times and availability under increasing transaction volumes. This must be attained within the current budget for hardware and software.

The mission statement should provide only company direction and commitment. The project's objectives and how-to information are provided by other levels of management and technical personnel in other steps of the plan.

Data center managers who do not have a mission statement from senior IS management must create one. They must also inform senior IS managers of the project's status as it progresses. One way or another, the data center must gain senior management's active support, or the automation project will turn into just another operations or systems task—such as performance monitoring—instead of a corporatewide mandate to use automation to improve all the corporation's information processing functions.

**Plan Objectives Ranked by Priority.** The automation plan must specify what tasks must be accomplished and the order in which they must be performed. These objectives can include:

- Improvement of the availability of data center services.
- Maintenance of data center personnel at current levels.
- Elimination of the center's third shift or of a weekend shift.
- Reduction of the number of consoles.
- Remote operation of a data center.
- Reduction of console message traffic by 80%.
- Standardization of policies.
- Creation of a focal point for operations.
- Simplification of command structures.
- Balancing of workloads to make use of all computer resources.
- Integration of network management system and subsystem automation.
- Automation of the management of IMS or CICS.

**Project Audit.** To achieve a concrete sense of the necessary scope of the automation project, plan developers must conduct an audit to determine the following:

- What is the current status of data center automation?
  —What hardware and software does it have?
  —What has been done to automate data center operations?
- What are the goals of the current automation project?
- How much effort and time can be spent on this project?
- How can the benefits of this project be maximized with minimal effort?

Exhibit II-9-2 is an audit checklist of one of the major areas for automation in data centers using MVS systems. A data center manager should use this checklist or others modeled on it to audit each system and subsystem that is a candidate for automation. The manager should then rank these systems and subsystems according to the order in which they should be automated. Viewed together, the information in these checklists gives the data center manager a broad picture of what in their facilities should be automated, the order in which this automation should occur (both among systems and among functions within systems), the effort necessary to automate, and what the result of automation will be.

The data center manager may someday decide to automate functions that were not chosen for automation on these checklists. This is not a problem; such a decision simply takes the data center to a more advanced stage of automation.

**Skills Audit.** Many operator skills used today to manage a data center will not be needed when data center operations are automated. New skills will be required instead. The data center manager must therefore plan now to train, outsource, or hire personnel with these new skills.

Exhibits II-9-3 and II-9-4 are sample forms that data center managers can use to take stock of those skills that will and will not be required and those that will be needed to a reduced extent after automation. Before starting on automation project, the data center manager should audit the skills and people in the data center organization—both those that are available and those that will be needed. This information is necessary to complete the automation plan.

## STEP TWO: LEARNING THE PRODUCT

An automation product usually has many capabilities. To become familiar with them, the data center manager should review the product's documentation. Following a demonstration script is also a useful way to learn about a product's features.

A data center manager who decides to evaluate two products should create a detailed list of the tasks that each product must automate. (For example, a data center manager who highly values IMS may include questions about how each product's IMS automated operator interface exit works, the operator productivity tools that the products offer, and how the tools interface with the data center's performance tools.) The manager should give this list

| Automation Area | Already Automated (Yes/No/Some) | Requires Automation (Yes/No) | Effort Required | Order of Implementation[1] | Priority (1–10)[2] |
|---|---|---|---|---|---|
| Message Management | Some | Yes | Minimal | 1 | 1 |
| Simplified Automated Responses | No | Yes | Minimal | 2 | 1 |
| IPL Automation | Some | Yes | Minimal–Maximum | 6 | 2 |
| Automation of Operational Procedures | Some | Yes | Minimal–Medium | 9 | 2 |
| Automation of Time-Initiated Events | No | Yes | Minimal–Medium | 7 | 2 |
| Automation of Subsystem Start-Up and Shutdown | Some | Yes | Minimal–Medium | 8 | 2 |
| Automation of System Recovery | No | Yes | Medium–Maximum | 11 | 5 |
| Automation of Problem Diagnosis and Solution | No | Yes | Minimal–Maximum | 12 | 7 |
| Automation of Problem Notification | No | Yes | Minimal | 5 | 1 |
| Console Consolidation | No | Yes | Minimal | 4 | 1 |
| Alert Management | No | Yes | Minimal–Medium | 3 | 1 |
| Remote Operation | No | No | Minimal–Medium | — | — |
| Automation of Problem Documenting | No | No | Minimal–Medium | — | — |
| Proactive Management Integration with Performance Monitors | No | Yes | Minimal–Maximum | 10 | 5 |

**Exhibit II-9-2. Sample Automation Audit Checklist for MVS Systems**

Notes:
1. Minimal   Completed in 1–2 days
   Medium   Completed in 5–6 days
   Maximum   Depends on user requirements
2. The order of implementation should be determined by considering the effort required and the priority.

163

| Skills or Tasks | Who Is Affected? |
|---|---|
| *Jobs* | |
| Console monitors | John Doe, Fred Jones |
| Print pool handlers | Jane Smith, Alex Elliot |
| *Tasks* | |
| Exception performance monitoring | Joe Field |
| Manual change control procedures | Nancy Wright |

**Exhibit II-9-3. Sample Skills Audit Form for Skills or Tasks That Will Change**

to each product's vendor along with a time by which the vendors must respond to the manager. The vendors' responses to the list may help the manager choose between the products.

Once the data center manager has selected the product to accomplish the objectives defined in step one of the automation project, the manager should install the product in a test system and train all personnel on the product. Then, the manager should move on to step three.

## STEP THREE: ANALYZING AND AUTOMATING MESSAGES

Message rates have been skyrocketing. Each additional million instructions per second involves an additional two or more messages per second on the console. Fortunately, automation can eliminate most of this traffic.

To undertand the company's need for message management and simple message automation, the data center manager should perform the following tasks:

- Analyze messages for suppression.
- Analyze messages for the automation of simple replies.
- Analyze messages for message rewording.
- Analyze network messages.
- Analyze messages for console consolidation (i.e., alert management).
- Analyze command procedures to simplify them.

During each of these tasks, the data center manager should seek the input of various sources, such as operators, operations supervisors, applications personnel, technical support, technical services, and the help desk.

Because of the number of people who should be consulted about the

| Task Required | Skills Required | Who can perform? Is help needed? |
|---|---|---|
| Project administrators | • Familiarity with operations, automation, applications, and systems<br>• Management and organization skills<br>• Ability to coordinate between operating systems and applications<br>• Ability to conduct meetings | Help needed |
| Report writers | • Basic programming skills<br>• Fourth generation language (e.g., CLIST or REXX) programming skills | Fred Jones |
| Procedure documenters | • Knowledge of procedures<br>• Knowledge of flow chart<br>• Organization skills<br>• Writing skills | All operators |
| Task organizers | • Ability to maintain schedules<br>• Ability to match skills and tasks | Alex Elliot |
| Automation code testers | • Conscious of quality<br>• Familiarity with operation procedures<br>• Ability to write test plans | Jane Smith |
| Change control developers | • Ability to develop procedures for change control policy<br>• Ability to enforce change control policy | Nancy Wright |
| Idea gatherers | • Ability to determine how automation can improve company operations | Task force needed |

**Exhibit II-9-4. Sample Skills Audit Form for Tasks Requiring New Skills**

nature and sources of company messages, the data center manager should consider setting up a series of meetings to discuss messages and their automation. Face-to-face meetings can strongly contribute to the success of automation projects. The manager must determine the attendance and format of each meeting.

Once step three has been completed, the amount of traffic coming across the console should be reduced by 60% to 90%. Now the manager can move on to step four.

## STEP FOUR: AUTOMATING PROCEDURES

During this step, the data center manager examines the procedures by which data center activities are conducted in order to eliminate or automate them. Automating the execution of routine procedures can:

- Reduce the need for personnel during certain periods of activity.
- Reduce system and subsystem outages.
- Reduce the occurrence of problems stemming from operator errors.

Operator errors result from complex procedures followed incorrectly, syntax errors, and slow responses to error messages. Putting routine procedures into a precoded procedure and making them readily accessible or executing them automatically can solve these problems.

An operators' procedure or run book is an excellent souce of information on these procedures. If no such book exists, a little more work may be required. Someone must compile the unofficial procedures being used to manage the data center.

Next, the data center manager must eliminate unnecessary procedures, identify procedures that can benefit from automation or from reduction to a few keystrokes, and match those procedures requiring automation (including those procedures yet to be developed) with the people responsible for coding and documentation.

Procedures can be automated in three ways. First, if a sample product exists in the automation product's solution offering, the data center manager can choose to customize the procedure, modify the procedure, designate an employee to modify it, or ask outside support to modify it. Second, if the product offers no similar procedure, the data center manager can choose to convert this procedure from the operations procedure book into an automation procedure, ask the employee responsible for developing the procedure to automate it, or ask outside support to automate it. If a manual procedure is not documented and no similar procedure exists in the automation product's solution offering, the data center manager can designate an operator to automate it, ask the employee responsible for developing this procedure to automate it, or call in outside support.

## STEP FIVE: AUTOMATING FUNCTIONS THAT CANNOT BE ACCOMPLISHED FROM THE HOST

Some aspects of automated operations cannot be performed from the host because it is not running or because necessary resources are not readily available on it. These functions are performed by an outboard workstation running on a microcomputer. An outboard can provide one or more of the following automation functions:

- Automation of IPL and IML.
- Heartbeat checking.
- Pager support.
- Remote operation.
- Environmental monitoring.
- Supplemental workstation functions.
- Remote dial-up for support purposes.

A data center manager who wants to automate functions on an outboard must understand its hardware needs. Many of the tasks in the foregoing list require the use of microcomputer boards. The cost of an outboard with a full complement of microcomputer boards can range from $5,000 to $10,000, and the price of two or three outboards can exceed that of mainframe automation software.

Before acquiring an outboard, data center managers should research their needs carefully. Important questions to consider include the following:

- What are the general hardware requirements for the outboard (e.g., CPU, memory, disk space)?
- How is code created on it?
- What language is used?
- Where is the code executed?
- How easy is it to use?
- How many connections does it have; what is its growth potential?

## STEP SIX: REDUCING OUTAGES

Because it may be impossible to completely eliminate system or subsystem outages, a realistic data center manager may choose simply to try to detect and recover from them as quickly as possible. To meet this goal, the manager needs an automation product with a continuous state manager.

The continuous state manager allows the data center manager to build a model of the expected state of subsystems at any moment in time. When the state of a system in operation does not match the expected state of its model system, the automation product compares the two and takes a previously defined action. A continuous state manager thus frees operations staff from manually monitoring CICS, IMS, or other subsystems. The manager performs this task automatically according to the continuous state manager's preset instructions.

In addition to implementing an automation product with a continuous state manager, data centers managers who wish to reduce system outages should understand what problems in their organizations cause outages. Managers who do not know should try to find out.

## STEP SEVEN: AUTOMATING PERFORMANCE

Although a system may issue warning messages for such problems as a console buffer shortage, it does not warn of all potential performing problems. A better source of this information is a performance manager. Not only do performance managers issue messages that warn of potentially critical problems, they can also authorize outside services to collect the additional information required to accurately diagnose them. By using a performance manager along with an automation product, the data center manager can therefore automate the analysis and solution of critical and complex performance problems.

Performance monitors provide two types of messages that notify the automation product of performance problems. The first indicates when a system does not meet a response time objective. The second indicates when resources are not performing according to expectations. The implementation of performance monitors, therefore, allows automation products to increase throughput and manage service levels proactively.

### One Task at a Time

A message indicating that a response time objective has been exceeded usually indicates a performance problem. Data center managers should therefore automate the response to messages indicating resource performance problems first. By doing so, managers minimize their messages for service-level exceptions, because they have automated the resolution of a problem that might have delayed response times.

Because some solutions to performance problems are quite complex, data center managers should consider implementing performance automation in two stages, especially if their time or resources are limited. The first stage is to ensure that warning messages are very visible so personnel can immediately respond to them.

The second stage is to install automation that reacts to messages. This reaction could be as simple as alerting a specific person responsible for the problem area or automatically starting data monitoring of the problem area to collect information for later review. Or the reaction can be much more sophisticated, involving additional analysis and action based on this analysis.

The next task is to identify all the important messages that are generated by the performance manager warning services and the course of actions that should be taken in response to each message. Possible courses of action for any of these messages include the following:

- Variable modifications to a solution in the solution pack.
- Development of a new solution.
- Creation of an alert to be routed to a central terminal.
- Creation of an alert and a follow-up procedure or solution.
- Routing a message to a TSO user.
- Phoning a beeper.

Of course, some combination of all of these actions is also possible.

When reviewing possible courses of action, data center managers should identify those that require too much effort to be implemented at the current time. Managers should schedule the implementation of these solutions in the future. They should also identify messages that indicate problems for which they do not anticipate automating solutions for now but on which they would like to have documentation for further reference.

Clearly, automating performance is a complicated, multistage process. A form that data center managers can use to organize this process is presented in Exhibit II-9-5.

Many performance problems can be minimized or prevented from becoming critical if prompt action is taken when a performance monitor product's warnings are detected. On this form, the data center manager should list the messages that the data center's performance monitor uses to indicate potential service degradation.

Then for each message, the manager should review all vendor documentation to see whether an automated solution has already been provided. If it has not, the manager should identify what automated action should be taken. To decide this, the manager should ask the following questions:

- Does the message indicate a problem that should be solved?
- Does it need only an alert?
- Does it need a solution and an alert?
- What system ID should the alert be routed to?
- Should a user be notified?
  —At the user's working terminal?
  —By beeper?
- Who should develop the solution?

## STEP EIGHT: AUTOMATING RECOVERY

There are two important points to consider when planning for systems recovery. The first is that automation does fail. People forget this fact until there is an automation failure. Then panic sets in as personnel rush around trying to recover from it.

The second point is the loss of operating skills a data center suffers

Date_____

Company_____                    Location_____

Department_____                 System/Subsystem_____

| Performance Manager ID (Msg-ID) | Automation Procedure (name) | Needs Solution Y/N ME* | SYSID (name) | Needs Operator Notification (i.e. Alert) Y/N | Route User (user ID) | Page # (phone #) | Person Responsible for Solution (name) |
|---|---|---|---|---|---|---|---|
| PWSCPU01 | PWSCPU01 | N | PWSCPU01 | | Processor CPU usage is high; prompt operator for action. | | |
| Time | | | | | Balances work loads on a single system. | | |
| Initiated | | N | | | | | |
| | none | Y | | Y | | | Tim Smith |
| CICS Manager ID FT095W | FT095W and CPE00NC | N | | | File degradation analysis. | | |
| FT019W | FT019W | N | FT019W | | Automatic purge of CICS MANAGER recorder files. | | |
| Time | | | | | Dynamic priority management of | | |
| Initiated | Query | N | | | CICS dispatching queues. | | |

**Note:**
ME   Monitoring by Exception. This requires a simple solution of automatically starting and logging diagnostic data.

**Exhibit II-9-5. Sample Performance Automation Task Form for Increasing Throughput and Managing Service Levels**

when it becomes automated. An operator in a nonautomated environment may perform an IPL several times a month. In an automated environment, the operator may never do an IPL unless there is a failure. How can an operator who never does IPLs be expected to then do one?

The solution to these problems is for the data center manager to have an operations automation development methodology in place before writing automation routines, implementing a vendor's solutions, or building rules.

Oddly enough, advanced automation requires more commitment to documentation and audit requirements than do traditional methods of operating a data center. Automation has been touted as eliminating the need for operator documentation, but in reality, the information maintained in programmed solutions is much more complicated than the simple human procedures it was written to replace. Luckily, the audit requirements are much simpler to enforce in a well-automated data center than they are in a center managed exclusively by human operators.

## STEP NINE: ENTERPRISEWIDE AUTOMATION

The last step in this process is the biggest and the most complex to complete. In it, data center managers apply the steps they took to automate their data centers' mainframes to the automation of all data center systems.

To do this, a manager needs an automation product different from the one that automates the mainframe. This product should allow the manager not only to manage hardware and software by such important vendors as IBM Corp., Digital Equipment Corp., and Hewlett-Packard Co., but to integrate the management of these platforms from one central location.

The implementation of such an advanced automation solution requires additional capabilities in the automation package. They include the following:

- The ability to communicate between systems.
- An alert management facility to facilitate the collection of alarms or warnings.
- The means to automate processes without using a mainframe.
- An easy-to-use, open systems procedural interface to other systems.
- Scalability for growth.
- Sufficient processing power to manage large networks and the devices on them.
- Flexibility and ease of use.

## SUMMARY

In recent years, information systems have grown in size, speed, and complexity. They can perform an incredible variety of work on many different platforms. The operations environment has therefore become increasingly complicated and prone to operating errors.

However, major advances have been made in the area of proactive systems automation, and automation software is available for most environments that run in a data center. The next stage of preventive automation will be yet another step toward predictive systems that act as automated systems managers. Vendors will have to ensure that these automation solutions can be implemented without the need for major programming efforts on the part of the implementation staff.

Every day, increasingly complex forms of automation are introduced to the marketplace, and companies find additional sources of information to process. The combination of large amounts of data and complicated installation requirements offers a new challenge to the vendors of automation products—a challenge they must accept to survive if they want their products to be selected for the sophisticated automation tasks of the next decade.

# Section III
# Data Center Controls

T here is no question that issues such as strategic planning, implementing new technology, and human resources management are crucial aspects of a data center manager's responsibilities. But, in reality, the primary role is still ensuring that the data center runs effectively and efficiently on a daily basis. This may not be glamorous, but it is certainly critical.

Many elements are involved in the daily operations of the data center. Some certainly more important than others, but they are all necessary for the successful achievement of the data center's goals to provide the best support possible to its customers. This section looks at several of these key data center control areas and offers some suggestions about how to improve operations.

Given the interest in outsourcing often expressed by senior management, today's data center managers often find that they are in the position of justifying the data center's continued existence. There is such a demand for reducing costs today that, often, senior management does not fully understand or appreciate the role the data center plays. To be able to indicate how well the data center is doing, there must be some type of reporting mechanism in place. Chapter III-1, "Developing a Data Center Reporting System," specifically addresses this issue and offers positive ideas about how to develop an accurate reporting system.

From a user perspective, the data center gets measured on one major point—providing reliable service. To ensure such a goal is met, the data center manager must ensure the data center environment is continuously stable and that any problems encountered are corrected immediately and, wherever possible, prevented from happening again. Therefore, implementing an effective change control system must be a top priority for the data center manager. Chapter III-2, "Update on Change Control and Problem Tracking Systems," provides guidelines and suggestions for implementing such a system.

Improved productivity is a major goal of most organizations today. Improved productivity means more tasks can be accomplished with the same, or even fewer, personnel. Thus, the data center manager must continually look for ways to improve overall productivity. Chapter III-3, "Improving Productivity by Implementing a Tape Workstation Environment," discusses a current technology approach to a classic area of data center operations—tape management.

Much of what takes place in the data center on a daily basis may be quite mundane. Nonetheless, the tasks are all important. Ensuring the effective backup of the company's data is another major responsibility of the data center manager. Chapter III-4, "File Retention and Backup," discusses one of these mundane tasks, and provides the data center manager with some excellent ideas regarding this area of responsibility.

# III-1

# Developing a Data Center Reporting System

*JOHN P. MURRAY*

T he data center manager faces an ongoing challenge in managing the data center as a business function; changing business conditions have caused that need to become more urgent in recent years. There are two reasons for this increased urgency. First, the available processing hardware and software options have proliferated dramatically. Second, the move to reduce—or at least control—data center expense as effectively as possible has become a primary issue in many installations. To respond to the pressure to manage more effectively, the data center manager must become a more adept business manager. In addition to increasing their business skills, data center managers must demonstrate the success of their management.

The data center manager's ability to prove that effective management is in place must be backed with factual data. Increasingly, the data center has to become an integral part of the overall business. As integration levels increase, the management of the function must deal with facts instead of with guesses, identifying instances of improved performance and using that information to strengthen the position of both the data center function and the data center manager. Managers who do not have this ability or who are not willing to begin the process of moving to such an environment are in a vulnerable position.

## PROTECTING THE DATA CENTER AGAINST OUTSOURCING

The recent rise of the outsourcing of data center operations has increased the potential vulnerability of even the most effective data center manager. Outsourcing has gained popularity in response to concerns on the part of senior management about data center expense and effectiveness. Two valid questions are: Is outsourcing an appropriate answer to the concerns of senior management? Are these concerns valid? The data center manager should be able to answer them when they arise.

Outsourcing has become a force within the IS industry and is likely to continue to influence the industry for some time. A data center manager who has adopted a businesslike approach to the management of the function is better able to counter any moves to outsourcing. The interest of senior management in controlling data center expense is understandable; a data center operation, even given the dramatic reductions in the cost of raw computing power, still represents a sizable budget item in most organizations. When the issue of expense reduction and control comes up, the data center therefore is an immediate target.

The data center manager must be prepared to counter the subjective arguments posed by the outsourcing organization. The manager should therefore give serious consideration to implementing a monitoring and reporting system to demonstrate the effectiveness of the data center. The facts about data center performance generated by such a system can help to counter any claims by outsourcers that they could do the job more effectively and to mitigate any attacks on the data center manager's credibility. The data center must be managed effectively for the reporting system to provide facts that support the manager's claims of superior performance.

Another subjective set of decisions is often made about hardware. The data center hardware resource is finite. Users' demand upon the hardware resource is by contrast infinite. In any strong business enterprise, the demand for data center resources is constantly growing. The data center manager should have two goals concerning the management of the hardware resources. The first is to obtain the maximum productivity from the installed hardware. The second is to carry out the planning necessary to provide for future growth. Data center managers must be able to anticipate the growth of the resource needs. Senior management must be made aware of those needs so the appropriate funding is available to provide those resources.

As with performance measures, this information must be based on facts not on speculation. A reporting system can provide the facts needed to make successful hardware decisions. Data center managers face serious rivals among data center options, such as outsourcing and client/server processing environments. Data center managers who continue to rely upon intuition and guesswork in the face of these options will encounter great difficulty in trying to convince senior management that they have effective solutions to data center problems.

## DEVELOPING THE REPORTING SYSTEM

The purpose of the reporting system is to document what is occurring in the data center. These reports should be used to highlight areas of strength and weakness and to lay the basis for changes to improve the environment. The reports should:

- Document current data center resource use and develop a historical record of what occurs with resource use for a period of at least a year.
- Develop additional material that can be used as the basis of forecast

anticipated changes in the processing environment over the coming months. This process should provide the ability to make estimates for at least 18 months with a high level of confidence and for up to 36 months with a reasonable level of confidence.

Given the rapid pace of change in technology, the intention should be not to attempt to provide definitive answers for the future but to provide information for considering the various options as the requirements of the business and the technology change. No one can completely forecast what will occur. However, having a clear understanding of where the data center is at a given time provides the basis for making reasonable judgments about the future.

Developing and using the reporting system effectively (i.e., the appropriate reports are in place and are regularly produced and distributed) has an immediate positive effect by enabling the data center manager to move to factual rather than emotional assessments of the service provided by the data center. A data center is a high-visibility function; so many people throughout the organization depend upon the services of the data center that any disruption in service can create considerable difficulty.

When problems arise, the actual degree of the difficulty can become distorted. Too often the data center manager is forced to deal with such statements as The system is always down, The system is slow, or from the development section, We never get enough resources for adequate testing. Unless the manager can produce accurate information about the performance of the system, it is almost impossible to counter such statements. Even if the reports show that the service levels are unacceptable, at least everyone will be working from facts instead of emotion.

Obviously in this case, the data center manager should take steps to improve the situation immediately. However, when the reports are put into use, organizations frequently discover that the performance of the data center, even in the early stages of the project, is better than had been supposed.

## DEVELOPING THE PROCESS

The data center reporting systems should be designed to generate reports that are consistent, timely, and structured toward the development of a historical data base. The data base is used to track performance and to provide material for the development of forecasting models. Those models can eventually be used to manage the growth of data center hardware requirements over time.

The first stage in the overall process should be to assess the current performance of the data center. The assessment should consist of identifying the current use of the installed hardware resources as well as the level—if any—of excess processing capacity available. Then, the requirement for a reporting system can be addressed. In identifying the current use of installed hardware resources, the idea is to develop the processing baseline—that is, the current level of demand on data center resource. This is the basis for identifying any usable excess capacity in the system. This process can be used to find a realistic processing level—that is, the highest level of processing load the system can accommodate before being adversely affected. The material developed should enable the data center manager to plan for and provide increased processing power as required and before the demand becomes critical.

The second question addressed the reporting system currently in place. If there is no reporting system, the task is to build a system that meets the needs of the installation. If a system is in place, it should be reviewed to determine whether the data is correct and whether it is sufficiently comprehensive. Circumstances change, and what may have been an adequate or even a useful reporting system several years ago may not be appropriate today. If the data center already has such a system, the first step should be to identify what, if any, of the existing system can be incorporated in the new system.

Data center reporting systems should be implemented with the needs of both the data center and the organization in mind. The system should be designed to provide sufficient detail to adequately inform anyone with an interest in the information. However, there should not be so much detail that the reports become difficult to understand and use. Two sets of reports are necessary. One should be a set of nontechnical reports that can be readily understood by data center customers as well as by senior management. The second set should contain more detail and have a technical orientation. These reports are used by the data center management and the technical support group. These reports can then be used to analyze current resource use to establish a basis for the development of the forecasting models. The intent is to be in position to present well-documented, factual cases for increasing the data center hardware resources when the need arises. Again, this is a case of moving from the emotional to the factual.

The second set of reports also provides details that are used to fine tune or optimize the performance of existing hardware. In addition, the reports provide information the data center manager needs to make the adjustments required to meet changing processing demands. Those demands can include increased resources to accommodate new applications or for increased transactions in existing systems.

## IDENTIFYING THE ITEMS TO BE MEASURED

The reports should be comprehensive and practical. Effective mainframe measurement packages can produce extensive data about data center use of a variety of resource components. Initially, it is advisable and usually more effective to capture as much data as practical, because it is likely that at least some crucial questions will not be apparent in the beginning of the process.

Having plenty of data from the start provides the ability to answer these questions when they arise. However, over time, the amount of data required and the number of reports produced can be reduced as appropriate.

The data required depends on the particular requirements of a given installation. However, a basic set of reports is necessary for most installations. The following sections describe these core reports and their functions. In addition, an example of each report, currently being used to manage a medium-sized data center in an insurance operation, is included.

## Mainframe Resource Use

This report is illustrated in Exhibit III-1-1. A basic tenet of any data center must be to ensure adequate processing resources. The term *adequate* should be understood to mean sufficient resources not only to handle current processing demands without stress but to allow for temporary increase in the processing load.

Many data centers, as a part of their charter, work to maximize the use of the data center resources. These installations routinely operate as close to 100% of capacity as possible. Although this may seem a sound business practice, it can be a shortsighted approach.

Because the expense associated with managing such an installation is inordinately high, the time employees spend trying to juggle resources offsets any savings gained from delaying the acquisition of appropriate hardware. The problems of scheduling, reruns, shifting disk storage loads, and poor data center service levels usually exceed any savings in hardware expense.

Because the expense associated with an increase in hardware resources is easily calculated, avoiding that cost can be seen as controlling expenses. However, the cost to the data center in operating too close to maximum capacity generates frustration, unnecessary additional effort, and perhaps some overtime costs. Although these costs are not as easily identified or quantified, they can have a substantial effect on the data center.

These reports focus on the total availability of the system. Because the processing demands in all installations are different, this chapter offers some general suggestions as opposed to specific goals. The availability of the system should be reported monthly. Current data center hardware is sufficiently sophisticated that the mean time to failure for most components is measured in years. Although hardware failure should no longer be an important availability issue, it does occur.

Other items that affect the availability of data center hardware resources include operating software failures, operator error, applications program difficulties, and power failure. Even though sound data center management can go a long way toward mitigating these failures, they do occur occasionally, even in the most effectively managed installations. They should be addressed when they occur.

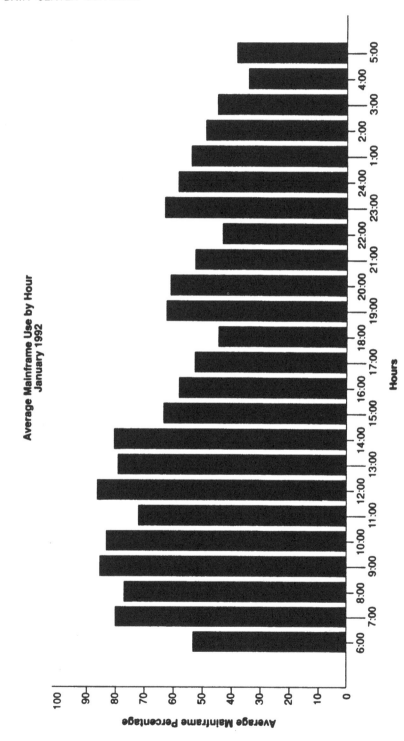

Average Mainframe Use by Hour
January 1992

Exhibit III-1-1. Sample Mainframe Use Report

Recognition and acknowledgement of these failures enables the data center manager to present an accurate picture of what has occurred as it relates to the established data center service levels and to the availability of the hardware resources. In addition, highlighting these problems helps to ensure that they receive appropriate attention.

## Online Processing Environment

Reports here indicate online system response times (see Exhibit III-1-2) and overall online system availability (see Exhibit III-1-3). Consistent processing response times should be maintained across the entire online network. Like hardware availability, the response times must fall within the agreed-upon service levels. Establishing and maintaining online response-time standards should be mandatory, and a reporting system can summarize these times to enforce or demonstrate compliance with the standards. Response-time requirements should weigh the legitimate concerns of the departments that will use the system against the expense associated with increasing the speed of the system. The goal should be to meet the actual needs of the users in the most cost-effective manner possible.

Usually, the affected departments attempt to obtain the fastest response times possible. Should a standard response time of less than two second 80% of the time be established when three seconds would be adequate? The issue may seem minor, but the consequences can be significant. First, there may be a considerable expense associated with the delivery of faster response time—it may, for example, require a CPU upgrade.

Another concern is the data center's ability to maintain fast response times as the processing load grows. Less than two seconds response time at least 80% of the time may be easily accomplished at the moment, but what about six months from now? Once the user community becomes accustomed to a certain level of response time, it will be less accepting of anything slower.

## Transaction Rates—Batch and Online

Reports on transaction rates must distinguish between batch and online processing because the demands and management techniques for each are different. In addition, the interests of those who rely on the different production environments are not necessarily the same. Because of its higher level of visibility and the continuous increase in its use throughout the IS community, the online processing environment usually gets the most attention in many data centers.

Transaction rate reports should help the data center manager determine whether the applications development group is receiving sufficient processing resources. The two aspects of online processing that require attention are the immediate, daily entry of data and production of reports to operate the business and the longer-term concerns of the work carried out by the members of the applications development group.

| Region | Transactions | Average Second | Less Than 1 Second | Less Than 2 Seconds | Less Than 5 Seconds | Less Than 10 Seconds | More Than 10 Seconds |
|---|---|---|---|---|---|---|---|
| California | 682,254 | 1.2 | 54.2% | 90.7% | 99.5% | 99.9% | 0.1% |
| Freeport | 1,137,683 | 1.0 | 65.8% | 93.5% | 99.6% | 99.9% | 0.1% |
| Indiana | 214,999 | 1.5 | 56.5% | 85.4% | 98.4% | 99.3% | 0.7% |
| Northwest | 683,365 | 1.0 | 67.0% | 93.8% | 99.4% | 99.9% | 0.1% |
| Southwest | 490,749 | 1.9 | 32.9% | 65.0% | 92.5% | 97.1% | 2.9% |
| Midwest Claims Park Center | 197,861 | 1.1 | 64.5% | 91.0% | 99.2% | 99.8% | 0.2% |
| Midwest Premium and Home Office | 428,721 | 0.3 | 94.5% | 98.0% | 99.8% | 99.8% | 0.2% |
| Total | 3,835,632 | 1.1 | 62.7% | 89.5% | 98.6% | 99.5% | 0.5% |

Average Window: 1 Hour and 13 Minutes
Total Response Time Incidents: 1
Slow Response Time Percentage: .07%

**Exhibit III-1-2. Sample Online System Response Time Report**

## Online System Availability Summary
### January 1992

| Region | Claims | | Premium | |
|---|---|---|---|---|
| | Weekdays Goal = 98% | Weekends Goal = 75% | Weekdays Goal = 98% | Weekends Goal = 75% |
| California | 99.83% | 100.00% | 99.83% | 100.00% |
| Freeport | 99.92% | 100.00% | 99.92% | 100.00% |
| Indiana | 99.94% | 100.00% | N/A | N/A |
| Northwest | 99.94% | 100.00% | N/A | N/A |
| Southwest | 96.69% | 100.00% | N/A | N/A |
| Midwest Claims Park Center | 99.94% | 100.00% | N/A | N/A |
| Midwest Premium and Home Office | 99.94% | 100.00% | 99.94% | 100.00% |
| | Weekday Claim Average 99.38% | Weekend Claim Average 100.00% | Weekday Premium Average 99.90% | Weekend Premium Average 100.00% |

**Availability Standards**
Weekdays Monday–Friday 6:00 AM—8:00 PM CST
Weekdays Saturday–Sunday 6:00 AM—7:00 PM CST

**Exhibit III-1-3. Sample Online System Availability Report**

183

Concern about meeting the demands of the applications development group should involve both the online and the batch processing environments. In many installations, a large portion of the testing for development is carried out in the batch processing cycles. However, although the batch environment is usually the more stable and therefore easier to manage, the data center manager must ensure that a reasonable portion of both the online and the batch processing resources are consistently available to the development group.

## Jobs Processed

Both batch and online jobs processed should be addressed by the reporting system (see Exhibit III-1-4). Growth of the mainframe processing load often occurs subtly. Although there may be little noticeable growth from day to day, over time the processing load is likely to grow considerably. The reason, particularly in installations experiencing some level of growth, is that activities that affect mainframe resources occur simultaneously in many areas. In this circumstance, attempting to identify and monitor all occurrences without some automated system is all but impossible. The assistance of an automated system cannot obviate all surprise; however, the system can provide the ability to track the areas of growth and measure what is occurring.

Growth in the processing load can come from any number of sources. Online transaction rates can rise as business increase or as new or enhanced versions of existing systems are implemented. The testing load from the applications development group may increase. Data base processing systems require increased hardware resources compared to non-data base systems. That circumstances is even more severe in installations that allow substantial user department inquiries.

The trend toward data base processing, coupled with the increased use of data center hardware resources by people in other departments, will continue to grow. A data center manager cannot afford to be forced to request an unplanned increase in hardware resources. The effective monitoring of the hardware resources can help the data center manager avoid such an unpleasant circumstance.

## Application Program Tests and Compiles

Two aspects of the capture and recording of data associated with the applications testing environment are of interest to the data center manager: the capability to identify the amount of resource being used to meet the demands of the development section and to decide whether the demands are growing, and the capability to provide the development manager with data about the testing and compiling activity in the section. In many installations, it becomes a habit to use the data center resources to debug source code. The programmer

**Batch and Online Jobs Processed by Month**

| | January | December | November | October | September | August | 6 Month Average |
|---|---|---|---|---|---|---|---|
| Production | 6519 | 4301 | 3930 | 4263 | 3734 | 3978 | 4454 |
| Model | 1480 | 1138 | 1371 | 1792 | 1556 | 1388 | 1454 |
| Test | 811 | 268 | 291 | 224 | 159 | 139 | 315 |
| Online Processing | 5340 | 4902 | 4505 | 5022 | 4264 | 4574 | 4768 |
| Programmer Testing | 6134 | 4673 | 4816 | 5302 | 4651 | 3527 | 4850 |
| Production Control | — | — | — | 670 | 278 | 435 | — |
| Systems Software | 4314 | 3140 | 3258 | 3648 | 2632 | 1875 | 3144 |
| Nonconforming Job Names | 701 | 915 | 2785 | 1517 | 2728 | 4376 | 2170 |
| Totals | 25,299 | 19,337 | 21,477 | 22,438 | 20,002 | 20,292 | 21,474 |
| | | | | | | | |
| Production Reruns | 147 | 153 | 108 | 111 | 101 | 99 | 119 |
| Production Rerun Percentage | 2.3% | 3.5% | 2.7% | 2.6% | 2.7% | 2.4% | 2.7% |
| Abnormal Termination | 1563 | 1406 | 1780 | 1637 | 1390 | 1392 | 1528 |

**Exhibit III-1-4. Sample Job Accounting and Reporting System**

185

compiles a program, corrects the identified errors, and recompiles again until the code is clean. Spending time desk-checking the program before compiling saves machine cycles and provides the programmer with an improved understanding of the code. Although it can be difficult for the data center manager to convey this message, facts from the reporting system can be used to support the contention that too many resources are being used.

## Jobs That Must Be Rerun

The purpose of the job reruns report (see Exhibit III-1-5), unless the incidence of reruns is high, should not be primarily to address the area of the resources used to accommodate those reruns but to address other issues. The first issue concerns the cause of the reruns. The data center manager should question why those applications are being rerun. As that question is pursued, such topics as job control language ( JCL), errors, inadequate operator instructions, incorrect dates, or other management issues arise. As those issues are recognized, the appropriate steps can be taken to make the necessary corrections.

The topic of production reruns is one that must have more than a cursory examination. There are several pragmatic reasons for paying attention to the issue. The place to begin is with a precise definition of what constitutes a rerun. For the purpose of this chapter, reruns are production jobs processed more than their scheduled number of times in any given period of time.

Once the guidelines for the recoding of reruns have been established, a monthly examination of the details of the rerun reports should be conducted. The examination may reveal rerun patterns; some jobs create substantial problems.

| System | Number of Jobs | Elapsed Time (HH:MM:SS) | CPU Time (HH:MM:SS) | Lines Printed |
|---|---|---|---|---|
| | | December 1991 Production Reruns | | |
| Premium | 38 | 19:13:29 | 03:10:10 | 219 |
| Claims | 77 | 00:54:03 | 00:02:31 | 384 |
| Underwriting | 11 | 00:14:53 | 00:00:15 | 636 |
| Stats | 02 | 01:39:40 | 00:13:95 | 0 |
| Commissions | 15 | 01:27:12 | 00:01:42 | 27641 |
| Accounts Payable | 06 | 00:24:07 | 00:01:12 | 0 |
| Agency | 02 | 00:24:45 | 00:02:00 | 138 |
| Loss Ratios | 02 | 00:02:49 | 00:00:00 | 0 |
| Total | 153 | 24:20:58 | 03:28:35 | 29018 |

**Exhibit III-1-5. Sample Report on Job Reruns**

The more likely causes for the reruns include:

- Incorrect data entry.
- Weak of nonexistent program edits.
- Programming errors.
- Inadequate documentation.
- Incorrect JCL or operator actions.

With the detail from the rerun reports, the causes of those reruns that are creating processing difficulty can be found and corrected. Not only does this improve the data center operation, it can in time provide the basis for an improvement in the quality of the IS department's products. The data center manager should develop a process to track and correct those production jobs that consistently create rerun problems.

### Presenting the Data

Once the data has been identified, a process can be established to capture that data. The next issue is the method of presentation of the data. It is advisable to move the raw data from the job accounting system to a microcomputer-based system (e.g., Lotus) that allows for the presentation of the material in graphic form. Using this approach puts the material in a format easily understood by nontechnical personnel. It also provides an opportunity for the data center to be seen as taking a businesslike approach to the issue.

## DEVELOPING SERVICE LEVELS

When data center managers are confident that the resource use data is accurate, they should then focus on the issue of service levels. Working with the use data, the data center manager can decide on a set of reasonable service levels to which the data center can make a commitment.

Obviously, care is required in this area. The agreed-upon service levels must be readily attainable under typical working conditions. As part of the agreement, the data center manager must be willing to take responsibility for the service levels that are not met. When that occurs, the data center manager has to identify the cause of the problem and take the required steps to keep the circumstance from recurring.

When agreement on the content of the service levels has been reached, the performance of the data center concerning those levels must be published monthly. In an operation as vulnerable as the data center, that circumstance must be anticipated. The goal is not to overemphasize levels that are missed occasionally. The issue is that the data center manager is willing to acknowledge the problem when it arises and to show the commitment to rectify it.

Those who use the services of the data center are sometimes skeptical about the data center's concern with issues that bear upon their work. The effective use of service levels can help to improve that aspect of the data center services.

## SUMMARY

Too often data centers find themselves caught in a trap when it comes to providing the resources required to maintain the necessary level of processing power. The management of the installation may know—or have a strong feeling—that increased power will be required. However, it sometimes happens that there is little substantial evidence upon which to base that feeling.

Data center managers find themselves in the unfortunate position of pleading for increased processing power under extreme pressure, not realizing that current hardware resources may be completely consumed. When this occurs, there is an immediate need to take some action. This circumstance does not cast the data center manager in the best possible light and should be avoided. The data center manager must maintain appropriate control of the hardware resources at all times. Providing a constant analysis of the use of the resources and sound estimates of when the requirement for additions is likely to occur is simply efficient business practice. A well-developed data center reporting system is part of this.

Having kept the appropriate management informed of the status of data center use does not, of course, ensure support. Although the managers receive the reports, they may not understand the material or may simply ignore the content of those reports. The important point is that the data center manager had fulfilled a responsibility to report on the data center through the production and distribution of these reports.

Successful management of the data center is contingent upon having sufficient information to understand events as they occur. The use of that information to monitor the progress of the function and to plan for future growth improves both the actual management of the data center and its image.

# III-2
# Update on Change Control and Problem Tracking Systems

*THOMAS FLEISHMAN*

T he explosive growth of information systems technology has been accompanied by an increase in the number of users whose daily activities are closely associated with and dependent on the IS function. In many cases, user activity involves complex online functions directly dependent on the availability of the computing resource. In the past, users seldom noticed such events as equipment changes, equipment outages, unsuccessful software installations, or untimely data. These events are now more visible to users than in the past, and they can cause significant service problems by interrupting online processing, which in turn disrupts the organization's business operation. Therefore, it is important to control such events to maintain the service levels required by users.

Determining baseline service levels and anticipating the effect that changes will have on these levels is one method of achieving user satisfaction. For example, the data center manager and the user community might agree that system availability at the terminal level is to be maintained at 98.5% for all online systems. If that level is barely maintained in a given period (e.g., a certain month), and if a major change is proposed that could reduce system availability below the baseline level during that period, that change (if not critical) could be postponed until the following month.

This chapter discusses the need for controlling changes in the data center and provides recommendations for implementing change control and problem tracking systems, usually referred to as systems managment. These systems (i.e., as covered in this chapter) are not usable for controlling or tracking user requests for enhancements to production sytems. It is assumed that such changes have been thoroughly tested before installation. The change control process beings when the treated enhancement is to be incorporated into the production environment. Initial requests for changes should be handled by some form of work request or project control process responsible for scheduling all projects and resources.

## THE CHANGE CONTROL PROCESS

Experience in large, complex data centers has shown that a significant correlation exists between changes in the data center and subsequent interruptions or disruptions in service. A formal change control system—which identifies, evaluates, and coordinates required changes—can minimize such performance problems. The need for a change control system is reinforced by the following factors:

- *Volume of changes.* As the size, complexity, and strategic importance of the computing environment increases, the number of required corresponding changes also increases—in some cases, proportionally; in others, exponentially. If uncontrolled, the volume of changes can quickly become unmanageable, resulting in a processing environment that is unstable and unable to meet the service levels required by and demanded by users.
- *Ranking of changes.* As the volume of requested changes increases, so too will their scope and magnitude. A ranking process is recommended to help determine which changes must be installed and which can be deferred, combined, or eliminated to minimize the probability of service interruptions to users.
- *Visibility of changes.* In an uncontrolled environment, certain systems or components are often the object of recurrent change. A change control system helps identify such systems or components and facilitates corrective action.
- *Coordination of changes.* A change control system identifies changes that depend on other factors so that their installation can be coordinated.
- *Reduction of impact.* A formal change control system can reduce the impact of required changes and help avoid serious problems and major outages.
- *Historical records.* Formal change control procedures facilitate the maintenance of historical records, which help managers identify software systems and hardware components that require repeated changes. The records also help the data center manager institute problem tracking for added control by establishing such procedures as component failure impact analysis, which assesses the impact of failure in all identified components in the processing environment.

### Definition of Change

The misconception that only major changes (e.g., migrating to a new operating system or installing a new online system) should be formally controlled prevents the fostering of effective change control management. Even such basic changes as installing an electrical outlet, moving a software module from a test to a production library, or increasing air-conditioning capacity should be monitored through the change control process because there is always a risk, however slight, that the change could disrupt service levels. In this context, a change is defined as any activity that can potentially degrade or interrupt service to users.

## Step-By-Step Procedures

The change control process comprises a series of steps aimed at providing the user with maximum system stability and availability. These steps are initiation, review, approval, scheduling, coordination, implementation, and follow-up audit. They are described in the following sections.

**Initiation.** The first step of the change control process is initiation of the change request. Anyone who requests a change should be required to submit a formal request form that performs the following functions:

- *Communication.* That is to notify those concerned that a change is being requested.
- *Recording.* This is to provide documented input to a change history log.
- *Impact analysis.* This is to determine the scope and expected impact of the proposed change.
- *Coordination.* This is to describe requisite and related activities that must be performed by other departments or personnel in order to implement the change.
- *Contingency planning.* This is to describe specific contingency or back-out procedures to be invoked and how these will be managed if the change is unsuccessful.

**Review.** All change requests should be directed to a central committee where they are reviewed for clarity and completeness as well as for conformity with existing formats and standards. Exhibit III-2-1 is an example of a typical change request form. This form is the major vehicle for the review process.

**Approval.** After the change request has been reviewed, it must be approved. The authorization or rejection of a proposed change should be the responsibility of a change control committee that represents the following groups:

- Application development.
- Software or technical support.
- Communications (WANs, LANs, and data and voice).
- Production (or computer) operations.
- Production control.
- Users (in appropriate cases).
- Data base and data administration.

With the rapid growth of online systems as an integral and critical component of the daily operation of many businesses (including airlines, banks, brokerage houses, and medical care facilities, among others), a new function

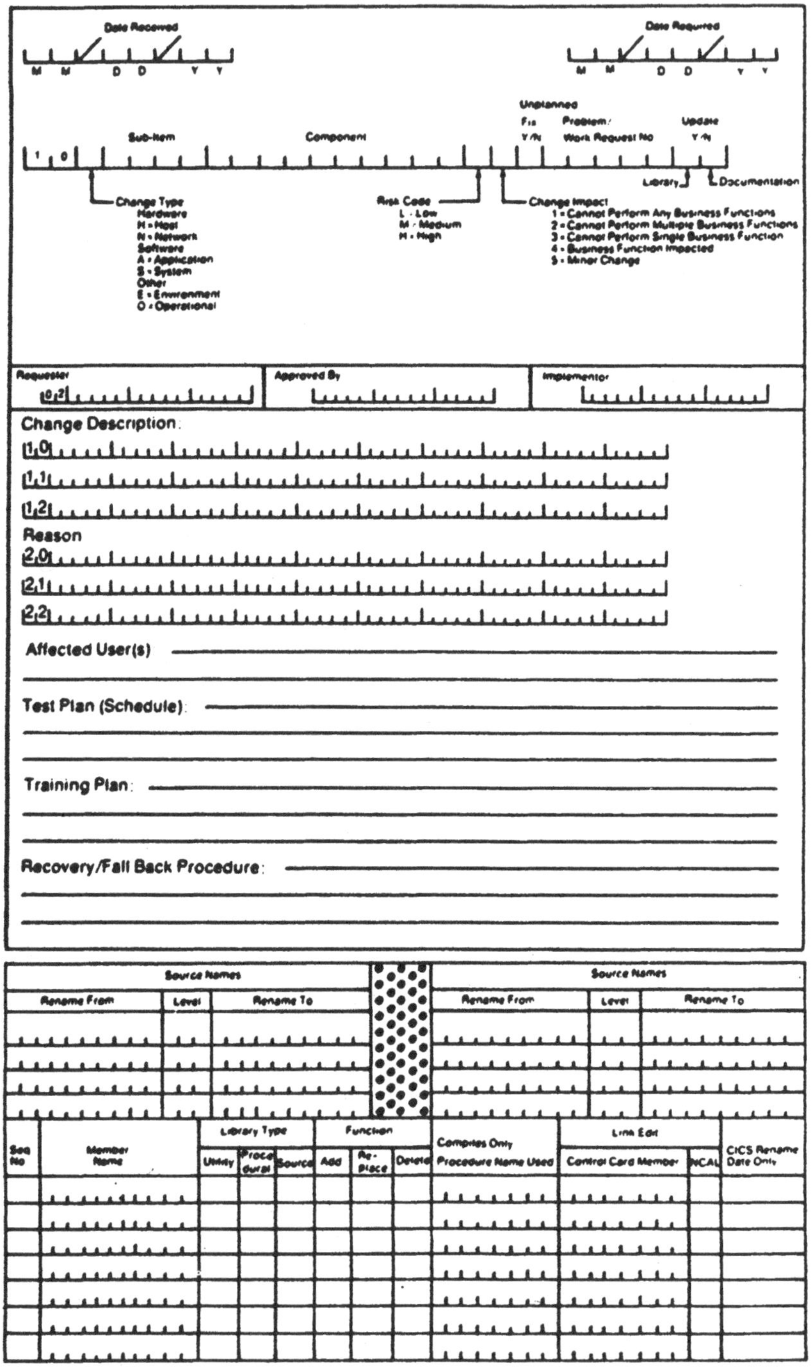

**Exhibit III-2-1. Sample Production System Change Request**

that affects the change control process has evolved in many of these organizations. This function is called service level management, and its mission is to formally establish, track, monitor, measure, and report on information systems' service levels and the adherence of such service levels to the specified benchmarks. Representatives from this function are key members of the change control committee. If an organization's structure and size allow, the service level management function should report to a neutral entity within the IS department, and a service level management staff member should chair the change control committee.

Another major manifestation of the growth of strategic online systems and the organizational and technical changes that accompany such growth has been the emergence of the communications systems function and its convergence with the traditional IS department. The criticality of networks to support online systems and attendant business practices is readily evident and needs to substantive elaboration in this chapter.

The globalization of business, which is such a popular topic in many current business publications, requires an even greater dependence on networks in conjunction with providing computing resources to users in various parts of the world. Regardless of whether or not the communications systems function is part of the IS department, the communications function must have major representation on the change control committee because of its vital role in the maintenance of service levels to the entire user community.

**Scheduling.** After the change has been approved, it must be scheduled. By scheduling a change properly, the data center manager can ensure that:

- Several changes are not targeted for the same period.
- Adequate task planning can occur.
- All involved personnel can be notified of the proposed change.
- The resources required to effect the change can be made available at the required times.
- The change does not conflict with other activities outside of the change control area.

**Coordination.** The purpose of this step is to alert all involved or affected parties to the proposed change. Involved personnel should hold at least one meeting to:

- Fully discuss the change.
- Expose and resolve any conflicts and misunderstandings.
- Establish and agree on priorities.
- Develop a written change agenda for distribution to management and all areas potentially affected by the proposed change.

**Implementation.** After agreement has been reached concerning the change, a standard methodology should be used for implementation. For example, the methodology might state that nonemergency changes to financial applications can be made only on the second or fourth Tuesday of the month, and nonemergency changes to systems software (e.g., MVS, CICS, IMS, TSO) can be made only on the first Sunday of each month. In addition, the implementation standards should explicitly state that only a specific group can implement production changes, thereby assigning accountability for the change process.

**Follow-up Audit.** The last step of the change control process should be an audit to review changes that have been implemented. The audit function can:

- Compare the actual results of the change with the change request form and note any discrepancies.
- Aid in tracking changes made to production systems, systems software, and other modules, libraries, and utilities.
- Satisfy corporate internal audit requirements regarding changes in sensitive or proprietary data files.

## Reporting Function

The reporting function is a key component of the change control process. For effective performance of this function, a change history file and some automated control over change-related data are necessary. The file should contain a composite list of all changes made to hardware, software, or the processing environment. The change history file may be archived, but it should not be destroyed.

In most installations, the volume of data that must be managed as part of the change control process is massive. If the data is handled manually, the results may be unsatisfactory and the personnel costs excessive or, in some cases, prohibitive. Therefore, some level of automation is necessary for effective data manipulation and storage.

When the change control process is introduced, decisions must be made regarding the volume and level of reporting to be used. Exhibit III-2-2 depicts a reporting structure currently being implemented in a large, multi-CPU installation supporting an extensive batch work load and an online user network with more than 10,000 workstations, terminals, and printers. Alhtough the set of reports in Exhibit III-2-2 is relatively small, the need for a complete change history file and an automated method for handling data and producing reports is clear.

This particular organization has created the position of change control coordinator as part of the service level management function. This employee plays a major role on the change control committee. The job description for this position is provided in Exhibit III-2-3.

**Daily Change Control Reports**

| Report | Recipients | Purpose |
|---|---|---|
| Change activity | Change requestor, change coordinator | Feedback and activity summary for all changes in programs |
| Changes implemented | Managers, change coordinator | Daily log of implemented changes |
| Scheduled changes | Managers, change coordinator | Preview of changes scheduled for the next seven days |

**Weekly Change Control Reports**

| Report | Recipients | Purpose |
|---|---|---|
| Complete change schedule | Managers, change coordinator | Identification of changes approved and scheduled |
| Change summary (type) | Managers, change coordinator | Summary of changes by types (e.g., hardware, software) |
| Change summary (system) | Director, managers, change coordinator | Summary of changes made to applications and control software |
| Change summary (emergency) | Director, managers, change coordinator | Summary of all nonscheduled and emergency charges implemented |

**Monthly Change Control Reports**

| Report | Recipients | Purpose |
|---|---|---|
| Change summary | Director, managers, change coordinator | Summary of changes by type, requestor, system risk, and impact |

**Exhibit III-2-2. Sample Change Control Reporting Structure**

## IMPLEMENTATION CONSIDERATIONS

As an organization prepares to implement change control procedures, several additional considerations must be addressed. For example, any control procedure is effective only if it is applicable to the specific installation and organization. A procedure that is successful in one installation may be ineffective in another. Therefore, data center managers who wish to implement a change control system must be thoroughly familiar with the organization involved, the role of information technology in the organization, the nature and importance of the organization's automated systems, and the manner in which they support the organization.

The development of a change control system is a sensitive procedure that should not be undertaken without a detailed implementation plan. When implemented, the system will inevitably uncover weaknesses in various functions, systems, and departments involved in the process. Unless the data center manager is aware of this problem, the change control process can degenerate into a forum for accusations and recriminations that can disrupt data center and user operations. The issues that should be considered in the implementation plans are described in the following sections.

### Overview of Responsibilities
- Analyzes each change request to ensure that no conflicts exist with other requests
- Interacts with IS personnel to develop a scheduled date for each change request
- Monitors all change requests to ensure timely implementation
- Is a member of, and reports any conflicts to, the change control committee
- Is responsible for the maintenance of change files and production libraries

### Detailed Responsibilities
- Coordinates all changes in the production environment concerning online and batch systems through the use of appropriate forms
- Monitors and logs progress of changes to ensure that scheduled dates are met; if a scheduled date cannot be met, ensures that all affected areas are notified of any schedule changes
- Reviews all change requests to ensure that the requested dates are feasible; schedules requests that have little impact on the production environment; reports to the change control committee for scheduling of those changes that conflict with other requests or that significantly affect the production environment
- Maintains the change file to ensure that all historical data is correct and up to date
- Ensures that all change request entries are removed from the change file when implemented
- Provides special reports to the change control committee or management on request
- Moves all test programs to production libraries on the scheduled date and controls the production libraries' passwords
- Forwards to the change control committee all problem reports resulting from a previous change request
- Interacts with the technical standards group (if one exists) when a change request warrants a technical announcement or bulletin

### Qualifications
- Ability to communicate and work effectively with all levels of IS, communications, and user personnel
- Strong oral and written communication skills
- Three to five years experience in information systems, including at least one year of hands-on JCL experience
- Working knowledge of procedures for maintaining computerized files and data bases
- Understanding of the user community and its use of, and dependence on, computing services

**Exhibit III-2-3. Sample Job Description for Change Control Coordinator**

---

**Management Commitment.** If management is not truly committed to the establishment, maintenance, and measurement of user service levels and to managing change, the data center manager should not try to implement a change control program. Management commitment must include an understanding of the philosophy behind change control and its potential impact on the various departments affected. In addition, management must recognize that effective change control requires significant resources in terms of time, hardware, software, and personnel.

**Reporting Relationships.** Organizational reporting relationships must be defined during the early stages of implementation. Although the change control function may report to the IS manager, the data center manager, or the technical support manager, it is advisable that a separate, neutral service level management organization be established for this purpose. The definition of line reporting relationships depends on the size of the organization and the level of expertise, interest, and commitment of the personnel involved.

**Change Committee Chairperson.** Reporting relationships depend on who is selected as committee chairperson. In general, it is advisable to appoint a high-level staff member from the service level management organization as the chairperson.

**Resource Requirements.** The implementation plan should define the personnel resources required for the change control process, including meeting time, staff work, and management. In addition, if a software package is required for data collection and reporting, planners must decide who will develop the package, or if a package is purchased, who will install and maintain it.

**Logistical Issues.** If the organization is geographically dispersed, the impact on change control meetings, implementation of changes, delivery of reports, and management of the function must be determined.

## PROBLEM TRACKING

The implementation of the change control process should be followed by the development and implementation of a problem tracking system. The change control process forms the foundation for problem tracking through the formalization of procedures and the compilation of data on changes in hardware, software, and the processing environment. Problem tracking is aimed at identifying and collecting detailed information on any occurrence that interrupts the computing resource at the user level.

The problem tracking system can be an automated system capable of tracking both changes and problems. A single center for trouble reporting should be established (e.g., the network control center in the data center). All hardware and software problems should be reported to network control, which is responsible for obtaining the essential descriptive details of the problem (e.g., terminal identification, hardware component serial number and address, application software system identification, transaction identification, or operating software system identification) along with any other information that can help identify and resolve the problem. After the data has been obtained, it is entered into the automated tracking system, and the problem is then assigned to the proper department for resolution.

The compilation of this data provides an invaluable tool for management. For example, the information can be used to:

- Control vendor performance.
- Evaluate the impact of changes to the computing environment.

197

- Tack application software stability.
- Track operating system software stability.
- Monitor hardware component history.
- Assist in hardware maintenance control decisions.

Change control and problem tracking are logically linked and are needed for effective data center management.

**Automated Systems.** The availability of automated systems has improved during the past few years and has facilitated the implementation of change control, problem tracking, and service level management of both the IS and communications environments. The following software products are some examples of the availability of vendor-developed tools for systems management. This list is by no means exhaustive nor should any endorsement be inferred; it is provided as a guide, and data center managers are encouraged to research these as well as other products to determine which best fit their organization's requirements:

- Change control and problem tracking:
  —Info Management/Info MVS from IBM Corp.
  —CA-Newman from Computer Associates International, Inc.
  —Network Management System 3 from Peregrine Systems, Inc.
- Service level management
  —Net Spy from Duquesne Systems.
  —Mazdamon from Computer Associates.
  —Infinet from Infinet.
  —Net Alert from Boole & Babbage, Inc.
  —System View Netview from IBM Corp.
  —Best from BGS Systems, Inc.

Because most available change control and problem tracking systems are currently mainframe oriented, and because of the consolidations among the software firms that address the mainframe utility software market, not many other automated tools are available. As the client/server architecture evolves and becomes a more extensive platform on which major production-level systems are developed, utility software for network management or security (to name a few) is likely to become more available and prevalent. Again, however, data center managers are encouraged to conduct a search for change control or problem tracking software for the specific computing platforms represented in their environments. Such a search is easily performed through any library or software vendor directory.

## SUMMARY

The development and installation of change control, problem tracking, and service level management systems is strongly recommended. However, to be successful, these tools must have both management and organizational commitment. In addition, planners must use detailed project plans (including estimates of required resources and specifications for reporting relationships) for development and implementation. When these issues are successfully addressed, change control and problem tracking can help the data center maintain a high level of service to the user community.

# III-3

# Improving Productivity by Implementing a Tape Workstation Environment

*DANIEL F. SCHULTE • GEORGE W. ZOBRIST*

M agnetic tape has gone through several transformations to reach its current level of sophistication. With each transformation, the speed and reliability of tape processing has increased considerably. For all practical purposes, a tape library can operate at one of three levels of efficiency: the standard environment, the working tape library, and the workstation. The standard environment offers the lowest level of efficiency because the tape media and hardware are stored in physically separate locations. The working library—the middle level of efficiency—is an additional library located near the tape drives. The workstation concept—the highest level of efficiency—subdivides a consolidated tape media and hardware environment into separate entities that have exclusive media and hardware resources. This chapter discusses the tape library in terms of these scenarios.

## THE STANDARD TAPE LIBRARY AND OPERATIONS ENVIRONMENT

Although organizations may differ in their strategies for maintaining tape resources, tape processing tasks and problems are very similar. These similarities permit the definition of a standard tape library and operations environment.

The logical structure of a tape environment includes several separate entities. The two major items are the tape library and the tape drive area. In general, the library and the tape drive reside in different sections of the building. In addition to the main tape library, one or more off-premise library vaults might exist, mainly for disaster recovery purposes.

A smaller entity of the logical structure of tape operations is the tape cleaning and evaluation area. This area handles tapes that have caused I/O errors or become otherwise unusable. In most operations, tapes must be transferred to areas outside the data center either because they must be stored in an off-premise storage vault or because information on the magnetic tape must be communicated to persons outside the organization. The data center also receives tapes returning from off-premise storage, satellite processing centers, and outside organizations. To effectively manage the movement of tapes, a shipping and receiving area usually acts as a go-between for the data center and outside sources.

## Tape Operations Tasks

The daily routine of a tape operations environment includes many tasks. The primary responsibility of tape operations is to satisfy tape-mount requests so that the data on tape can be processed. Keeping track of what data is on each tape and which tapes are eligible for output is usually handled by an automated tape management system. This system may have hooks in the operating system that obtain control when a data set is created on tape, or it may be part of the operating system itself. At the point of control, all pertinent characteristics of the data are logged in a tape management catalog. A catalog inquiry can identify the contents of any tape in the library at any time.

Another daily task of tape operations is determining which tapes can be used for output. These scratch tapes contain either no data or data that has expired. The automated tape management system saves much time in this area because the tape management catalog contains the expiration date of each tape in the library.

A common activity in many data centers is the prestaging of tapes. In some cases, advanced notice is given that a certain job requires the use of specific tapes.

Many support tasks affect the time required to mount a tape; this chapter outlines a method to improve productivity by tuning tape operations. The emphasis is on minimizing nonproductive activities so that the tape operations environment becomes a highly tuned process.

## THE WORKING LIBRARY

Practical experience has shown that after a data set has been created or accessed on tape, it is likely to be reused as input within the next 24 hours. Considering the overlap of automated applications, this is a reasonable assumption. Many applications have grown so large and complex that it is not uncommon for one application to use data created by another.

To accommodate this need, it is possible to create an additional tape library that resides very near the tape drives. This working library would be comparatively small in relation to the main library and would house only tapes that have been created or read within the last 24 hours. Under this scheme, a considerable percentage of the tapes requested for mounting would reside in this library. Because the working library is located next to the tape drives, less time is required for an operator to retrieve and mount the tape. Any reduction in tape mounting time enhances the efficiency of the entire data center.

To create a working tape library, operators must log the date and time of last use for each tape in the library. For environments without an automated tape management system, the manual effort required to track the date and time of last use would probably offset any potential gains in efficiency. However, most tape management systems feature the ability to post the last-use date and time after a tape is mounted.

With this feature, an operator immediately files a tape in the working library instead of in the main library after removing the tape from the drive. When a particular tape is requested for mounting, the operator tries to locate the tape first in the working library and then in the main library. Each day, a reverse pull is required to move any tapes not recently used back to the main library. A simple program can be written to identify these tapes in the tape management catalog.

After the initial installation, two actions are necessary to retain an efficient working library environment. First, each tape must be filed in the working library after removal from a tape drive. This allows faster access to the newly created data if the tape is requested within the next 24 hours. Second, the reverse pull must be run daily to purge the working library of older tapes. If this is not done regularly and punctually, the working library becomes an unwieldy second library. With daily tape movement between the two libraries, the working library should remain small and should increase the efficiency of tape operations.

## THE WORKSTATION ENVIRONMENT

In medium- and large-scale tape environments, media and hardware are usually housed in separate areas of the data center because of building space constraints and security considerations. The introduction of cartridge tape technology to a data center, however, offers an opportunity to abandon the concept of separately housed media and hardware.

Compared with previous tape technology, the overall size of cartridge media and hardware is vastly reduced. This reduction allows most data centers to house both tape media and hardware in the space that previously contained only the tape hardware. The working library concept partially brought media and hardware together, but the cartridge technology allows full exploitation of this concept ( in addition to improved tape processing reliabilty and performance). The benefits obtained from consolidating media and hardware are substantial; the most obvious is the time reduction for tape-mount requests.

The consolidation of media and hardware (i.e., libraries and tape drives) allows the formation of a new operations environment that was previously impractical for large tape operations. This new environment uses the concept of separate and independent tape workstations within the overall tape operation. The goal of the use of workstations is to reduce the nonproductive activities associated with mounting tapes. For example, in most operations, the majority of tape operator activity consists of walking to and from the tape library to search for requested media. The reduction of walking and searching results in lower mount-pending times and increased efficiency.

Another benefit is that the use of workstations addresses the problems involving the size of the tape library. Implementation of tape workstations can overcome the degraded efficiency resulting from consistent annual growth of the tape library. The workstation environment divides a consolidated media and hardware operation into distinct entities, each functioning as an independent tape operation with separate media and hardware resources. As a result, a large tape operation is broken down into two or more smaller tape operations.

Each operation division is assigned a number of tape drives and a range of tapes. The objective is to assign a tape attendant to a workstation and eliminate the need for that attendant to leave the workstation. In theory, a tape-mount request will never be issued for a volume that does not reside in the same workstation as the allocated tape drive.

Of paramount importance is the transparency of this scenario to both the user and the workstation attendant. There are no job control language requirements for the users and the attendant's productivity is increased because most tape-mount requests can be satisfied with a volume located within the workstation.

The benefits obtained from workstation implementation are substantial. First, tape volume retrieval and refiling time are reduced. Instead of the original large tape library, a tape attendant works with a smaller, personal library. The number of volume serials (volsers) that an attendant is responsible for is smaller, which reduces the time required to locate a volume.

Second, all volumes are housed within a short distance of the tape drives. This reduces the amount of walking required to retrieve a tape; in addition, the library becomes the easiest place to store a tape when it is not on a drive, decreasing the number of lost tapes and simplifying the identification of scratch tapes. Most important, workstations promote productivity and improve the quality of work life for tape attendants. These factors are no longer mutually exclusive.

## Workstation Implementation

The implementation of workstations for a tape operation assumes that the required systems software packages are in place. (This software is discussed later in this chapter.) After installation of the required software, the workstation parameter library members must be created and maintained.

Creation of the parameter library members requires visualization of the tape operations area as logical clusters of tape drives and cartridges. Standard editing techniques are used to create the parameter library members that describe these clusters to the control software. An example and description of these members (e.g., TMOSCROO, TMONSMOO) is provided later in this section.

In creating parameter library members, the first item of concern is the number of workstations required for a particular tape operation. The number of workstations depends on the amount of productivity expected from a tape attendant. This could vary greatly among organizations, depending on the emphasis placed on efficient tape activity. In addition, productivity levels vary among tape attendants, so the data center manager must exercise care when determining the number of workstations. After an appropriate number is determined, the data center manager simply divides it into the total number of volumes in the tape library to arrive at the number of volumes within a workstation.

The resulting physical environment should be arranged as follows:

- Each workstation should be arranged so that the average walking distance from any volser in a workstation to any drive in the same workstation is minimized.
- The number, length, and placement of media racks should remain consistent from one workstation to another so that an attendant who is moved to another workstation need not learn a new system.
- Workstations should be conveniently positioned so that one attendant could easily cover two workstations during slow periods or breaks.

These three concepts should guide the physical placement of resources to achieve the lowest possible mount-pending times.

When the data center manager has established a mental picture of the workstation environment, the parameter library members representing this picture must be constructed for each system CPU. At initialization, these parameters are scanned and a map of the environment is built in each CPU. In this way each system has invisible boundaries defined for each workstation and will attempt to prevent tape activity from crossing those boundaries.

**An Example of Workstation Implementation.** The tape operations of a particular data center might have 32 tape drives and 20,000 tape volumes. After studying tape attendant productivity, the data center manager might decide to divide operations into two workstations.

To define this environment for the system, two parameter library members are required. The first member (TMOSCROO) defines the volser ranges for tape pools, and the second (TMONSMOO) defines the mount rules to be used. The TMOSCROO member separates the tape library into pools 1 and 2, ranging in volsers from 000000 through 009999 and from 010000 through 019999, respectively. This has basically divided the library into two entities, with 10,000 tapes each. The TMONSMOO member has divided the pool of tape drives into two sections containing 16 drives each. In addition, the rules have indicated that tape pool 1 belongs to the range of drives with addresses of 240 to 24F and that tape pool 2 belongs to the range of drives with addresses of 250 to 25F.

As discussed earlier, the allocation of tape resources is based on device priority for scratch tapes and volser priority for input tapes. For example, using the workstation assignment rules given for the sample environment, if a scratch tape were required for a job using drive 243, the system mount request message would be modified to indicate that a scratch from the pool 1 range should be mounted (i.e., a scratch tape with a volume serial in the range of 000000 through 009999). After a tape is mounted, checks are initiated to ensure that the tape was indeed available for scratch and that its volser was in the requested range. If the checks fail, the mounted tape is rejected and the modified system mount request message is reissued. In the same manner, scratch-mount requests are processed for the other 15 drives within workstation 1 (i.e., pool 1). Scratch requests for drives 250 to 25F are handled similarly, except that the mount request and mount verification are done from the pool 2 range (i.e., volsers 010000 through 019999).

As mentioned, a volser priority scheme is used for input tape requests. If a job required the use of volser 015000, drives 250 to 25F would have preference for allocation. Before allocation, the system scans the **TMOSCROO** member parameter to determine which volume pool the volser belongs to. In this case, the volume pool is 2. A scan of the **TMONSMOO** member reveals that drives 250 to 25F are to be used for this pool of tapes. An attempt is then made to allocate a drive from this range. If no drives are available in this range, a drive outside the range is allocated. This is known as workstation crossover, which is discussed later in this section.

An operational option is requried to increase the flexibility of workstations. This option deals with scratch tape availability. In the sample data center described, the tape library was divided into two pools. If a scratch tape from pool 1 were requested and one from pool 2 were mounted, the volume would be rejected and the mount message reissued. This check is valid for accidental mounting but does not address the possibility that no scratch tapes remain in pool 1. A quick resolution is needed to prevent the delay of tape activity on the 240 to 24F range of drives.

The solution is a system command that can enable or disable the volume serial range check for scratch mounts. In this situation, the check can be disabled to allow scratch mounting from any workstation. The volume serial check can remain disabled until scratches are available from pool 1. This option also permits a smaller data center to direct input tapes to the nearest drive without being required to manage multiple scratch pools. The option is most important to the tape librarian, who sees the potential catastrophe of depleting scartch tapes within a particular pool.

**Crossover.** In some situations, a tape volume must be mounted outside its own workstation. This is know as workstation crossover and must be mini-mized to ensure the highest possible efficiency. One source of crossover is outside tapes, which are tapes received from outside vendors or satellite data processing centers. This type of crossover is unavoidable, and it poses no major problem because outside tapes usually represent a very small percentage of the total number of tape mounts.

Another source of crossover is the unnecessary extended use of the volume serial check disable. This permits scratch tapes from any workstation to be mounted and causes crossover later for multivolume files. If a file is created and spans multiple volumes that reside in different workstations, crossover occurs when this file is called for input. The first volume of the file will be requested from the proper workstation, but subsequent volumes may reside in other workstations because of the volume serial check disable when the file was created. With the volume serial check enabled, all multivolume files should reside on volsers from the same workstation.

The final type of crossover results from unit affinity and prevents the allocation of unneeded tape drives. If a user wishes to process multiple tape files serially, only one tape drive is needed at any given moment, so only one is allocated. This prevents idle drives from being unavailable to other users. Because of unit affinity, the first tape is requested from a drive in its workstation, but subsequent tapes could reside in any other workstation on the floor. Although unit affinity can cause crossover, it is a very resourceful technique.

## Systems Software Packages

The three software components used to support the workstation environment in the sample data center are CA-1/MVS (Tape Management System, from Computer Associates International, Inc.), MIM (Multi-Image Allocation Component of Multi-Image Manager from Legent Corp.), and, as an option, TDS (Tape Display System, written by Southwestern Bell Telephone Co). CA-1/MVS and MIM are established systems software packages that interface with the operating system to provide a mechanism for workstation capability. If either MIM or CA-1/MVS is absent from the operating environment, any substitute software or operating system user modifications that have been applied to achieve workstation capability must interface with the operating system in a similar manner.

CA-1/MVS, as distributed by the vendor, supports the pooling of tapes through data set name or job name. By modifying the CA-1/MVS source code, the data center manager can establish the capability to pool tapes by tape drive device address. Although CA-1/MVS release 5.0 does not allow pooling by device address, future support of this feature is under consideration by the vendor. When CA-1/MVS is initialized on each system, the workstation boundaries are mapped out in each system. These mapping tables are then referenced by CA-1/MVS and MIM for each incident of tape activity. The extent of the CA-1/MVS role for workstations appears very simple. Each time a scratch tape is requested on a particular drive address, CA-1/MVS scans the workstation map to see which pool of tapes corresponds to that drive. After a pool is determined, the system tape-mount request message is modified to reflect the proper pool of tapes. CA-1/MVS also ensures that multivolume data sets reside on volumes that all being to the same pool. Any subsequent tapes mounted for a spanned data set must belong to the same pool as that of the first volume of the data set.

The role of MIM in the workstation environment is more complex. An optional user exit controls the allocation of tape drive. The exit receives a list of devices eligible for allocation and is permitted to trim the list, if desired. When a request for an input tape is issued, the exit scans the workstation mapping tables and uses the specified input volume serial number to determine which tape drive addresses are applicable. The eligible device list is then trimmed to exclude those that are not applicable for the specified volume serial number. The trimmed list is then returned to MIM so it can select one of the remaining devices for allocation. If the list has been trimmed to nothing (i.e., if no drives are available in that workstation), MIM allocates a drive from the original list that was passed to the exit.

For drives that are requested for output, the exit does not modify the original eligible device list. In this manner, regular system device selection occurs for output tapes. The eligible device list is modified only when an output data set requires multiple tape drives. The first drive is chosen by system device selection, but the exit attempts to select subsequent drives from the same workstation that the first drive resided on.

The final component of workstation software is TDS. The use of TDS is optional, but the features provided can further enhance the benefits of workstations. Usually, an attendant views tape-mount messages on a system console. These messages remain highlighted on the screen until the mount is completed. One difficulty is that the attendant sees mount messages for all workstations and must ignore the mounts that are the responsibility of other workstation attendants. TDS can monitor the status of as many as 42 tape drives on a single terminal screen. Each TDS terminal can be defined to display the status of a selected number of tape drives (e.g., those in a given workstation). At any instant, an attendant can scan the current status of all drives within a particular workstation. Each drive entry on the screen displays the system and job name of the drive allocated as well as the volume serial number of the tape. Drives that have mounts pending are highlighted to provide easy readability.

The objective of TDS is to allow quick and easy reference, which tape attendants can use to determine what outstanding tape-mount requests are in their areas. The less time attendants use to determine tape activity in their areas, the more time they have to satisfy tape-mount requests.

## SUMMARY

Aside from the obvious benefit of minimizing the walking distance required to mount a tape, other benefits are obtained from implementing a tape workstation environment. With the consolidation of tape media and hardware, the only two places that an active tape can be located are on a tape drive or in its storage rack slot. Workstation implementation also reduces the distance traveled to refile a tape after it is used. In addition, multiple-volume files are localized in a smaller region than before, making it easier to retrieve the entire data file when it is required. In an environment that does not use workstations, the multiple volumes could be scattered anywhere in the tape library.

All of the potential benfits of workstation implementation serve to achieve the overall objective, which is to reduce the nonproductive tasks associated with mounting tapes. The higher productivity level attained affects not only the efficiency of tape operations but the entire data center, resulting in better service for users, at a lower cost.

# III-4
# File Retention and Backup

*BRYAN WILKINSON*

W hen data was stored solely on paper, information was often duplicated and distributed to several locations. If one source of the information was destroyed, most of the data could be reconstructed from the alternative sources.

In a centralized data processing environment, an organization's current and historical data, and the programs that process this data, are stored on magnetic media in a central library. Although centralization offers certain advantages, it also exposes the organization to the risk of losing all of its data and processing capacity in the event of a major accident. In addition, files stored on magnetic media are more susceptible to damage than files stored on paper. For example, if a disk, reel, or cartridge is dropped, the data it stores could be destroyed; dropped papers require only resorting. In the event of fire, the glue binding ferrite particles to tapes, disks, and diskettes begins to dissolve at temperatures as low as 125°F; paper begins to burn at 451°F. Therefore, a fire-retardant vault designed for paper files provides only limited protection for magnetic media. Magnetic files are also susceptible to tape crimping or stretching, disk deformation, head crashes, viruses, and magnetic erasure.

Furthermore, when mainframes were the sole source of computer power, retention and backup procedures could be enforced. Copies of all files and programs could be conveniently kept in a central library. Copies of essential files and programs could be kept in a secure off-site location. Automated tape management systems were developed to facilitate proper file retention and backup.

Microcomputers and local area networks (LANs) have greatly complicated data storage and backup. Vital information is often stored on hard disks and diskettes that are scattered throughout an organization. The data center manager may have little or no authority or control over such distributed data. Furthermore, in environments in which data is transmitted by way of electronic data interchange, the data may reside only on magnetic media; there may be no input forms, no documentation, and no printed output. If a microcomputer's hard disk is damaged by physical accident or malicious mischief, the data is lost if the user has not followed proper backup procedures. If a diskette is lost or damaged through mishandling, the data is lost if no duplicates exist. This chapter explains how these problems can be minimized with proper file retention and backup procedures.

## FILE BACKUP

The most common causes of file damage or destruction are operational errors, natural disasters, and sabotage. The proper backing up of files considerably lessens the adverse impact of such occurrences. The following sections discuss causes of damage and their effect on file integrity in both centralized and decentralized computing environments.

### Operational Errors

In a centralized processing environment, more files are lost or damaged because of human error than for any other reason; the most common errors are probably unintentional scratches. Inadvertent scratches can occur when unlabeled tapes are being labeled, filed, pulled, and mounted. Labeling tapes does not necessarily prevent accidental scratches. Although most mainframe operating systems have an option that permits a retention date or period to be placed in the label, this capability is not always used, thereby making it impossible for the operating system to detect a tape that must not be scratched. With some operating systems, the operator can ignore the warning console message and write over a tape even when a retention period is specified in the internal label. An operator or user can also erase of incorrectly alter a file by entering a transaction that overwrites the file or by failing to save the file.

Updating the wrong generation of a master file can also destroy data. Both the operator and user are responsible for this error. The operator mounts the wrong generation of the file and ignores warning messages from the operating system; the user fails to notice the problem when reviewing the reports. If the error is not detected until after the transaction or the proper version of the master file has been scratched, it can be extremely costly and nearly impossible to correct. Additional updating problems can occur when an update period covers more than one transaction tape. A given tape can be used more than once or not at all. Without externally generated control totals, such errors are almost impossible to detect.

Unlike tape files, disk and diskette files have no automatic backup capabilities. A special operational procedure is necessary to copy the file. This problem is complicated by the update-in-place process used with disk and diskette files. If the system fails during an update, the operations manager must determine how much was accepted by the system to avoid duplicate updating. The use of a data base by several applications compounds the seriousness of losing a file.

Online systems present a special problem when input is not recorded on hard copy. If a file is accidentally destroyed, reconstruction may be impossible unless a tape or another disk copy was made during data collection. With online updating, transaction logs in the form of journal tapes can provide a valuable source of backup. Program, software, and equipment malfunctions can also destroy or alter data and therefore necessitate file reconstruction.

Another operational error is the improper handling of magnetic media. If, for example, an unprotected tape reel is grasped by the outer edge rather than at the hub, the tape can be crimped and made unreadable. Destroyed or degraded files must be restored, which requires file backup.

An automated tape management system can minimize some operational errors, especially if a computer center uses many tape files. Proper file retention and backup standards and procedures are other solutions to operational problems.

## Microcomputer File Backup

An increasing amount of data is stored on microcomputers or downloaded from mainframes and then maintained on microcomputers. These computers are usually operated by people who are relatively inexperienced with data handling procedures. As a result, files have a greater chance of being lost or damaged. The data center manager should ensure that all microcomputer users know and understand the following basic precautions:

- If the microcomputer has a hard disk, the heads of the disk drive should be positioned over a nonsensitive area of the disk before the computer is moved—This is usually done running a **PARK** routine. Many portable microcomputers also feature a headlock capability, which provides the same protection.
- If a large file is being created, it should be saved periodically during the creation process.
- Two files should not be created with the same name unless the older version is no longer desired—the new file will overwrite the old.
- File names should print in a standard location on output documents.
- Diskettes should be kept in protective envelopes and storage containers when not in use.
- No portion of the diskette's magnetic surface should be touched.
- Diskettes should not be bent or squeezed.
- Diskettes should be kept away from smoke, liquids, grease, motors, magnets, telephone, display monitors, extreme temperatures and humidity, and direct sunlight.
- Diskettes should be removed from disk drives before the system is shut off.
- Only felt-tip pens should be used to write on $5^1/_4$-inch diskette labels.
- Paper clips and staples should not be used on diskettes.
- Diskettes should not be cleaned.

## Natural Disasters

Operational errors usually destroy only a limited number of files; disasters can damage an entire library. Fire is the most common disaster threatening a data center. The data center environment creates its own fire hazards (e.g., high voltages and easily combustible paper dust). Fire melts or burns disk packs, diskettes, and tape cartridge and reels, as well as the glue that binds the ferrite particles to the medium. Media damaged by smoke are unreadable until cleaned. If water is used to extinguish the fire, the files must be dried before they can be used.

Microcomputers are vulnerable to such localized disasters as small fires, power surges, electrical shorts, or collapsing desks. This is reason enough for regularly backing up the hard disk using diskettes, tape streamers, or Bernoulli boxes; by uploading to a mainframe, or by using another backup method.

Although other natural disasters—earthquakes, hurricanes, tornadoes, and floods—might not destroy the files, a medium is rendered unusable until it is cleaned, tested, and refiled. Magnetic files must be backed up and stored in a location that is not exposed to the same threat of natural disaster as the central data library is to ensure the organization's ability to recover these files in the event of a natural disaster.

## Sabotage and Theft

Sabotage of files or programs can include magnetic erasure and physical abuse. In addition, programs can be altered to erase or modify files when a specified event occurs, and external tape labels can be interchanged, requiring the files to be reidentified. Anyone with physical, program, or online access can sabotage files and programs. An effective approach to protecting files from disaster and sabotage is off-site backup.

Microcomputer users should be warned about using bulletin board programs, programs obtained from friends, and programs purchased from people who do not have a well-established reputation in the computer industry. Such programs can carry viruses, worms, or Trojan horse programs that can wipe out or alter files or deplete a computer's resources. If the microcomputer is linked to a mainframe, there is the added hazard that the problem instruction set could be transmitted to the mainframe, where the problems it causes could be magnified and spread. It is recommended that someone well versed in programming review new microcomputer programs or that the programs be vetted by antiviral software before they are used.

In addition, microcomputers have increased the threat of file loss through theft. Microcomputer file libraries are usually not behind locked doors. Diskettes are easy to conceal. People steal diskettes, not only for the data on them, but to use on their home computers. If the diskettes are stolen, the files are gone if no backups exist.

## FILE RETENTION REGULATIONS

The Internal Revenue Service requires that adequate record retention facilities be available for storing tapes, printouts, and all applicable supporting documents. Because this procedure was issued in 1964, before the widespread use of disks, it refers only to tapes. A 1971 IRS procedure, however, states that punched cards, magnetic tapes, disks, and other machine-sensible media must be retained for as long as their contents may be regulated by the administration of internal revenue law. If punched cards are used only as input and the information is duplicated on magnetic media, the cards need not be retained. The IRS has also developed audit programs that can be performed through the computer by using files retained on magnetic media.

There are about 3,000 federal statutes and regulations governing the retention of records. Not all of the records covered by these regulations have been automated, but many have. A digest of these regulations, called *Guide to Record Retention Requirements in the Code of Federal Regulations,* is available from the US Government Printing Office. These regulations can be grouped in the following categories:

- Accounting and fiscal.
- Administrating.
- Advertising.
- Corporate.
- Executive.
- Insurance.
- Legal.
- Manufacturing.
- Personnel.
- Plant and property.
- Purchasing.
- Research and development.
- Sales and marketing.
- Taxation.
- Traffic.

Although many of these records might not be automated, those that are can be retained economically on magnetic media. State-regulated organizations (e.g., banks and insurance firms) must also satisfy state file-retention requirements because audit software is used to expedite and expand state audits.

## EDP AUDIT REQUIREMENTS

Auditors must be able to verify that programs are operating properly and that magnetic file data is accurately represented by the tab listings for audit. In addition, they must confirm an organization's ability to recover from a disaster

or an operational error. Auditors can impose retention and backup requirements on data processing by requesting that specific files—usually year-end
files for important financial systems and transactions—be kept for testing.

## Retention and Backup Standards

Generally, the absence of file retention and backup standards means that the
system designers probably decide which files are retained and backed up;
consequently, too few or too many file generations may be retained. Each
situation is costly and illustrates the need for file retention and backup standards. Standards should be established for local and disaster recovery backup
and legal file retention requirements (see Exhibit III-4-1). The sources of
information and approaches to file storage vary according to these requirements.

**Local Recovery.** The data center manager provides information about
local recovery requirements. Responsibilities include detailing the types of
operational errors that affect file or program integrity and documenting how
and when a problem was detected and what steps were taken to restore file
or program integrity. The causes and consequences of any situation in which
integrity cannot be restored must be thoroughly investigated. Constraints on
restoration should be listed, and steps that can simplify or improve restoration
should be examined. When files are updated online or data is collected through
communications networks, the individual most familiar with data communications should provide the same type of information for communications failures.

Users who prepare input should be questioned about the disposition of
original input documents and data transmission sheets. This information is
particularly important when data is entered online with no paper documentation for backup. The data entry supervisor should be questioned to determine
the cost and time required to reenter the average quantity of input for one
processing cycle (i.e., one transaction file).

The programming manager should be consulted about problems associated
with restoring application programs and other software files. Particular attention should be paid to the recovery of packaged programs that have been
modified in-house. It is important to determine the availability of procedural
documentation needed to restore the programs. The programming manager
should provide the same information for the operating system and its various
subroutines.

Microcomputer users should be questioned about the types of data in
their files. Such data is increasingly of the type usually stored on the mainframe
and centrally maintained. If there is data of this type, the problems and costs
associated with its loss must be considered.

**Disaster Recovery.** Some of the information needed to establish disaster

I. Purposes
  A. Retention
  B. Backup
II. Policies
  A. Existing files
  B. New systems and files
III. Standards
  A. Basic retention and backup schedules (time and location)
    1. Operating systems
    2. Software packages
    3. Application programs
    4. Master files
    5. Transaction files
    6. Work files
    7. Documentation
      a. System
      b. Program
      c. File
    8. Input documents
    9. Other material
  B. Retention and backup schedule approvals
    1. Retention
    2. Disaster backup
    3. Operational problems backup
  C. Security considerations
    1. Company private data and programs
    2. Government-classified data
    3. Customer files
  D. Use of retention periods in file header labels
  E. Storage location
    1. Backup
    2. Retention
  F. Transportation of files to and from off-site storage location
  G. Procedural documentation
    1. For users
    2. For MIS
  H. Periodic tests of the usability of the backup and retained materials
IV. Appendix
  The appendix should provide an item-by-item schedule of all material whose retention and backup schedules differ from the basic schedule.

**Exhibit III-4-1. Outline for Developing Standards**

recovery backup standards is collected during the local recovery survey. Additional data can be obtained from reviews of a file inventory that identifies the files of each department with the organization. Department managers should review the inventory on a file-by-file basis to specify which files are vital to operations and must be reconstructed, department documents from which files can be restored, and the maximum time limit for recreating each file (assuming that the disaster occurred at the worst possible time). The IS manager should review all application programs, software packages, and operating system files. If several departments maintain organizational data bases, it may be necessary to recreate data at the data element level of the file.

Although all this information may not be needed to develop retention and backup standards, it does provide justification for developing and enforcing the standards. The information can also be used to establish backup and recovery procedures.

**Legal Requirements.** Retention requirements are set by the IRS, other government regulatory agencies, and departments within the organization. The controller is generally responsible for meeting the legal requirements and therefore should be consulted when it is being determined which files must be retained and for how long. The IRS recognizes that not all magnetic files can be maintained for long periods because of cost and volume and therefore has found that the appropriate method of determining record retention needs is to evaluate each system and current retention policies. If the IRS has not reviewed organizational retention policies, the controller should ensure that such an evaluation is made. If the IRS has identified what should be retained and for how long, this information should be incorporated into the retention standards. The retained files should be periodically inventoried to confirm that the standards are being followed.

Department managers must be familiar with the other federal and state guidelines that apply to their files. In addition, record retention requirements established by users, senior management, EDP auditing, and other departments must be enforced. Differences between the requirements specified by the users and those demand appropriate by the auditors should be resolved.

## STORAGE LOCATIONS

For efficient operation, files are usually stored in the computer room or an adjacent tape library. Microcomputer users who back up their files usually store the backups near the microcomputer. As protection against disaster, sabotage, or theft, a duplicate copy of important files should be stored off site. Various facilities can be used for this purpose:

- *Commercial off-site storage facilities.* These are useful for an organization with hundreds of files to be stored.
- *Moving and storage companies.* Several of these organizations use part of their warehouses to store magnetic files.
- *Bank safe-deposit boxes.* The size and cost of safe-deposit boxes make them appropriate for only a small number of files. Access to safe-deposit boxes may be limited to banking hours.
- *IS facilities of another organization.* This alternative provides an environment with proper temperature and humidity controls. Unauthorized

access can be prevented by keeping the files in a locked facility that can only be opened by an employee of the customer organization.

- *Remote corporate buildings.* This approach is probably the least costly.

## Off-Site Storage Selection

Several factors should be considered during the selection of an off-site storage location:

- *Availability.* Backup files should be available 24 hours a day. Bank safe-deposit boxes present accessibility problems.
- *Access.* File access should be limited to a few employees. Individuals outside the organization should not have file access.
- *Physical security.* Fire safeguards (e.g., heat and smoke detectors and automatic fire extinguishers) that will not damage the files should be installed. The storage facility should be located and built to minimize damage from disasters. On-site and off-site facilities should not be concurrently vulnerable to the same disaster.
- *Environmental controls.* The proper temperature and humidity should be maintained continuously, including weekends and holidays.
- *Identifiability.* If a storage facility is used that is not part of the organization, there must be a method of distinguishing and identifying the material that belongs to the organization. If this is not done and the storage company declares bankruptcy, a bankruptcy court will seize and hold the files.
- *Storage requirement flexibility.* A facility should be able to meet the organization's current and future storage needs. It must be determined whether increased storage requirements will require the organization to use different locations in the building, purchase additional equipment, or pay for remodeling.
- *Cost.* This factor should be considered only after all other requirements have been satisfied. Compared with the reconstruction of files, any form of off-site storage is a less expensive alternative.

## Storage Contracts

If a commercial storage facility, bank, or warehouse is selected as a storage location, the proposed lease should be reviewed by legal counsel. The lease should specify the lessor's file protection responsibilities and the recourse for appropriate indemnification of file damage or loss.

If the data center of another organization is used for storage, a written agreement should identify the legal owner of the file, stipulate access rights, and define the liability of the organization providing the storage facility (or its insurer) if the files are accidentally or deliberately destroyed while on its premises. Legal counsel should review the proposed agreement to verify its appropriateness and validity. If the other organization refuses to sign an acceptable written agreement, use of the proposal facility should be approved by the senior management of the organization wishing to obtain off-site storage.

### Transportation Considerations

The method of transporting files to and from the off-site storage facility should be considered carefully. Because magnetic media can be damaged by excessive heat, jarring, and mishandling, files should be packed in protective containers. Logs of all material stored off site should be maintained, and if a commercial transportation service is used, a packing slip should accompany each file.

### OPERATIONAL CONSIDERATIONS

Proper off-site backup can shorten disaster recovery time and simplify the process. Because backup takes time and costs money, the frequency of backup should depend on how long the organization can continue to function without up-to-date data. In some operations, the answer may be no time. In such cases, the data must be captured simultaneously on two or more remotely located computers. If the answer is one week, weekly backup of master files and daily backup of transaction files should be adequate.

Frequency of backup depends on the type of application. For example, most manufacturing companies first used computers for financial data. In such cases, the company could manage for a week or two without the usual computer-produced reports. Now, many production applications are running so that production lines are scheduled, material is bought, and product status is determined using online automated systems. Off-site backup is often needed in these situations.

A standard approach to backup is to require a minimum of three generations of each master file, with the oldest generation being off site. Transaction tapes needed to bring the off-site version up to current status would be taken off site daily, weekly, or monthly, depending on the frequency or volatility of the update. Some organizations maintain their permanent-hold (usually year-end) tapes at the off-site location if the off-site storage location is more secure or spacious than the organization's storage area.

In a VSI or MVS environment, the system catalog should be backed up for off-site storage. When the catalog matches the tapes at off-site storage, recovery is much easier; it is unnecessary to modify job controls to specify volume and serial numbers or absolute generations. Instead, restore jobs can refer to the relative generation number with a symbolic parameter that is easily modified.

Many data centers use reel numbers instead of labels on tapes that are managed by a tape management software package. Even when external labels are on the tapes, finding a particular tape among hundreds or even thousands can be next to impossible. Therefore, it is strongly recommended that a complete listing of tapes to be sent to off-site storage be prepared just before pickup and that the list be sent off site with the tapes. The list should include the tape volume and serial number, the date and time that it was created, and the data set names of every file on each tape. Automated tape management systems can produce such a list quickly and easily, and the list is important enough to justify the labor of producing it manually if no tape management system is in use.

## SPECIAL FILE ACCESS PROBLEMS

Special file access problems complicate file retention and backup procedures. For example, if customer, classified, trade-secret, and sensitive data are processed in an online environment, a security software package must limit file access. The following sections address other access considerations for such files.

**Customer Files.** If an organization performs processing for other entities, it must access their files and programs. Customer agreements should be reviewed to determine the organization's contractual liability. Standards and procedures should have safeguards that minimize the possibility of lost or altered files. The customer should agree in writing to proposed backup and retention schedules.

**Classified Data.** Files with a government security classification must be stored and transported according to government regulations. The data center operator and the auditor should review these limitations to verify their enforcement.

**Trade Secrets.** Trade secrets are programs, formulas, and processes that given an organization a competitive edge. Methods of handling and protecting trade secrets are specified by state law and therefore vary. Several requirements, however, are basic to maintaining trade secrets:

- A trade secret and its associated material must be physically secured and designated as company confidential.
- The information cannot be published or made available to the public.
- If the material must be disclosed to someone outside the organization, this individual must be advised of the trade secret and must agree to maintain its confidentiality.
- A permanent record should be maintained of the material's location when it is not in the usual storage location.

Senior management must designate which files or programs represent trade secrets, and the data center manager and auditor should ensure that an organization's retention and backup standards and practices meet state and internal requirements. The standards and practices should be reviewed with legal counsel to ensure adequate control.

**Sensitive Data.** Financial, payroll, and similar accounting information is generally considered confidential, with access limited to specific employees. Such data may be found on both hard disks and diskettes. If the data is on hard disk, access to that computer must be limited. If the data is also on diskette and is not encrypted, the handling and storage of the diskette (including its off-site storage) must be controlled. The data center manager must determine which files contain sensitive information, who is permitted access to each of these files, and how such access is controlled. Access control should be specified in the appropriate standards and procedure.

## BACKUP USABILITY

Although the proper files may be retained and backed up, procedures must be established to maintain and test backup file usability.

One problem occurs when files that are to be retained for several years are stored on tape. Unfortunately, gravitational pull usually deforms tapes that are unused for a year or longer. A standard technique to prevent this problem is to rewind unused backup tapes every 6 to 12 months. If this practice is not being followed, the readability of the older tapes should be verified through a tape-to-print program.

If there is no standard on file retention, or if the standard is not followed, the proper versions of files, transactions, and programs may not be retained. To detect this problem, the data center manager can inventory the files at the backup location and compare this listing to the standard. A more useful but difficult approach is to use the files and programs at the backup site (instead of those at the data center) to process one or more applications. This method determines whether the standards are adequate and are being adhered to and whether operators know the procedures for using the backup material. Even if this technique fails to make these determinations, the processing pinpoints unexpected problems that could arise in an actual emergency and reemphasizes the need for workable emergency procedures.

## ACTION PLAN

To ensure effective file retention and backup, the data center manager should:

- Determine file exposure.
- Determine the government record retention requirements that affect the organization.
- Compare current record retention standards with exposures and requirements.
- Identify and evaluate local recovery problems and their solutions.
- Review the organizational understanding of potential problems, proposed solutions, and legal requirements for record retention.
- Inspect and evaluate off-site storage.

- Review off-site storage agreements.
- Inspect and evaluate the facilities used to transport files to the off-site location.
- Determine special file access restrictions.
- Evaluate the usability of backup files.
- Prepare recommendations based on reviews and evaluations.

# III-5
# Checklists for Reviewing MVS Data Center Controls

*RONALD G. EARLES • WILLIAM A. YARBERRY, JR.*

A s organizations streamline operations to improve their competitive position or reduce costs, data center managers must identify and eliminate inefficiencies in the data center. The process of identifying and correcting processing inefficiencies in a data center is often referred to as tuning the data center. Though this process can be time-consuming, it can often result in a significant saving for the organization. For example, tuning a data center with a large mainframe could delay a hardware upgrade for six months to a year. However, the net result could be a saving of several million dollars. In many cases, EDP auditors are asked to look for ways to improve data center efficiency. This article explores how data center managers alone or with EDP auditors can eliminate processing inefficiencies by targeting potential weak spots and initiating corrective measures.

## EVALUATING SYSTEMS PERFORMANCE

Because many data center managers have concentrated on providing users with functional support and maintaining the technical environment to provide sufficient resources to support operations (e.g., ensuring enough DASD is available for new applications), processing efficiency has often become a secondary consideration. As a result, there may be numerous opportunities to improve data center operations. It is in the data center manager's best interest to review existing systems in order to identify areas of low productivity and suggest and implement corrective measures.

Because the investigation of systems performance is highly technical and vendor specific, the data center manager may need to engage outside consultants or in-house auditors to assist in the performance review. In selecting a consultant, the data center manager should determine whether the potential consultant has experience in tuning applications or operating systems. Systems tuning is a specialty within the field of systems consulting; a general background in data processing does not necessarily provide sufficient expertise. The data center manager should also determine whether the consultant's experience is current and includes the operating system used in the organization. The consultant should have hands-on experience with performance measurement software and be familiar with online data monitoring.

## ESTABLISHING SERVICE-LEVEL OBJECTIVES

Before evaluating systems performance, the data center manager must determine the level of processing service required by the organization within its resource and cost constraints. Once established, these service objectives form the basis for evaluating the effectiveness of data center operations. Specifically, they provide users and data center management with accepted criteria for measuring performance. Without such quantitative measures, the perception of service can be unduly influenced by random events, such as spikes in response time or sudden changes in volume.

To review service-level objectives, the data center manager should first verify that formal service-level agreements have been developed, issued, and implemented. These agreements must be consistent with the organization's goals and objectives. For example, if most work is done in batch mode, online response time should not be given undue weight in evaluating system performance. The data center manager must also ensure that the agreements specify the exact quantitative measures to be employed in the assessment. Such measures might include system response time (for CICS, data base, and TSO transactions), the rate of on-time report delivery, the rate at which the batch turnaround schedule is met, and the number of help desk calls resolved in a 24-hour period.

The technical definition of service levels must be correct. For example, including short, medium, and long TSO transactions in a single composite average may distort the true picture of performance. Furthermore, performance measurements should be taken within the same time period (usually during regular working hours) to ensure that averages are not skewed and that comparisons of performance data are meaningful.

## PERFORMANCE MEASUREMENT TOOLS

Having established the review objectives, the data center manager should next identify the systems performance software available for the environment. These software tools can be broken down into the following general categories:

- *Statistical analysis.* Statistical software is used to identify trends and patterns in large volumes of data. A powerful statistical package (e.g., SAS Institute's SAS) may be required. Typically, the package is used to evaluate raw data from online monitors.
- *Resource measurement.* This type of software is used to measure such resources as CPU time, DASD transfer, wall clock time, queue time, tape and cartridge transfer, number of transactions processed, and storage

utilization. Software packages are available from operating system and third-party vendors.

- *Graphics.* Charts and graphs facilitate the analysis of the results of performance tests. Typically, test results report on large quantities of data; historical trends may not be apparent from direct review of the raw data. A pictorial representation of the data can be used to graphically illustrate historical trends, current variance, and other patterns.

## MVS System Monitors

The primary tools for measuring performance of an MVS system are its IBM system monitors, the System Management Facility (SMF), and the Resource Measurement Facility (RMF). In some cases, these measurement tools themselves must be tuned so that system overhead does not exceed reasonable limits.

**System Management Facility (SMF).** SMF is the major source of information about job-related processing for an MVS system. SMF can be used to monitor billing, job resource consumption, data set activity, system resource use, system security, and system availability. In addition, programmers can write system program exits to generate additional SMF records that report on user-defined areas of interest. Because SMF records report on system activity at a detail level, the volume of SMF records generated per day can be very large (e.g., half a million records for a large data center or more if all record types are turned on).

To ensure the effective use of SMF at the data center, the data center manager must:

- *Determine whether only necessary SMF records are being created.* If an SMF record type is not used for analysis, it should not be written. Redundant record types should be eliminated. For example, job-related information is contained in type-30 records; type-4 and type-5 records contain similar information and should be eliminated through use of the **SMFPRMOO** member of **SYS1.PARMLIB**.
- *Determine how long SMF information is retained.* Trending requires retention of data for a minimum of 12 months; however, summary records can be created to reduce required storage volume.
- *Determine whether the SMF records are being properly transferred to tape cartridge or other long-term storage media.* SMF records can be lost if the disk-based data sets used to store them are full. It is necessary that auditors should examine the timestamps of records to verify that there are no gaps among SMF records.

**Resource Measurement Facility (RMF).** RMF generates measurement data from the MVS work load using time-interval accounting. Whereas

SMF data represents a single task performed, RMF data represents an accumulation of all batch, online, and TSO tasks performed for that time interval.

RMF identifies global problems, such as input/output contention, excessive CPU use, and poor disk management. To ensure that RMF is used effectively, the data center manager should:

- Verify that RMF records are generated and retained in the correct record format (e.g., record type 72).
- Analyze reports generated from the RMF system. The data center manager should refer to the IBM RMF manuals or attend an RMF course.
- Track performance of data center components. For example, does the IBM-3390 disk access rate significantly exceed the recommended 30 milliseconds on a consistent basis? If so, determine whether all files for a frequently accessed system have been placed on the same pack; it has been shown that this practice can result in poor access rates.

## PERFORMANCE OF THE EFFICIENCY AUDIT

Having identified service-level objectives and the required performance measurement tools, the data center manager is now ready to conduct the efficiency review. The various components of system processing that are to be reviewed include:

- Overall processing work load.
- Application-based processes.
- Batch processes.
- Data transfer and storage.
- VSAM data sets.
- CICS.
- Data bases.
- System development processes, procedures, and training.

### Work Load Leveling

The processing work load of an MVS data center consists of batch, online, and TSO processes. Processing overhead, including MVS operating system processes and storage management processes such as full-pack backups and data set migrations, consumes much of the total CPU capacity.

Exhibit III-5-1 presents a typical pattern of CPU consumption during a 24-hour period. Capacity planners often evaluate processing requirements based on peak demand rather than total demand. Techniques that can be used to level this work load include:

- Shifting as much batch processing as possible to nonpeak hours (called zones by capacity planners).
- Staggering the development staff's workday to include underused time periods, such as the lunch hour.

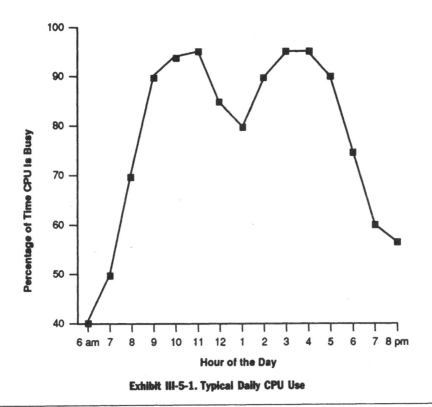

**Exhibit III-5-1. Typical Daily CPU Use**

- Reducing the frequency of processing utility functions during hours of peak demand. For example, IBM's storage manager, DFHSM, may run every 15 minutes to compress old data sets. During peak periods, this frequency could be reduced.
- Reviewing the processing demand placed on the system by the data center's performance monitors. These tools are significant consumers of processing resources. For example, the MICS monitor can aggregate performance data at the detail, weekly, monthly, and yearly levels. If data is reported only at the summary level, however, the data center manager can eliminate more detailed levels of aggregation, thereby reducing storage and processing costs.
- Using workstations for data entry and validation and uploading to the mainframe after peak hours.

## Tuning Application-Based Processes

It is more difficult to tune the system by tuning specific applications than by making global changes to JCL or system parameters. Typically, there are many application programs; modifying them requires specific knowledge of each application. For example, if an application accesses a large file both sequentially and randomly, the file's optimum block size depends on the frequency of access in each mode. If the file is usually processed sequentially, a large block size is more efficient, whereas, if access is mostly random, a small block size reduces I/O operations and processing time.

To review applications efficiency, the data center manager should:

- *Examine run frequencies.* In some cases, reports are run more frequently than necessary. For example, jobs that should be run only on request are sometimes run daily so that they will be available when needed.
- *Examine the 100 most processing-intensive production jobs.* Incremental improvements in the processing of large jobs can improve overall application efficiency. These large jobs can usually be identified by ranking production jobs according to CPU time consumed (using MICS or SMF data as input to a reporting program).

## Tuning Batch Processes

Most batch processes can be performed during nonpeak processing hours, such as at night or on weekends. The efficiency of batch processing becomes a more important concern for those jobs that must run during peak hours (e.g., a nightly job that continues into the morning). To review batch efficiency, the data center manager should:

- *Analyze batch runs for delays when accessing a data set.* Delays can be caused by file, device, string, or path contentions. Techniques for reducing contention include moving data sets to different packs and staggering execution of jobs requiring the same data set.
- *Analyze the selection of storage media.* A batch job that must access a large number of data sets stored on tape can experience delays caused by device contention.
- *Review the number of initiators for batch processing.* A low number of operator initiators can result in excessive job queue time.
- *Analyze the system resource priority assigned to batch job classes.* Low priority can result in a job being swapped out for an inappropriate amount of time.
- *Review jobs for proper allocation of buffers.* Buffers determine the number of records that can be read with one I/O operation. Increasing buffer size increases transfer rates for sequentially accessed files.

## Tuning Data Transfer and Storage

More than half the efficiencies to be gained in a data center relate to the storage and transfer of data. To improve throughput and storage management, the data center manager should:

- *Ensure that the most efficient utilities are being used for backing up files.* Commonly used utilities, such as IEBGENER, are not particularly efficient for backups. Newer utilities, such as the IBM DFDSS, typically require less than half the CPU time of IEBGENER (see Exhibit III-5-2 for a comparison of three utilities). DFDSS can be used to back up data sets as well as full storage packs.
- *Store large sequential files on tape rather than disk to improve access time.* After a tape has been mounted, a sequential file can be read four to five times faster than the same file stored on disk. However, several factors limit the usefulness of tape storage: only one application can access the file at a time; instantaneous access to specific records is not supported; and file size should exceed 60M bytes. A tape cartridge typically holds about 160M bytes of data. A comparison of the relative cost of transferring sequential data from tape and disk is shown in Exhibit III-5-3.
- *Use high blocking factors when appropriate.* The higher the blocking factor, the greater the number of logical records that can be obtained per physical read of the storage media. A large blocking factor also compresses more data into the same storage space. However, large block sizes are not always appropriate; for example, a high blocking factor should not be used for files that are accessed nonsequentially.

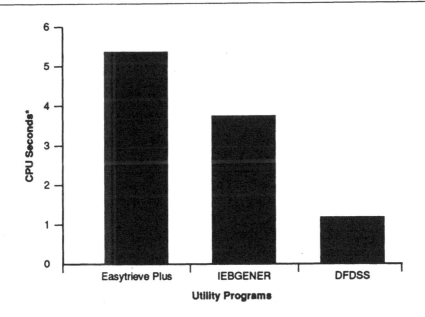

Note:
*Time each program takes to copy 500,000 records.

Exhibit III-5-2. Benchmark Test of Backup Utilities

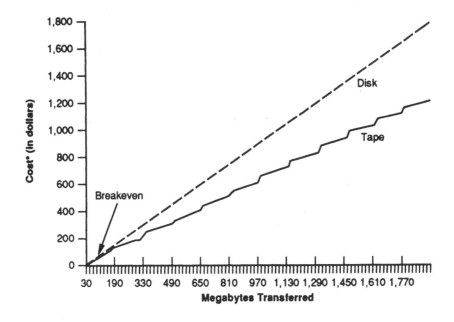

**Key:**
— — Disk costs
——— Tape costs

**Note:**
*Assumes transfer of data twice per day over a 90-day period.

**Exhibit III-5-3. Comparative Cost of Transferring Sequential Data Stored on Tape and Disk Using Easytrieve Plus**

## Tuning VSAM Data Sets

More options must be specified when allocating VSAM data sets than sequential data sets. If these options are set incorrectly, performance can degrade sharply. The data center manager should verify that the following techniques for tuning VSAM data sets are practiced:

- *Allocating files in cylinders rather than tracks.* Allocating space in cylinders can increase performance. Control intervals of 512K bytes should be allocated.
- *Minimizing the total number of extents allocated to the data set.* Extents are allocated to ensure sufficient storage on a volume with insufficient contiguous space. Many extents can increase processing overhead and CPU time.
- *Minimizing the number of control area (CA) splits in the data set.* CA split processing increases processing time and degrades online performance. The **CA FREESPACE** parameter can be used to control CA splitting.

- *Minimizing the number of control interval (CI) splits in the data set.* Although CI splits do not affect performance as dramatically as CA splits, many CI splits may force CA splits to occur. The **CI FREESPACE** parameter can be used to control CI splitting.

- *Using VSAM cluster parameters, such as* **IMBED, REPLICATE,** *and* **SPANNED,** *properly.* The **IMBED** parameter inserts the sequence set index records on the first track of the control area that it references. **IMBED** reduces the seek time required to retrieve data control intervals. The **REPLICATE** parameter causes each index record to be stored on its own track, reducing rotational delay. The costs of using these parameters include higher disk storage requirements and inefficient use of cache controllers for disk devices. The **SPANNED** parameter permits data records to be stored in more than one data control interval. The **SPANNED** option should be avoided because it increases processing times, disk space requirements, and buffer requirements.

- *Sorting sequential data files before loading them on their corresponding VSAM data sets.* This reduces the number of CA and CI splits, improves disk space use, and decreases CPU processing time.

- *Allocating the proper number of index and data buffers required for batch processing VSAM data sets.* This reduces job run time and limits physical I/O operations.

- *Reviewing inactive VSAM data sets.* Inactive files can be identified. File creation date, characteristics, and activity can be listed.

## Tuning CICS Processes

CICS must be tuned for maximum processing performance and resource use. (Such products are rarely tuned by the vendor for a specific installation.) To ensure efficient CICS processing, the data center manager should:

- Ensure that VSAM data sets used by CICS-based systems have been tuned. Improperly allocated or tuned VSAM data sets can degrade CICS performance.

- Verify that CICS tables and the parameters used to establish a CICS region are consistent with VSAM allocations.

- Review the use of local shared resource versus nonshared resource buffering to ensure efficient access to data.

- Ensure that an appropriate number of DASD strings have been allocated to each CICS region. The manager should analyze each region's performance statistics for wait-of-string conditions that indicate string contention.

- Check that buffers are allocated as follows: 512K-byte buffers should be allocated in multiples of 8, 1,024K-byte buffers in multiples of 4, and 2,048K-byte buffers in multiples of 2. This improves virtual storage efficiency.

- Verify that regular monitoring and tuning of CICS regions is performed.

Monitoring tools, such as Landmark's The Monitor, greatly simplifies performance analysis.

## Tuning Data Base Applications

Data base applications usually consume a large percentage of system resources. To ensure data base efficiency, the data center manager should check that these steps are followed:

- Review of performance reports created by the data base management system (DBMS) on a regular basis.
- Design and implementation of application systems to minimize demand on processing resources and maximize performance within the constraints of the DBMS. For example, a program designed to update a record using a direct access key might, in fact, sequentially read all data base records until it finds the desired record because of an improper data base call statement.
- Use of planned redundancy to decrease processing time or excessive I/O. Unplanned redundancy should be avoided.
- Determination and implementation of the optimal amount and mix of system resources required for maximum performance of the DBMS. The resources to be specified include memory and buffer size, tasking priorities and storage devices. For example, high-speed cache controllers must be used on disk devices serving data base files.

## Tuning Systems Development Processes and Procedures

In some organizations, TSO and batch processing devoted to systems development can consume a third of resources not devoted to operating system overhead. The quality of systems development can be reduced if resources are scarce—for example, an insufficient number of test runs executed during the development cycle. Several techniques can be used to reduce resource consumption and increase the value of resources used. Among these are to:

- *Transfer development activities such as programming and testing from the mainframe to workstations.* After syntax errors and basic logic problems have been debugged on the workstation, the programs can be ported back to the mainframe. Compilers for microcomputer versions of third- and fourth-generation programming languages are available. CICS and data base simulation software enable stimulation of online mainframe code.
- *Perform system testing using a small subset of production data sets.* An integrated test facility is useful for development. Commercial test data generators can be used to create small test data bases. The auditor should verify that system developers are, for the most part, using small sets of test data rather than full copies of production data during system testing.

If the appropriate naming conventions have been followed to distinguish test files from production files, an effective audit test is to compare the storage allocated for test files to that for production files.

- *Set compile options for optimum performance before placing programs into production.* For example, COBOL debug features should be turned off. This technique can reduce CPU time as much as 25%.
- *Include a vigorous processing efficiency review during systems development.* Developers are usually concerned more about system functioning than system performance. Typically, performance becomes an issue only if service to the end user degrades noticeably. Inefficient practices should be identified in the review process and eliminated.
- *Prototype all large projects.* Users should be shown functioning screens, examples of data, and the relationships of information before the detailed design to ensure that they understand and agree with the design approach. If incorrect design specifications are not detected before the detailed design phase, many resources will be consumed later in the project to correct these design errors.

### Tuning Development Staff Performance

The most effective time for improving the performance of application systems is during development. The modification of systems after they have been implemented is both expensive and risky. Management should provide the training and tools to ensure that developers know how to develop systems that conserve resources. If management holds developers to a reasonable standard for the development of efficient systems, the waste can be eliminated.

To evaluate the effectiveness of an efficiency program, the data center manager should ensure that the development and production staff are provided adequate training courses and materials related to systems performance and that they are given sufficient time for study. In addition, estimates of resource consumption that were made during development should be compared with actual consumption after implementation.

### SUMMARY

A review of data center efficiency can result in significant savings for the organization. Given the processing inefficiency of most data centers, there are substantial opportunities to reduce resource consumption and improve service to users. A thorough review may be more successful if an EDP auditor is assigned to the project.

To evaluate data center efficiency, the data center manager should first identify service-level objectives consistent with the organization's goals and environment. The manager should then identify the performance monitoring and analytical tools required to perform the review. A thorough data center review will include an evaluation of various system components, including application-based processes, batch processes, data transfer and storage management, VSAM data set allocations, and CICS and data base processes. The data center manager should also evaluate system work load levels and the impact of development activities on overall system performance.

# III-6

# Understanding Computer Negligence and Liability

*EDWARD H. FREEMAN*

O ne of the major misconceptions regarding information technology is the myth of computer error. Computers are inanimate objects; they can act only on the logic that has been programmed by humans. Although computer hardware occasionally fails, the only loss from such occurrences is time. Most so-called computer errors can be traced to some form of human error.

Despite its complexity, computer hardware typically performs with high reliability. Hardware may cease operating, but it seldom gives erroneous results. On the other hand, software packages typically contain at least a few logical flaws. Due to time constraints, programmers often put software into operation even though they suspect that problems may develop. To further complicate matters, a system might be infected with a virus. Finally, computer system errors can be caused by the mistakes of people who develop or maintain the system as well as those who enter data into the system. Although most software includes subroutines that check for data entry errors, some errors may escape detection and cause problems at run time.

When computer-generated information is faulty or incomplete, serious financial or personal losses may result. For example, a computer error that resulted in an excessive dose of radiation was cited as the cause of death in a cancer patient. Computer error nearly started World War III several years ago when a Department of Defense computer falsely reported a missile alert. Such errors may be the results of negligent actions by the software developer, hardware manufacturer, or some other party.

This chapter discusses the traditional theories of negligence and how the courts have related these concepts to computer applications and security. It outlines the responsibilities of the various parties and defines what is necessary to prove or disprove charges of computer negligence. Associated issues, such as malpractice and strict liability, are discussed. Examples from court cases are given, and specific, practical steps that an organization can take to reduce or prevent potential problems are offered.

## NEGLIGENCE

Negligence is conduct that falls below the standard of care set by law for the protection of others against unreasonable risk of harm. Matters of negligence are judged by the results of the actions in question. The intent of the negligent party makes no difference; usually the negligence is inadvertent—not malicious.

To recover for negligence, a plaintiff must prove a legally recognized injury of some monetary value. The following factors are required to begin an action for negligence:

- *Duty.* In the relationship with the plaintiff, the defendant must have a legal duty to act according to certain standards, and to avoid unreasonable risks to others.
- *Breach.* The defendant's actions must fail to conform to that duty.
- *Actual cause.* The plaintiff must show that the defendant's negligence caused the injuries—without the defendant's negligence, the injuries would not have occurred.
- *Proximate cause.* The plaintiff must demonstrate a close causal link between the defendant's negligence and the harm suffered by the plaintiff.
- *Actual damage.* The plaintiff must show that damages resulted from the defendant's actions.

These factors are discussed in the following sections.

## Duty

An organization or individual often has a legal responsibility, or duty, to act with reasonable care toward other parties. For example, a motorist has a duty to drive with reasonable care, according to a standard of conduct. Anyone who cannot adhere to this standard for any reason has a duty to stay off the road. Even though two drivers are total strangers, each has a duty to the other. A driver who speeds and causes an accident may be liable for the other motorist's injuries.

Under certain circumstances, a duty does not exist and individual actions are not negligent. For example, if person A is walking near a lake and sees person B drowning, person A has no legal duty to person B. Although the failure to help may be considered morally reprehensible, person A is not negligent in a legal sense. Similarly, a landlord might not be liable if a trespasser or robber trips on the stairs and breaks a leg.

If a duty exists, the major difficulty in testing a claim of negligence is the determination of the standard of care by which a party's actions or lack of action are to be measured. The traditional negligence standard is the care that reasonable person would have exercised under similar circumstances. The law recognizes a higher standard of care when parties hold themselves to be professionals, because they have a higher level of skill in their field.

There has been considerable discussion in the courts as to whether IS professionals are subject to this higher professional standard of conduct. Because programmers, unlike physicians, accountants, engineers, and architects, have no standardized licensing and educational requirements, the courts have not yet created a class of computer malpractice. Without uniform standards, the determination of a standard level of skill in an IS professional remains too subjective and is impractical.

This does not mean that IS professionals are free from any responsibility to provide accurate, reliable products. Like individuals in other trades, IS professionals are held to a standard of care. Traditional negligence and contract claims can be made against them.

## Breach of Duty of Reasonable Care

After an IS professional is held to a specific standard of reasonable care, the second element of a negligence action is to show whether the IS professional acted in such a manner as to prevent harm to another by this standard of care. Failure to meet this requirement is known as breach of duty and the breach does not have to be intentional.

Breach of duty can occur only if reasonable care is absent. Reasonable care is usually interpreted to mean the care that a prudent person—in these circumstances, prudent IS professional—would have exercised. The obvious danger in this standard is that the typical judge and jury may not have the technical background needed to determine reasonable care. They might lack the technical expertise necessary to evaluate the system design decisions of IS professionals. Even if the software worked exactly as intended, the court might determine that it was designed improperly for its purposes. As a result, the user or designer would be held liable for damages to another party injured by the system's perceived inadequacies.

Such a situation occurred in a 1981 Pennsylvania case, *FJS Electronics v. Fidelity Bank.* Fidelity Bank's procedure for stopping payment on a check required that a customer give the exact amount of the check to be stopped. The bank's computer program was designed to key in on three sets of numbers on the bottom of each check: the bank's federal reserve number, the account number, and the amount of the check. Every digit on the check had to match the stop-payment request before the computer would pull the check.

The president of FJS Electronics, a bank customer, requested that Fidelity stop payment on check number 896. Although FJS's president had been instructed to be precise, he told the bank that the amount of the check was $1,844.48 when the correct amount was 1,844.98. Because of the $.50 difference, Fidelity's system did not stop payment on the check. The check was paid and FJS brought suit to recover the $1,844.98 mistakenly paid out of its account.

Fidelity argued that its procedure for stopping payment on a check required absolute accuracy in that information provided by the customer. Fidelity claimed that FJS was aware of this procedure and was, therefore, responsible for the error. The court refused to accept this argument, concluding that when the bank decided to provide this service using such an inflexible system, it assumed the risk that the system would fail to stop a check. FJS was therefore awarded damages for its losses.

This case shows that the use of a computer in business does not change an organization's duty of reasonable care in its daily operations. The court ruled that the computer could have been programmed to process stop-payment requests on checks with an amount that was within a reasonable range of the amount stated on the request. To ensure accuracy, Fidelity could have manually verified the pulled checks. The bank's failure to install a more flexible, error-tolerant system inevitably led to problems.

**Overreliance on Computer Data.** An organization should refrain from overreliance on computer output. Many businesses use computers to handle the bulk of their record keeping and decision-making procedures. The courts are increasingly concluding that no matter how a computer system makes its errors, overreliance on computer output can be a source of liability for negligence.

An example of such overreliance occurred in *Ford Motor Credit Co. v. Swarens.* Swarens bought an automobile on credit from Ford and made his monthly payments in a timely manner. After a few months, a computer error informed collection agents that Swarens had fallen behind on his payments. Ford repossessed the car and later resold it, even after Swarens showed Ford's repossession agents his canceled checks. Swarens sued for the value of the car, and Ford did not contest. Swarens also sued for punitive damages, which are awarded when the court hopes to deter misconduct by the defendant. The court awarded punitive damages.

Another case also illustrates the computer user's responsibility to avoid overreliance on computer-generated information. On January 4, a bank's customer used an automatic teller machine to deposit $608. The machine incorrectly imprinted March 4 as the date of the deposit. During April, the customer received notice of an overdraft, discovered the error, and informed the bank. The bank's officers agreed to credit the customer's account, but told him that an investigation would follow. The customer then went on vacation. A week later, the bank filed criminal charges against the customer for felony theft. The customer was arrested while on vacation and spent two days in jail.

In May, both parties discovered the erroneous deposit slip. The bank offered to dismiss the criminal charges, with the condition that the customer release the bank from any civil liability. The customer refused to do so and was acquitted of any criminal activity. He then filed suit alleging intentional infliction of emotional distress and abuse of process. The case was eventually settled out of court for more than $50,000.

These cases demonstrate that a computer user must act reasonably in interpreting computer-generated information. If a prudent person could be expected to evaluate computer-generated information before using it, the courts will impose a duty of human intervention. The user must take reasonable care to allow for human intervention or be liable for any resulting harm.

**Res Ipsa Loquitur.** In cases of alleged computer negligence, it is often difficult for the plaintiff to prove that the defendant's conduct was a breach of duty. The doctrine of res ipsa loquitur (i.e., the matter speaks for itself) allows the court to assume that negligence occurred, on the basis of certain facts and conditions. Specifically, if the event is of a type that ordinarily does not occur unless someone has been negligent, the court will assume that the defendant was negligent. In such cases, the defendant must prove there was no negligence.

To apply the doctrine of res ipsa loquitur, three requirements must be met:

- The event must be of the type that does not usually occur without someone's negligence.
- The event must be caused by a factor within the exclusive control of the defendant.
- The event must not have been due to any voluntary or contributory action of the injured party.

Res ipsa loquitur simply allows the plaintiff to show that the event occurred and to create an inference that the defendant was probably negligent, without showing precisely how the defendant behaved.

In an 1863 case, the plaintiff was walking in the street past the defendant's shop. A barrel of flour fell on the plaintiff from a window above the shop. There was no other evidence. The court held that the accident itself was evidence of negligence. Without the doctrine of res ipsa loquitur, the pedestrian would have been required to show that the shop owner's negligence caused the barrel to fall. Because the court applied the doctrine of res ipsa loquitur, the shop owner had to prove that his negligence did not cause the flour barrel to fall.

Computer errors often meet the requirements for applying the res ipsa loquitur doctrine. Computer errors typically occur through negligence (e.g., software errors, incorrect input, hardware defects). The computer is usually within the exclusive control of the user. The injured party usually has no control over any aspect of the situation.

A recent Tennessee case explored the use of res ipsa loquitur in computer matters. The plaintiff alleged that a fire in its place of business was caused by a defect in a computer sold by the defendant, a computer manufacturer. An expert witness testified to the following facts:

- The fire originated at a computer terminal on a work table in an office of one of the plaintiffs.
- The only source for the ignition of the fire on the table was the computer equipment.
- The electrical outlets were still intact.
- The wiring that fed those outlets did not malfunction.
- The origin of the fire was not at the floor level.

The court accepted the fact that a computer would not ordinarily ignite and cause a fire, and by the rule of res ipsa loquitur, the plaintiff's claim was accepted. When the res ipsa loquitur doctrine is applied, the defendant may still rebut the plaintiff's claims, but the burden of proof has been transferred from the plaintiff to the defendant.

The relevance of the res ipsa loquitur doctrine to computer errors has not yet been completely resolved by the courts. The doctrine is more likely to be applied when the plaintiff is an innocent bystander and was not involved in any way in the development and operation of the computer system.

**Respondeat Superior.** The doctrine of respondeat superior makes an employer liable for negligence committed by an employee within the scope of that person's employment. When employees are negligent, they are rarely included as defendants. The employer organization is usually the defendant because it is wealthier and more able to pay a cash judgment.

It may be useful to include employees as defendants in negligence matters, though they will probably be unable to contribute substantially to any settlement. If the relationship between the employee and the employer has soured, the employee may be willing to testify against the employer in exchange for a release from liability. Conversely, the defendant may choose to add the employee as a third-party defendant. Such actions should be taken only after consultation with legal counsel and computer experts.

### Actual Cause

After the plaintiff has shown that the defendant has a duty to act with reasonable care and that the defendant behaved in a negligent manner, the plaintiff must show that the defendant's behavior caused the plaintiff's injuries. A but-for test usually determines the presence of this element: But for the defendant's action, would the harm have occurred? If so, the causation-in-fact requirement (i.e., actual cause) is satisfied.

Actual cause or causation becomes an issue when several parties have been negligent and the plaintiff cannot prove whose negligence directly caused the injury. In a classic case, *Summers v. Tice,* the plaintiff and the two defendants were members of a hunting party. Both defendants fired negligently and simultaneously, and the plaintiff was shot in the eye. It was not known from which gun the bullet was fired. The court held that the two defendants were jointly liable for the plaintiff's injury.

It is not yet clear how the courts would decide this issue if it arose in a computer context. The technical complexity of most computer negligence cases often makes it impossible to determine whose negligence actually caused the damage. Deciding which error was the cause in fact of the injury would be the primary issue in court. If actual cause cannot be shown, the court might find that neither party is liable. More likely, the court would use the *Summers* doctrine and find both parties jointly liable.

## Proximate Cause

Proof of negligence also requires that the damages were proximately caused by the defendant's conduct—that it was foreseeable that the defendant's conduct would lead to the harm. This requirement sets limits on otherwise open-ended liability for errors. The proximate cause element is usually satisfied if an injury is of a type that would be a foreseeable result of the defendant's negligence or if there is a direct sequential relationship between the breach and the injury.

If the plaintiff is injured by some remote circumstances caused by the defendant's negligence, should the defendant be held liable? This question was posed in a famous 1928 New York case, *Palsgraf v. Long Island R.R.*

In *Palsgraf*, a man was running to board the defendant's train. He stumbled and was about to fall. One of the defendant's employees tried to push him onto the train and dislodged a package from the passenger's arms. The package contained fireworks, which exploded when they were dropped. The shock of the explosion toppled some scales at the other end of the platform. The falling scales injured the plaintiff.

The court held that the defendant's employee was negligent in his actions. His conduct, however, did not involve any foreseeable risk to the plaintiff, who was standing far away. The key issue was whether the defendant's negligence was sufficient to make the defendant liable to the plaintiff, who was injured by an extremely remote and bizarre coincidence.

In a split decision, the court held that the defendant was not liable. Most of the *Palsgraf* court phrased its ruling in duty, rather than foreseeability, asking whether the defendant had a duty of care to the plaintiff. Even the dissenting judges, who held that the defendant was liable, recognized a need to restrict the defendant's liability at a point short of all possible outcomes that might stem from his negligent conduct.

A generalized formula for determining proximate cause probably cannot be developed. The matter must be determined case by case, according to an undefinable standard of fairness. It may or may not be foreseeable that third parties would rely on erroneous information furnished by a computer system. The analysis provided by *Palsgraf* might guide the court, but the court will decide each case on its own merits.

One court's logical analysis of foreseeability and causation in computer matters occured in *Akins v. District of Columbia*. The plaintiff was the victim of an armed robbery in Washington, DC. At the time of the robbery, the assailant was out on bond for previous armed robberies. Because an IBM computer failed to operate at the time of the assailant's two previous arraignments, the arraignment judges did not have a complete report of his arrest and conviction record. As a result, the arraignment judges released the assailant once on his own recognizance, and later on a $3,000 bond. The victim brought a negligence suit against the District of Columbia, the Pretrial Screening Agency (PSA), which is supposed to maintain and update criminal records, and IBM.

By itself, the perpetrator's criminal assault of the plaintiff might be considered a remotely foreseeable result of computer failure at the courthouse. However, the court noted the PSA's intervening failure to retrieve manually the perpetrator's record, and the discretionary decisions of the arraignment judges. IBM's negligence could not be characterized as a proximate cause of the plaintiff's injuries. Because IBM's actions did not have enough of a causal relationship with the plaintiff's injuries, the court found that there was no negligence and denied the plaintiff's claim against IBM.

## DAMAGES

Finally, a negligence claim requires that the plaintiff has suffered damages as a result of the defendant's breach of duty. The damage does not have to be physical or monetary. An injury to the plaintiff's reputation could be sufficient to recover for monetary damages. The threat of future injury or near-miss situations, in which injury might have occurred but did not, is not sufficient to sustain an action for negligence.

## STRICT LIABILITY

In some cases, the courts will hold a defendant liable for damages without requiring the plaintiff to show fault. Strict liability occurs most often in product liability cases. A person who is injured by a defective product does not need to prove how the manufacturer was negligent in producing the product. It is sufficient for the plaintiff to prove that the manufacturer produced a defective product that injured the consumer.

Relatively few cases involving computer programs have been decided on the basis of strict liability. The key is whether computer programs are products, a term that usually refers to tangible items. Negligence and strict liability restrictions are more clearly applicable in cases involving computer hardware than in those involving software products, especially if the use of hardware causes physical damages. In *Austin's of Monroe Inc. v. Brown*, a restaurant sued a hardware manufacturer, but software caused the damages. The hardware was not defective, and the court denied the claim. Strict liability for computer errors eventually may be accepted by the courts, but standard methods of proving negligence are currently the norm in such matters.

## FAILURE TO USE MODERN TECHNOLOGY

Computers have become accepted tools for doing business. Accordingly, an organization may be placed at risk because it is not using up-to-date technology. If a court finds that damages could have been avoided by the use of modern and accepted technology, a defendant's failure to use such technology might breach the defendant's duty to exercise reasonable care. For example, such applications as railroad switching, air traffic control, and medical diagnosis may give rise to liability claims if modern technology is not used.

This necessity of using up-to-date technology was recognized by the courts as early as 1932. *The T.J. Hooper* case involved two tugboats that were towing barges containing cargo. Both barges sank in a gale. Evidence presented at trial showed that the tugboat pilots could have learned about the storm and taken proper precautions if radios had been installed on board.

At the time, few tugboats had radios. Nevertheless, the *Hooper* court decided that this fact did not conclusively prove that the tugboat owner was not negligent in failing to install them, and the tugboat owner was found liable for the lost cargo.

How does the *Hooper* doctrine apply to computer technology? Even if computers are not ordinarily used in an industry, an organization may still be liable if it fails to use state-of-the-art computer technology. The following factors should be considered when determining whether nonuse of technology is negligent:

- The cost of the technology must bear a reasonable relationship to the harm that might be suffered if it is not used.
- Computers must have received a level of acceptance in regard to this particular application.
- The technology must be reliable and readily available.

## DEFENSES AGAINST NEGLIGENCE CLAIMS

When faced with a claim of computer negligence, defendants can assert several claims in their own defense. If successful, such defenses may introduce facts and points of law that can counter the plaintiff's allegations of negligent conduct. These defenses are described in the following sections.

### Contributory and Comparative Negligence

The essence of the contributory negligence defense is that plaintiffs are barred from any recovery if they were negligent in any way and that negligence contributed to their injuries. This rather harsh doctrine has been changed in most states with the adoption of comparative negligence. Under comparative negligence, the court calculates each party's proportional fault and allows recovery for only that portion of damage that was not caused by the injured party's own negligence.

In a hypothetical example, the defendant was injured because the plaintiff was negligent in its use of computer security. The court determined that the damages to the injured party were $10,000. The court then determined that the plaintiff was 20% responsible and the defendant was 80% responsible. Under comparative negligence, the plaintiff would receive $8,000 or 80% of the $10,000 in damages. This is in sharp contrast to contributory negligence, under which the plaintiff—who was 20% responsible—would recover nothing.

The defense of contributory or comparative negligence implies that the injured party in some way caused the injury. In cases involving computer negligence, unless the plaintiff actually had access to the computer system, the only reasonable way in which an injured party could be contributorily negligent would be by supplying erroneous input data.

Two examples involving Citibank Corp. demonstrate the courts' logical reasoning in cases involving alleged contributory negligence. In *Judd v. Citibank*, the plaintiff claimed that a third party made unauthorized withdrawals from her checking account, using an automated teller machine. The plaintiff produced evidence that she was at work when the withdrawals were made. Citibank countered with evidence of stringent security precautions programmed into the system, but admitted that in certain instances, the computer had malfunctioned. The issue was whether Citibank's computer printouts were somehow in error or whether the plaintiff had been contributorily negligent by allowing another person to use her card and by divulging her personal identification number. The court held for the plaintiff, finding that she had proved that she was not contributorily negligent.

In a similar but unrelated matter, the court allowed recovery by the plaintiff for an initial unauthorized withdrawal from an automated teller machine, stating that the bank had failed to show that the plaintiff was negligent. However, the plaintiff was not allowed recovery for subsequent unauthorized withdrawals. The evidence established contributory negligence because the plaintiff knew about the first unauthorized withdrawal but failed to notify the bank.

## Assumption of Risk of Harm

Arguing that the injured party assumed the risk of injury is another defense to negligence. A party assumes the risk of certain harm by voluntarily consenting to take the chance that harm will occur, despite being aware of such risk. When an assumption of risk is shown, the plaintiff is, under traditional common law principles, completely barred from recovery.

A computer user might be able to take advantage of this defense if the injured party knows the nature and extent of a risk of injury before being exposed to that risk. This situation can occur when a contractual relationship exists between the parties.

In contracts with other businesses, a clause limiting liability may help relieve the IS organization of some liability. Contractual protection of this type is limited in its application, however, because courts may not accept contract language that absolves a party from any liability whatsoever, especially in personal injury cases. The court may honor a clause limiting the amount of liability (e.g., to a refund of purchase price) but may not honor a clause by which the other party, who has little or no control over the computer, bears the entire risk of error.

The doctrine of assumption of risk is based on the concept that both parties had equal bargaining power and voluntarily agreed to the terms of the contract. Courts may find that a party's contractual assumption of risk was not voluntary if the other party possessed considerably more bargaining power. Contract clauses that shift responsibility away from the negligent party will probably be ineffective under such circumstances, especially if the injured party is a consumer.

### Statute of Limitations

A frequent defense in negligence actions involves the statute of limitations. Under statutes of limitations, plaintiffs are barred from pursuing court actions after a specified period of time has passed. Such laws are enacted on the basis of the following beliefs:

- There is a point in time beyond which a prospective defendant should no longer need to worry about the possibility of and defending against a claim of negligence.
- The law disapproves of stale evidence.
- Plaintiffs who delay bringing action for an unreasonable amount of time should forfeit their claims.

One aspect of the statute of limitations has troubled courts for many years: If a plaintiff does not discover an injury until long after the defendant's negligent act occurred, does the statute of limitations start to run at the time of the negligent act, at the time of its discovery, or at the time when the plaintiff should have been aware of the negligent act? Until recently, courts almost always held that the statute started to run as soon as the negligent act was committed. If a plaintiff did not discover an injury until after the statute term had expired, any claim was denied. However, many courts have recently refused to continue this injustice under certain circumstances.

In one such case, *St. Louis Home Insulators v. Burroughs,* the plaintiff signed a contract for the purchase of five software packages to be delivered in 1977 and 1978. The defendant delivered three of the five systems during 1977 and early 1978. After encountering problems with the quality of these systems, the plaintiff refused delivery of the last two systems. The defendant made repeated attempts to correct the problems but failed to do so. The plaintiff terminated the project in 1978.

In 1983, the plaintiff filed suit, claiming negligent misrepresentation, fraud, and breach of warranty. The defendant claimed that the statute of limitations had expired and that the plaintiff's suit should be dismissed. The court noted that the plaintiff knew as early as March 1978 that the software program was not operating properly and could not be made to do so. As such, the plaintiff no longer had a cause of action because the applicable statute of limitations on the claim had expired. In computer negligence matters, the time period of the statute of limitations begins when the plaintiff should be aware that a problem exists.

## SUMMARY

Most computer negligence can be traced directly to human error. Consequently, an IS organization's efforts to minimize the chance of being sued for computer negligence begin with its personnel. They should be thoroughly trained to act professionally, think for themselves, and know when vendors and contractors are not meeting their obligations.

# Section IV
# Systems Planning

P lanning for the effective use of hardware and software within the data center has always been a major responsibility of the data center manager. It has also always been a challenge. Today, however, not only is it still a major responsibility, the challenge is even greater. There are many reasons for this situation, including

- A merging of hardware and software based on new technology.
- Increased pressure from corporate management to control IS costs.
- Increased pressure to achieve not only the data center's goals, but the company's business goals.
- The continued rapid introduction of new technologies and management approaches, such as client/server computing.
- The introduction of new development tools and approaches, such as object-oriented programming.

To fulfill their systems planning role, data center managers must remain aware and knowledgeable of the many changes taking place in the hardware and software environment. This section examines some of the key areas of change.

The concept of client/server computing has moved rapidly to the forefront of systems planning. Its promise is to provide greater distributed processing power at reduced cost. Although this promise is true in some cases, implementing client/server computing has proved to be a major challenge.

To plan for client/server computing and to determine whether it is appropriate for their organization, data center managers must understand the basic concepts. Chapter IV-1, "A Primer on Client/Server Technology," provides an overview of the basic concepts behind the client/server architecture. These concepts are applied in Chapter IV-2, "Managing Hardware in a Client/Server Environment".

As mentioned, implementing client/server technology is a complex and difficult task. However, because of senior management demands to reduce costs and improve IS service and support, it is rapidly becoming a requirement for the data center manager to understand and implement client/server computing. Chapter IV-3, "Preparing to Implement Client/Server Solutions," discusses the technical issues involved and provides recommendations for organizing such a project.

Another focus of corporate management today is reengineering—the re-building of an organization's business processes to improve competitiveness, productivity, and cost structure. This concept directly involves IS and the data center manager, because many internal business processes are tied directly to the use of information systems. Chapter IV-4, "Implementing Business Process Reengineering: A Case Study," provides an excellent study of how reengineering was implemented at a major corporation, how the IS organization was involved, the changes that were made, and the lessons that were learned.

In the area of hardware, disk storage continues to be of major interest. In today's competitive business environment, decisions must be made quickly. Sound decisions require quick access to current information. As a result, corporations must maintain large data bases. A real revolution in on-line storage capacity is occurring with the introduction of optical disk technology. Chapter IV-5, "An Update on Optical Disk Systems," provides an overview of the technology, its impact, and the promise it holds for providing dramatic increases in storage capacity at a fraction of the cost of current storage technology.

The data center manager must be aware of new applications development tools and methodologies, because these advancements can have a major effect on the overall operation of the data center as new systems are developed and put into production. Chapter IV-6, "Planning for Object-Oriented Systems," provides insight into a concept and methodology being used to develop an entirely new generation of information systems based on an object-oriented approach.

As we have discussed earlier, implementing a client/server computing strategy is a complex undertaking and there are many considerations which must be taken into account. Chapter IV-7, "Lessons From Three Client/Server Implementations," provides some real-life lessons regarding the implementation of a client/server architecture, the things that can go wrong, and how to avoid them.

It should be apparent by now that a client/server strategy represents a significant departure from many of the "classic" approaches to computing. As a result, the impact of such change on an organization are going to be significant. Knowing how to effectively manage such change may mean the difference between a successful implementation of client/server and failure. Chapter IV-8, "Using Client/Server Technology to Enable Change," provides a first-hand look at how this change can be managed successfully.

# IV-1
# A Primer on Client/Server Technology

*LAYNE C. BRADLEY*

T oday, the information systems field appears to be in complete confusion. Data center managers are being inundated with demands from many different directions. Their companies' management is demanding that more systems and support be provided with less resources. Users continue to demand new systems and improved customer support. Hardware and software vendors are releasing new products and services at such a rate that data center managers cannot even evaluate them, much less decide whether they are appropriate for their organizations.

The information systems field is going through a major structural change. Microcomputer and local area network (LAN) technology has dramatically shifted the source of computing power and the design approach for new applications. The problem facing data center managers is to determine if and how this new source of computing should be integrated into their organizations. To make such a determination, they must first understand this new technology.

Most of this confusion currently stems from the client/server concept. The confusion exists because there does not seem to be a single, clearly delineated definition of client/server computing. Depending on the vendor, client/server is a management concept, a new technology, an entirely new set of tools to be used in applications development, or a combination of all three. The client/server concept encompasses all three aspects. Therefore, data center managers must understand each facet in some detail and when each is applicable. To facilitate this understanding, this chapter discusses the various aspects of the client/server concept. For the purpose of this chapter, client/server computing is defined as the use of technology and procedures to move all or the majority of applications systems from mainframes and minicomputers to smaller, faster, and less expensive networks of personal computers, with the intent of dramatically reducing information systems expenditures.

## THE BUSINESS CASE FOR CLIENT/SERVER COMPUTING

As with most technology today, there are significant business issues driving the client/server concept. These business issues include:

- Increased competition.
- Shrinking product life cycles.
- Importance of customer service.
- Proliferation of personal computers.
- Need to increase productivity.

## Increased Competition

During the last few years, businesses in the US have been restructuring. Because of several factors, it is becoming increasingly difficult for companies to continue to operate as they have in the past and remain profitable. Such factors as the use of cheaper foreign labor, government regulations, increased taxes, and the economic rise of Third World countries have put tremendous pressure on the ability of large US corporations to compete effectively. Competition today must be viewed not only from the perspective of the US market but from that of the global market.

Companies have had to learn how to operate in a global marketplace in order to compete. Thus, they have had to reduce large, expensive overhead structures. A significant amount of downsizing—massive reductions in staff—has occurred and is continuing. From the corporation's point of view, this approach has both benefits and disadvantages. Reducing the number of employees, as well as employees' salaries and benefits, can improve profit margins, at least for a period of time.

However, because of such technology available today as personal computers, fax machines, and cellular telephones, many former employees have become competitors in the global marketplace. In 1993, 40 million people were running businesses out of their homes. Many have developed successful companies. The competition cycle is growing rapidly.

Because of these competitive pressures, companies must be able to identify and respond immediately to competitive threats. Ignoring a new competitor, a new product, or a new marketing approach could be fatal to the survival of a company.

## Shrinking Product Life Cycles

Historically, consumer product life cycles were as long as three or four years, from initial design to delivery of the product to the market. Today, it is not unusual to find product life cycles as short as 18 months. In the software industry, for example, product life cycles can be as short as only three months. Therefore, to be successful, a company must be able to get its products to market as quickly as possible. Simply having a good product is no longer enough to guarantee success. A company must get its products into the hands of customers quickly, or the customers will choose a competitor. Consumers in the 1990s are more discriminating and demanding. Customer loyalty is fleeting, and companies must work harder than ever to maintain it.

## Importance of Customer Service

Consumers demand personal attention and are looking for quality products. They also demand products and services that are tailored to their specific needs. To be successful today, companies must focus on and meet specific individual consumer needs.

Because of changing consumer attitudes, companies cannot take customers for granted. Customer loyalty is no longer guaranteed, and only those companies that are able to provide outstanding customer service will remain successful.

## Proliferation of Personal Computers

New developments in technology have placed enormous computer processing and communications capabilities into the hands of individuals. Even very small companies or individuals can often compete equally, or even in a superior manner, with large corporations by using PCs, modems, and LANs. Because their overhead is usually much lower, small companies often enjoy a significant cost advantage.

## Need to Improve Productivity

Because of these current business conditions, US companies have had to improve productivity. To ensure a competitive cost advantage or at least to be able to operate at the same level as competitors, a company must improve productivity. Usually, this involves finding ways of doing more work with fewer people. Of course, merely reducing staff is no guarantee of improved productivity. New ways to accomplish tasks provide a better guarantee. Looking for these new ways is the basic goal of reengineering. Many US companies are now engaged in reengineering efforts, and information systems play a very important role in these efforts.

## Business Benefits of Client/Server Computing

Competitive pressures have forced many companies to downsize in order to control costs, reduce expenses, and increase profits. Downsizing can range from a relatively small reduction in staff to a major overhaul that includes discontinuing products, closing facilities, and massive layoffs of employees. In previous years, IS staff were not greatly affected by layoffs, but because of the large expenditures made on information systems, the IS staff has become a target for downsizing. In the basic client/server model, applications from large, expensive mainframes are moved to smaller and less expensive networks of file servers and personal computers; thus, client/server computing is often seen by senior management as a way to drastically reduce IS costs while continuing to provide needed IS services. However, this strategy does not always work out as management planned.

## CLIENT/SERVER ISSUES FOR IS

Because of the increasingly close relationship between information systems and business activities, the challenges that face the business become challenges that face the IS group. Much turmoil experienced in the IS industry today is related to its efforts to manage challenges created by business conditions. These challenges are discussed in the following sections.

### More Work with Fewer Resources

As businesses continue to come under greater competitive pressure, prices and profit margins often fall. Many companies have developed large, structured, expensive IS organizations that they can no longer support on smaller profits. Thus, efforts to cut expenses often result in large layoffs of IS employees. However, the requirements for staying in business and competing effectively do not necessarily change. Therefore, companies demand even more of their IS groups as resources shrink. IS groups are therefore faced with the challenge to perform effectively under such conditions. Those that do not meet the challenge could possibly be replaced by outsourcing.

### Client/Server Technology

The introduction of networking and file servers has greatly changed the way microcomputers are used in business. In many organizations microcomputers and mainframes are connected by LANs—a common client/server layout. The combination of a mainframe and client/server network provides companies with a great deal of computing power and flexibility. This structure can enable the distribution of systems and data bases throughout a network as well as provide control and security. However, many client/server networks use only powerful PCs and file servers. These systems can provide significant computing power themselves, but for many applications a mainframe is needed.

## CLIENT/SERVER ARCHITECTURE

Although today's hardware and software technology permit flexibility in designing networks, there are two basic client/server topologies. The names of these topologies are *two-tiered* and *three-tiered.*

In a two-tiered topology, microcomputers are connected directly to a mainframe, which acts as the server see (Exhibit IV-1-1). In this topology, the bulk of applications and data bases reside directly on the mainframe. Communications software is used to connect PCs and the mainframe. Microcomputer users download information, manipulate it, and upload it to the mainframe. In addition, microcomputer users often store and run certain applications that do not reside on the mainframe. The two-tiered structure is part of the natural evolution of personal computing.

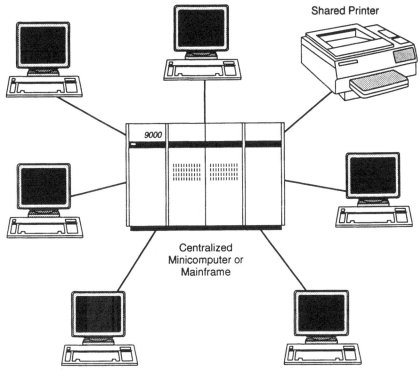

Shared Printer

9000

Centralized
Minicomputer or
Mainframe

**Exhibit IV-1-1. A Two-Tiered Topology for Client/Server Computing**

As shown in Exhibit IV-1-2, the three-tiered topology is a LAN of microcomputers connected to a file server, which is connected to a mainframe or a minicomputer. This structure provides much greater distributed data base and computing capability. Depending on the application, the LAN file server can either store its own separate data bases or download data bases from the mainframe to microcomputer.

This configuration can free up a great deal of processing power on the mainframe because fewer microcomputers are connected directly to it and computing is done at the server level. By using this architecture, companies take maximum advantage of the investment they have in their mainframes while taking advantage of the distributed processing capabilities provided by client/server technology. The three-tiered topology and variations are preferred.

## LANS IN CLIENT/SERVER COMPUTING

Because LAN technology has played such an enabling role in the development of client/server computing, data center managers must be familiar with the

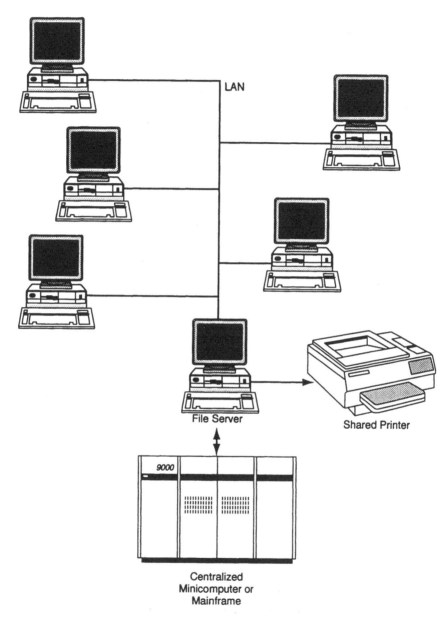

Exhibit IV-1-2. A Three-Tiered Topology for Client/Server Computing

basic elements of LANs. The following sections cover the most important aspects of LANs in client/server systems.

## LAN Topologies

There are three basic LAN configurations, but developments in LAN technology enable flexibility in the design of actual networks. Many different variations on the basic topologies meet the needs of a particular application. The following sections cover the basic LAN topologies.

**Bus Topology.** Exhibit IV-1-3 illustrates the LAN bus topology. In this configuration, microcomputers are connected to a cable in a linear fashion. This is the simplest type of LAN to design. It has two primary advantages. First, it is relatively easy to install. Second, it is comparatively inexpensive, because the amount of cable required is limited. The cable is run through the work group and new computers are simply added when needed. Another advantage of the bus topology is that new computers can be easily added. A LAN cable connection is used to plug new computers into the network. The cost for each node (i.e., each computer) connected to the LAN can be less than $500.

**Ring Topology.** In this configuration, nodes are connected to a cable that forms a closed loop (see Exhibit IV-1-4). A single continuous path joins each computer. The primary advantage of this topology is performance. In this configuration, data flows continuously through a loop at high speed. One of the most popular forms of the ring topology is known as a token ring. In a token ring, a software token (i.e., polling mechanism) goes around the ring,

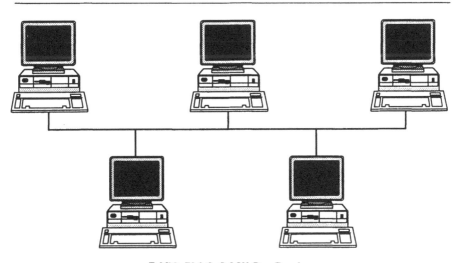

**Exhibit IV-1-3. A LAN Bus Topology**

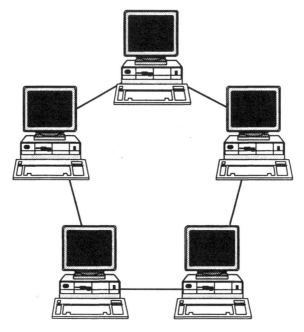

**Exhibit IV-1-4. A LAN Ring Topology**

and each node places information on it and passes it to a specific node in the network. This approach is efficient and enables the high speed transfer of data. A disadvantage of the ring topology is that nodes depend on each other. If one node breaks down, the loop is broken. (There are, however, ways to remedy this situation.) If a single node fails in a bus-topology LAN, however, this failure should not affect the other nodes on the bus.

**Star Topology.** The third basic LAN topology is the star (see Exhibit IV-1-5). In this configuration, one node is in the center of the network and cables connect it to all other nodes in the network. The central node acts as a communications controller for all other nodes in the network. The advantage of this topology is that it is relatively easy to install. The primary disadvantage is the dependence of the network on the central node. If it fails, the network is rendered inoperable. Depending on its capacity and the volume of traffic on the network, the central node also can become a bottleneck and degrade network performance.

### The Advantages of LANs

Local area networks are popular for a number of reasons, including:

- *Reliability.* Devices can be attached to the LAN to provide redundancy and backup.

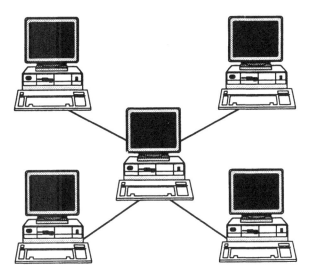

**Exhibit IV-1-5. A LAN Star Topology**

---

- *Ease of modification.* LANs consist primarily of cable, so devices can be easily added or deleted from the network by connecting or disconnecting them from the cable.
- *LANs are self-contained.* LANs are controlled by the organization that installs them and there is no dependence on outside carriers.
- *Flexibility.* There are many different ways to design and implement LANs to meet an organization's needs.
- *Cost.* Because nodes can share other devices on the network (e.g., printers and storage devices), costs can be kept to a minimum.
- *Expansibility.* Nodes and other devices can be easily added without major restructuring of the network.
- *Connectivity.* LANs enable nodes to easily communicate with other nodes in the same or another network.
- *Standardization.* By creating LANs, organizations can standardize hardware and software, thereby promoting efficiency and controlling costs.

## CLIENT/SERVER APPLICATIONS DEVELOPMENT

There are three basic approaches to applications development in a client/server environment. First, a migration plan can be developed that moves all or most of the existing applications from the mainframe to the client/server architecture. Although corporate management often favors this approach because of anticipated cost savings, this approach is very difficult to carry out successfully.

Many companies that have attempted this migration have found that the transition costs eliminated any short-term savings. Often, the client/server system does not have enough computing power to support all applications. Many such migration projects have been abandoned before completion.

The second application development approach is to develop all new applications for the client/server architecture while older applications are maintained on the mainframe until they are phased out. Many applications are suited for operation in a client/server environment, but some are not and an IS organization must try to force-fit the application. Again, this approach is often difficult, expensive, and unsuccessful.

The third approach is a hybrid. That is, applications are developed for the environment for which they are best suited—the mainframe, client/server, or both. Many new applications are being developed to be distributed across both the mainframe and the LAN. This third approach can provide the most flexibility; existing systems are maintained on the mainframe and new ones are developed for the environment that is most efficient and cost-effective.

In the next few years, development tools will be significantly improved for developing applications in the client/server environment. Graphical user interfaces (GUIs), object-oriented programming, and query languages are designed to allow greater ease and flexibility in the development of major applications. Query languages, for example, give users greater capabilities to create not only reports but subsystems using data base structures of major applications.

## Data Base Applications

An area of great interest in client/server computing is distributing data bases. Traditionally, a primary function of a mainframe was to process large corporate data bases. The power of the mainframe was needed to access, retrieve, manipulate, and store large amounts of data. The development of the client/server architecture has resulted in the capability not only to distribute processing from the mainframe to the server but to distribute major portions of data bases.

Data base designers can now distribute data bases across multiple platforms (i.e., the mainframe and the file server). Network configurations can be designed that connect dedicated data base file servers to communications and control servers, which are connected to a mainframe. This approach enables a data base to be placed closer to users and distributes administrative computing associated with processing and manipulating data bases. Thus, greater performance can be achieved throughout the network.

A value of the client/server architecture is its transparency to users. Where a data base is located does not matter to users. They simply make appropriate data base requests, which are handled appropriately by a file server, mainframe, or both.

## SUMMARY

Like any new technology, client/server computing has its advantages and disadvantages. Over time, client/server concepts, development methodologies, and technology, as well as hardware and software will be further developed and improved, and eventually become standard. In the meantime, data center managers should be aware of the current capabilities and limitations of client/server computing.

Client/server computing has three primary advantages:

- Costs are reduced because either mainframes are eliminated or new, additional ones are not required.
- Functions, efficiency, and computing speed are increased by distributing information across the client/server system.
- Organizations depend less on proprietary systems provided by traditional hardware vendors.

Client/server computing also has its disadvantages:

- There is a lack of available skilled IS personnel who understand network design, implementation, and management.
- A distributed environment is more difficult to secure and control.
- Current server technology is still somewhat limited, and existing servers often lack the computing power required to drive large networks.
- Existing client/server network, communications, and applications development tools are limited.
- Effectively interconnecting multiplatform environments is difficult.
- The cost of implementing and moving to a client/server environment is often much greater than anticipated.

The greatest weakness in the client/server architecture is probably systems management. During the past 30 years, many sophisticated tools have been developed for managing mainframe systems environments. These tools monitor and tune performance, manage storage, back up and restore operations, and manage networks. In contrast, IS managers often must develop their own tools to move ahead with their client/server projects. This challenge and the difficulties posed by operating across multiple platforms make client/server implementation projects complex and challenging.

There is no question that client/server computing holds great promise for the future. In the meantime, data center managers should learn all they can about this new technology and understand it as thoroughly as possible in order to assist both IS and corporate management in making informed decisions. For example, cost should not be the only factor in moving to client/server computing. By learning more about client/server computing, data center managers increase their value to their organizations as well as add to their skills and experience—both critical factors to career advancement in today's competitive business environment.

# IV-2
# Managing Hardware in a Client/Server Environment

*JOHN P. MURRAY*

M any believe that client/server computing is less expensive than processing data on a mainframe. Client/server computing can ultimately be
less costly, but moving to a client/server environment requires a considerable
up-front investment. Data center managers must analyze this investment to
present senior management with an accurate picture of the expense of moving
to client/server computing. Estimates of implementation costs, lacking an objective analysis of all the issues involved, are almost always lower than actual
costs. Preparing senior management for the true cost of client/server computing makes good business sense.

A key issue in moving to client/server computing for data center managers
is the use of hardware. The important questions concerning the management
of the hardware resources are not only about the client/server environment,
but about the mainframe environment during the transition to client/server
computing. The answers to these questions carry long-term consequences for
the organization.

Data center managers should be aware of the negative consequences of
rushing into client/server computing and bring these risks to the attention of
senior management. The potential to incur excessive project expense is only
one risk. Others include:

- The complete failure of the client/server project.
- Disruption of customer service.
- Selection of the wrong technology, which might necessitate starting the
  project over again.
- Declining morale throughout the organization.

Rather than try to forestall the introduction of client/server technology,
data center managers should present a realistic appraisal of the expense and
risks associated with the move to client/server computing. By rushing into
client/server computing, an organization can increase expense rather than
reduce it. The watchword for moving to client/server computing is planning.
Data center managers must actively participate in planning the move to client/

server computing. This chapter discusses hardware issues that data center managers must consider as part of a well-thought-out plan for moving to client/server computing.

## INITIAL HARDWARE COSTS

Hardware is the largest single expense in the move to client/server computing. This hardware includes:

- File servers.
- Workstations.
- File backup equipment.
- Printers.

A client/server system is often linked to a mainframe, and this connection requires such equipment as bridges, routers, and gateways.

### Mainframe Costs

The expense associated with the current data center mainframe is not the baseline cost for the client/server environment. For example, additional software must be added to the mainframe operating system to handle the transfer of data between the mainframe and the client/server hardware. Additional hardware and software may also be required to accommodate the transfer of mainframe data.

The adequacy of the installed mainframe's processing capacity also must be carefully considered. Because of additional software loaded onto it, the mainframe may not be able to accommodate data transfers to and from the client/server environment, and the mainframe may have to be upgraded. Such an upgrade must be calculated into the cost of the transition.

During the transition and afterward, at least the current mainframe expense will have to be carried as well as the cost of client/server hardware. Therefore, the total hardware-related expense increases rather than decreases. There are many sound business reasons for moving to a client/server environment, but an immediate savings in data center hardware costs is not one of them.

### Client/Server Costs

Although the cost of client/server hardware is less than the price of a mainframe with comparable processing power, the total cost of a transition to client/server processing is still substantial. The total expense may shock senior managers who are responsible for approving expenditures. Data center managers are responsible for providing senior management with accurate information about the cost of moving to client/server computing. Identifying these expenses requires hard work and careful investigation.

## ANTICIPATING GROWTH

Data center managers should ensure that the proposed hardware can handle rapid growth. Excess capacity does not have to be installed at the outset of a project, but provisions for future growth must be made. The budget for a client/server project must include funds for the purchase of increased processing capacity when required. An effective approach involves incremental increases in processing capacity.

There are several reasons for taking this phased approach. One is avoiding additional expense. Another is a lack of experience in determining the level of processing capacity required of a client/server system.

### Estimating Future Client/Server Needs

There are various methods for estimating requirements, but many of these methods produce nothing more than educated guesses. Because client/server technology is still new, many of the tools and methods used for client/server capacity planning and response time are still immature, though vendors are constantly improving methods for forecasting client/server capacity loading. Data center managers should include growth figures in any client/server capacity planning model. The most effective approach is to double or triple the original estimate. Data center managers should not bet their careers on currently available client/server capacity forecasting tools.

Because of rapid changes in PC technology, work load processing capacities should not be underestimated. New PC software often requires more processing power than previous versions. Although the additional expense of a new or advanced version of a software product must be considered, the decision to acquire the new software may not rest with the data center manager. However, data center managers should anticipate the growth of the client/server system. If department managers cannot purchase more powerful software because the cost of the additional hardware required to run that software was not adequately anticipated, data center managers will find themselves open to criticism. Also, if additional processing capacity has not been adequately anticipated, data center service levels will be lowered or senior management will have to be asked for additional money. Neither situation bodes well for any data center manager.

Data center managers also must understand different client/server configurations. Costs differ if a mainframe does the majority of processing (i.e., a host-based system) or if most of the processing is done by the workstation or server (i.e., a two- or three-tiered system).

Data center managers have been able to successfully forecast mainframe work load capacities. The combined use of forecasting tools, experience, and intuition has enabled organizations to address mainframe work load growth. However, it has taken some data center managers a long time to learn how to avoid running out of processing power and presenting senior management with unplanned demands for more funds. Because of rapid growth of processing demands in many client/server environments, the topic of adequate hardware expense forecasting and control is often a highly charged, emotional issue. Data center managers must explore the use of techniques for forecasting hardware capacity requirements in client/server environments.

## DEVELOPING STANDARDS FOR MANAGING CLIENT/SERVER HARDWARE

Data center managers must establish a set of hardware standards to be used in forming decisions about hardware purchases and use. These standards should be based on the criteria examined in the following sections.

### State of Technology

Moving to and maintaining a state-of-the-art environment is a practical business decision for those companies that want to use client/server computing. To develop that type of environment, state-of-the-art microcomputer hardware and software must be made available within the organization.

### Redundancy

Redundancy can affect expense, data center service levels, and customer service because redundancy involves systems availability and network response time. Because client/server hardware costs less than traditional mainframe hardware, data center managers should push for hardware redundancy.

Redundancy can be provided at the server level by duplicating the number of servers and disk mirroring, which double the cost of the server hardware. However, that cost must be weighed against the value of the organization's ability to continue computing in the case of a server failure. Another way to provide redundancy is to purchase spare servers and extra disk capacity. One or more extra servers that meet the data center's standards are purchased and stored for future use. If a server fails, the data center staff can quickly install a spare server to bring the LAN back online as quickly as possible. This process is not as effective as the use of fully redundant servers, and it causes a higher level of disruption. However, if expense is a constraint to full redundancy, a spare server is a reasonable alternative.

### Expense

Although it is important to control data center costs, purchasing hardware that is less than state of the art is not cost effective. For example, assume that an organization purchased 386-based microcomputers at a time when 486-based models were becoming more popular and the price of 386 hardware was declining. Within a few months, new versions of applications software were released offering increased productivity and effectiveness. Although the managers in several departments of the organization want to use these new releases, the newly acquired 386 microcomputers cannot accommodate the new software.

In such a situation, a data center manager has three options, none of which is attractive. First, it may be possible to upgrade the 386 units, but the net cost of the upgrade may be greater than the purchase price of the 486 units. The second option is to find a use for the 386 machines in other departments and to purchase some new 486 units. The third option is for the data center manager to admit that because the wrong units were purchased, it is not possible to accommodate the new applications software.

## Inventory Control

In many client/server sites, no staff member has more than a vague notion about the number and types of PCs installed. Although some information about an organization's microcomputers can be obtained by consulting the fixed asset records in its accounting department, a data center manager should develop and maintain sound microcomputers inventory records. At a minimum, a microcomputer inventory record should contain the following information:

- Make, model, and size of each microprocessor.
- Date of purchase.
- Cost of purchase and depreciation schedule.
- The location of the unit.
- The department and the name of the person who uses the PC.
- Serial number.

Inventory records need to be developed and accurately maintained in the data center for two reasons. First, microcomputers can easily be moved or stolen, and inventory records can ensure that all microcomputers can be accounted for and have a better chance of recovery if stolen. Second, microcomputer inventory records enable the data center to place in other departments microcomputers that one department has replaced. This reuse of microcomputer hardware is not only a sound business practice but can improve the reputation of the data center.

## Controlling Microcomputer Purchases

A data center manager should identify no more than two microcomputer hardware vendors with which the organization will do business. The simple issue of compatibility can become complex if an organization mixes microcomputer vendors. Also, a data center manager should select vendors that have a good chance of remaining in business. To control the microcomputer hardware selection process, senior management must agree that all microcomputer hardware purchases must be approved by the data center manager.

## Hardware Portability and Scalability

The ability to shift various pieces of processing hardware (e.g., workstations and servers) from one location to another provides great flexibility in having processing power wherever it may be needed. The ability to scale up hardware incrementally as more server processing power is needed provides increased flexibility and controls expense. Also, because of rapid advances in processing power, usually at less overall cost, moving the existing server to some other location in the company and replacing it with a larger unit can prove to be a sound business decision.

The development and implementation of data center microcomputer standards mark the start of controlling microcomputer hardware. In anticipation of resistance to the enforcement of the standards, data center managers should gain the support of senior managers before the standards are published. Senior management's authority is needed to overcome any such resistance. Some organizations are currently attempting to deal with the failure in enforcing data center microcomputer standards and have realized the value of such standards.

## CLIENT/SERVER INFRASTRUCTURE EXPENSES

Another aspect of client/server hardware costs are infrastructure expenses involved in moving to client/server processing. These expenses are tied to physically preparing a facility where the hardware will be located. Infrastructure issues to be considered include:

- Is the area appropriately wired to accommodate the placement of additional workstations and servers? If not, what actions must be taken to prepare for the client/server hardware?
- What standards should be set for the wiring of the location? The wiring that is installed should meet the anticipated growth of user demands as well as accommodate the demands of new technology. Because the largest expense in wiring is not the cost of the wire but the labor associated with its installation, an organization should prepare for this expense. Also, some network response and reliability issues concern wiring. For example, higher capacity wiring improves the likelihood of acceptable performance.
- Can the installed telephone switch handle both current and probable future demands for increased communications capability? Part of the planning process for the client/server environment should be to carry out telephone traffic studies. On the basis of those studies, increases in traffic demand during the next several years should be predicted.
- Although server hardware usually does not require a great deal of space, the hardware should be located in a secure area where access can be restricted. Also, there must be a provision for adequate wiring closet space for each LAN installed. These closets, which may occupy the same area as the server hardware, must be designed to limit access.

## ACTION PLAN

Although experienced data center managers readily understand the hardware issues involved in the management of a mainframe environment, moving to a client/server system presents new challenges and opportunities. Much knowledge about appropriately managing client/server systems will be gained through trial and error. Necessary management tools will become available over time, just as they have for mainframes. In the meantime, data center managers are advised to take a cautious approach in the development of a client/server environment.

Controlling client/server hardware expense, and developing, implementing, and enforcing appropriate hardware standards are mandatory. Some of the same battles that were fought in building strong mainframe data center functions will be fought again. Establishing an effective client/server environment is not easy, data center managers who do the job right will find it worth the effort.

# IV-3
# Preparing to Implement Client/Server Solutions

*HUGH W. RYAN*

D uring the past 25 years, no computing technology has emerged as quickly and grown to such a dominant position in providing business solutions as client/server computing. This is evident in the emergence of the new leading vendors in the computing field and in the decline in the influence of older vendors. Systems integrators and consultants are in the first wave of new client/server applications; many report that a growing percentage of their work involves client/server solutions. For example, in 1993, 40% of the work of Andersen Consulting was based on client/server computing. Client/server technology is a development that IS professionals must follow, understand, and develop skills in. This chapter discusses the structure for client/server computing and presents steps for implementing client/server business solutions.

## STRUCTURE FOR CLIENT/SERVER COMPUTING

Client/server computing is a style of computing that involves multiple processors—one of which is usually a workstation—over which complete business transactions are processed. The typical structure for client/server computing is discussed from three perspectives:

- System software, hardware, and network.
- Data.
- Processing.

### System Software, Hardware, and Network—Evolving Client/Server Environments

Exhibit IV-3-1 shows the typical hardware and network configuration in a client/server solution. According to the definition, workstations provide the business user with other workstations on a local area network (LAN). The workstation is also usually connected on the LAN to a work group server that provides data base server capabilities to the workstations. This work group server or another server provides support in communicating to other work groups and to the enterprise machine.

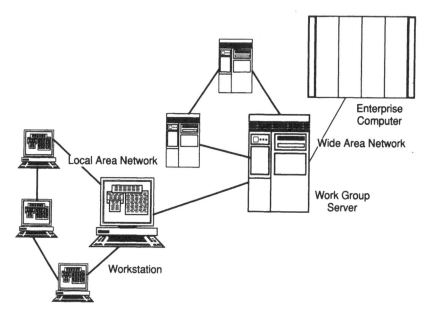

**Exhibit IV-3-1. Typical System Software, Hardware, and Network Configuration in a Client/Server Environment**

An intrinsic part of the client/server solution is the enterprise computer, which is usually the mainframe or a minicomputer. Typically the connection to the enterprise machine occurs through the use of a wide area network (WAN).

There are, of course, many variations on this theme. One is that the workstation will change in form during the next few years. For example, personal digital assistants, such as Apple's Newton, may be used as mobile workstations in the future. Another variable is the intermediate work group server, which is often a widely debated element in client/server computing. (The next sections on data and processing allocation explain the need for an intermediate work group server in client/server business solutions.) The form of the enterprise computer is also likely to change as traditional mainframe computing technology is replaced by more powerful but much less expensive processors that use reduced instruction set computing (RISC). The network may change as well, with client/server being a driving force for mobile computing. Many of the traditional wiring approaches for networks could be replaced by wireless technology, for both local and wide area networks.

Client/server hardware and network computing technology will change in form and behavior as solutions become more pervasive. However, the roles of these processors and networks will remain stable.

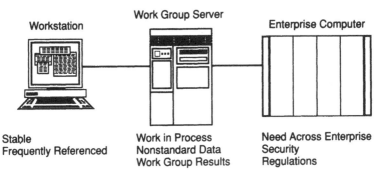

Exhibit IV-3-2. Typical Data Allocation in a Client/Server Environment

## Data Perspective

Exhibit IV-3-2 shows a typical data allocation in a client/server business solution. If the workstation has a disk, the application usually involves stable, frequently referenced information. For example, in an auto insurance underwriting application, there are rating tables and a list of the automobile types that are covered. Both represent data that would be frequently referenced in the process of underwriting an insurance application. Placing the data on the workstation contributes to the overall processing speed by allowing fast access to the data. It may also contribute to the stability of the application by not requiring access of the data over one or more networks that may be subject to variable and unpredictable loads.

On the intermediate processor, multiple types of data reside. This includes what might be termed work-in-process data, or data that is built up in the process of doing a business transaction until the transaction is complete. Nontraditional data, such as image and voice, is also included.

Finally, the enterprise machine contains the data that must be shared across the enterprise. The auto insurance policy is an example of such data. The claim is made at some site other than that at which the policy was written. If the insurance policy resides on the enterprise machine, whoever in the enterprise needs the information has access to it.

## Processing Perspective

Exhibit IV-3-3 portrays a typical processing allocation in a client/server environment. On the workstation is the processing that controls the flow of the application. To use the insurance example again, if the agent decides to move from descriptions of autos to be covered to specific types of coverage by automobile, the processing logic to do this would reside on the workstation.

The intermediate processor does the processing that directs the flow of work through the office. Thus, if a receptionist in the insurance office takes

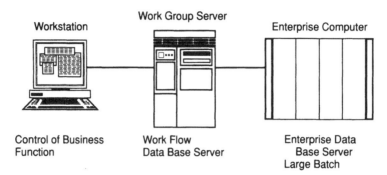

**Exhibit IV-3-3. Processing Allocation in a Client/Server Environment**

initial information on customers and determines that they are interested in buying life insurance, the logic to move this data to the appropriate underwriter would reside on the local office server.

The enterprise processor in this description serves as a data base server to the enterprise, supplying data where and when it is needed across the enterprise. In addition, the processing of large batch applications such as cycle billing seem to fit best on this processor.

## ISSUES IN IMPLEMENTING CLIENT/SERVER COMPUTING

It is probably safe to say that in the move to client/server computing, the issues associated with successful implementation are not always thought through carefully. Client/server computing involves distributed data and processing; therefore, client/server applications represent a more difficult problem to implement than traditional computing.

There are six key areas of concern for organizations that are implementing client/server applications, and each covers a broad set of issues. The key areas are:

- Change management.
- Technology architecture decisions.
- Delivery of infrastructure.
- Systems management.
- Network delivery.
- Site implementation.

### Change Management

The cost and difficulty of client/server computing can be justified only if the organization is, in some fundamental way, changing the business process. Business process reinvention (also known as business process reengineering) reflects changes in roles, responsibilities, and rules. For any organization attempting the implementation of client/server computing, it is an essential consideration.

To define the reinvented business process, the first thing needed is an understanding of the business, the information technology, and what the technology can do for the business. The organization must analyze the business process and each of its steps, asking why and how the steps and the overall process contribute to the business, before a reinvented process emerges.

The most difficult part of reinventing business process is getting the user to accept the reinvented business process. Inherent in business process redesign is that the business users must change their behavior to work with the reinvented system. Therefore, an extensive change management effort must be undertaken.

There are various life cycles for implementing a change management effort. Exhibit IV-3-4 gives a conceptual overview of such an effort. The business user moves through several stages over time to acceptance of the reinvented business process. Change management begins well in advance of user training.

**User Awareness.** The first stage is to build awareness of the reinvented business process. This means helping the business user understand what the system is about, why it must be changed, and at a superficial level, how the reinvented business process will work. This stage is often accomplished by

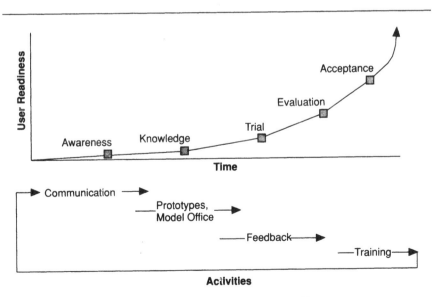

**Exhibit IV-3-4. The Change Management Curve**

communication through a series of presentations on the process, demonstrations of prototypes, and extensive written and verbal communication on the new business process. These early communication efforts must be led by a business user who has the respect of the business organization. Without this, the typical IS person has a credibility problem in advising business users on the need to do things differently.

**User Knowledge.** Awareness building is followed by an effort to build knowledge of the proposed reinvented business process. This process is a more intensive effort to ensure that the user understands how the system behaves and how the user will behave with it. A model office is useful at this stage. A model office includes a complete simulation of the proposed work environment. The business user can go through significant parts of the workday and deal with specific parts of the new business process.

**Trial and Evaluation.** Business users need to test the reinvented business process against their knowledge of the business and what the business needs to be effective. It is imperative that the change management and systems-building teams listen to the business users' concerns about the reinvented business process and understand the problems. The teams must think carefully about whether the issues that users raise are a reflection of the current view of how work is done or are in fact a real shortfall of the reinvented process.

If the problem relates to users' reluctance to change, there must be more effort to explain why the new way is the answer for the future. However, if the systems builders determine that there is a need to change the planned reinvented process, changes must be undertaken. The business users who wanted the change must review and evaluate it to ensure that it addresses their concerns. This is a way for users to see that they are a part of the systems-building process and can have an impact when they have real concerns. This perspective may be invaluable in enhancing the credibility of the systems-building team.

Although strategies vary depending on the size of the user population, the change management effort should attempt to move as many business users as possible through this process. The business users should have credibility as businesspeople and they must be asked to communicate their experiences and their perspectives of the system to the rest of the business community.

**User Training.** As this testing and revision process begins to stabilize, in terms of additional changes, the training effort can be built. However, training should not be started too early, because if done before the user has built a knowledge and understanding of the system, it can give users the impression that their input will not be used.

## Change Management and Training for IS

A change management process for the IS person is as valid as a concern as for the business user. The objective of the change management effort in the case of the IS staff member is to complete the learning curve in the application of client/server computing. This effort tends to be overlooked or treated in an ad hoc fashion. This is unfortunate because client/server technology can succeed only if systems personnel are well informed.

One approach to developing training for IS personnel is dubbed the "rules, schools, and tools" method. The first step to building new skills for IS personnel is to define the overall methodology used for development. This methodology defines how systems are to be developed in a client/server environment to the point of tasks, steps, and deliverables. It defines the roles of designer, programmer, architect, and project manager.

With the rules in place, it is possible to define the training required by role and then go through a process of selection, purchase, or building of required training to execution of the actual training. In addition, as the rules are established, it becomes more logical to define criteria for selection and opportunities for building the tools to be used as part of the systems-building effort for future client/server environments. If the rules are not well defined, the selection process can lead to a set of discrete tools that are difficult to integrate and share across the entire development process.

The amount of training depends on the individual's background and the rules selected. It is reasonable to expect programmers to need two to four weeks of training, designers one to three weeks, and architects one to four weeks. Project managers may need one to two weeks of training. Training can run from $1,000 to $4,000 per person. IS management should plan on one to two weeks of skills upgrading when going forward with this technology.

**Training Costs.** Another issue is how to account for training costs. Companies use several strategies. One is to ignore the costs and hope in some way they go unnoticed. Although this seems unwise, many sites try to do just that. Inevitably, what happens is that training is not done or is done inadequately, with subsequent loss of effectiveness of the personnel.

A second approach is to have a formal training budget that treats skill upgrades as part of doing business in a technology area. The advantage to this method is that it allows IS to focus on and control the cost of skill upgrades. It allows the organization to implement a program for the IS department, which can ensure a consistent and high-quality training program. Such an effort also creates a sense of the IS department working as a team to meet the shift to a new technology. The problem with this approach is that when a large technology shift such as that to client/server is undertaken, the costs to build skills in the IS department can be so high that they may be questioned and perhaps denied.

A third strategy is to make the cost of learning a part of the business case for the application that is prompting the move to client/server. Because these costs are typically only for the team members committed to the project, they are often smaller and more acceptable as an overall amount. In addition, the costs can be made a part of the business case for the application and thus can have a direct payback. The issues associated with such an approach are that it may not be fair to ask one project to absorb all of the costs associated with training people when that knowledge can be used across subsequent projects, or the training received may be project-specific and may not address the full range of training required for client/server competence. The fact that only team members are trained can also create an "us versus them" situation in which some people seem favored and others do not.

Decisions on how to pay for training depend on site specifics. The key point is that significant training is required for the move to client/server technology. The enterprise committing to this technology must plan on the investment in developing personnel if it is to succeed at the effort.

## Technology Architecture Decisions

One of the most common questions companies have when moving to client/server computing centers on what technology to select, and it is also one of the most difficult issues to resolve. Exhibit IV-3-5 provides a framework in which to evaluate the technology decisions. This exhibit portrays, at a high level, the concept of a layered technical architecture. Fundamental technology decisions are needed to define a technology architecture and to address the following:

- Platform and networking.
- Operating systems software.
- Networking software.
- Data base management systems.
- Graphical user interface.

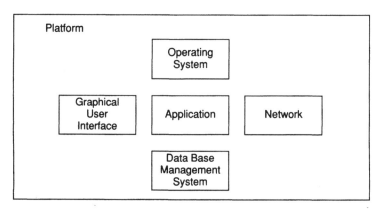

**Exhibit IV-3-5. The Technology Architecture Framework**

After these decisions have been made, the next step is a set of decisions on development tools and systems management approaches. These decisions in turn lead to a development architecture and a systems management architecture.

These decisions are difficult to make because in an open systems environment, there are four to five hardware vendors, an equal number of networking vendors, two to three operating system strategies, four to five data base management system (DBMS) vendors, and two to three graphical user interface (GUI) vendors from which to choose. The number of possible combinations of solutions in this case could exceed 1,000. At a minimum, IS should focus on those components that affect the enterprise's ability to interoperate, or share data across departments. If possible, IS should define, at the enterprise level, those components that allow departments to share information.

For example, mixed hardware such as RISC processors and CISC processors can present ongoing problems in sharing data because of basic dissimilarities in bit patterns. Different networks in different departments present ongoing problems when those departments want to share data. Different data base management systems present basic problems when there is a desire to access one department's information from another department. In each case, a means can be found to circumvent these problems, and systems integrators are widely involved in solving them. However, if IS sets basic guidelines on what constitutes a consistent technical architecture, it does not need to find workarounds.

Most enterprises end up with incompatible technical architectures. Many factors contribute to this situation, including legacy decisions. IS personnel contribute to the problem when they take too long to come to a decision on technical architecture and, as a result, the end-user community goes ahead without IS involvement. Therefore, the major reason to focus on interoperability as a criterion for technology decisions is to define a minimal subset of all the decisions so that they can be made more quickly.

## Delivery of Infrastructure

When making decisions on the technical architecture, IS must begin thinking in terms of what reusable components the enterprise must build to make the technical architecture usable by developers and business users. These enterprise-built reusable components are what is meant by infrastructure.

In a traditional IS shop, guidelines for designers and programmers are often referred to as the programming standards. An equivalent is needed for client/server computing. Indeed, the equivalent may be even more critical because often the designers and programmers do not have the client/server experience to fill in the gaps.

Some of these standards are addressed by the methodology decision, but many are not. For example, standards for the input/output design of applications using GUI may be needed. Programming and design standards for workstation environments may be required. Time and effort can be saved if a consistent layered architecture, such as shown in Exhibit IV-3-6, is used. Such an architecture must be established, defined, and explained to developers as a consistent framework for all developers to use. As this infrastructure is defined, there follows a need to select or build tools to provide the components and to develop designer and programmer guidelines and training in how to use the infrastructure.

## Systems Management

Systems management addresses the ongoing operation of the client/server application when in production. Systems management should start with and be driven by the definition of service level agreements. These agreements are, effectively, commitments to meet certain levels of overall system performance, reliability, and recovery from problems. The starting point is framing these service-level agreements. With the agreements defined, those parts of the systems management environment that specifically contribute to meeting and confirming conformance to service-level agreements receive the first attention in delivering systems management.

The typical activities that are associated with systems management in a client/server environment include, but are not limited to, the following:

- Configuration management, which involves managing components found in the application and the status and version of these components.
- Activation and execution of components of the client/server application. This activity can include bringing up online and batch components and the activation and execution of service components such as the data base management system.
- Determination of fault status, assessment of reasons for failure, and the initiation of recovery from failure.
- Help desk facilities to answer inquiries from the user and system communities on problems, questions, and steps to recover from problems.

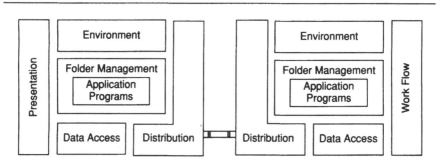

**Exhibit IV-3-6. Infrastructure Architecture for Client/Server Environment**

- Determination of performance reliability and, potentially, assessment relative to service management contracts.
- Vendor contract management and associated contacts and payments.

Although this list is not complete, it is representative of the range of issues to be addressed when starting with a service-level orientation. Among client/server solutions, there are currently few, and mostly limited, prepackaged software solutions available to the systems builder. In comparison, traditional computing offers rather extensive solutions often as a part of the system software.

The cost of preparing solutions for systems management in a client/server environment is high. Experience suggests that 10% to 40% of the development budget for initial client/server solutions should be devoted to the delivery of the system management facilities.

**Help Desks.** On the low end of this range, a strong help desk facility can be built. In traditional environments, the help desk is used to collect and route problems with some sort of minimal problem analysis/resolution role. In a client/server environment, a relatively complete analysis of the problem may be required as the problem occurs. Immediate analysis is needed for at least three reasons. First, the problem is frequently due to events on the client computer. There are few if any tools to capture status and playback of events on this machine. Once the client has rebooted, all traces of actions and events are often lost. Thus, the detailed analysis must be done while the situation exists.

Second, client/server applications have a rich set of interactions and it may be essential to find out at the time the problem occurs what steps the business user went through while they are fresh in the user's mind. Finally, a client/server application is probably deeply embedded in the business flow; to get the user working again, it may be essential that the help desk go through a complete assessment and recovery while the user is on the phone seeking assistance. The help desk staff should be required to have a thorough understanding of the application and how it is applied in the business process.

In this proactive role, the help desk should be viewed as a problem manager having the authority to contact IS and operations personnel and the ability to direct their work to correcting the problem. This approach raises many questions about who has authority for the direction of personnel. The issues must be resolved in favor of what best supports the business user in need of assistance.

High-end solutions include sophisticated software for the detection and isolation of problems. Although only limited software solutions are available at this time, there is reason to believe that much more complete solutions will become available from vendors during the next few years. Thus, to avoid investing in systems software solutions that are overtaken by vendor products, IS should focus on the lower end of the scale and, specifically, the delivery of a highly effective help desk facility and tools to upgrade the applications and overall configuration.

## Network Delivery

In the client/server architecture in Exhibit IV-3-1, the question is: Where is the computer in this architecture? The answer is that it is all the computers. The network is the platform. Client/server computing is as much a communications solution as it is a computing solution, so there must be as much focus on the network side as on the computing solution.

The difficulty is twofold. First, the typical information processing person is not strong in networking knowledge and design. For many years, the proprietary networks associated with traditional technology were largely the domain of the network specialist; the IS person simply provided the network specialist with requirements while the specialist did what was required to meet the needs.

At the same time, the network specialist is confronted with a new set of terms and concepts for modern networking technology. In addition, the network has such a profound impact on the capabilities of the client/server solution that network specialists must be brought into the design process much earlier. Often they are the ones to say yes or no to a functional requirement on the basis of the networking capabilities.

The actual delivery of the network may require greater lead time to assemble and integrate the required components as compared with earlier proprietary solutions, in which the network components usually arrived from the vendor with assurance that the vendor would integrate them after assembly. In a client/server environment, usually components from different vendors are being integrated to support the network and resolution of problems falls to the integrator. There may also be a need to upgrade the overall network, which can greatly lengthen delivery time frames. Even as the components are assembled and tested, it is common to encounter transient problems that take extended time to resolve. When the network goes into production, there still may be a need for ongoing network problem solving to make the network stable.

## Site Preparation and Installation

Site-related work refers to:

- The process of reviewing sites, assessing what is required to prepare them for installation of the client/server solution.
- The process of readying and installing the sites.
- The process of testing an installed site to ensure that it works as expected.
- Ongoing maintenance of an inventory of the site and its status for running the application.

These efforts may not be directly related to client/server computing, yet most sites involved in the first-time application of client/server technology to business problems encounter significant and difficult problems in this stage. If hundreds of sites require significant upgrades, site installation and upgrade may be the single largest line item in the development budget and may require the longest lead time.

If the enterprise has already installed client/server applications, site-related work may be less of an issue. But for first-time applications, it is necessary to assess the site's suitability to run a client/server application. This assessment should address all aspects of site preparedness, including power, air conditioning, and possibly the installation of physical wiring. Some potential problems may seem obscure. For example, at one manufacturing site, a stamping process created a heavy vibration that required additional protection for disk drives. Another site was next to a radio station that posed a problem with electromagnetic fields.

These problems must be recognized and resolved before the purchase and installation of hardware and software. In addition, sites should be tracked because in the process of building the system, the initial survey/assessment may become outdated.

Arrangements must be made to have carpenters, electricians, and air conditioning specialists come to each site to make any necessary changes. Often, complex negotiations and ongoing contract management are needed to find parties qualified to do this work. A building contractor may be retained to see the work that is to be done. When many sites are involved, a management challenge arises for which the organization might have little competence. It is worthwhile to consider outsourcing the site upgrades to companies that specialize in this effort.

## ORGANIZING FOR SUCCESSFUL CLIENT/SERVER ENGAGEMENTS

Exhibit IV-3-7 is a planning chart in which each box suggests a work segment to be done to address the previously discussed issues in implementing a client/server solution. The arrows and lines suggest a relative sequence and interdependency of the efforts. The completion of a segment usually means that a major work deliverable has been completed.

The diagram is complex because there are a complex set of interrelated problems that must be dealt with as a whole. At the same time, the exhibit is still at a conceptual level, because it does not show all the interrelationships or the actual work tasks to be done.

To provide a frame of reference, the work segments labeled Design Applications and Implement Applications represent the basic process of designing and building the application systems. Full life cycle methodologies for this effort in a traditional environment may span 700 to 1,000 pages—and that is just one component of the total systems effort.

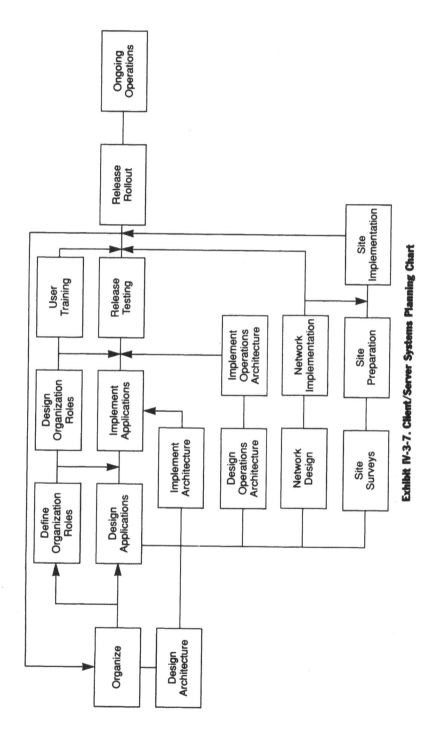

Exhibit IV-3-7. Client/Server Systems Planning Chart

## Making Change Happen When It Is Needed

The boxes across the top of Exhibit IV-3-7 pertain to organization roles and user training; these work segments address the change management issues of getting the business user to work with the new client/server system. The first major segment of work is to define the new business organization. The next work segment is to design the specific work roles in terms of daily tasks and deliverables. Finally, training is defined that ensures that the business user can take on and fulfill the new roles.

Change management includes ensuring user awareness, knowledge, and trials and evaluation of the reinvented work process, and it is one of the most challenging and creative jobs to be found in the process of building systems today. The real difficulty is defining where the responsibilities for change management end and where the role of the systems designers begins. There can be an overlap between what the change management personnel and the systems-building personnel define. In essence, both groups are making commitments on what the system will do. It is important that these work efforts be coordinated. The key to avoiding the potential overlap is to have the change management and systems people sit down and resolve what each group will deliver.

## Technical Architecture Design

The Design Architecture work segment refers to the many decisions on hardware, systems software, and networking. The decisions made in the work segment Implement Architecture form the basis for building the infrastructure of tools, standards, and methodology that the systems builders need.

Included in the technical architecture decisions are:

- Going-in positions on hardware platforms to be allocated by site.
- Associated decisions of operating systems, GUIs, and network strategy.
- Decisions related to the DBMS and development tools and languages.
- Positions on the intent to provide support for the developer and user. For example, will the design environment be highly integrated with the implementation environment? Will a repository strategy be used? What facilities and capabilities are to be provided with regard to testing? What capabilities are to be provided with regard to training and help facilities?

Without these initial decisions, progress on all other application and business issues is difficult. At the same time, once these decisions have been made, they must be reevaluated as experience and time passes.

## Getting the Systems Management In Place

The Design Operations Architecture and Implement Operations Architecture work segments (see Exhibit IV-3-7) address the steps needed to get the systems management approach in place.

Design Operations Architecture should begin after the technical architecture decisions have been made and as the functional capabilities and requirements of the application are beginning to be defined. Information on functional capabilities is needed to help determine service-level agreements. The service-level agreement is key to defining the overall systems management architecture.

When the decisions on the overall systems management architecture have been made, implementation work begins. This is often a matter of purchasing individual tools and integrating them. Included in this effort is the definition of help desk features and the beginning of training and actual implementation of the help desk.

### Client/Server Is Communications

The tasks of network design and implementation also must be performed in order to deliver a client/server business solution. The Network Design and Network Implementation work segments should begin once the functional capabilities of the application are known.

Client/server computing demands a much tighter integration of network and systems design and building compared with traditional development. Careful attention should be paid to the evolving network design and how extensive an upgrade is needed from current capabilities.

### Having Someplace to Put the Client/Server Application

The tasks at the bottom of Exhibit IV-3-7—site surveys, preparation, and implementation—include steps for preparing the physical premises for a review of the client/server application. Specifics vary, but plans should be made to survey every site to assess its suitability to run a client/server application. Change management efforts and the site upgrade work must also be coordinated.

### Make Sure It Works

A final work segment worth noting is Release Testing. This work is needed in client/server environments to ensure that all the components previously described come together as a system and work. By definition, client/server systems run in the business environment, perhaps thousands of miles away from the systems developers. Furthermore, if an organization bases a new business process on the system, the business could then become critically dependent on the system. Releasing a less than completely tested system would be damaging.

Tests are needed to ensure that the application works as a whole, that the infrastructure and technical architecture to be released is the one that applications have been running on, and that the installation procedures are usable by someone at the local site. Any emergency procedures or error recovery procedures should be tested to determine whether they are understandable and workable by people at the local site. End-to-end performance must be addressed at this time to ensure that the service-level agreements can be met. In addition, operations and help desk procedures should be tested to ensure that they do what is expected. Release testing can make a significant contribution to the ongoing reliability and usability of the system; at the same time, it is not a trivial effort. IS can expect to plan a two to-three-month test cycle in release testing.

## Just In Time Adds Tension

A key concept in the framework is the just-in-time delivery of components of the parallel work segments. Ideally, people like to do work in a sequential fashion; in today's business environment this is not practical. Furthermore, it is more efficient to have results shared between the work segments as the work proceeds. As a result, all the work segments shown in Exhibit IV-3-7 should be performed in parallel.

This just-in-time approach, in which several teams must be kept tied together and working as a whole, is a major challenge. To manage the overall effort, a program management strategy must evolve that ensures that individual efforts are proceeding according to an overall plan and that the deliveries from each team meet expectations in terms of quality and timeliness.

## The Value of Moving to the Right Answer

There is a return arrow at the top of Exhibit IV-3-7 that signifies that the adoption of client/server computing requires an iterative approach. It is essential in this environment to get the application delivered to the user. Inherent in adopting a new business process is the unanticipated impact it will have on the business user. Also inherent in the use of client/server computing is the rapid evolution of technology. Iterations provide the opportunity to rethink architectures to determine whether previous decisions and approaches have aged and are no longer valid.

Iterations must be done quickly. According to one view, iterations should be done in six months or less; however, it is difficult to get all of these parallel efforts organized and drawn to a conclusion in six months. A more practical approach is a 12- to 18-month cycle for each iteration, considering the number of parallel work efforts involved.

## ACTION PLAN

For IS, the course of action depends on where the organization is in the application of client/server technology. For the site just beginning the application of client/server technology, the following suggestions are made; IS managers should:

- Choose applications that would benefit from the distinct technology features of client/server computing, such as its ability to put processing where it is needed and the communications capability that is an inherent part of client/server applications. Publicize that the application will be a first delivery of processing capability in a client/server environment. Ensure real and lasting commitment from the business community for the application.
- Build a team with skills in client/server technology. This can be done through the use of training for in-house personnel and by retaining outside expertise. Ensure that users with credibility in the business world are committed to the effort.
- Organize an effort according to the planning chart shown in Exhibit IV-3-7. Time and resources are needed to ensure the following:
  —The change management team defines the reinvented business process and begins the work activities shown in Exhibit IV-3-4.
  —The technical team defines a technical architecture addressing the execution components of Exhibit IV-3-6.
  —The design of the application to support the reinvented business process is begun and coordinated with the change management effort.
  —As business worker requirements for performance and reliability under the reinvented business process begin to appear, a systems management effort should be initiated to build the systems management capability that can determine whether these needs are being met over time.
  —A network design effort is started that brings online the network required to support the effort.
  —As required, the site evaluation, installation, and delivery effort should be planned so the sites are ready to run the client/server application as it is implemented.
  —A program management effort can be instituted to ensure that all these strands of work deliver the components needed on a timely basis and at a sufficient level of quality to make for an acceptable application.

Client/server computing appears to provide the next level of technology that organizations need to solve the problems of reinventing business processes. At the same time, it is a more complex and inherently more difficulty technology than traditional computing to successfully implement. It is safe to say that business problems demand that IS address and contain these risks to advance the value of business computing.

# IV-4

# Implementing Business Process Reengineering: A Case Study

*FAY DONOHUE-ROLFE • JEROME KANTER • MARK C. KELLEY*

H ealth care and health care costs have become a national priority. The current economic environment, an aging population, and the advances in extensive and expensive medical treatment are having a revolutionary impact on companies in the health insurance field. There are many more options, choices, and combination packages as well as ever-changing government and state regulations and programs. Like many industries, the health insurance field is going through a volatile deregulation phase.

The 1990 annual report of Massachusetts Blue Cross and Blue Shield set the stage for a business process reengineering effort to create a new company, one that is open to change, able to react quickly and aggressively, able to offer an integrated line of health plans in a coordinated manner, and competitive in both benefit costs and administrative costs. This case study describes how information technology was used in the company's effort to reengineer its organization and, in particular, its approach to marketing. The experience draws lessons for the IS department and its involvement in business process reengineering programs initiated by business management.

## COMPANY BACKGROUND

Massachusetts Blue Cross and Blue Shield is an old-line company in the health care field. It offers health maintenance organzation (HMO) plans, preferred provider organization (PPO) plans, and traditional health plans. Premiums earned in 1990, when the reengineering program began, were in excess of $3 billion. The company employs some 6,000 people.

Starting out in a highly regulated portion of the industry, the company operates in a rapidly changing environment with new competitors, new products and services, and ever-increasing demands from its customers. In addition to such broad-based competitors as Aetna, John Hancock, Prudential, and various HMOs, there are niche players, including organizations that assume benefit management for a company and provide other services. The companies they service expect a reduced rate from their insurers.

Massachusetts Blue Cross was experiencing an eroding market, declining sales, and strained service levels. It had a high cost structure and an organization that reflected a traditional hierarchical business with multiple layers of management. The combination of a heightened competitive structure and reduced sales effectiveness because of an inability to reach new markets was having a marked business impact. The company was losing members within its accounts as well as entire accounts.

## The Marketing Organization

The marketing organization was based on geographical territory within Massachusetts. A salesperson might have 300 accounts ranging from companies having 1 to 4 members, to small businesses with 5 to 24 members, to larger accounts. The salespeople had complete cognizance over their territory, servicing accounts, acquiring new business, and retaining existing business. Customer contract has traditionally been through the salespeople, who make frequent calls and handle all questions and matters of their clients either in person, over the phone, or in writing.

At the start of 1990, there were 140 salespeople and a support staff of more than 300. The marketing organization was organized into seven regional sales offices ranging from 15 to 60 employees, with several levels of management. A sales office handled multibillion-dollar high-technology companies as well as local business that fell into its territory. The seven regional offices were organized strictly by geographic territory. The other groups with direct sales responsibilities were the national accounts sales office, which sold to certain large and designated Massachusetts corporations, and separate offices for two extremely large accounts, General Electric and NYNEX. Four other groups—marketing communications, advertising, sales and service training, and marketing information systems—provided support to the sales offices.

## The IT Support Infrastructure

The technical computer infrastructure that supported the sales offices was a carryforward from the traditional centralized mainframe environment (see Exhibit IV-4-1a). In the case of Massachusetts Blue Cross/Blue Shield (BC/BS), there were two incompatible mainframes and two incompatible minicomputers. One mainframe housed the master data base for companies, institutions, and individual members. This system was used to calculate rates, enroll and bill new and current customers, and process renewals of existing customers. The other mainframe processed claims from groups, individuals, doctors, and hospitals. One of the minicomputers was installed to handle the new HMO and PPO insurance while the other was used for accessing marketing data bases and prospect information (a system known as Marketrieve).

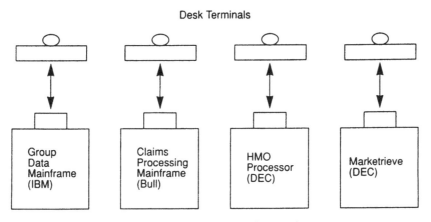

a. Centralized Mainframe Approach

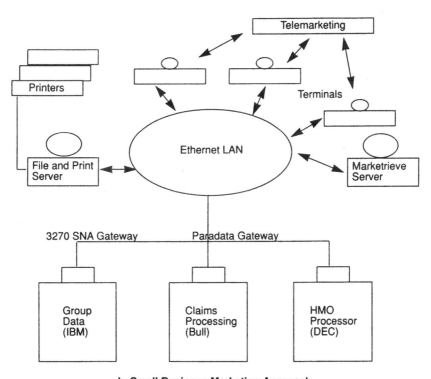

b. Small Business Marketing Approach

**Exhibit IV-4-1. IT Support Infrastructure Before and After Reengineering**

These systems progressed over the years from primarily a batch COBOL orientation to an online mode with terminals (not personal computers) installed in the sales offices. The terminals connected to the claims mainframe were on each desk, but there were only one or two terminals per office connected to the group data mainframe. There were even fewer terminals for the HMO processor. The different security access codes and protocols for the mainframes and minicomputers resulted in a specialization among the office staff.

Questions concerning claims, membership, enrollments, and rates were routed to the sales office handling the account. As might be expected in this technical environment, few if any calls can be answered on the spot if access to one or more mainframes is required. If a particular salesperson or administrator is not available, the call must be returned later. Processing a service call can require multiple hand-offs to different administrators. In essence, although the systems have online terminals, the process is still essentially batch oriented. A major effort has been under way by the central IS department to replace the two mainframes with a single unit that would handle both group data and claims processing, but this has proved difficult and costly to implement.

### The Small Business Marketing Group

An initial study area in the change initiative was the small business market segment, defined as companies with 5 to 24 employees. Small account losses had been averaging 14% a year. Senior management realized that new business practices were a necessity for survival. The need was compelling and changes had to be made quickly, according to the findings of an in-depth consultant study done at the end of the previous year.

### THE DECISION TO REENGINEER

External pressures drove the small business marketing project. First, the consultants had senior management attention. By mid-1990, the marketing vice-president knew that January 1991 would be a high renewal month and crucial period for sales. Presentations of 1990 results were scheduled to be made to senior management and the board of directors at year's end. Marketing wanted a success story to tell by that time. The marketing VP evaluated options and decided to spin off small business accounts to a separate sales force that would use telemarketing techniques.

This change involved breaking several deep-seated corporate tenets. Telemarketing and teleservicing were culturally unacceptable to Massachusetts Blue Cross. The strong assumptions were that health insurance is too complex to sell over the phone and relationship selling is essential. A key ingredient was a sales force dedicated to a specific market segment, breaking down the long-standing geographic territory concept for new business sales. A crucial part of the new strategy was a customer focus; indeed "customer driven" became the battle cry throughout the project.

From the start, the project was business driven. Marketing took the initiative, conducting customer and prospect surveys that showed that a direct sales force was not needed if policy information was available on an accurate and timely basis by telephone. The marketers knew enough about telemarketing to realize it could be the technological enabler; however, the change required a major organizational shift as well as major information technology shift to support the new business concepts.

## REENGINEERING THE ORGANIZATION

The decision to proceed was made by July 1990 and was quickly followed by a $2 million budget (indicating the project had senior-level support). The time frame was seven weeks for the new department to become operational. The marketing director was appointed director for the project. The project director had a solid grasp of the conceptual, strategic, and practical elements of the program and the ability to implement plans. The seven-week time period was a significant constraint in initiating the project.

### The Self-Managed Work Team Model

Exhibit IV-4-2 represents the new sales department organization with the spin off of the small business marketing office. The small business office was originally given responsibility for sales and support to small companies having 5 to 24 people, but this was later expanded to include companies with 1 to 4 people and extended to companies with 25 employees. The remaining accounts were organized into five regional offices; national accounts were combined in a single unit, as were the four support units. Not only were the direct reports to the VP of marketing reduced to four, but the organization levels within the units were reduced and simplified. Five levels of management were truncated into two.

By September, 20 people were hired for the new department. Four team leaders were designated. The project director delegated the recruitment and hiring of the people so that the project director only reviewed finalists after they had been screened. The people were chosen on the basis of their sales abilities (not necessarily insurance) and their experience with telemarketing. The stated objective was to hire and train leaders, not managers, who could facilitate self-managed work teams. The goals were to reengineer people, systems, and attitude: to empower people to act, and to provide the technology base they needed. The 20 people started a six-week training program, focusing on product, process, and the information systems that would play a vital role in the new marketing approach.

Senior management made a substantial investment to accommodate the major cultural change by providing an extensive education program, both up front and continuing. Currently, the department allocates one day a week (after-hours time) for a training session. Team communications and team

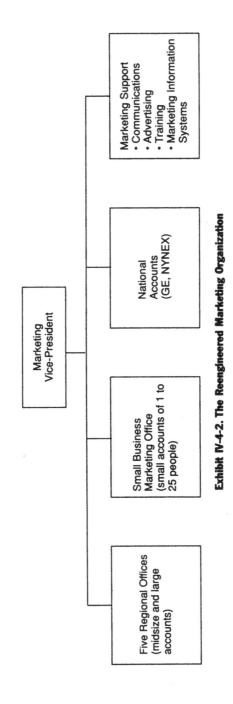

**Exhibit IV-4-2. The Reengineered Marketing Organization**

building, which promotes the individual review of one another's work while suggesting alternate ways of accomplishing work, are important elements of the new organization. Work and results are shared. On the sales floor, for example, graphs of performance versus quota and other key indicators of group performance are displayed. In addition, the first-ever incentive system has been established.

## REENGINEERING THE TECHNOLOGY

In concert with the staff, the project director, who before the program started had never used a personal computer, created the systems requirements. The project director assigned an internal IS specialist who had been a member of an experimental four-person telemarketing unit that was eventually disbanded. However, the IS specialist's experience was limited to spreadsheet and word processing software.

The small business marketing group gave its requirements to several outside vendors who were hands-on implements, rather than to the traditional planners and consultants. The official in-house IS response was to develop an RFP, but this would take too long. The IS department worked with the project director on the evaluation and selection of the vendor; from that point on, it was a team proposition.

### Line Management Leadership

The project director relied on IS because of the complex interconnections that the new system would have with the existing data bases. The real challenge was to have a single IBM-compatible terminal with a Windows interface capable of tapping into the available information from the two disparate mainframes and the two minicomputer systems. In addition, the 20 telemarketers needed to be linked by a local area network (LAN) to share current information on a client/server type architecture. The project direct selected the graphical interface Windows as the common interface (at the consultant's recommendation) rather than opening up the decision on interface selection, because that would potentially jeopardize the deadline. The new system was scheduled to be in operation by the end of October 1990.

The systems designer assigned to assist and provide the central IS resources needed by the small business group expressed concern at the beginning and skepticism that the project could be carried out. At first, the support from the IS group was limited because it already had a sizable work backlog. The central IS group had been working on a multiyear, $50 million project to combine the two mainframe systems onto a single integrated platform, and to completely realign IT to the business. Five years later and many millions of dollars over budget, the project was still far from completion. With this history, it was difficult for the system designer to believe that a project directed by department people with scant computer background and involving several technologies new to the company could meet successful completion within seven weeks.

IS acknowledged, however, the benefits of the system, both from what the application could do from a business standpoint and also from a pure IS cost perspective. Replacing four terminals with one would have a significant impact on hardware and software costs, training, and support. However, numerous problems occurred during the course of the implementation.

## The Reengineered Systems

An Ethernet LAN was installed that allowed direct linkage using Windows 3.0 into both the group data mainframe and claims mainframe (see Exhibit IV-4-1b) and the HMO minicomputer (implemented subsequent to the October 1990 start-up). In addition, the Marketrieve system, which was acquired from a software company, was modified from its previous use and was connected to the LAN. The files are tailored for Massachusetts businesses. All sales representatives use this file and add their notes on individual prospects to afford continuity for themselves and their colleagues as the sales campaign unfolds. These files are accessible by anyone on the LAN and have been instrumental in the highly successful new business sales produced by small business marketing group.

In addition to accessing the two mainframes and the minicomputer, the group has its own server that allows the sharing of five laser printers and other resources, including E-mail, word processing, spreadsheets, and data bases. Because of the instant access from the desk workstation to the various remote data bases and to notes that have been appended to the individual account file from previous calls and contacts, any of the sales and support people can handle an inquiry. If everyone is on the phone at a particular time, the caller has the option of waiting or leaving a voice message.

Exhibit IV-4-1b appears more complex than the original architecture (Exhibit IV-4-1a), but to the user, a transformation has occurred in simplicity and ease of use. The complex interconnectivity is transparent to the user.

## PROJECT OUTCOME: GREATER EFFECTIVENESS AT LOWER COST

The results of the new dedicated telemarketing sales team with rapid access to account information have been impressive. Previously, an inquiry may have gone through six people before a response was made, now one person handles the inquiry and in a far more expeditious manner.

By the end of 1990, according to the annual report, the small business group made almost 13,000 prospect calls. Sales totaled 73 new medical groups and 13 new dental groups, representing a total of 1,001 members. The unit established itself as an important contributor to the company's future success.

Results continue to be impressive, both on the qualitative side and the quantitative side. A year later, in the small business market there was a cost saving of $4.7 million (costs of running the old process less cost of the re-engineered process) or 62%, a sales increase of 24%, a sales-retention increase of 6%, with total additional revenue of $22 million. The group made 86,000 prospect calls in 1991, a figure equal to the previous five years. Quality of service has also improved. Calls are recorded and timed. No caller waits longer than 45 seconds and 90% of the inquiries are resolved in one call of five to eight minutes. Those calls that require correspondence are handled in less than five days.

### Organizational and Operational Results

A walk through the 15th floor of the Massachusetts BC/BS building, where the small business marketing group operates, reveals an open office environ-ment with individual cubicles for managers, team leaders, and customer service representatives. There is little to distinguish who is who, based on office size or location. There are no technicians or IT professionals on site, although the LAN network is quite complex. One of the team leaders acts as the IT liaison and local network manager. All network or technical questions go to this individual, who now handles about 80% of the problems. Other problems are routed to another IT liaison in the personal computer applications area, situated on another floor.

The horizon of the small business marketing group keeps expanding and the entrepreneurial spirit has become more pervasive. The group continually searches for opportunities to improve its existing business and for new areas to apply telemarketing/teleservicing skills. It is a classic case of what can happen when the individual is empowered.

Technically, the group is in the process of installing fax capability at the workstation to reduce the time away from the phone. Another development is to enhance the client-server to have more of the customer data available locally instead of having to access the mainframe. However, the accomplish-ments made in such a short period are a strong motivator to the small business marketing group that these extensions will materialize.

## LESSONS LEARNED FOR THE INFORMATION SYSTEMS ORGANIZATION

It is interesting to review the role of IS (or its lack of a role) in this example of business process reengineering. Although there is a large central IS organization at Massachusetts Blue Cross/Blue Shield, there was scant participation by IS professionals in the implementation. The central IS group was preoccupied with a major conversion of its old legacy systems onto a new hardware/software platform. The impetus for reengineering was initiated and led by the functional department, in this case, the small business marketing group.

## Business Goals Drive IS Development

The first lesson learned is that the leadership for reengineering must come from those closest to the business process affected. The marketing group dealt directly with outside consultants and software developers; there was only one central IS participant in the project. In retrospect, greater IS involvement would have alleviated problems that later arose in connecting to the central system. In this case, IS missed the opportunity to recognize the scope and importance of the new approach and to become more actively involved.

The driving force in this example, as it is in most cases, is the need to become business competitive. Information technology is the enabler not the driver. The technology used need not be the most advanced technology on the market; many successful users of IT apply common technology uncommonly well. This is not a case study about technology; it is about business change in the way a company markets its product. Information technology has enabled the company to tap into systems that were 20 years old and to use telemarketing, which though common in the overall industry, represented a major cultural business change to Massachusetts Blue Cross.

## Timely Delivery

Another lesson learned is that line departments often set goals that seem impossible to meet, yet somehow the job gets done. Often this means arranging alliances with third parties using rapid application development approaches. Business and competitive pressures require that product cycle times be reduced. If American businesses have learned anything from the Japanese business model and from total quality management (TQM), it is that the design-to-delivery cycle of products must be compressed. This holds for IS products, particularly as information technology becomes more embedded in the business.

## Redefining the IS Role

Though applications can be implemented by line departments quickly and often effectively, there is still a valuable role that IS must play. Rapidly produced programs often lack the industrial-strength qualities needed when the application moves into mainstream operation. Security, backup, documentation to incorporate the inevitable changes that occur, linkage with other systems, and error controls are just a few of these elements. Massachusetts Blue Cross/Blue Shield found that many of these problems did arise and could have been avoided with IS involvement.

Another important lesson is for IS to build an architecture that can respond to changing business needs, exemplified by the small business marketing group. The original system could not incorporate the changes necessitated by the switch to telemarketing. It was built on separate and disparate data bases. A major outside effort was required, and even then the user interface was not a completely smooth or transparent one. A future architecture must have the flexibility to easily adapt to changing business conditions and demands.

The key to success is increasingly built around alliances; alliances with outsourcers, software developers, and consultants outside the company, and alliances with operating departments and business units within the company. IS can no longer be a back-office superstructure.

The small business marketing group typifies business departments that are accomplishing work that sometimes IS claims is impossible. Technologies such as client-servers, graphical user interfaces, and a plethora of improving application software packages have become the enablers. Business managers want to see immediate response to their problems and they seek control of the resources necessary to see it happen. Whereas the central IS group may experience a priority problem, a line department does not.

## SUMMARY

This chapter gives an example of a company taking a high-risk course of action that it thought the business environment and the changing competitive dynamics warranted. The company proceeded to break with tradition and to reengineer the organization and its approach to marketing. One of the most important changes was the fundamental precept of empowering people to act on their own.

Information technology enabled the change. The implementation involved the installation of a department client-server, which together with a department LAN and the use of telemarketing and teleservicing, gave salespeople shared access to relevant and current information about their customers and prospects. Included in the rapid formation of a new department and a new approach to doing business was a time frame and schedule that demanded action and decision. It is a classic example of a line department-led transformation that was supported and enabled by a transformation in the use of technology. This case study illustrates that a solid business/technology partnership can reengineer a company to improve its competitive position.

# IV-5
# An Update On Optical Disk Systems

*GILBERT HELD*

O ptical storage technology, which became commercially available during the late 1980s seems certain to capture a significant share of the computer storage market. This optimistic projection is based on the technology's ability to provide a data storage capacity much greater than conventional magnetic media at a fraction of the cost per stored byte.

The data center manager concerned with evolving technologies should understand optical disk systems and how they can be most effectively used. This article examines the three primary types of optical disk systems and a hybrid system and their current and expected uses. It discusses the primary applications best suited for each type of system and the constraints and limitations of each system type.

## SYSTEM TYPES

Optical disk systems can be divided into three basic categories: read-only, write-once/read-many, and erasable. These systems are similar in that they all contain a laser source, a disk, and a positioning mechanism to move a recording, reading, or read/write head (depending on the system type) to a defined position on the disk.

### Compact Disk Read-Only Memory Systems

The read-only optical disk system was pioneered by Sony Corp. and N.V. Philips. Because of the size of the medium—4.7 inches in diameter—and because prerecorded data on the disk can only be read, this system is best known as compact disk read-only memory (CD-ROM).

The operation of a CD-ROM system is based on the creation of a prerecorded optical disk containing the data to be read by the system. In creating the prerecorded medium, a laser beam is used to burn tiny indentations approximately one micron wide (about 50 times thinner than a human hair) into a plastic coated disk. Binary data represented by 1s and 0s is coded by the presence or absence of a dent on the disk. When the disk is inserted into a

CD-ROM system, a low-power laser detects the presence or absence of the dents by illuminating the disk and detecting the difference in reflection caused by dent and nondent areas.

In 1984, Sony and N.V. Philips announced a CD-ROM data structure that has become a de facto standard for the physical recording of data on a read-only optical disk (see Exhibit IV-5-1). According to the recording format, 270,000 blocks of information are contained on a single side of the disk; the actual user data per block is limited to 2,048 bytes. As a result, the CD-ROM disk's recording capacity is approximately 550M bytes for a 4.7-inch diameter disk. In 1991, a 3.5-inch diameter disk with a data storage capacity of 128M bytes was standardized. This new diskette format was designed primarily for portable applications (e.g., a built-in CD-ROM drive in a laptop or notebook computer or as a standalone portable CD-ROM system that includes a small keyboard and LCD display).

Unlike an audio compact disk, in which a few misplaced 1s and 0s might not be noticed, a single incorrect digit in a data retrieval situation could result in catastrophe. To prevent such an occurrence, the CD-ROM format includes a sophisticated error correction technique based on a Reed Solomon code. This code reduces the probability of an uncorrected bit error to approximately $10^{-12}$. (In communications, a bit error rate of $10^{-6}$ is considered acceptable.)

Because CD-ROM disks must be prerecorded, the mastering process is a potential obstacle to certain types of use. Until recently, an installation that wished to distribute data on CD-ROM media had to first generate a magnetic tape according to a predefined format to create a master disk and then press that disk to create the number of copies the user desired. Until 1989, the mastering process often resulted in a three-to-five-week delivery delay of the required CD-ROM disks. Therefore, this technique was not well suited to dynamic data.

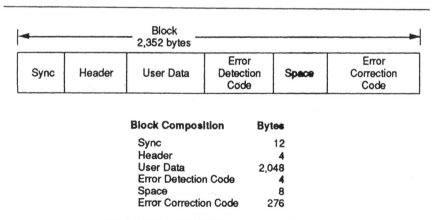

**Exhibit IV-5-1. CD-ROM Data Structure Format**

In 1989, several vendors introduced CD-ROM preprocessing mastering systems for use on microcomputers that used the Intel 80386 microprocessors, including the Compaq 386 and the IBM PS/2 Model 70. Each micro-based mastering system includes a small magnetic tape unit connected to the micro-computer, special software, and a removable disk cartridge system. Large data bases to be mastered can be supplied on either magnetic tape or a series of removable disk cartridges.

The software supplied with the system allows the end user to specify various methods by which the data base is indexed for search and retrieval purposes. Once the index method is specified, the program software allows the user to select the magnetic tape or disk cartridge system for output. Then, the software processes the data base and builds the index—a process that can require several days of processing time on an Intel 80386-based microcomputer.

Once an indexed tape or series of cartridges is produced it can be express mailed to a mastering center. Because the indexing has already been performed, the mastering center can use the tape or disk cartridges directly to manufacture the number of CD-ROM disks requested. As a result of the preprocessing, the three-to-five week delivery delay of the requested CD-ROM disks can be reduced to a three-to-five-day delay.

In 1991, a revolution in the development of CD-ROM data bases began with the introduction of Sony Corp.'s CD-Write Once system. The hybrid CD-ROM player, which is the heart of the CD-Write Once System, includes a write-once optical drive that enables a master disk to be created. When used with an 80486 microprocessor-based computer and appropriate software, the CD-Write Once System enables small quantities of large data bases to be mastered on site. This eliminates shipping tape or disk cartridges to a commercial organization and waiting three to five days to examine the resulting product. The CD-Write Once System can also be used for prototyping operations, thus eliminating the time-consuming and expensive trial-and-error process in developing certain types of CD-ROM data bases.

Because CD-ROM information cannot be altered, its use is limited to the distribution of information that is relatively stable or that represents historical data. Currently, CD-ROM drive manufacturers are targeting their products toward microcomputer and minicomputer systems. In late 1990, several vendors introduced 3.5-inch disk systems that can be installed in laptop computers, providing business travelers with access to hundreds of millions of bytes of information through the use of miniature CD-ROM disk weighing less than 1/10 of an ounce. Furthermore, the cost of CD-ROM drives has declined from approximately $800 to between $250 and $500 per system, which makes them very affordable.

**Applications.** The primary application of CD-ROM systems is microcomputer users searching large data bases. For example, widely used applications that have achieved a considerable level of sales include the *Grolier Electronic Encyclopedia* (Grolier Inc, Danbury CT), publication data bases sold to libraries, and shareware software. On one CD-ROM, the *Grolier Electronic Encyclopedia* contains all 21 volumes of the *Academic American Encyclopedia* (Grolier Inc). Included with the diskette is software that provides a menu system on the user's microcomputer that simplifies search requests, allowing the user to specify a single word or to concatenate search words to reduce the number of articles retrieved on the basis of specified search parameters.

Data bases sold to libraries on CD-ROM include catalogs of books and various publications in print. At these libraries, a microcomputer connected to a CD-ROM drive can be used instead of expensive online search capability or card catalogs. In addition to being more economical, the microcomputer software can expedite searches by processing user requests instantly. Microcomputer users can now also purchase 600M bytes of shareware programs on one CD-ROM disk for less than $100.

**Recent Developments.** Sony and N.V. Philips announced an extension to their CD-ROM format that provides automated graphics and digitized audio. This format, known as compact disk interactive (CD-I), is compatible with CD-ROM; any data base recorded in CD-ROM format will work on the CD-I drives, which reached the consumer market in early 1992. This is reassuring for organizations interested in distributing one or more of the following data base candidates in CD-ROM text format:

- Forms, policies, and procedures.
- Financial reports.
- Internal manuals.
- Legal abstracts.
- Medical abstracts.
- Store catalogs.
- Travel directories.
- Clip art.

However, CD-I disks will not work with CD-ROM disk systems. Organizations that require or could use the capability to incorporate graphics and audio into a data base for interactive instruction or other applications may wish to defer purchasing CD-ROM systems until CD-I systems become readily available.

The key difference between CD-I and CD-ROM is the ability of CD-I to store digitized voice and video as well as data. Because digitized video requires a large amount of storage, less than 15 minutes of video images can be stored on one disk. Because of this recording limit, General Electric Co. (GE) developed a system called Digital Video Interactive (DVI), which uses extensive data compression technology to store 60 minutes of video on one CD-ROM disk. In 1989, GE sold its DVI division to Intel, which is continuing to develop this technology.

**Media Production Costs.** By 1990, approximately 10 companies were mastering and replicating CD-ROM disks. Typical costs ranged from $2,000 to

$3,000 for mastering the disk and from $2 to $3 per disk, depending on the quantity ordered. A unit cost of $2 per disk required the replication of at least 1,000 disks; users can expect the total cost, including the amortization of the mastering process, to range from $4 to $5 per disk in quantities of 1,000. The cost per CD-ROM disk may increase to between $40 to $50 per disk when only 100 disks are replicated. A quantity of 10 replications would substantially escalate the cost to between $200 to $300 per disk.

The preceding costs are based on the use of an outside vendor to master and replicate CD-ROM disks. If an organization wants to quickly master a limited number of CD-ROM disks, the purchase of a CD-Write Once System and blank media is a possible solution. The retail price of the Sony CD-Write Once System was approximately $10,000 in early 1992, while a blank disk costs approximately $25. Therefore, the actual cost per disk depends on the distribution of the cost of the system over the number of masters created and the cost per disk. For example, if a company plans to distribute 50 master disks quarterly and expects the CD-Write Once player to last five years, the player's cost is amortized as $2,000 per year. The cost of the disks is multiplied by the number of disks distributed per year. In this example the disk cost would be $25 × 50 × 4, or $5,000. When this amount is added to the amortized CD-Write Once System cost, the annual cost becomes $7,000. Dividing that amount by 200 disks per year results in a per-disk cost of $35.

These cost estimates suggest that custom-mastered CD-ROM disks are economical only when the data base is relatively stable and the distribution list is extensive, or if prototyping or a rapid distribution of a limited number of master copies of a disk are required. If any of these criteria varies, write-once/read-many (WORM) optical disks may be more economical and offer users increased storage potential.

## WORM Optical Disk Systems

The WORM optical medium and disk system predate read-only systems. Originally known as direct-read-after-write (DRAW), these systems were initially confined to the laboratory.

Early WORM media were produced using rare-earth materials and such low-melting-point alloys as tellurium and selenium. The laser in the WORM drive recorded data onto the disk by physically melting the media to form an indentation representing a 1 bit. Once data was recorded onto the optical medium, the WORM system read it by illuminating an area on the disk with the same laser operating at a lower power to generate different reflections between the previously created indentations and nonmelted areas.

The volatility of the materials used in the media, however, caused them to be destroyed by exposure to oxygen or water vapor. In addition, the reflection of the melted areas from the laser illumination did not vary appreciably from nonmelted areas on the disk. Sophisticated electronics were therefore required to denote the difference between melted and nonmelted reflection areas. Although the WORM disk was eventually coated with either glass or plastic to seal the medium from the effect of an atmospheric reaction (i.e., to raise the life of the medium), WORM system electronics remained highly complex.

In 1982, 3 M developed the concept of using a high-power laser to preformat WORM disks, a process that resulted in the generation of a series of blisters on the disk. The blisters were formed by the thermal activity of the laser's light beam on a layer of a new type of WORM medium designed to produce a small amount of gas in reaction to the laser's heat. When the preformatted disks were placed in a WORM drive, the laser in the drive produced enough heat to burst the prerecorded bubbles to generate digital 1s. The burst bubbles provide a high contrast area and are much more easily recognized by the drive's electronics during the reading process. Several WORM drive manufacturers have since designed systems based on similar techniques. An added benefit of the 3M technique was an increase in the life of the WORM media.

**Technical Specifications.** Most WORM drives operate with 5¼- and 12-inch-diameter disks, though a few have been built to operate with 8- and 14-inch diameter disks. The most popular WORM disk systems operate with a 12-inch-diameter disk and provide a storage capacity of 1G byte for a single-sided drive using single-sided media. The dual-sided drive using dual-sided media provides a total capacity of 2G bytes per disk.

Disks used with WORM systems are manufactured as platters and cartridges. Because no de facto recording standards existed for WORM systems until recently (in contrast to CD-ROM systems), data recorded on the American National Standards Institute (ANSI) promulgated standards for 12-inch-diameter disks, and standards for 5¼-inch diskettes are expected to be promulgated in the near future.

All 12-inch-diameter WORM systems incorporate a small computer systems interface (SCSI), an intelligent interface that uses such high-level macro commands as **READ BLOCK** in the protocol. Most minicomputer systems are compatible with SCSI, and several third-party vendors have developed SCSI adapter boards for the Apple II series and IBM PC, PS/2, and compatible computers. These adapter boards enable WORM systems to be interfaced to most small and medium-sized computers.

An SCSI interface permits multiple devices to be connected to a common controller; several WORM system manufacturers therefore permit between four- and eight-disk systems to be accessed through one controller. This enables microcomputer and minicomputer systems to access up to 16G bytes of online storage—more than 80 times the storage capacity offered by IBM for its top-of-the-line PS/2 microcomputer.

**Applications.** Two primary application areas for WORM systems are archival and secure data storage. Because data can be written onto a WORM disk only once, this medium is well suited for maintaining a historical record of financial transactions as they occur. WORM systems can be used effectively in various application areas, including:

- Archival storage.
- Secure data storage.
- Small-scale disk mastering.
- Engineering drawing and document distribution.
- Fixed-disk backup.
- Local area network server.

WORM systems may also be used effectively for mastering a small quantity of WORM disks for distribution to other departments in an organization, similar to the use of the previously described Sony Corp. CD-Write Once System. A single-sided WORM cartridge typically costs slightly less than $100; organizations can replicate 20 copies of a data base for approximately the one-time mastering fee for CD-ROM disks. In addition, users can perform the replication process with a WORM system directly, thereby avoiding the turnaround delay associated with commercial CD-ROM mastering and replication services.

In addition to the distribution of engineering drawings and documents mentioned, other storage-intensive applications may be suitable for WORM systems (e.g., a fingerprint identification system). The California Department of Justice currently operates a WORM system with the fingerprints of 390,000 people recorded onto a write-once disk.

WORM systems may also be used for fixed-disk backup and as local area network servers. With a media cost of approximately 1¢ per 100,000 bytes, a WORM system provides an inexpensive mechanism for the backup of fixed-disk storage on a periodic basis. In addition, WORM systems are effective as local area network servers because the programs stored on a local area network are usually stable, and the changing data files they use may require only a fraction of a WORM system's storage capacity.

### Erasable Optical Disk Systems

Although erasable optical disk systems have been developed as laboratory prototypes since 1981, commercial systems are only now reaching the market. Erasable systems are based on a magnetooptic recording technique. This technique relies on a phenomenon called the Faraday effect, in which a polarized beam of light is rotated after being reflected off a magnetized surface.

Because magnetic material loses its magnetism when heated above a certain temperature, using a laser to heat magnetic spots on a disk changes its reflection, which can be measured during a read cycle. Similarly, during another write cycle, the magnetic spots can be heated to another temperature to regain the magnetism, which then rotates a polarized beam of light a predefined amount. This rotation can be measured during a read cycle by measuring the rotation of the polarized light.

The first commercial erasable disks to reach the market were incorporated into the NeXT computer. These 5¼-inch drives were manufactured by Cannon Inc. for NeXT and were quickly followed by drives from Sony Corp. and Verbatim Corp. The Sony and Verbatim drives have a storage capacity of 600M bytes, and each meets the proposed standards of ANSI and the International Standards Organization (ISO), while the Cannon drive uses a proprietary recording technique. Although the retail price of the Sony and Verbatim drives each exceeded $3,000, their costs are expected to substantially decline over the next few years as volume production increases.

Although several manufacturers introduced different recording techniques that delayed standardization of 5¼-inch drives, a series of 3.5-inch-drive developments resulted in the rapid standardization of this format to provide users with 128M bytes of removable storage. By early 1992 IBM, Acumen, MicroNet Technology, and Pinnacle Micro were actively marketing 3.5-inch erasable optical drives for use with microcomputers. At a retail price of approximately $2,000, a 3.5-inch erasable optical drive costs almost as much as three 200M-byte magnetic SCSI drives. The cost of a removable magnetic cartridge is approximately $60, and when added to the cost of a 200M-byte SCSI drive, it results in a cost of about $3 per megabyte of storage. In comparison, an erasable optical drive with one disk costs about $15 per megabyte. By the time six optical disks are in use, however, the cost has been reduced to less than $3 per megabyte. This results in an increase in the use of erasable optical media and a decrease in its unit storage cost. The amount of data that can be stored makes an erasable disk drive an economically feasible alternative to removable magnetic media.

## SUMMARY

CD-ROM and WORM systems provide alternatives to implementing communications access to large, storage-intensive applications on a centralized mainframe. Increases in the storage capacity of CD-ROM systems by the introduction of multiple disk playing systems provides microcomputer and minicomputer users with access to 3G bytes of read-only information. With this in mind, the data center manager might want to consider which applications can be developed on microcomputer or minicomputer systems interfaced to CD-ROM and WORM systems. Storage-intensive applications with a stable data base that can be updated on a defined schedule (e.g., monthly or quarterly) may be optimum candidates for CD-ROM and WORM systems. Once such applications are identified, the characteristics of each system must be considered with respect to the application.

The comparison of major CD-ROM and WORM system characteristics shown in Exhibit IV-5-2 can be used to help identify applications best suited for a microcomputer or minicomputer connected to either type of optical disk. In addition to new applications, some existing applications operating on a

| Characteristics | CD-ROM | WORM |
|---|---|---|
| Unit Data Storage (G Bytes) | 0.5 | 1–2 |
| System Data Storage (G Bytes) | 3 | 8–16 |
| Mastering Time | 3 to 5 days | Immediate |
| Number of Disks for Economical Distribution | Usually greater than 100 | Usually less than 100 |

**Exhibit IV-5-2. System Characteristics: CD-ROM Versus WORM**

corporate mainframe may be better suited to an optical disk-based system. One example is an organization's personnel system linked to 20 manufacturing plants by expensive communications facilities.

If the master personnel file is updated monthly, this application might be a suitable candidate for a WORM-based system. The IS department could master 20 copies of a WORM disk and mail the optical disks to each manufacturing plant, where they could be used with a minicomputer or microcomputer attached to a WORM system. The cost of existing communications facilities to access the personnel file must be compared with the cost of providing each plant with an optical disk system and sending an optical disk to each plant every month. Implementing such a system may also free the centralized computer to perform other tasks. All aspects of an application should be examined to identify potential cost reductions or the availability of storage and processing capability that may be obtained from moving applications onto optical disk systems.

The use of erasable optical disk systems can be justified as a storage economy measure. As previously indicated, the breakeven point is based on the use of a sufficient number of removable disks, after which additional storage requirements make an optical disk economical. It is economically beneficial to analyze the cost of erasable optical storage against removable magnetic media before selecting an erasable storage mechanism.

# IV-6
# Planning for Object-Oriented Systems

*JOHN E. GESSFORD*

F or many users, Macintosh icons were an introduction to object-oriented systems. Each icon had behavioral as well as visual characteristics. Users learned about an icon more often by interacting with it than by reading about it. More important, users found it easy to think of the computer as being composed of a collection of objects that came to life when the system was turned on.

The Windows system, a product of Microsoft Corp., brought the concept of an object, called a window, to the much larger group of IBM PC users. Because Windows is capable of managing multiple windows simultaneously, it can manage the transfer of an object from one window to another.

IBM's description of its Application Development Cycle (AD/Cycle) and Repository Management System, which is intended to automate applications software development, shows clear evidence of object orientation. The repository is designed to store not only definitions and descriptions of data but also a definition of the programs that can access that data. Applications programming that is organized by the data that it operates on is presumed.

This way of structuring software is the hallmark of object-oriented programming. A major objective of the joint venture between Apple Computer, Inc. and IBM, announced in 1991, is to create an object-oriented operating system that will be an alternative to Microsoft Windows and OS/2. This alliance will strongly influence the way a large portion of the computer industry's efforts and resources will be spent in the coming years. It seems certain that the dominant operating systems of the future will be object-oriented.

## THE NEED FOR OBJECT-ORIENTED APPLICATIONS PLANNING

If the hardware, operating system, and applications software all incorporate object-oriented principles, the method of analyzing and designing business applications probably should also be object-oriented. The fact that program specifications, which are a result of analysis and design, need to be object-oriented if the programming is to be object-oriented strongly suggests that a complete object-oriented approach is needed. Comparing a set of traditional program specifications with a set of object-oriented programs to determine whether the specifications are satisfied can prove to be a difficult task. Different parts of the traditional, procedurally oriented program specification are satisfied by different program modules (i.e., methods) in the object-oriented system.

This change in planning methodology represents a quantum leap. Small adjustments to the traditional method of systems analysis and design do not work. The legions trained in structured analysis and design methods during the past two decades find this change difficult to accept. Even today, many large applications software development departments are attempting to accommodate object-oriented software specification demands by adopting hybrid planning systems.

Hybrid planning usually begins with a structured decomposition of the relevant business procedures and data flow diagramming of these procedures; objects are then defined in terms of the functions and data stores of these data flow diagrams. Identifying the objects in this way is a poorly defined and complex process that tends to yield abstract objects that are often only arbitrary groupings of program modules.

Fortunately, the majority of applications software developers are not constrained by structured methods because, for the most part, they have no formal method of analysis and design. They simply obtain performance specifications from those who will use the system and then write the application programs. The first version the developers come up with may be called a prototype; a subsequent version is implemented, and the system is then refined for the rest of its life by what is euphemistically called maintenance programming.

Those who take this ad hoc approach, however, risk creating even more low-quality, expensive software with AD/Cycle and other new computer-aided software engineering (CASE) tools than they have in the past. This is because the traditional method of systems development—the applications software project—leads to distinct, incompatible systems unless the individual projects are governed by a more comprehensive plan. The object-oriented approach requires an investment in an infrastructure of businesswide standards to create a full accurate computer simulation of the objects vital to the business. Management's understanding of this necessity is requisite to ensure that appropriate attention and resources will be devoted to establishing and maintaining this infrastructure of information systems standards.

## THE ESSENCE OF OBJECT-ORIENTED PLANNING

The object is the atomic unit in an object-oriented approach. The planning activities of systems analysis and design should be based on this fact. Rather than treat the need for object-oriented software specifications as an exogenous condition to be accommodated by the planning method, the planning should focus on objects from the start.

The starting point in systems analysis should be object identification, not procedure analysis. The objects that system users need to know about and work with should be the focus of attention. Only after these objects are identified and classified should other considerations come into play.

The classification of objects of vital importance to a business is the purpose of entity-relationship (ER) analysis. The entity types identified by this analysis are object classes to be included in the object-oriented business information systems being planned. In addition, ER analysis models the relationships between entity types that should be simulated by the system and the information about entity types and relationships that is needed to run the business effectively.

The basic purpose of systems design should be to plan a simulation of the classes of objects identified through ER analysis. A real-time simulation system is needed to show management the condition of the business at any time. Ultimately, after a series of development projects, the entire business can be simulated as a collection of objects that are created, evolve, interact, and finally cease to exist as far as the business is concerned.

The object simulation viewpoint defines and organizes the procedures of the systems in an entirely different way than the traditional input-process-output view of information systems. The object-oriented approach is to define the procedures needed to simulate the objects of each class. In contrast, the input-process-output approach organizes the data (i.e., objects) according to the business procedures that use the data.

Because applications software projects are defined in terms of automating specific business functions, the input-process-output approach is more compatible with traditional systems development than is the object-oriented approach to planning. The object-oriented approach is not compatible with project-by-project systems development unless the objects have first been modeled from a businesswide perspective. If standard data object classes are not defined businesswide, incomplete, conflicting, and incompatible object simulations will give misleading information to management, customers, and others who use the system.

Object-oriented systems design should begin with the object classes and relationships identified as part of the system in the analysis phase. With rare exceptions, standardized processing procedures should be applied to automatically create the software needed to capture, process, display, and print object information of interest to systems users.

## Avoiding the Very Large Systems Syndrome

The need for leadership in developing object-oriented business information systems is imperative. As explained, a lack of leadership usually results in disparate systems because a project-by-project approach to development is taken without businesswide information systems standards.

A businesswide set of information systems standards requires senior management involvement. Only senior management can create an environment in which individual systems development initiatives can be harmonized and share object simulation software. It is important to note, however, that too much high-level involvement is possible. If senior management tries to micromanage systems development, the very large systems syndrome is experienced. It is easy to fall into the trap of thinking that the solution to incompatible systems is one large system. In the case of information systems, there is considerable evidence that this apparent solution is faulty. What seems to be a straightforward solution to the problem of fragmented systems turns into a quagmire in many cases. Very large information systems lead to uncontrollable development expenses and defective systems.

One example of the very large systems approach is IBM's Business Systems Planning (BSP) methodology, which was introduced during the early 1970s, just after the first data base management systems were developed (the most recently revised version of BSP was published in 1984). BSP is an elaborate methodology that has been used by many companies, and variations on it are used by many systems consulting organizations today.

BSP studies have been conducted in hundreds of organizations. One survey of organizations that had completed BSP projects indicated, however, that the results have been disappointing in terms of eliminating incompatible systems, though some positive benefits were noted. The following three conclusions about BSP can be drawn from this survey and other evidence:

- The BSP methodology requires more time and resources than the results justify. The multiyear systems development plan is too detailed in view of the uncertainties an organization faces over the time period encompassed by the plan.
- The top-down approach is helpful to the IS manager in the organization. One reason is that senior management provides a clearer picture of the systems and data needed to effectively run the business than do people at lower levels in the organization.
- The BSP approach results in a plan for data bases that is too vague to ensure compatibility among systems.

The first conclusion points to the main reason why the very large systems approach fails. The life of a modern organization is too dynamic. The systems plans made today are inappropriate for the organization in the future, when the resources to build the system become available. A more flexible and results-oriented way of defining systems is needed.

The second conclusion supports the proposition that senior management involvement in systems planning is needed to align that planning with the strategic needs of the company. This is one clear benefit of the top-down approach of BSP.

The last conclusion indicates that the methodology must be extended to include the establishment of a high-level data administration function that can develop data specifications that will ensure systems compatibility. The function must be executed from a high-level position to ensure complete cooperation.

## NINE STEPS TO OBJECT-ORIENTED SYSTEMS

An approach to managing information systems allows senior-level management involvement yet avoids very large systems commitments. In this approach, different aspects of systems are managed at different organizational levels. Some aspects are managed organizationwide, others businesswide, and others on an application-by-application basis. (The distinction between organizationwide and businesswide is based on the conception of a legal organization engaged in more than one line of business.)

The organizationwide and businesswide management of certain aspects creates the environment within which compatible applications systems can be developed. The systems aspects that are managed organizationwide and businesswide should determine whether systems are compatible or vital to the strategic plans of the organization. All other aspects are best managed on an applications project basis.

This approach is summarized in Exhibit IV-6-1; nine steps, from clarifying strategic goals to implementing the information systems, are shown. The first four steps have a businesswide scope. An organizationwide scope is recommended for the fifth step. The last four steps are taken on an application-by-application basis.

This approach is a variation on the information engineering (IE) methodology defined by James Martin. The first five steps accomplish many of the same results achieved by the planning and analysis phases of the IE methodology. These five steps work in a simpler, more flexible way, however. Two complicated techniques in the IE approach—affinity analysis and process diagramming—are omitted from the methodology described here.

### Step 1: Clarifying the Strategy and Goals

Clarifying the strategy and goals of a business is an important first step in aligning the information systems of the business with its goals. A clear statement of purpose and explicit strategic plans for achieving that purpose may directly identify some information systems needs. Information systems may even be identified that play a vital role in a strategy.

Objectives and the strategies to achieve them also provide the rationale for the functional model developed in step 2, which is used to systematically identify information systems requirements. An understanding of corporate strategy is needed to set systems development priorities.

Step 1 can be taken only by the senior management of an organization. Only as these leaders adopt a strategy and specific goals should they be allowed to influence the way resources are used, including resources devoted

| Step | Management Involved | Scope | Data Sources | Software Used |
|------|---------------------|-------|--------------|---------------|
| 1. Clarify the strategy and goals | Senior management | Businesswide | Investment and policy proposals Organizational data | Strategic planning support system |
| 2. Define a functional model | Senior management and data administrator | Businesswide | Business strategy Management discussions | Repository |
| 3. Identify functional experts | Human resource management and data administrator | Businesswide | Organization chart Job classifications Employee data | Repository |
| 4. Define the businesswide information structure | Functional experts and data administrator | Businesswide | Reports Transactions Existing information structure | Repository |
| 5. Establish the computing environment | Senior and IS management | Organizationwide | Platform, DBMS, and CASE tool information | Operating system DBMS CASE tools |
| 6. Design the application | Systems analyst and users | Application by application | Systems requirements Prototype screens | CASE design tool |
| 7. Establish the physical data base | Data base administrator | Businesswide | Conceptual data base DBMS documentation | Repository DBMS |
| 8. Generate software | Programmer | Application by application | Systems design CASE coding tool requirements | CASE coding tool |
| 9. Implement the system | Testers, documentation writers, trainers, and users | Application by application | Systems design Applications software | Applications software |

**Exhibit IV-6-1. Steps from Strategy to Information Systems**

SOURCE: J.E. Gessford, *How to Build Business-wide Databases* (New York: John Wiley & Sons, 1991).

316

to information systems. Others in the organization should provide strategic ideas through policy or investment proposals and provide suggestions for solving problems. It remains up to senior management, however, to accept these ideas for the organization.

The procedures and schedule for strategic planning may vary from one organization to another. Approaches that involve a broad cross section of the organization generally promote a participative style of management. An information system that facilitates the formulation, communication, and evaluation of goal suggestions from across the organization (labeled a strategic planning support system in Exhibit IV-6-1) can be helpful in making such approaches more effective.

## Step 2: Defining a Functional Model

The functional model of a business defines what must be done to achieve the strategic goals. It is a form of strategic planning that breaks down the overall activity of fulfilling the purposes of the organization into the required actions and decision making.

Because it is part of strategic planning, a functional model is appropriately defined by senior managers who understand the organizational purposes and plans to be fulfilled. A data administrator can offer assistance in formulating the model in a way that is compatible with a type of software package and data base that the information engineering methodology terms a system encyclopedia and that IBM calls a repository system. This system can be used to record the functional model and link it to the other plans developed in steps 3 and 4. A repository allows information about the functions and their subfunctions to be entered into an information system and then displayed or printed in various formats.

When the major functions have been identified, further definition and subdivision of them can be done by experts in each function (step 4). For example, marketing is often a major function required by the strategy of the organization; the definition and subdivision of marketing is best left to marketing experts, or should at least be done in consultation with such experts.

## Step 3: Identifying Functional Experts

The functional model is not an organization chart, but it can be described in terms of the jobs and positions in the organization. An analysis of how the functional model relates to the organization must be made to identify who should determine the data requirements of each function and subfunction. In most cases, someone who is executing the function is best qualified to serve as the functional expert.

This analysis can provide some equally important side benefits to those responsible for human resource (i.e., personnel) management. By comparing job descriptions with the definitions of the functional model, misalignments with respect to the organization's strategic goals can be detected. Functions not provided for in the organizational structure (or being performed redundantly) are identified.

Ideally, the repository system should provide the information needed to make this analysis. The fact that the information is useful to both personnel and information systems management points to a need for cooperation and sharing that has not been traditionally recognized by the management of either of these departments.

## Step 4: Defining the Businesswide Information Structure

The term *information structure* is used to designate a plan that is not a complete conceptual data base that can serve as the framework of the conceptual data base. (The term *conceptual data base* is used to denote a complete definition of the data needed by the organization.) The information structure defines the entity types about which the business needs data, but not all the specific types of data required. Relationships between entity types are also defined in an information structure.

The functional experts and data administrator work together to characterize data requirements in terms of an information structure. The functional expert describes transactions, queries, and reports that are important to the function. The data administrator abstracts from the descriptions the entity types and relationships involved.

The reports, queries, and transactions, as well as the entity types and relationships that they imply, should be defined in the repository system. To the extent that the report, query, and transaction descriptions are complete, attributes of entity types can be recorded as well; however, attribute specifications should not be considered final until step 7 has been completed.

The execution of step 4 by the data administrator should be businesswide so that data definition standards can be set up to govern all references to data in all software purchased or developed. This is the prerequisite for automatic data sharing without special import-export programs. Exhibit IV-6-2 illustrates how the results of step 4 are used in the development of integrated systems. The data base concept, shown in the upper-left corner of Exhibit IV-6-2, guides the development of an integrated set of data bases that all information systems of the business can use. The development of the integrated data bases from the results of step 4 is the responsibility of the data administration function.

The objective in this fourth step is limited to information structure definition, rather than the conceptual data base definition, so that the step can be accomplished businesswide within a few months. To obtain a complete data base definition would require a far more detailed analysis and could take years. Identifying the entity types gives the data administrator a basis for evolving the conceptual data base definition over a period of years as applications development projects are undertaken. The businesswide information structure

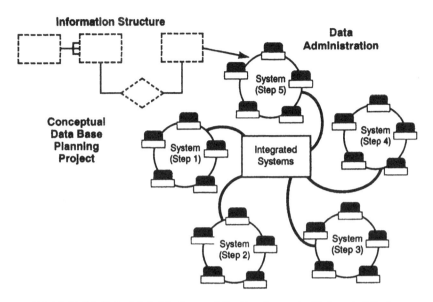

**Exhibit IV-6-2. Data Administration and the Development of Integrated Systems**

linked to the functional model provides an overview of who needs what types of data in the organization.

## Step 5: Establishing the Computing Environment

To gain the full benefit of the first four steps, an automated approach must be taken for the remaining steps. Otherwise, the businesswide plans will be obsolete before the systems to implement them can be developed. This is one reason why properly designed CASE tools are so important. They can automate the design of applications systems, the creation and testing of applications programs, and the preparation of training and reference materials.

A CASE tool is designed to work with a certain operating system. It may generate code that makes calls to a certain type of data base management system (DBMS) and network control system as well. The operating system, DBMS, and network control system usually have certain access control systems and require specific hardware to function. Consequently, standards for CASE, DBMS, the operating system, data networking, security, and computer hardware must be established, roughly in that order. Hardware should not be selected first. This common mistake often excludes the best CASE, DBMS, and operating system alternatives from consideration.

These aspects of the information systems standards are needed to ensure integrated systems and businesswide conceptual data bases. Without these organizationwide standards, the systems developed will be more or less incompatible and training and maintenance expenses will be greater than necessary.

The setting of these standards is of strategic importance and therefore needs to be done by senior management. Because there are technical as well as business issues involved, IS professionals should participate in the decision-making process. The business and technical leaders of the organization must reach a consensus on these decisions.

## Step 6: Designing the Application

The definition of an application and its feasibility, the formulation of system performance requirements, and the detailed design of the system are included in this step. Step 5 represents that part of applications development that front-end CASE tools are commonly designed to automate. It does not include the businesswide or organizationwide planning of steps 1 through 5.

Usually a systems analyst works with potential users in accomplishing this step (sophisticated users may prefer to design applications themselves, however). Rapid application development (RAD) techniques and tools, including prototyping, help to facilitate communication between developers and system users during this step.

This step is greatly simplified if an object-oriented approach is taken and a businesswide information structure is available as described in step 4. For each entity type (and certain relationships) involved in the application, a data object class can be defined. For each screen and report to be included in the system, a window object class or report object class can be defined. Then, for each object class, standard programs required to simulate objects of the class can be specified. Each computer program is dedicated to simulating a certain behavior of object of a single class. The entity types and relationships identified in step 4 can therefore be directly translated into design objects in step 6. The part of the businesswide information structure that a given application uses should be fleshed out at this time so that it constitutes a conceptual data base. This process must be performed before a physical data base can be developed. The process should take into account any attributes of the entity types involved in the application that other future applications will require.

## Step 7: Establishing the Physical Data Base

The planning and creation of physical data base files should be done on a businesswide basis. It may be that every application should have its own physical data base, though transaction processing times and data communications costs can be significantly reduced by storing certain data in a different data base or more than one data base.

In managing physical data bases, it is also important to satisfy security requirements and to consider the cost of providing adequate technical support to ensure that files are not corrupted. A file containing thousands of transactions or data on thousands of customers represents an important asset of the business, even though it is not an asset in the accounting system. These considerations tend to favor a centralized approach to physical data base management.

Physical data bases should be established and managed by a data base administrator who is responsible for maintaining the organization's data resources. This individual works with the systems analyst in defining a view of the data associated with each entity type and relationship that is relevant to a particular application. The data base administrator then maps that view to the data definitions of one or more physical data bases.

## Step 8: Generating Software

Using a CASE approach provides the biggest payoff in code generation, traditionally the most expensive and least controllable step. The system designed with CASE tools can be coded automatically using a code generator designed to work from the design specifications created by the CASE design tool. Consequently, the programmer is removed from direct applications programming, and the time and cost of coding are thereby cut dramatically. Higher-quality code is also obtained, which means the code testing and debugging cycle is brought under control.

## Step 9: Implementing the System

The final step includes preparing user documentation, training the users, and pilot testing the new system in an operational environment. This is a difficult step to manage because each phase often reveals omissions and misunderstandings from previous phases and steps; therefore, iterative processes are involved.

The importance of performing this final step well is commonly underestimated. Failure to properly test and document a new system and train its users can be as fatal to the success of the system as poor design or an inadequate DBMS. If the system's users do not understand a feature of the system, they will not use it, and it may as well have been excluded. Poorly trained users are usually frustrated users, who soon blame all their troubles on the system.

Step 9 should be executed by system user experts, not programmer-analysts. Individuals familiar with the business function but not the computer system are most likely to detect operational deficiencies during testing and to provide thorough training and documentation. Programmers usually take too many details about the system for granted.

## BENEFITS OF BUSINESSWIDE MANAGEMENT OF OBJECTS

The benefits of preparing for object-oriented systems using the method described are not merely technical and qualitative. In an increasingly fast-paced, electronic business world, object-oriented systems are quantitative and central to business survival.

The major reason for coordinating references to objects (i.e., data) across an organization is the same as for establishing standards for communication between army, navy, and air force units engaged in battle against a common enemy. It is not enough that different parts of the organization share a common goal. They must also work from a common base of information, or they will be uncoordinated and will end up blaming one another for failures.

The way in which goals, information, and resources interact to determine what an organization accomplishes needs to be better understood. In one sense, information is a resource because it enables workers to effectively execute the functions that need to be performed to achieve the goals of the organization. Yet information is different from other resources in the way it shapes goals and guides the use of other resources. Information is not just another resource.

Information shared and communicated is probably the best means for coordinating the daily work of different departments in an organization. The goals of the organization determine the departments that are needed, and they can be used to set up measures of performance and incentives for individual managers as well as for the organization as a whole. However, it takes shared information to coordinate hourly and daily the work of different parts of an organization.

The natural tendency of individual managers to develop information systems customized to the needs of their departments leads to an incompatible collection of systems that inhibit the sharing of information. Each department develops its own version of what needs to be done to achieve the goals of the business. The result is misunderstandings and uncoordinated responses to the needs of customers and suppliers.

To obtain fast, coordinated organizational responses to customer requests, information systems that transcend both interorganizational and intraorganizational boundaries are needed. Such systems can deliver the information each person in the organization needs to work with others in achieving the goals of the organization.

The underlying drive to develop information systems clearly should and does come from those who stand to benefit directly from the use of them. Too often, this drive comes from units far down in the organization. Such initiatives lead to many separate, narrowly defined systems suited to the needs of the individual department. The manager who is in a position to make an information system profitable and commits to doing so is usually the one who gets the funds.

Senior management must decide how it should exert a countervailing force for coordination and integration of information systems. In cases in which senior management has simply taken over systems development, the result has been very large systems, which have been defined by one prominent consultant as projects that are never completed. A more effective approach is one that creates an environment within which the proactive manager builds systems. This environment channels the primary creative forces in ways that create systems that transcend organizational boundaries.

A more coordinated and responsive organization is the major reason for creating businesswide guidelines for object-oriented systems development. There are, however, other advantages to be gained by this approach.

**Access to More Data.** In a shared data base, all the data is available to each user group that has a valid need (and the appropriate access codes) to access the data. This assumes an adequate data communications system is in place.

**Shared Programs.** Business functions performed at multiple locations can use the same applications software if they use the same data base design (or the same data base), so the cost of developing and maintaining programs can be spread over multiple sites.

**Use of Compatible Purchased Software.** Two or more software packages that use the same commands (e.g., SQL commands) to access a data base, and that are able to access data bases that have the same design, can share data. Purchased software that does not meet these two characteristics results in independent data bases that can be shared only by importing and exporting data, which is a complex and slow process.

**Reduced Data Capture Expense.** When data is shared, it needs to be keyed in only once. Product descriptions, for example, need not be entered separately into sales, purchasing, manufacturing, inventory, engineering, and other systems. If product descriptions are shared by these systems, they can be entered once and accessed by all these systems. Independent applications systems usually have independent data capture modules, so there is much duplication of both data entry and data storage.

**Reduced Data Expense.** To the extent that two or more applications are using the same physical data base, only one copy of the data (instead of two or more) needs to be held in online storage (usually disk storage).

**Avoidance of Inconsistent Data.** When two executives at a meeting present contradictory data on the same subject, a great deal of expensive professional time can be consumed in reconciling the data. The discrepancy is often the result of a technical difference in the way updates to the data base are handled in the two applications systems.

**Improved Interface Between Systems.** The output of one system is often input for another system. For example, the output of a computer-aided design (CAD) system in engineering is a product definition that must be reviewed by the manufacturing engineers if the product is to be produced in-house. Unless design and manufacturing engineering have integrated data bases, a data capture (or data conversion) operation must be performed before production planning analysis can take place.

Information systems departments generally have not been able to develop systems that share a common data base, according to a survey conducted by the Sloan School of Management. What they commonly do is extract data from the files of separate systems and put it into an information center data base that is accessible to managers and analysts. This provides access to more data—one of the advantages from data sharing listed—but it fails to provide the other advantages. If maintaining a duplicate data base is worthwhile because of the access it provides, the greater benefits of real systems integration must certainly be worthwhile if a workable way to build such systems is available.

## SUMMARY

A new generation of information systems is emerging that is shaped by an object-oriented approach to design. Object-oriented systems are relatively inexpensive and easy to work with, and when combined with CASE tools that make customized systems easy to generate, they are likely to lead to a proliferation of microcomputer-based systems in most organizations.

The planning of business applications must change to be compatible with object-oriented systems. In implementing new planning methods, there is an opportunity to define organizationwide standards that will make all information systems adhere to the standards coordinated and integrated with respect to data access. Establishing such standards, however, requires business leadership.

Business management has an opportunity to make better use of computers by exercising more leadership in the development of systems. More technical expertise is not the critical factor. Leadership in creating an environment that fosters systems that are compatible and that share data is the vital factor. Without this leadership, a patchwork of disparate information systems is inevitable.

The managerial approach taken to establish systems that share data must avoid the very large system syndrome. Difficulties arise if systems development efforts are too centralized. Experience provides ample evidence of the fallacy of trying to centrally plan and manage information resources as one big system. Business is simply too dynamic and multifaceted for that strategy to be practical.

The most promising systems development strategy is one in which senior management supports the establishment of a businesswide definition of data resources and an organizationwide set of standards for the computing environment. The development of individual applications within this environment can be left to individual departmental managers and professional staff members.

# IV-7
# Lessons From Three Client/ Server Implementations

*JOHN LEVIS • PETER VON SCHILLING*

L ike many of today's advanced technology concepts, client/server computing seems to have many definitions. Essentially, client/server computing
is a software-based architecture that enables distributed computing resources
on a network to share common resources among groups of users at intelligent
workstations. This definition high-lights the four fundamental building blocks
in a client/server architecture.

## FOUR BUILDING BLOCKS OF CLIENT/SERVER ARCHITECTURE

First, intelligent workstations (i.e., clients) act as the user entry point into the
client/server environment. To be a client, a workstation must be intelligent
because it must have processing capabilities and make requests to common
resources. Second, common resources, or servers, perform a set of special
tasks for any other device requesting their services. Third, networks connect
the workstations with common resources. Last, and perhaps most important,
software applications tie the other three components together to form the
client/server architecture (see Exhibit IV-7-1).

The feature that distinguishes client/server from other technology architectures is that it contains cooperative processing capabilities, which physically
split the processing performed by the client from that performed by the server
while presenting a single logical picture to the user. Exhibit IV-7-2 illustrates
a typical dialogue between clients and servers.

## INDUSTRY AND BUSINESS FACTORS

Client/server has emerged as a significant computing architecture as a result
of several industry factors, one of which is the continuous improvements
in price/performance ratios of desktop computers. Powered by an Intel 486
processor, a PC can provide 5 MIPS (millions of instructions per second),
roughly the same computer power as that of a small IBM mainframe. The
difference is that the 486 PC can sit on a desktop in any office, whereas the
mainframe needs a controlled environment and a support team.

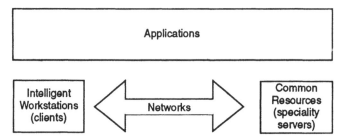

**Exhibit IV-7-1. The Four Building Blocks of Client/Server Computing**

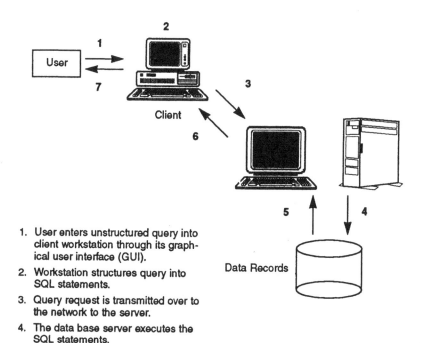

1. User enters unstructured query into client workstation through its graphical user interface (GUI).
2. Workstation structures query into SQL statements.
3. Query request is transmitted over to the network to the server.
4. The data base server executes the SQL statements.
5. The server accepts the results of the query.
6. The raw data is transmitted back to the client.
7. The client formats the query as requested by the user and presents it using the GUI.

**Exhibit IV-7-2. Typical Client/Server Dialogue**

Economic conditions, along with the move toward downsizing all aspects of the organization to refocus them into core business functions, have also contributed to the evolution of client/server architectures. The traditional IS department with its large annual operating budget is often high on the list of functions to be refocused. As IS departments downsize, the client/server architecture becomes a new way of distributing computing technology to users while providing at least the same level of functionality and, at the same time, reducing the associated overhead.

The trend toward niche products in the hardware and software market-places is another factor. In the past, hardware and software products were intended to be all things to all people. This led to technology environments in which each component performed several tasks adequately but few tasks really well. With the introduction of specialty products such as graphical user interfaces (GUIs) designed to provide a consistent look and feel to applications, companies can improve the collective performance of their technologies. The solution that has emerged to address these issues is client/server computing.

## EXPECTED BENEFITS FROM CLIENT/SERVER

For client/server computing to appeal to the mainstream organizations, the investment must offer benefits. The benefits realized to date are not well documented. For this reason, it is perhaps best to look at the expected benefits of client/server technology to determine its potential value.

Client/server is considered a way to reduce the operating costs of IS departments. The hardware that is used typically requires less sophisticated environments and fewer high-priced support personnel. In the extreme case, the overhead of a corporate data center could be eliminated through the implementation of client/server architectures.

There is also potential for a better return on technology investments because the technology can be used in an optimal manner. The niche products on the market can be configured to leverage each other's strengths, thus ensuring greater value from their acquisition.

Client/server computing allows greater access to corporate data and information. In traditional architectures, data is maintained in highly protected centralized data structures. During the 1980s, when there was a move to provide more access to this data, it was discovered that even the most advanced data base management systems operating on the fastest central processors could not satisfy user requests for data. By distributing the tools to access the data, client/server can increase user access to corporate data.

Finally, companies expect client/server to provide the flexibility needed to maintain a state-of-the-art technology environment. In traditional architectures, the replacement of existing hardware or software can disrupt the entire environment. Support staff and users need retraining, applications may require upgrading, and in general, the environment becomes unstable for a period of

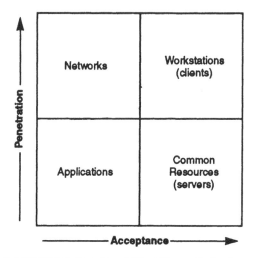

**Exhibit IV-7-3. Maturity of Client/Server Technology**

time. As a result, many companies are reluctant to make such changes. In a client/server architecture, however, only small pieces of the environment must be replaced, thus reducing the impact of such changes.

**Market Status.** Clearly, client/server technology has substantial potential benefits if implemented correctly. However, the success of client/server computing first of all depends on how well the building blocks become accepted in the marketplace. In Exhibit IV-7-3, each of the four components of a client/server system is plotted on a graph measuring its market penetration on the vertical axis and its acceptance (with respect to standards) on the horizontal axis. Applications are by far the most immature building block. At present, the lack of applications designed for client/server environments is limiting its acceptance.

Industry trends and theoretical benefits will not, by themselves, convince a company to adopt client/server technology. The following case studies demonstrate the motivations of three companies for implementing client/server and the obstacles that surfaced in the process.

## CASE STUDY 1: GOVERNMENT

One organization that has committed itself to the implementation of client/server technology is a government authority mandated to construct and operate a new airport in Asia. AirCo is a newly formed authority with one basic goal: to construct a world-class, state-of-the-art airport by June 1997.

The initial mandate of the IT department was to provide computing resources to the growing staff to support analysis and document processing. The department also recognized that eventually the technology requirements of the organization would become more diverse. With no established technology environment, management decided that the most appropriate architecture for the company would be client/server.

The organization is projected to grow from an initial staff of three to nearly 1,000 employees. An estimated 70% of the staff will need access to basic computing resources. Client/server provides a framework that allows the IT department to build the technology coverage from the ground up in small, incremental blocks. The basic objective is to expand the technology environment at the same pace as the organization's expansion, so that the staff/technology ratio remains roughly constant. Traditional mainframe-based architectures cannot achieve this because of the high capital costs associated with large-scale central processors.

Client/server is seen as meeting AirCo's medium- and long-term need for departmental applications to share corporate data. In many ways, AirCo views itself as a property developer that is conducting a series of mutually dependent projects so it can complete the airport. The project teams need to share information, not just departmentally but on a corporate scale, to achieve the required level of coordination. A client/server architecture is well suited to meet this requirement.

Because AirCo is expanding to multiple locations, the technology environment should be relatively self-sufficient. Relying on access to a central processor in AirCo's head office location would be risky. A client/server architecture, by its very nature as a distributed technology environment, minimizes this risk. Configuring the network to minimize remote location dependence on the head office limits the risks associated with remote computing.

The eventual size of the organization once the airport becomes operational is an unknown variable. Therefore, the IT department needs an architecture that can expand or contract with the size of the organization without affecting the applications and data residing within it. IT management believes that the modularity of client/server provides the needed flexibility.

## Progress

In the first year, intelligent workstations in the form of 386-based desktops were distributed along with a standard complement of word processing, spreadsheet, and presentation software running under a GUI environment. Once workstations were in place, they were interconnected to a LAN to share printing resources. The first client/server application—a human resources management system with UNIX server components and DOS client components—has been implemented with positive results. Now that the hardware and communications infrastructure is in place, the pace of client/server application implementation is expected to accelerate, provided that such packages can be found.

## Problems Encountered

Despite the general success of the plan, AirCo's IT department has encountered several problems, some technological in nature and some not. The first problem is the lack of generally accepted standards in networking. AirCo went to great lengths to ensure that the UNIX servers it planned to install would be accessible from its DOS-based GUI, because the two protocols involved, TCP/IP and Novell NCP, were different. In addition, care was needed to ensure that the network electronics could support both protocols over different media (e.g., twisted copper wire, optical fiber, and microwave). AirCo must continuously retest the hardware and software it acquires to ensure compatibility. Vendor support for client/server has not reached the point at which the expected benefit of plug-and-play components can be realized.

The second major obstacle encountered is the lack of true client/server application packages. Many software vendors claim that their products are designed for client/server computing, but after conducting thorough searches for various packages, the systems delivery group found few that followed the client/server model. Although conventional applications can operate on the installed technology, the authority cannot fully realize the benefits of its approach until a broader range of client/server packages is available.

The third problem did not directly involve technology. Instead, AirCo discovered that the organization as a whole could not accept the responsibilities associated with client/server. Even though many members of the staff had been recruited from companies in which technology was integral to the business processes, the delegation of administrative policies and procedures that accompanies client/server computing was too demanding for them. As a result, some departments were unable to outgrow their dependence on the IT department.

This case study illustrates that even in a new technology environment, the implementation of client/server technology is not without its difficulties.

## CASE STUDY 2: FINANCE

FinCo is a large, international financial services and life insurance company. Unlike the organization in first case study, FinCo has no overall plan for client/server but rather sees it as one of the many technology options available.

FinCo has a solidly entrenched IT environment and considers itself a technology follower, implementing only proven technology. The corporate mainframe is the primary platform for core business applications. Microcomputers have not yet reached a significant penetration in the user community, despite the fact that control over IT decisions is decentralized. The corporate IT department, created just three years ago, is responsible for the head office data center, the communications infrastructure, and technical support of the development environment. The divisions are responsible for applications development, workstation, and LAN technology decisions. Not surprisingly, the divisions have different ideas about the direction the company should be taking with information technology. Constrained by these factors, the company's efforts to implement client/server computing are just beginning.

### Motivation

Because FinCo does not have an explicit plan for implementing a client/server architecture across all its divisions, the corporate IT department has set a goal of implementing client/server computing on the assumption that the company will, in the long term, migrate to client/server technology. Several factors motivate the corporate IT department to choose this goal.

The primary motivating factor is the need to leverage the investment in large, mission-critical applications and mainframes. Any one of the division's core business applications would cost in the order of $20 million to develop and implement. Implementing a client/server architecture that leverages this investment is of key importance.

A second motivating factor is to realize the full benefits of using intelligent workstations. Corporate IT believes that the intelligent workstation with a GUI increases productivity, reduces training costs, and provides users with a single point of access to information resources. Because mainframe applications do not support GUI features, another architecture is required.

Because two divisions had previously selected nonmainframe platforms for their core business applications, a third motivating factor is the belief that client/server can be used to integrate the company's various islands of technology into an overall architecture.

### Progress

FinCo has initiated a pilot project to implement a distributed workstation-based development environment. Not only will this project provide FinCo's staff with experience in client/server implementation, it is also expected to reduce mainframe use, emphasizing one of the major benefits of client/server computing.

### Problems Encountered

The major obstacles for the company are the absence of a comprehensive strategic plan for incorporating client/server computing, the existence of organizational barriers to creating and implementing a distributed technology environment, and the high level of investment in current technology and core business systems.

The first two obstacles are the most critical. Clearly, FinCo needs to create a comprehensive plan to implement a client/server architecture. Furthermore, this plan needs the endorsement of senior management to influence the technology acquisition decisions of the business units. FinCo may have difficulty progressing with the implementation as long as business units are free to set workstations and networking standards independently from one another.

The high level of investment in the existing mainframe and resident core business systems may prohibit FinCo from implementing a complete client/server architecture. Instead, the company needs to design an architecture that delivers major benefits while attempting to maximize the investment in current technology—a not-so-easy task.

This case study illustrates how the absence of a client/server plan and the lack of centralized standards are major obstacles in implementing client/server.

## CASE STUDY 3: LIFE INSURANCE

InsurCo is successfully maintaining sales revenue and carefully monitoring expenses to sustain profitability in the competitive domestic life insurance market. At the initiative of the president, new IS management was hired two years ago with the mandate to realize a better return on technology investment. As a first step, the new IS management developed a long-range strategic plan to move InsurCo from its traditional mainframe platform to a client/server architecture that would best meet the company's changing information technology needs.

### Motivation

A client/server architecture is expected to enable InsurCo to distribute applications from the central IS department to the units that own them. With application processing residing in the business units, the business units will be able to make better business decisions about their requirements.

Like FinCo, InsurCo has a major investment in the corporate data center and mission-critical systems and cannot afford to replace its entire IT architecture. Client/server technology provides the mechanism to supplement the core business systems with more advanced applications. In this way, the company's IT architecture can evolve to one based on client/server.

IS management also realized that the business units needed applications faster than the current IS organization could provide them. Client/server applications require smaller development teams and result in quicker development of applications. Client/server facilitates the development of discrete data base applications in small autonomous units. Therefore, client/server reduces lead times to develop applications, allowing business units to make more effective use of technology.

### Progress

When IS started implementing client/server computing, one of its first initiatives was to centralize technology decisions. A second step was the creation of a network group to develop an enterprise network plan and to build such expertise within the company. This step allowed IS management to make effective decisions regarding specific network and workstation technologies with its new centralized control. In addition to moving application processing to the business units, client/server provides the ability to centrally manage the data and the environment across business units, thereby realizing economies of scale.

InsurCo had already determined that implementing client/server reduces costs. By avoiding the next mainframe upgrade and reducing operations staff, the company has realized a 30% decrease in its annual IS budget. These savings have allowed the company to fund the new client/server technology.

IS management developed an IT strategic plan based on client/server technology. In starting to implement the enterprise network plan, InsurCo was able to build individual network components with the full confidence that they would all work together as the network expanded. There are now 150 users on the network platform, some of whom use both the mainframe-based core business systems as well as supplemental client/server applications. In fact, the core business applications of two of the three InsurCo divisions have already evolved to be fully client/server in nature.

## Problems Encountered

While making significant progress over a two-year period, InsurCo has encountered three major problems. One obstacle is the lack of mature products to support a diverse and complex client/server computing environment. This environment demands tools for network management, security, and backup to control applications and data. Especially in the microcomputer networking market, tools are not robust enough to meet InsurCo's requirements.

Another major obstacle is the shortage of people with the skills to implement client/server technology—that is, people with technical skills in each of the four building block technologies. Client/server computing is also forcing a change in the profile of IS resources. Client/server applications development emphasizes the front-end identification of user requirements and the back-end implementation. The result is a greater need for business analysts and systems integrators and less demand for systems analysts and programmers. The availability of such resources for in-house IS staffs is limited because software houses and systems integrators gobble up the few skilled people who are available.

InsurCo's last major obstacle is the absence of a client/server development methodology. The modular characteristic of client/server means that there are three options to each development decision: reuse, buy, or build. Therefore, the IS department's role must evolve from a developer of systems to that of a systems integrator. The traditional development methodology is inadequate because more emphasis is needed on implementation considerations, such as backup and recovery of data on a distributed network. The marketplace has not yet developed methodologies that support client/server.

In summary, this case study highlights a company that has made significant progress in surmounting an entrenched information technology environment to implement client/server. However, the company continues to face some major obstacles.

## OVERCOMING THE BARRIERS TO IMPLEMENTATION

The problems encountered by each of the companies profiled can be classified into three categories. The first consists of technology-related problems, including those dealing with standards and the availability of client/server application packages. The second is associated with the IS infrastructure of a company, such as the existence of a clear client/server plan and the centralization of technology standards. The third is made up of obstacles in the organization as a whole, such as the attitude and capabilities of the user community. Together, these three categories form a triangular barrier to the successful implementation of client/server (see Exhibit IV-7-4). The challenge facing most companies implementing client/server is to collapse the three sides of the triangle in a coordinated fashion.

**Technology Barriers.** Probably the first barrier to collapse will be the technology barrier, because it will be torn down by the vendors. The critical success factor for companies that are waiting for additional products to emerge

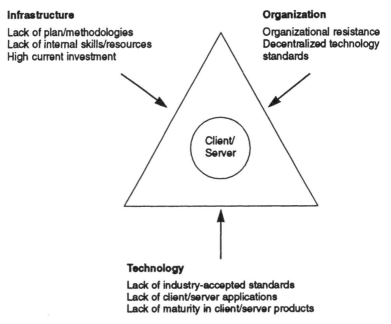

**Infrastructure**
Lack of plan/methodologies
Lack of internal skills/resources
High current investment

**Organization**
Organizational resistance
Decentralized technology
standards

Client/
Server

**Technology**
Lack of industry-accepted standards
Lack of client/server applications
Lack of maturity in client/server products

**Exhibit IV-7-4. Barriers to Client/Server Computing**

is to make technology decisions based on industry-accepted standards. Investing in proprietary hardware or software simply because vendors now offer client/server packages could limit the company in the long term.

**Infrastructure Requirements.** While the IS industry is knocking down the technology barrier, companies can focus on the more difficult infrastructure barriers. In each of the three cases, the initiative for moving to client/server computing came from top levels in the organization. This senior management support is important for success because it is at this level that infrastructure-related decisions—such as creation of strategies, commitment of plans, and allocation of resources—are made.

As seen in case studies 1 and 3, an important tool in overcoming the infrastructure barrier is a definitive strategic plan for implementing client/server technology. Whether it is the tactical approach used by InsurCo or the more strategic appproach used by AirCo depends on the state of a company's application environment. If the company has a considerable investment in existing business systems and technology, it may choose the tactical approach, concentrating on implementing client/server one application at a time. Companies with little or no investment in core applications can take a more top-down approach by introducing client/server across the entire organization (see Exhibit IV-7-5). Regardless of the approach, an important step is to devise a plan that clearly states what initiatives will be taken, when, and by whom.

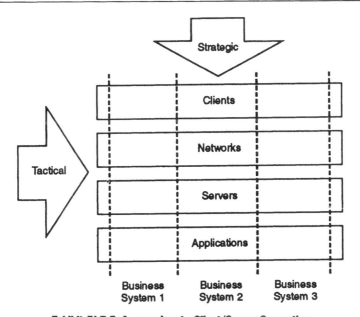

**Exhibit IV-7-5. Approaches to Client/Server Computing**

Once the plan is in place, it must be carried out. However, as InsurCo has learned, finding staff with the necessary skills and experience in client/server technology is a big part of the problem. One way of punching a hole in this part of the infrastructure barrier is to bring in experienced resources from outside the organization. Many systems integrators and consulting firms are building strong client/server resource pools; companies can use these firms as a way of initiating their client/server plans while transferring knowledge to their internal staff.

**Organizational Barriers.** The third and potentially most difficult barrier to overcome is the attitude of the organization as a whole to a new computing environment. A company may be either unprepared or unreceptive to changes brought about by client/server technology. These changes range from the technological (e.g., adopting GUIs) to the procedural, with the delegation of application administration to the user community. AirCo continues to find this to be the most significant of the three barriers and has attacked it by investing heavily in education and training.

In the case of FinCo, the organization barrier manifests itself in the form of distributed responsibility for establishing technology standards. This can make the implementation of client/server exceedingly difficult unless the standards are the same. These standards, if adhered to, can ensure that the technology acquired by non-IS departments can be integrated into a client/server architecture.

## SUMMARY

Of course, the relative strength of each of the major barriers to client/server computing varies from company to company. For example, the infrastructure barrier is almost nonexistent at AirCo, whereas it is almost insurmountable for FinCo. Before a company can make any serious movements in the direction of client/server, it must assess the strength of the barriers it faces and determine what resources are required to collapse them.

# IV-8

# Using Client/Server Technology to Enable Change: A Case Study

*DONALD SAELENS • STUART NELSON*

T he nation's capital is full of talk of making government more responsive to its constituents. The Minnesota Department of Revenue (DOR) is ahead of the game. For Minnesota businesses, a redesigned sales tax system will mean fewer dollars spent on lawyers and accountants to help them comply with the state's sales and use tax laws. For the state, the project is expected to enable the DOR to resolve delinquent accounts in fewer than 90 days (instead of as many as two years) and reduce the number of paper tax returns it receives.

This case study describes the reengineering project and its targeted changes in the department's mainframe-based systems and in the DOR's functional orientation. The IS management principles guiding the client/server development effort are also shared.

## FAILINGS OF A RIGID SYSTEM

As the state's tax- and revenue-collecting arm, the DOR has frequent and direct contact with Minnesota businesses and citizens. Under the old system, DOR employees operated within a compliance process that offered no systematic capability for accommodating exceptions or responding to changing business practices and demographics.

Continuous changes in the state's complex sales and use tax laws often left businesses confused about how to comply with the law. They simply received their tax forms in the mail with directions to file and pay. When they called for help, they found DOR employees hard to reach or unable to answer their questions because they did not have the appropriate information readily available. As a result, businesses ended up sending in the wrong returns, the incorrect payment, or nothing at all.

The state sales tax system is one of three major tax systems under the

DOR's jurisdiction (the others are income and property) serving 151,000 businesses and administering more than $2 billion in sales and use taxes annually. The sales tax system was originally created in the late 1960s as a temporary measure. Over the years, the tax became permanent; businesses also sprang up in the state, and many companies evolved into new lines of business. The tax system and the DOR fell out of sync with the times and with business growth, reaching the breaking point in the late 1980s. Employees could no longer trust the taxpayer data because maintaining updated information on all businesses was virtually impossible. In addition, it took months to properly process returns. The agency had trouble effectively dealing with problems and questions taxpayers had about their returns and payment.

The chief contributor to these problems was the DOR's computer system, built more than 25 years ago. Although the business environment changed over the years, the agency was constrained by the computer. Employees could not apply common sense to case management because the computer set the parameters. As a result, many good suggestions from employees on how to improve the process could not be accommodated because all cases had to be made to conform to the computer.

Another problem that hamstrung the agency was its functional orientation. Employees were charged with narrowly focused tasks—auditing, data entry, and payment processing, for example. This job design, which contributed to employees' inability to address taxpayer concerns outside of their area of expertise, was reinforced by the DOR's criteria for judging and rewarding employees. Instead of measuring employee performance with an eye toward the entire sales tax process, the agency emphasized the accomplishment of individual tasks and activities.

These inefficiencies took a toll on the state's bank account. Because the DOR could not swiftly identify taxpayer problems, many businesses—more than 13,000 in 1992—paid less than they should have or nothing at all. Problems in collecting this revenue were further compounded by the fact that more than half of the delinquent companies were no longer in business. Because of inaccurate information in the agency's computer, employees found it difficult to know who was in business and who was not. Because every delinquent case represents revenue potentially lost to the state, the DOR needed to make it easier for companies to file (and file correctly), and it had to give employees the tools and means to reduce the time it takes to track down and collect taxes from nonfilers.

## THE REENGINEERING PLAN

The agency began by redefining its mission and its image among taxpayers. In addition to holding regular meetings of top officials, the DOR solicited input from employees and taxpayers. The result of the two-year strategic planning process, the agency's first, was a comprehensive business plan and a succinct mission statement: to win compliance with Minnesota's revenue system.

What's unique about this mission statement is how it positions the agency in relation to taxpayers. Embodied in the new mission statement is a philosophical shift from demanding compliance to winning it. This new philosophy places equal emphasis on making it easy for people to file and pay the right amount of taxes, helping them understand what is expected of them, and enabling them to choose the right option for compliance that best fits their needs.

To reach this goal, changes were targeted in the department's mainframe-based systems and the DOR's functional orientation. Among the other constraints the agency faced were increasing workload, a declining cost/benefit ratio, and the end of several years of budget growth.

The agency had already received funding to replace the 1960s computer system, and DOR executives wanted to ensure that it was invested intelligently. After reviewing the challenges, the agency decided that rather than reautomating the current inefficient work processes, it should apply its funding to a complete reeningeering of the sales tax system.

The overall reengineering project involved three phases:

- *Phase 1—vision and strategy.* In January 1991, the DOR assessed the sales tax system business processes and established targets that would bring significant improvements in performance.
- *Phase 2—business process redesign.* In October 1991, teams used the targets established during phase 1 as the basis for creating and then developing the redesigned business processes.
- *Phase 3–development and implementation.* In August 1992, the final phase began involving the development, testing, and implementation of appropriate information systems, job designs, and management systems.

## PROCESS REDESIGN FOR CUSTOMER SERVICE

With the support of the highest levels of DOR leadership, the project team—which was composed of representatives from all areas of the agency, as well as several external consultants—redesigned the sales tax system's six key processes: taxpayer registration and profiling, sales and use tax filing, filing processing, ensuring compliance accuracy, ensuring payment, and performance information dissemination. (The information technology support for each of the redesigned processes is discussed later.) All processes cross divisional lines within the organization.

The result of this process redesign effort is a significantly streamlined sales tax system, the heart of which is the taxpayer registration and profiling process. Because many of the problems the DOR experienced in the past stemmed from its lack of timely and accurate taxpayer information, the new process was designed to handle greatly expanded registration options available to taxpayers and more detailed information about companies' operations.

Today, when a taxpayer registers, a unique, customized profile is created in the system's data base. This profile—which can be updated by any DOR employee or even by the taxpayer—collects and stores pertinent company information, including the type of business the company is involved in, how long it has been operating, its location, and its relationship with the DOR. In addition, taxpayers can register in several different ways (e.g., phone, fax, or mail) and can be accommodated regardless of whether they are filing permanently, seasonally, or just once.

DOR employees can now send customized return forms to taxpayers instead of generic forms. Another advantage of the customized taxpayer profile is that it allows the agency to be proactive in supplying businesses with tailored education and service options. Using information from the profile, the DOR can inform taxpayers of industry-specific educational offerings or potential law changes.

### Process Improvements

Before the process redesign, a taxpayer with payment problems was continually handed off to different employees, each of whom handled a small portion of the case. Now, most delinquent taxpayers can be assigned to one DOR employee who follows the case through to completion or resolution. Employees are empowered to make decisions throughout the process to resolve cases more quickly and to take accelerated enforcement action to ensure that every case is resolved within 90 days. The future work load of cases for businesses still operating is expected to improve significantly. Today's volume is 5,700 cases with an average age of 20 months and a balance of $3,500. By interceding early, DOR employees will be able to ensure that the state receives the revenue due more quickly and that the process does not become a burden on the taxpayer.

The greatest opportunity for improved efficiency is in the area of filing processing. Each year, the agency receives approximately 900,000 paper returns filed by Minnesota businesses. Every one of these returns must be received in the mailroom, opened, sorted, and routed. The information on the returns is entered manually into the computer by a team of employees, after which the team microfilms the returns for future reference. The DOR expects to reduce the number of paper returns it receives to 600,000 because many more taxpayers will qualify for quarterly or annual filing, and because state and local option tax returns have been combined. Initially, high-dollar businesses will be required to file and pay electronically; by 1995, the agency plans to further trim the number of paper returns it handles because 95% of businesses, regardless of dollar volume, will have the option to file electronically.

## INFORMATION SYSTEMS DECISIONS

Crucial to the success of the redesigned processes is the information technology developed to support them. The agency's 25-year-old mainframe system, patched numerous times throughout the years, could no longer deliver the performance necessary for DOR employees to be effective. Therefore, the team designed and build a completely new system, based on a client/server architecture that would be flexible enough to meet the needs of the redesigned environment.

Technological underpinnings of the system are Macintoshes and Windows-based microcomputers that are linked by local area networks to both a mini-server and the agency's legacy mainframe. This technology provides users with a much more friendly environment in which to operate. The client/server architecture brings processing power and critical information to employees' desktops. It can also easily accommodate the multitude of exceptions and differences that DOR employees encounter from taxpayers as large as Northwest Airlines to those as small as traditional mom-and-pop businesses.

In addition to the technology, several other factors contributed to the project's success. First was the fact that the agency's IS department was involved from the beginning of the project, not brought in at the tail end to build supporting systems in a vacuum. IS was also represented on the executive steering committee. This provided the opportunity for a better understanding among the IS staff of what the users needed to do their jobs more effectively.

Another factor was the set of IS management principles relating to, among other things, technology infrastructure, applications development, and data that the project team devised to guide itself through the project. These principles, listed in Exhibit IV-8-1, helped to keep team members focused on their mission.

Finally, the team selected a proprietary accelerated applications development methodology that makes extensive use of pilots and prototyping. The team thus avoided spending two years defining requirements and then pushing the system onto users all at once. The resulting system closely reflects users' true requirements (and was more readily accepted by employees). The methodology promotes the use of timeboxing, which limits the amount of time available for a task, a design iteration, a work session, or even an entire development project. The project team was able to define, design, and implement applications in 12 months.

## THE INFORMATION TECHNOLOGY CHANGES

The redesign effort resulted in significant changes to the way the DOR conducts business. Without the appropriate enabling technology, however, the improved operations would exist only on paper. The following sections discuss the major changes enacted in the agency's six key processes and how information technology was applied to make these changes a reality.

**Taxpayer Registration and Profiling.** The redesigned registration and profiling process expands the registration options available to taxpayers as

### Infrastructure

- It is important to make networked intelligent workstations available on every knowledge worker's desk.
- Cooperative processing will be implemented in a client/server architecture, with each platform handling what it does best.
- DOR will use an open systems architecture and avoid close, proprietary architectures.
- Mainframe systems will not be modified beyond what is necessary to support existing data.

### Applications Development

- Pilots and prototyping are to be used to help us learn and apply new ways to deliver information products.
- The underlying information technologies will be transparent to the user.
- Applications will be written to operate on or as close to the workstation as possible.
- Development will occur on IBM and compatible equipment, not on Macintoshes.

### Data

- Information will be located at the level that will best facilitate its shared access.
- Existing data will continue to be stored and maintained on the mainframe. New data will be stored and maintained on the client/server platform.
- Data redundancy will be avoided except in cases of performance.
- Data will be transmitted electronically whenever feasible.

**Exhibit IV-8-1. DOR's Guiding Principles**

---

well as the information about their operations. To support this new process, the project team developed the following:

- New registration screens, expanded taxpayer profile data base structure, and follow-up structure.
- A process to synchronize the new taxpayer data base with existing mainframe systems.
- A system to distribute and manage the disbursement of available taxpayer identification numbers.
- A system to accommodate taxpayers' electronic access to and update capability of their profile information.

**Sales and Use Tax Filing.** New filing cycles have been established; returns can be customized; and taxpayers can have options concerning the method they use to file and remit sales and use taxes. To address these changes, the team developed:

- A new flexible sales tax system to create customized, computer-readable sales tax returns based on a taxpayer's profile.
- A 24-hour touchtone computer response and personal computer bulletin.
- Software for customers' use in filing, paying, and requesting information on sales and use taxes.

In addition, the team upgraded the existing workstations to accommodate responses to and interactions with taxpayers and modified the core tax system on the mainframe to handle individual use tax reporting.

**Filing Processing.** The actual processing of the tax returns received by the agency presented several challenges to the project team. To satisfy new mandates—for example, that critical tax return information be available online on the day of arrival (with the balance of that information being available within seven calendar days), that filing information must be 98% accurate, and that tax remittances be deposited immediately—the team implemented an imaging and scanning system to capture filing and payment information and developed interfaces between the core sales tax system and other existing systems.

**Ensuring Compliance Accuracy.** The profile information obtained during the registration process is used by the agency to customize its services to taxpayers on the basis of their needs and compliance history. To provide access to such information, the team developed:

- Software for electronic links to taxpayers.
- A compliance screening data base with an automatic update from transaction data bases.
- Statistical applications and expert systems to identify candidates for specific compliance actions.
- A workflow management and case preparation system to automatically assign and track compliance activities.

**Ensuring Payment.** This process is divided into accounts receivable resolution and registered nonfiler resolution. In the new process, delinquent taxpayers are to be assigned to one DOR employee who has discretion in choosing how to deal with them. The goal is to resolve all cases within 90 days of identification. The process is supported by LANs that provide access to the workflow management system as well as other information systems and offer a place to record case activity for future reference in assistance with case resolution.

**Performance Information Dissemination.** As part of the process redesign, new measures have been instituted to monitor the department's progress in winning compliance. To help management in applying these measures, the project team developed automated performance measurement capabilities and links in all new information systems, and created and installed a technological infrastructure to support the development and operation of the online systems containing the sales tax performance measures.

## ORGANIZATIONAL IMPACT

As can be expected, an effort of this magnitude has profound implications for the organization, particularly the IS department, which had typically taken the lead in enacting change. The project generated a considerable amount of uneasiness among the IS staff, especially certain technology specialists who faced a completely new technological environment and new job responsibilities. It was important for the top levels of the organization to provide assurance to these employees.

One of the biggest challenges the project team faced was approaching the redesign of jobs with the same openness of mind used in redesigning the processes. When it comes to the human perspective, friends and colleagues are involved. These issues cannot be circumvented, because it doesn't help the organization or its employees to adapt to the changes if they are.

Project leaders initially thought they could gain employee acceptance of the new system if they just communicated to employees what was happening. The team quickly discovered that communication is not enough; people actually have to start doing the new work and using the new technology as soon as possible.

One of the ways this was accomplished was by instituting a technology lab in which employees could feel safe to experiment and make mistakes. Although communication about what the organization is trying to accomplish alleviates some concerns employees have about new technology, there's no substitute for hands-on experience.

On a broader scale, all DOR employees experienced firsthand how information technology could be used to break down organizational barriers and draw people together. One of the earliest deliverables of the project was an integrated infrastructure of 500 workstations equipped with groupware products. Within four to five days of installing the application, employees who were formerly not allowed to communicate with each other were in touch by electronic mail, and DOR leadership could communicate directly and immediately with all employees.

Lotus Notes was installed as a departmentwide tool for team members in the sales tax reeningeering project. Discussion data bases were established for the individual teams that focused on the separate business processes that made up the overall sales tax system. These data bases were used to share ideas and concepts and to coordinate information across teams. In addition, data bases were established to track project issues and their resolution, as well as to document decisions that could be referred to as needed by any member of the project.

## WAS IT WORTH THE EFFORT?

The project has undoubtedly been stressful and complex for DOR employees, demanding a lot of energy, time, and brainpower from the entire DOR staff during the past two years. The outcome benefits both the taxpayers and the agency. For taxpayers, the new system not only makes it easier to comply with the tax laws, but it will also reduce their cost of compliance. If they have questions about taxes, businesses know where to go for help, and they can get that help much more quickly and completely than before. In addition to being given instructions on what they must do to comply, they are asked what changes would help them comply more easily. Businesses are encouraged to participate in the policy-making process to ensure that sound, realistic policies are created.

For DOR employees, the reengineered environment and new technology give them the flexibility to be creative in how they approach their work. Instead of single-function jobs, employees have multifunctional responsibilities. Rather than focusing inward on information flow, employees emphasize an external customer view. They are no longer handcuffed to a rigid method of dealing with taxpayers largely because the new client/server system supports the new processes and provides everyone with instant access to important information.

The project is nearly completed, and those involved plan to take some time to reflect on what went right, what went wrong, and how the DOR can best capitalize on the new system. The agency's next step is to consolidate its gains and make sure that the new systems it put in place work and work well. That includes taking steps to institutionalize the new system. By making sure that all aspects of the project—human, process, and technical—are continually nurtured, the DOR is reinforcing the attitudes, behavior, and practices needed to support the new processes and structures. It is also prepared to make ongoing process improvements to ensure that the system remains pertinent, flexible, and effective.

# Section V
# Network Technology

When mainframe networks were originally developed, their primary purpose was the sharing of work loads between systems. As networks evolved, they allowed users to communicate with the mainframe, as well as each other, to share information. With the introduction of local area networks (LANs) to link microprocessors together, processing capability was distributed from the mainframe throughout the organization, even to the desktops of individual users.

In the 1990s, the network has become the backbone of many corporations. Without an effective network, many businesses would cease to exist. The complexity of today's network is enormous. LANs can be linked to other LANs, which, in turn, can be connected to mainframes and other LANs. Although the flexibility for expanding networks has contributed greatly to the growth of many corporations, designing, implementing, managing, and securing these networks has become a daunting task. This section addresses a wide range of issues associated with today's networks.

As with all other areas of information systems, network technology continues to change at a rapid pace. The data center manager must be aware of the current state of network design technology. Chapter V-1, "Enterprise Network Design Technology," reviews the current state of network design technology, emphasizing software, network optimization, and system performance.

It may be that the complexity of managing today's extensive networks is rapidly moving beyond the capabilities of network management personnel. Therefore, new tools must be developed and new management practices put into effect. Chapter V-2, "An Expert Operating System that Manages Multinetwork Communications," addresses the concept of using expert systems technology to manage large-scale networks.

Simply designing and building networks is only the first step in effective network management. Because the network is such an integral part of the business for many corporations, providing security for the network is a major responsibility of all those personnel associated with managing the network. Chapter V-3, "Securing Distributed Data Networks," and Chapter V-4, "Distributed Network Security," discuss the issues that must be addressed to provide secure network operations.

Many data center managers now have direct responsibility for their companies' LANs. Ensuring the reliability and availability of these LANs is a major concern for the data center manager. Chapter V-5, "The Data Center Manager's Guide to Ensuring LAN Reliability and Availability," provides practical advice for fulfilling this responsibility.

Data center managers often become so involved in the intricate details of implementing and managing a network that they overlook necessary controls that must be maintained to ensure the continued effectiveness of the network. Chapter V-6, "Auditing LANs," provides the data center manager with an auditor's view of the types of controls that should be in place for a LAN. Following the author's advice can give the data center manager a great deal of confidence that the LAN is being managed as effectively, and securely, as possible.

# V-1
# Enterprise Network Design Technology

*ROSHAN L. SHARMA*

N etwork design is an important but neglected component of the network management process. Part of the reason for its neglect is that it is a highly multidisciplinary field, and it can intimidate even the most experienced manager. All network design efforts involve several distinct, quite different tasks. A data base is created that describes the customer premise equipment and the communication facilities serving all network locations. The end-to-end multi-hour traffic flows between all network locations are modeled. End-to-end performance requirements for all forms of communication are defined. Traffic growth for the life cycle of the network system is modeled. Several networks, all using available technologies, are designed. The best network design, based on cost, cutover considerations, and performance, is selected. The performance of the network after cutover is tested. The analytical tools are updated and preparations are made for the next design cycle. The results of the process are documented.

Consideration of these tasks suggests that a data center manager needs a combination of perseverance, traffic engineering knowledge, an understanding of (and access to) user-friendly, interactive design tools, electrical engineering skills, and marketing savvy (to convince senior management of the new network's value). The knowledge required to perform these tasks far exceeds that demanded of any other corporate officer.

## DATA BASE

The first task is by far the most time-consuming. A relational data base should at least list the 10-digit telephone numbers, associated vertical and horizontal coordinates, all customer premises equipment (each record should include the vendor's name, date of installation, and single point-of-contact), the use level of each piece of equipment, type and number of communications facilities serving each location, and the points-of-presence of local exchange carriers and other common carriers along with their vertical and horizontal coordinates.

## TRAFFIC FLOW, PERFORMANCE REQUIREMENTS, NETWORK GROWTH

The next three tasks quantify traffic for all hours and all types of communications between all significant pairs of locations, based on the principles of traffic engineering. This set of tasks also includes the creation of meaningful models of traffic growth for the next applicable life cycle.

## NETWORK DESIGN

The design of several possible networks requires the availability of a user-friendly, state-of-the-art, computer-based network design tool that can generate strategic network alternatives in an iterative fashion and that can accommodate emerging communications technologies. The lack of such a tool is probably the most significant reason that managers neglect the network design effort. Consequently, the design of many enterprise networks is based on engineering dogma or the designer's hunches, or a design inherited from the previous management is used. In addition, many enterprise networks are transformed slowly during their lifetime into unrecognizable and severely unoptimized entities, particularly compared with the networks that could result from the use of new communications technologies. Strategic and tactical network planners estimate that enterprises can reduce monthly network management costs by 40% if networks are designed with modern design software and the managers consider cost-effective emerging technologies.

## SELECTION, SELLING THE NETWORK, POSTCUTOVER PERIOD

Selecting and selling the best solution to management is an art mastered primarily through experience; an emphasis on life cycle costs and savings analyses is generally effective. Testing the performance of the system during the postcutover period and documenting the results validates and can also improve the software package's analytical tools.

## MODERN ENTERPRISE NEEDS

An enterprise must introduce new products or services just to stay abreast of its competitors. Some enterprises (e.g., the regional Bell operating companies and state and federal governments) must maintain cost-effective networks whose administration and management satisfy legislative requirements and the scrutiny of public utility commissions.

Digital transmission technology is making available new communications facilities (e.g., T1, fractional T1, fractional T3, privately owned digital microwave, and fiber optics). Architectures for hybrid networks (employing, for example, frame relay, switched multimegabit data service, asynchronous transfer mode) are either available now or soon will be. Reasonably priced customer premises equipment based on digital multiplexers for access control either at all customer locations or on nodes attached to the backbone network can now be purchased. The hybrid networks that can be implemented using this equipment and the new services and architectures can lead to considerable cost savings over existing networks.

Corporate strategic planners engaged in network design should understand the needs of a modern enterprise. A typical strategic planning cycle lasts three to five years and entails the continual evaluation of the goals and needs of the enterprise and its competitors and an understanding of new communications technologies, customer premises equipment, and networking standards. The goal of a communications strategy is to deploy these technologies cost-effectively and enhance the productivity of a network's users. A strategic planning group should work closely with the IS department and should have access to all the necessary resources and tools.

## OUTSOURCING

Experience shows that a strategic planning group can succeed only if the enterprise does not use outsourcing. No outside consultant or company can fully understand the demands of the marketplace, the structure of the IS department, and network operations. Only the internal strategic planning group can do that. Outsourcing companies have their own bottom line considerations, and these may run counter to the interests of their customers.

## NETWORK DESIGN TOOLS

A network design tool should enable the designer to work in a manner similar to the pencil and paper (sometimes known as back-of-the-envelope) methods used in the past for simpler voice-only networks. A user-friendly tool should help the strategic planning group obtain feasible network approximations iteratively and interactively. The following examples illustrate situations that require the design tool to deliver either rapid modeling and designing or quick conceptual solutions.

## Example 1

An enterprise has 25 locations interconnected by a single-level T1 voice network, as depicted in Exhibit V-1-1. What will happen if these same locations are served by a two-level hierarchical network with uniform routing over T1 links? Network design software shows that for the two-level hierarchical network (see Exhibit V-1-2) a three-switch design is the optimum solution. Monthly transmission costs fall from $248,162 with the existing single-level network to $151,239 for the new configuration.

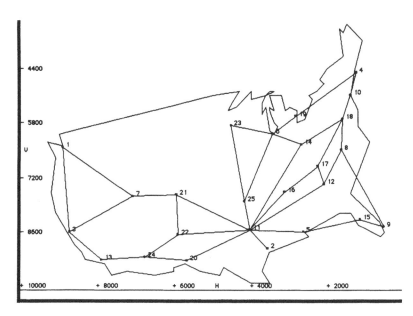

**Notes:**
Monthly access line costs: $248,162.
Monthly trunking costs: $0.
Total monthly access line and trunking costs: $248,162.

**Exhibit V-1-1. Existing 25-Node T1 Network Topology**

---

## Example 2

An enterprise has an efficient, optimized two-level, 41-node data network with three switches arranged in a star topology (see Exhibit V-1-3). The existing traffic loads are accommodated on 9,600-bps lines. Can any cost saving be realized by substituting a three-level network with the same topology, seven concentrators, and two tandem switches? The configuration solution is illustrated in Exhibit V-1-4, where it is shown that monthly costs can be reduced from $29,616 to $23,169.

## Example 3

An enterprise anticipates a 20-fold increase in traffic over a 41-node 9,600-bps link data network (e.g., either network depicted in Exhibits V-1-3 and V-1-4) when computer-aided design and computer-aided manufacturing (CAD/CAM) and electronic data interchange (EDI) applications are introduced. What are the optimum network topologies if the 9,600-bps links are replaced by 56,000-bps facilities? Exhibit V-1-5 shows a star topology configuration to handle the increased line speed, and Exhibit V-1-6 arranges the network in a multidrop topology.

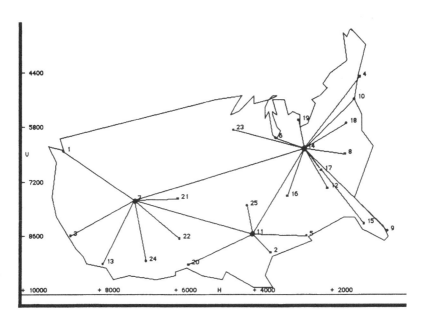

**Notes:**
* Represents a switch.

Monthly access line costs: $127,551.
Monthly trunking costs: $23,688.
Monthly access line and trunking costs: $151,239.

**Exhibit V-1-2. Proposed Two-Level T1 Network with Three Switches**

## MAJOR NETWORK DESIGN ISSUES

Current literature dealing with networking is often confusing, being characterized by buzzwords, hype, and the presentation of too many solutions with no
single solution for a particular class of user. Some articles recommend that an
enterprise network employ only virtual lines; other articles advocate the use
of both private leased lines and virtual facilities. LAN design articles do not
clarify the merits of optimizing a LAN for its intended department's use versus
optimizing it for interconnection, through frame relay or other WAN services,
with other LANs. New types of technologies and new network architectures
are described, but the readers are left to assess the usefulness of the new
facilities in respect to their own enterprises.

The network design process is basically concerned with two issues: topological optimization (the way network nodes are connected to one another
while satisfying a limited number of design and performance constraints)
and system performance (end-to-end connection and response times, path
congestion, and link availability).

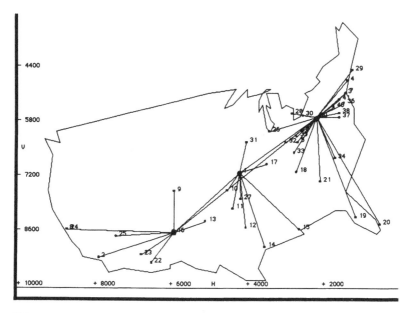

**Notes:**
Monthly access line costs: $26,805.
Monthly trunking costs: $2,811.
Monthly access line and trunking costs: $29,616.
Monthly cost to move one megabit of data: 80.82 cents.

**Exhibit V-1-3. A Two-Level Data Network with Three Switches**

---

Issues related to system performance are most affected by network topology. Recurring network cost is another important consideration and is also determined by the network's topology.

Network design tools provide approximations to performance questions. Precise, closed-form solutions for end to-end system performance are very difficult to obtain. Solutions based on computer simulations apply only to a specialized set of initial network conditions and then only when calculations reach statistical equilibrium. Proving out the network by testing is becoming difficult because of the extremely low error rates and fast response times the tests must document. Articles that discuss LAN interconnection ignore the difficulties that the interconnection of voice networks caused network designers during the 1970s.

## THE OLD NETWORK DESIGN TECHNOLOGY

Previous generations of network design technology are characterized by the use of specialized tools for voice, data, and video networks. They usually run

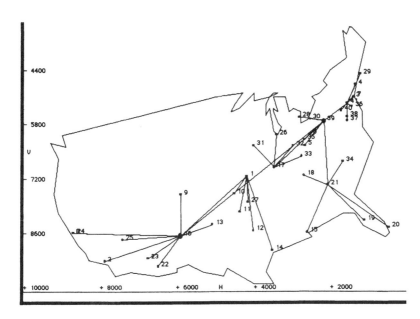

**Notes:**
For level 1 (7 concentrators):
    Monthly access line costs: $23,169.
    Trunking costs: $0.
    Total cost to move one megabit of data: 85.81 cents.
For levels 2 and 3 (2 switches):
    Monthly access line costs: $26,666.
    Trunking costs: $1,096.
    Total cost to move one megabit of data: 76.37 cents.

**Exhibit V-1-4. A Three-Level Proposed Data Network with Two Switches and Seven Concentrators**

---

on mainframes, distancing the network designer from the host processor, and making the software expensive to license and use. The jobs are invariably batch processed and the results become available, after a processing delay, in printout form. Each change of a design parameter or study of a new technology entails another delay. The absence of graphics causes additional delays in interpreting results.

## Tariffs

The old design technology also requires the use of an extensive tariff data base. These tariffs have been increasing in number and changing quite rapidly since the divestiture of AT&T in 1984. The complexity of the tariff data base is the main reason mainframes are used. If such a data base is incorporated into a minicomputer or a minicomputer-based workstation, sizable processing delays occur.

355

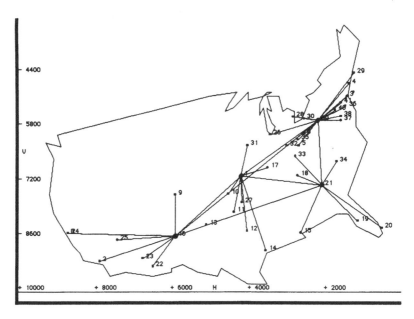

**Notes:**
Monthly access line costs: $54,511.
Monthly trunking costs: $12,683.
Monthly access line and trunking costs: $67,194.
Monthly cost to move one megabit of data: 9.16 cents.

**Exhibit V-1-5. A Proposed Two-Level Data Network with Four Switches in a Star Topology**

Because enterprise networks are designed or planned for a future period, exact tariff accuracy is unnecessary. In addition, because network topologies do not change with changes in any given tariff (they change only with varying design parameters and technologies), a simplified set of existing or new tariffs can be used and excellent network optimization results obtained quickly even on a desktop workstation. At a later time, these topologies can be analyzed for cost using one of the many available personal computer line pricer products. This two-step approach separates the network design algorithms and the tariff data base. The network design package should not require updating just because a tariff changed slightly.

## Design Tools

A useful design package should be an intuitive tool in the hands of an expert network designer. Network design tools based on the older technology are not interactive or user friendly. Lacking an acceptable graphical user interface, they require a long training and familiarization period.

Network design tools based on older technology are not flexible enough to handle the multilevel network hierarchies made possible by new customer

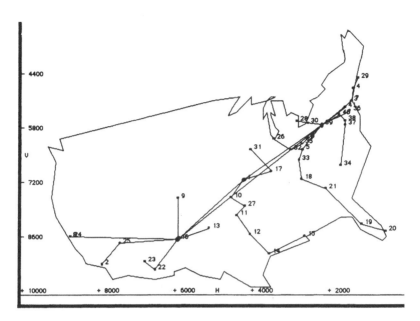

**Notes:**
Monthly access line costs: $59,913.
Monthly trunking costs: $8,702.
Monthly access line and trunking costs: $68,615.
Monthly cost to move one megabit of data: 9.36 cents.

**Exhibit V-1-6. A Proposed Two-Level Data Network with Three Switches in a Multidrop Topology**

premises equipment (e.g., low-cost multiplexers, voice and data compression units, tandem switches, and bridges, routers, and gateways), leased or fully owned digital transmission facilities (e.g., T1, fractional T1, T3, fiber, and digital microwave), and network architectures based on virtual services (e.g., X.25, fast packet, frame relay, and SMDS). Handling of mixed topologies through the process of topological superimposition is also generally not allowed with the older design tools.

## NEWER NETWORK DESIGN TECHNOLOGIES

Older network design packages did not produce detailed end-to-end performance models for the various architectures previously mentioned, but neither do the newer ones. End-to-end performance evaluation for controlled situations have always been the province of university or private research laboratories. Network design packages use simplifications of operational environments. Problems occur only when users of these network design packages treat the

| Vendor | Package | Advantages | Disadvantages |
|---|---|---|---|
| The Aries Group-MPSG Rockville MD (301) 840-0800 | Separate voice and data packages | Well-tested for voice networks | Host-based, old technology |
| BGS Systems Waltham MA (617) 891-0000 | BEST/1 Series | Best for SNA networks | Host-based, old technology |
| Comware Systems, Inc. New York NY (212) 686-5558 | NODE1 (voice) | User-friendly | Voice networks only |
| Connections Telecommunications Brockton MA (508) 584-8885 | Distributed network design system | Well-tested | Separate voice and data |
| Economics and Technology, Inc. Boston MA (800) 225-2496 | Network planning workbench | Integrated voice and data and hierarchical networks | Single-node, backbone only |
| HTL Telemanagement, Ltd. Burtonsville MD (800) 225-5485 | Several voice and data modules | Good for voice | Separate voice and data, no graphics |
| JBA, Inc. Louisville TX (214) 436-8334 | Hybrid network design system | One of the best for voice | Slow on a microcomputer |
| Network Design & Analysis Markham Ontario (800) 337-4234 | AUTONET Designer (data only) | Very thorough in modeling | No hierarchical data networks |
| Network Analysis Center, Inc. Syosset NY (516) 364-2255 | Mind (data) | Well-tested | Best for data |
| Quintessential Solutions, Inc. San Diego CA (619) 280-7535 | Network designer module | User-defined tariffs | Data networks only |
| Racal-Datacom Boxborough MA (800) 722-2555 | Network resource planning tool (data) | Highly modular | Expensive |
| Telecom Network Science Dallas TX (214) 691-6790 | ECONETS | Integrated voice and data and automated call distribution | Manually entered tariffs only |

**Exhibit V-1-7. Currently Available Network Design Tools**

resulting performance metrics as if they were exact descriptions of real networks.

Software packages are available for simulating system performance and can evaluate, for example, LANs (voice or data) and WANs (which consist of interconnected LANs). However, the simulation program has to reflect the exact network topology and the underlying communications protocols, and it must be completely debugged before the performance metrics (e.g., throughput and end-to-end response times) can be evaluated. Simulation of a typical enterprise network requires considerable run-time; so simulation tools are not interactive. For the same reason, computer simulation is not an ideal method for discovering an optimum network topology.

Iterative, user-friendly, interactive design tools are available for several current workstation platforms. Many of these tools can compute end-to-end connect and response times for unusual operational conditions; some provide special tools for analyzing system security and reliability.

Even the use of the intuitive graphical user interfaces does not eliminate the need for an expert network designer or architect. Because the designer works by repeatedly changing system variables in order to observe the effect on the network, the design package is useful only if it provides solutions rapidly. To allow this during the topological optimization phase, it is necessary to reduce or eliminate reliance on the mainframe or a detailed tariff data base.

Some vendors make available to their customers remote access to the vendor's host-resident network design software. However, delays and high communications costs tend to discourage this practice. Exhibit V-1-7 lists some well-known network design tools available today, along with some advantages and disadvantages of each.

## SUMMARY

The time-consuming tasks involved in the process of network design are often the reason it is overlooked or neglected by many managers. Consequently, companies that do not maintain efficient, cost-effective networks capable of handling constant change may have trouble staying abreast of their competition. To facilitate network design, today's strategic planners can use a variety of interactive desktop tools to help them optimize their network's topology.

# V-2
# An Expert Operating System That Manages Multinetwork Communications

*YEMMANUR JAYACHANDRA • HAL SANDERS • GITA JAYACHANDRA*

A wave of technology following the tide of organizational divestiture has swept through corporate communications networks, replacing the previously pervasive Bell System's centralized networks with multivendor distributed networks. Managing these networks requires real-time surveillance and control to ensure that all their components operate efficiently and reliably. A system for managing these large, diverse, multivendor networks is long overdue.

According to industry literature, network technology is entering its fifth generation. The characteristics of each generation are:

- *First generation.* These networks use a shared transmission facility.
- *Second generation.* These are switched utility networks of data and voice.
- *Third generation.* These are standardized architecture networks, including the Tymnet and Telenet X.25 networks, IBM System Network Architecture (SNA) networks, Northern Telecom SL-1 private automatic branch exchange (PABX), IBM and Rolm computerized PABX, and AT&T S/85 PABX.
- *Fourth generation.* These are fully interoperable application networks, including the manufacturing automation protocol and technical office protocol (MAP/TOP), IBM System Application Architecture (SAA), OSI file-transfer access management service (FTAM), and CCITT recommendation X.400 message-handling service.
- *Fifth generation.* These networks use new and proposed standards and protocols, including the broadband integrated switched digital network (B-ISDN), synchronous optical network transport (SONET), Bellcore switched multimegabit data service (SMDS), ANSI fiber distributed data interface (FDDI), and IEEE 802.6 metropolitan area network.

During the next decade, all five generations of network technologies will coexist in network environments. Given the current and emerging network technology, the cost of network operations and management for a three-year period could far exceed the capital appropriation cost of the networks themselves, and the qualified IS professionals to operate them could become increasingly scarce and expensive. The cost of a labor-saving expert system for integrated and interoperable multinetwork administration and control could easily be justified. Modeling the thought processes of a team of human experts, a prototype extended network expert operating system (ENEOS) at the Bank of America in San Francisco is helping manage multivendor, multinetwork communications facilities.

## ENEOS DESIGN

The ENEOS architecture was designed to manage networks of multiple and arbitrary types and topologies and consists of seven knowledge bases, more than 16 units, 200 frames, 380 operating rules, and 65 LISP procedures. It is an easily maintainable expert system capable of autonomously operating various corporate networks and can be easily upgraded to accommodate emerging fifth-generation technologies that contain embedded management channels and protocols.

The ENEOS elements use parallel processing to operate in real time and are partially distributed. A finite inference frame processor engine, the key component of ENEOS, organizes its collection of rules into frames. The finite inference frame processor performs parallel rule processing at high speeds byusing frames as case or situation inferences. The use of a frame-based inference engine gives ENEOS the following capabilities and features:

- End-to-end connection management through several heterogeneous networks (e.g., public and private local area, wide area, and metropolitan area networks with multivendor facilities and semiautonomous operations).
- Self-learning, self-reconfiguring, self-improving, and self-repairing algorithms for fault-tolerant and autonomous operations.
- Mechanisms for adapting to internal and external environmental changes or problems by deducing tasks and reorganizing, and for the parallel execution of expert programs for optimal, self-preserving network operations.
- Real-time expert system control for trouble-free voice, video, and data communications.
- The use of standard, high-level human-machine and machine-network protocols with flexible interface adaptations to accommodate such current and emerging management channels as SONET's embedded operating channel and T1/T3 data channels.
- A uniform intelligent user interface that prompts the user for input and suggests actions for optimal network operations.

These features enable ENEOS to:

- Provide online network servicing, including in-service tests and controls, ensuring maximum uptime and minimal service outages.
- Measure, with loopback capability, the bit-error rate, the error-free seconds, and the line-signal-to-noise characteristics of any desired line segment.
- Use CCITT B-ISDN specifications to control signals and catastrophic degradation.
- Identify the cause of gradual or catastrophic degradation.
- Perform self-repair operations by reconfiguring with alternate or backup facilities where available.
- Advise the network administrator regarding repair and recovery procedures when manual operations are required.

ENEOS can inject various stress and monitoring signals into a pseudochannel (e.g., the embedded operating channel of the SONET, the extended super frame data channel of T1 links, and the management channel of proprietary networks). ENEOS then uses an expert module to analyze the measured test data, identify the most likely cause of events, and decide to take appropriate actions on the relevant network elements.

An ENEOS network operating environment (see Exhibit V-2-1) involves multiple ENEOSs to ensure reliability and to survive throughout the network; each ENEOS controls its own local network. At any given time, however, only one ENEOS can exercise global control, although all ENEOS elements are physically identical.

An important attribute of ENEOS is its ability to recognize multivendor, multigeneration networks and to adapt its operations to manage them. On a real-time basis, given a global network view, ENEOS can do the following for network management:

- *Configuration.* Reporting network status, including bandwidth management information and autorouting and rerouting.
- *Problem-resolution.* Performing comprehensive diagnostics and reporting all problems, noting status and resolution.
- *Change.* Executing changes in links, circuits, and nodes and reporting prior and pending moves and changes.
- *Performance oversight.* Combining the reporting of alarms with the use of circuit-connection details.
- *Security.* Keeping out unauthorized users.

ENEOS can also perform the following offline network management functions:

- Asset management to track network assets inventory (e.g., workstations, file-servers, printers and servers, modems, multiplexers, channel service units, circuits, leased lines, and hosts) and generate inventory reports.
- Customized billing and accounting and generation of appropriate reports.

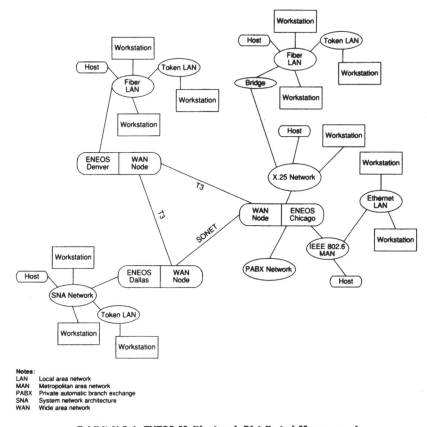

**Notes:**
LAN    Local area network
MAN    Metropolitan area network
PABX   Private automatic branch exchange
SNA    System network architecture
WAN    Wide area network

**Exhibit V-2-1. ENEOS Multinetwork Distributed Management**

---

- Network administration, expansion and modification, and resource allocation.

## PROTOCOLS AND STANDARDS

Large business networks consist of elements that range from host computers, workstations, and terminals, to front-end communications processors, multiplexers, statistical multiplexers, channel service units, and wideband and narrowband leased lines that use terrestrial fiber-optic cables, copperwires, and microwave satellite transmissions. No single vendor can supply all of these network elements.

There are many popular methods of network control and operation, including subdividing large and complex networks into smaller networks or installing them separately to geographic region, vendor or equipment type, or application type. Current network management methods are based on six product categories: modems, LANs, PABXs, T1/T3 multiplexers, host-based management systems, and public inter- and intra-LATA WAN-based management systems covering the spectrum of all the other management systems (see Exhibit V-2-2).

National and international committees are developing standards for network protocols and messages. Some of the more important of these are the ANSI X3T5 standard for OSI management and the Exchange Carriers Standards Association's T1M1.5 standard for SONET management and maintenance. Important de facto standards created by dominant vendors include the IBM NetView and AT&T Unified Network Management System and network management and operation standards. ENEOS incorporates these standards as well as significant enhancements. Exhibit V-2-3 lists the OSI network management layers and the protocols that have been adopted in ENEOS.

ENEOS integrates an installed base of subdivided networks into a cooperative network that uses expert system applications, broadening the scope of the emerging OSI network management standards. ENEOS extends its services to multinetworks with three basic modules: the presentation adaptation and learning module, the function adaptation and learning module, and the interface adaptation and learning module (see Exhibit V-2-4).

## ARCHITECTURE

ENEOS models the thought processes of a team of human experts when it assesses the current network environment and determines the most reasonable solution to any problem, choosing from a pool of existing possibilities. For ENEOS to support online management with a global network perspective, its architecture had to include stringent real-time capabilities.

ENEOS is vulnerable to damage, however, like any network element. To

| 1. Host-Based Management | | | |
|---|---|---|---|
| 2. Modem-Based Management | 3. LAN-Based Management | 4. PABX-Based Management | 5. T1/T3 Multiplexer-Based Management |
| 6. Public Inter- and Intra-LATA WAN-Based Management | | | |

**Note:**
LATA   Local access and transport area

**Exhibit V-2-2. Network Management Methods Organized by Product Categories**

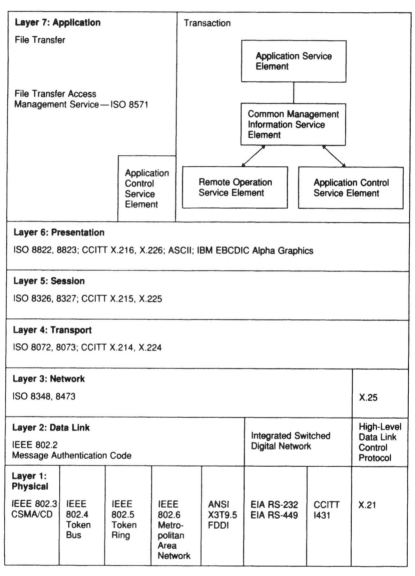

**Exhibit V-2-3. OSI Layer Services and Protocols Adopted by ENEOS**

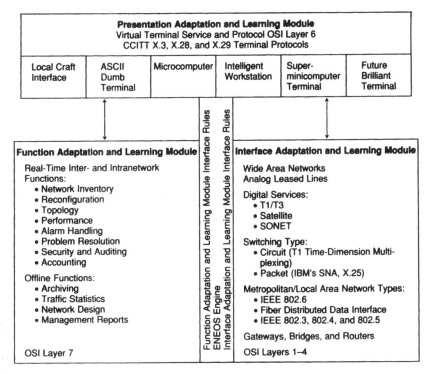

| Presentation Adaptation and Learning Module | | | | | |
| --- | --- | --- | --- | --- | --- |
| Virtual Terminal Service and Protocol OSI Layer 6 | | | | | |
| CCITT X.3, X.28, and X.29 Terminal Protocols | | | | | |
| Local Craft Interface | ASCII Dumb Terminal | Microcomputer | Intelligent Workstation | Super- minicomputer Terminal | Future Brilliant Terminal |

**Function Adaptation and Learning Module**

Real-Time Inter- and Intranetwork Functions:
- Network Inventory
- Reconfiguration
- Topology
- Performance
- Alarm Handling
- Problem Resolution
- Security and Auditing
- Accounting

Offline Functions:
- Archiving
- Traffic Statistics
- Network Design
- Management Reports

OSI Layer 7

Function Adaptation and Learning Module Interface Rules

Interface Adaptation and Learning Module Interface Rules

Function Adaptation and Learning Module
ENEOS Engine
Interface Adaptation and Learning Module

**Interface Adaptation and Learning Module**

Wide Area Networks
Analog Leased Lines

Digital Services:
- T1/T3
- Satellite
- SONET

Switching Type:
- Circuit (T1 Time-Dimension Multi- plexing)
- Packet (IBM's SNA, X.25)

Metropolitan/Local Area Network Types:
- IEEE 802.6
- Fiber Distributed Data Interface
- IEEE 802.3, 802.4, and 802.5

Gateways, Bridges, and Routers

OSI Layers 1–4

**Exhibit V-2-4. ENEOS Extended Services for Multinetwork Integrated Management**

ensure continued operation in the event of damage, the ENEOS architecture allows the cloning and replication of ENEOS functions at alternate ENEOS sites. One ENEOS is elected as a master according to certain election rules; it then controls the global network operations with continuous help from the other ENEOS elements that have local control of their respective domain networks (see Exhibit V-2-1). If the master ENEOS is disabled, a second ENEOS is elected as a master to provide continuous control of global network operations, avoiding communication outages. If a local ENEOS fails, the nearest ENEOS assumes control of the domain. Exhibit V-2-5 shows an architectural functional block diagram for ENEOS.

Multiple networks can be managed through either a centralized system or a distributed system with several linked expert systems. ENEOS uses a distributed approach because—through smaller mass-produced processors—it provides more computing power than a centralized approach can. In a distributed approach, expert system modules can be applied wherever needed throughout the system by working in parallel with local processors, thereby reducing the chances of a failure at a single point.

The disadvantages of a distributed processing approach include overhead

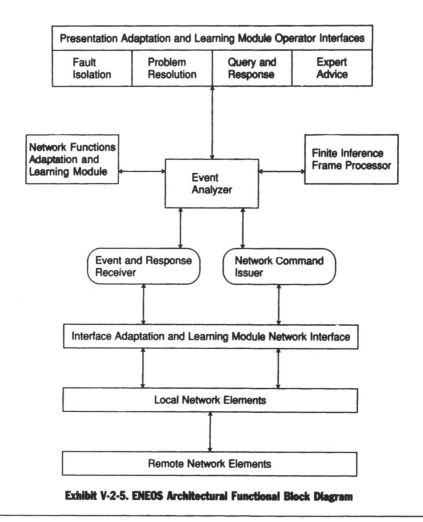

**Exhibit V-2-5. ENEOS Architectural Functional Block Diagram**

for cooperative communications among the ENEOS entities, complex election rules for choosing a master ENEOS to control global operations, complex timing and synchronization for coordinating subordinate and master ENEOS entities, and the amount of bandwidth for the management channels. These disadvantages are gradually being eliminated by development of fast processors, inexpensive bandwidth, and sophisticated expert system technologies.

## EVENT ANALYZER

As shown in Exhibit V-2-5, the ENEOS event analyzer collects data on events as they are generated by network elements and their components. This analyzer gathers and interprets raw data intelligently, simulating a team of human experts. Its output is either an operational command to a network element, accompanied by an alarm, or simply a status report for the operator. When ENEOS encounters a problem, the system activates audio and visual alarms.

In large networks, event analyzers perform several complex tasks. An abnormal condition triggers many events, each of which provides information that can help identify and resolve the overall problem. A single event is generally not significant, but a group of events taken together can be critical, depending on its patterns.

Correlating events for problem determination and analysis is not a straight-forward task; it is affected by time correlation, event attenuation, redundant events, location correlation, partial data, and multiple problems. These factors are explained in the following sections.

### Time Correlation

A particular problem may cause other events to occur during a finite time period at unpredictable intervals that range from microseconds to days. Isolating and characterizing a problem that involves a degrading component may take days, and the frequency of events can have a critical bearing on the problem. For example, one frame slip on a T1 line during a day may not be serious, but 10 frame slips an hour can be quite serious.

### Event Attenuation

Events generated by some types of problems may not be communicated. Examples are jitter (i.e., short-term variations in signal interval phases commonly caused by nonlinear transmission circuit elements) and wander (i.e., long-term variations in signal phase intervals) in T1 lines resulting from intermediate repeaters and cross-connect systems that use large buffers. Error-correction codes processed at intermediate network elements can also go unreported.

### Redundant Events

Some events occur as a consequence of other events and provide no new information; they may even be reported after the problem has been resolved. This type of event should be masked in the system to avoid distractions while the cause of the problem is being isolated.

### Location Correlation

An abnormal problem can have consequences in other network components. In this situation, a problem must be determined from related events that are reported by other properly functioning components.

## Partial Data

Problem resolution often proceeds despite incomplete data. Data is gathered incrementally as more events are reported over time. In some cases, event analysis does not always produce a definite conclusion; events can be lost, mutilated, or not reported because of damaged network elements, or false events can be conveyed as a result of noisy communications. The ENEOS event analyzer generates hypotheses about a given problem, analyzing additional events as they occur and using this information to revise and refine the hypothesis. The inference processor must allow the system to make plausible revisions. Occasionally, the absence of events may be highly significant and should also be processed by the inference engine. For example, if events indicating a faulty component or degraded signal stop occurring, any hypothesis regarding a faulty component or degraded signal should be abandoned.

## Multiple Problems

A large network usually has some independent problems that are pending resolution. Events generated by these problems are mixed with events caused by the problem. The inference processor should be able to separate such a mixture of events, assigning priorities to the problems according to their severity.

## KNOWLEDGE BASES

An expert system's knowledge base contains items called objects. ENEOS's knowledge base contains such objects as corporate networks, gateways, specific network types, sites, nodes, ports, paths, links, intermediate multiplexers, repeaters, front-end controllers, and terminal types. Ad hoc collections of objects are created as needed for resolving particular problems. See Exhibit V-2-6 for a condensed taxonomy of ENEOS objects and parameters. Objects and their associated measurements performed or acquired during a problem-resolution session are listed in Exhibit V-2-7.

Network element operators manipulate network objects through a combination of heuristics, test commands, and algorithms, triggering the actions needed for problem resolution. When operations are applied to objects, they may produce children and grandchildren within the hierarchy of objects and sets. Operators' properties characterize their domains and ranges in the network object taxonomy; they also have procedures that can generate presentation-layer descriptions of icons, tables, charts, and graphic displays. Operators can trigger further actions in network elements that assist in problem resolution (e.g., rerouting traffic through an alternate path to by pass a failed element).

## Object Orientation

Object-oriented knowledge bases, data bases, and programming are state-of-the-art AI concepts, offering significant advantages over conventional program-

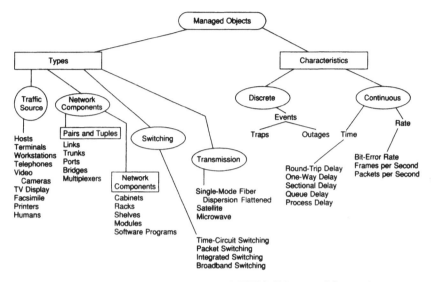

**Exhibit V-2-6. Condensed Taxonomy of ENEOS Objects and Parameters**

ming techniques. In ENEOS, objects communicate with one another by sending and receiving messages. An object consists of a collection of information and the protocols needed to manipulate it.

The knowledge base consists of factual, algorithmic, and heuristic knowledge. Examples of factual knowledge in the ENEOS knowledge base are:

- Transmission media, including single-mode dark fiber in dispersion-flattened and polarization-preserving formats and transmitter lasers (e.g., thermo electric cooled, distributed feedback, and Faby-Perot lasers).
- Switching and connectivity frames and rules.
- Test commands and invocation rules.
- Electrical and optical test definitions, including noninvasive optical time domain reflectometry and stress signal tests.
- Test thresholds and limits.

The declarative knowledge of network elements and communication paths consists of three entities: sets of network element classes, classes of network elements, and instances of network element classes in which each element is represented as a frame.

Frame-based knowledge representation provides a system with deep knowledge because of the complex structures within the frames. Rule-based knowledge systems, however, provide only surface knowledge because of the limited way information can be presented. A typical frame describing an instance of a specific entity contains the following information:

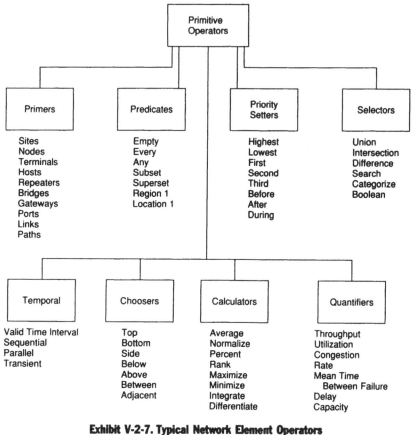

**Exhibit V-2-7. Typical Network Element Operators**

---

- Element class and hierarchy.
- Functional description.
- Structural description.
- Behavioral description.
- Legal operations, including test, preventive, corrective, and adaptive procedures.
- Bandwidth resource management procedures.
- Routing algorithms and procedures.
- Set of possible instantiations.
- Failure rate.
- Repair and maintenance procedures.

One of ENEOS's most essential tasks is instantiating these types of frames. (See Exhibit V-2-8 for a simple instantiated frame.)

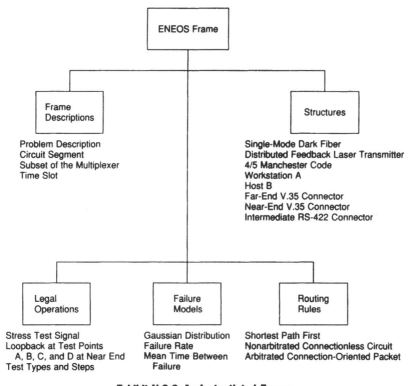

**Exhibit V-2-8. An Instantiated Frame**

A specific instance of a class of network elements could have two terminals—workstation A and host B—specified in the frames as communicating in connectionless packet mode. By establishing the communications mode between the terminals, ENEOS creates a direct correspondence between the relationships in a given situation, facilitating the natural presentation of global network knowledge.

All knowledge that is to be processed must be represented in frames. Because the operations and manipulations of these frames are expressed as specialized procedures, ENEOS uses factual knowledge of such network elements as the state of communicating terminals, communications protocols, connection mode, links, and time slots in a time multiplexer.

Naming a frame helps control the proper matches of the restricted variables, allowing ENEOS to derive all the test points and test operations for a given problem resolution. In a frame-based procedure, a frame stored in the knowledge base is selected and matched against the collected data to predict the structure of the data.

Using frame-based rather than rule-based processing provides real-time parallel processing capabilities in ENEOS (e.g., how ENEOS relates alarms). A frame is selected with many alarms pointing to other objects and their relationships. The alarms are classified according to their level in the hierarchy of network components that are sending the alarms; this level number is added to the alarm-signal knowledge base. The frame with the highest alarm level is the master frame, and the matching process is performed according to ENEOS's procedures. Alarm-data collection, processing, and matching must be done in real time for meaningful network-management operations to occur. Coding these procedures, therefore, requires real-time considerations.

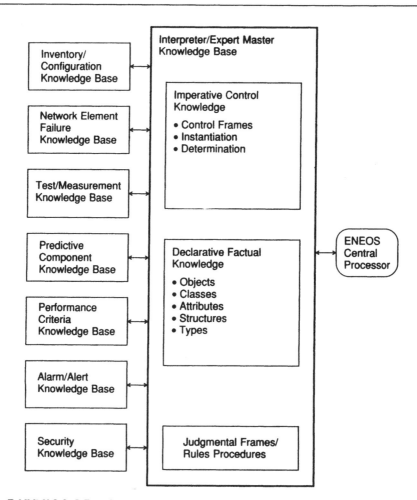

**Exhibit V-2-9. A Functional Block Diagram of the ENEOS Finite Inference Frame Processor**

## FINITE INFERENCE FRAME PROCESSOR

Inference generation in ENEOS is performed in the finite inference frame processor. As noted, this processor is the key component of ENEOS; its functional block diagram is shown in Exhibit V-2-9. The design of all the knowledge bases in the finite inference frame processor is similar to that of the interpreter knowledge base, shown in the central box in Exhibit V-2-9. The design of the knowledge base is an important aspect of the finite inference frame processor.

### Knowledge-Base Design

Stanford University researchers B. Buchanan and E. H. Shortpiffe, pioneers in expert systems technology, have designed several expert systems capable of performing medical diagnostics: EMYCIN, MYCIN, and NEOMYCIN. The most important design principle of relevance to ENEOS to come from the MYCIN project is that all control knowledge should be represented abstractly and separately from the domain knowledge on which it operates. Control knowledge, like rule-clause ordering, specifies when and how a program should perform such operations as pursuing a goal, acquiring data, focusing on an object, and making an inference.

### SUMMARY

In ENEOS, the knowledge bases and the associated inference engine of the finite inference frame processor have separate components for encoding control knowledge, factual knowledge, and judgmental rules. The inference engine applies the judgmental rules according to the embedded control procedures that define distinct control steps. The control knowledge, coded through an applicative and imperative programming language, defines the control actions that will be executed in a multitask environment. The separate encoding of the control knowledge allows ENEOS to generate inferences that are readily intelligible, explainable, modifiable, and upgradable.

To provide a transparent presentation of both control knowledge and factual knowledge, the knowledge bases in ENEOS are organized in distinct frames that contain an ordered rule structure of separately encoded control blocks. Factual knowledge is coded with network-defined objects, class types, legal-value hierarchies, class instances, and attributes. The imperative control knowledge cooperates with the structures of the declarative factual knowledge to provide built-in control.

# V-3
# Securing Distributed Data Networks

*NATHAN J. MULLER*

Protecting vital corporate information from unauthorized access has always been a concern for organizations. Security is a paramount issue with electronic data interchange (EDI) and electronic funds transfer (EFT) applications that involve financial transactions and monetary payments.

Security measures for EDI and other messaging systems are basically the same as for other automated information systems. Major considerations are message integrity and source authentication as well as access control for the microcomputers, minicomputers, and mainframes that handle various portions of the applications.

To the user of such systems, the application and data appear to reside locally; however, each application component and individual user has access to—and sometimes control over—the corporate data residing on various hosts and storage devices. Such openness invites misuse and requires a degree of administration to enforce security procedures.

The ease of use and ready accessibility that have made local area networks (LANs) so popular have also made them vulnerable to security violations. Because LAN resources are distributed throughout the organization, access can be obtained at many points within the network, including unattended wire rooms and closets. Aside from taking precautions to control the physical environment, an organization should periodically evaluate the accessibility of all shared network resources. Distributed environments are usually not controlled by common management structures and authorities. Furthermore, distributed environments constantly evolve in unpredictable directions, further complicating the implementation of centralized security procedures.

## ACCESS CONTROLS FOR SHARED DATA BASES

Access controls are needed to prevent unauthorized local access to the network and to control remote access through dial-up ports. The three minimum levels of user access usually assigned are: public, private, and shared access. Public access allows all users to have read-only access to file information. Private access gives specific users read-and-write file access, whereas shared access allows all users to read and write to files.

Perhaps the most difficult application to secure is the shared data base environment offered by LANs. When a company offers network access to one or more data bases, it must restrict and control all user query operations. Each data base should have a protective key; or series of steps, known only to those individuals entitled to access the data. To ensure that intruders cannot duplicate the data from the system files, users should first have to sign on with passwords and then prove that they are entitled to the data requested. Passwords should have a minimum of six or seven characters; passwords with fewer characters are too easily broken by brute-force guessing.

Plaintext passwords are especially vulnerable on LANs because each guess increases the chance of unauthorized entry by a factor of $1 \times n$, where $n$ equals the number of passwords on the LAN. A user ID should be suspended after a certain number of passwords have been entered to reduce the chance of a trial- and-error procedure being used to successfully access the operating system. In addition, to help track any inconsistencies, the IS security function should obtain a daily printout of the keys and passwords used.

### Password Protection

To maintain confidentiality, passwords should be difficult to guess or discover with random keyboard combinations. The most effective password is one that is long and obscure yet easily remembered by the workstation user. Changing passwords frequently and using a multilevel password-protection scheme can also help ensure confidentiality.

There are two systems of password protection that organizations can employ to maintain security: hierarchical and specific. With hierarchical passwords, users employ a defined password to gain access to a designated security level, as well as all lower levels. With specific passwords, however, users can access only the intended level. Although specific-level passwords offer greater security, they require that a senior, trusted employee have multiple passwords in order to access the many data bases and associated levels used daily. Password levels, especially specific levels, also make the task of network management more complex.

LAN administrators (who may be from the IS group or a functional department) must select and implement a particular password security method; they must also ensure that the connected workstations play an active role in supporting password use. For example, when a user enters the password, the monitor should automatically blank out all key entries to minimize the risk of exposing the password to casual observers. The LAN administrator can also install password routines that do not display any information on the screen or that sound an audible alarm and lock the keyboard after a specified number of failed entry attempts. In addition, the LAN administrator should survey the password master file, keep the file on disk, change any infrequently used passwords, and review risks periodically whenever a breach of security is suspected.

## Distributed Authentication and Authorization

As with traditional mainframe and minicomputer systems, the security features of the operating system are crucial to network security. LAN software usually offers log-on security, which requires a user to enter a password to access the system. Most passwords identify the user and associate the user with a specific workstation and perhaps a designated shift, work group, or department. Passwords provide a minimum level of security and do not require special equipment, such as keys or card readers.

Reliance on passwords has drawbacks, however. Chief among them is that users do not always maintain password confidentiality—nor does the network itself. The danger of focusing only on passwords is that after any intruders get through this security shield, they have free rein and may be able to access any resource on the network, including connections to EDI gateways and other electronic messaging systems that provide access to the stored files of the organization's creditors and trading partners.

Authentication services provide an effective way to implement password protection in the distributed environment. As an alternative to requiring every computer to store and manage the passwords of all users, an authentication service stores a unique number (or key) that corresponds to each user's password. The authentication server knows all of the passwords on the network and checks them on behalf of the clients. When a user wants to access a network resource, the authentication service checks the submitted password against the key assigned to that user. If the password and the key match, the authentication service verifies to the network resource that users are who they claim to be.

Authentication services can also be configured to perform a variety of useful access functions. Not only can they verify the separate identities of two users, they can set up a verified channel over which the two users can exchange messages, requests, or data.

Related to authentication services are authorization services. Once unique identities and a means of verifying them have been established, distributed security requires a mechanism that allows legitimate users to gain access to the services they need but shuts out others. Access control lists (ACLs), widely used in standalone systems, are the basis for distributed authorization services. When a user accesses a resource, the authorization service checks that person's identity against the resource's ACL to determine the user's clearance to perform an operation or to access privileges, and either clears the access request or rejects it.

There are two levels of authorization: discretionary control and mandatory control. Discretionary access control allows privilege levels to be defined (if desired) for users in the environment. Mandatory access control requires that privileges be defined for every user and resource in the environment. Mandatory access controls add an implementation cost and can be complicated to administer; however, they may actually be more cost-effective than enforcing and managing such controls manually or through centralized procedures.

## Key and Card Systems

The simplest key systems require users to insert a key in a lock to turn on the computer. Some vendors market external hard disks, keyboards, and modem switches incorporating key locks. With lock-and-key systems, however, intruders can pick the lock or duplicate the keys. To help minimize this threat, security personnel should keep keys in a secure cabinet where the keys can be checked out and their use can be monitored.

LAN administrators can also employ a magnetic card-reading system to control access to workstations. Card systems offer more flexibility than simple key systems in that they allow users to access data from any available workstation simply by inserting a card into a reader attached to the workstation; most banking ATMs use this type of security, combined with access codes and personal identification numbers (PINs). The card key system allows access-level definition for each user rather than for each workstation.

These cards are more difficult to duplicate than metal keys. Whereas lost keys can be copied and returned without ever being reported as missing, the loss of a magnetic card is generally reported promptly. If users plan to take cards out of the building, the cards should not contain a company logo, street address, or anything that could identify the company. A simple printed statement to mail the card to a post office box is sufficient. The LAN administrator should reserve a post office box for this purpose, listing it under a fictitious company to maintain complete security.

Although cards with magnetic stripes are the most popular, other types—bar-code, plastic, and proximity cards—are also available. Some companies favor plastic cards with magnetics embedded in the core for employee entrance control as well as workstation control. Although cards encoded with bar codes for optical readers may be chosen, they are relatively easy to duplicate. Proximity cards, which can be read by radio frequency at distances ranging from a few inches to 10 feet, may be unsuitable for offices in which the workstations may be close together.

LAN administrators should not issue the same card for both workstation identification and access to other areas of the company. The workstation deserves a higher level of security and closer control of card distribution than company-access cards. The IS department can also choose smart cards as possible security alternatives. These devices, which contain embedded microprocessors, accommodate a range of security tasks, including performing online encryption, recording a time-on/time-off log, and providing password identification. Such devices offer a viable security option for both local and remote access control. The major drawback of both key and card systems is that access control can (willingly or unwillingly) transfer to someone other than the authorized user.

## SECURING DISTRIBUTED DEVICES AND FILES

In addition to controlling access to data bases, LAN managers should evaluate all shared resources that can be accessed through the network (e.g., applications, directories, or corporate files) and should implement some type of access restriction for each. Other security measures that can be employed, often in combination, include:

- Diskette and drive controls.
- Data encryption.
- Callback systems.
- Network operating systems with built-in security features.

### Diskette and Drive Controls

LAN security is weakest at the point of entry. Removable disks are vulnerable to physical theft, unauthorized access, false data, and viruses. To avoid theft and unauthorized copying of removable diskettes, data cartridges, and hard drives, these items should be stored in a locked cabinet; critical diskettes (e.g., backup copies of sensitive files) can be stored in the corporate safe. Users should create several backup copies of sensitive files weekly or daily to provide a reliable source of archived data for restoral in the event of a system failure.

Backup copies of data help to prevent the spread of computer worms and viruses. If an infected diskette should contaminate network resources, multiple backup copies made before the virus infection occurred are available to restore the affected files, application programs, data bases, and operating systems.

A removable hard disk is ideal for transferring large files between machines, for archiving and backup tasks, and for use as a secondary storage device. Some removable drives are entirely self-contained; others are removable cartridges that contain only the disk itself. Removable cartridges are best for applications in which security and long-term portability are the most important considerations.

Disk-locking programs are available to prevent program diskettes from operating properly if copied or used with an unauthorized host computer. LAN administrators can protect data diskettes and files with passwords or modify them so that they allow access to data only when used with a specific program disk.

Eliminating access to removable diskettes provides the highest level of protection against data theft. A bar placed over the diskette drive can prevent intruders from removing diskettes or completely removing the drive from the computer. Keyboard locks are another option to prevent access to the hard disk.

Another method of securing diskette copying activities is to employ diskless workstations. A diskless workstation allows users to store all information on the network server or local hard disk, thereby eliminating the need for diskettes. These workstations offer several potential benefits from a security standpoint. They eliminate the possibility of diskette theft, unauthorized copying, or concealing information downloaded from the host computer. The absence of diskette drives also lessens the risk of introducing a virus into the network through infected input devices.

The environment in which diskless workstations operate presents another security benefit. Networks composed of these workstations rely on a centralized storage medium, such as a network file server, to boot an operating system and launch applications, download information, and generate hard copy on network printers. The diskless workstation usually houses local RAM storage and a microprocessor chip (e.g., an Intel 80386) that processes the information after it has been downloaded from the server. In this configuration, the diskless workstation assumes a dual role. First, it returns the information processing capability of a typical microcomputer. Second, it assumes a role in the network configuration that is similar to that of a host-dependent dumb terminal, relying on the file server to store, distribute, and print information.

For many organizations, diskless workstations may be impractical. If they are selected, however, the secure placement of printers, terminals, and file servers, as well as the placement of users with access to those resources, must be examined. This security procedure ensures that a user assigned to a diskless workstation cannot copy or print information stored on a standard LAN workstation with a nearby printer.

In the final analysis, the type of disk storage facility required depends on the duties of each workstation user. Therefore, a variety of safeguards should be in place to accommodate the differing needs of users.

## Data Encryption

Data encryption, also known as cryptography, is a method of scrambling information to disguise its original meaning. The concept of cryptography is simple: two communicating devices are programmed to use the same scheme to code and decode messages. Encryption provides the only practical means of protecting information transmitted over dispersed communications networks. Because intruders cannot read encrypted data, the information is not vulnerable to passive or active attack.

When implemented along with error detection and correction, encryption offers a highly effective and inexpensive way to secure communications links. For example, file encryption with decryption at the user workstation adds security to both the file server and the transmission medium. The data is secure from other workstations, illegal taps, and interception of spurious electromagnetic radiation.

Because common carriers use a variety of media that radiate signals—including unshielded copper lines, microwaves, and satellites—data encryption should be implemented whenever sensitive data is transmitted through the public data network, as in EDI and EFT, for example. Although either the hardware or software can perform encryption, hardware-based encryption provides more speed and security, because an intruder who is skilled in programming will not usually be able to interfere with the encryption hardware. Online encryption requires the installation of encryption and decryption units at both ends of the communications link.

Cryptographic methods involve the use of an encryption key, a string of characters used in conjunction with an algorithm to scramble and unscramble messages. For example, if intruders know the algorithm, they will be unable to decode the scrambled information unless they also know the specific encryption key. The more characters the key contains, the more difficulty an intruder encounters when attempting to breach security. The strength of a cryptographic system lies in the quality and secrecy of the keys selected.

Another encryption method, public key systems, offers a relatively high degree of security. Public key encryption techniques use a two-part key structure to eliminate the problem of sharing a single encryption-decryption key. This technology permits users to encode data files with a public key that is associated with a specific user. The public key can encrypt but not decrypt a file. A private key, associated with each set of public keys, enables users to decrypt files. The key used to decrypt a file is associated with, and available to, only a single user; this minimizes the likelihood that a key will be copied or discovered by unauthorized users. Furthermore, because the decryption key is valid for only one user, it cannot be used to decrypt files intended for a different user. There is no need to keep the public keys secret or to risk compromising private keys by transmitting them between various users.

Presently, encryption methods offer the only practical means for protecting information transmitted through complex communications networks using telephone lines, microwaves, or satellites. Users must select an encryption system that ensures a sufficiently complex encryption algorithm to present an effective obstacle to would-be intruders. The encryption method selected must be weighed against the need for data security as well as the cost factors, including the cost of decreased data throughout and overall system performance. Moreover, encryption is not a panacea. It adds overhead, especially when implemented by software. Data can still be lost if the encryption key is forgotten or the data file is maliciously or accidentally deleted.

## Callback Systems

Callback security systems, which are commonly used with password and ID security schemes, control remote dial-up access to hosts and LAN servers through modems. These systems usually employ an interactive process between a sending and receiving modem. The answering modem requests the caller's identification, disconnects the call, verifies the caller's identification against the user directory, and then calls back the authorized modem at the number matching the caller's identification.

Callback security ensures that data communication occurs only between authorized devices. The degree of security that callback modems provide is questionable because of the widespread use of such telephone functions as call forwarding. It is also possible for a knowledgeable intruder to stay online and intercept the return call from the answering modem. In addition, callback security may be inappropriate for some networks, because it assumes that users always call from the same telephone number. Traveling employees and users who must connect to the LAN through a switchboard cannot use this technique.

Neither passwords nor callback modems provide complete security for remote communications. The difficulties inherent in remote authentication make a combined security method imperative. Two identification methods (e.g., callback modems combined with data encryption) may be more effective than a single method.

Another approach combines password security with the callback feature. With this technique, the password is verified and the inbound call is disconnected. The security system then calls the remote user at a predetermined telephone number to enter the pass-data mode. If a hacker breaks the password, the security system will call back a secure location, thereby denying the hacker access. This system is effective but very slow and is limited to a finite number of stored telephone numbers.

These approaches rely upon establishing links to a central site device, such as a front-end processor or communications controller. In all cases, security is implemented through the use of ASCII passwords or DTMF tones after the modem handshake. Security procedures can be implemented before the modem handshaking sequence, rather than after it, to effectively eliminate the access opportunity from potential intruders. In addition to saving time, this method uses a precision high-speed analog security sequence that cannot be detectable even by advanced line monitoring equipment.

## NETWORK OPERATING SYSTEMS SECURITY

Security is to a large extent dependent on the LAN operating system. Network operating system developers have tried to build in features, such as log-on passwords and access rights, that make it possible to exert some control over these problems, but LANs still have holes. Some third-party developers have created monitoring and security programs, but these also have limitations.

Most network operating systems simply divide the server's memory into sections, called volumes, allowing the LAN manager to assign different levels of user access to particular parts of the same resource. Some network operating systems (e.g., Novell's NetWare) offer several additional levels of security. For example, access to a directory is determined by a combination of user and directory access rights. Other features include audit trails that record which users log on to the network and the programs and resources they access.

Auditing systems can detect intruders impersonating authorized users and assist in network recovery in the event of an attack. Networks that do not have adequate built-in network operating system security can be enhanced with encryption or access-control software. Some third-party software products offer enhanced auditing features designed to make security administration easier. Using the software's auditing capabilities, network managers can quickly compile a list of users as well as the network access rights each has been given—a task that can otherwise take hours.

## Accountability

Auditing services give users the means to enforce accountability in a distributed environment or to do a back-track analysis to discover the source of a security breach or a data base integrity compromise. There are two factors to consider when deciding to implement distributed auditing services: the cost of auditing and the administrative interface to distributed auditing.

Auditing services in a distributed system usually record more information than standalone auditing systems. In a distributed environment, it is often useful to record authentication and authorization information along with data describing significant activities. The result is larger logs and a greater cost in terms of system overhead—from 10% to 12%, depending on how logs are implemented and tuned on individual servers.

It is not difficult to log information about system activities in a distributed environment. What is difficult is coordinating the auditing services and using the collected information. To date, no vendor provides a solution that makes it possible to manage multiple distributed auditing services from a central location.

## Virus Protection

Among the dangers of inadequate network security are the alteration and destruction of valuable records and whole data bases by worms and viruses introduced into the network through unauthorized programs brought into the workplace by unknowing users. Worms and viruses are usually differentiated according to their degree of transferability. A virus, for example, limits its damage to the LAN workstation through which it entered and is transported by external action, such as by sharing diskettes. Worms are self-replicating and move by their own initiative to different network nodes.

Virus protection is a necessity because computer viruses can have a multiplier effect on sensitive network resources. If a standalone microcomputer becomes infected, there is little chance that the virus will spread to other machines, unless diskettes are shared. If a mainframe is infected, the damage can be more severe, but there still is only one system to restore.

When a virus invades a LAN, however, the damage can be far-reaching. Diskettes used to boot servers are a prime source of LAN infections. Because workstations communicate with the network file server to obtain shared programs and data files, a virus can spread rapidly to every computer that accesses the server.

To protect against a catastrophic virus attack, network managers should implement internal barriers between connecting systems. These barriers (e.g., different encryption codes for separate programs or network devices) cannot completely insulate a network from a virus attack; however, they restrict damage only to that area of the network where the virus has entered. If a LAN subsystem is only a pass-through from a data source to a major interior system, a virus can be detected and blocked from entering the interior system. The technique involves making hash totals at the input and output of the subsystem and matching them. If a virus has intervened, the totals will not match and the data should be blocked from passage. Networks that can be accessed by dial-up lines should have a barrier (e.g., an encryption change) at the second entry port or interface in a multisystem network.

Borrowed or secondhand programs represent the most frequent source of virus infection. Companies should consult a reputable dealer and make sure that the vendor's seal is intact on the package before purchasing or using any diskette software. Companies that purchase secondhand software should verify that the supplier has tested the software for viruses; they should then retest the software (using one or more of the many virus detection packages available) before loading it onto the network. When the programs are loaded onto the network, companies should monitor the size of directory files for any unexplainable changes and maintain archives versions and hard copies of the files for purposes of comparison.

Some antivirus data security software packages only identify changes being made to files; others identify and remove viruses and repair the damage the viruses inflict. Boot sector viruses locate themselves on the first sector of a floppy disk, whereas file viruses invade executable files. Antivirus software can identify and eliminate viruses before the damage occurs. Some packages disinfect files, boot sectors, and memory without harming the infected portions of the system. As yet, no product can guarantee complete protection against a virus attack, and new types of viruses are constantly being discovered.

## THE NETWORK SECURITY PLAN

With security issues becoming increasingly important among businesses of all types and sizes, it is wise to have a security plan in place. The plan's extensiveness is directly proportional to the network's complexity. At a minimum, the plan should address the following:

- Access levels and definitions.
- Rules for access (e.g., password policy and volume access).
- Work groups and how they fit into the network's access rules.
- Physical installation and access guidelines, including approved add-in security protection.
- Accountability guidelines.
- Internetwork connections and access requirements.
- Levels of administration and accountability.
- Periodic software upgrade, auditing, and installation policies.

The security plan should have the power of a corporate policy, signed and authorized by management's highest level. Department heads should administer the plan. Every user should be required to read and sign off on the plan. Security plans should be reviewed and revised at least annually, perhaps more frequently if employee turnover is a problem.

The ideal network security plan must protect against the theft, alteration, and interception of network information. It should also deter theft or vandalism of equipment, the duplication or resale of programs, and unauthorized use of computer time by wiretapping or unauthorized dial-up. Companies should first implement procedures to deter unauthorized users who may be tempted to breach the system. When properly implemented, such deterrents bolster confidence in the integrity of the organization and its information assets, assuring management, staff, customers, and trading partners that the system is safe and dependable.

When deterrence fails and an intruder attempts to breach the system, the preventive techniques described in this chapter can guard against further damage. Companies should choose one or more security methods that offer password control, data encryption, alarms to notify network managers of a security breach, and audit trails to locate the source of the breach. Companies should design a security plan that can expand to accommodate network growth and take into account the increasing sensitivity of data applications.

## SUMMARY

In the past, most companies were concerned more with the nuts-and-bolts aspects of interactive communication and resource sharing than with security issues. Consequently, the design of most network operating systems reflected these priorities. With the increase in virus and worm attacks, however, many organizations want their network operating systems to incorporate protective measures that both provide and restrict access to information. Vendors are beginning to upgrade existing operating systems with advanced network security features.

When the distributed networking environment is examined, layer upon layer of risk can be found, especially with the implementation of EDI and EFT systems that convey sensitive financial transactions. Absolute protection of network resources from intruders may be too expensive and impose too much overhead to be practical. It is therefore essential to weigh the risks against the costs when deciding what security measures to implement.

# V-4
# Distributed Network Security

*IRA HERTZOFF*

D uring the 1980s, distributed processing was performed by a client using files and programs stored on a server. Today, distributed processing is split between the server and client to offer desktop power, more efficient network resource use, and better control of network traffic. As these open systems grow in importance, securing them becomes a networkwide process as opposed to a node-based operation.

Clients on networks supporting structured query language (SQL) data base servers can access a common data base. Transparent access to data shared between applications and to data bases on multiple servers is provided by widely used front ends (e.g., Lotus 1-2-3, Paradox, and Excel). Applications are vulnerable to misuse and manipulation because access tools are well known and commonly available.

In the layered networks of the 1990s, mission-critical data is stored on corporate hosts; local data is stored on multifunctional servers providing back-end SQL data base services; and dissimilar clients run multiple front-end applications. Numerous paths into the network permit access to data from both internal and external sources. Distributed networks can be penetrated from remote locations and their security seriously compromised if a single node is accessible. Distributed network security now depends on how the desktop computer is used and how desktop power is managed. No operation is safe unless all connected operations are secure—protecting only the host is no longer sufficient.

## THE NEED FOR PROTECTION

Appropriate procedures and techniques are necessary to protect the network from external or internal manipulation of its programs, data, and resources. An effective security program protects a network from physical destruction, unauthorized modification, or disclosure of software and records.

## Risk Analysis

Balancing costs and benefits is essential in a security plan. If a risk is overlooked and inadvertently assumed or retained, the enterprise is exposed to losses that the data center manager should have protected the system against. If the potential loss or frequency of a loss is incorrectly estimated, the protection decision, though technically correct, may be inappropriate for the enterprise.

The first step toward balancing costs and benefits is to conduct a formal risk analysis using the network's configuration data base. If a configuration data base does not exist, one must be developed; it is the repository for network resource information. By applying risk analysis to this information, the data center manager identifies the assets exposed to loss, the relative frequency of such losses, and their estimated dollar amounts. This risk profile allows the data center manager to rank potential risks by potential cost.

When resources are limited, it is better to allocate dollars to procedural tools than to bunkerlike control centers that protect against only the uncommon disaster. It is better to strengthen the network than to build disaster plans for failure recovery. Risk analysis rates dissimilar events by their dollar costs to allow consistent risk comparison and evaluation.

High-technology network penetration is a glamorous subject and certainly a possible threat, but low-tech penetration is much more common and much more dangerous. Intruders who take advantage of procedural weaknesses represent a greater threat to distributed networks than do industrial spies with, for example, emissions-sensing devices. Protection costs should be balanced against risk reality. The data center manager can offer cost-effective protection against real risks by carefully rating the problems that can occur. If the maximum potential risk is from a disgruntled employee, the data center manager should not specify distributed network security measures to protect against a resourceful and determined adversary (e.g., an unfriendly government).

## THE PROTECTION DECISION

There are three ways to protect a network against risk: self-insurance or risk retention, insurance against economic loss, and installation of security measures. These methods are discussed in the following sections.

### Insurance

Protection measures should be selected with the assistance of the corporate risk or insurance manager. Large enterprises commonly self-insure for minor risks, obtain outside insurance against larger risks, and use security measures when they are less expensive than insurance. Insurance is a proven method of managing risk and should always be part of a network security plan. A corporation can elect to risk an event and make no insurance or security provisions; if this is a planned rather than accidental decision, it is a valid approach.

## Security Measures

Distributed networks require three types of protection: disaster recovery, physical security, and data security. Because these areas overlap, a single well-selected security measure can offer protection in more than one. Distributed networks, because their elements are geographically separated, are inherently protected against physical destruction. Distributed networks do not require the complex backup procedures for disasters that single-site operations must have, because the distributed architecture is based on distributed servers and because the data center staff is trained to automatically back up files.

Geographically distributed systems pose security risks because processing does not take place in physically secure computer rooms, desktop computer users can create openings into the network, and software can be introduced into the network from many workstations. Preventing viruses, worms, and the unauthorized copying of software and files requires proper administrative procedures.

## SECURITY MECHANISMS

The distributed network needs in-depth protection involving multiple layers of defenses. Any single security measure can be improperly installed, be bypassed, or have flaws; the use of multiple security measures protects against weaknesses in any individual measure (see Exhibit V-4-1). The risk of simultaneous failure of multiple measures is the product of the risk of failure of individual components.

Unplanned shutdowns and restarts of any programmable network device must be considered a breach of security and investigated. In particular, operating system restarts should not be allowed or accepted as normal operating practice.

### The Auditor's Role

The effectiveness of any security plan must be proved by ongoing reviews conducted by technically competent auditors. To ensure their independence, these auditors must not have any other operating responsibilities. If there is no existing program for conducting audits and training auditors or if the existing program is inadequate, an effective program should be established.

### Security Ratings

The Department of Defense National Computer Security Center establishes security requirements, standards, and test procedures for defense and federal governmental operations and for industrial computer security. Its standards, which are compiled in the Orange Book, represent the test procedures that software and hardware must pass to gain an acceptable security rating (see Exhibit V-4-2).

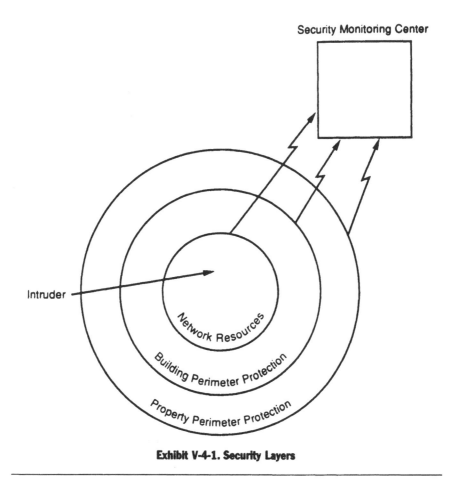

**Exhibit V-4-1. Security Layers**

## Multilevel Processing Security

Because various classes of work are usually performed on the same network, processes requiring different levels of security interact. (When all work on a network is at the same security level, processes do not need to be compartmentalized to prevent a user from accessing another user's data.) Security requires that these processes interact only in a known, predictable, and authorized manner. The Orange Book standards establish this manner for single machines and, by extension, for distributed network processing when secure and insecure processes are mixed.

## Secure Processing over an Insecure Network

The public telephone network and many private communications facilities are inherently insecure. The telephone network is universal (with many points of

Secure System Classifications

A. Verified Design (B3 requirements and proofs)

B. Mandatory Protection
   B3: Security Domains (B2 requirements and a small kernel)
   B2: Structured Protection (B1 requirements and a modular kernel)
   B1: Labeled Security Protection (C2 requirements and security labels)

C. Discretionary Protection
   C2: Structured Protection (C1 requirements and audit trails)
   C1: Discretionary Security (discretionary access control)

D. Minimal Protection

**Exhibit V-4-2. Department of Defense Orange Book Ratings**

---

access and exit) and has well-known security weaknesses. Any secure process that operates over such links must use handshaking techniques to verify that only the desired parties are in communication. Cryptographic techniques applied to the data can ensure that data cannot be interpreted if it is intercepted.

## Risks of LANs as Gateways to Hosts

When a LAN is used as a front end to a secure mainframe, a serious LAN security breach will compromise the mainframe's security. Such breaches can occur because both secure and insecure operating systems run on the same network and because of the nature of workstation intelligence. A user can program a personal computer to set up a connection through the LAN to secure host data bases. Anyone with physical, logical, or remote control access to that personal computer can log into the host as a user. Gateways should be evaluated by how they support network management and security.

## LAN Security

Many LAN security systems are inadequate because they were designed for work group automation and are the product of a single-user design mentality. One indication of a poor LAN operating system is the availability of many add-on security products. Access rights tools should be an integral part of the operating system.

The use of LANs as host gateways is economical, but many LAN operating systems expose host passwords by letting them reside in buffers or making them available for decoding by protocol analyzers. In both LAN token-ring and Ethernet networks, each station sees all LAN traffic. A true star topology is therefore superior. Personal computer-based LANs suffer from the weaknesses of their DOS operating system and are prone to virus and worm attacks. Diskless workstations prevent users from loading unauthorized software. Requiring users to load local operating system software from the network reduces the risk of infection.

## DISASTER RECOVERY

A network must function under all normal and anticipated abnormal conditions and must be robust enough to survive the unexpected. The data center manager must provide the systems, staff, and procedures necessary to ensure that a disaster—intentional or otherwise—does not cripple the organization. As mission-critical applications become more time-dependent, the acceptable time for restoration of service is decreasing.

Accurate recordkeeping in a configuration control data base with connectivity information is fundamental. This type of network management can be the core of a disaster plan generated as the network control staff performs daily operations. Problem management tools can simulate outages, and change control tools can track recovery operations. Data center managers responsible for maintaining distributed networks must integrate disaster planning into their daily operations—not as a separate project but as a large problem that requires immediate action and resolution.

### Reserve Capacity

To protect data against disaster, the data center manager can, at different locations, place multiple servers with reserve capacities so that each server can absorb additional work loads as necessary. This dual-operating capability should be part of installation planning so that critical applications operate at two or more sites.

Disaster recovery of a distributed network is a network process. Under both normal and abnormal conditions, the network should use its interconnections and facilities to support recovery of failing network elements. SQL data bases, mirror-imaged at different points on distributed client-server networks, can be designed to allow automatic recovery.

## THE NETWORK AS A BACKUP SYSTEM

With enough network bandwidth, critical files can be stored on several servers. Provisions to switch network control should be made if a disaster disables the primary control point. In large networks, management domains must be established and plans developed for switching control if a domain management point is unavailable. The swapping of network control should be a normal and periodic procedure familiar to the staff at all sites.

The process of restoring an operation includes recognizing that a disaster has occurred. This function is best handled by the network management center. Incomplete information generated by inadequate tools can delay action until the problem becomes uncontainable. Disaster recovery resources should enhance the network management system rather than create disaster recovery systems that operate in parallel.

## Backup Types

Backups are file copies used to protect against errors; they are recycled on a regular schedule. (Archival backups may be retained permanently.) The process of recycling media is called rotation. Backup media can be recycled on a generation basis or on a longer cycle. A distributed network with enough bandwidth can be backed up to a server in a central location. Central backup ensures that remote devices are backed up according to plan and taken off site.

## PHYSICAL SECURITY

A network's physical security can be penetrated and its security seriously compromised in many ways, for example, through the destruction of or damage to buildings, cables, switches, power sources, computer hardware, computer files, and programs.

### Seals

Security seals are attached to equipment to detect tampering or entry. A damaged seal indicates that a unit has been opened. Managers of large networks should use prenumbered, bar-coded seals. Each seal number should be recorded in a data base and assigned to a technician. The number on the seal should be then linked to a specific machine or component.

When a seal is broken during an authorized repair, a new seal should be installed and the number linked to the old seal number, the repair technician, and the actions taken. This approach keeps the configuration data base current. It allows the data center manager to positively identify each component, which technician worked on it, and whether it was altered by anyone—authorized or unauthorized—from the state recorded in the configuration data base.

### Hot Work: Flame, Electrical, and Plumbing Service Control

Effective security practice requires any employee or contractor working on critical systems to obtain proper clearance—a hot work permit or license. The license ensures that responsible managers know when work that can cause a fire or cut power or water is being performed. Permits should be required for all work on communications lines and power sources and for construction that can affect lines. In some cases, a prudent manager may assign a staff member to follow the worker with a fire extinguisher. Avoiding a halon dump or extended downtime makes this precaution a wise investment.

## CONTROL OF EXECUTABLE CODE

The data center manager should control the loading onto the network of all executable code to reduce the risk of infection from computer viruses and worms and from unauthorized modification of programs. On a distributed network, all paths that can result in code execution must be blocked, including unintended paths. On a DOS machine, for example, using the **Type** command on a text file with embedded ANSI.sys commands results in execution of the commands. In this case, a text editor is safer than using **Type** when checking suspect files. Other unintended paths include service diagnostic disks that can carry viruses and worms from machine to machine; problems can also be caused by a failure to maintain a network operating system software at current revision levels.

### Remote Library Control

Effective security practice requires valuable assets to be concentrated and placed in a protected environment. To protect executable code and programs, data center managers must ensure that all network programs are kept in program libraries, which are stored in directories with controlled access.

Authorization to make changes or add programs to the library and the ability to authorize such changes should be assigned to different individuals. Activity journals on each file must be kept to verify accountability. Library data structures should be maintained to improve management insight and control.

## ACCESS CONTROL

Access controls limit a particular user's access to specific network resources. One method is to request information that only one person knows (e.g., a password). User IDs, authorization tables, and access rights lists can also be used to control access. Such controls (as audit trails and alarms) are essential to protect against authorized users and should be implemented in the software that controls the program library as well as in the software that prevents unauthorized access to production data. Various access control methods are discussed in the following sections.

### Handshaking

Network users should be informed of the last use of their ID and password when they log on to the network. They should report any suspicious activity to management or be held responsible for the results of this activity.

### Lockwords

Lockwords permit users with knowledge of the file code to access that file without verifying their identity. Multiple resources require multiple lockwords, a problem that, on some LANs, is counteracted by writing batch files to issue lockwords. This practice results in very poor security, and it is difficult to change lockwords. The use of lockword security is unacceptable and is particularly dangerous when LAN gateways to hosts are used.

### Passwords

Passwords use access control as their primary security mechanism. Password secrecy is needed to prevent system access, but passwords can be compromised in many ways, the easiest being user carelessness. Procedural controls on the contents of passwords—restrictions on using common words or names—and forcing users to periodically change their passwords are essential. Real-time monitoring of log-ons to discern the use of password detection programs should be continuous, as should logging of successful attempts into an audit trail.

## COMMUNICATIONS SECURITY

Data interception is a concern in organizations with valuable or sensitive data. Data can be intercepted by wiretapping or emission sensing, by unauthorized access to data, and by authorized or unauthorized terminals. Communications security is the key to protecting against data interception. To be effective, communications security must be enforced in five areas: line, transmission, cryptography, emissions, and technical. These areas are discussed in the following sections.

### Line Security

Line security involves protecting telephone lines against wiretapping or other types of interception and employs the same techniques used for protecting voice conversations against interception. Often, PBXs and other premises-based equipment are not properly protected. Intruders can enter them in the supervisor mode and, with the right resources, capture and analyze their data streams for user IDs and passwords. The intruders can then use these identifications to gain access to the network.

The data center manager should double-check that PBX security is adequate. Because protocol analyzers and other diagnostic devices can discover passwords and cryptographic keys, their use should be restricted. It is preferable to employ high-level diagnostic programs to identify failing components.

### Transmission Security

Transmission security is the protection of network communications against their interception by workstations authorized to access the network but not particular data. It provides protection against the use of authorized devices for unauthorized purposes.

### Cryptographic Security

Cryptographic security protects the keys, encryption software, and hardware used for encoding transmissions. The cryptographic system must operate at a level higher than the highest-level information the system protects. Just as a lock does not protect against a stolen key, cryptography does not protect against a lost or intercepted cryptographic key.

## Emissions Security

Emissions security protects against the interception of computer emissions (e.g., electrical fluctuations, radiation, or other modulations), by an adversary who can determine what is being processed. This risk is posed primarily by an adversary who is both resourceful and determined (e.g., a foreign government). Emissions-suppressed equipment and cables are available to protect against it.

Optical fiber does not radiate much and is not prone to emission leakage and interception. Light does leak at cable bends, however, and emissions can be read by interception equipment that is very close to the cable. However, the skill required for tapping optical fiber is very high and the risk of discovery is great. Fiber is useful in areas prone to electrical storms because it is nonconductive and can isolate equipment from voltage surges.

## Technical Security

Technical security is a broad phase used to describe protection against non-computer intrusion devices. Some known devices include:

- Microphones or free-space transmitters (e.g., radio taps).
- Devices built into equipment (e.g., modulators).
- Carrier-current bugging equipment (e.g., power-line modulators).
- Visual or optical surveillance equipment (e.g., video cameras).
- Telephone bugging devices (e.g., infinity transmitters).

## DANGERS OF PRIVATE SECURITY

Coordinated networkwide security is necessary to protect against the conversion of corporate resources to private use. It is difficult to determine whether user-developed security measures are adequate or well implemented, and networkwide measures are needed to ensure that the network is not vulnerable to its users.

## Control of Client/Server Processes

Host-to-host links over the public network require multilevel security, which must be provided with access controls. Network services needing multilevel security are mail, file transfer, and remote log-on. Network applications should be usable without modification.

In UNIX, for example, users should have access to any network application usually provided on the UNIX host. The objective is to create a user-transparent wall around network applications that permits initial setup of the connection to another host but does not allow application-to-host communication until security is ensured for both systems. Users must be allowed to enter passwords, but password interception must be prevented. A verified trusted path mechanism, with network accesses that are audited at the called host, is desirable.

## NETWORK MANAGEMENT INTEGRATION

Network management control centers are similar to central station burglar alarm control centers. Alarms in both are forwarded to central monitoring points where computer programs either take action on them or display recommendations, for action. Network management control centers monitor line conditions and check for device failures. Message displays indicate if, for example, there is an outage, an intruder is testing passwords, or unauthorized access has been detected.

## NEW RISKS

As network management interfaces are standardized according to internationally accepted models, the possibility of an attack on the management system increases. Reconfiguring routers can effectively destroy communications. In assessing the security of the network management system, the data center manager should ask:

- What are its message authentication procedures?
- Should network control messages be encrypted?
- How are trusted users controlled within the system?
- How are external messages from linked networks validated?

### Protecting Against Trusted Users

Perhaps the most difficult security problem is caused by authorized users doing unauthorized work. Every authorized user should sign a standard statement indicating that access to the network is granted for approved business purposes only, that they will limit their use to those purposes, and that they will adhere to network security practices.

The audit trail and trend analysis of audit logs are used to detect use changes of authorized users. This is a task for independent, technically competent auditors who should periodically review use patterns. However, this is primarily an after-the-event check. To turn it into a deterrent, these audits must be publicized, along with the corporation's intention to prosecute when users convert network resources to their own use.

### The Super-User Problem

Most security systems have a super-user who can start and stop it. The ID and password of the super-user should be used only when absolutely essential—in other words, the person or persons having super-user authority should also have less powerful rights under a different ID and password. Super-user IDs and passwords should never be used when a less dangerous method of completing a task exists.

## Network Administration

The policy of separating IDs for security management from IDs for daily use also applies to network administrators. On LANs, a log-on from a machine with a corrupted hard disk can propagate through the network if the user has management privileges. This risk can be minimized by restricting where and how the management ID is used. It is safest to execute management tasks from a console, not a workstation.

## Viruses, Worms, and Contaminated Hard Disks

Conditions that do not seriously affect mainframes (e.g., viruses and worms) are hazardous to distributed networks if proper procedures are not followed. Total protection is impossible, but the risks can be controlled. The key is to control how executable code gets on the network. This can be done by restricting the ports of program entry to the minimum, installing quality-control mechanisms, and educating end users.

Control of unintended portals is more difficult. Software must be kept at current release levels, and new software must be audited before installation. Users with administrative rights must be instructed to protect their boot diskettes and to avoid logging on from unknown machines when using their administrative rights. When practical, administrative users should work only at their terminals.

## SUMMARY

The prerequisite for distributed network security is a stable, well-managed network. To achieve this, data center managers must ensure comprehensive data security as hardware and software implementation decisions are made and as network processes migrate from host-to-terminal environments to peer-to-peer environments (in which computer resources are often located in open user areas under the control of nontechnical managers).

# V-5
# The Data Center Manager's Guide to Ensuring LAN Reliability and Availability

*NATHAN J. MULLER*

In many businesses, LANs have displaced older, paper-based methods of doing work, and these organizations now depend on the reliability and availability of their networks for daily operations. A LAN's reliability is a measure of its capacity to operate despite failures in communications links and equipment. Availability is a measure of performance; it refers to the LAN's capacity to meet the communications needs of its users. On a LAN with high availability, services are provided immediately; on a LAN with low availability, users have to wait for network access, or network response is poor. This chapter discusses some of the technologies that contribute to LAN reliability and availability. By applying them, data center managers can ensure that their networks enhance company productivity, not detract from it.

Discussions in this chapter refer to LANs according to their topology. Simple versions of the basic LAN topologies are shown in Exhibit V-5-1.

## RELIABILITY

Star topologies score high in LAN reliability. The loss of a link on a star network prevents communication between the hub and the node attached to that link, but all other nodes operate normally. The hub is the weak link; the reliability of the network depends on the reliability of the central hub, and if the hub malfunctions, all nodes go down. If a peripheral node fails, only that node is affected.

A ring network topology, in its pure form, offers poor reliability during both node and link failures. In ring networks, link segments connect adjacent nodes to each other. Each node passes the data it receives to the adjacent node. The loss of one link not only cuts off one node but can bring down the entire network. To improve the reliability of a ring network, the data center manager can add redundant links between nodes and bypass circuitry in the nodes. This course of action, however, is very expensive.

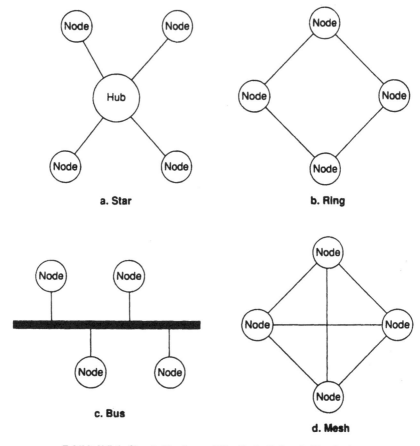

**a. Star**

**b. Ring**

**c. Bus**

**d. Mesh**

**Exhibit V-5-1. Simple Versions of the Basic Network Topologies**

Although link failures also cause problems on a bus network, a node failure will not bring it down. A redundant link for each segment increases the reliability of the network, but as with ring topologies, it raises the cost.

Mesh topologies are used on internetworks, which connect geographically separated LANs. Mesh networks are the most reliable because they always provide more than one route between nodes. However, this route diversity is achieved by adding more physical links and the equipment (e.g., routers) to support them, which again raises the cost of these networks.

## AVAILABILITY

Availability is a measure of a LAN's capacity to support all users who wish to access it. A network that is highly available provides services immediately to users, whereas a network that suffers from low availability typically forces users to wait for access or degrades overall network performance when it supports too many users at the same time.

Availability on a bus network depends on its load, length, and access control protocol. Under a light load, availability is virtually assured for any user who wishes access. As the load increases, however, so does the probability of information collisions. When a collision occurs, the transmitting nodes stop and attempt to transmit after a short interval. The chance of collisions also increases with bus length.

A mesh topology's multiple paths make it the most reliable of networks. In addition, because it provides the highest degree of interconnectivity between users, this type of network is always available.

The capacity of a network based on a star topology is limited to the capacity of the central hub. Under heavy load conditions, users can be denied access. However, hubs equipped with multiple processors can provide improved access in high-demand networks.

Although the ring topology does not provide the same degree of availability as a mesh topology does, it is an improvement over the star topology. Ring availability is lower than a mesh network's because each node on a ring must wait to receive permission before transmitting data. As the number of nodes on the ring increases, the time interval allotted to each station for transmission decreases.

## ACCESS METHODS

All LANs share media, but the way they do so is determined by their access method. A network's access method plays a key role in determining its reliability and availability.

### Bus

Ethernet, the major type of bus topology, is contention-based, which means that nodes compete with each other for access to the network. Each terminal listens to the network to determine whether it is idle. Upon sensing that no traffic is currently on the line, the terminal is free to transmit. The trouble with this access method is that several terminals may try to transmit simultaneously, causing a data collision. The more terminals connected to the network, the higher the probability that such collisions will occur.

To avoid a loss of data, transceivers listen as they send, comparing what is sent with what is heard. If they are not the same, a collision has occurred. The transceiver notifies the attached node with a collision signal and sends error messages onto the Ethernet so that all nodes know of the collision.

Because packets travel at nearly the speed of light over coaxial cable, collisions may appear to be unlikely. In fact, during the very brief interval that it takes for a packet to traverse the network, terminals at the far end cannot know that the network is in use. This collision window imposes a practical limit on the length of a bus network that does not use repeaters. In its 802.3 standard for Ethernets, the Institute of Electrical and Electronic Engineers recognizes 2,500 meters as the maximum bus length, regardless of data rate or cable type.

Ethernet is relatively simple to implement; therefore, it typically costs less than other types of network do. Because each node functions independently, the failure of one does not disrupt the operation of the others, and nodes may be added or removed without disrupting the network. Ethernet is media independent, functioning well over twisted-pair wire, coaxial cable, and optical fiber. The choice of media depends on desired data rate, range, and immunity to interference from external sources of electrical noise.

## Ring

The token-ring network uses a more efficient topology. Logically, the network forms a ring; however, it may be physically configured as a star. A token consisting of several bytes of data (also referred to as a packet) circulates around the ring, giving each terminal in sequence a chance to put information on the network. This token-passing access method ensures all terminals an equal share of network time.

To transmit, a station captures the token, adds a data packet to it, and then reinserts the token on the ring. Each station in turn receives the packet, but only the addressee retains the data in it, and only the station that put the packet on the ring can remove it. Because each terminal regenerates data packets and the token, token-ring networks do not have the size and distance limitations of Ethernets.

A further advantage of token-ring networks is that traffic can be assigned different priorities. A station can transmit a token only if it has traffic equal to or higher in priority than the priority indicator embedded in the token.

The token ring is not without liabilities. Special procedures must be followed to add a terminal to the network without breaking the ring and to ensure that the new station is recognized by the others and is granted a proportionate share of network time. Because failed repeater circuits in a node can break the ring, bringing down the whole network, each station must be equipped with bypass circuitry.

A logical token ring can be wired as a star. If bypass circuitry is used with this configuration, failures of network equipment can more easily be corrected than if the bypass circuits are in the nodes. Each node is wired to a centrally located panel, which contains the bypass circuits. If a nodal or link failure occurs, the bypass circuit is activated, preventing the ring from being broken. Centralizing the bypass circuits in this way also facilitates moves and changes as well as fault isolation, because identifying connections at a central point is much easier than performing traces between offices and floors.

Anomalies on a token-ring network can tie it up until someone figures out the problem. If a terminal fails before it has passed the token, the whole network goes down until a new token is inserted. The token may even be corrupted by noise so that it is unrecognizable to the stations. The network can also be disrupted by the occasional appearance of two tokens or by the presence of continuously circulating data packets. The latter can occur when data is sent and the originating terminal fails before it can remove the packet from the ring.

To ensure network availability, one terminal is typically designated as the control station to continuously monitor network operations and do such necessary housecleaning as reinserting lost tokens, taking extra tokens off the network, or disposing of "lost" packets. Each station is equipped with control circuitry, so that the first station detecting the failure of the control station assumes responsibility for network supervision. Such protective measures complicate the network and add to its cost.

## Star

In a network based on the star topology, network devices are connected to a central hub. This topology is familiar in the office environment, where each telephone is ultimately tied into the PBX. Another example of a star network entails several terminals sharing a single host. The star and the ring network share a key disadvantage in that the failure of a single critical node can result in the failure of the entire network, unless provisions are made for hardware redundancy or bypass. In the star topology, the critical point, of course, is the central node.

An example of a LAN product that uses the star topology is AT&T's Datakit. In this system, all the network interface units and interconnecting media are contained within a single cabinet to which the individual stations are connected through twisted-pair wiring. The system looks very much like a PBX, but it implements data communications. AT&T also offers StarLAN, which operates at 1M bps, and StarLAN 10, which operates at 10M bps. AT&T originally developed StarLAN to satisfy the need for a low-cost, easy-to-install local area network that would offer more configuration flexibility than IBM's Token Ring.

Unlike a bus or ring network, in which intelligence is distributed throughout the system, the star network concentrates all of the intelligence required to run the network at a central hub. In the case of AT&T's StarLAN, the hub is a minicomputer. The failure of one terminal on the star network does not affect the operation of the others unless, of course, the faulty terminal happens to be the hub. Because network intelligence is centralized at the hub, safeguards must be taken to protect it from catastrophic failure. Such measures may include an uninterruptible power supply, an alternative computer on hot standby, or use of a fault-tolerant computer with redundant subsystems built into it.

Other steps may be taken to minimize the effects of a hub outage. For example, file servers in front of the hub may permit limited communication among the terminals connected to it. With such an arrangement, users can not communicate with terminals not connected to the server, but they can access files stored in the assigned disk area of the server.

## EQUIPMENT RESTORAL CAPABILITIES

A variety of types of equipment can help restore service on a disrupted LAN.

### Data Switches

Data switches—also known as port-selection or port-contention devices—have been used in mainframe computer environments since the early 1970s. They permit terminals to share a relatively limited number of computer ports on one or more hosts or the hosts' associated peripherals. Data switches have evolved from relatively simple port-selection and port-contention devices to sophisticated communications controllers capable of managing access to LANs and WANs and of initiating restoral procedures.

Unlike matrix switches, which provide permanent connections, data switches establish connections dynamically to users as needed. Such sophistication offers an economical migration path to LANs. For LAN users, the data switch makes an efficient LAN server or gateway to packet and T1 networks.

Terminals may be connected to the data switch in several ways. The most reliable connection is a direct connection by RS-232C cabling, at distances as far as 50 feet. For distances of one to two miles, between buildings for example, terminals may be connected to the data switch by line drivers or local multiplexers. Some vendors have integrated these devices into their data switches as optional plug-in cards. Terminal-to-switch connections may also use twisted-pair wiring, whereas remote connections may be achieved over dial-up phone lines.

Today's data switches have enough built-in redundancy to virtually eliminate the data switch as a single point of network failure. Not only is control logic concentrated on a single processor card, but optional redundant logic allows some data switches to automatically activate an optional secondary processor card if the first one fails. Configuration instructions are automatically copied into the standby card on cutover, eliminating the need for manual reentry.

Some manufacturers offer redundant power supplies that plug into the switch and activate automatically on failure of the primary power supply. To prevent unnecessary downtime, the faulty power supply module may even be safely replaced with another plug-in unit while the data switch is in operation.

The redundant or split backplane protects the switch from damage that can occur from the failure of components connected to the bus. In the event of a failure on the bus, the switch automatically cuts over to the spare backplane to maintain uninterrupted operation.

Some data switches perform continuous background diagnostic procedures so that faulty channels can be disabled automatically. If a requested port is out of service, a message notifies the user that the port is unavailable. When the appropriate channel board is replaced, the data switch automatically reenables it. Of course, a terminal keyboard can be used to disable a port from a terminal for any reason.

If the primary route is busy or out of service, the dynamic rerouting capability of some data switches allows users to reach any node on the network without performing manual reroutes. The process is entirely transparent to the user.

Data switches with built-in data rate conversion capability eliminate the need to match terminals with computer ports; each computer port can be set at its highest rate. The buffer in the data switch performs rate conversion for any device that operates at a rate different from its assigned port. Users do not have to be concerned about speed at all, and data center managers do not have to waste time changing the transmission speeds of computer ports to accommodate lower-speed devices. A computer port set at 19.2K bps can send data to a much slower printer.

For reliable data rate conversion (i.e., with no loss of data) connecting devices must provide flow control. When XON/XOFF is used for flow control, for example, the switch buffer is prevented from overflowing during data rate conversion. When the buffer is in danger of overflowing, an XOFF signal is sent to the computer, telling it to suspend transmission. When the buffer clears, an XON signal is sent to the computer, telling it to resume transmission. These settings are also used for reformatting character structures, enabling devices of different manufacturers to communicate with each other through the data switch.

These features and levels of redundancy are especially important for data switches because they are usually configured in the center of star-type networks. The data switch is potentially the only point of failure that could bring down the entire network. The modularity of today's data switches provide an economical method of network protection.

## LAN Servers

Distributing LAN resources protects users against the loss of information and the downtime that users of a centralized network experience when it fails. Servers are used to decentralize LAN functions, including security and data protection, network management, and resource accounting.

Moreover, the use of specialized devices as servers permits the integration of diagnostic and maintenance capabilities not found in general-purpose microcomputers. Among these capabilities are error detection and correction, soft controller error detection and correction, and automatic shutdown in case of catastrophic error. Some servers include such management functions as remote console capabilities.

Protecting data at the server has become a critical concern. Some servers store multiple gigabytes of data; loss of this much data or even damage to it can have disastrous consequences. There are several ways to configure a server to minimize data loss, depending on the level of fault tolerance desired and the available budget. Server drives can be unmirrored, mirrored, or duplexed, or a redundant array of inexpensive disks (RAID) can be used.

An unmirrored server configuration entails the use of one disk drive and one disk channel, which includes the controller, a power supply, and interface cabling. This is the basic configuration of most servers. It's advantage is chiefly cost; the user pays only for one disk and disk channel. The disadvantage of this configuration is that a failure in the drive or anywhere on the disk channel can cause the temporary or permanent loss of the stored data.

The mirrored server configuration entails the use of two hard disks of similar size, as well as a single disk channel over which the two disks can be mirrored. In this configuration, all data written to one disk is automatically copied onto the other. If one of the disks fails, the other takes over, thus protecting the data and assuring all users of access to the data. The server's operating system issues an alarm when one of the mirrored disks needs replacing.

The disadvantage of this configuration is that both disks use the same channel and controller. If either the channel or the controller fails, both disks become inoperative. Furthermore, because the disk channel and controller are shared, writes to the disks must be performed sequentially; that is, after the write has been made to one disk, a write is made to the other disk. This process can degrade overall server performance under heavy loads.

In disk duplexing, multiple disk drives are installed with separate disk channels for each set of drives. If a malfunction occurs anywhere along a disk channel, normal operation continues on the remaining channel and drives. Because each disk drive uses a separate disk channel, write operations are performed simultaneously, a performance advantage over servers using disk mirroring.

Disk duplexing also offers a performance advantage in read operations. Read requests are given to both drives. The drive that is closest to the information answers the request, and the request given to the other drive is cancelled. In addition, the duplexed disks share multiple read requests for concurrent access.

The disadvantage of disk duplexing is the extra cost involved for multiple hard disk drives (also required for disk mirroring) and for the additional disk channels and controller hardware. However, this cost must be weighed against the replacement cost of lost information, plus costs that accrue from the interruption of critical operations and from lost business opportunities. Compared to them, the investment of a few hundred or even a few thousand dollars is negligible.

An emerging method of data protection uses RAID, or many small disks instead of a single large one. Distributing data across disks offers protection from a crash that could cause the loss of all data if it were stored on a single shared disk. Multiple disks also ease disk I/O bottlenecks, thereby improving information throughput.

For various technical reasons, current RAID solutions are not yet widely viewed as an option. RAID manufacturers, for example, have not yet perfected the means to put enough storage capacity (i.e., in the gigabyte range) onto $5^1/_4$- and $3^1/_2$-inch drives. Intelligent controllers that direct the placement and retrieval of data must still be refined, and RAID devices must also come down in price to compete with conventional disk storage.

However, RAID may yet evolve to perform the massive storage chores of the advanced fiber-optic networks that will be introduced by IBM and other computer manufacturers during the 1990s. IBM is a committed proponent of RAID. Its RAID-3 configuration for the RS/6000 workstation includes as many as 40 $5^1/_4$-inch enhanced small device interface disk drives operating at a sustained data rate of 18M bytes per second. Prices for RAID-3 begin at about $113,000.

## Bridges

The bridge is a protocol-independent interconnection device that operates at the data link layer. To be more specific, a bridge interconnects at the media access control (MAC) sublayer and routes by using the logical link control sublayer. In working below the communications protocols, the bridge can interconnect LANs that use diverse communications protocols. As long as a bridge operates at the MAC layer, it does not need to perform protocol conversion. It monitors all traffic on the subnets that it links. In reading packets, it looks only for the MAC-layer source and destination address to determine where the packet is going. This means that a bridge can interconnect DECnet, TCP/IP, or XNS networks without concern for higher-level protocols. Unless LAN protocols are the same, however, bridging alone cannot ensure that applications from one network interoperate with applications on another.

As the user population of a LAN grows, performance can suffer because an increasing number of users must contend for the same amount of bandwidth. This can be quite frustrating to the user who merely wants to send a message or print a document. Bridges are useful for partitioning sprawling LANs into discrete subnetworks that are easier to control and manage. Through the use of bridges, similar devices, protocols, and transmission media can be grouped together into communities of interest. This partitioning can eliminate congestion and improve the response time of the entire network. Bridges can also make adding, moving, and changing devices on the network much easier, because the effect on only the subnetwork need be considered. Finally, partitioning makes problems easier to diagnose and isolate while enhancing overall security.

There are two types of bridges: dumb and smart. Dumb bridges must be told which addresses are local and which are remote to filter packets. Smart bridges, also called learning bridges, can figure out address locations by themselves. Such bridges have distinct learning modes for intraLAN traffic and interLAN traffic. IntraLAN traffic requires that the bridge identify each device on the LAN. Some bridges accomplish this within several seconds, even for LANs with several hundred terminals. The locations at remote devices are automatically determined by a process referred to as flooding. A bridge broadcasts to all locations the first packet it receives with an unknown destination address. When it receives a reply from the remote device, it updates its routing table.

Learning bridges are also used on networks that have many bridges and several paths that traffic can follow between nodes. In this environment, it is possible for some packets to be duplicated, or endlessly looped between bridges. A smart bridge incorporates the spanning tree algorithm or some other proprietary routing algorithm (IBM uses source routing but has indicated it will also offer the spanning tree algorithm) to detect loops and shut down the redundant alternative path. If an active link fails, the smart bridge can detect the failure and activate an idle link automatically.

A bridge that is an integral part of a T1 multiplexer is under the control of the integrated network management system. Available bandwidth can be allocated either for LAN-to-LAN communications or for voice or data communications as needed. The integral bridge allows the multiplexer's existing management system to monitor and collect error and use statistics. Furthermore, the bridge's filtering capabilities allow the data center manager to restrict the types of packets that go out over the bridge, thus alleviating traffic bottlenecks.

### Routers

The traditional router is a device that is similar to a bridge in that both provide filtering and bridging between subnetworks. Whereas bridges operate at the physical and data link layers, routers join LANs at a higher level: the network layer. Routers take data formatted for LAN protocols, convert it for wide-area packet network protocols, and then perform the process in reverse at the remote location.

Whereas bridges are transparent to network protocols and are used for point-to-point connections between LANs, routers can be used to build complex internetworks. Routers also offer the highest degree of redundancy and fault tolerance, providing congestion control in conjunction with end nodes to ensure that packets traversing large internets do not experience critical errors that can cause host sessions to time out.

Routing is intended to make the most efficient use of a network by sending data over the most available and direct route between nodes. Routers devise their own routing tables, which can adapt quickly to changes in network traffic, thereby balancing the load. Routers can also detect changes in the network to avoid congested or inoperative links. However, not all routers can use more than one path concurrently; some even cause loop problems.

Nevertheless, routers allow the partitioning of networks for tighter access control by eliminating the broadcast requirement of faster, cheaper, but less reliable bridges. Bridges are less reliable than routers because they deliver packets of data on a best-effort basis, which can result in lost data unless the host computer protocol provides error protection. In contrast, routers can provide flow control and more comprehensive error protection.

Recognizing the value of routers for network reliability, vendors of intelligent wiring hubs are now offering router modules that fit into their hub chassis. The router-on-a-card strategy promotes a tight coupling of the device's network management with the hub vendor's network management system, usually the simple network management protocol (SNMP). With SNMP, devices from other manufacturers can be managed from the hub; because the router shares the hub's power supply, it does not introduce another potential point of network failure.

Another advantage of choosing a router module rather than a standalone version is that it eliminates the need to change the physical configuration of an existing LAN. With a standalone router at a central location, the user must run another riser cable from the router and add another port. This may cost much more than adding a module to an existing box.

Hubs now have such advanced management capabilities as protocol and traffic analyses, distributed network management, comprehensive port control, and relational data bases that archive historical information on network performance, store an inventory of interconnected devices, and keep service vendor contact information. These new hubs considerably enhance network reliability. Ultimately, the hub vendors will interface their equipment to enterprise management systems such as IBM's NetView and AT&T's Accumaster Integrator.

Some high-end hub vendors have introduced reduced instruction set computing (RISC) architectures to help users avoid the transmission bottlenecks that can result from embedding more and more internet functions into the hub. The move to RISC increases throughput for routing, bridging, and connectivity to high-speed LAN backbones, such as the fiber distributed data interface (FDDI). With such hubs, it is even possible to use a high-speed backbone to connect several FDDI rings. All of this capacity is made available at the port.

## Intelligent Wiring Hubs

A fault anywhere in the cabling of a bus or ring network can bring it down, and this weakness is compounded by the inability of these networks to identify the location of a failure from a central administration point. These shortcomings led to the development of the intelligent wiring hub. This device physically rewires bus and ring networks into star networks while logically maintaining their Ethernet or token-ring characteristics. Cabling faults affect only the link's node; more important, the intelligent hub provides a centralized point for network administration and control.

Installing an intelligent wiring hub saves costs in several ways. Because unshielded twisted-pair wiring is used, there is no need to install new cabling. Redundant links are unnecessary, and bypass circuitry at every drop location is no longer needed to ensure network reliability.

A fully redundant backbone can be installed to interconnect LANs. Backbone redundancy can be achieved at two levels: cable and hub. A secondary physical cable links all of the hubs to protect the network in case one of the cables experiences a break. To protect the network against hub failure, a standby hub must be cabled into the network.

The flexibility of the hub architecture lends itself to variable degrees of fault tolerance, depending on the criticality of the applications being run. For example, workstations running noncritical applications can share the same link to the same LAN module at the hub. Although this arrangement is economical, a failure in the LAN module would put all of the workstations on that link out of commission. A slightly higher degree of fault tolerance can be achieved by distributing the workstations among two LAN modules and links. That way, the failure of one module would affect only half the number of workstations. A one-to-one correspondence of workstations to modules offers an even greater level of fault tolerance, because the failure of one module affects only the workstation connected to it. Of course, this is also a more expensive solution.

Sometimes a mission-critical application demands the highest level of fault tolerance. This can be achieved by connecting the workstation running the application to two LAN modules at the hub, with separate links. A transceiver is used to split the links at the workstation (the ultimate in fault tolerance would be achieved by connecting one of those links to a different hub).

An intelligent wiring hub's subsystems are appropriate points for built-in redundancy. The hub's management system can enhance the fault tolerance of the control logic, backplane, and power supply by monitoring their operation and reporting any anomalies. With the power supply, for example, this monitoring can include hotspot detection and fan diagnostics to identify trouble before it disrupts hub operation. If the main power supply fails, the redundant unit switches over automatically or under management control, without disrupting the network.

## IMPACT ON SERVICE SELECTION

Interconnecting LANs over a wide area network requires the installation of devices that connect them to a carrier's network. The selection of appropriate hardware can reduce the need for these services; for example, if the hardware is capable of error correction, the carrier's network need not perform this vital function.

X.25 packet networks, often used for LAN interconnection, have such substantial error correction capabilities that any node on these networks can request a retransmission of errored data from the node that sent it. At the time X.25 networks were set up, errors had to be detected and corrected within the network because most end-user equipment did not have enough intelligence and spare processing power to perform this task.

With much of the public network now converted to inherently reliable digital switching and transmission, there is less need for error protection. Today's intelligent end devices are adept at handling error control and diverse protocols. Consequently, the communications protocol used over the network may be scaled down to its bare essentials, permitting an optimal balance of efficiency and throughput. This is the idea behind frame relay and the reason frame relay services are rapidly becoming the preferred means for interconnecting LANs.

## SUMMARY

Many companies depend on LANs for much of their processing needs. These networks must be reliable and fast. Fortunately, data center managers with responsibility for the effective functioning of these LANs can choose among many strategies and devices to make this job easier.

# V-6
# Auditing LANs

*PAUL CULLEN*

L ocal area networks (LANs) enable users to efficiently share information while allowing them to maintain individual control of processing. PC LAN applications provide good price/performance but must be reviewed so that they get the maximum return. This distribution of processing power is part of a growing end-user computing trend that brings the management of internal controls out of centralized information processing and shifts the responsibility to the end users who are not proficient with controlling processing. In addition, PC LAN vendors focus on product capabilities rather than controls. Thus, controls have typically taken a back seat in the development of LAN applications, resulting in critical applications being implemented without adequate controls in the areas of security, contingency planning, and change control. Data center managers and users are faced with the challenge of assessing risk and implementing controls in a new arena. Auditing PC LANs begins with an understanding of the standards and practices established by management and with the risk inherent in the applications running on the LANs.

## UNDERSTANDING THE PROCESSING ENVIRONMENT

PC LAN processing controls should be based on standards developed by user and data center management. These standards define the practices and controls adopted by management to ensure that processing is performed with a prudent level of risk. Standards should be developed in data security, systems development, program change control, problem management, and disaster recovery planning. Early DOS-based PC LANs had limited control capabilities, and frequently separate standards needed to be developed. These standards focused on manual controls, limited data security controls, and the assessment of risk to determine whether high-risk applications should even run in a PC LAN environment. Recent releases of LAN software, such as IBM Corp.'s OS/2 LAN Manager and Novell, Inc.'s Netware, have made improvements in logical security and system recovery, making their features similar to those found in mainframe environments. This reduces and sometimes eliminates the need for separate PC LAN standards.

The data center manager must work with the EDP auditor to develop a picture of the audit environment, including understanding the business functions and information flows and storage.

## Evaluating the Risk

PC LAN controls should be implemented on the basis of the risk inherent in the application. Risk should be assessed in information confidentiality, loss of data and software, and processing integrity. Users typically confuse applications with the software used to run the application. A typical error would be that Lotus spreadsheet software is an application that could be easily replaced. This does not consider the consequences of errors in the spreadsheets or the effort required to reconstruct a spreadsheet if it is lost. In addition, users have frequently assumed that mainframe and minicomputer applications were of high risk and applications running on PC LANs held little risk. This paradigm is changing as LAN applications have been developed for financial reporting, processing payroll, and handling banking transactions. Auditors must verify that PC LAN application risks have been accurately assessed and that controls are in place to address the risks.

For example, Exhibit V-6-1 presents a simplified risk analysis table showing risks and related controls. The following sections describe audit program steps that can be taken to ensure that risks are properly assessed and controls are in place to address those risks.

## Audit Program Steps

The audit program steps in this chapter begin with the auditor obtaining an overview of the PC LAN, including how it is used and managed. The first step is to identify the LAN administrator and the designated backup. This person is responsible for resolving LAN problems, adding new users to the LAN, making changes to LAN software, and backing up programs and data to ensure that the applications could be recovered in the event of a disaster.

The next step deals with reviewing what the LAN is used for. Here, the auditor documents the applications as well as the risks and exposures associated with the applications. The risks inherent in the LAN applications determine

| Risks | Related Controls |
|---|---|
| Inappropriate Disclosure of Information | Physical Security PC LAN Logical Security |
| Loss of Data or Software | Contingency Plan |
| Processing Errors | Edits Checks, Test Plans |

**Exhibit V-6-1. Risk Analysis Table**

the necessary controls and resulting audit procedures required to verify the adequacy and effectiveness of those controls.

The auditor should also review the network system manuals to determine the systems capabilities. This would provide a basis for possible recommendations. In addition, the auditor should review the use of LAN monitoring equipment and capabilities. Many types of equipment are available to monitor LAN traffic for tuning operations and diagnosing problems. The exposure with these products is that they also can view and capture sensitive data being transmitted across the network. Although these are necessary tools to be used in LAN administration, their use should be properly controlled by authorized individuals.

Gateways are used to connect networks running on different architectures. They are commonly used to connect LANs to mainframes. PCs on the LAN can then act like smart terminals, allowing users to have mainframe sessions. Some gateway products can capture data flowing from the PC to the mainframe, and there is the potential for sensitive information, such as passwords and other confidential data, to be captured. Gateways should be physically secure and restricted only to authorized individuals.

The auditor also should determine whether public domain or shareware software is being used. This software may not be properly licensed, and the company may be infringing on a copyright by using it. In addition, public domain software is arguably more likely to contain computer viruses that could infect and destroy data in individual PCs or an entire LAN.

Finally, a review should be performed to determine the inventory and fixed assets process for controlling hardware and software. PC LAN equipment consists of expensive and typically marketable fixed assets and should be controlled to prevent loss or theft. The inventory review should include tracing equipment and software to inventory records and license agreements to verify their accuracy and to verify that license agreements and copyrights are not being violated.

### The Audit Objective

The audit objective is to determine whether a process is established for planning, organizing, directing, and controlling the activities related to the LAN.

### Risks

The risks include:

- Inappropriate disclosure of confidential information because of inappropriate data security controls.
- Loss of hardware, data, or software because of viruses or inappropriate fixed-asset controls.

417

## Steps

The specific audit steps include:

1. Identifying the LAN administrator and designated backup.
2. Reviewing what the LAN is used for (e.g., application systems, data, files, documents, spreadsheets).
3. Identifying what data is stored on the server and workstations.
4. Documenting the LAN hardware and software. Can it provide the level of access control necessary for the applications and data used on the LAN? Are additional products used to improve LAN security and operations?
5. Determining whether LAN monitoring equipment is used for problem resolution. If so, is this equipment secure to prevent the inappropriate capture or disclosure of sensitive information?
6. Determining whether public domain or shareware software is used on the LAN. If so, is there virus detection and prevention?
7. Determining whether an inventory of hardware is kept and whether there is a process for physically controlling the assets.
8. Determining whether there is a written policy and enforcement process regarding copyright infringement.

## DATA SECURITY

The purpose of this module is to determine whether the LAN applications and data are adequately secured. To begin with, the layout of the LAN should be documented, and physical security over the PC LAN should be evaluated to determine logical controls required to compensate for weaknesses in physical security.

Dial-access capabilities should also be controlled. Many companies believe that LAN operating system security alone is not adequate to control dial access, which could allow access to anyone with a PC, modem, and software. PC products allow a user to dial into a LAN workstation from any location and control the workstation, which removes the ability to rely on physical security. Additional features, such as callback or encryption modems, should be considered to improve dial-access security.

The auditor also must understand the access controls available within the LAN operating system. This typically begins with a review of the administrators manual for the PC operating system.

Security can be cumbersome if a log-on is required for the personal computer, the network operating system, the application, and the mainframe interface. Vendors are beginning to work together to interface log-ons to provide integrated PC, LAN, and mainframe security solutions. This trend will likely continue and become more refined as processing is distributed in the end-user computing environment.

The auditor should next identify the particular platform on which processing is performed and where data is stored. Application software and data can be stored on the PC workstation, LAN server, or mainframe. In addition, the application software itself can provide for internal security. This situation creates the potential for up to four data security functions—workstation, LAN operating system, mainframe, and application security. The auditor must assess the strengths and weaknesses of each of these platforms to ensure that the applications programs and data are adequately secure, based on corporate standards and risk assessment.

The final steps in this section refer to the administration processes for adding new users, reviewing access capabilities, approving new access, and removing access when it is no longer needed. These steps are the same for PC LAN-based systems as they are for applications processing on other platforms. The reporting features may differ, however, as was discussed previously.

## The Audit Objective

The audit objective is to determine whether the systems and data on the LAN are adequately secure, considering the nature of the data and LAN system capabilities.

## Risks

The risks include the loss or inappropriate disclosure of critical or sensitive information because of inadequate or ineffective data security controls.

## Audit Steps

The specific audit steps include:

1. Documenting the physical layout of the LAN:
   —What physical units have access to the LAN? Is access to all nodes on the LAN physically controlled?
   —Is dial-up access to workstations or servers allowed? If so, are products such as Microcom, Inc.'s Carbon Copy used?
   —Are the logical access controls implemented on the LAN system documented?
   —How do workstations access data? Determine who has access to the servers' logical drives.
2. Documenting the LAN security administration process:
   —Is there a process for authorizing new users, authorizing and updating user access capabilities, and deleting access when it is no longer needed?
   —Is there a user listing and a periodic review process established to ensure that access capabilities remain commensurate with job accountabilities?

## A DATA SECURITY TESTING OVERVIEW

The purpose of this section is to verify that access capabilities are authorized and appropriate based on the user's job function. This section begins with the review of log-on password protection.

Passwords can be scripted in .bat files, logging on the workstation when it is started. Then, everyone who has access to the workstation can access the LAN. If passwords are not encrypted, as is true with early LAN systems or possibly application software, users who can access the password file can have all access on the system. The auditor must also determine whether the LAN software allows for peer-to-peer network capabilities. If so, logical access controls over each PC through the network must be assessed. If the network allows access only to a dedicated server, the auditor only needs to identify the servers and review network logical access controls over the servers. There are software packages, such as Brightwork Development, Inc.'s Netremote, that enable administrators to access and control a user's workstation, typically for problem resolution. The use of these packages and controls preventing inappropriate access must be evaluated for their adequacy and effectiveness.

The final steps in this section are to review access capabilities and verify that they are appropriate, based on job function. This includes reviewing user IDs and the groups and resources to which they have access, tracing them to authorized individuals, and verifying their appropriateness. Administrator capabilities and supervisory authority should be limited, as they permit access to all system resources.

### The Audit Objective

The audit objective is to determine whether the systems and data on the LAN are adequately secured, considering the nature of the data and LAN system capabilities.

### Access Testing

Access testing includes the following steps:

1. Determining whether passwords are printed during log-on.
2. Determining whether the password file is encrypted.
3. Determining whether there is violation and access capability reporting.
4. Determining whether file access passwords can be properly controlled if file security is based on passwords. What is the process for distributing and periodically changing file access passwords?
5. Determining whether workstation drives can be accessed from other workstations.
6. Determining whether access control can be based on user or group IDs.
7. Reviewing access capabilities on the PC and LAN server.
   —Tracing IDs to an organization chart to verify that the ID belongs to a valid employee.

—Tracing access capabilities to employee functions to verify that the level of access is appropriate. Access controls should be tested for the various levels of access—read-only or write-and-update.

### Security Administration Testing

Security administration testing involves listing user IDs with administrator authority if such a capability exists. It should be verified that the administrative capability is limited and appropriate for the individual's job function.

### PROBLEM MANAGEMENT

The purpose of this module is to determine whether PC LAN system problems are being recorded, analyzed, and resolved.

The DOS operating system does not have an automated error-tracking file system similar to mainframe systems, such as IBM's System Management Facility (SMF). Thus, there are no automated problem logs for the early DOS-based LANs. Other networks, such as Novell's Netware, OS/2 LAN Manager and LAN Server, and certain implementations of UNIX, do have logging capabilities for operating system and hardware errors. Exhibit V-6-2 presents a sample file server error log that shows operating system errors and bad log-ins. Application software and user errors, however, would not be logged. Therefore, LAN administrators should keep a manual or automated log of all problems, including:

- User.
- Application.
- Operating system.
- Hardware errors.

This log should contain the date the problem occurred, the problem description, length of downtime, priority of resolution, actions taken to resolve the problem, and date the problem was resolved. The problem log should be

---

7/5/93 3:56:05 PM Severity = 0.
1.1.60 Bindery open requested by the SERVER

7/5/93 4:17:19 PM Severity = 0.
1.1.62 Bindery close requested by the SERVER

7/5/93 4:17:20 PM Severity = 4.
1.1.72 SERVER TTS shut down
     because backout volums SYS was dismounted

7/5/93 4:38:39 PM Severity = 0.
1.1.60 Bindery open requested by the SERVER

**Exhibit V-6-2. Sample File Server Error Log**

analyzed on a periodic basis to find weaknesses in testing, hardware reliability, and user training requirements. Another concern is whether problems are resolved within the appropriate time frames. For critical time frame applications, companies may need to contract for LAN equipment support within specified time frames and have backup equipment to ensure that the network is performing according to business needs. In addition, a complete problem log can show problem trends with hardware, operating system software, application software, and communications software.

### The Audit Objective

The audit objective is to determine whether the LAN system has a problem-reporting tracking and resolution process.

### Risks

The risks include unresolved errors or inefficient processing because of inadequate problem management controls.

### Steps

The specific audit steps include:

1. Documenting the process used for tracking and reporting problems:
   —How are problems identified, tracked, rates for severity, and resolved?
   —Is there a process for problem history and trend analysis?
   —Is there a process for reviewing the criteria for assigning resolution deadlines for problems?
2. Obtaining and reviewing the problem listing. LAN users should be questioned regarding LAN problems to see that they are recorded.
3. Reviewing open problems to see that they have been resolved in a timely manner.
4. Reviewing closed problems and verifying with users that they are in fact properly resolved.

## CHANGE MANAGEMENT

The purpose of this module is to determine whether system changes are authorized, tested, documented, communicated, and controlled. A process should also be in place to ensure that production source and executable code are synchronized and secured in order to prevent inappropriate program alteration and to be able to reconstruct the system files. PC LAN operating systems typically do not have the change management facilities that are found in mainframe systems. Therefore, LAN administrators manually control production code on restricted subdirectories on the LAN servers. Once a change has been tested and approved, an independent party should move the code to a restricted library on the server or distribute the software to workstations. This process would ensure the integrity of the software version that is running in production and that unauthorized changes are not introduced into the system.

PC LAN software is also frequently developed by software vendors outside the company. Because users are not involved in program development, they do not feel the need to test the software. User acceptance testing, however, should be performed before each PC LAN software release is propagated to ensure that the system is performing according to user expectations and to prevent the corruption of user files.

The auditor should review the process for unit, system, and user acceptance testing. There should be evidence showing that users have signed off approving the change, that the systems documentation was updated, and that the risk factors were updated if appropriate.

### The Audit Objective

The audit objective is to determine whether a system is in place to ensure that changes on the LAN are properly authorized, documented, communicated, and controlled.

### Risks

The risks include:

- Fraud and embezzlement resulting from unauthorized change.
- Incorrect or incomplete information caused by improperly installed changes.
- Business interruptions caused by improper change coordination.

### Steps

The specific audit steps include:

- Documenting the process used for authorizing, communicating, and documenting changes to the LAN systems and applications.
- Documenting who makes the changes and how programs and files are managed during the change process.
- Verifying that there is a separation of duties.
- Documenting the change testing process.
- Reviewing test plans to ensure that they are complete and that any inadequate test results have been resolved.
- Documenting the change fallback process, which would enable a system to use the previous version of the software to facilitate the recovery of the system in the event of an error (i.e., backing out a change).
- Reviewing directories on the workstations and servers to verify that production programs and data are adequately secure to prevent inappropriate alteration.

- Verifying that production source and executable software are synchronized to provide the ability to reconstruct the processing environment in the event of problems.
- Reviewing the process for updating systems documentation for each change.
- Reviewing documentation to verify that it is current.

## DISASTER RECOVERY AND CONTINGENCY PREPAREDNESS

Disaster recovery planning is basically no different for PC LAN systems than for any other systems. The business unit must identify the risk of the applications and the time frame required for recovery. Based on this assessment, a disaster recovery plan should be developed identifying who will be responsible for recovering the system, where recovery will be performed, and what equipment is required for recovery, including communications equipment. Backups of workstation and server programs and data are frequently kept in the form of backup tapes. A common approach is for users to back up workstation data to the server and then back up the server to tape. The backup tapes should be kept in a secure off-site location, and the frequency of the backups should be assessed based on how often the data is updated and the amount of effort required to reconstruct the files. The security of the off-site location is critical for PC LAN systems because logical security provided by the LAN operating system does not protect data on backup tapes.

The disaster recovery plan should be tested to ensure that it is sufficient to recover all critical functions. This test should include recovery from the backup tapes to verify that the backup process is effective.

### The Audit Objective

The audit objectives are to determine the adequacy of contingency and disaster recovery planning, which ensures the timely business recovery from possible major disasters, and to determine whether all required documentation, data files, and recovery materials are stored in a secured off-site location that is readily available in the event of a disaster.

### Risks

The risks include the interruption of information processing business caused by inadequate recovery procedures.

### Steps

The specific audit steps include:

1. Documenting the backup and recovery process:
   —Has the area documented the time frame required for recovery and

the critical software, data, and hardware to be used in the event of a disaster?

—What is the process for backing up LAN workstations and servers?

—What is the frequency of backups?

—Has recovery been tested?

—What hardware and software are used for the backup process?

—Is redundancy built into the system to avoid downtime for systems that need high availability (e.g., are there duplicate disk drives and servers to be used as a fallback)?

2. Reviewing procedures for off-site storage of essential software, documentation, and data.
3. Verifying that the backup media is properly stored in an off-site location.
4. Verifying that the media is effectively secured.

## SYSTEMS DEVELOPMENT AND PROJECT MANAGEMENT

This module is also basically the same for PC LAN systems as it is for other systems and is closely related to the change control module previously discussed. The module may need to be tailored for certain situations. PC LAN software development is often done in groups of small data bases in purchased packages or by contract programmers. The area may not have a development staff similar to one found in mainframe applications. A development methodology, project management, and user involvement and training, however, should be used for PC LAN systems development, as with the development of any other systems.

Strategic planning should be performed to ensure that the LAN systems and applications are compatible with the corporation's wide area networks and technology direction. The systems strategic plan should be based on the business units' plans. In addition, the operating system and hardware should provide for migration to future platforms. This is a difficult issue because the future of operating systems, such as DOS and OS/2, is arguably not certain, and it is difficult to decide which LAN operating system and hardware provides the best migration path for the future. The auditor should review the systems development methodology for inclusion of critical elements.

Other concerns regarding the development of PC LAN systems include a cost/benefit analysis to ensure that the payback from the system justifies its cost as well as competitive bidding to ensure that the prices paid for the hardware and software are reasonable considering this highly competitive market and that the purchases are properly approved by an appropriate level of management. Finally, if software is developed by vendors or contract programmers, copyrights and software ownership must be clearly defined.

### Audit Objectives

The audit objectives are to determine whether LAN systems are developed to fulfill user requirements in a cost-effective manner that allows for adequate system growth and to determine whether there is a process for setting priorities for LAN projects.

## Risks

The risks include projects that do not meet specifications and the cost and time overruns caused by inefficient planning and budgeting.

## Steps

The specific audit steps include:

1. Documenting the planning process for LAN systems:
   —Has management devised a strategic plan for the development of applications and the selection of the optimum processing platform based on user requirements?
   —Was a cost/benefit analysis performed?
   —Is there evidence of user management approval?
2. Reviewing the project management process used for systems development, including project budgets, schedules, timekeeping, and issue tracking.
3. Verifying that purchases were cost-effective through the use of competitive bids, vendor analysis, and thorough requests for information.
4. Documenting the process for user training and involvement in LAN systems development.
5. Reviewing and evaluating the systems development documentation, including evidence of approvals and cost/benefit analysis.
6. Verifying that copyrights have been registered for new software.

## PROCESSING INTEGRITY

Processing integrity for PC LAN-based systems has some unique control concerns in addition to the basic input, processing, and output controls that apply to all application systems. Users typically install applications on a PC LAN platform because it is a low-cost alternative to mainframe development. The ability for the PC LAN application to grow on this platform is limited, however, particularly for DOS-based systems. Equipment should be benchmark tested before it is propagated to ensure that it has enough capacity.

Another concern for PC LAN-based systems is the control over concurrent updates; that is, the ability to prevent two people from updating the same file or record at the same time. This can be controlled by the LAN operating system and by the application software. LAN servers typically fail in one of two ways. First, they can be too restrictive by preventing two or more people from accessing the same disk drive or subdirectory at the same time. This can obviously be inefficient when the desire is to share data. The second way LANs can fail is by letting two or more individuals into the same file or even the same record but not preventing the loss of one person's update or the destruction of a file.

Another concern regarding PC LAN applications is that they are typically used to process data that is distributed by downloading it from a mainframe or minicomputer environment. Processes need to be developed to ensure that the distributed data bases are current and that users are all working from the same data.

### The Objective

The objective is to determine the adequacy and effectiveness of controls to ensure the integrity of data maintained on the PC LAN network.

### Risks

The risks include:

- Inaccurate processing.
- Unauthorized transactions.
- Inefficient processing.
- Lost or duplicated transactions.

### Steps

The specific audit steps include:

1. Reviewing system capability and user procedures for editing input data, accurate processing, and reconciliation of output. The input, processing, and output controls are not unique to the PC LAN platform and are not covered in this chapter.
2. Interviewing the LAN administrator regarding the consideration given to the controls in place to prevent concurrent updates of data.
3. Reviewing software manuals to verify that controls are in place.
4. Reviewing procedures relating to the cataloging and updating of application programs.
5. Reviewing program documentation for accuracy and currency. Are system operating instructions documented?
6. Verifying that the equipment has been adequately tested, including benchmark testing to ensure that the systems have adequate capacity for the number of users and transaction volume.
7. Verifying that processes are in place to ensure that distributed data bases are current.

### SUMMARY

High-risk applications are being developed on PC LAN platforms. Data center and user management must assess the risk of these applications and implement appropriate controls. Auditors must verify that this assessment is performed and that adequate and effective controls are established based on the application risk. Although the steps required for assessing PC LAN controls are basically the same as those for assessing controls on most platforms, they should be tailored to match the unique characteristics of the PC LAN platform. The steps included in this chapter provide a starting point for the development of an audit program required to assess controls on this important platform.

# Section VI
# Contingency Planning

The primary mission of the data center manager is to ensure the continuous operation of the data center facilities in support of the business operations of the company. The word *continuous* is the focus of this section. There are many challenges to ensuring that the data center functions continuously. Hardware, software, and human errors occur every day. These errors usually have little, if any, major effect on operations. Today's information systems have levels of built-in redundancy that are designed to eliminate, or at least minimize, the impact of errors.

However, systems may become inoperative for relatively short periods of time. Although this may be an inconvenience, it usually poses no major problems for the company. At still other times, outages may occur that are more serious, and could require several hours or days to resolve. In these cases, the data center manager must take steps to ensure the continuity of operations in some manner, until the outage has been corrected.

Finally, the data center itself could suffer damage serious enough to put it out of operation for a substantial period of time, or even permanently. In this case, the data center manager must put into effect a plan that allows for the recovery from a disaster. For many years, the possibility of such a situation required data center managers to develop disaster recovery plans. Often, these were merely paper plans—that is, they were designed to answer the questions of outside auditors, but, in reality, their chances of being implemented were marginal. An entire industry was built around disaster recovery planning, as vendors established hot sites and cold sites and consulting services designed to help data center managers develop workable disaster recovery plans. Over the years, numerous disasters, such as fires, earthquakes, and floods, have proved that such plans, when carefully and realistically developed, can be implemented successfully.

Because of the growing dependence on information systems, companies have come to realize that, as important as it is, recovery of the data center is only one aspect of the overall recovery of the company following a disaster. Thus, the concept of business continuity planning has developed. The data center manager must understand this concept and how the data center disaster recovery plan fits into the overall company business recovery plan. In some cases, data center managers, because of their expertise in this area, have been the ones to encourage their companies to develop overall business recovery plans and have been actively involved in assisting the company in their development.

Chapter VI-1, "Overview of Business Continuity Planning," discusses the concepts of business continuity planning. The author stresses that such a plan involves the active participation of all functional units in the organization. Several methods associated with this type of planning are addressed and the author provides a detailed sample plan that the data center manager can use in discussing the development of a plan with senior management.

Once the data center manager has gained an overall understanding of the basic concepts of business continuity planning, the next step is to understand the approaches used in developing such a plan. A comprehensive plan must include not only large systems recovery but the recovery and testing of midrange systems, networks, and work groups. Chapter VI-2, "Strategies for Developing and Testing Business Continuity Plans," describes the steps in this process. The chapter covers the specific stages of the plan development and provides recommendations and basic guidelines for a test plan.

One of the major considerations of a business recovery plan is assessing the impact of a disaster on the business. Before a plan can be developed in detail, a comprehensive impact study must be undertaken. Chapter VI-3, "A Business Impact Analysis for Disaster Recovery," addresses in detail those areas an auditor should consider when assessing the impact of a major system outage on an organization. With this guidance, data center managers can conduct their own in-depth impact analysis as part of the overall business recovery plan development project.

The scope of the data center's operations often extend beyond the physical data center itself. The rapid development of computer networks has provided greater processing capability for end users. Often, the data center is one node in a large, complex network that can even extend globally. As a result, ensuring the successful continued operation of the data center may not be enough. The data center manager must ensure the network continues to operate successfully in order to ensure the survival of the company itself. Network disaster recovery is an extremely challenging task. Chapter VI-4, "Network Disaster Recovery Planning," discusses the myriad details involved in developing a network recovery plan and offers practical suggestions concerning the development of such a plan.

Although it is certainly important to understand the concepts associated with disaster recovery planning, the task of developing an effective plan is often beyond the experience, or available time, of the data center manager. Knowing when and how to select an outside consultant to assist in developing a plan can often mean the difference between having a real plan rather than one that merely satisfies legal or audit requirements. Chapter VI-5, "Disaster Recovery Planning Tools and Management Options," provides suggestions for selecting an outside consultant, examines the tools available for developing a disaster recovery plan and provides advice as to when it is appropriate to use each one.

Though it may seem somewhat mundane when compared to developing an overall disaster recovery plan, ensuring the data center has an effective uninterruptible power system (UPS) is a major responsibility of the data center manager. Often, the UPS can prevent a major outage. A major component of a UPS is the type of battery that is used with it. This may seem to be a minor point, but many data center managers have simply assumed that all batteries are the same, much to their dismay when the UPS failed to operate correctly. Chapter VI-6, "Selecting and Maintaining UPS Battery Systems," provides information regarding how the data center manager can prevent such a situation from occurring.

# VI-1
# Overview of Business Continuity Planning

*SALLY MEGLATHERY*

C orporate business continuity planning specifies the methodology, structure, discipline, and procedures needed to back up and recover functional units struck by a catastrophe. Therefore, every functional unit must accept responsibility for developing and implementing the business continuity plan, and the plan must have the total support of management.

Strategically, senior management must ensure the development of a policy stating that the company will recover from any type of outage. Such recovery requires high-level commitment to the policy from all levels of management. Tactically, however, middle management implements the policy and the plan and is responsible for the daily operation of the plan. For management and the functional units to participate, they must have a comprehensive methodology to guide them in their actions and activities. This chapter discusses methods of developing a corporate business continuity plan.

## PROJECT PLANNING

There are numerous reasons for developing a total business continuity plan. Some of the most compelling are legal and regulatory requirements. Consideration must be given to the following when developing the plan:

- Are there any federal statutes or regulations applicable to the business which would apply to disasters relating to the business?
- Are there any state statutes or regulations applicable to the business which would apply to disasters relating to the business?
- What contract requirements (e.g., labor contracts, insurance agreements, mortgages, loans, or other financial documents) should be addressed by the plan?
- Are there any common-law considerations, such as claims against directors and officers raised by shareholders and others? Could there be negligence claims against the company for property damage or injuries to customers or business visitors?

Before beginning development of the business continuity plan, management should identify a business continuity project team. The project team is responsible for developing the business continuity plan and designing procedures and reporting techniques to support overall project management. In addition, the project team should identify individuals from senior management to review and approve the work performed by the project team.

Although the makeup of the project team will vary among companies, the following departments should be represented on the team:

- Real estate and facilities.
- Security.
- Human resources.
- Information systems.
- Communications.
- Technology, planning, and development.

Additional departments may also be represented. A business continuity manager should be delegated for the team.

## DEVELOPING THE PLAN

The plan that is developed must ensure that any disaster will have a minimum impact on the company. The plan should address the company's reasons for establishing the plan, the functional area of the company's business that the plan will cover, and what staff or materials are in place or should be in place for the plan to function. The following sections discuss the requirements of the business continuity plan, the various elements of the plan, and the scope of the plan.

### Plan Requirements

Although most plans address the need to continue data processing operations and to support critical operations during a crisis, most plans fail to consider loss of other functional units within the organization. Data processing generally initiates the need for disaster recovery planning; however, it is now recognized that recovering data centers alone cannot ensure the continuing health of the organization. Companies must address corporate division and department business continuity planning as well. In fact, planning should be done for all essential functional units of the organization.

The plan must be comprehensive; it must deal with the broadest range of disasters possible. There should be a basic plan with additional procedures for specific hazards (e.g., earthquakes, fires, or exposure to hazardous materials). The plan should preserve the integrity of the business, not individual items or goals.

The plan must contain sufficient detail so that its users will know what procedures to follow, how to perform these activities, and the resources that will be available. The plan should contain action steps that have been decided on and agreed to in advance. Both the response to the immediate disaster and the recovery and continuance of business operations and functions must be specified.

The plan must be owned by the organization. Key personnel must participate in identifying priorities, determining alternative strategies, negotiating agreements, and assembling necessary materials. The plan should be reviewed on a periodic basis or when circumstances change. It should be periodically tested with a defined testing program to ensure that it remains effective and up to date.

## Plan Elements

The plan itself has five major elements:

- Risk and business impact analysis.
- Alternative analysis.
- Response and recovery planning and plan documentation.
- Plan publication and testing.
- Training and implementation.

These are discussed in the following sections.

**Risk and Business Impact Analysis.** Before the plan is written, the hazards that may affect the company's facilities must be identified and their potential impact determined. It is also necessary to identify and rank the major business functions and the resources necessary to carry out those functions, and to identify the potential impact of the hazards on the critical business functions and operations. This helps determine the maximum allowable downtime for individual business functions and operations. From there, the minimum resource and personnel needs and time frames in which they will be needed can be identified. Finally, consideration of emergency operating procedures and strategies can begin.

**Alternative Analysis.** Using the risk and business impact analysis as a base, consideration is given to the internal and external alternatives available for continuation of each function within the necessary time frames. These alternatives should be chosen on the basis of their cost, benefits, and feasibility. The alternatives considered should include not only those that are currently available but those that can be developed.

**Response and Recovery Planning and Plan Documentation.** This involves the development and documentation of the procedures to be used to activate the plan (by declaration or event), move specific functions to the alternative or backup facility, maintain operations at that site while the primary site is being restored or a new permanent site prepared, and return operations to the primary site or another permanent location. The plan must identify ways to procure alternative resources to carry out business activities; determine responsibilities and notification procedures for the company, vendors, customers, and others; and detail recovery strategies and responsibilities.

**Plan Publication and Testing.** The plan must be reviewed and agreed to by senior management and all departments. It must then be documented and distributed to key personnel with additional copies secured off site. Individual sections of the plan should be distributed to those who will be involved with its activation and operation.

The plan should contain a schedule for periodic review and updating. The only way to assess the adequacy of the plan before a disaster occurs is with a program of periodic tests. The tests used will vary from conceptual walk-throughs to actual relocation of specific departments or business functions.

**Training and Implementation.** Employees should understand what is expected of them in a disaster and what their roles will be in the recovery process. This is achieved with a training and education program, which should be conducted before the plan is implemented.

### The Scope of the Plan

All key personnel should be identified in the business continuity plan and given specific assignments. Common terminology should be defined in the plan document to avoid confusion at the time the plan is put into effect. In addition, the plan should interface with the IS disaster recovery plan. Budgets should be prepared for the initial costs of developing the plan and for the costs of maintaining the plan.

The scope of the business continuity plan should include the features discussed in the following sections.

**A Vital Records Program.** The plan should help establish an information valuation program to determine which records should be retained and for how long. In addition, there should be a methodology for ensuring that critical records are retained off site.

**Security Requirements.** The plan defines what security measures must be in place in the event of a disaster and what security measures are necessary for an off-site location. It also states who has access to each location.

**Accounting Procedures.** Procedures must be put in place to facilitate the acquisition of needed replacement parts and to properly account for the costs of recovery. This in turn facilitates the filing of insurance claims, among other benefits.

**Insurance Requirements.** The plan should define what insurance claims must be filed and give guidelines on working with risk managers to file a claim. One of the benefits of developing the business continuity plan is that insurance requirements are specifically defined.

**Interdepartmental Interfaces.** Interfaces between divisions and departments must be defined in the business continuity plan.

**Backup, Recovery, and Restoration Strategies.** All critical data, files, and documents should be backed up and stored off site. Recovery procedures should be documented in the business continuity plan, defining the steps necessary to recover the information that was lost. Restoration may require recreating the lost data, files, or documents rather than recovering with a backup. Procedures for such restoration must be documented.

**Plan Maintenance and Testing.** Once implemented, the plan must be tested regularly to ensure that it is up-to-date. The plan should include a maintenance and testing schedule as well as a methodology for testing the plan to ensure that it is operating as expected.

## IDENTIFYING CRITICAL RESOURCES

Not all activities within an organization are critical at the time of a catastrophe. The management disaster decision team identifies those operations that it deems critical to the organization. This determination is based on several specific factors, including the time at which the disaster occurs, legal and regulatory requirements, the amount of time that availability is lost, the company's public image, loss of market share, loss of revenue, the type of service loss (e.g., administrative, executive, or financial), and deadline requirements.

In addition, the plan should account for the facilities, equipment, materials, and supplies needed to adequately perform required tasks. Voice and data communications are particularly critical and should be given proper consideration.

For example, personnel are vital to the success of the recovery, and their comfort and support should be given special attention. Supplies and forms should be maintained off site so that a supply is readily available in times of emergency. In addition, transportation can easily be disrupted in times of emergency, and transportation to an off-site location may not be readily available. Therefore, transportation to the main site or an off-site location must be planned if employees are to arrive at the designated stations in a timely manner.

Spare parts and units for power and environmental systems (e.g., air conditioners, fans, and heaters) should be available at the central business location. The engineering staff should have spare parts on hand for replacing broken parts. A backup unit should be available to replace the disabled units. When that is not possible or when the outage is outside the control of the company (e.g., the loss of a telephone company's central office or a power company's power station), the company must be prepared to move to its off-site location.

A vital record is any document that is necessary to ensure the survival of the business. To ensure the preservation and availability of vital records, all corporate documents should be classified as to their importance (e.g., essential, valuable, important, or nonessential). Corporate recordkeeping policies as well as retention requirements based on legal or regulatory requirements should be documented. The source document should be controlled and protected. In addition, there should be backup procedures for the documents, and a copy of them should be maintained at the off-site location.

Documentation, policies, procedures, and standards should be available in hard copy and should be accessible in both main and off-site locations. A disaster recovery plan has no value if the disaster recovery team cannot locate a copy of it.

## ORGANIZING THE PROJECT

The business continuity plan should be prefaced with a mission statement or purpose. This can be incorporated into the introductory section of the plan. All departments and functions involved in the project must understand the need for the plan, agree to participate in its implementation, and be committed to enforcing the plan.

The departments and functions that participate in the project vary among companies. In most companies, however, senior management must be kept up to date and is responsible for making most key decisions. The audit department oversees the entire process, ensuring that controls are enforced. When a disaster strikes, the building and facilities staff determine any losses and necessary repairs, and the public relations and marketing staffs calm customers and reassure them that the company is all right. A legal staff helps protect the company from litigation, negotiates purchase contracts, and enforces contracts.

The human resources department is usually responsible for keeping all employees informed during and after a disaster, particularly in union shops. In addition, this staff often serves as the go-between for employees and management.

When it is necessary to replace equipment or parts, the purchasing department acquires the necessary components at the best possible price, and the financial or accounting department controls costs and purchases. The engineering department ensures that the companies are properly ordered and installed.

At some level, all disasters have an impact on data processing. Therefore, the IS department must be kept up-to-date and should participate in the recovery procedures. The operations department ensures that the company continues to run as smoothly as possible.

Depending on the company's business, the following departments might also be included in the business continuity planning process:

- Manufacturing.
- Research and development.
- Warehouse and distribution.
- Customer service.
- Field support services.

Representatives from these business areas can identify the functional, management, and support operations of the company in the initial phases of the project, while gathering information for the plan. As a result, critical divisions and departments that support the organization in times of catastrophe are identified.

In any company, the business continuity plan cannot be developed without the commitment and assistance of management and departmental staff. A considerable amount of coordination is also required, both within the company and between any external resources or consultants and company personnel. To facilitate this, it is recommended that different planning teams and functions be created. The size, number, and type of teams used are determined by the size of the company and by the computing environment. The following are various options, ranging from senior-level management teams on down:

- *The management decision-making team.* This team consists of senior management. It is responsible for making major decisions about the continuity plan and about whether or not to move off site after a disaster.
- *The business continuity steering committee.* This committee provides overall management of the project. It establishes and controls policies, standards, and procedures, and it defines the organization of the departments and other participants to ensure cohesive planning groups. This committee should include members of operations, IS, and finance. The actual composition of the team can be agreed on at the initiation of the project.
- *The business continuity planning coordinator.* This individual provides day-to-day coordination of the project and typically works with external resources or consultants. This person must be able to commit sufficient time to the project to ensure that it is completed within the agreed time frame.
- *The management operations team.* This team consists of line managers who are responsible for managing the day-to-day operations after a disaster occurs. They advise the management decision-making team and report decisions down through their respective areas.
- *Department coordinators.* These individuals are responsible for providing information on their department's operations, completing forms, and developing draft plans. Related departments can be grouped under one coordinator; other departments may have their own individual coordinators.

The time required of these individuals increases with each phase of plan development.

- *The emergency operations team.* This team consists of those people who are responsible for ensuring that operations keep running in the off-site environment.
- *The damage assessment and postinvestigation team.* This team is responsible for evaluating damages to the facility and determining the cost to restore operations. It should consist of those people in charge of facilities and operations.
- *The reconstruction team.* This team consists primarily of facilities personnel. It is responsible for managing restoration activities.

It is recommended that at least a business continuity steering committee, a business continuity planning coordinator, and department coordinators be appointed.

It is important that departmental employees involved in developing the plan for their departments be aware of the reasons for developing the plan, the project organization, what is expected of them during the project, and the tools and information that will be provided to assist them in their work. This can be achieved by holding one or more group business continuity training meetings to discuss these points. During these meetings, any software that will be used should be demonstrated and all questionnaires and forms to be used in developing the plan should be explained in detail.

The following sections discuss the responsibilities of the various teams that may be involved in business continuity planning.

## The Disaster Decision-Making Team

The disaster decision-making team is primarily responsible for notifying the board of directors, regulatory bodies, regional companies, local companies, international bodies, and the media as required. This team may make these notifications itself or delegate the work.

In addition, members of this team make the final business decisions regarding whether the plan should go into effect, whether to move operations to the off-site location or continue business at the main site, and even whether to continue conducting business at all. Should the plan be put into effect, the team is kept up to date through management operations teams, the business continuity coordinator, and those functional areas reporting to the team that are in charge of handling areas of the disaster.

All recovery activities are submitted to this team for review; however, all disaster containment activities are handled on site as the events take place. Steps taken to contain the disaster are reported back to this team through the management operations team, as they occur if possible or after the fact if not. All major decisions regarding expenditures of funds are made by this team.

## The Business Continuity Steering Committee and Planning Coordinator

The business continuity steering committee is responsible for establishing and controlling policies, standards, and procedures and for defining the structure of the project to ensure that the departments and other participants work together cohesively. In addition, the committee reviews, approves, and coordinates the plans developed by the participating groups.

In the event of a disaster, this committee serves as a facilitator, responsible for providing transportation to the backup facilities, if required; notifying affected personnel and families of the status of the disaster; providing cash for needed travel or emergency items; securing the affected areas, the business resumption control center, and the backup site; escorting personnel, if necessary; and presenting a carefully formatted release to the media and affected personnel as to the status of operations and personnel. Several areas are represented on the business continuity steering committee during the disaster, to ensure that basic necessities are made available to support those individuals working to recover the business.

The size of the business continuity steering committee depends on the extent of the disaster and the recovery needs. The following departments should be consulted in forming the committee:

- Purchasing.
- Human resources.
- Communications.
- Auditing.
- Finance and accounting.
- Transportation and amenities.
- Facilities.
- Security.
- Public relations.
- Risk management and insurance.
- Administrative services.
- Operations.
- Information systems.

The business continuity planning coordinator interfaces with the business continuity steering committee to ensure a smooth and successful transition to each phase of the plan. In addition, the coordinator acts as team manager for the management operations team, discussed in the following section.

## The Management Operations Team

The management operations team is responsible for coordinating all emergency operations teams. When management decides that the business continuity plan is to be implemented, these team members (or their alternates) contact the emergency operations team members to advise them of the disaster declaration.

They then report to the business resumption control center to begin damage assessment. Once at the disaster site, the management operations team monitors the emergency operations team's progress and acts as overall manager for all emergency operations teams activated by the operational group.

The management operations team forwards all requests for space, equipment, supplies, and additional human resources support to the department coordinator. The team members report daily on the status of all emergency operations to the business resumption coordinator for the management operations team.

The management operations team is primarily responsible for determining the extent of the disaster, relocating at the business resumption control center, and notifying emergency operations team managers and department coordinators. In addition, the team monitors recovery progress, and compliance with the business resumption plan during recovery and reports on recovery status to the business resumption coordinator, who in turn reports to the company president as required.

## The Department Coordinators Team

The department coordinators team is composed of members from all functional areas. Each department coordinator acts as chairperson for his or her department's emergency operations team. In addition, the department coordinator manages the management disaster decision team and the business continuity steering committee. He or she communicates all of the department's needs and the department's status.

Department coordinators have access to the business resumption control center and attend strategic planning meetings. When a disaster occurs, they contact all emergency operations team managers and coordinate recovery efforts. Department coordinators submit written requests for equipment or supplies as soon as needs are made known to the business continuity steering committee.

Perhaps most important, the department coordinators monitor recovery operations. In this capacity, they receive and communicate status reports, receive daily reports from all emergency operations team managers, request additional human resources support as necessary, and maintain a log of the department's status and progress. In addition, the department coordinators communicate all decisions made by the management disaster decision team to affected managers within the department.

## The Emergency Operations Team

The members of the emergency operations team are responsible for the smooth transition to the prearranged emergency backup center, continued operations, emergency procedures, notification of users, requisition of equipment and supplies, and a return to normal processing. Each member of the team should designate an alternate in case the primary team member is unavailable when a disaster occurs.

The size of the emergency operations team depends on the extent of the disaster and operating needs. The responsibilities of the team members include forwarding requests to the business continuity steering committee for transportation to the alternative facilities, if required, and for notification of key employees, affected families, and any employees who were off duty at the time of the disaster. In addition, the emergency operations team makes requests for first aid, supplies, mail or courier service, replacement of software or equipment, temporary workers, additional security or communications measures, backup power, and documentation. Team members also work with the data processing operations and communications departments.

Each emergency operations team has a team manager and a backup manager, who report to the department coordinator. The team manager is responsible for coordinating the recovery effect. The managers participate in the damage assessment meeting to determine the extent of the damage. The manager gives daily status reports regarding recovery and ongoing operations to the business resumption coordinator.

### The Damage Assessment and Postinvestigation Team

The damage assessment team reports directly to the management operations team and notifies it of the extent of damage. After damages have been assessed, this team functions as a postinvestigation team to determine the cause of the disaster. In some cases, the cause is obvious (e.g., an earthquake), but in many cases it is not. For example, in the case of a fire, the origin of the fire must be determined as well as how to prevent such a fire from happening again.

### The Reconstruction Team

The reconstruction team is composed of those departments required to restore the damaged site. It should include all departments associated with building services as well as representatives from the damaged areas.

The reconstruction team's responsibilities include both temporary and long-term reconstruction efforts. From the initial damage assessment to final reconstruction of the damaged area, the reconstruction team directs and coordinates efforts to bring about a smooth, efficient reconstruction of the damaged areas.

### PREPARING THE PLAN

In preparing the plan, members of the business continuity project team must assemble documentation about their specific functional area and operating environment. In addition, they must identify critical performance requirements and rank the tasks within their jobs according to priority.

Departments that rely heavily on computer processing must explain in detail how their operations interface with each other and are supported by data processing. The needed information can be gathered from:

- Organizational charts.
- Job descriptions.
- Procedures manuals.
- Technical support requirements.
- Existing disaster recovery or business continuity plans.
- Risk analyses.
- Business impact analyses.
- Vulnerability assessments.

Questionnaires can be used successfully to gather information that can provide a foundation for the strategies that must be developed in the planning process. Although questionnaires should be customized for individual projects, they should always provide the basic information presented in Exhibit VI-1-1.

---

☐ Description of departmental operations.
☐ Functions that support those operations.
☐ Peak operating times.
☐ Impact of department downtime.
☐ Recovery priorities and time frames for departmental functions.
☐ Staffing requirements under normal circumstances and in an emergency.
☐ Computer support for both departmental operations and individual functions. (This should cover both centralized and decentralized computer operations.)
☐ Site requirements for both normal and emergency operations.
☐ Equipment needed (and the vendors of that equipment).
☐ Office and other supplies (and the vendors).
☐ Critical records needed and their backup and recovery requirements.
☐ Priority ranking of departmental functions.
☐ Name and address of alternative-site vendor.
☐ List of responsibilities and home telephone numbers of key personnel.
☐ Emergency telephone numbers (e.g., fire and police departments).
☐ Critical forms (number, names, and average use).
☐ Special equipment specifications.
☐ Area user list.
☐ Vendor backup contracts.
☐ Critical functions and assumptions (e.g., individuals might assume that they will have access to backup files).
☐ Minimum equipment and space requirements.

**Exhibit VI-1-1. Checklist of Basic Information Required on Business Continuity Planning Questionnaires**

Departments should be asked to complete the questionnaire after the initial training meeting. The completed form should be returned to the department coordinator and any external consultants for review. The department coordinator and external consultants should review the answers with the department manager and the employee who completed the form to clarify, amend, and confirm the information.

The completed questionnaires should be compared to determine the priority of departmental functions, the impact relative to specific time frames, and the minimum resources needed to maintain the company's critical functions. This information is helpful when considering alternative or backup sites that will be needed.

All of the information obtained in these early phases of plan development is integrated into the business continuity plan. Plan development is designed to integrate or provide interfaces between sections of the data processing plan and the corporate business continuity plan. In addition, the plan incorporates any emergency procedures and provides references to any applicable sections of existing data center and departmental standards and procedures manuals.

The prompt recovery of an organization's corporate and functional operations from a loss of capability depends on the availability of a broad spectrum of resources. The procedures necessary to restore operations—initially in temporary facilities and later in the original or another permanent location—are detailed in the plan.

Each of the functional units prepares its plan on the basis of the outline provided by the plan coordinators (see the sample outline provided in Exhibit VI-1-2). The outline can be modified to suit the needs of the individual units. Although the plan discussed in this section addresses disaster backup and recovery from a worst-case scenario, less severe or even short-term interruptions can also be planned for by using subsets of the overall plan.

## BUSINESS CONTINUITY PLANNING SOFTWARE

Several contingency planning and risk analysis software packages are currently on the market. It is not practical to list and evaluate them because that list is constantly changing. However, certain criteria should be used during the software package selection process.

For example, ease of use and the number of installations or users are important when the company is selecting any software package, as are the frequency and availability of updates, the quality of documentation and vendor support, the reputation of the vendor, and the amount of training the vendor provides. The usability of output should also be considered. Specific to contingency planning, the software should be evaluated in terms of whether it provides total business continuity planning assistance or simply data center recovery.

CONTINGENCY PLANNING

I. Introduction
    a. Executive overview or summary
    b. Organizational overview
    c. Minimum requirements
    d. General categories of disasters and contingencies
II. Responsibilities of the Disaster Decision-Making Team
III. Responsibilities of the Business Continuity Coordinator and the Business Continuity Steering Committee
IV. Responsibilities of the Management Operations Team
V. Responsibilities of the Department Coordinators Team
VI. Responsibilities of the Emergency Operations Team
VII. Responsibilities of the Damage Assessment and Postinvestigation Team
VIII. Responsibilities of the Reconstruction Team
IX. General Issues
    a. Awareness of critical events
    b. Notification of relevant persons
    c. Diagnosis of the cause, severity, and expected duration of the event
    d. Coordination of emergency response
    e. Communications
    f. Investigation and analysis of the event
X. The Corporate Recovery Plan (corporatewide outage)
    a. Organization and staffing
    b. Arrangements with vendors, contractors, and other organizations
    c. Backup and recovery plans
        1. Information and communications systems
        2. Hardware
        3. Site
        4. Location of business resumption control center
XI. The Operational Area Recovery Plan (based on functional areas)
    a. Responsibilities of the backup operations team
    b. Responsibilities of the emergency operation team
    c. Responsibilities of the reconstructions team
    d. General issues
    e. Priority ranking of functions
    f. Name and address of alternative-site vendor
    g. List of responsibilities and home telephone numbers of key personnel
    h. Emergency telephone numbers (e.g., fire and police departments)
    i. Critical forms (number, names, and average use)
    j. Special equipment specifications
    k. Area user list (ranked according to priority)
    l. Copy of vendor backup contract
    m. Critical functions and assumptions (e.g., individuals may assume that they will have access to backup files)
    n. Minimum equipment and space requirements
    o. Appendixes (same as Section XV)
XII. Emergency Notification
    a. General categories of disasters and contingencies
    b. Immediate evacuation
    c. Fire emergency procedures
    d. Telephone bomb threat procedures
        1. Bomb search procedures
        2. General alert for bomb threats
    e. Medical emergencies
    f. Civil disorder

**Exhibit VI-1-2. Sample Outline of Business Continuity Plan**

      g. Severe weather or threat of a natural disaster
      h. Extortion and terrorist threats
      i. Building and equipment emergencies (e.g., loss of power)
      j. Notification
         1. Company closings for a disaster
         2. Activating the business resumption control center
         3. Access control procedures
      k. Company closings for early release of employees (e.g., because of an impending storm)
      l. Major milestones in the notification process
      m. Backup sites

XIII. Testing the Business Continuity Plan
      a. Methodology for testing the plan
      b. Determination of frequency of testing

XIV. Business Resumption Plan Maintenance
      a. Procedures for updating the plan
         1. Areas that require regular review
         2. Areas that require occasional review
      b. Frequency of review for updates
         1. Areas that require regular review
         2. Areas that require occasional review

XV. Appendixes
      A. Special Resources for Business Resumption
      B. Special Guidelines for Managers Dealing with Disaster-Related Stress
      C. Disaster Recovery for Microcomputers
      D. Inventory Control Form and Instructions
      E. Equipment Requirements
      F. Decision Matrices
      G. Critical Time Periods (daily or seasonal)
      H. Cross-Training Requirements and Responsibilities Matrix
      I. Typical Resources Allocation Plan (TRAP) Charts
      J. Test Schedules
      K. Test Worksheets
      L. Preparedness Overview
      M. Network Diagrams
      N. Off-Site Storage Inventories
      O. Critical Functions
      P. Staff Emergency Contact Information
      Q. Vendor Emergency Contact Information
      R. Vendor Contracts
      S. Emergency Organizational Charts
      T. Management Succession List
      U. Agreements for Alternative Work Space
      V. Temporary Agencies
      W. Functional Systems Overview
      X. Emergency Telephone Numbers
      Y. Control of Building Contents (e.g., equipment and supplies)
      Z. Special Salvage Vendors
      AA. Purchasing Department's List of Vendors
      BB. Procedures for Preserving Damaged Records
      CC. List of Personnel Who Need Access to the Plan
      DD. Notification Sequence
      EE. Organizational Chart for Business Resumption Command Center
      FF. Emergency Medical Information
      GG. Emergency Housing Information

**Exhibit VI-1-2.** *(continued)*

HH. Emergency Transportation Information
II. Business Resumption Control Center Notification
JJ. User Area Notification

**Note:**
* For simplicity, this section of the outline shows a general building outage recovery plan that is used for all locations. Some organizations may find it necessary to have a separate recovery plan for each location.

**Exhibit VI-1-2.** *(continued)*

---

## ACTION PLAN

For each company, the business continuity plan should cover all types of disaster situations. Procedures should be focused on getting the system running again within an acceptable time frame. The cause of the downtime is not important except in cases of regional disasters (e.g., earthquakes) or such specific hazards as a toxic spill. Special procedures should be included in the plan for these types of disasters.

The recovery strategies and procedures should be organized according to business functions. Strategies and procedures should be sufficiently detailed to enable company personnel to understand what is expected of them and how they should complete their responsibilities. However, strategies and procedures should be sufficiently flexible to permit changes should circumstances warrant them. Procedures should cover the maintenance of critical functions in an emergency mode as well as restoration of the primary facility or relocation to another permanent location.

The plan must specify the priority of recovery activities. It is impractical to determine during an emergency the order in which recovery procedures are to be conducted.

Personnel from the departments covered by the plan should be involved in its development from the start. These departments will be the users of the plan and therefore should play an integral part in its development.

The plan should be reviewed and updated on a regular basis; a plan is only as effective as its maintenance and updating program. Changes in departmental or company operations can quickly render a plan obsolete. A thorough maintenance and updating program prevents this.

Development of a business continuity plan may seem like a long and tedious process with no immediate benefit to the company. However, over the long term, a well-developed and well-maintained plan can help ensure that the company stays in business when a disaster strikes.

# VI-2
# Strategies for Developing and Testing Business Continuity Plans

*KENNETH A. SMITH*

C omprehensive business resumption planning is growing beyond the walls of the data center. Business's growing dependence on multiple computing platforms and increasingly sophisticated communications networks is making companies more vulnerable to disaster. Actual disasters are highlighting the importance and vulnerability of distributed computing systems, even while mainframe recovery is becoming more reliable. Business continuity plans must address these evolving integrated and networked business environments.

Public awareness of the need for comprehensive business recovery is on the rise as well, probably largely because of the increase in major regional catastrophes during the past few years. The public sector is also getting involved, with increasing federal, state, and local government participation in comprehensive disaster planning.

Companies are reacting to this need by developing enterprisewide disaster recovery plans but are discovering a host of problems associated with comprehensive business recovery planning. These plans require far more participation on the part of management and support organizations than mainframe recovery planning. The scope is no longer limited to recovery; plans must integrate with existing disaster prevention and mitigation programs. These companywide resumption plans are costly to develop and maintain and are frequently prolonged, problematic, and unsuccessful.

Fortunately, there have been successes from which data center management can learn. This chapter presents some of the lessons learned, including some of the tools, techniques, and strategies that have proved effective.

## COMPREHENSIVE BUSINESS RECOVERY STRATEGIES

Successful recovery from disease often depends on workable and timely alternative operating recovery strategies. A well-known set of recovery strategies, including some simple and relatively inexpensive commercial products and services, has made recovery planning feasible for large-scale mainframes and midrange computers. New solutions are becoming increasingly available for small computer configurations and business resumption (e.g., work group) recovery. These evolving solutions are based on experiences gained from a multitude of single-site and regional disasters.

Formal recovery planning and testing is an essential part of the total recovery solution. Companies that develop, maintain, and regularly test their business resumption plans recover far better and faster than those that are not prepared.

Exhibit VI-2-1 illustrates the scope needed for a companywide business continuity program. Business resumption should be thought of as an on-going program, much like existing avoidance programs (e.g. security) and loss-mitigation programs (e.g. insurance).

Resumption planning is moving into departmental work groups. Executive management and the support organizations are also taking part in business resumption through integrated crisis incident management planning.

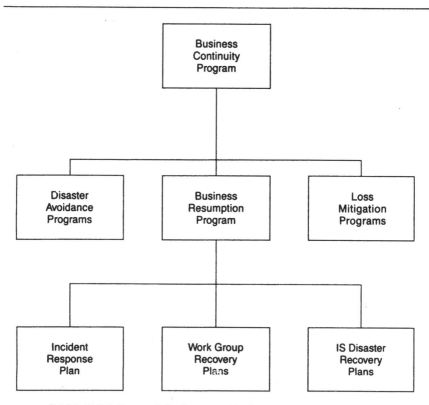

**Exhibit VI-2-1. Scope of the Companywide Business Continuity Program**

Numerous planning tools and strategies are available to help companies develop plans. The tools include commercially available software, consulting services, and several public-domain information sources. These tools and services are invaluable in reducing the effort, elapsed time, and cost involved in developing business resumption plans.

Before discussing how to develop a plan, it would be useful to review the available strategies for both computer and work group recovery. The following sections examine these strategies.

## Mainframe Systems

The choice of which mainframe recovery strategy to follow is based primarily on business recovery timing requirements, cost, and reliability. Hot sites are fast becoming the recovery strategy of choice for companies requiring rapid recovery. The commercial hot site is second only to an internally owned redundant site in terms of reliability and timing, and usually at less than 10% to 30% of the annual cost. In some areas (e.g., disaster support and telecommunications infrastructure), hot sites can actually provide a more reliable strategy than an internally owned redundant facility.

The potential strategies for mainframe and midrange computer recovery (discussed in the next section) are listed in Exhibit IV-2-2. Most organizations use multiple strategies, depending on the severity of the disaster and expected outage duration. During planning, different strategies may be identified for different applications, depending on the potential business consequences.

The recovery time frames in Exhibit VI-2-2 do not imply either minimum or maximum times; these figures represent actual company experiences following disaster. For example, in two recorded examples of a total data center loss, the rebuilding time was 6 months for one company and 12 months for the other. Most recoveries using commercial hot sites have been accomplished within 8 to 24 hours.

When costs for mainframe recovery strategies are analyzed, it is important to realistically estimate personnel and equipment costs. In addition, the strategies should be planned out over a minimum three-to-five year period to ensure that the cost of maintaining and upgrading equipment is considered. Equipment resources for mainframe strategies should be defined at a fairly detailed level, because the cost of the incidental infrastructure and network can significantly affect actual costs.

Evaluating potential hot-site or cold-site recovery vendors is less clear-cut. Quality of service is most important but difficult to evaluate. Decisions are often made on the basis of technical and pricing criteria.

Exhibit VI-2-3 presents a checklist itemizing several issues that may be used to evaluate disaster recovery vendors. The checklist may also be used in deciding whether to adopt an internal or an external solution.

| Strategy | Recovery Time Frame | Advantages | Disadvantages |
|---|---|---|---|
| Repair or Rebuild at Time of Disaster | 6–12 months | • Least cost | • Time to recover, reliability, and testability |
| Cold Site (private or commercial) | 1–6 weeks | • Cost-effective<br>• Time to recover | • Testability<br>• Detail plans are difficult to maintain<br>• Long-term maintenance costs |
| Reciprocal Agreement | 1–3 days | • Useful for specialized equipment in low-volume applications | • Not legally acceptable in some environments<br>• Testability |
| Service Bureau | 1–3 days | • For contingency planning (e.g. backup microfilm) | • Not available in large CPU environments |
| Shippable or Transportable Equipment | 1–3 days | • Useful for midrange computing | • Logistical difficulties in regional disaster recovery |
| Commercial Hot Site | Less than 1 day | • Testability<br>• Availability of skilled personnel | • Regional disaster risk |
| Redundant Facility | Less than 1 day | • Greatest reliability | • Most expensive<br>• Long-term commitment and integrity |

**Exhibit VI-2-2. Mainframe and Midrange Recovery Strategies**

## Midrange Systems

Effective business resumption planning requires that midrange systems be evaluated with the same thoroughness used with mainframes. The criticality of the midrange applications is frequently underestimated. For example, an analysis of one financial institution found that all securities investment records had been moved to a midrange system previously limited to word processing. Because it was viewed as office support, this system's data was not protected off site. Its loss would have meant serious if not irreparable damage to this company and its investors.

Midrange systems share the same list of potential recovery strategies as mainframes. In addition, shippable and transportable recovery alternatives may be feasible. Shippable strategies are available for recovery of several specific hardware environments, including DEC/VAX, IBM AS/400, and UNISYS.

| Questions | Vendor 1 | | Vendor 2 | | Vendor 3 | |
|---|---|---|---|---|---|---|
| **Section 1: Business Issues** | | | | | | |
| How many years has the vendor supplied disaster recovery services to the commercial marketplace? | | | | | | |
| What percentage of the vendor's business is in disaster recovery? | % | | % | | % | |
| Can the vendor's contract be assigned or transferred without the subscriber's consent? | Yes | No | Yes | No | Yes | No |
| Does the vendor provide an audited, ongoing technology exchange program? | Yes | No | Yes | No | Yes | No |
| Does the vendor provide an annual survey of subscriber satisfaction and critical components? | Yes | No | Yes | No | Yes | No |
| Are non-mainframe recovery solutions available at the primary hot-site facility? | Yes | No | Yes | No | Yes | No |
| Does the vendor provide an account management approach or philosophy? | Yes | No | Yes | No | Yes | No |
| Is there easy access to the vendor's facility? Is there sufficient, secure parking? | Yes | No | Yes | No | Yes | No |
| Can the subscriber notify the vendor of a potential disaster without incurring hot-site declaration fees? | Yes | No | Yes | No | Yes | No |
| Does the vendor have a proven track record of having restored every declared disaster within 24 hours, including full network restoration and application processing? | Yes | No | Yes | No | Yes | No |
| Has the vendor ever lost a customer subsequent to the customer's declaring a disaster? If yes, attach a list of those customers. | Yes | No | Yes | No | Yes | No |
| Does the vendor provide hot site-related services, including remote bulk printing, mailing, and inserting services? | Yes | No | Yes | No | Yes | No |
| Does the vendor have a proven, proactive crisis management approach in place? | Yes | No | Yes | No | Yes | No |

**Exhibit VI-2-3. Alternative-Site Vendor Comparison Checklist**

| Questions | Vendor 1 | | Vendor 2 | | Vendor 3 | |
|---|---|---|---|---|---|---|
| **Section 2: Contractual Commitment** | | | | | | |
| Does the vendor contractually accept full liability for all direct damages caused by its negligent or intentional acts, without monetary limit? | Yes | No | Yes | No | Yes | No |
| What is the limit on the liability for direct damages? | | | | | | |
| What is the statute of limitations on claims made by the subscriber? | | | | | | |
| Does the vendor contractually guarantee comprehensive technical support to the subscriber during recovery operations? | Yes | No | Yes | No | Yes | No |
| Will the vendor pretest the subscriber's operating system, network control programs, and communications circuits outside of the subscriber's test shifts? | Yes | No | Yes | No | Yes | No |
| **Section 3: Audit** | | | | | | |
| Does the vendor contractually give the subscriber the right to audit the recovery center? | Yes | No | Yes | No | Yes | No |
| Will the vendor contractually guarantee to have its disaster recovery facilities and contracts regularly reviewed by an independent, third-party auditor to verify compliance with all contractual commitments made? If yes, have the vendor provide a copy of the current audit. If no, why not? | Yes | No | Yes | No | Yes | No |
| Will the vendor allow any regulatory authority having jurisdiction over the subscriber to inspect the recovery center? If no, why not? | Yes | No | Yes | No | Yes | No |
| **Section 4: Backup Network** | | | | | | |
| Are the subscriber's circuits connected on a full-time basis to the front-end processors? | Yes | No | Yes | No | Yes | No |
| Are the subscriber's circuits immediately switchable (using a matrix switch) to:<br>• All other front ends within the primary recovery center? | Yes | No | Yes | No | Yes | No |

**Exhibit VI-2-3.** *(continued)*

| Questions | Vendor 1 | | Vendor 2 | | Vendor 3 | |
|---|---|---|---|---|---|---|
| • All other front ends within the secondary recovery centers? | Yes | No | Yes | No | Yes | No |
| • The primary cold site? | Yes | No | Yes | No | Yes | No |
| • All other vendor-provided cold sites? | Yes | No | Yes | No | Yes | No |
| Can the subscriber perform comprehensive network testing at the secondary recovery centers? | Yes | No | Yes | No | Yes | No |
| Can the subscriber test remotely from any subscriber-designated remote location using a channel-attached or equivalent system console? | Yes | No | Yes | No | Yes | No |
| Can the subscriber perform IPLs from a remote system console? | Yes | No | Yes | No | Yes | No |
| What are the vendor's fees for backup network consulting? | | | | | | |
| How many central offices support the vendor's recovery center? | | | | | | |
| How many AT&T points of presence are directly accessible to and from the vendor's hot-site? | | | | | | |
| Which common carriers are currently providing service to the vendor's hot site? | | | | | | |
| Is diverse local loop routing available at the hot site? | Yes | No | Yes | No | Yes | No |
| Are multiple vendors providing local loop routing to and from the hot site? | Yes | No | Yes | No | Yes | No |
| Does the vendor have diverse access capacity for: | | | | | | |
| • T3 access? | Yes | No | Yes | No | Yes | No |
| • Accunet Reserve T1 access? | Yes | No | Yes | No | Yes | No |
| • Accunet Reserve Switched 56K-bps access? | Yes | No | Yes | No | Yes | No |
| • 9.6K-bps access? | Yes | No | Yes | No | Yes | No |

**Exhibit VI-2-3.** *(continued)*

| Questions | Vendor 1 | | Vendor 2 | | Vendor 3 | |
|---|---|---|---|---|---|---|
| • Live dial tones available for disaster recovery? | Yes | No | Yes | No | Yes | No |
| **Section 5: Access Rights**<br>What are the subscriber's rights of access to the hot-site facility (e.g., guaranteed access or standby access)?<br><br>If standby access (first come, first served), can the subscriber be denied access in the event of a multiple disaster? | Yes | No | Yes | No | Yes | No |
| Does the subscriber need to declare a disaster in order to be guaranteed access to the recovery center? | Yes | No | Yes | No | Yes | No |
| Has the vendor ever allowed a company that is not a hot-site customer to recover from a disaster? | Yes | No | Yes | No | Yes | No |
| Will the vendor allow a company that is not a hot-site customer to recover at the time of a disaster? If so, how does the vendor guarantee recovery for hot-site customers? | Yes | No | Yes | No | Yes | No |
| Does the vendor contractually limit the number of subscribers per hot site? | Yes | No | Yes | No | Yes | No |
| Can the subscriber verify the limitation of subscribers per hot site? | Yes | No | Yes | No | Yes | No |
| Are any of the vendor's hot sites located in an area susceptible to floods, hurricanes, or earthquakes? | Yes | No | Yes | No | Yes | No |
| Will the vendor contractually limit the number of subscribers per building? If so, how many? | Yes | No | Yes | No | Yes | No |
| Does the vendor contractually guarantee access to the hot site immediately upon disaster declaration? | Yes | No | Yes | No | Yes | No |
| Does the vendor provide a cold site at the primary recovery center? | Yes | No | Yes | No | Yes | No |
| If so, how many square feet does it have? | ____ sq. ft. | | ____ sq. ft. | | ____ sq. ft. | |

**Exhibit VI-2-3.** *(continued)*

| Questions | Vendor 1 | | Vendor 2 | | Vendor 3 | |
|---|---|---|---|---|---|---|
| Is the vendor's cold site capable of immediately supporting the installation of multiple CPU configurations? | Yes | No | Yes | No | Yes | No |
| If so, how many and what type? | | | | | | |
| Does the vendor provide any subscriber with greater rights than any other subscriber? | Yes | No | Yes | No | Yes | No |
| Can the vendor provide a list of all customers that have preemptive hot-site access rights? If yes, attach a list of them. | Yes | No | Yes | No | Yes | No |
| **Section 6: Technical Issues**<br>Does the vendor use physical or logical partitioning of hot-site CPUs to support customer processing? | | | | | | |
| If physical partitioning is used to partition the vendor's hot-site CPUs, what is the maximum number of subscribers per CPU partition? | | | | | | |
| If logical partitioning is used to partition the vendor's hot-site CPUs:<br>• What is the maximum number of partitions per CPU? | | | | | | |
| • What is the contractual limit of customers per partition? | | | | | | |
| • Does the vendor provide additional resources to accommodate hardware partitioning (e.g., IBM's PR/SM)? | Yes | No | Yes | No | Yes | No |
| • How does the vendor resolve problems associated with testing multiple subscribers simultaneously on the same mainframe? | | | | | | |

**Exhibit VI-2-3. *(continued)***

Cold-site and repair or replacement recovery timeframes can be much shorter for midrange systems (e.g., days instead of weeks), because many systems do not require extensive facility conditioning. However, care should be taken to ensure that this is true for specific systems. Some systems are documented as not needing significant conditioning but do not perform well in nonconditioned environments.

| Questions | Vendor 1 | Vendor 2 | Vendor 3 |
|---|---|---|---|
| What is the exact physical or logical hardware configuration to be provided to the subscriber:<br><br>• How many megabytes of central storage are dedicated to the customer? | | | |
| • How many megabytes of expanded storage are dedicated to the customer? | | | |
| • How many channels are dedicated to the customer? | | | |
| Does the vendor supply a comprehensive electronic vaulting program? | Yes    No | Yes    No | Yes    No |

**Exhibit VI-2-3. (continued)**

Special considerations should be given to turnkey systems. Turnkey software vendors often do not package disaster recovery backup and off-site rotation with their systems. On the other hand, other turnkey vendors provide disaster recovery strategies as an auxiliary or additional cost service.

Companies using midrange systems frequently have mixed hardware and network platforms requiring a variety of recovery strategies and vendors. When recovery strategies are being evaluated, some cost savings can be realized if all of the midrange systems are considered at the same time. Another planning consideration unique to the midrange environment is the limited availability of in-house technical expertise. Recovery at the time of the disaster often requires people with extensive skills in networking, environmental conditioning, and systems support. A single hardware vendor may not be able to supply these skills in the mixed platform environments.

In an evaluation of the recovery timing strategy, special attention should be given to recovery timing issues on midrange systems. Some platforms are notoriously slow in restoring data.

## Work Group Systems

The computer recovery strategies can be borrowed and adapted to work group recovery planning. However, the optimum choices frequently differ because of the different technical and logistical issues involved. As a result, numerous commercially available products and services are becoming available for work group recovery.

The goal of work group recovery planning is to re-establish essential day-to-day business functions before the consequential effects occur. To accomplish this, most organizations find it necessary to relocate their employees to an alternative location or to relocate the work itself. Exhibit VI-2-4 lists the most common work group strategies.

In addition to these alternative operating strategies, work group planning has some unique and difficult computer recovery challenges. Businesses' dependence on desktop computing is growing far faster and with less control then did their dependence on mainframe and midrange systems. Disaster experiences are showing that many businesses are absolutely dependent on these systems and that the degree of disaster awareness and preparation is seriously and dangerously lacking.

## Desktop Computers and Local Area Networks

Currently, the most common method of information protection is to back up data at a file server level and accept the business risk of the loss of microcomputer workstation data. In actual disasters, many companies have been found to be inadequately protecting their microcomputer-based information. The ultimate solution for desktop and local area network (LAN) information recovery rests in two major areas: standards and standards enforcement.

Planning for LAN recovery is made more difficult by the absence of standardized backup devices. Unlike mainframes and minicomputers, no backup media (e.g. no equivalent to standard mainframe 9-track tape) has been accepted industrywide. Backup device technology changes frequently and is not always downward compatible. Some companies have found it difficult to acquire older compatible technology at the time of a disaster. Redundant equipment and meticulous testing may be the only feasible solution.

The two most common hardware recovery alternatives for individual workstations are replacement at the time of the disaster and having shippable microcomputers. Ordering, packaging, assembling, and installing workstations is a long and labor-intensive process during recovery. Use of commercial shippable microcomputers is becoming more common because of the prepackaging of these systems. In addition, some disaster recovery vendors are providing LAN capability as part of the shippable offering.

Unfortunately, solutions for file server configurations are less clear-cut. Because these customized machine configurations are frequently not stocked in quantity by local computer suppliers, replacement can be quite difficult. Internal reciprocal and redundant options are being used for the file servers. One network software company and some recovery vendors are also making file servers available as a shippable alternative. This reduces the redundant hardware requirements to a backup device and software.

Technological obsolescence must be considered in any long-term LAN recovery strategy. Equipment purchases and stored off site (e.g., redundant

| Strategy | Recovery Time Frame | Advantages | Disadvantages | Comments |
|---|---|---|---|---|
| Repair or Rebuild at Time of Disaster | 1–3 days | • Ongoing cost for office space and equipment | • Availability risk<br>• Limited availability of special equipment and space | Rent space an...<br>replacement e... |
| Shippable or Transportable Equipment | 1–3 days | • Ease of use<br>• Reliability | • Ongoing cost | Use commerci...<br>and services |
| Hot Site or Cold Site | Immediate | • Testability | • Availability in regional disaster | Use commerci...<br>office space |
| Reciprocal Agreement | 1–3 days | • Useful for specialized equipment in low-volume applications | • Limited application capacity | Arrange office s...<br>(internal) and s...<br>facilities (exter... |
| Service Bureau | 1–3 days | • Useful for daily contingency planning | • Not available for large CPU environments | Use commerci...<br>(e.g., print sho...<br>microfilm comp... |
| Redundant Facility | Immediate | • Greatest reliability | • High cost<br>• Long-term commitment and integrity | Internal use on... |

**Exhibit VI-2-4. Work Group Recovery Strategies**

strategy) rapidly becomes obsolete. Reciprocal agreements require that hardware remain compatible over time, which is often difficult.

An even more difficult planning consideration is network wiring. Companies are wiring their buildings with special network facilities (e.g., IBM Token Ring and EtherNet), making relocation to dissimilar facilities difficult. Companies with multiple facilities (e.g., campus environments) can sometimes use reciprocal arrangements if capacities are sufficient. In the absence of these facilities or in a regional disaster, shippable microcomputers that include preinstalled network capabilities are the safest alternative.

Lack of industry-standard communications hardware is a problem in local and wide area network recovery, making rapid replacement at the time of the disaster risky. Several shippable products (e.g., shippable bridges and gateways) are commercially available to assist local and wide area network recovery. When these tools are unavailable, stockpiling of redundant equipment is usually the only recourse.

## Wide Area Networks

Disaster recovery planning for wide area networks (WANs) is still in its infancy. Even though few companies are addressing recovery of WANs, these networks are often installed to support vital business missions. For example, they are being installed to support such mission-critical functions as LAN-resident business applications, electronic data interchange (EDI), and gateways to mainframes.

Recovery of a WAN is primarily a network planning issue. Wide area networks are typically connected using communications lines with massive bandwidth capabilities (e.g., 56 Kbps or more). Typically, the same type of network solutions for large mainframe-based networks are available for WAN connections. Unfortunately, that massive bandwidth can also equate to large network expense.

## Networking

That the communications infrastructure (both voice and data) is essential to daily business operations is well understood and accepted. Business impact studies have shown that networks must be restored in most locations at near-full production capacities, usually in a very short time. Some companies have found that the need for voice and data communications is actually higher than normal during a disaster.

Network recovery strategy decisions are driven by business timing requirements, choice of alternative processing decisions for computer recovery, work group recovery, and cost. The technical strategies and the menu of products and services are far too complicated to discuss here; however, the network strategy planning criteria are quite simple to describe.

Simply stated, network recovery strategies should address all technology and facilities required to reestablish connectivity. This includes person-to-person, person-to-computer, and computer-to-computer connections. All network components should be addressed and appropriate strategies decided on. For most components, the same recovery strategies previously described for computer and work group recovery can be applied.

The following sections discuss some of the special requirements of work group facilities and communications equipment.

**Work Group Facility.** Loss of a work group facility requires replacing all equivalent network components. These include telephones, terminals, control units, modems, LAN network wiring, and the PBX. These may be obtained at time of disaster using replacement or shippable strategies. They may already be in place in an existing redundant, reciprocal, or commercial hot-site or cold-site facility. The same set of planning issues and network disaster recovery strategies can be employed.

**Access to Communications.** A disaster may affect the communications infrastructure outside the work group facility (e.g. loss of phone lines or a central office). In this case, an entirely different set of strategies comes into play.

Two possible recovery strategies can be used: relocating to an alternative facility in which the infrastructure is in place or reconnecting to the surviving infrastructure through alternative facilities. Because of timing, these alternative communications facilities are usually redundant and can be quite expensive.

### Electronic Vaulting

Electronic vaulting has gained wide attention during the past couple of years as an emerging disaster recovery strategy. Electronic vaulting allows critical information to be stored off site through means of a network transfer rather than traditional backup and off-site rotation. Electronic vaulting brings two major benefits: decreased loss of data and shortened recovery windows.

Electronic vaulting is currently available. Commercial disaster recovery vendors provide both remote transaction journaling and data base shadowing services. Several companies with multiple computer sites are using electronic vaulting internally on a variety of computer platforms. Electronic archiving is becoming fairly common in the microcomputer area. Although use has been limited because of significant hardware and communications costs, these costs are expected to decline, making electronic vaulting more attractive in the future.

Until the costs become more reasonable and standardized technology is in place, however, electronic vaulting will be limited to selected applications needing its unique benefits. The business impact analysis process helps determine when this strategy is justified.

## A DEVELOPMENT APPROACH

Presented in Exhibit VI-2-5 is a graphical representation of a simple but effective three-phase approach for developing a business resumption plan. The foundation phase of the development methodology is identification of disaster recovery business requirements. Once these requirements are fully understood, appropriate recovery strategy planning can be conducted. Finally, detailed resumption plans, or action plans, may be developed and documented. All three of these recovery phases involve the surrounding elements of personnel, recovery, resources, and planned recovery action.

### Project Planning and Management

Before the first planning phase can be initiated, some thought should be given to project planning and management. Two of the first crucial activities within project planning are clearly defining the scope of the project and enlisting management support.

In larger companies (e.g., those with more than 500 to 1,000 employees), the sheer magnitude of the task may justify staging work group recovery planning. Usually computer disaster recovery planning should be done before or at the same time as work group recovery planning. The business requirements phase helps identify the areas that need to be planned first as determined by the consequences of losing those organizations.

Important business decisions must be made during the planning process regarding preparedness and eventual recovery issues. Active management support throughout the planning process is essential if the planning project is to be successful.

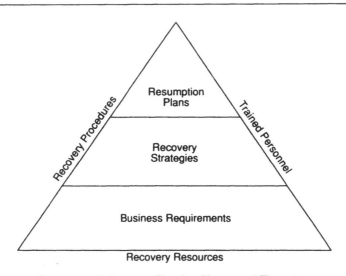

**Exhibit VI-2-5. Recovery Planning Phases and Elements**

The success of the project is affected by selection of the development project team and distribution of planning responsibilities. Care should be taken to select a qualified project leader. The skills needed for an effective project manager or business resumption planner include:

- Extensive large project management skills.
- A thorough understanding of records and data protection concepts.
- A basic understanding of network concepts and recovery capabilities.
- Outstanding communication skills, both written and verbal.
- Knowledge of business resumption concepts.

Delegating responsibility for planning to individual work groups usually is not practical. Because of the learning curve and documentation skills, it is more cost-effective to lend a specific work group these skills in the form of a qualified project manager. In addition, many recovery planning decisions involve centralized strategy planning (e.g., determining how the voice network will be recovered or how the replacement of office equipment and departmental computers will be replaced), which would be better managed by a centralized project team.

On the other hand, some planning activities are more effective conducted at the individual work group level. For example, inventorying of equipment resources, identifying minimum acceptable configurations, and identifying specific implementation requirements are all handled best by departmental management. Responsibility for maintaining the recovery capability must remain the individual work group's responsibility because it must use the plan when a disaster occurs.

The following sections discuss the three phases of developing the business resumption plan.

### Defining the Business Requirements

Once the project plan has been developed, actual business resumption planning can begin. The first and most essential step in this process is to gain an understanding of the business recovery requirements—that is, determining which functions must be recovered and when.

The business impact is often intuitively obvious without a formal analysis. For example, loss of a reservation system is a catastrophic event to an airline company. Other businesses and functions may need to conduct a formal business impact analysis to quantify the potential impact and timing requirements. In either case, it is necessary to understand the consequences and timing of the negative business impact of a disaster to each work group. Most of the negative effects on the business develop in spurts over time. For example, an outage of a few hours may be acceptable, but cessation of business operations for a few days may be intolerable.

The business impact may be quantified in tangible values, such as revenue (e.g., income), loss of assets (e.g., warehouse shrinkage), or lost sales (e.g., underwriting support). The impact may also be intangible, affecting such areas as company reputation, client satisfaction, and employee morale.

Gathering and analyzing business impact information and the current level of preparedness is best done by the project management team working with work group management. Care should be exercised to identify the appropriate level of management; the size of the organization often dictates the level of analysis. Questionnaires should be used sparingly; besides the obvious difficulty in getting responses, questionnaire responses almost always miss unique characteristics and effects on some work groups.

### Selecting Appropriate Recovery Strategies

Once the business recovery timing requirements are understood, the choice of an appropriate recovery strategy becomes a business risk issue rather than an emotional issue. Recovery strategies vary by cost and the speed at which business operations can be resumed. Recovery strategies providing very fast recovery (e.g., redundant facilities) are usually expensive. At the other end of the scale, strategies for replacement at the time of the disaster may lower ongoing costs but can take considerably longer. The choice of recovery strategies must weigh the potential impact from loss of the business functions, relative timing of the impact, and the cost of protection compared to the business risk.

Once the business recovery timing requirements are understood, a company can immediately eliminate those strategies that do not meet the business needs. The remaining strategies can then be analyzed on the basis of their relative merits and costs, resulting in an informed business decision.

It is important to note that companies always make a decision about recovery strategies. Companies without a formal recovery plan have implicitly chosen to use either a repair and rebuilt strategy or a do not recover strategy, depending on how successful they are at identifying and storing essential data off site.

It is important to determine all strategies, not just the alternative computer processing strategy. For example, recovery of the voice network, the level of detailed planning, and the degree of training are all strategy issues that must be considered. As these recovery strategy decisions are weighed and decisions made (either explicitly or implicitly), these decisions should be documented along with the reasons for reaching the decision. Finally, any resulting exposures should be documented.

### Developing Detailed Resumption Plans

The final phase of business resumption planning is the detailed resumption planning. Planning must address all three recovery elements: personnel, recovery resources, and recovery actions. A common mistake is to focus on personnel and recovery resource planning and to overlook planning and documenting the actual business resumption activities needed to resume operations.

Planning is best done in a series of working sessions conducted jointly by the project team and work group management. Testing is an integral part of the development process. Each of the following steps represents a work group planning session:

- Step 1: Formulating the strategy.
- Step 2: Analyzing the implementation.
- Step 3: Validating the implementation.
- Step 4: Approving the recovery plans.

The project team may assist the work groups in carrying out these steps. In addition, the project team is responsible for much of the preparatory work for these steps, because these team members have more knowledge of disaster recovery and more experience in writing plans. The work groups bring special knowledge of their particular areas to the planning process. The following sections discuss these steps in more detail.

**Formulating the Strategy.** The work group must review the business requirements and high-level recovery strategies and then formulate implementation plans and strategies. As a result of this planning session, recovery management and logistical issues will be defined and documented.

**Analyzing the Implementation.** A work-flow analysis is a useful tool with which to conduct this planning. By reviewing how work is processed on a daily basis, the work group can identify which recovery actions would be required to recreate this environment in an alternative operating location.

Detailed planning should identify those individuals responsible for managing the recovery process. In addition, any key technical resources (internal or external) necessary for effecting recovery should be identified and documented within the recovery plan.

Logistical arrangements and administrative activities must be clearly documented in a plan. A frequent complaint of companies recovering from a disaster is that the logistical and administrative activities, particularly in regard to personnel, are inadequately planned.

Testing should be considered in planning the recovery activities. Resources should be documented in such a way that their presence may be validated during exercises. Information resources (e.g., vendor contacts and emergency phone numbers) should be usable during exercises.

**Validating the Implementation.** Once plans have been defined and documented, they should be validated through testing. This can be done in a manual exercise of the plan, comparing the plan's recovery actions against a hypothetical disaster scenario. Following this validation, iterative implementation planning sessions may be required.

**Approving the Recovery Plans.** In each step, recovery strategies, actions, and resources are documented. As a final step, the plans should be formally reviewed, accepted, and turned over from the project team to the respective work groups.

## TESTING THE PLAN

There is no surer way to turn a disaster recovery manual into waste paper than to fail to frequently and periodically test the plan. Testing is critical in the development and ongoing maintenance of business resumption plans.

There are five important reasons why business resumption plans should be tested periodically. These reasons apply equally to traditional mainframe and midrange planning and work group recovery planning. The reasons are:

- Testing proves whether the recovery plan works and whether it can meet the business's recovery requirements.
- Testing the plan identifies the weak links in the plan, allowing them to be corrected before the plan is actually needed.
- Testing the plan is the primary employee training tool. Frequent testing of the plan enhances employees' familiarity with the strategies and implementation process and also raises general awareness levels.
- Periodic testing is necessary to comply with legal and regulatory requirements for many organizations. Although this is especially relevant in the banking industry and some insurance companies, it is fast becoming a de facto regulatory requirement for all industries.
- Testing is a prudent business practice. The testing program protects the initial development investment, reduces ongoing maintenance costs, and protects the company by ensuring that the plan will work when a disaster occurs.

Testing is a universal term used in the disaster recovery industry. Unfortunately, testing has a negative pass/fail connotation carried over from school days. The term *testing* would be better replaced by such terms as *exercising* or *rehearsing*. Finding problems during a test should not be viewed as failure when it is really the basic reason for conducting the exercise. Attention should be focused on the positive, not the punitive. For the testing program to be successful, this attitude should be carefully communicated to employees.

### Testing Approaches

An effective testing program requires different types of tests to cost-effectively examine all components of the plan. For the purposes of this discussion, testing can be categorized into four types:

- *Desk checking or auditing.* The availability of required recovery resources can be validated through an audit or desk check approach. This type of test should be used periodically to verify stored, off-site resources and the availability of planned time-of-disaster acquisitions. Unfortunately, desk checking or auditing is limited to validating the existence of resources and may not adequately identify whether other resources are required.

- *Simulations by walkthroughs.* Personnel training and resource validation can be performed by bringing recovery participants together and conducting a simulated exercise or plan. A hypothetical scenario is presented, and the participants jointly review the recovery procedures but do not actually invoke recovery plans. This type of exercise is easy to conduct, inexpensive, and effective in verifying that the correct resources are identified. More important, this testing approach helps train recovery personnel and validate the recovery actions through peer appraisal.
- *Real-time testing.* Real-time testing is frequently done on the mainframe or hot-site backup plan and is gaining popularity in work group recovery planning. Real-time testing provides the greatest degree of assurance but is the most time-consuming and expensive approach. If only limited real-time testing is planned, priority should be given to high-risk areas.
- *Mock surprise testing.* Surprise tests are a variation of the other three approaches but with the added dimension of being unanticipated. This type of test is frequently discussed but rarely used. The inconvenience for personnel and the negative feelings it generates tend to outweigh its advantages. The benefits derived from a mock surprise disaster can be achieved by careful attention and implementation of controls to avoid the possibility of cheating during planned exercises.

These testing approaches can be combined into an unlimited variety of tests. For example, walkthroughs can be extended by actually performing some recovery activities (e.g., notifying vendors). Training facility equipment can be used to test replace-at-time-of-disaster strategies, alleviating the need to actually purchase replacement computers, desks, tables, and chairs.

## A Matrix Approach to Testing

An orderly and organized approach to testing is necessary to ensure that all recovery strategies and components are being adequately validated. A matrix approach may be used to ensure that all plan components were adequately considered, as determined by their level of importance (e.g., business impact) and risk (e.g., reliability and complexity of recovery strategy). The matrix presented in Exhibit VI-2-6 illustrates this concept.

In this approach, one or more tests are identified for each component of the plan. The organization can develop a long-range (e.g., two-year) test program during which each element and component of the plan is verified or validated. The test program can then be reviewed and revised periodically

| PLAN RECOVERY COMPONENTS \ TEST PLAN | Type of Test | Frequency of Testing | Comments |
|---|---|---|---|
| Crisis Management Plans | | | |
| Data Center • Phase 1 | | | |
| • Phase 2 | | | |
| • Phase 3 | | | |
| Work Group 1 | | | |
| Work Group 2 | | | |
| ⋮ Work Group *n* | | | |

**Exhibit VI-2-6. Test Planning Matrix**

(e.g., annually) on the basis of testing results, identified exposures, and training requirements.

Work groups testing approaches and frequency depend on the complexity of the organization. For ease of testing and awareness purposes, some plans may be separated and tested by phase (e.g., test alert notification and alternative-site restoration). In general, technical resources (e.g., computer systems or network recovery) require frequent real-time testing. Work group computing needs occasional real-time testing to ensure that the recovery strategies work when they are needed.

Some departments (e.g., outside sales and long-term strategic planning) have fairly low risk in recovery, allowing less rigorous testing to be done. Process-oriented departments (e.g., order processing, credit and collections, and plant scheduling) have greater risk and recovery complexities, justifying more frequent personnel training and recovery testing.

## Conducting the Test: Guidelines and Techniques

There are several important ground rules that must be followed in developing a testing program. These are discussed in the following sections.

**Limit Test Preparation.** Test preparation should be limited to developing a test disaster scenario, scheduling test dates and times, and defining any exceptions to the plan. Exceptions should be limited to defining the test scope (e.g., testing only the notification component) or resource acquisition (e.g., substituting a training center for rented office space). Actual testing should follow the documented recovery procedures.

**Avoid Cheating.** An independent observer should be identified for each recovery test. Controls should be put in place to ensure that only resources identified in the recovery plans are used for the recovery effort. Exceptions to the recovery plan should be noted for subsequent follow-up. The object of limiting cheating is not to be punitive but to ensure that all activities and essential resources have been identified and will be available at time of disaster.

**Document and Communicate Test Results.** The results of the recovery test should always be documented, including follow-up activities, when possible. Corrective actions should be identified, responsibilities defined, and dates set.

Test results should be communicated to the participants and management in a positive manner. Successes should be clearly documented and recognition given to those contributing to the success. Likewise, identified problems should be stated in a positive manner with emphasis on the corrective actions.

**Test Information Reconstruction.** Difficulties in data restoration and recreation are usually discovered only through real-time testing. The off-site storage facility should be periodically audited to ensure that backups are present and safely stored. The ability to restore should be tested using the actual off-site backup media. When information recreation depends on other facilities (e.g., paper in branch offices or microfilm at the off-site vault), the ability to access this information should be verified. Sufficient volume should be tested to ensure that recovery actions are effective at production volumes.

## ACTION PLAN

To develop an effective and comprehensive business resumption plan, companies should take advantage of the lessons learned from other companies and should approach disaster planning from a business perspective as well as a technical perspective. The course of action depends on the status of the organization's current disaster recovery plans and business priorities.

The following steps summarize how a company should expand its current plans into a comprehensive business resumption plan:

1. Conducting realistic and critical evaluation of the current recovery program. This evaluation should clearly define the status of the entire business resumption plan scope, including incident crisis management, computer disaster recovery, and work group business resumption.
2. Developing a project plan to expand the current program, using the development guidelines presented in this chapter. This involves:
—Analyzing the business's recovery requirements.

—Adopting appropriate recovery strategies to meet the recovery requirements.

—Developing detailed recovery plans necessary to implement the proposed recovery strategies.

3. Developing an ongoing testing, training, and maintenance program for the business resumption plan.

# VI-3
# A Business Impact Analysis for Disaster Recovery

*KEN DOUGHTY*

A disaster recovery plan is essential in today's business world, in which computerized information systems play a vital role. The US Controller of Currency formally recognized this through the enactment of legislation that required federally chartered financial institutions to have a demonstrable disaster recovery plan as of January 1, 1989.

Data center managers and EDP auditors have long recognized the potential risk that their organizations are exposed to should they lose their information processing capabilities. The EDP Auditors Foundation has included the evaluation of the organization's disaster recovery plan capability in *Control Objectives* (April 1990, Section 3.5.1). The Institute of Internal Auditors (IIA) has also recognized the potential risk. In *Statements of Professional Practice of Internal Auditors*, Section 330, the IIA requires the internal auditor to review the means of safeguarding the organization's assets.

To comply with these various requirements, the data center manager and EDP auditors should perform a business impact analysis to identify whether the organization should invest financial and human resources in developing a disaster recovery plan capability. A disaster recovery plan is defined for the purposes of this chapter as a plan of action that details the duties, responsibilities, and tasks to be undertaken by personnel in the recovery of the information processing function in the event of a disaster. A business impact analysis is defined for the purposes of this chapter as the determination of the expected loss, both financial and nonfinancial, that can arise from the loss of computing resources from the likelihood of various risks.

The business impact analysis identifies the nature of the organization's business, how and what it uses to accomplish its objectives, which computer functions are critical to its survival, and what risks the organization is exposed to and determines the expected loss from a computer disaster. The information gathered during the business impact analysis is crucial for the disaster recovery plan and may also be used by management for future planning purposes for:

- Hardware and software purchases.
- Financial and human resources planning.

- Project scheduling and implementation.
- Operations.

The business impact analysis involves six phases:

1. Examining the environmental (i.e., physical) controls of the organization's computers.
2. Identifying critical applications.
3. Estimating the value of the assets to be protected.
4. Quantifying the estimated disaster loss.
5. Determining the critical timeliness for recovery.
6. Preparing the business impact analysis report.

## PHASE 1: EXAMINING THE ENVIRONMENTAL CONTROLS OF THE ORGANIZATION'S COMPUTERS

The EDP auditor can perform this important function because the auditor has been trained in the area of risk management.

### Step 1: Reviewing Internal Controls

The EDP auditor should review the organization's computer operations to identify the threats and hazards the operations are exposed to, including:

- Fire.
- Water.
- Power supply failures.
- Security breaches.
- Electrical interference.

The EDP auditor should also examine which controls are in operation to minimize those risks (e.g., fire prevention systems, positive drainage, a power conditioner, and cipher pads).

The review should include not only the organization's data center but the local area networks (LANs) within the organization. The growth of LANs has required the EDP auditor to look at this area, because the risks and exposures can have a major impact on the organization's overall operations. The types of threats and exposures for LANs are:

- File server failure by fire, water, or malicious damage.
- Printer failure by fire or malicious damage.
- Line failure by fire, water, or malicious damage.
- Accidental or malicious damage to software or data.

To perform the review, the auditor should use an internal control questionnaire with references to relevant standards to provide guidance on the minimum physical environmental controls for the organization's data center or LANs. A sample internal control questionnaire is provided in Exhibit VI-3-1.

| Risk | Consider | Yes | No | NA | Comments |
|---|---|---|---|---|---|
| Fire | **Location and Surroundings**<br>Data center is located in an environmentally secure area, away from:<br>• Heavy industry.<br>• Chemicals.<br>• Major road, rail, or air corridor.<br>• Congested buildings.<br>Data center is isolated from fire hazards posed by:<br>• Cafeteria.<br>• Chemical storage area.<br>• Paper storage area.<br>• Garage.<br>• Major plant and equipment.<br><br>**Construction**<br>Noncombustible material has been used in construction of data center, including the:<br>• Walls.<br>• Floor.<br>• Ceiling.<br>Computer room walls extend above false ceiling to roof to prevent fire from spreading.<br>Roof is sealed to prevent water ingress from above.<br>Subfloor is concrete with suitable drainage.<br>All electrical wiring placed in conduits in:<br>• Ceiling.<br>• Subfloor, which is also suitably grounded.<br>Sufficient and appropriate smoke and heat detectors are located in the:<br>• Ceiling.<br>• Subfloor.<br>An adequate fire suppression system is in place that uses:<br>• Halon.<br>• Sprinklers.<br>• Fire hoses.<br>Any glass in partitions is reinforced.<br><br>**Equipment**<br>There are sufficient and appropriate portable fire extinguishers using:<br>• Carbon dioxide.<br>• Halon.<br>• Foam.<br>Fire detection and suppression systems are regularly checked, including:<br>• Halon gas cylinder pressure.<br>• Sprinkler heads.<br>• Portable extinguisher pressure.<br>Audible alarm mechanism has been installed that:<br>• Covers all work areas and computer room.<br>• Is regularly tested.<br>Smoke and heat detectors are identified by suitable markers in the:<br>• Ceiling.<br>• Subfloor. | | | | |

**Exhibit VI-3-1. Sample Internal Control Questionnaire**

| Risk | Consider | Yes | No | NA | Comments |
|------|----------|-----|----|----|----------|
| | Smoke and heat detection mechanisms are centrally connected through:<br>• A centrally supervised control panel.<br>• Security personnel.<br>• Fire department.<br>Smoke detection equipment automatically shuts down the air-conditioning system and critical equipment.<br>Air-conditioning system heat sensors automatically shut down the CPU.<br>Air-conditioning system failure automatically shuts down the CPU. | | | | |
| | **Management**<br>Exits and evacuation routes are clearly marked.<br>Curtains and furniture are noncombustible.<br>Stationery and cleaning supplies are stored outside the computer room.<br>Fire procedures are:<br>• Documented.<br>• Complete.<br>• Up to date.<br>• Prominently displayed.<br>• Included in new staff induction.<br>The fire department is aware of the location of the data center.<br>The fire department can gain swift emergency access outside regular work hours.<br>A nonsmoking policy is strictly enforced.<br>Emergency power-down procedures are:<br>• Documented.<br>• Complete.<br>• Assigned to specific personnel.<br>• Up to date.<br>• Readily accessible.<br>• Regularly tested.<br>• Included in new operator training.<br>The staff is cross-trained in emergency power-down procedures.<br>Fire procedure responsibilities have been assigned.<br>Fire procedure training is provided.<br>Fire drills are conducted regularly.<br>Fire procedures contain:<br>• Rerun routines.<br>• Sprinkler shut-off routines and maps.<br>Computer facilities are separated to minimize the impact of fire, including:<br>• CPU.<br>• Communications.<br>• Printer area.<br>• Tape and disk libraries.<br>• Backup files.<br>• Program and application library.<br>• Operations procedures.<br>• Control procedures.<br>• Report distribution.<br>Space and ventilation between equipment is adequate.<br>Humidity control and monitoring equipment is in place. | | | | |
| Water | **Location and Surroundings**<br>The data center is located in an environmentally secure area, away from:<br>• Water courses.<br>• Flood zones. | | | | |

**Exhibit VI-3-1.** *(continued)*

| Risk | Consider | Yes | No | NA | Comments |
|------|----------|-----|----|----|----------|
| | **Construction**<br>Water pipes are not directed through the computer room.<br>Subfloor drainage is adequate.<br>The air conditioner is suitably protected through:<br>• Sealed and minimum-length water pipes.<br>• Subfloor drainage.<br>Exterior windows and doors are adequately sealed.<br>The floor above the data center is watertight.<br>A dry-head sprinkler system is in place.<br>Raised subfloor electrical junction boxes are used.<br><br>**Equipment**<br>Water pipes are regularly inspected.<br>Air-conditioner water pipes are regularly inspected.<br>The sprinkler system is regularly inspected.<br><br>**Management**<br>Only authorized inspection and maintenance work is permitted. | | | | |
| Elec-trical | **Construction**<br>Dedicated lines and circuits are used for the data center.<br>An alternative power supply is in place.<br>Future expansion capability is 'adequate.<br>Power connection points are secure.<br><br>**Equipment**<br>The power supply is protected from:<br>• Spikes.<br>• Brownouts.<br>• Blackouts.<br>The alternative power supply is regularly tested.<br><br>**Management**<br>Only authorized inspection and maintenance work is permitted.<br>Wiring diagrams are:<br>• Up to date.<br>• Readily accessible.<br>Emergency power-down procedures are:<br>• Documented.<br>• Complete.<br>• Assigned to specific personnel.<br>• Up to date.<br>• Readily accessible.<br>• Regularly tested.<br>• Included in new staff training.<br>The staff is cross-trained in emergency power-down procedures. | | | | |
| Pollu-tants | **Construction**<br>Air-conditioning and ventilation ducts are suitably screened.<br><br>**Equipment**<br>A regular cleaning schedule is adhered to for:<br>• The computer room.<br>• Equipment surfaces.<br>• The subfloor.<br>• Wastepaper receptacles emptied outside the computer room.<br>Paper bursting and shredding take place outside the computer room. | | | | |

**Exhibit VI-3-1. (continued)**

| Risk | Consider | Yes | No | NA | Comments |
|------|----------|-----|----|----|----------|
| | Report generation and distribution occurs outside the computer room. Antistatic and antidust mats are: <br> • At all entrances. <br> • Regularly replaced. <br> Damaged ceiling tiles are replaced. | | | | |
| | **Management** <br> No food, drink, or smoking is allowed in the computer room. <br> Chemicals and cleaning agents are not stored in the computer room. | | | | |

**Exhibit VI-3-1. *(continued)***

## Step 2: Testing Internal Controls

The controls identified in step 1 should be tested to ensure that they are operational and maintained. Data center managers and EDP auditors often presume that the controls are operational even though they may never have been independently tested when installed or retested since installation. Testing can involve arranging for the organization that installed and maintains the equipment to perform the testing under audit supervision.

The auditor must obtain not only support from the data center manager to perform the tests but approval from senior management to incur the expenditure. The auditors need to convince management of the value of testing the controls to ensure that they are operational. The major selling point is the worst-case scenario (i.e., destruction of the data center or LAN if the controls are not operational).

The auditor must ensure that regular preventive maintenance has been performed and obtain documentary evidence confirming that maintenance has been carried out. Audit evidence can be obtained by reviewing the maintenance schedules and service logs located on site.

## Step 3: Verifying Review Findings

After the review has been carried out, the EDP auditor must discuss the review findings with the data center manager to ensure that such findings are correct and that the recommended course of action to rectify the control weakness is appropriate. Further, the EDP auditor must obtain the data center manager's commitment to the implementation of the recommendations, with a timetable for implementation.

## PHASE 2: IDENTIFYING THE CRITICAL APPLICATIONS

The EDP auditor should perform the following steps to identify the organization's critical applications.

## Step 1: Performing a Preliminary Survey

The EDP auditor should perform a preliminary survey of the applications currently available to users to determine:

- The number of applications currently in operation.
- Each application's name.
- The version number of each application.
- The date each application was brought into production.
- The relative size of each application (i.e., the number of programs within the application).
- Links with other applications.

The profiles of the applications can be obtained from the IS department. The profiles are required to determine whether the applications are critical to the organization's business and because those applications may have an impact on the likely success of the plan. For example, a critical application can have links to other applications that are not critical. If these links were severed during the disaster recovery period and had not been considered in the planning, it is highly likely that the recovery process is in danger of failing. Often the links are hidden because of poor planning, spaghetti programming, and a lack of documentation.

## Step 2: Identifying Users

Once the application profiles have been obtained, the next process to be carried out is to identify the major users of the information processing facilities. The data center can assist the EDP auditors in this endeavor by providing the desired statistics. If there is some resistance in providing the data, the EDP auditor can outline the benefits to be gained by the data center, which include assisting data center planning in the areas of:

- Capacity planning.
- Demand management.
- Software maintenance.

The statistics that can be used to identify the major users are:

- CPU resource use.
- Time logged on.
- Disk space used.
- Memory use.
- Applications used.
- The number of times a program has been executed by users.
- The number of reports generated.

## Step 3: Analyzing the Data

Once the statistics become available, the data should be analyzed. The analysis should focus on identifying the major users, the applications they use, and the frequency of use. The EDP auditor must be aware, however, that some applications have little use or are used only at certain times of the year (e.g., for budgeting purposes), but they may be essential to the operations of the organization.

## Step 4: Preparing a Business Impact Analysis Questionnaire

After careful analysis, the data center manager and the EDP auditor should prepare a questionnaire with appropriate instructions for the users to complete (a sample questionnaire is provided in Exhibit VI-3-2). The questionnaire must be endorsed by senior management with an appropriate memorandum to department heads to ensure that the questionnaire is filled out accurately and completely and to verify that it will be used only for the purpose of determining whether the organization should invest in disaster recovery planning.

It is essential that this is clearly stated; otherwise, department heads may believe there is a hidden agenda attached to the questionnaire. The questionnaire should be distributed to the organization's department heads with a specified return date.

## Step 5: Determining the Results

Once the questionnaire has been returned, the data center manager and the EDP auditor must evaluate and collate the results as well as identify:

- Those users who stated that specific computer applications were critical for their operations.
- The type of processing performed.
- The number of users.
- The processing cycle and the timing of the cycle within the department.
- The work load (including fluctuations and time period).
- The impact on financial and human resources of the loss of the computer (e.g., one hour, half-day, one day).
- The critical time frame and estimation of total loss.
- The maximum period the department can operate without computer operations.
- The estimated amount of resources required to clear any backlog.
- Any arrangements or contingencies in place in the event of a disaster and the cost of such arrangement.
- What applications are essential for the day-to-day operations of the department.

From the evaluation of the answers to the questionnaire, the auditor may need to clarify and substantiate the answers given by interviewing the department management. This would include:

- Verifying that the computer applications stated as critical are in fact critical to the operation of their area of responsibility.
- Clarifying any ambiguous answers given in response to the questionnaire.

**User Department:**

_____

**Department Manager:**

_____

**Brief Description of Business Functions:**

_____

_____

_____

_____

*On a separate page, please provide the following information:*

**Section 1: Application Systems**

1. List the application systems used in your department.
2. Write a brief description of each application. Include in this description its general purpose, the number of users, and the type of functions performed (e.g., data entry, inquiry, and report generation).
3. Specify for each type of function performed the volume of transactions and dollar value for the following time periods:
   - 24 hours.
   - 48 hours.
   - 7 days.
   - 14 days.
   - 21 days.
   - 30 days.
4. Provide the frequency of use (e.g., daily, weekly, or monthly) and variations of use (including peak loads) for each function.
5. Provide details of normal hours of operation and any variations due to seasonal conditions (e.g., year-end).
6. Provide details of the programs used from the menu system and frequency of use.
7. List the details of any reports or transaction listings generated for each application.
8. If the application system passes information from one system to another, please provide details of:
   - The name of the system.
   - The type of transactions.
   - The volume of transactions.
   - The dollar value of transactions.

**Section 2: Financial Impact**

1. Describe the likely impact a computer disaster (i.e., unavailability of each application system) would have on your department for each of the follow-

**Exhibit VI-3-2. Sample Business Impact Analysis Questionnaire**

481

ing for the time periods 24 hours, 48 hours, 7 days, 14 days, 21 days, and 30 days:
- Cash flow (dollar values).
- Revenue collection and generation (dollar values).
- Accounts payable (dollar values).
- Production costs.
2. Describe the contractual obligations that would be affected and quantify the exposure (dollar values); this includes:
- Trade union agreements.
- Contracts with suppliers.
- Contracts with clients.
- Government legislation.
3. Describe the likely impact on the organization's image in the business sector and the local community.

### Section 3: Management Information and Control

1. List the management controls that would be affected by the unavailability of the computer in your department.
2. List the daily operational functions that would be affected. Please quantify your answer with examples.
3. Describe the impact the disaster would have on management decision making in your department. Please quantify your answer with examples.
4. List the management reports that would be affected by the unavailability of the system.
5. Describe any other management functions that would be affected.

### Section 4: Operational Impact

1. Detail the impact on the service level provided to other departments' and organizations' clients.
2. Describe the impact on management reporting.
3. Provide an estimate of productivity loss both in worker days and dollar value for 24 hours, 48 hours, 7 days, 14 days, 21 days, and 30 days.
4. Provide an estimate of the number of hours, days, or weeks that could pass before unavailability of the application system would affect your department. Please provide details to support your estimate.

### Section 5: Postrecovery

1. Provide details of how the backlog of data would be collected and processed.
2. If it were not feasible to recover the backlog of information, please provide an estimate of the impact on the operations in your department.
3. If the application system was available for a minimal number of hours per day, week, or month during recovery, provide an estimate of the minimum processing period needed to support your department operations.

**Exhibit VI-3-2.** *(continued)*

- Ascertaining whether management has given any consideration as to how it would maintain its operational functions in the event of a computer disaster.
- Determining whether alternative sources of daily information are available outside the computer system.
- Verifying that the costs stated in the reply would actually be incurred if the computer system were unavailable for a given period. This estimate should relate specifically for each application identified as critical to the department's operations.
- Determining what additional resources would be required by management to provide a reasonable, though reduced, operational capacity in the absence of computer support.
- Determining whether management has given any consideration to how its source documents would be stored for reprocessing purposes when computer operations have been restored.

Senior management must be consulted during this phase because it has a greater appreciation of what functional operation is essential for the survival of the organization. The EDP auditor may find that senior management disagrees with the assessment made by the major users that the application is critical. Consensus is important to ensure that only those applications that are truly critical are considered for the purposes of disaster recovery planning. The results of the survey also provide a strong guide on the type of disaster recovery plan strategy that would be appropriate for the organization (e.g., hot site, cold site, off the shelf).

## PHASE 3: ESTIMATING THE VALUE OF ASSETS TO BE PROTECTED

The survey provides information on the likely effect, including an estimate of the financial impact, that the disaster may have on the operational areas of the organization. The EDP auditor now should estimate the value of the organization's investment in its information processing facilities. This includes the hardware and software as well as the vlaue of the information stored on the computer.

The questionnaire seeks to determine the value (expressed in dollars) of the information assets. This may present a problem to the users; however, it is essential that some value be provided to facilitate an estimate of the overall value of the organization's information assets. The value of tangible assets (i.e., hardware and software) can be obtained from the accounting records. Consideration should be given, however, to valuing the tangible assets at replacement cost rather than the value at the time of original purchase or development.

## Step 1: Information

Determining a value for the organization's information is somewhat subjective, because it depends on management's perception of what it considers to be of value to the business. There are some information benchmarks that can be used by management to place an estimate on the value of the data, including:

- Debtors:
  - —Amount outstanding.
  - —Debtor's name and address.
- Creditors:
  - —Amount owing.
  - —Creditor's name and address.
- Marketing data:
  - —Clients.
  - —Sales, including demographics.
  - —Market share per product.
  - —Product mix.
- Production data:
  - —Cost per unit over time.
  - —Waste.
  - —Machine idle time.
  - —Breakdowns.
- Human resources data:
  - —Sick leave.
  - —Staff turnover.
  - —Payroll data.
- Insurance data:
  - —Workers' compensation claims.
  - —Public liability claims.
  - —Product liability claims.
- Financial data:
  - —Profit and loss.
  - —Cash flow.
  - —Investment (current and fixed).
  - —Return on investment.
  - —Budgeting.
  - —Purchases.
  - —Capital expenditure.
  - —Liabilities (current and noncurrent).
  - —Inventory.

Departmental managers, in consultat' n with senior management, should be able to provide an estimate of the value of information stored on the organization's computer system. The EDP auditor should collate the estimates of value for hardware, software, and data for the report to management.

### Step 2: Hardware

Although the cost/performance ratio of hardware has decreased, the cost of hardware maintenance has increased significantly. Therefore, the cost hardware maintenance must be a factor in calculating the replacement cost.

Another concern is whether the hardware is software dependent and whether it is available through the hardware vendor or in the secondhand market. Additional costs will be incurred if the software cannot be ported to another hardware platform. The EDP auditor, in consultation with the organization's senior financial officer and data center manager, should determine a value for the hardware.

### Step 3: Software

Determining the value for software is difficult, especially if it was developed in-house. Often, the cost in the accounting records reflects only the historical cost from the initial development and may not include the cost of any enhancements that have been performed.

Another consideration in determining a value for software is the cost to redevelop the software with recent changes in technology. Therefore, in determining a value for software, consideration must be given to the cost of the purchase of new development tools and staff training. The IS manager should be able to provide, in consultation with the senior financial officer, an estimate of the value of the software.

### PHASE 4: QUANTIFYING THE ESTIMATED DISASTER LOSS

After interviewing the managers and reviewing the information provided, the EDP auditor may need to consider the concept of probability to determine the likelihood of a disaster situation occurring and relate this to management's estimate of the expected loss from a disaster. For example, the probability of a 747 jumbo jet striking the organization's data center would be extremely low, unless the data center were in a high-rise building on the flight path to an airport. The expected loss, however, would be extremely high.

There are several methodologies available to assist in estimating the expected loss from a specific event. For example, one method of evaluating security risk requires every file or data set in an application to be evaluated to estimate the impact of breaches of file integrity. In organizations with a large number of data bases, however, it may be appropriate to vary the method by adopting a simplified model of the applications that have been determined to be critical.

For each application evaluated, an average annual cost should be calculated for each of the risk considered. These risks are:

- Disclosure of the file.
- Destruction of the file.
- Modification of the file.

The cost calculation has two components:

- The likelihood of the risk's occurrence, which is estimated in orders of magnitude, ranging from once in 300 years (magnitude 1), through once in 30 years (magnitude 2), and so on to 100 times a day (magnitude 8).
- The magnitude of the dollar impact of each occurrence; this is estimated from $10 (magnitude 1), $100 (magnitude 2), to $10 million (magnitude 7).

The annual cost is calculated as follows. If $p$ is the magnitude assigned to the likelihood of occurrence and $v$ is the magnitude assigned to the dollar impact, the annual cost in dollars is determined by referring to Exhibit VI-3-3. For example, a specified risk is likely to occur once in three years, so that $p = 3$. Its cost impact is of the order of $100,000 per occurrence, so that $v = 5$. By referring to the exhibit for $p = 3$, $v = 5$, the auditor finds the answer to be $30,000, an estimate of the average annual cost of the risk.

Another methodology facilitates the estimation of the annual cost for the likelihood of various risks that may cause the loss of computing capability. The overall objective is to quantify the estimated loss in terms that management can readily understand and accept, including:

- The direct financial impact on the organization's cash flow and profit and loss for a given time period.
- The direct financial loss flowing from a loss of market share or client base.

| Value of v | Value of p | | | | | | | |
|---|---|---|---|---|---|---|---|---|
| | 1 | 2 | 3 | 4 | 5 | 6 | 7 | 8 |
| 1 | | | | | 300 | 3K | 30K | 300K |
| 2 | | | | 300 | 3K | 30K | 300K | 3M |
| 3 | | | 300 | 3K | 30K | 300K | 3M | 30M |
| 4 | | 300 | 3K | 30K | 300K | 3M | 30M | 300M |
| 5 | 300 | 3K | 30K | 300K | 3M | 30M | 300M | |
| 6 | 3K | 30K | 300K | 3M | 30M | 300M | | |
| 7 | 30K | 300K | 3M | 30M | 300M | | | |

**Exhibit VI-3-3. Annual Cost in Dollars**

- The indirect loss of influence on the direction of the market.
- Loss of investment opportunity.
- Indirect loss of the organization's reputation or goodwill with existing and prospective clients, financial institutions, shareholders, staff, and other interested parties.
- Financial penalties that can be imposed from government agencies for failing to provide reports by a set date.

## PHASE 5: DETERMINING THE CRITICAL TIMELINESS FOR RECOVERY

Applications identified as critical by line management in its response to the questionnaire must be confirmed by senior management, because there may be a difference of opinion between line and senior management as to what applications or computer functions are essential and the timing of the recovery. To attain consensus, the EDP auditor may have to chair a meeting between line and senior management to determine those applications or computer functions that are essential to the organization and the timing of their recovery. Once consensus has been reached between line and senior management on the critical applications, critical timeliness for recovery must be determined (i.e., when does the computer system have to be operational to resume operations to ensure the survival of the organization?)

For each critical application, a recovery timing criterion should be determined. For example:

- *Payroll.* Recovery should be within one payroll period for each category of employee.
- *Sales and inventory.* Recovery should be within seven days.
- *Computer-aided design and drafting.* Recovery should be within 14 days.
- *Accounts receivable.* Recovery should be within one accounting cycle.

Timing is important because it will facilitate the decision on what type of disaster recovery plan strategy will be implemented to meet management's timing recovery objective.

## PHASE 6: PREPARING THE BUSINESS IMPACT ANALYSIS REPORT

From the analysis undertaken, the results must determine how much the organization should invest in disaster recovery planning, or the hard-won reputation of the EDP auditor will be damaged. Therefore, the report to management must be a document that will not only be clear and concise in the information to be conveyed but provide a constructive and objective comment on the risks and exposures the organization faces.

The report should be a selling document that can convince management of the need for a disaster recovery plan and gain commitment to provide resources for the development and maintenance of the plan. The contents of the report should be discussed with line and senior management before its release to ensure that there are no errors. Any errors will detract from the objective of providing senior management with a detailed analysis of the organization's exposure from a computer disaster and its likely impact on business operations.

A summary of the risks and exposures must be highlighted in the executive summary in terms that senior management understands. For example, an estimated loss of $2 million in gross revenue per week will occur if the data center is detroyed by fire and is not operational within seven days. Further, the manual systems will not be able to function after 36 hours because of the volume of work and the complexity of the tasks performed in providing services to the organization's customers.

## SUMMARY

Senior management does not usually realize the organization's dependence on its computerized information systems. Therefore, the data center manager and the EDP auditor have the responsibility of identifying the risks of loss and clarifying exposures resulting from a computer disaster in terms that senior management understands (i.e., dollars and cents).

Management often realizes the value of investing in a disaster recovery plan only when a real disaster occurs. To ensure that management understands the need to consider investing resources in a disaster recovery plan, the data center manager and the EDP auditor need to perform a business impact analysis. A sales effort is needed to convince management to invest the time and resources in performing the business impact analysis. Without the initial investment, there can be no disaster recovery plan.

# VI-4
# Network Disaster Recovery Planning

*NATHAN J. MULLER*

A lthough strategies for protecting computer resources from potential disaster are receiving an increasing share of attention these days, the lion's share of concern should instead be given to the links between hosts and terminals. Digital facilities are sensitive to a variety of anomalies that can degrade performance, resulting in transmission errors, retransmission delays, and, at worst, prolonged power failures.

Because there are many more links than host computers, there are more opportunities for failure on the network than in the hosts themselves. Consequently, a disaster recovery plan that takes into account such backup methods as the use of hot sites or cold sites without giving due consideration to link-restoral methods ignores a significant area of potential problems.

Fortunately, corporations can use several methods that help protect their data networks against prolonged downtime and data loss. These methods differ mostly in cost and efficiency.

## NETWORK RELIABILITY

A reliable network continues operations despite the failure of a critical element. In the case of a failed link, a reliable network can continue to support applications over an alternative link with unused or spare channel capacity. The mesh topology, for example, is reliable because it provides a diversity of routes; however, route diversity entails adding more physical links to the network, which typically inflates the cost of networking.

### Component Reliability

**Star Topology.** With respect to link failures, the star topology is highly reliable. Although the loss of a link prevents communications between the hub and the affected node, all other nodes continue to operate as before unless the hub suffers a malfunction.

The hub is the weak link in the star topology; the reliability of the network depends on the reliability of the central hub. To ensure a high degree of reliability, the hub has redundant subsystems as critical points: the control logic, backplane, and power supply. The hub's management system can enhance the fault tolerance of these redundant subsystems by monitoring their operation and reporting anomalies. With the power supply, for example, monitoring may include hotspot detection and fan diagnostics that identify trouble before it disrupts hub operation. Upon the failure of the main power supply, the redundant unit switches over automatically or under management control without disrupting the network.

The flexibility of the hub architecture lends itself to variable degrees of fault tolerance, depending on the criticality of the applications. For example, workstations running noncritical applications may share a link to the same local area network (LAN) module at the hub. Although this configuration might seem economical, it is disadvantageous in that a failure in the LAN module would put all the workstations on that link out of commission. A slightly higher degree of fault tolerance may be achieved by distributing the workstations among two LAN modules and links. That way, the failure of one module would affect only half the number of workstations. A one-to-one correspondence of workstations to modules offers an even greater level of fault tolerance, because the failure of one module affects only the workstation connected to it; however, this configuration is also a more expensive solution.

A critical application may demand the highest level of fault tolerance. This can be achieved by connecting the workstation to two LAN modules at the hub with separate links. The ultimate in fault tolerance can be achieved by connecting one of those links to a different hub. In this arrangement, a transceiver is used to split the links from the application's host computer, enabling each link to connect with a different module in the hub or to a different hub. All of these levels of fault tolerance are summarized in Exhibit VI-4-1.

**Ring Topology.** In its pure form, the ring topology offers poor reliability to both node and link failures. The ring uses link segments to connect adjacent nodes. Each node is actively involved in the transmissions of other nodes through token passing. The token is received by each node and passed onto the adjacent node. The loss of a link not only results in the loss of a node but brings down the entire network as well. Improvement of the reliability of the ring topology requires adding redundant links between nodes as well as bypass circuitry. Adding such components, however, makes the ring topology less cost-effective.

**Bus Topology.** The bus topology also provides poor reliability. If the link fails, that entire segment of the network is rendered useless. If a node fails, on the other hand, the rest of the network continues to operate. A redundant link for each segment increases the reliability of the bus topology but at extra cost.

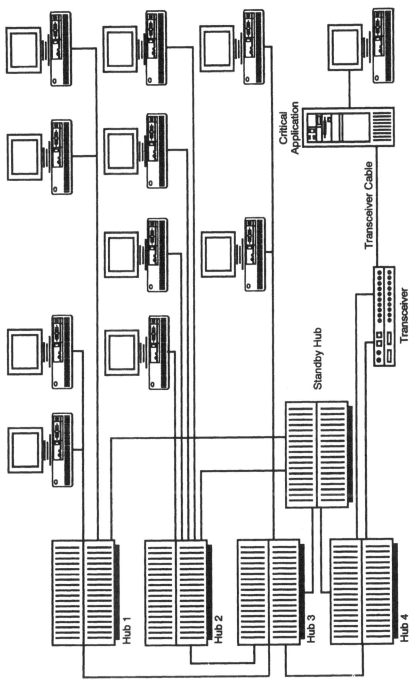

**Exhibit VI-4-1. Fault Tolerance of the Hub Architecture**

## NETWORK AVAILABILITY

Availability is a measure of performance dealing with the LAN's ability to support all users who wish to access it. A network that is highly available provides services immediately to users, whereas a network that suffers from low availability typically forces users to wait for access.

### Availability of Components

Availability on the bus topology depends on load, the access control protocol used, and length of the bus. With a light load, availability is virtually ensured for any user who wishes to access the network. As the load increases, however, so does the chance of collisions. When a collision occurs, the transmitting nodes back off and try again after a short interval. The chance of collisions also increases with bus length.

With its multiple paths, a mesh topology (a variation of the bus topology) provides the highest degree of interconnectivity, which implies that the network is always available to users who require access.

A network based on a star topology can support only what the central hub can handle. In any case, the hub can handle only one request at a time, which can shut out many users under heavy load conditions. Hubs equipped with multiple processors can alleviate this situation somewhat, but even with multiple processors, there is not usually a one-to-one correspondence between users and processors. Such a system could be cost-prohibitive.

The ring topology does not provide the same degree of availability as does a mesh topology but still represents an improvement over the star topology. The ring has a lower measure of availability than the mesh topology because each node on the ring must wait for the token before transmitting data. As the number of nodes on the ring increases, the time interval allotted for transmission decreases.

## METHODS OF PROTECTION

In today's distributed computing environments, with so much information traversing corporate networks, it is imperative that information systems managers be acquainted with the available protection methods to ensure uninterrupted data flow. On a wide area network (WAN), the choices include carrier-provided redundancy and protection services, customer-controlled reconfiguration, bandwidth on demand using ISDN, and dial backup. On the local area network, the choices include various recovery and reconfiguration procedures, the use of fault-tolerant servers and wiring hubs, and the implementation of redundant arrays of inexpensive disks. All these methods are discussed in detail in the following sections.

## Tariffed Redundancy and Protection

Among the traditional methods for protecting WAN facilities are the tariffed redundancy and protection services offered by such interexchange carriers as AT&T Co., MCI Communications Corp., and US Sprint Communications Co.

A reliable method for minimizing downtime on the WAN is to have redundant lines ready and waiting. When a link goes down, the standby facility can be activated until the source of the failure is determined and appropriate action taken to restore service. Having duplicate facilities is a prohibitively expensive option for most businesses because monthly charges accrue whether or not the facilities are used.

To minimize the effects of failed facilities on the same route, AT&T, for example, offers two special routing methods in conjunction with its digital and analog service offerings: diversity and avoidance.

**Diversity.** Diversity is available for ACCUNET T1.5, ACCUNET Spectrum of Digital Services (ASDS), 56K-bps Dataphone Digital Service (DDS), and voicegrade private lines. With diversity routing, designated groups of interoffice channels (i.e., AT&T's portion of the circuit) are furnished over physically separate routes. Each route entails installation and routing charges. A custom option for diversity furnishes the interoffice channels partially or entirely over physically separated routes when separate facilities are available. In this case, AT&T applies a special routing charge to each channel.

**Avoidance.** The avoidance option allows the customer to have a channel avoid a specified geographic area. In this way, the customer can minimize potential impairments such as delay, which might be exacerbated by long, circuitous routes. It also enables the customer to avoid potential points of congestion in high-use corridors, which can block traffic. This option also gives customers the means to avoid high-risk environments that can be prone to damage from floods, earthquakes, and hurricanes.

## Further Protective Capabilities

Although special routing can minimize the damage resulting from failed facilities by allowing some channels to remain available to handle priority traffic, special routing makes no provision for restoring failed facilities. AT&T has attempted to address this issue with its automatic protection capability and network protection capability.

**Automatic Protection Capability.** Automatic protection capability is an office function that protects against failure for a local channel (or other access) for the ACCUNET T1.5 and ACCUNET T45 services. Protection of interoffice channels is provided on a one-to-one basis through the use of a switching arrangement that automatically switches to the spare channel when the working channel fails. To implement this capability, a separate local access channel must be ordered to serve as the spare and compatible automatic switching equipment must be provided by the customer at its premises.

**Network Protection Capability.** Whereas AT&T's automatic protection capability protects against failures of a local access channel, its network protection capability is designed to protect against the failure of an interoffice channel. Protection is furnished through the use of a switching arrangement that automatically switches the customer's channel to a separately routed fiber-optic channel on failure of the primary channel.

For both ACCUNET T1.5 and ACCUNET T45, an installation charge is incurred for the network protection capability. For the amount of protection promised, however, it may not be worth the cost, because most, if not all, of AT&T's interoffice channels are automatically protected, whether or not they use the network protection capability. When AT&T circuits go down, traffic is automatically switched to alternative routes.

## Dial Backup

Over the years, dial backup units have come into widespread use for rerouting modem and digital data set transmissions around failed facilities. Dial backup units are certainly more economical than leasing redundant facilities or using reserved service or satellite sharing arrangements.

This method entails installing a standalone device or an optional modem card that allows data communication to be temporarily transferred to the public switched network. When the primary line fails, operation over the dial backup network can be manually or automatically initiated. At the remote site, the calls are answered automatically by the dial backup unit. When the handshake and security sequence is completed and the dial backup connection is established, the flow of data resumes. On recovery of the failed line, dial backup is terminated in one of two ways: by a central site attendant, who manually releases the backup switch on the dial backup unit; or, when in the automatic mode, the dial backup unit reestablishes the leased line connection and disconnects the dial network call upon detection of acceptable signal quality.

## Rerouting on T1 Lines

To support applications requiring a full T1, dial backup over the public switched network is available with AT&T's ACCUNET T1.5 reserved service. With this service, a dedicated T1 facility is brought online after the customer requests it with a phone call. An hour or more may elapse before the reserved line is finally cut over by AT&T. This option may be acceptable under certain conditions, however, as a possible course to loss of network availability for an indeterminate period. This is an effective alternative for the customer who has presubscribed to the ACCUNET T1.5 reserved service. If the customer

494

has not presubscribed, this service is not a suitable alternative for routing traffic around failed facilities, if only because the local access facilities must already be in place at each end of the circuit.

### Customer-Controlled Reconfiguration

Management capabilities, such as customer-controlled reconfiguration available using AT&T's Digital Access and Crossconnect System (DACS), can be a means to route around failed facilities. Briefly, the DACS is a routing device; it is not a switch that can be used to set up calls (i.e., a PBX switch) or for performing alternative routing (i.e., a multiplexer switch). The DACS was originally designed to automate the process of circuit provisioning. With customer-controlled reconfiguration, circuit provisioning is under user control from an on-premise management terminal.

With customer-controlled reconfiguration, however, a failed facility may take a half hour or more to restore its operations, depending on the complexity of the reconfiguration. This relatively long period is necessary because the carrier needs time to establish the paths specified by the subscriber through use of a dial-up connection.

A recovery time of 30 minutes may seem tolerable for voice traffic (where the public switched network itself is a backup vehicle), but data subscribers may need to implement alternative routing more quickly. Therefore, AT&T's DACS and customer-controlled reconfiguration service (and the similar offerings of other carriers) are typically used to remedy a long-term failure rather than to rapidly restore service on failed lines.

### ISDN Facilities

T1 multiplexers offer many more functions than does DACS with customer-controlled reconfiguration. In fact, the instantaneous restoral of high-capacity facilities on today's global networks calls for a T1 networking multiplexer with an advanced transport management system.

An ISDN-equipped T1 networking multiplexer offers yet another efficient and economical means to back up T1 and fractional T1 facilities. With ISDN, the typical time required for call setup is from three to 10 seconds. An appropriately equipped T1 multiplexer permits traffic to be rerouted from a failing T1 line to an ISDN facility in a matter of seconds rather than in hours or days, as is required by other recovery methods.

**Advantages of ISDN.** Using ISDN facilities is also more economical than other methods, including the ACCUNET T1.5 reserved service. With the reserved service, the user pays a flat fee for a dedicated interoffice circuit over a certain length of time, including the time when the circuit remains unused. With ISDN, the user pays for the primary rate local access channels and pays for the interoffice channels only when they are used because these charges are time and distance dependent—like ordinary telephone calls.

With AT&T's offering of the high-capacity H0 (384K-bps) and H11 (1.544M-bps) ISDN channels, users can avail themselves of the ISDN for backing up fractional or full T1 lines rather than pay for idle lines that may be used only occasionally during recovery. This is accomplished through a T1 multiplexer's capability to implement intelligent automatic rerouting, which ensures the connectivity of critical applications in an information-intensive business environment.

When confronted with congestion or impending circuit failure, the intelligent automatic rerouting system calculates rerouting on the basis of each likely failure. During a failure, the system automatically recalculates optimal routing, based on current network conditions. After restoration, the system again automatically calculates the most effective rerouting, should a second failure occur on the network. In this way, the system is always ready to handle the next emergency.

Because applications require different grades of service to continue operating efficiently during line failures, circuits must be routed to the best path for each application, not just switched to available bandwidth. This ensures that the network continues to support all applications with the best response times.

To avoid service denial during rerouting, voice transmissions can be automatically compressed with compression algorithms to use less bandwidth. This can free up enough bandwidth to support all applications, including voice and data.

## DDS Dial Backup

Despite carrier claims of 99.5% availability on digital data services (DDS), this seemingly impressive figure still leaves room for 44 hours of annual downtime. This amount of downtime can be very costly, especially to financial institutions, whose daily operations depend heavily on the proper operation of their networks. A large financial services firm, for example, can lose as much as $200 million if its network becomes inoperative for only an hour.

An organization that cannot afford the 44 hours of annual downtime might consider a digital data set with the ability to "heal" interruptions in transmission. Should the primary facility fail, communication can be quickly reestablished over the public switched network by the data set's built-in modem and integral single-cell dial backup unit.

Sensing loss of energy on the line, the dial-backup unit automatically dials the remote unit, which sets up a connection through the public switched network. Data is then rerouted from the leased facility to the dial-up circuit. If the normal DDS operating rate is 19.2K bps, dial restoration entails a fallback to 9.6K bps. For all other DDS rates—2.4K, 4.8K, and 9.6K bps—the transmission speed remains the same in the dial-backup mode. Downspeeding is not necessary.

While in the dial backup mode, the unit continues to monitor the failed facility for the return of energy, which indicates an active line. Sensing that service has been restored, the unit reestablished communication over it. The dial-up connection is then dropped.

## RECOVERY OPTIONS FOR LANS

The local area network is a data-intensive environment requiring special precautions to safeguard one of the organization's most valuable assets—information.

The procedural aspect of minimizing data loss entails the implementation of manual or automated methods for backing up all data on the LAN to avoid the tedious and costly process of re-creating vast amounts of information. The equipment aspect of minimizing data loss entails the use of redundant circuitry, components, and subsystems that are activated automatically when various LAN devices fail, thereby preventing data loss and maintaining network reliability.

In the simplest terms, a LAN is a conduit or family of conduits linking various communications devices. The conduits may consist of ordinary telephone station wire from each device on the network, which connect in a wire closet to a backbone coaxial cable and possibly to a fiber link between buildings.

Connections to the LAN are achieved with network interface units that plug into each device on the network, enabling them to communicate with other devices on the LAN that use the same communications protocol. These interface units may be pooled at a server to permit access on a dedicated or contention basis. Various special-purpose LAN servers are available to facilitate resource sharing and protocol conversions among different computers and LANs.

### Recovery and Reconfiguration

In addition to the ability to respond to errors in transmissions by detection and correction, other important aspects of LAN operation are recovery and reconfiguration. Recovery deals with bringing the LAN back to a stable condition after an error, and reconfiguration is the mechanism by which operation is restored after a failure.

LAN reconfigurations involve mechanisms to restore service upon loss of a link or network interface unit. To recover or reconfigure the network after failures or faults requires that the network possess mechanisms to detect that an error or fault has occurred and to determine how to minimize the effect on the system's performance. Generally, these mechanisms provide:

- Performance monitoring.
- Fault location.
- Network management.

- System availability management.
- Configuration management.

These mechanisms work in concert to detect and isolate errors, determine errors' effects on the system, and remedy these errors to bring the network to a stable state with minimal impact on network availability.

**Reconfiguration.** Reconfiguration is an error management scheme used to bypass major failures of network components. This process entails detecting the occurrence of an error condition that cannot be corrected by the usual means. Once it is determined that an error has occurred, its impact on the network is assessed so that an appropriate reconfiguration can be formulated and implemented. In this way, operations can continue under a new configuration.

**Error Detection.** Error detection is augmented by logging systems that track failures over a period of time. This information is examined to determine whether occurring trends may adversely affect network performance. This information, for example, might reveal that a particular component is continually causing errors to be inserted onto the network, or the monitoring system might detect that a component on the network has failed.

**Configuration Assessment Component.** The component of the reconfiguration system that does this is typically referred to as the configuration assessment component. It uses information about the current system configuration (including connectivity, component placement, paths, and flows) and maps information onto the failed component. This information is analyzed to indicate how that particular failure is affecting the system and to isolate the cause of the failure. Once this assessment has been performed, a solution can be worked out and implemented.

The solution may consist of reconfiguring most of the operational processes to avoid the source of the error. The solution determination component examines the configuration and the affected hardware or software components, determines how to move resources around to bring the network back to an operational state or indicates what must be eliminated because of the failure, and identifies network components that must be serviced.

**Function Criticality.** The determination of the most effective course of action is based on the criticality of keeping certain functions of the network operating and maintaining the resources available to do this. In some environments, nothing can be done to restore service because of device limitations (e.g., lack of redundant subsystem components) or the lack of spare bandwidth. In such cases, about all that can be done is to indicate to the servicing agent what must be corrected and keep users apprised of the situation.

**Implementation of the Configuration.** Once an alternative configuration has been determined, the reconfiguration system implements it. In most cases, this involves rerouting transmissions, moving and restarting processes from failed devices, and reinitializing software that has failed because of an intermittent error condition. In some cases, however, nothing may need to be done except notifying affected users that the failure is not severe enough to warrant system reconfiguration.

For wide area networks, connections among LANs may be accomplished over leased lines with a variety of devices, typically bridges and routers. An advantage of using routers to interconnect LANs over the wide area network is that they permit the building of large mesh networks. With mesh networks, the routers can steer traffic around points of congestion or failure and balance the traffic load across the remaining links.

## Restoral Capabilities of LAN Servers

Sharing resources distributed over the LAN can better protect users against the loss of information and unnecessary downtime than can a network with all of its resources centralized as a single location. The vehicle for resource sharing is the server, which constitutes the heart of the LAN. It is the tool that the network administrator uses to satisfy the needs of users. The server gives the LAN its features, including those for security and data protection as well as those for network management and resource accounting.

**Types of Servers.** The server determines the friendliness of the user interface and governs the number of users that share the network at one time. It resides in one or more networking cards that are typically added to microcomputers or workstations and may vary in processing power and memory capacity. However, servers are programs that provide services more than they are specific pieces of hardware. In addition, various types of servers are designed to share limited LAN resources—for example, laser printers, hard disks, and RAM mass memory. More impressive than the actual shared hardware are the functions provided by servers. Aside from file servers and communications servers, there are image and fax servers, electronic mail servers, printer servers, SQL servers, and various other specialized servers.

The addition of multiple special-purpose servers provides the capability, connectivity, and processing power not provided by the network operating system and file server alone. A single multiprocessor server combined with a network operating system designed to exploit its capabilities, such as UNIX, provides enough throughput to support five to ten times the number of users and applications as a microcomputer that is used as a server. New bus and cache designs make it possible for the server to make full use of several processors at once, without the usual performance bottlenecks that slow application speed.

**Server Characteristics.** Distributing resources in this way minimizes the disruption to productivity that would result if all the resources were centralized and a failure were to occur. Moreover, the use of such specialized devices as servers permits the integration of diagnostic and maintenance capabilities not found in general-purpose microcomputers. Among these capabilities are error detection and correction, soft controller error detection and correction, and automatic shutdown in case of catastrophic error. Some servers include integral management functions (e.g., remote console capabilities). The multiprocessing capabilities of specialized servers provide the power necessary to support the system overhead that all these sophisticated capabilities require.

Aside from physical faults on the network, there are various causes for lost or erroneous data. A software failure on the host, for example, can cause write errors to the user or server disk. Application software errors may generate incorrect value, or faults, on the disk, itself. Power surges can corrupt data, and power failures can shut down sessions, wiping out data that has not yet been saved to disk. Viruses and worms that are brought into the LAN from external bulletin boards, shareware, and careless user uploads are a relatively new problem. User mistakes can also introduce errors into data or eliminate entire files. Although careful system administration and strict adherence to security procedures are usually sufficient to eliminate most of these problems, they do not eliminate the need for backup and archival storage.

**Backup Procedures.** Many organizations follow traditional file backup procedures that can be implemented across the LAN. Some of these procedures include performing file backups at night—full backups if possible, incremental backups otherwise. Archival backups of all disk drives are typically performed at least monthly; multiple daily saves of critical data bases may be warranted in some cases. The more data users already have stored on their hard disks, the longer it takes to save. For this reason, LAN managers encourage users to off-load unneeded files and consolidate file fragments with utility software to conserve disk space as well as to improve overall LAN performance during backups. Some LAN managers have installed automatic archiving facilities that will move files from users' hard disks to a backup data base if they have not been opened in the last 90 days.

Retrieving files from archival storage is typically not an easy matter; users forget file names, the date the file was backed up, or in which directory the file was originally stored. In the future, users can expect to see intelligent file backup servers that permit files to be identified by textual content. Graphics files, too, will be retrieved without the name, backup date, or location of the file. In this case, the intelligent file backup system will compare bit patterns from a sample graphic with the bit patterns of archived files to locate the right file for retrieval.

As the amount of stored information increases, there will be the need for LAN backup systems that address such strategic concerns as tape administration, disaster recovery, and the automatic movement of files up and down a hierarchy of network storage devices. Such capabilities portend the emergence of a new area of LAN development, which might be referred to as system storage management.

## Levels of Fault Tolerance

Protecting data at the server has become a critical concern for most network managers; after all, a failure at the server can result in lost or destroyed data. Considering that some servers can hold vast quantities of data in the gigabyte range, loss or damage can have disastrous consequences for an information-intensive organization.

Depending on the level of fault tolerance desired and the price the organization is willing to pay, the server may be configured in several ways: unmirrored, mirrored, or duplexed.

**Unmirrored Servers.** An unmirrored server configuration entails the use of one disk drive and one disk channel, which includes the controller, a power supply, and interface cabling, as shown in Exhibit VI-4-2. This is the basic configuration of most servers. The advantage is chiefly one of cost: the user pays only for one disk and disk channel. The disadvantage of this configuration is that a failure in either the drive or anywhere on the disk channel could cause temporary or permanent loss of the stored data.

**Mirrored Servers.** The mirrored server configuration entails the use of two hard disks of similar size. There is also a single-disk channel over which the two disks can be mirrored together (see Exhibit VI-4-3). In this configuration, all data written to one disk is then automatically copied onto the other disk. If one disk fails, the other takes over, thus protecting the data and assuring all users of access to the data. The server's operating system issues an alarm notifying the network manager that one of the mirrored disks is in need of replacement.

The disadvantage of this configuration is that both disks use the same channel and controller. If a failure occurs on the channel or controller, both disks become inoperative. Because the same disk channel and controller are shared, the writes to the disks must be performed sequentially—that is, after the write is made to one disk, a write is made to the other disk. This can degrade overall server performance under heavy loads.

**Disk Duplexing.** In disk duplexing, multiple disk drives are installed with separate disk channels for each set of drives (see Exhibit VI-4-4). If a malfunction occurs anywhere along a disk channel, normal operation continues on the remaining channel and drives. Because each disk uses a separate disk channel, write operations are performed simultaneously, offering a performance advantage over servers using disk mirroring.

Disk duplexing also offers a performance advantage in read operations.

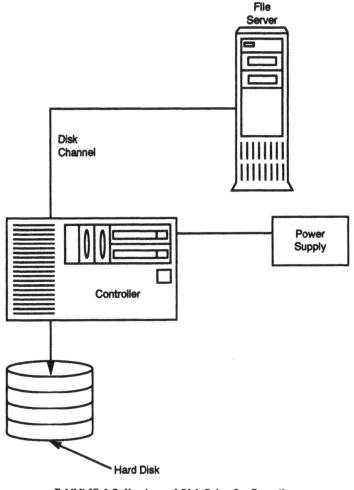

**Exhibit VI-4-2. Unmirrored Disk Drive Configuration**

Read requests are given to both drives. The drive that is closest to the information will respond and answer the request. The second request given to the other drive is canceled. In addition, the duplexed disks share multiple read requests for concurrent access.

The disadvantage of disk duplexing is the extra cost for multiple hard disk drives (also required for disk mirroring) as well as for the additional disk channels and controller hardware. However, the added cost for these components must be weighed against the replacement cost of lost information plus costs that accrue from the interruption of critical operations and lost business opportunities. Faced with these consequences, an organization might

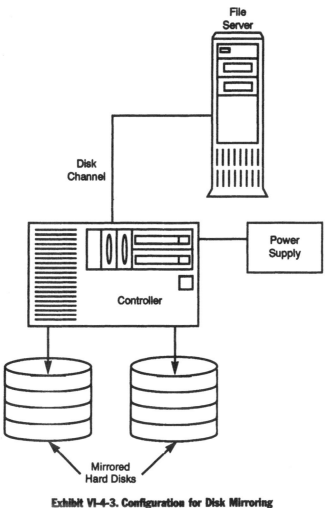

**File
Server**

**Disk
Channel**

**Power
Supply**

**Controller**

**Mirrored
Hard Disks**

**Exhibit VI-4-3. Configuration for Disk Mirroring**

---

discover that the investment of a few hundred or even a few thousand dollars to safeguard valuable data is negligible.

## Redundant Arrays of Inexpensive Disks

An emerging method of data protection on the LAN is redundant arrays of inexpensive disks (RAID). Instead of risking all of its data on one high-capacity disk, the organization distributes the data across multiple smaller disks, offering protection from a crash that could wipe out all data on a single-shared disk (see Exhibit VI-4-5). Other benefits of RAID include:

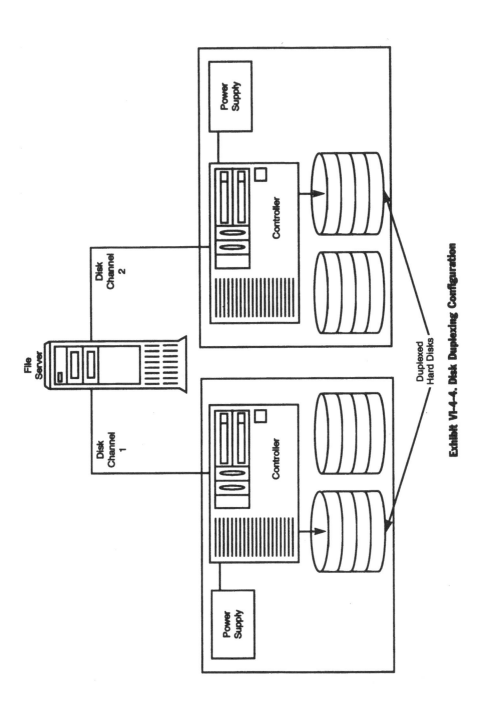

**Exhibit VI-4-4. Disk Duplexing Configuration**

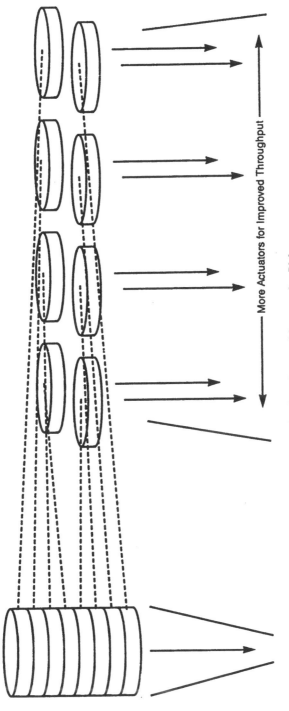

Exhibit VI-4-5. Redundant Arrays of Inexpensive Disks

- Increased storage capacity per logical disk volume.
- High data transfer or I/O rates that improve information throughput.
- Lower cost per megabyte of storage.
- Improved use of data center floor space.

RAID products can be grouped into at least six categories:

- RAID-0 products are technically not RAID products at all, because they do not offer parity or error-correction data to provide redundancy in case of system failure.
- RAID-1 products duplicate data that is stored on separate disk drives. Also called mirroring, this approach ensures that critical files will be available in case of individual disk drive failures.
- RAID-2 products distribute the code used for error detection and correction across additional disk drives. This is not a widely used approach, because the error detection function is already built into most disk drives and their controllers. RAID-2 products are needlessly redundant.
- RAID-3 products store user data in parallel across multiple disks. Error-correction data is stored on a dedicated parity disk. This array functions as one large logical drive and is ideally suited to supporting applications that require high data transfer rates for reading and writing large files.
- RAID-4 products store and retrieve data using independent writes and reads to several drives. Error-correction data is stored on a dedicated parity drive.
- RAID-5 products interleave user data and parity data, which are than distributed across several disks. There is no dedicated parity drive. This configuration is suited for applications that require a high number of I/O operations per second, such as transaction processing tasks that involve writing and reading large numbers of small data blocks at random disk locations.

Some vendors are creating enhanced array configurations that involve caching schemes to increase performance. Users should evaluate the available alternatives, based on their applications needs. A RAID-0 configuration may be appropriate for protecting applications requiring high data rates or very large files. If continuous availability is a requirement, fault tolerance becomes more important, in which case RAID-1 is an effective solution but RAID-5 is more economical. If the preferred RAID configuration involves reduced performance in write-intensive applications, some vendors offer optimization software that fine tunes performance, depending on the applications mix.

**RAID as a Future Solution**

Prospective clients should consider that RAID may be a future rather than current solution to the storage needs of the computing environment. Standard disk drives have become more reliable since the late 1980s, when RAID was first proposed. In addition, for a variety of technical reasons, current RAID solutions are not widely viewed by potential users as a feasible option.

RAID manufacturers, for example, have not yet perfected the means to put enough storage capacity (in the gigabyte range) onto the smaller 5¹/₄- and 3¹/₂-inch drives. Intelligent controllers that direct the placement and retrieval of data to and from the drives must be refined. RAID devices must also decrease in price to compete with conventional disk storage.

IBM is a committed proponent of RAID. Its RAID-3 configuration for the RS/6000 workstation includes as many as 40 5¹/₄-inch enhanced small device interface (ESDI) disk drives operating at a sustained data rate of 18M bytes per second. Prices for RAID-3 begin at about $113,000.

RAID may yet evolve to become the answer to the massive storage chores implied by the advanced fiber-optic network architectures that will be introduced in the mid-1990s. Theoretically and practically, the disk array may be the only means to achieve sufficient reliability in such data-intensive environments.

## SUMMARY

The methods mentioned in this chapter are only a few of the many network and data protection options available from carriers and equipment vendors. With more and more businesses becoming aware of the strategic value of their networks, these capabilities are significantly important to organizations. A variety of link restoration and data protection methods can provide effective ways to meet the diverse requirements of today's information-intensive corporations that are both efficient and economical. Choosing wisely from among the available alternatives ensures that companies are not forced into making cost/benefit trade-offs that jeopardize their information networks and, ultimately, their competitive positions.

# VI-5
# Disaster Recovery Planning Tools and Management Options

*JON WILLIAM TOIGO*

A n effective disaster recovery plan can be developed either by a disaster recovery consultant or by in-house personnel. Consultants can offer considerable expertise and experience and, in some cases, help overcome internal obstacles to the plan's development. The cost of consultant-developed plans, however, is more than most small and medium-sized organizations can afford. In addition, this makes in-house disaster recovery planning an interesting option. There is an increasing body of literature to help novices understand and implement disaster recovery planning. In addition, several software packages have been developed to aid in plan development and maintenance. This chapter examines the advantages and disadvantages of both approaches to disaster recovery planning.

## THE CONSULTANT OPTION

Several factors support a decision to hire a consultant. Experienced consultants bring a set of proven tools to the project, which may mean the quick development of an effective plan. A practiced consultant understands the effective construction of a disaster recovery plan, asks the right questions, and typically knows who is who in the disaster recovery products and services industry. Consultants who work in a specific industry often tailor a methodology for disaster recovery planning to that industry, which reduces the amount of time needed to learn new skills and helps speed development. Further, consultants bring a fresh perspective to the process, spotting important recovery requirements that may be overlooked by employees.

Consultants are expensive, however. Ironically, this may be an advantage in some cases. Disaster recovery planning requires the interaction of users and information systems personnel. In many large IS operations, fractious functions (e.g., programming and systems operations) must cooperate. Frequently, the only way to have all parties work together efficiently is to impress upon them the considerable cost of the consultant. Similarly, because senior management has made an investment in the consultant's plan, it may be less inclined to withdraw the support needed to implement the plan.

However, many myths surround consultant-driven plans. Many managers believe that because consultant plans are written by experts, they are more effective than those developed in-house. With the disaster recovery information and tools available to all contingency planners, however, even novice planners can develop an efficacious plan.

Another fiction is that only consultant plans are executed successfully. Although this used to be the rule, in the past few years there have been numerous instances of successful recoveries in organizations that developed their plans in-house. Along those same lines, many managers believe that auditors will accept only consultant plans; in fact, as long as the plan has been fully tested and demonstrated to be effective, auditors will accept it.

There is a common but false belief that employees of an organization using consultants do not need to be involved in developing the recovery plan. At a minimum, any organization should have at least one employee work with the consultant to develop the plan. If the consultant works entirely alone, the plan will not work because staff members will not understand their part in it.

### Selecting the Right Consultant

To guard against making a contract with the wrong consultant, the data center manager should take five initial steps. They are discussed in the following paragraphs.

**Obtaining Qualifications.** It is important to request in advance the name and background of the consultant who will provide disaster recovery services. Which organizations has the consultant served? Were these clients satisfied with the job? An inexperienced consultant, even one who is in contact with more experienced professionals, should be avoided. The ideal consultant possesses a solid grasp of information systems, understands the specific requirements of the client's business, and has developed satisfactory disaster recovery plans for at least two other organizations.

**Requesting a Plan Proposal.** The consultant should submit a proposal that details the phases, tasks, and milestones of the planning project. Most consultants work from generic methodologies that they can adapt to specific client requirements. With the increasing availability of commercial products for planning and managing contingency planning and disaster recovery projects, consultants can no longer portray their work as mysterious or otherwise beyond the reach of nonpractitioners.

**Validating Proposed Time and Cost Estimates.** A consultant cannot develop meaningful time and cost estimates unless consulting services are packaged as a fixed-price contract. The data center manager should be particularly wary if the consultant quotes exact costs or completion times without having assessed the organization's requirements.

Estimates provided by the consultant can be of value to the data center manager in several ways. For example, valid time and cost estimates are useful benchmarks for comparing the proposals of various consultants, especially if each estimate is made on the basis of similar projects for comparable businesses. To ensure that the data presented in each proposal is as accurate as possible, the manager should verify that all predictable costs, including the consultant's travel and lodging, are reflected in the estimated cost.

**Negotiating Cost.** Initially, consultants often market their premium service, offering the less expensive shared-responsibility approaches only if they sense they may be pricing themselves out of a contract. Faced with the prospect of losing business, a consultant can be notably creative in finding cost-saving measures. In one case, the cost of the plan development was cut by putting corporate word processing at the consultant's disposal to take care of all documentation and by designating one of the staff members to work full time with the consultant, replacing the assistant called for. Other managers have purchased a consultant's microcomputer-based disaster recovery planning tool, contracting with the consultant only for the initial analysis and data collection. The result: substantial cost reductions.

**Assessing the Consultant's Relationships with Vendors.** Many consulting firms have formal and informal relationships with vendors of disaster recovery products and services. In fact, some consultants argue that it is partly their extensive knowledge of and contacts within the industry that qualify them for the rates they command. These relationships can, in some cases, benefit the client organization. The client may thereby qualify for a discount on a fire protection system, off-site storage, or the use of a hot site.

The potential for misuse of these relationships is also present. An unethical consultant may be willing to forgo the objective analysis of client requirements and recommend a product or service for which the consultant receives compensation. Therefore, it is important to know with whom the consultant has marketing agreements and how these agreements may translate into cost advantages. Most vendors will openly disclose special arrangements, particularly when they profit a potential client and, in the process, improve the marketability of their service.

## THE IN-HOUSE OPTION

For many organizations, the use of consulting services is a luxury, a cost over and above the already expensive disaster recovery planning project that they must undertake to satisfy legal and audit requirements. Others take the view that any reasonably intelligent employee, equipped with management support and the technical details of an organization's system and network operations, can develop a competent disaster recovery capability.

The problems faced by organizations that elect to develop a contingency plan using in-house personnel are fourfold. First, many novice planners lack fundamental knowledge about the scope of disaster recovery planning. This problem is reflected by the inordinate amount of time spent by the novice planner who creates disaster scenarios and strategies for coping with them, or by the lengthy, theoretical dissertations on disaster recovery found in many internally developed plans.

The second problem confronting many do-it-yourself planners involves procedure. Procedural difficulties arise from efforts to collect information from departmental managers and from outside agencies (e.g., fire department representatives, local civil emergency planners, and utility and telephone companies). Managers or planners who do not know the appropriate questions to ask or how to effectively manage interviews confront major obstacles to plan development.

Vendor management is the third problem. If the planners can surmount the problems of scope and procedure and develop an understanding of the needs and exposures that disaster recovery planning must address, they may still be thwarted by their lack of knowledge of commercially available products and services that help reduce exposure. Even if planners have a general knowledge of products and services, they may know little or nothing about product pricing or about the contracts that govern delivery of promised commodities.

Finally, there is a problem of plan articulation. The way a planner assembles information about systems, exposures, and recovery strategies into a disaster recovery plan document determines how useful the plan will be in an actual emergency and how difficult the plan will be to maintain. A well-written plan is structured so that only pertinent sections are given to recovery teams in an emergency and so that plan procedures can be implemented readily. The plan should be structured to be updated easily as the names of vendor contacts, recovery team members, details of systems and network hardware, and software configurations change over time.

A partial solution to these difficulties is to use one of the numerous, commercially available disaster recovery planning tools: software packages typically designed for use on a microcomputer. Sometimes irreverently referred to as canned plans, these applications can provide scope, procedure, and format to disaster recovery planning projects.

## WORD PROCESSOR-DRIVEN TOOLS VERSUS DATA BASE-DRIVEN TOOLS

Disaster recovery planning tools come in a variety of forms. Some are simply boilerplate text documents, sold on diskette in ASCII format. The user imports this plan into a word processor, and the plan can be modified or customized using word processor editing functions. Another type of packaged plan is data base driven. Both types of plans offer distinct benefits and are discussed in the following sections.

## Word Processor-Driven Tools

There are several advantages of these plans, one of them being that the in-house planner can use familiar software (i.e., the word processor), which reduces the learning curve that frequently delays plan development. In addition, a text plan may be readily expanded to incorporate disaster recovery planning for user departments, for branch offices, or to account for other requirements that may not be part of the generic plan. Finally, word processor-driven plans are easy to maintain using the global search-and-replace function that is part of most business word processors.

Once customized, the word processed plan is printed as is any text document. The format and the content of the plan can be redesigned to resemble other business plans or to accommodate company standards relating to document preparation.

## Data Base-Driven Tools

Another type of plan is data base driven. The generic portion of the plan is incorporated into the fields on the data entry screens, and the data requested from the user is specific and detailed. As the data is entered onto the screens, several relational data bases are compiled containing information about systems, networks, and personnel. Then, through the use of vendor-supplied queries and programs, the disaster recovery plan is printed out as a series of reports.

Advantages of this approach to planning tool design are the enhanced organization and management of data derived from a data base structure. For example, all data pertaining to recovery teams (e.g., the names and emergency telephone numbers of each team member) is located in a single data base, making it easier to update the information regarding such matters as employee turnover or changes of telephone numbers.

Other vendors have developed planning tools that integrate enhanced data base software applications (e.g., project management software) with a generic disaster recovery plan, claiming the combination supports not only plan development and maintenance but implementation. One such package provides decision support software that can be used during a disaster to collect data on the progress of the recovery effort.

## CRITERIA FOR SELECTING DISASTER RECOVERY PLANNING TOOLS

Regardless of the mode of presentation employed, the primary determinant of the microcomputer-based disaster recovery planning tool's effectiveness is the generic plan that it provides. Although this built-in plan is neither right nor wrong, it may be more or less appropriate to a specific organization and its disaster recovery planning requirements. Several planning tools should be evaluated by an in-house contingency planner before one is selected.

The in-house contingency planner should outline various criteria to aid in evaluating packages (as well as consultant-developed plans). Some criteria are suggested by the following questions, and these criteria are outlined briefly in the product evaluation checklist in Exhibit VI-5-1.

**Does the Tool Provide the Means for Developing a Disaster Recovery Plan for the Entire Organization?** If disaster recovery planning is to be comprehensive, the selected planning tool must be able to handle plans for the recovery of more than hardware, software, and electronically stored data (e.g., telecommunications recovery) and for the restoration of company operations to an acceptable level. Most planning tools do not provide this capability in their generic, noncustomized form, despite vendor claims to the contrary. The contingency planner should determine, in advance, the degree to which the plan can be modified to meet the organization's needs.

**Does the Planning Tool Require Adoption of an Approach to Recovery Planning That Differs from Methodologies Used in Other Planning Activities?** Effective disaster recovery planning differs little from other types of business planning. Objectives are developed, tasks are derived from objectives, and criteria are set forth to gauge task and objective fulfillment. An experienced planner can use basic project management skills to develop and maintain an effective contingency plan; novice planners, however, may need more than a generic project management software package to develop their first plans. The package that a novice planner uses should not deviate drastically from a basic project management approach. If a manual is required just to understand the plan's methodology, it is probably not the most appropriate plan.

**Is the Planning Tool Comprehensive?** At a minimum, the essential sections in the plan are:

- *The action plan.* This is the order in which recovery activities must be undertaken to result in speedy disaster recovery.
- *Plan activities.* These are the tasks that must be undertaken in a recovery situation. They should be ranked in order of importance and related to an action plan.
- *Recovery teams and the notification directory.* The planning tool should have a location for recording the names of company personnel who will participate in recovery, as well as a list of telephone numbers for all personnel who must be notified in the event of a disaster.
- *Vendor information and contact directory.* The planning tool should provide a location for recording information about all vendors who will

| Product Identification | Yes | No | Comments |
|---|---|---|---|
| **Product Name:** _____ | | | |
| **Vendor:** _____ | | | |
| **Address:** _____ | | | |
| _____ | | | |
| **Price:** _____ | | | |
| **Scope** Data Center Only Companywide Corporationwide | | | |
| **Methodology** Project Management (if No, state other) | | | |
| **Plan Description** (Check Yes if feature is provided) Generic Plan Action Plan Plan Activities Recovery Team Directory Vendor Information Equipment Inventories Records and Locations Network Descriptions System Descriptions Company Information | | | |
| **User-Friendliness** (Check Yes if feature is provided) User Interface (menus, windows, or mouse) Help Screens (contextual) Input Methods (nonredundant data entry, batch mode) Output Methods (diversity of reports, query language) | | | |

**Exhibit VI-5-1. Disaster Recovery Planning Tools Evaluation Checklist**

provide products or services during a disaster and the names and telephone numbers of vendor contacts.

- *Records requirements and locations.* The plan should include sections detailing the locations and types of vital records stored off site and the procedures for accessing them during recovery.

- *Equipment inventories.* An inventory of systems hardware and other equipment should be maintained in the plan, both for insurance purposes and for use as a checklist in plan testing.
- *Communications networks, line, and equipment requirements.* The plan should provide a description of network operations and communications line and equipment and of services recovery requirements.
- *Application systems software and hardware requirements.* This section should provide system descriptions and should list the hardware necessary for operations and for meeting user hardware organizations.
- *Company information.* Information regarding an organization's lawyers, insurance policies, and lines of credit should be maintained in the plan document.

**Is the Package User-Friendly?** An excellent disaster recovery planning application should be as user-friendly as any other software package. In fact, given the specialized work of the package, the planning tool should be even more user-friendly. Some of the factors that contribute to user friendliness are:

- *The user interface.* Complex packages should require less expertise from the user. This rule of thumb applies to nearly all applications. A well-designed package should provide menus, displays, and straightforward escape routes. Mouse controls may also be desirable, though system portability is reduced if a fallback to cursor control is unavailable.
- *Help screens.* Contextual help screens are a definite advantage. Printed manuals are not as useful as help screens that can be invoked from anywhere in the program to explain how to avoid or repair errors and list available options.
- *Tutorials or samples.* A disaster recovery planning tool should give the user an idea of what an actual disaser recovery plan looks like. The microcomputer-based tool should come equipped with a sample that the user can modify to accommodate the organization's requirements.
- *Input.* Data input should be as simple as possible. This is a key issue in determining which type of planning package—word processor-driven or data base-driven—is best for a specific environment. The plan should be organized to reduce or eliminate redundant data entry. In addition, it may be useful if the planning tool allows the importation of outside files through batch conversion or some other method, because some of the information needed for the plan may have been assembled in another form or for another purpose and importing files will reduce duplicate entry.
- *Output.* The planning tool should be able to output an actual plan. The plan should be divided into sections by subject or task, and its form should be flexible enough to accommodate documentation standards.

**What Is the Pedigree of the Planning Tool?** Many disaster recovery planning tools were developed by consulting firms for the consultant's use at client sites. In some cases, the package was subsequently licensed for use by the client, who then maintained the plan. Consulting firms began to customize their planning tools for disaster recovery backup facility vendors and their clients. Finally, direct sales to the client became a lucrative source of business for consulting firms. Hence, many tested, reliable planning tools were originally used to develop actual plans for specific organizations. Untested planning tools may produce inadequate plans, a fact discovered only after testing or—in the worst case—in an actual disaster. Therefore, the pedigree of the plan is extremely important.

These considerations aid in the selection of the best disaster recovery planning tool for a particular organization. In addition, the price of the planning tool, the availability of telephone support, and other factors that contribute to the selection of any software package are also important.

Exhibit VI-5-2 provides a list of disaster recovery planning tool vendors and their products. Most vendors offer demonstration copies of their software for evaluation.

## WHAT PLANNING TOOLS DO NOT PROVIDE

Disaster recovery planning tools can aid the in-house planner in many ways. They can provide an example of the structure of a plan, which may be unavailable from other sources. From this base, the planner can build and customize. Most tools also provide emergency action plans for reacting to disasters of varying destructive potential. This helps to set limits on the endless creation of scenarios that often strangles novice planners' efforts. Planning tools underscore the information that the planner must acquire. Knowing what questions to ask and having a format for entering responses can speed project completion.

However, disaster recovery planning tools are also limited in what they can provide. For example, no planning tool can provide the in-house planner with the skills needed to obtain the cooperation of departmental managers in assessing those systems that are critical. Planning tools do not provide planners with the skills required to evaluate vendor offerings, to negotiate contracts for hot-site services, or to develop effective off-site storage plans. Nor can a planning tool convince senior management of the need for disaster recovery planning.

On the other hand, planning tools can be used to articulate a plan for business recovery, a plan that can be tested, refined, and maintained. An effective tool will pay for itself in the time saved in maintaining the plan. This is arguably the greatest benefit disaster recovery planning tools can offer.

## SOURCES OF INFORMATION ON PLANNING TOOLS

Generally, the best sources of information about disaster recovery planning and tools are professional contingency planning associations. The number of

**AIM/SAFE 2000**
Advanced Information Management, Inc.
12940 Harbor Dr.
Woodbridge VA 22192
(703) 643-1002

**Basic Recovery**
Computer Solutions, Inc.
397 Park Ave.
Orange NJ 07050
(201) 672-6000

**ComPas (Comdisco Plan Automation System)**
Comdisco Disaster Recovery Services
6111 North River Rd.
Rosemont IL 60018
(708) 518-5670

**Corporate Recovery**
Executive Compumetrics, Inc.
PO Box 95
Tinley Park IL 60477
(800) 368-3324
(708) 687-1150

**Customized Disaster Survival Manual**
Disaster Survival Planning, Inc.
669 Pacific Cove Dr.
Port Hueneme CA 93041
(805) 984-9547

**Disaster Recovery 2000**
Disaster Recovery Services, Inc.
427 Pine Ave.
Suite 201
Loma Beach CA 90802
(310) 432-0559

**DP/90 Plus**
SunGard Planning Solutions, Inc.
1285 Drummers Lane
Wayne PA 19087
(800) 247-7832
(215) 341-8700

**DPS-30 Disaster Planning System**
Arel Technologies, Inc.
1557 Coonrapids Blvd.
Suite 200
Minneapolis MN 55433
(612) 755-6901

**DRS**
TAMP Computer Systems, Inc.
1732 Remson Ave.
Merrick NY 11566
(516) 623-2038

**HOTSITE Recovery Plan**
HOTSITE
110 MacKenan Dr.
Cary NC 27511
(919) 460-1234

**Information Security Policies Made Easy**
Information Integrity/Baseline Software
PO Box 1219
Sausalito CA 94966
(415) 332-7763

**Living Disaster Recovery Planning System (LDRPS)**
Strohl Systems
500 N. Gulph Rd.
Suite 500
King of Prussia PA 19406
(215) 768-4120

**NCR 911 Disaster Recovery Planning System**
NCR Corp.
1700 South Patterson Blvd., SDC-3
Dayton OH 45479
(800) 626-3495

**Recovery Architect**
Dataguard Recovery Services, Inc.
PO Box 37144
Louisville KY 40233-7144
(502) 426-3434
(800) 325-3977

**Recovery/1**
Computer Performance, Inc.
68 Hartford Turnpike
PO Box 718
Tolland CT 06084
(203) 872-1672

**Recovery PAC**
**Recovery PAC II**
Computer Security Consultants, Inc.
590 Danbury Rd.
Ridgefield CT 06877
(203) 431-8720

**REXSYS**
Recovery Management, Inc.
435 King St.
PO Box 327
Littleton MA 10460
(508) 486-8866

**Exhibit VI-5-2. Microcomputer-Based Planning Tools**

**RPS (Recovery Planning System)**
Contemporary Computer Services, Inc.
200 Knickerbocker Ave.
Bohemia NY 11716
(516) 563-8880

**Total Recovery Planning System
(TRPS)**
CHI/COR Information Management, Inc.
300 South Wacker Dr.
Chicago IL 60606
(800) 448-8777
(312) 322-0150

**Exhibit VI-5-2.** *(continued)*

---

these organizations has increased dramatically over the past several years, and membership is booming.

Most contingency planning group members are disaster recovery or security planners from organizations within a specific geographic region. Members exchange ideas and information openly about their situations and offer advice and solutions from their own experiences. These groups can be valuable sources of new techniques and methods of plan development—from pitching the plan to management, to deciding on the best records-salvaging strategy. Many associations are self-appointed watchdogs over the essentially unpoliced disaster recovery industry. The groups invite vendors to demonstrate products and provide insight into their particular expertise. In addition, most disaster recovery groups do not allow their vendors to interfere with candid appraisals of products and services, including disaster recovery planning tools.

## SUMMARY

Because of the costs associated with contracting a disaster recovery consultant, many organizations choose to develop a contingency plan in-house, either by using planning tools or by using a consultant for the initial stages of the development. Either choice is valid, but disaster recovery planning tools do not provide a comprehensive solution to an organization's disaster recovery planning needs. Only by careful study of the literature of disaster recovery planning and by interacting with other disaster recovery planners can novice planners obtain the competence to develop effective recovery capabilities for their firms. On the other hand, planning tools can be a useful adjunct in plan development activities by providing an example of plan format and by exposing the user to the plan's unique approach and method.

# VI-6
# Selecting and Maintaining UPS Battery Systems

*DAVID D. ITTNER*

A ll batteries are not alike. They differ depending on their application. Trade-offs must be made because for all the advantages any one battery provides, there are corresponding disadvantages. Battery size, life, capacity, watering frequency, maintenance, load duration, and operating environment are all considerations when selecting a battery.

Understanding the characteristics of the battery system is important insurance for the data center manager to guarantee continued uptime. The reliability of the computer system is contingent on the reliability of the power system, including the backup generator, uninterruptible power supply (UPS) system, and battery system. The data center manager should have a thorough knowledge of the battery system used to ensure optimum performance. This chapter provides general guidelines for and information about UPS batteries; however, standards vary among battery types and manufacturers. Therefore, the manufacturer's specifications should be viewed as the final authority for any UPS battery system.

## OPERATING CHARACTERISTICS

Most data centers today use a UPS system designed to support the computer system during utility power fluctuations and short duration discharges. If a power failure occurs, the battery supplies critical power to the UPS system, which in turn provides power for the system to operate. If the power failure remains, the load then can be shut down in a controlled manner. The system maintains information and damage is avoided.

A backup generator alone is not enough to ensure uninterrupted uptime. Before it can effectively take over, the generator needs time to start up and maintain speed. This results in a temporary power loss and subsequent system damage. A battery is necessary to support the UPS system and maintain power while the generator activates. The UPS batteries must support that load long enough for the backup generator to come online or for personnel to perform an orderly shut down of the computer.

Standard data center specifications for a UPS battery call for:

- Low watering intervals.
- A 77° operating temperature.
- The smallest possible size.
- 240–480 volts DC (120–240 cells).
- A 15-minute discharge rate.
- A 1.250 specific gravity.
- A 10–20 year nominal life expectancy.

The reasons the industry adopted these standards and the options available are discussed in the following sections.

**Watering Intervals.** Adding water to batteries is a costly, time-consuming job. Therefore, frequent watering intervals always have been a major complaint about storage batteries. The typical stationary battery used in the US is the flooded, or well cell, two-volt nominal lead acid battery. However, experimentation with batteries made with calcium alloys has shown that they require less watering than batteries made with antimony, but there are trade-offs to consider. Calcium alloy batteries are less tolerant of high temperatures and may not provide an equivalent life cycle. They also may require a higher float voltage to maintain their state of charge. Despite these disadvantages, reduced watering maintenance makes calcium batteries the best UPS battery choice for most data centers.

**Operating Temperatures.** Temperature extremes are a major factor affecting a battery's performance and life. Operating at lower extremes will increase life, yet decrease capacity. Higher temperatures slightly increase capacity but decreases life. A 20-year battery operating at 92°F will reduce its life expectancy by half; at 105°F, the battery's life shortens to five years. Low temperatures do not have such an extreme effect, but the data center manager should know that run time is significantly reduced in low temperatures. The ideal operating temperature for both battery life and capacity is 77°F. The data center manager must control the battery environment to provide an even, year-round temperature for optimum performance.

**Battery Size and Shape.** The data center manager often must consider space limitations when selecting a battery. Batteries designed to provide the most power in the smallest package usually are the best choice. Taller cells, multicell jars, and stacked racks help conserve space while providing the required power.

**Voltage Versus Current.** The actual units of power required to power electrical equipment are watts. To determine the wattage that a battery provides, the voltage (which can be increased by connecting cells in a series) should be multiplied by the amperage (which can be increased by providing more surfaced area of the plate, usually by adding plates or making the plates bigger within a cell). The voltage and amperage must balance properly to achieve the desired wattage. Voltage must remain as high as possible to avoid the increased cable size and line loss that occurs with high amperage. On the other hand, high voltage increases the chance for electric shock and ground tracking, thus requiring an increase in amperage. Therefore, the typical limit is a 480 vdc (volts direct current) nominal buss.

**Rate of Discharge.** Rate of discharge usually is determined by the individual facility's need for backup time. Most data centers plan for a 15-minute battery backup at full load. If the data center is not supported by an engine generator, the battery allows the data center to operate for five minutes. If power does not come back on within that time, an orderly shut down can be performed with the remaining battery power.

**Specific Gravity.** Maximizing battery life and capacity are vital concerns in ensuring computer power reliability. Proper proportions of sulfuric acid and water (called electrolyte) are essential to battery life because too much of either will destroy the cell. Specific gravity measures these proportions. Maintaining a high specific gravity gets the most power out of a cell. Lower gravity allows a lower float voltage and can extend life. The typical flooded cell high rate UPS battery uses 1.250 specific gravity electrolyte, whereas standard, stationary batteries operate at 1.215 specific gravity. Valve-regulated lead acid (VRLA), also called sealed or maintenance-free, batteries are now using higher gravities with electrolyte in the 1.300 range.

**Life Expectancy.** Battery life is an important consideration when selecting a battery system. Batteries have traditionally been warranted in years. This worked well for long-duration batteries that were rarely cycled, such as telecommunications batteries. However, UPS batteries are subject to many short-duration discharges. Purchasers often are unaware that their UPS batteries probably will not reach the rated life expectancy because the batteries are frequently used and complete numerous cycles. Although manufacturers still warrant their batteries with a 10- to 20-year life span, they now refer to the number of cycles as an overriding factor influencing the warranties.

## BATTERY MAINTENANCE

After selecting the appropriate battery, the data center manager may be responsible for determining what maintenance activities are necessary to ensure uptime. Although a battery technician may perform these activities, the data center manager should be aware of and familiar with factors that influence the need for maintenance. They are discussed in the following sections.

### Proper Charging

*Float charge* is the term used to describe the continuous charge that maintains a battery at an optimum state of charge without overcharging it. Although

| Nominal Specific Gravity | Antimony Volts per Cell | Calcium Volts per Cell |
|---|---|---|
| 1.215 Standard | 2.15 to 2.323 | 2.17 to 2.26 |
| 1.250 Medium | 2.25 to 2.30 | 2.25 to 2.30 |
| 1.300 High | Not Used | 2.33 to 2.38 |

**Exhibit VI-6-1. Recommended Float Charge Rates**

charging instructions vary according to the manufacturer, Exhibit VI-6-1 provides a guide to recommended float charge rates.

Cell voltages and gravities may vary, indicating that the float charge is not sufficient to keep the battery fully charged. An equalize charge must be provided to bring the cell voltages and specific gravity back to a uniform state. The time required to equalize depends on the battery's state of charge, the equalize charge rate applied, the specific gravity, and the lead alloy used (i.e., antimony or calcium). Exhibit VI-6-2 provides a general guide to recommended rates and times, though some may vary by manufacturer.

Some precautions must be taken during equalizing. Because of an increased release of potentially explosive gases, this process requires proper ventilation. In addition, fluid levels may rise during equalizing, in which case,

| Volts per Cell | Antimony 1.215 | Calcium 1.215 | Calcium 1.250 | Calcium 1.300 |
|---|---|---|---|---|
| 2.24 | 100 | 225 | — | — |
| 2.27 | 70 | 165 | — | — |
| 2.30 | 50 | 105 | — | — |
| 2.33 | 35 | 75 | 110 | — |
| 2.36 | 25 | 50 | 80 | 1.25 |
| 2.39 | — | 35 | 55 | 90 |
| 2.42 | — | 25 | 40 | 60 |
| 1.45 | — | — | 28 | 45 |
| 2.48 | — | — | — | 30 |

**Exhibit VI-6-2. Recommended Minimum Hours of Equalize Charge**

the electrolyte must be removed to keep the cells from overflowing. This electrolyte should be saved to add back after the levels recede. Cell temperature should be kept as close to normal as possible and should never exceed 100°F.

### Storage Considerations

Occasionally, the data center manager may need to store the UPS batteries, such as during a move or before initialization of a new system. Lead acid storage batteries may be held for several months without a float charge only if the data center manager:

- Stores them in a fully charged condition. Recharge should be performed within the following time frames:
  —Antimony. Three months at 77°F
  —Calcium. Six months at 77°F
  —VRLA. Six months at 77°F
- Stores them in a cool environment to restrict local action (i.e., self loss).
- Maintains low humidity in the storage place to inhibit corrosion and oxidation of leaded surfaces.

Batteries can be stored for longer periods. To prevent permanent damage, however, they must be brought back to full charge before storing or be float charged continuously until returned to service.

### Cycling

Excessive cycling reduces the calendar life span of a battery. The data center manager must be aware of this effect on battery life to prevent unexpected downtime. Cycling is the complete discharge and recharge of a battery. This usually occurs when the battery supports a full load for the battery's rated duration or during a capacity test. However, any discharge, for any duration, accumulates and reduces battery life. Purchasers should be aware that battery manufacturers recommend performing full load capacity testing no more than once every 12 months. A battery system must not cycle more than necessary. The data center manager must understand that frequent load testing will dramatically reduce the life of the battery.

### BATTERY INSPECTIONS

The Institute of Electrical and Electronic Engineers (IEEE) has established guidelines for the maintenance of flooded cell batteries. An adaptation of those guidelines follows. This program, recommended for data centers, consists of 12 scheduled preventive maintenance inspections per year. The eight monthly inspections can be performed in-house, but the data center manager should engage a battery professional for the more comprehensive quarterly and annual inspections.

The eight monthly inspections should consist of the following 10 steps:

1. Inspecting the appearance of the battery and battery room for cleanliness and cleaning as required.
2. Measuring and recording the total battery float voltage and charging current.
3. Inspecting electrolyte levels and adjusting them if necessary.
4. Visually inspecting jars and covers for cracks and leaks and cleaning and repairing or replacing cells as necessary.
5. Visually inspecting for evidence of corrosion and cleaning if necessary.
6. Measuring and recording the ambient temperature and adjusting it if necessary.
7. Verifying the condition of the ventilation equipment if applicable.
8. Measuring and recording the pilot cell voltage.
9. Measuring and recording the pilot cell's specific gravity and electrolyte temperature.
10. Maintaining records of detailed written reports noting any deficiencies and corrective action taken.

Three quarterly inspections should consist of steps 1–10 plus:

11. Verifying the integrity of the battery rack.
12. Measuring and recording the specific gravity of all cells.
13. Measuring and recording a random group (i.e., at least 10% of the system) of representative cell temperatures.
14. Measuring and recording the float voltage of all cells.
15. Randomly checking the torque on 10% of the interunit connectors.
16. Randomly checking and recording 10% of the battery connections' resistances, using a calibrated digital micro-ohmmeter.
17. Measuring and recording the internal resistance (or impedance) of all VRLA batteries.

One annual inspection should consist of steps 1–17 plus:

18. Retorquing all bolted battery connections to the battery manufacturer's specifications.
19. Measuring and recording all bolted battery connection resistances in micro-ohms.

## BATTERY INSPECTION GUIDELINES

The following paragraphs describe some guidelines to follow when inspecting batteries at the data center.

**Cleaning.** When dirt and dust accumulate, the outside of the cell should be wiped with a damp cloth. If electrolyte spills on cell tops, it should be neutralized with a solution of one pound of baking soda mixed with one gallon of water. After the fizzing stops (following application of the soda solution), the residue should be cleaned with a damp cloth.

**Watering Recommendations.** As electrochemical devices, batteries "gas" under charge, breaking down the electrolyte into sulfur, hydrogen and oxygen. Some of the hydrogen and oxygen do not recombine into water. Instead, they evaporate from the cell and must be replaced. (Under the proper charge, calcium alloy class should be watered only once or twice a year.) Cells should be refilled with an approved distilled or deionized water. To reduce the potential of cell contamination, pure water should be used. The cells should be refilled to the high-level mark when the fluid falls below the low-level mark. Cells that have been taken off charge for an extended time should never be watered. They may overflow when placed on charge and gassing begins. Cells that are off charge should not be watered because the water will not mix with the electrolyte.

**Corrosion.** Because corrosion is a normal chemical action of batteries, it is difficult to eliminate, even with post seals and corrosion-resistant grease. Any corrosion found on the battery should be attended to immediately to stop spreading and deterioration of the post connection. The corrosion should be removed, the electrolyte neutralized, and the surface cleaned of all lead peroxide. The surface can be recoated with grease.

**Voltage Readings.** A pilot cell is any representative cell used as a benchmark. Individual pilot cell readings should be taken with a calibrated digital voltmeter, to the second decimal place (i.e., 2.25 vdc). On most VRLA batteries, the intercell connections are enclosed and voltage readings must be taken in groups. These unit readings should be recorded and kept as a permanent record for future reference, evaluation, and warranty purposes. Individual readings must not vary more than $+/-.05$ vdc. If deviations occur, further readings must be taken to determine whether cells are bad or equalization is necessary.

**Specific Gravity Readings.** A hydrometer measures specific gravity. This device draws a sample of electrolyte into a tube. The point at which the electrolyte touches a float within the glass designates the specific gravity. To ensure an accurate reading, the proper amount of electrolyte must be drawn and the float must not be at the top or bottom of the tube. Although readings typically vary slightly from cell to cell, a healthy battery system should have all readings within 10 (.010) points of the manufacturer's nominal operating range. A wide range of readings may indicate the need for an equalized charge.

**Retorquing.** The makeup of the posts, connectors, and hardware determines the frequency of retorquing. The IEEE recommends one retorquing annually, for all systems, to be performed only with an inch-pound torque wrench. The manufacturer's specifications should be adhered to because overtorquing may cause significant, irreparable damage to the battery.

**Battery Connection Resistance.** One of the many operating and maintenance considerations that a data center manager must face for stationary batteries is that of connection resistance. Connection integrity plays an important part in the successful and safe operation of a stationary battery. Resistances that exceed a safe limit can result in poor performance or possibly catastrophic failure. A terminal can even melt down during a discharge. This can occur in a fraction of a second if a proper connection and large amounts of current are present. In addition, this item is not under warranty by the manufacturer because the manufacturer has no control over the making of battery cell field connections. It is up to the installer initially, and the end user thereafter, to ensure the integrity of these connections. Connection resistance must be monitored effectively.

The actual resistance between the cable and lead-plated copper interconnectors is expressed in micro-ohms. It is measured with a micro-ohmmeter, also known as a digital low resistance ohmmeter. When connection resistance exceeds the maximum recommended values stated in IEEE 450, appropriate steps must be taken to bring the resistance back within the guideline. Some values may exceed 20% of the system average. Those connections should be disassembled and inspected to identify the cause of the problem. In most cases, corrosion at the connection point is the cause, and cleaning and neutralizing intercell connectors and preparing contacting services solves this problem. A less frequent cause is loose or poorly torqued hardware. In extreme cases, the connection hardware may require replacement and resurfacing of the cell post or terminal.

### Impedance—Internal Resistance Measurements

Because data center managers cannot routinely monitor individual cell voltage, specific gravity, or electrolyte levels, sufficient guidelines have not always been available to gauge the VRLA battery condition. Testing the battery's internal resistance (i.e., impedance) now fills that void.

Impedance indicates approximate capacity. A capacity test, at the rate for which the battery is sized, is the only way to determine capacity with close to 100% accuracy. However, a capacity test takes time and equipment and requires taking the system offline. It also adds one more cycle to the battery, further reducing its life. Impedance measurements can be performed quickly, online, and with no detrimental effects on the battery's life. Impedance testing can also be used on parallel systems. Most online UPS systems induce enough alternating current (AC) ripple current on the battery to determine the impedance without the use of a separate power supply. If the current is one amp or greater, it is sufficient. If less than one amp, an outside power source is needed to perform this function.

To obtain impedance, this known current is put through the battery. The AC voltage present on each unit is measured and the impedance is calculated by the following formula:

$$Z = E/l$$

where:

$Z$ = the calculated impedance
$E$ = the measured AC voltage of one unit
$l$ = the measured AC current (amps)

Any impedance that is excessively above average is suspect. High impedance requires further investigation, and it may be necessary to replace the battery. If a unit is suspect, the manufacturer should be consulted for a final determination.

## SERVICE

Choosing a battery service provider can be a difficult task. The competition is vast, and no licensing or certification is required. Many service companies follow their own guidelines instead of the IEEE standard.

The data center manager must determine the scope of work the particular data center will adopt and what services will be performed in-house. Data center electrical personnel usually can perform the eight monthly inspections. The quarterly and annual inspections are more involved, however, and are commonly left to a professional battery service company.

When reviewing quotes from service companies, the purchaser must confirm that he or she is comparing apples with apples. The scope of work must be the same and must meet the data center's requirements. The operator should verify whether corrective work, parts, and cells are included. A premium for night and weekend work could greatly affect the value of the service. The servicer should have the experience and resources to diagnose problems and perform major corrective work when required. A strong working relationship between the battery service provider and the UPS service provider ensures the best possible operation of the complete UPS system.

## SUMMARY

To maintain the most reliable UPS, battery, and generator system possible, the data center manager should understand the limitations of the battery and should:

---

Institute of Electrical and Electronic Engineers, Inc. (New York)
- IEEE Recommended Practice for Maintenance, Testing and Replacement of Large Lead Storage Batteries for Generating Stations and Substations ANSI/IEEE Standard 450-1987

Yuasa/Exide, Inc. (Raleigh NC)
- Stationary Lead Acid Battery Systems—Section 50.900
- Stationary Battery Installation & Operation Manual—Section 58.00

**Exhibit VI-6-3. Further Sources of Information**

- Choose the best battery for individual needs according to the operating environment.
- Maintain 77°F for optimum life and capacity.
- Not cycle the battery any more than necessary.
- Initiate a comprehensive battery maintenance program.
- Plan for the replacement of the system a few years early.

Exhibit VI-6-3 shows recommended sources of further information on UPS batteries.

# Section VII
# Human Resource Management

The phrase *human resource management* might seem to suggest a very cold approach to interacting with data center personnel. In reality, it is an appropriate concept. For many years, the management of personnel was known as personnel administration. This term created an image of a purely mechanistic approach to handling the affairs of employees. Human resource management, on the other hand, implies that people are a major resource and managing them effectively is a primary responsibility of the data center manager.

The data center environment is undergoing dramatic changes. This is certainly true with regard to hardware and software, and there is often a tendency to focus on the technology environment. However, the real revolutionary change that is occurring in the data center involves its organization, mission, and approach to managing personnel.

Due to the significant changes occurring in today's corporations, such as downsizing and reengineering, data center managers are in the difficult position of trying to adapt to new technology, such as client/server, while dealing with the organizational issues that are facing the rest of the corporation. This section examines several of the major organizational trends affecting the data center, and provides guidance for dealing with issues of career planning and motivation of data center personnel.

IS groups are not immune to the widespread structural and organizational changes that are affecting many corporations. Downsizing and outsourcing are forcing complete restructuring of IS and the data center. Chapter VII-1, "New Organizational Styles for the IS Department," provides strategies for changing the IS organizational structure, integrating total quality management, and establishing a customer-focused cultue.

One of the new management approaches sweeping the US is reengineering. This term has many connotations, but its basic philosophy is completely rebuilding business processes to reflect today's highly competitive environment. Chapter VII-2, "Reengineering IS Professionals," describes how IS professionals can reengineer themselves to ensure that they continue to provide added value to their organizations.

Today, the term *career* has a much different meaning than it did even a few years ago. Once, a career implied a long-term relationship with a single employer, eventually leading to retirement. This is no longer the case. It is likely that individuals will work for many different employers. To improve their chances for successful and rewarding careers. IS professionals need to understand the changing environment and how to adapt to it. Chapter VII-3, "Career Planning: A New Set of Rules," provides insight into these issues.

Managing change is always difficult. Managing technology change is quite different than managing people during such technology change. Although it may be apparent to the data center manager that major change is taking place in the role and operation of the data center, it may not be as readily apparent to data center personnel. Even if the changes are recognized, employees may have great difficulty coping with them. Data center managers must help their employees adapt to necessary changes. Chapter VII-4, "Systems Change: Managing Resistance from Data Center Personnel," provides guidelines for managing changes.

One of the important changes taking place in the data center today is that much greater emphasis is being placed on the data center operations. Merely being a skilled technician is no longer sufficient to guarantee a successful career. Rather, understanding business fundamentals and concepts and being able to communicate them effectively is increasingly important. Effective interpersonal skills are mandatory. Chapter VII-5, "Managing Technical Professionals in Dynamic Data Center Environments," provides insight into this important role of the data center manager.

Employee motivation is an essential element of effective human resource management. Data center managers are in a unique management situation. On one hand, data center managers must find ways to keep employees motivated despite such threats as downsizing, reduced budgets, and outsourcing. At the same time, corporate management demands improved productivity—a difficult challenge in the best of times. Chapter VII-6, "Increasing Productivity and Job Satisfaction by Motivating Employees," provides methods to assist the data center manager in dealing with this difficult issue.

In any profession, having someone more experienced to act as a guide can be a major career booster for an employee. The idea of a mentor has been around for a long time. The technical nature of the job rarely affords an information systems professional the opportunity to learn many of the business skills that are required for success in today's corporations. Chapter VII-7, "Mentoring As a Career Strategy," provides some guidelines for the data center manager to use when considering the idea of mentoring.

There are many reasons why major systems implementations fail. More often than not, however, the failure to effectively implement the idea of change into an organization is a chief cause. Becoming skilled at managing changes in organizations may be one of the most important skills today's data center manager can become proficient at. Chapter VII-8, "How to Manage A Changed

Organization," provides the data center manager with some ideas to consider with regard to this important issue.

Career planning continues to be a major issue for the data center manager. Given today's business environment, it is often difficult for data center employees to determine their career paths. Providing such guidance is the responsibility of the data center manager, to a great extent. Chapter VII-9, "Career Paths for data center professionals," provides the data center manager with some guidelines for structuring employees' careers and provides advice on how best to communicate such guidelines.

# VII-1
# New Organizational Styles for the IS Department

*MADELINE WEISS*

For many organizations, continuous improvement and rapid response to market needs are a way of life. Because of these pressures, few organizations are able to provide the long-term security of traditional careers. Whereas mergers and acquisitions were rampant a few years ago, the current trend is toward corporate downsizings and restructurings that lead to the creation of a just-in-time work force or to the outsourcing of services or entire departments. Organizations have higher expectations for quality, productivity, and commitment from their remaining employees. At the same time, employees expect more satisfying jobs and greater input into decision making.

These trends hold true not only for organizations as a whole but for the IS departments within them. IS must support the organization's use of information technology with agility and innovation. Some IS departments are converting from chargeback systems to staff services for sale, and others can anticipate pressure from their organizations to do so. In effect, with staff services for sale, business units outsource work to IS, which must compete with outside IS service providers. To compete effectively, IS departments must produce high-quality products and services with fewer resources.

## STRATEGIES TO ACHIEVE A NEW ORGANIZATIONAL STYLE

Leading-edge IS organizations are responding to these trends by adopting a number of successful strategies, including:

- Flattening the management hierarchy.
- Adopting total quality management.
- Establishing empowered, customer-focused organization cultures and structures.

This chapter addresses these strategies.

## FLATTENING THE MANAGEMENT HIERARCHY

Over the past few years, Weiss Associates, Inc., has conducted organization simulations with IS managers and professionals. In each case, participants are divided into three categories—top, middle, and bottom—arbitrarily. Instructions to each group are intentionally vague. Invariably, the same dynamics emerge: Those at the top feel isolated; those in the middle feel like useless go-betweens and messengers; and those at the bottom feel frustrated, powerless, and angry. No matter how open they try to be, the top and middle categories are mistrusted by participants at the bottom, and nothing is ever accomplished. Discussions after the simulation always focus on how bureaucratic chains of command stand in the way of agility and innovation—to say nothing of how they create frustration and anger.

For decades, IS departments have emulated the management style of their organizations, which is based on a management model of bureaucracy that is 50 years old. The model prescribes clear systems of hierarchical relationships with precise direction and close supervision by cascading layers of managers who collect information and prepare reports for higher-level managers. The result is an expensive pyramid of supervisory managers who keep the business humming (not blazing) and reward themselves with generous salaries and high status.

Times are changing. IS professionals are highly educated and can direct their own activities. Most are highly motivated (before the organizational hierarchy discourages them) and want considerable autonomy in their work. Communications are rapid. Organizations cannot wait for bureaucratic hierarchies to make decisions. They need answers from flexible, responsive, committed professionals on the frontline, who are closest to their customers' ever-changing needs.

Some leading-edge IS departments are modifying their management hierarchies to substantially reduce administrative costs and enhance service, responsiveness, and innovation. Following are some examples:

- The IS organization at Medtronic, Inc., a manufacturer of medical devices, reduced its management hierarchy to one level between IS professionals (organized in self-managing teams) and the vice-president for corporate services.
- In applications development at Armstrong World Industries, Inc., approximately 80 IS professionals (also organized in self-managing teams) report to one IS manager.
- In three departments of Corning, Inc.'s IS division, only one management level separates IS professionals (also organized in self-managing teams) from the IS senior vice-president.

In these flatter organizations, everyone accepts ownership for delivering quality products and services. Remaining managers focus their energy and time on setting and communicating visions, coaching, mentoring, and providing resources to IS professionals.

## ADOPTING TOTAL QUALITY MANAGEMENT

Organizations recognize the need to establish systems and practices that motivate, support, and enable members to consistently design, produce, and deliver quality offerings that meet or exceed customer requirements. Although each organization's approach to establishing a quality environment varies, certain common elements underlie the variations: leadership, information and analysis, planning, human resources use, quality assurance of products and services, quality results, and customer satisfaction. These elements are the seven basic criteria for the Malcolm Baldrige National Quality Award. Leading IS organizations incorporate these seven elements into their culture.

## Leadership

Senior IS managers create, communicate, and manage daily through clear visions of where their organizations are headed in terms of technology leadership, customer service, and IS staff work life.

## Information and Analysis

The IS department seeks information on customer satisfaction through surveys, interviews, and informal exchanges, analyzing feedback to determine how to serve its customers better.

## Planning

The IS department takes responsibility for understanding customer requirements for information technology and developing plans for meeting and even anticipating those requirements.

## Human Resources Use

IS professionals are encouraged to grow by learning and using new skills and knowledge. There is a recognition that customer relations mirror staff relations because well-respected and satisfied staff members treat their customers well.

## Quality Assurance of Products and Services

IS members have accountability and skills for continuously improving their delivery of quality products and services.

## Quality Results

There are quantitative and qualitative measures of quality based on overall IS quality goals. IS members recognize that customers are the ultimate arbiters of quality.

## Customer Satisfaction

The IS department stays close to its customers in order to understand changing requirements and ensure that they are met, if not exceeded.

## ESTABLISHING EMPOWERED, CUSTOMER-FOCUSED CULTURES AND STRUCTURES

Other forward-thinking IS departments have gone beyond flattening the hierarchy and establishing total quality management processes. By thinking creatively about relationships between people, work, technology, and information, some corporate IS departments are developing work systems capable of achieving significantly higher levels of sustained performance. These work systems frequently include empowered, customer-focused cultures and structures, many of which are characterized by self-managing teams.

### Characteristics of Self-Management

Self-managing teams, known alternatively as self-directed teams or clusters, are groups of people who work interdependently with responsibility, authority, and accountability toward accomplishing a common mission with little or no supervision. Mature teams view themselves as managing and operating their own business. Following are examples of teams in IS departments:

- Applications development teams at Medtronic, Inc., are responsible for developing systems for their customers' businesses (e.g., marketing or manufacturing).
- Applications development teams at Armstrong World Industries are responsible for developing common world-class systems for their assigned business process (e.g., customer billing, production and distribution management, or manufacturing management) and installing these systems in various Armstrong divisions (e.g., floor products and ceiling products).
- The operations services team at Corning, Inc., runs all corporate mainframe and midrange computers.
- The help-line services team at Corning, Inc., handles calls from internal customers (i.e., Corning employees) on services spanning the mainframe, midrange systems, microcomputers, and networks.
- The data administration team at LTV Steel Company, Inc., which is physically dispersed across different locations, is responsible for all data administration functions for the corporation.
- Technical services teams in IBM's southeast region Information and Telecommunication Systems Services organization are responsible for supporting eight IBM manufacturing sites in the southeastern US.

Mature self-managing teams usually:

- Create their business plans.
- Schedule their work.
- Anticipate and resolve daily problems and make decisions related to the team's functioning.
- Allocate projects and tasks to team members.

- Coordinate with other teams and units.
- Set their own objectives.
- Evaluate team members' performance and recommend salary increases, promotions, and other rewards.
- Train team members or arrange for training.
- Select new team members.
- Set and manage their own budgets.
- Correct team members who do not contribute their fair share to the team's performance.
- Recommend termination of team members if needed.
- Continually search for new ways of enhancing customer service and productivity.

Managers in organizations with self-managing teams concentrate their time and effort on creating an environment where individuals are secure in using their authority. They also manage by results (rather than telling teams how to achieve results), coach team members, and break down barriers to empowerment that have built up over decades. Organizations with self-managing teams are profoundly different from traditional ones. The paradigm shift is from control to commitment and coaching. Exhibit VII-1-1 describes some key differences in these paradigms.

## Impact on the Organization and Individuals

Although self-managing teams in IS departments are relatively new, the impact on both the IS department and its service to customers throughout the organization has been noteworthy in many cases. These organizations experience improved customer satisfaction because of greater flexibility, responsiveness, and higher-quality products and services. Team members are better positioned to understand customer requirements and move quickly to meet them, and team members feel empowered to approach anyone in the organization to solve problems and provide excellent service.

In most IS departments, increased customer service carries a higher price tag. However, where self-managing teams have taken hold, costs have been reduced, principally by eliminating management layers and positions and by redeploying people to other needed positions within IS and the organization. Time is not wasted working through supervisors or managers, and team members develop a sense of personal responsibility to their customers. Moreover, newly acquired financial knowledge and business perspectives also help team members feel strong ownership for the IS business. In addition, individuals have been shown to acquire and continue to demonstrate skills and leadership beyond IS managers' expectations.

## Case Study: Corning, Inc.

Some organizations are already realizing the positive impact of self-managing on the IS department and its services.

| Old Paradigm | New Paradigm |
|---|---|
| Supervisor or manager control | Commitment and coaching by supervisor or manager |
| Many levels of management | Flat organization |
| Directive decision making | Consensus decision making |
| Competitive | Cooperative |
| "Tell me what to do." | "How can we work smarter?" |
| Low risk-taking | Innovation |
| Reacting to change | Seizing opportunities |
| "We'll think about it and set up a committee to study it." | "We'll do it faster than the competition." |
| Internal-organization driven | Customer driven |
| Rules-bound and slow | Flexible and fast |
| Doing things right | Doing the right things |
| "I only work here." | "I am the organization." |
| Exercising power over staff | Empowered staff |
| If it's not broke, don't fix it. | Continuous improvement |
| Acceptable quality and service | World-class quality and service |
| Status counts | Ability and contribution count more than status |
| Rewards reflect time in job and what people know | Rewards reflect real contributions |

**Exhibit VII-1-1. Different Attitudes Required in an Empowered, Customer-Focused Organization**

---

**Improved Customer Satisfaction and Higher-Quality Products and Services.** The help-line services team at Corning, which handles almost 3,000 calls a month from internal customers, upgraded the help line from a mediocre to a premier service. Team members sought additional education so they could expand services from mainframe to midrange systems and microcomputers. The percentage of calls resolved on the spot is more than 90%, compared to 75% when the help line started in July 1988. Customer satisfaction has jumped from 78% to 100%.

To ensure it has the data for continuous improvement, the team has started initiatives to measure quality, including monthly surveys of selected customers, tracking of call handling and abandonment, follow-up calls the day after customers are helped, and informal lunch-hour focus groups. After noticing a trend toward increased call volumes and abandon rates, the team proposed converting another budgeted (exempt) position into an additional help-line (nonexempt) position. Management agreed and noted the team's initiative.

Improvements were not limited to the team's own boundaries. Instead, the team initiated regular working sessions with teams in the network services department to resolve long-standing coordination and communication problems. Team members across departments help each other. After major network changes or outages, network services team members provide information and answer questions alongside help-line services team members.

**Higher Productivity and Lower Costs.** Corning points to annual savings of more than $500,000 because of fewer management levels. The company is making better use of existing people and providing them with greater opportunities to learn and apply new skills and knowledge.

When the operations team at Corning acquired new tape cartridge technology, a vendor submitted a proposal to create internal and external labels on the cartridges for $45,000. Team members decided to do the job themselves at a cost of only $500 in overtime and temporary help.

In a benchmark study conducted by an outside firm, Corning's computer utility was cited as among the best in its class. According to the study, Corning runs its data center with 29% fewer persons than the average for the MIPS group. The operations staff has the greatest difference with 48% fewer persons. The study noted that cost per person is 11% lower in operations and 4% lower in technical services than the MIPS and industry groups.

Champion International Corp. participated in another benchmark study. According to this study, staff productivity in Champion's data center (composed of self-managing teams) is 32% better than the best-of-the-best organizations in its reference group, staff size is 21% lower, and costs and service are world class.

**Enhanced Teamwork and Problem Solving.** Traditionally known as back-office personnel, Corning's IBM technical services people used to interact with their customers only when requested to do so. In contrast, they now work as active partners with customers to identify and solve problems. This change began with the control organization at Corning, which asked the IBM technical services team to help solve performance problems during critical period closings. The solutions implemented improved the process. Furthermore, team members, buoyed by their success, proactively approached other customers they serve and sought to resolve long-standing problems. Their current success rate to date: not only do they meet with customers to fix problems, but they attend periodic customer reviews, using these opportunities to discover ways of contributing to plans.

Corning's VAX technical services team explored inefficiencies in carrying out team functions. After careful analysis, they redesigned their work process using Corning's IMPACT (Improved Method for Process Analysis of Cost-Time) methodology. Instead of using generalists to perform all functions on their own VAX systems, specialists strive to become experts on particular aspects of all systems. Duplication of effort has been reduced and the team has been able to support an expanding portfolio of VAX systems without a commensurate increase in its own membership.

**Increased Opportunity to Develop and Demonstrate Skills and Leadership.** Team members who previously kept to themselves now believe they can make a difference beyond their own individual jobs. In addition to contributing substantially to their own teams, they become influential participants in the overall management of IS. Some of the biggest contributors of time, creativity, and energy to IS-wide quality improvement teams are self-managing team members.

Network consulting team members at Corning have taken on responsibilities previously reserved for managers. For example, Corning has changed its primary telecommunications services vendor—a change that should result in savings in the millions of dollars. An analyst on this team played a major role in negotiating the contract.

In many ways, the most important result is that people are growing, learning, and developing. Because IS departments are in the service business, IS professionals who are committed, energetic, skillful, and highly knowledgeable hold the key to success.

## KEY SUCCESS FACTORS

Experience so far confirms several key success factors for implementing empowerment strategies in the IS department.

### Start with a Vision and Measurable Goals

IS leaders must demonstrate true leadership in stating and promoting the IS department's vision of the desired new work system. They must also establish clear goals for reaching that vision as well as measurement systems to track goal achievement. Although managing by the numbers is an integral part of total quality management, IS departments that establish self-managing teams must be even more vigorous in their measurements because managers are less involved in daily decisions. Results of measurements must be shared with teams.

### Ensure Management's Support and Willingness to Take Risks

This new work system leads to changes in roles, relationships, management styles, and work flows. Senior managers must continue to demonstrate their commitment and willingness to take the risks inherent in such major changes, such as sharing power and information. When managers pay lip service to empowerment but fail to nurture an environment that supports empowered behavior, others in the organization quickly become cynical.

If senior IS managers publicly commit to empowerment, people will quickly flag management actions that are not consistent. In one case an IS senior vice-president was admonished in public for not accepting the recommendations of a quality improvement team empowered to identify applications development methodologies for the IS department.

IS managers must learn to modify their thinking and behavior in order to sustain major cultural change. They must transform themselves from command and control managers into true leaders who give self-managing teams responsibility, accountability, and authority for delivering first-class customer service.

They must also learn to be barrier busters. During this time of transition, many practices and systems throughout organizations are not yet geared to the empowerment level of IS teams. For example, supervisory signatures are often expected for job descriptions, expense reports, and other administrative actions. Many company senior managers are not yet comfortable receiving phone calls directly from team members. IS managers have to reduce the many subtle and unwitting barriers to empowerment.

## Pay Attention to Middle Managers and Supervisors

It is not uncommon for middle managers and supervisors to view announcements of impending empowered work systems with suspicion, uncertainty, and resistance. Some view the change as a threat to power, influence, and importance over which they have minimal control. Realizing that their repertoire of management skills (often developed after years of experience and struggle) are about to become at least in part obsolete, they question their ability to master new coaching and facilitating skills. These managers and supervisors need support from their managers and peers, especially those who are further along in their transitions. Training in new skills can help. Training should include skills in setting boundaries (e.g., about team decisions, objectives, and budgets) and communicating them. Coaches have to set limits and back off as sound judgment in decision making is demonstrated.

## Involve Staff in All Phases of the Project

In addition to building commitment and ownership, involvement ensures that plans incorporate valuable insights and experience of those who do the work. Moreover, active involvement helps team members internalize new team concepts. For example, before operations became a self-managing team at Corning, the operations supervisor asked if the team would take over the responsibility for being on call on weekends. This responsibility was being rotated among various IS managers. The first response was the traditional one: weekend duty was a supervisor's job. The second response, from another operator, recognized that the team was assuming many supervisory responsibilities and would lose credibility if it did not also assume this one. At that point a key aspect of the new self-managing team was internalized by all team members.

### Effectively Communicate

Uncertainty accompanies significant work system changes. Communication is a strong antidote. IS managers can address uncertainty at the onset by communicating their commitment not to terminate people as a result of the new work system. In addition, those involved with the design of the new work system must keep communication flowing to all who have a stake in the new system. Communication involves regular briefings, information lunch sessions, rollout meetings, and the distribution of minutes.

### Educate Everyone Involved

Education and training must continue to be high priorities. Educating managers in how to take a leadership role in an empowered organization is critical to success. Managers must learn how to coach and facilitate rather than direct. They must understand how teams develop over time and how they can facilitate that growth. Team members must also be educated in how teams develop over time and how to work effectively in a team environment. Education in team skills, as well as technical and business skills, must be an ongoing activity among team members. Formal seminars should continue to be held on relevant subjects. More important, team members learn by doing on the job—with guidance from their managers and advisors.

### Develop a Reward System that Promotes Success

Many IS departments have an extensive system of rewards for recognizing individual accomplishments in improving quality. Because the system focuses on the individual, it must be augmented with rewards for team accomplishment. In some IS departments with self-managing teams, rewards are based on meeting both individual and team objectives. Teams evaluate themselves as a whole on how well team objectives were met at the end of the yearly performance cycle. In more mature teams, members conduct performance evaluations of individuals as well. Some IS departments are exploring additional ways of formally and informally rewarding team performance, including gain-sharing programs.

### ACTION PLAN

IS departments successful in establishing and sustaining empowered, customer-focused organizations with self-managing teams have used structural approaches to designing and establishing teams. Although each organization's approach is somewhat different, they have in common certain design principles and strategies.

## Seven Design Principles

Seven design principles have proven essential in a range of projects and initiatives.

**Design Starts from Outside the Organization.** Because the core purpose of redesign is to enable people to produce and deliver products and services that meet customer requirements in the context of changing environments, design must start from outside the organization or unit, beginning with customers and their requirements and then moving back to the work and organizational processes.

**Teams Are the Basic Organizational Building Blocks.** Rather than focus on how to break down work into the smallest units that can be performed by an individual, the goal is to design units or teams around whole pieces of work—complete products, services, or processes. Within the context of clear customer requirements, teams are empowered to design and manage their own work processes and are given the resources they need (i.e. time, money, information, decision-making authority) to do so.

**Direction and Goals Are Clearly Specified.** Although there is great latitude in determining how teams will accomplish their missions, there is a great need for clarity about the requirements of the output. Therefore, empowered teams need clear missions, defined output requirements, and agreed-on measures of performance.

**Social and Technical Systems Are Interlinked.** Design must achieve joint optimization of technical elements (i.e., work flow, specific technologies employed, movement of information, and work processes) with social ones.

**Information Must Be Easily Accessible.** Members of teams need timely access to information about the environment, the output, work processes, problems, organizational directions, and results.

**Human Resources Practices Must Be Supportive.** Many human resources policies and practices reflect the 50-year-old bureaucracy model, with its emphasis on control, uniformity, and inspection. New work designs require such human resources practices as team hiring and firing, peer evaluation, minimization of rank and hierarchy, and team-based compensation systems.

**Work Units Need the Capacity to Reconfigure Themselves.** Because organizations and work units are being redesigned to anticipate or respond to environmental requirements and conditions, work units must be capable of reconfiguring themselves based on their learning—that is, by collecting information, reflecting on the consequences of their actions, and gaining new insights.

## Steering Committees and Design Teams

Choosing effective strategies for developing empowered, customer-focused organizations using these design principles is at least as important as the principles themselves. A steering committee and design team should work closely throughout the process. Senior managers on the steering committee create the vision and then sponsor, guide, and support the change process. Those who will have to live with the new work system play an active part in creating it through participation on design teams. These teams are responsible for:

- Conducting benchmarking studies.
- Surveying customers and staff members to identify both what is going well and areas for improvement.
- Exploring anticipated changes in the organization's external and internal environment that may impact this project.
- Reviewing current work practices, systems, tools, and results.
- Recommending redesigned work practices, structures, systems, and tools to achieve the vision created by the steering team.
- Developing implementation plans, including measures for monitoring project success, and extensive training programs.
- Serving as change advocates and communicators.

Design team members are individuals who are part of the work system under study for various compelling reasons. For example, they may recognize that:

- Active involvement builds ownership and commitment.
- Involvement ensures that recommendations incorporate the valuable insights and experience of those who do the work.
- Involvement teaches work team members how to collect data, analyze their work system, and find ways to improve it—skills all work team members need in order to facilitate continuous improvement beyond this project.
- Active involvement helps team members internalize new team concepts.

This collaborative approach is clearly more time-consuming upfront than more traditional methods of having consultants or managers identify needed changes and then mandate them. However, this approach leads not only to more effective implementation by committed individuals who own their solutions, but to better long-term results.

Redesign and implementation are just the beginning. Existing teams require sustenance if continuous improvement is to become a way of life. Managers must meet regularly with teams to address issues and concerns. Teams must also evaluate their own performance frequently, making improvements as required to enhance customer service, quality, productivity, and work life. To do a self-evaluation, the team may explore such issues as: what the team has done well collectively, problems or potential areas for improvement for the team, and methods for addressing these problems or areas of improvement. In addition, formal assessments give a more objective, overall view of the organization's progress. They help put in perspective successes, while at the same time highlighting areas for improvement and suggestions for taking the next steps.

# VII-2
# Reengineering IS Professionals

*STEWART L. STOKES, JR.*

In some organizations, changes are reactive, designed to enable the organization to survive. In other cases, the changes are proactive, designed to enable the organization to reposition itself for its next stage of growth. In all cases, change poses threats and opportunities for IS professionals, for they too must change to survive and grow. They can do this best by being proactive and being prepared to continually reposition themselves as value-adding resources in the organization. Above all, IS professionals need to understand that they alone bear responsibility for their future.

For many IS professionals, this represents a departure from traditional career-path-planning expectations. The requirements for survival and success have shifted from a focus on being individual technical experts to becoming business partners. In short, IS professionals are at a crossroads. This chapter discusses issues and strategies that can help IS professionals to stay on top of their careers.

## CAREER OPPORTUNITIES AND THREATS

It has been said that where people stand on an issue depends on where they sit. The gulf between the individual cubicle and executive suite widens as changes overtake the organization. What could be a growth opportunity for the organization and its employees often deteriorates into a struggle for personal survival. The changes that result from corporate restructuring that represent opportunities to those on top are seen as threats by those on the bottom. Those in middle management seem to have the most to lose.

When many IS professionals talk about being change agents in their organizations, these are often code words for inflicting change on others. When it becomes their turn to be on the receiving end of change, IS professionals experience all the emotional wear and tear that change brings. Changes that threaten careers are seldom initially perceived as representing potential gains.

If people perceive that changes brought about by downsizing or outsourcing may be career-threatening, resulting in their losing more than they may gain, then they will prepare themselves psychologically to resist it (notwith-standing the rhetoric from the executive suite). If they perceive that a change may enhance their careers and well-being, then they will prepare themselves to support it.

The importance of perceived benefits is a critical success factor for change agents. Those who would be agents of change need to take every opportunity to sell the benefits of the new undertaking to everyone involved. The significance of change must be expressed in personal terms.

## PARTICIPATION IN REENGINEERING

Organization and personal changes are increasingly driven by process and technological reengineering: rethinking and remaking the enterprise. Whether or not its payoff exceeds its promise remains to be seen. To reengineer an organization is essentially a political process, and because reengineering represents a change for everyone it touches, it represents both individual opportunities and threats.

Reengineering means rethinking and altering the way an organization does business. It affects the organization's processes, jobs, intra- and inter-departmental relationships, structure, and most important, its organizational beliefs.

In organizational reengineering, every element in the status quo is challenged. Reengineering is about process management and processes become cross-functional. The creation of cross-functional teams involves the participation of IS professionals and their colleagues from the business units. Active participation on such collaborative teams requires the development of skills that may be unfamiliar and uncomfortable for those IS professionals who are accustomed to working alone or in small groups of colleagues. Collaborative teamwork also requires a high tolerance for ambiguity. Systems professionals usually prefer certainty, which is scarce during process reengineering.

Rethinking and reengineering the organization requires changing the perception the organization has of itself. It requires thinking horizontally instead of vertically—that is, thinking across the organization instead of in terms of a single department. This thinking requires a knowledge of the entire enterprise and how it works.

For IS professionals to participate successfully in reengineering projects, they need to change their perceptions of themselves from technical experts on vertical applications to business partners using technology to improve enterprisewide business processes. For example, such processes can involve an entire procurement to payable cycle, spanning several functional areas. Information technology becomes the enabler.

To be perceived by their clients as business partners, IS professionals must demonstrate a willingness and commitment to learn the businesses they serve. This means learning about such issues as:

- The company's objectives in terms of product strategy, revenue growth, focus, customers, geographical breakdown, and distribution channels.
- Company mission, business objectives, and long and short range strategy; business plans of strategic business areas; organizational functions and cross-functional activities; customer expectations.
- The information implications of business activities. (IS professionals cannot know these implications unless they understand the business activities themselves.)
- Culture, processes, and politics, all of which are required for IS to be accepted as a vital part of the business.

Because of the demands of reengineering and the pressure to become business partners, IS professionals must also rethink their own career development and redefine what is required to remain effective in their work in the coming years. Systems professionals have always been highly achievement-oriented, and research has repeatedly shown that those making a career in IS lead their colleagues in other business departments in their need to achieve. This high level of achievement motivation can be beneficial as career insurance.

## RESPONSIBILITIES FOR PROFESSIONAL DEVELOPMENT

The question of whether to refocus and retrain employees or bring in new blood has been elevated in importance by the worldwide economic downturn and enterprisewide restructuring. Although both the enterprise and the individual have a role to play in providing the opportunities and resources IS professionals require to continue to grow and become true business partners, the emphasis has changed.

For many years, an implied contract existed between employee and employer, under which the employer had the long-term career growth interests of the employee in mind and would supply appropriate opportunities for its people to grow and advance in their jobs and careers. Human resource departments flourished, career paths were carved out, and training departments were created. IS personnel were included and an entire career field of IS training and education was born. People came to expect that they would receive a certain number of days of training per year (10 on average). This commitment to regular training was viewed as a major advantage when hiring and retaining IS talent. Upward mobility, in terms of rank, responsibility, and remuneration, came to be expected either in the form of promotions, with more people in the manager's span of control, or new and challenging technical assignments, with opportunities to learn and use new technologies.

With the business downturn, however, organizations have cut costs and are examining closely their patterns of spending and investment. Layoffs and budget constraints have affected IS so that existing career paths have become casualties. There are fewer opportunities for upward mobility, and fewer dollars and time for training and education. In many cases, the need for certain types of training lessened because organizations cut back purchases of hardware and software.

A key requirement for IS professionals—including managers—becomes the need for them to view themselves as value-adding resources. This means viewing themselves as products that deliver a bottom-line payoff to the organization. It represents a significant change in self-perception. People can be uncomfortable thinking of themselves as products, but the fact is that seasoned IS veterans may be candidates for early retirement if they have failed to keep pace with both evolving technology and the changing business needs of their organizations. Having $X$ years of experience is no longer viewed as a career asset; more often, IS professionals are perceived as having one year of experience $X$ times—which is a considerable career liability.

### The Politics of Reengineering

Because new business processes are cross-functional and enterprisewide, they may have no real owners. This makes the reengineering process inherently political. Reengineering requires rethinking and redefining the interfaces—those locations in the horizontal process flow where there are handoffs between departments, teams, and individuals. Multiple stakeholders emerge, including work groups and individuals. These constituencies have a stake, or a vested interest, in conditions as they are. The political process of influencing and persuading can become frustrating and time-consuming for those involved in the change process. If reengineering fails to deliver its promise potential, it is usually because of the political obstacles in its path, not because of problems with new technology.

Line managers in the functional areas and business units must drive the process. IS staff and information technology become the enablers. The IS department takes on the role of influencer, positioning itself and the IS staff as value-adding resources to the business managers who are rethinking the business processes. This requires that the business people perceive their IS colleagues to possess competencies that transcend the technical and include an understanding of business issues and interpersonal skills.

### Value-Adding Skill Sets

It is important for IS professionals to learn about the businesses they serve so that they might be better perceived as partners by their clients. Not all of their partners, however, feel a reciprocal need to learn a great deal about information systems. Business users may know how to do spreadsheets on the microcomputers but this is a far cry from their understanding their role and responsibilities in the systems development and operations process. Consequently, IS professionals may find themselves forming partnerships that are less than equal and require more new learning on their part than on their partner's.

The Boston Chapter of the Society for Information Management (SIM) has conducted research into the levels of expertise required of the next generation of IS professionals. Its study revealed movement away from several tasks and skill sets long considered essential. For example, two of the groups surveyed, IS practitioners and IS educators, agreed on the declining importance of such standbys as COBOL and operating systems knowledge. In their place, practitioners and educators see a growing emphasis on understanding the broader issues of analyzing business problems in user-driven, distributed computing environments in which information is treated as a strategic corporate resource. Furthermore, instead of concentrating on purchasing and tailoring applications software, tomorrow's IS professional will need to plan and manage enterprisewide information strategies. The orientation is shifting from a narrow departmental or functional focus to a broader, enterprisewide, cross-functional focus. This requires the acquisition of a wide range of managerial and interpersonal skills, plus business awareness and organization knowledge, that provides the context within which these new skills and competencies will be used.

The emphasis on reengineering cross-functional processes and systems is ratcheting up the importance of understanding behavioral issues. This knowledge includes the development of interpersonal, intrateam, and interteam skills, including influencing, negotiating, managing expectations, giving and receiving feedback, conflict resolution, coaching, consensus building, and coalition building.

### Being Accessible to Business Partners

For IS professionals to add value to their clients in business units, they have to be in close, continual contact with them. This contact must include opportunities for in-depth communication between IS managers and their peers, and among IS professionals and their colleagues in user departments. This contact and communication must be championed by senior management, for it is almost impossible for significant communication and understanding to happen in the middle and lower echelons if it is not present and visible at the top.

There are increasing numbers of ambitious IS professionals who are making the sacrifices necessary to maintain not only their technical currency, but also to gain the knowledge and understanding necessary to partner with their business-oriented peers and colleagues. This understanding includes strategies, products, markets, customers, channels of distribution, competitors (and their products and strategies), and of course, how information can, does, and should be supporting functional areas and business units. Coupled with this hard business information is the savvy about corporate power structures and politics, key people and departments, and formal and informal human networks, for it is through these channels that work gets done. IS professionals must gain access to these relationships if they are going to become value-adding business partners.

A key requirement for success today is visibility and more hours on the job. Many IS professionals are no strangers to long hours and hard work, but the bar for achievement and success is being raised higher. If there is a glass ceiling over the careers of IS professionals today, it exists for those who do not have business savvy and sophistication and who (for whatever reasons) are unable or unwilling to make the commitment to continuous learning and extended hours on the job.

## THE LEARNING ORGANIZATION: A MODEL FOR THE FUTURE

The only sustainable competitive advantage for individuals is their ability to learn. This is as true for organizations as it is for individuals. For learning to take place, risk must be encouraged. Risk opens up the possibility of failure, but some of our most effective learning comes through failure.

Individuals who are risk-averse may enjoy short-run security but they cut themselves off from longer-run opportunities for learning and improvement. Risk is always uncomfortable, but its quality of uncertainty is the driver for continuous personal improvement.

The same is true for organizations. Those enterprises that encourage risk and the entrepreneurial spirit learn the most about their environments. They also enhance their ability to survive. These organizations usually outdistance their more risk-averse competitors in the marketplace.

In his book *The Fifth Discipline,* Peter M. Senge defined the learning organization as "an organization that is continually expanding its capacity to create its future . . . adaptive learning (to survive) is joined by generative learning (to create). . . ." In the adaptive and generative organization, the vehicles for organizational learning are teams that coalesce around problems, needs, and issues. These teams can be ad hoc, coming together as needs arise and dissolving as needs are met. Team members are flexible, and do not seek to perpetuate the team beyond solving those problems that brought the team into existence in the first place.

The learning organization metaphor can be applied to individuals as well. Those persons who are both adaptive and generative, who adapt and create, can adopt self-directed learning techniques. Individuals—not their employers or organizations—hold the key to personal and economic security. It is through self-directed learning that individuals can exercise this responsibility. Those who take the initiative to plan their own career future and who accept the responsibility to seek out the training and education necessary to secure a career future are making the correct turn at the career crossroads.

## SELF-DIRECTED LEARNING: A PERSONAL SURVIVAL SKILL

Self-directed learning is learning for which the individual takes the initiative and bears the responsibility. As such, it represents a departure from the learning style with which most adults are familiar.

Most people grew up with an other-directed, dependent style of learning whereby someone else (e.g., teacher, employer, manager, or trainer) determined what was to be learned, when it was to be learned, how it was to be learned, and if it was learned correctly. The infrastructure that has traditionally provided IS-related training and education opportunities within the organization—the internal IS training department—is withering away, however. The individual stands at the crossroads with basically two choices: either wait for the doubtful return of those who might make learning opportunities available—a reactive strategy—or become proactive and seek out learning opportunities on one's own. The latter strategy is the best career insurance policy available.

As IS training staffs shrink, any decision to wait for supervisors or managers to provide learning opportunities and resources is a shaky strategy, because it is based on the questionable assumption that managers feel accountable for the career development of their people. The reality of career enhancement in the slow-growth environments of organizations today is that individuals must be self-directed in planning and implementing their own career development programs.

Self-directed learning is learning for which the individual:

- Takes the initiative to learn about problems the organization is facing.
- Accepts responsibility for developing personal learning objectives designed to help solve those problems.
- Establishes learning objectives that meet not only personal needs but contribute to meeting the learning needs of the IS staff and the organization as a whole.
- Locates learning resources, including people, materials, courses, conferences, professional associations, situations, and circumstances that provide learning opportunities.
- Uses these learning resources in disciplined, purposeful ways.
- Validates what is learned by working with those who understand the organization's problems and who possess relevant subject matter expertise.
- Tests what is learned to determine if the new knowledge and skills help to alleviate or solve the problems.
- Develops new learning objectives based on the outcomes of the previous learning experiences and the evolving situation.
- Continues the process of self-directed learning to meet the demands of new and changing requirements.

The traditional, other-directed learning model was effective because it enabled people to absorb a great deal of information. In some cases it prepared people to act upon that information. Unfortunately, it did not help them understand the most basic survival skill of all: how to learn on their own.

Self-directed learning is situation-centered learning. It is the structuring of learning experiences based on life-changing events and is predicated upon the belief that one's personal development is one's personal responsibility. The enterprise or organization and its managers and staff can and should be resources for continuing self-development, but the locus of responsibility rests with the individual.

## NINE STEPS TO SELF-DIRECTED LEARNING

Many IS professionals arrive at a mid-career plateau where they have advanced as far as they can go using their technical skills. To continue to grow in their careers they must develop new competencies outside the technical realm, primarily in the area of people skills. If they are fortunate, they may become aware of their arrival at a career plateau through a performance review discussion with their manager, or perhaps during conversations with a colleague. If they are not so fortunate, they may stumble upon this insight after watching some of their peers who possess the requisite organizational and business skills move past them.

There are nine stages, or steps, in the self-directed learning life cycle. These steps are applied to a common IS career crossroads dilemma to illustrate how IS professionals in question might benefit from their use.

### Career Development in a Matrix Environment

Many organizations are redeploying their systems analysts from the centralized IS department out into the business units. Working as business analysts, they operate in a matrix environment, one of the most challenging and frustrating of all organizational designs. A matrix is an organizational environment with dual chains of command; there is a direct link to the functional manager but also links to the client or customer. The client or customer relationship is the most important in terms of responsibility but the relationship with the functional manager is most important in terms of authority and accountability. To be successful in such an environment, the IS professional must be proficient in influencing and negotiating.

For IS professionals to make this career move successfully, they need information about the business unit and its mission, objectives, and strategies. This knowledge and these skills can be learned and developed. The resources are available, but to take advantage of them IS professionals must undertake self-directed learning, which requires a high degree of personal discipline and initiative. The context for the design of a self-directed learning experience is a learning life cycle consisting of the following nine steps.

**Step One.** The IS professional must understand as much as possible about the current and future direction and goals of the organization, as well as the changes that will be required if the goals are to be achieved. This step, in and of itself, requires that the professional actively gather information.

**Step Two.** Changes must be placed in a larger context (i.e., what is happening in the organization's industry and in the IS profession and computer field?). This also requires information gathering; however, the individual gains the insight required for self-directed learning decisions.

**Step Three.** Using what was learned from steps one and two, the IS professionals' next step is to determine as clearly as possible where they would like to be at some predetermined point in the future (i.e., in one or two years). An individual's next career objective needs to be expressed as clearly and as unambiguously as possible. The more precise the description, the better.

**Step Four.** With a career objective in mind, IS professionals need to determine the competencies required to attain that objective (i.e., what must they need to know, or be able to do to perform that job in an outstanding manner?). Because of the availability of talent, continuing career advancement and success may accrue to those who learn how to perform in a consistently outstanding manner.

**Step Five.** Professionals should assess, as objectively as possible, their current competency level and determine the gaps that exist between the competencies they possess and the competencies required to attain the career objective identified in step four. Steps four and five may also require some self-directed information gathering.

**Step Six.** Professionals must create learning objectives designed to enable them to close the competency gaps identified in step five. These learning objectives should:

- Be clear and unambiguous.
- Be expressed within a specific time frame.
- Be measurable.
- Be expressed in terms of cost—both out-of-pocket cost and opportunity cost. For example, if people attempt to achieve a personal objective, what will they have to give up or sacrifice?

The more a persons' objectives meet these criteria, the easier it will be to focus on the objectives and gather the resources to achieve them.

**Step Seven.** Professionals must locate learning resources and design learning experiences to accomplish their learning objectives. These are really two steps in one, but they are so intertwined as to be interchangeable. In some cases, an individual may design a learning experience and, in so doing, locate a suitable learning resource. For example, IS professionals who are gathering some first-hand experience in a particular business unit may discover someone from among user management who could become a temporary mentor.

Learning experiences can include informal but focused individual reading programs, small-group discussions on specific topics, participation in courses, and active involvement in professional association programs, perhaps by serving as a chapter officer. Other learning experiences and learning resources include such temporary assignments as:

- Short-term (i.e., one to three months) participation on a task force.
- Longer-term field assignments in branch offices.
- In the case of multinational organizations, assignments in overseas locations.

Task forces are increasingly popular as organizations rightsize and as IS departments attempt to do more work with less staff. A task force is a team of people brought together to accomplish a specific assignment. It is usually short-lived. Task forces often consist of people with specific and complementary competencies, and they may be extracurricular in nature. In other words, task force members may serve on their own time, with their primary responsibilities remaining their own jobs. The career benefits accruing from serving with people from different departments in the organization comes with the price of extra hours and additional effort.

Sometimes task force assignments may be of longer duration, even up to a year. In such cases, task force members relinquish their primary positions and work on the task force full-time. One organization formed a task force of seven IS professionals to work on temporary assignments for a year, at the end of which time all seven people returned to the IS department, but not necessarily to their former positions. Assignments ranged from assuming the role of an internal IS consultant to formulating an internal IS management development program. The rewards were considerable, but so were the risks. The only guarantees were a stimulating change-of-pace assignment for a year, with no loss of benefits or of seniority. The risk was that the participants' former positions might not be available; this was in fact the case for all of the seven, who afterward had to compete for new positions.

**Step Eight.** Results of the learning must be validated through applying the learning on the job, to determine the effectiveness of the learning experience. This sets the stage for the final step in the self-directed learning life cycle.

**Step Nine.** The IS professional must continually identify new or modified learning needs and begin the life cycle process again.

## ACTION PLAN

IS professionals examining their career must remember, first and foremost, that they bear primary responsibility for their own career development. This is a difficult reality for many highly competent and loyal systems people to accept yet it may be the best advice they ever received.

IS professionals are among the most highly trained, educated, and motivated in today's workforce. Their focus on the rapidly evolving technology is both an advantage and a disadvantage. It is an advantage because IS professionals are on the cutting edge of the technological advances that organizations must make if they are to remain competitive. It is a disadvantage because they can become so transfixed by the technological changes that they lose sight of the changing economic and organizational conditions that provide the basis for the changing technology in the first place.

To take charge of their careers, IS professionals can begin by following this course of action:

- Assuming responsibility for career growth and development.
- Focusing on what they want out of their careers; becoming explicit about what they do well and want to do more of in the future.
- Becoming disciplined students of not only their technical specialty but also of their organizations and their industry.
- Understanding what makes their organizations successful and concentrating their efforts upon aligning IS projects with these critical success factors.
- Seeking out key managers and professionals in the functional areas of the organization and building value-added partnerships with them.
- Reading widely; concentrating on those professional journals that contain industry-related information they can use as they build relationships with their internal customers, IS management, and senior line managers.
- Becoming active members of professional associations, not only those related to the IS function but also to those connected with their organization's industry. (IS professionals who are not joiners miss out on opportunities to learn about new issues and developments and to network with their peers and colleagues.)
- Becoming habitual self-directed learners; creating, finding, and using the many learning resources available.
- Being alert to opportunities for growth that are consistent with career goals. If a person's goal is to move into an IS management position, this may require saying yes to a transfer into a business unit and accepting interpersonal responsibilities while saying no to an opportunity to learn more about a technical specialty. The issue is to become increasingly clear about personal career aspirations, then to manage those aspirations accordingly.
- Becoming risk-takers. There is no career growth without risk.

IS professionals must adopt a proactive posture toward their personal career planning. Training, education, and professional development resources still exist, but it is the individual's responsibility to activate these resources. The core of this proactive posture is self-directed learning. The only sustainable competitive advantage for both individuals and organizations is their ability to learn, and self-directed learning is becoming more important as organizations change and individuals strive to survive.

# VII-3
# Career Planning:
# A New Set of Rules

*LAYNE C. BRADLEY*

G iven the rapid change and turmoil the information systems industry is experiencing during the 1990s, the idea of career planning might seem to be almost irrelevant. In the face of downsizing and outsourcing, merely keeping a job could be considered the extent of current career planning. In fact, the idea of a career now has a much different connotation than in the past.

Many data center managers might wonder whether they actually have a career anymore. Some have found themselves outsourced, downsized, or reengineered out of a job. Others who have so far escaped the sweeping management changes taking place in many corporations wonder how much longer they will be able to practice their chosen profession. This chapter provides data center managers with a better understanding of the changes that are taking place today, why they are taking place, and how to deal with them.

## DRAMATIC CHANGES

To better understand what is happening throughout the information systems industry, data center managers must first examine and understand the changes that are taking place not only in the economic and social structure of the US, but how these changes are occurring on a global scale. This background is needed to understand the impact these changes will have on the information systems industry and the data center manager.

Following World War II, the US was arguably the most powerful nation in the world. Because of the massive effort put together by government and industry to produce necessary war materials, the US possessed a tremendous industrial base.

While the US enjoyed such a strong industrial position, much of the world's industrial capability was completely devastated. As a result, the US quickly became the world leader in producing manufactured goods.

From the 1940s through the 1970s, the US dominated world business.

Successful companies became even more successful and new companies destined for success were started. Organizational structures, management approaches, and tools were developed and implemented around the core of the manufacturing base that had been created. During this time, corporate bureaucracies and hierarchical management structures proliferated.

Following World War II, pent-up demand in the US for goods and services, combined with the need for other nations to rebuild their economies and social structures, produced an ideal climate for US business growth. Almost any type of consumer product that could be made could be sold, both in the US and abroad. Many US companies developed into large international corporations.

During this time, many companies adopted a product-driven orientation. Customers were not necessarily considered during product development. Rather, companies designed and produced new products and services and then implemented marketing and advertising campaigns designed to convince consumers that they needed those products and services.

By the 1970s, many countries, most notably Japan and West Germany, had recovered from World War II and were making dramatic advances in developing their business and industrial bases. They were beginning to influence business on a much broader global scale. Slowly, the US began to lose its position as the world's business leader.

Much has been written about how US businesses failed to recognize and adapt to the changes that were taking place in the global marketplace. Because resources had been so scarce following World War II, such countries as Japan and West Germany had to develop companies with lean management structures, efficient operations, and work environments that fostered creative, innovative thinking. In addition, government and industry formed close alliances dedicated to improving social, economic, and political conditions in their countries. As these countries moved to expand their marketing boundaries, they saw the US as an ideal place to market their goods and services.

Perhaps the most important marketing strategy employed by these countries was involving consumers directly—making them part of the product design process. These companies simply asked customers what they wanted. Then they developed and produced high quality, cost-competitive products and services that met the customers' needs and wants. At a time when US producers basically determined what they thought customers needed and then tried to convince them of those needs, the customer-driven, high quality approach employed by these countries worked—often dramatically.

Because of US industry's inability or unwillingness to recognize and adopt this customer-driven, high quality focus, the US no longer enjoys overall leadership in many industries. As a result, many US corporations are struggling to recreate themselves in such a way that they can compete and survive. The results of this effort can be seen in the layoffs of huge numbers of workers. It appears that this situation will continue for some time to come.

Thus, from a business perspective, the world has become a global marketplace with many new strong players (and more to come). The US is no longer the dominant force in many markets. This situation continues to have a major effect on the careers of data center managers.

In addition to the global business issues that are affecting the US and the data center manager's career planning, another, even more important change is taking place—the ushering in of the information age.

## THE INFORMATION REVOLUTION

As computer technology developed during the 1950s and 1960s, many people expressed concern that computers were going to replace people and eliminate jobs. Unions often played on this fear in an attempt to negotiate stronger labor contracts that would protect their members from technology-related layoffs. In reality, these fears were unfounded. The introduction of the IBM 360 series of mainframe computers in the mid 1960s marked the beginning of the era of business data processing. Companies could develop practical business applications and obtain information more quickly than ever before. However, rather than eliminating jobs, the computer technology spawned an entire industry of information systems, software, telecommunications, systems analysis, and related fields.

From the 1960s to the early 1980s, the data processing industry matured. Along with the continuing development of technology, IS professionals created applications development methodologies and management techniques. Corporations built large data centers to accommodate their growing data processing needs. Often, these data centers were linked together to form massive computer networks.

During this period, the role of the data center manager also evolved. From initially being responsible for ensuring the hardware was operating, the range of the data center manager's responsibilities widened dramatically. Data center managers commanded a vast array of large, expensive technology with responsibility, for ensuring that the company's production systems were operational and that the necessary output from those systems was available on schedule.

Still, the information systems industry continued to grow and add people to meet growing demands. However, the introduction of the microcomputer in the early 1980s changed the nature of information processing in many corporations. Due in part to a high degree of frustration with corporate data processing departments and their inability to develop new application systems in a timely manner, corporate end users rushed to obtain microcomputers that could handle their information systems needs.

Although the implementation of microcomputer-based systems in companies has not been without trial and error learning by end users as well as information system professionals, PC-based systems have become a defacto standard. Advances in software and networking capabilities now provide users of PC-based systems with access to tremendous processing capabilities.

Because of the success of PC-based systems, companies are finding they can obtain significant productivity gains. This realization, combined with the pressures of global competition, is one of the driving forces behind the layoffs and downsizing taking place in the US today. The basic premise is simple— increased productivity, fewer people, reduced expenses. Unfortunately, information systems departments and data centers have not escaped this rapidly changing work environment.

## NEW STRATEGIES

With this new work environment and the turmoil being experienced in the information systems industry, the question becomes how to survive and prosper. The answer is that the data center manager must adopt a new set of career planning strategies.

It is necessary to accept that the current situation is permanent. Unfortunately, many IS professionals still view it as a temporary economic situation that will change once the economy begins to grow again. To the contrary, the changes taking place are dramatic and permanent—at least for the foreseeable future. To succeed, the data center manager must accept this fact and take advantage of the circumstances.

Data center managers must understand that simply being a highly skilled technician is no longer sufficient. Although technology is still important, it is rapidly becoming a commodity. Companies generally are no longer interested in technology for technology's sake, being leading-edge companies, or experimenting with new technologies merely to uncover potential applications. Rather, most companies are interested in using technology and systems only if they add value to the business. Adding value usually means increasing revenue, reducing expenses, reducing personnel, gaining a competitive edge, or moving new products to market faster. Thus, the data center manager must become recognized as someone capable of playing a key role in determining how new technology can add value to the company.

Data center managers must think not only in technical terms but also in business terms. While data center managers clearly will continue to have responsibility for managing the technical environment of the data center on a daily basis, they should not make that the sole focus of their jobs. All data center tasks should be approached from the perspective of how they can improve overall business operations. Improved efficiency, reduced cost, and higher productivity should be the primary focus for data center managers.

When dealing with corporate management, data center managers must think and talk in business terms, not technical ones. To be perceived as a business professional, the data center manager must learn to speak the language of business. In other words, it is essential to use such terms as cost-benefit analysis and return on investment when proposing new projects or plans for the data center. Corporate management now includes such positions as the Vice President of Information Systems or the Chief Information Officer.

These positions are gaining increased visibility and stature in many corporations. In many cases, however, they are also being filled with nontechnical executives from operational areas other than information systems. Thus, the data center manager could easily be reporting to an executive with little or no technical background. As a result, data center managers must be able to present their ideas from a business, rather than a technical, perspective.

To keep up with the rapid changes in technology, data center managers must expand their skills. For example, if the data center manager's skill set involves COBOL, DB2, and a centralized mainframe environment, it is time to broaden that skill set—quickly. The data center manager must become skilled in such technologies as LANs, client/server architecture, imaging, object-oriented programming, and wireless communications. Although mainframes will continue to be the hub of the data center for some time to come, their role is clearly changing and the data center manager must understand that changing role.

Data center managers also must improve their general business skills. At one time, it was unusual for a data center manager to have an MBA. Today, such a level of business acumen is almost mandatory. To have a successful IS career, the data center manager must become part of the business management team. IS is rapidly being absorbed by the business functions, and only those IS players with strong technical and business skills will achieve leadership roles in the company.

Data center managers must understand all aspects of the company. In the past, IS professionals often believed they could practice their particular skills anywhere. At one time, that view was reasonably accurate and not likely to create any career problems. However, given the current idea that systems must add value to the business, this approach is no longer acceptable. The current corporate view is that systems must add value, and data center managers can be certain their actions are in fact adding value only if they thoroughly understand the company's business.

Finally, data center managers must revise their concept of a career. It is becoming less likely that any individual will have a long-term career with a single company. Rather, a career will probably involve working for several companies, perhaps in different industries. Thus, data center managers must take responsibility for managing their own careers. They must remain knowledgeable of new technology, expand and maintain their business skills, and develop reputations as managers who can clearly combine business and technology skills to produce value for their employer. A data center manager who can do these things well will be in demand.

## CAREER PLANNING TIPS

The preceding section described the overall career planning strategies that data center managers must employ to be successful in the 1990s. The following sections describe specific actions that can be taken to maximize the effect of these strategies.

## Become Knowledgeable of the Company's Business

Many data center managers—particularly those who have held the position for some time—may believe they are knowledgeable of their company's operations. However, knowledge of the types of systems, the reports that are produced, and the recipients of those reports represents only a superficial understanding of the company's business. The Data Center Manager must understand the business as well as any other line manager.

The data center manager should meet with other key department managers on a regular basis, not to discuss information systems needs, but to find out what their jobs entail. The data center manager should understand their daily responsibilities, their business needs, the difficulties they face in meeting those needs, and where they see the company going.

Because of the competitive challenges discussed earlier in this chapter, many companies have assembled numerous study teams to investigate such issues as changing market conditions, competitor's actions, the impact of government regulations, product liability trends, and new product and manufacturing ideas. The data center manager should volunteer to join such study teams, even if they do not directly involve information systems. This activity will have two effects. First, it will give the data center manager a much clearer understanding of the issues facing the company and how they are being addressed. Second, it will position the data center manager as a team player and a business person interested in furthering the interests of the company.

Because many companies are operating with fewer employees than in the past, effective training and retention of outstanding employees is more important than ever. The data center manager should take advantage of any training the company offers that helps employees better understand the company, its position in the marketplace, and trends that are affecting it. Even in a era of reduced expenditures, many companies still offer tuition refund programs for appropriate college courses. If the company offers an opportunity to obtain a business degree, the data center manager who lacks such credentials should seize the opportunity.

Numerous seminars are available to help people understand and manage the changes that are taking place in society. Regardless of which business the data center manager is associated with, it is likely that industry experts offer relevant seminars. The data center manager should make every effort to attend such seminars in order to obtain the most current information available.

Finally, the data center manager must know where the company is headed. Specifically, data center managers must understand the company's long-term goals and strategic business plans. Although many companies fail to provide this type of information to all employees, data center managers can enhance their stature in the company by making it known that they are interested in such information and in becoming more knowledgeable of the company's business plans. Unfortunately, many data center managers never ask to receive such information and become known simply as computer experts.

## Thoroughly Evaluate Business Skills

To become a more effective business person, data center managers must first determine their current level of business skills. As mentioned, the data center manager who lacks a formal business education would be wise to consider obtaining one. Even data center managers who have obtained undergraduate degrees in business should consider pursuing a graduate-level degree. Although this is a major, time-consuming commitment, it can be tremendously beneficial from a long-term career planning perspective. Because many companies are assigning nontechnical people to senior management positions in IS, it should be clear that the emphasis is on a strong business background. Combining a strong technology background with effective business skills can give the data center manager a decided competitive edge for such positions.

As mentioned earlier, data center managers should attend seminars that provide sound, basic business skills. With the seemingly unlimited supply of business books available on the market today, data center managers should make it a habit to read such books regularly. For the cost-conscious IS professional, many book-of-the-month clubs provide the latest business books at reduced cost.

The data center manager should focus on developing strong skills in basic financial analysis, marketing, and oral and written communications. These skills are essential for business professionals in today's highly competitive global marketplace. Simply having a good idea is not sufficient. Today's business professional must be able to support that idea with a cost-benefit analysis, show how it can be profitably marketed, and communicate it effectively to senior management. Only those ideas that meet the company's goals for financial results and sales returns are accepted. Possessing these basic business skills can give the data center manager a definite advantage when competing for scarce resources in the company.

The data center manager must become comfortable with public speaking and giving presentations. This is essential for being perceived in the company as an effective business person. Skilled speakers will usually find themselves much in demand in the company. Rather than merely being part of a study team, they often find themselves in the role of team spokesperson. Being in such a position on important projects or study teams can increase visibility with senior management. Many college courses, seminars, books, tape programs, and organizations are available to help the data center manager develop skills in this area. Unfortunately, many business professionals lack effective presentation skills and take little initiative to improve themselves. However, poor speaking skills can severely limit career growth. Conversely, effective communication skills can often propel a career faster and farther than any other business skill.

### Remain Knowledgeable of Emerging Technologies

With all of the emphasis on becoming a skilled business professional, it is imperative that the data center manager remain knowledgeable of new technologies and how they can favorably impact the business. After all, this is the data center manager's primary responsibility in the company. Balancing this responsibility with the previously mentioned business-related activities is a challenging task. To be successful however, a data center manager must be able to perform this balancing act.

### Seek Out a Mentor in the Company

Many successful executives admit that much of their success results from having a mentor in the company—someone who was able to teach them about the business, the management structure, and the politics. There are usually senior managers who are willing to help the data center manager who is pursuing the goal of being perceived as a strong team player and a knowledgeable business person, not just a systems technician. The data center manager must be aggressive and seek out such individuals to ask for their help. Senior managers are always looking for bright, ambitious, dedicated individuals to help grow the company, and the data center managers can improve their chances of being perceived as one of these individuals by actively seeking counsel from senior managers.

### Be Known as an Innovator

The data center manager should develop a reputation as an innovator who is flexible, adaptable, and willing to change. Unfortunately, the stereotype in business of the typical IS manager is someone who is unwilling to change with the times and is much more interested in preserving the status quo with regard to systems, policies, and procedures. The data center manager should understand that the new role being established by business for the information systems professional is one of Change Manager. Such an individual views information systems as a critical part of the business, not just a backroom data processing function. A change manager also understands business and the company, has a grasp on new technologies, and can effectively integrate those technologies into the company. Data center managers who fail to adopt this new role could put their careers in jeopardy.

### Put the Customer First

One of the major trends in business today is to ensure that customers' needs are the absolute top priority for the company. Anything less is unacceptable. The driving force behind such management practices as reengineering, Total Quality Management, and even outsourcing is to ensure that everything the company does is focused entirely on the customer. There is no other reason for a company to exist. Unfortunately, many companies today are struggling because this was not the primary goal of the company. Today, companies that do not adopt such an approach are not likely to survive.

The same concept holds true for data center managers. They must ensure that the data center is truly meeting the customer's needs. Merely producing reports on a timely basis, which used to be the primary measure of the data center, is no longer valid. With the move toward personal computing, many customers are able to develop their own systems and reports. If the data center is not meeting customer needs, the data center manager must find out why. The data center manager should meet with customers regularly to find out how their needs are changing. When necessary, the data center manager must make changes in personnel, policies, procedures, training, and hardware and software platforms. To meet customer needs, the data center manager must become an internal information systems consultant who is recognized as an effective business person with technology knowledge not possessed by the customer. The data center manager must determine how the data center can add value to the company and to the customers. In short, the data center manager must develop a reputation as a customer-oriented problem-solver who can make things happen rather than merely following the rules.

## Accept That Career Planning is a Personal Responsibility

To succeed today and build a strong foundation for a sucessful long-term career, data center managers must understand and accept that career planning is now their personal responsibility. Long-term relationships with companies are no longer the norm.

Today, professionals are usually hired to accomplish specific tasks for specific periods of time. However, an individual who develops a reputation as a highly skilled business professional with a strong technology background may enjoy a long-term career with a single company. To be successful, data center managers must accept the fact that they may be required to change jobs more often than in the past. The data center manager should give maximum effort while employed with a particular company. Building a reputation as a skilled professional who can be counted on will ensure positive references when it becomes necessary to look for another position. The new rules of the career planning game for data center managers are:

- Accept personal responsibility for career planning.
- Set career goals.
- Be aggressive in pursuing those goals.
- Be committed to the company and put forth maximum effort.
- Develop skills and expertise that can be used by other companies, should the need or the opportunity arise.
- Become skilled in basic business disciplines.
- Don't become dated as a systems professional. Be aware of and become proficient in new technologies.

1. Become knowledgeable of the company's business.
   —Meet with key department managers. Learn what they do, and what they need to do their jobs better.
   —Volunteer to serve on company study teams—even if they do not directly involve IS.
   —Take advanatage of any training the company offers to help employees understand what the company does and the industry it belongs to.
   —Attend seminars oriented toward the company's particular industry.
   —Understand the company's long-term goals and strategic business plans.
2. Thoroughly evaluate business skills.
   —Consider returning to college for additional business education.
   —Attend seminars and read books that will develop business skills.
   —In particular, develop strong skills in basic financial analysis, marketing, and oral and written communications.
   —Improve public speaking skills by taking courses or joining organizations that can help improve those skills.
3. Become knowledgeable of emerging technologies that can benefit the company.
4. Seek out a mentor in the company. Learn more about the business, the management structure, and the politics. Develop a reputation as a knowledgeable business person—not just a technician.
5. Develop a reputation as an innovator. Be flexible, adaptable, and willing to change. Avoid being perceived as a typical IS manager who is unwilling to change with the times.
6. Put customer needs first. Seek out customers and make sure the data center is meeting their needs. If not, find out why. Make changes. Add value. Develop a reputation for being a customer-oriented problem-solver who can make things happen.
7. Above all, recognize that career planning is a personal responsibility. Long-term relationships with companies are becoming rarer. Understand and accept that people change jobs more often than in the past. Put forth maximum effort, but be sure to develop skills and expertise that can be used by other companies should the need, or the opportunity, arise. Do not become dated.

**Exhibit VII-3-1. Career Planning Tips**

---

- Build a reputation as a highly motivated, customer-oriented, problem-solving change agent.

## SUMMARY

The current business environment is highly challenging. It has been said that the changes that are currently being experienced are equal in scope and impact to those that took place during the Industrial Revolution. Clearly, technology and systems are helping drive those changes. Thus, there will continue to be a significant role for skilled data center managers, provided they are able to make themselves truly valuable to their employer. Exhibit VII-3-1 summarizes the career planning actions discussed in this chapter. It can serve as a reminder of the areas that are most important for career-oriented data center managers. Success has never come easy. But for today's data center manager, it can be an even more elusive goal.

# VII-4
# Systems Change: Managing Resistance from Data Center Personnel

*FRANK COLLINS • GARY MANN*

W hen changing a system, most data center managers anticipate dealing extensively with technical issues. Experienced managers, however, have learned that staff and end-user support is also essential to a successful systems change. They accordingly anticipate three types of staff response: active resistance that prevents the change, passive resistance that causes the change to fail, and open support that leads to collaboration between management and staff in implementing the change.

Open support from staff and end users is critical to implementation of the change, and managers must often work hard to gain it. To win this support, even from employees who actively oppose the change, managers must understand and anticipate employees' reactions. This chapter examines resistance to systems change by looking at job-related and personality-related factors as well as the role of management. The chapter concludes with some strategies designed to ensure employee support.

## SYSTEMS CHANGE PHASES

Significant systems change requires a formal plan. One such plan is the systems development life cycle, which has three distinct phases: definition, development, and implementation. In the definition phase, IS management and staff identify needs, analyze the feasibility of the change, and evaluate possible solutions. In the development phase, a solution is designed and the hardware and software needed to implement the solution are acquired, developed, and tested. In the implementation phase, conversion and implementation activities take place. This last phase is often followed by post-implementation reviews.

During all phases, but especially during the definition and implementation phases, there is a high degree of interaction among users, systems development personnel, and IS management. The amount of interaction among personnel is higher during definition and implementation than during development because developmental activities are more technical. It is during the phases in which management, systems personnel, and systems users must interact that resistance to change arises.

## STAFF RESISTANCE TO CHANGE

The phenomenon of resistance to change is well documented, and many examples of passive and active resistance have been recorded. These types of resistance are discussed in the following paragraphs.

**Passive Resistance.** This type of resistance involves withholding support and assistance or allowing failure to occur when intervention would bring success. Examples of passive resistance include situations in which a department manager does not publicly and firmly indicate support for the change, a terminal operator calls in sick on the day of an important system test, or a supervisor fails to stop employees from entering improperly coded data.

**Active Resistance.** This form of resistance involves taking specific measures to ensure that the change will fail. Examples of active resistance include situations in which a supervisor urges staff members not to cooperate with development personnel, a clerk intentionally inputs erroneous data into the new system, or a department head repeatedly requests a restudy of the system design in the hope of delaying or even scuttling a systems change.

### Causes of Resistance to Change

Although the specific causes of resistance vary with the situation, there are six common causes of resistance to a system change:

- Belief that the changed system will not be as effective or efficient as the old system.
- Anxiety that the changed system will threaten the employees' job security (i.e., a fear of layoffs, pay cuts, or less-frequent raises and promotions).
- Fear that the job after the change will be dull and less fulfilling or that employees will lose status among their colleagues
- Concern that the changed system will be too complex to understand.
- Fear of unforeseeable consequences the change might bring
- Dread of extra work and strain that may be incurred by the changed system.

In addition to these six general causes, the autonomy of some workers may pose a special problem for the IS staff. Some organizations consist of discrete, organizational subunits whose members often exhibit strong group identification and values that may conflict with the values of other organizational units.

For example, an engineering group might regard development personnel as outsiders who do not understand the group's needs or goals and who may undermine the existence of the group. Managers must be aware that the type of resistance this group demonstrates is particularly difficult to overcome and requires considerable skill to remedy. The approaches for eliminating resistance to change listed in a following section of this chapter, however, can still be helpful. Development personnel must also realize that this type of resistance is apt to be stronger than other types. When faced with this type of situation, the development staff members must remember that the group has a strong psychological need for control and autonomy, and development personnel must respect the group's needs.

## RESISTANCE FROM MANAGERS

Resistance to change is often perceived as coming only from lower-level personnel. Organizational managers, however, sometimes feel threatened by change and accordingly offer resistance. Although the causes of resistance listed in a previous section apply equally to personnel at all organizational levels, the following additional factors may cause managerial resistance:

- Apprehension that the changed system might diminish or eliminate the manager's exclusive access to information.
- Fear that the changed system might reduce the manager's authority.
- Concern that the changed system might reduce the manager's decision-making prerogatives.
- Fear that the changed system might consume a significant portion of the manager's resources, thereby precluding other preferred uses of these resources.
- An overall desire to protect territory (e.g., position and responsibilities).

Because managers have greater authority and influence, and because their resistance may likely increase their employees' resistance, managerial resistance to change can compound even further the difficulty in accomplishing a successful systems change.

## JOB-RELATED FACTORS AFFECTING STAFF RESISTANCE

Six job-related factors influence the degree to which employees resist a system change, thereby affecting the success of the change. These factors are:

- *Management's role.* This factor involves the extent to which management understands its role, expends resources, listens to personnel affected by change, and convinces them that job security is not endangered.
- *Management support.* The extent to which employees believe that management has provided active and positive change support plays an important role in the implementation of a systems change.
- *Personal advancement.* The extent to which employees believe that the

change will enhance their job satisfaction, chances for promotion, and salary also influences a systems change.

- *Job situation.* Whether IS staff believe that the change will benefit the organization and that their work load will be reduced as they adjust to the change is another critical factor.
- *Input appreciation.* The change's success is determined in part by the extent to which those affected by the change feel that they possess helpful information and can communicate this information to management and IS personnel.
- *Change complexity.* The degree of frustration employees feel regarding technical problems associated with the change, their uncertainty regarding the change, or their belief that management does not understand its role is also crucial to the change's success.

The first two factors—management role and management support—are most influential in bringing out a successful system change and therefore are discussed in detail in the following section. The remaining factors are only moderately important.

One study revealed that when management understood its role in the systems change process (i.e., what management should do to assist the change effort) and, more important, actively supported the change, resistance was significantly lower than when management did not understand its role and was passive. This study also showed that if employees believed that the change would positively affect their job satisfaction, potential for promotion, and salary, their resistance abated. In addition, if staff believed that the change was important to the organization and that they were free to express their views, they also supported the change.

The study also revealed that if management did not understand its role and acted passively toward change, user resistance was strong. Staff members look to management for a cue on how to react to change. If management does not visibly support the change, employees interpret management's apparent lack of support as disinterest or disapproval.

Furthermore, if employees believed the change would negatively affect their job security, they resisted the change. They also resisted if they felt that the change was not in the best interests of the organization. Finally, a lack of adequate channels of communication among users, management, and data center and development personnel exacerbated resistance.

## MANAGEMENT LEADERSHIP AND SUPPORT

Active management leadership is crucial to the success of a system change. To ensure success, management must:

- Demonstrate strong support for the change.
- Be attuned to the needs of those affected by the change.

- Provide training and guidance to reduce change complexity.
- Allay fears regarding job security, advancement potential, and the effect of the new system on working relationships.

By taking these actions, management demonstrates that it understands its role and supports change, thereby enhancing the chances of a success. In some situations, however, IS personnel's fears about job security may be justified, because their positions will be displaced by the new system. Although it may be impossible to eliminate resistance in that case, sensitivity, candor, and effort on the part of management to find other job opportunities can minimize resistance.

## PERSONALITY-RELATED FACTORS AFFECTING RESISTANCE

Effective change management requires not only management's support and understanding of its role in the change process but its understanding of the personality factors that influence change. Two personality characteristics—locus of control and attitude toward ambiguity—determine how much employee resistance is influenced by job-related factors. These personality characteristics influence all personnel involved with a systems change and can increase or decrease resistance.

### Locus of Control

Locus of control refers to people's perceived ability to control their destiny and involves two types of personnel: the internal type and the external type. Internal types believe that they control their future (i.e., their locus of control is internalized). External types, on the other hand, believe that external forces over which they have no or little control determine their future (i.e., their locus of control is externalized).

Internal types might be concerned by a system change but are unlikely to be unreasonably fearful. These types might welcome the change as an opportunity to mold their own and their organization's future. Internal types would not be fearful about protecting their current positions and responsibilities, because they believe they control their future. Internal types can play a positive role in a systems change; they can be proponents of a beneficial change. Internal types will likely want to be partners in developing a new system, becoming disposed to share insights into the new system and to take risks to make the change successful. Internal types who oppose the systems change, however, will show unrelenting resistance and take risks to halt or defeat the change. Therefore, IS managers should diligently seek the support of internal types.

External types can also present problems; they will likely fear a systems change. Changing from existing procedures and routines is frightening to these individuals, because change reinforces the idea that their future is in the hands

| | Locus of Control | |
| --- | --- | --- |
| Intolerance of Ambiguity | High External | Low Internal |
| High Intolerance | Strong reaction, rush to judgment | Most fearful of change |
| Low Intolerance | Strong reaction, steady | Not as fearful as above, passive |

**Exhibit VII-4-1. Relationships Between Locus of Control and Intolerance of Ambiguity**

of others. In talking to others, they will most likely rationalize their resistance. For example, they will say they oppose the change because it will not benefit the company or will waste time and money. This rationalization, however, covers their fear about the change. Managers must be aware of the motives of external types.

## Attitudes Toward Ambiguity

Intolerance of ambiguity can also increase resistance to change. Some individuals are comfortable with a high degree of uncertainty, whereas others require regularity and certainty. This characteristic can be displayed by both internal and external types. Internal types who show great intolerance of ambiguity will quickly pass judgment and take action to reestablish certainty; they react strongly. External types who display intolerance of ambiguity, however, will freeze momentarily or, in extreme cases, become totally immobilized. They are unable to take action because they believe that they have little control over events and their situation is therefore uncertain.

Individuals who have a decidedly external locus of control and a high intolerance of ambiguity will be most negatively affected by a systems change. They are most likely to leave the organization or to be ineffective in implementing the change. Those with an external locus of control and low intolerance of ambiguity are likely to be fearful and passive. The problems this type of individual presents are examined in the following section. Exhibit VII-4-1 represents the relationship between locus of control and intolerance of ambiguity.

## STRATEGIES FOR COMBATING RESISTANCE

A successful strategy for handling user resistance requires some knowledge of the psychological reasons for resistance. Research shows that attempts to change a resistant attitude through coercion or through an authoritarian approach typically strengthen the resistance. Simply insisting on the change does not work.

The most effective approach is to dispel some of the reasons behind resistance (e.g., the employees' fears). Development and data center personnel and management at the appropriate levels should take the following actions to dispel or forestall resistant attitudes and to effect a positive response to a systems change:

- Discussing the proposed change with those affected by it.
- Identifying opinion leaders (i.e., individual users who have significant influence on group attitudes) and enlisting senior management support for the system change.
- Clearly communicating the reasons for the change and its possible effects and encouraging user participation.
- Assigning a member of the technical staff to the user group.
- Marketing the change to user groups.

These actions are discussed further in the following paragraphs.

**Discussing the Change.** Data center and IS managers should hold discussions with IS staff, the user group, and user department managers to gain an understanding of employees' and the managers' attitudes and opinions concerning the existing system and the proposed change. These discussions should continue throughout the change process so that managers can identify and anticipate possible resistance. Although managers are not trained psychologists, they should try to identify in users the personality-related factors examined in the previous section.

**Identifying Opinion Leaders.** Data center and IS managers should also use these discussions to find opinion leaders of the employees. Candidate opinion leaders can be admired supervisors, long-time employees, or personnel with respected skills. Obtaining the support of such leaders is equally as important to the success of the system change as gaining support from senior management.

**Communicating Clearly and Encouraging Employee Participation.** Open lines of communication regarding the system change can alleviate many employee fears and resistance, particularly with external types and those intolerant of ambiguity. Effective communication also enables employees to become involved in planning and implementing the systems change. By participating in the planning and implementation of the change, personnel can develop a commitment to the project. Personnel with a highly internal locus of control will especially welcome the opportunity to participate.

**Assigning a Technical Staff Member to the Employee Group.** An effective way to enhance communication is to assign a technical staff member to the group. This individual reports to the group manager, even if the assignment is temporary. Thus, the group has a technically proficient member who can communicate the group's opinions to the IS staff.

**Marketing the Change.** The data center and development managers and the technical staff should realize that a system change must be marketed to employees to gain the commitment needed for a successful change. Often, resistance to change is merely a reluctant attitude toward change, and marketing the change often overcomes this reluctance, When marketing the change, the managers can refer to the improved efficiency or effectiveness of the system as a result of the change. The marketing approach can be used effectively to address some of the causes of resistance to change (e.g., perceived threats to job security and fear of an excessive work load).

## ACTION PLAN

IS management and systems development personnel can take action during any phase of a system change. The sooner action is taken, however, the greater the chances to reduce resistance, because staff begin to form attitudes toward the change in its early stages. As the change process enters its final stages, managers should continue to monitor and manage resistance to change.

One method to encourage support for the change is to foster the idea that problems with the existing system are shared by both management and staff. Managers can also gain staff support by soliciting employee views; this strategy is most effective during the planning phase. The more staff and user views are reflected in the identification of the problem, the more likely it is that they will respond positively to the change. In addition, staff and users often have useful suggestion about the systems change.

In the design phase, problem definition is often treated as part of requirements identification. Problem definition deserves more attention, however, because it can play an important role in gaining staff acceptance and support. By treating problem identification as a separate step, employees have the opportunity to formally express their concerns about existing systems problems and their support for any solutions.

Support from all personnel involved in a systems change is critical to the change's success. Inadequate attention to the attitudes of all affected personnel can foster resistance to change. The approach for combating resistance presented in this chapter can encourage staff acceptance and cooperation. Data center managers must be aware that technical competence cannot substitute for the behavioral skills associated with systems change.

# VII-5
# Managing Technical Professionals in Dynamic Data Center Environments

*NATHAN J. MULLER*

N ew as well as established companies in virtually any industry know that continuing success depends largely on technical expertise and marketing savvy, a powerful combination for attracting new business, retaining satisfied customers, and increasing market share. Currently, IS professionals are beginning to appreciate the role of computer resources and data networks in sustaining corporate competitive advantage.

To reap the full advantages of technology, however, IS managers can no longer afford to rely solely on technical expertise to bring corporate projects to successful completion. Interpersonal communication skills are equally important because they facilitate the problem-solving process and contribute to the making of better decisions. Too many inexperienced and experienced managers overlook the importance of finely honed communication skills, preferring instead to get by on technical expertise, business acumen, and common sense.

## MEETING THE CHALLENGE WITH INTERPERSONAL SKILLS

Managers in today's dynamic technical environments must be concerned with interpersonal communication skills to avoid becoming part of their staff's problem. Technical professionals frequently begin to discuss one problem, which only makes them aware of another (e.g., the frustration of not being heard or of not being respected). Thus, they are sidetracked from the original topic. When staff members are weighed down with such problems, their desire to excel is diminished. This may impinge on personal as well as organizational performance.

Whether the manager holds responsibility for an IS and data processing shop, engineering group, or software house, a manager's inability to handle people problems can have disastrous consequences. Poor managerial communication skills can create problems that stifle initiative and creativity, delay projects, and increase staff turnover—all of which can drive up costs. If the situation is allowed to continue, long-term corporate objectives may even be jeopardized.

## THE MANAGER'S CRITERIA FOR GAUGING SUCCESS

Generally, staff members in the technical environment are reluctant to come to grips with interpersonal relations: human emotions do not lend themselves to neat, clear-cut rules, nor do they lend themselves to easy diagnoses, fault isolation, and remediation. Compared to such challenges as systems integration, applications programming, or interconnecting LANs, dealing with human emotions is often viewed as a messy business that managers would rather ignore than confront.

## NECESSARY SKILLS

Despite the seeming untidiness of interpersonal communication, the process can be broken down into discrete stages, each of which requires specific skills to support. This chapter presents a model for the interpersonal communication process against which managers can evaluate their present adeptness and gauge their likelihood of success in dealing with present and future interpersonal challenges.

### Structuring the Setting

Problems with personnel relations usually surface in one of two ways: they are revealed by poor performance (e.g., lateness, sloppiness, or errors) or brought to the data center manager for arbitration after staff members have exhausted all other resources or reached an impasse. In such cases, problem resolution requires private meetings with the people involved to properly and completely address all issues and viewpoints. Other occasions can call for highly developed interpersonal communication skills, such as in project development, which necessitates the cooperation of many individuals to implement a project on time and under budget.

**Atmosphere.** In problem-solving meetings, the first element that requires attention is the setting. Ideally, during the initial meeting most of the information should come from staff members. The manager's responsibility at this point is to listen and ask probing questions to prompt answers that can help clarify the issues. The manager should avoid jumping to conclusions, questioning actions or motives, belittling others, or casting blame. Such actions not only confuse the issues but create undercurrents of discontent that will be difficult to surmount later.

Because many people relate information in a casual, indirect way, the manager must engage in active listening, note taking, and requests for clarification. Only after relevant information has been gathered from the primary source or sources can it be developed and analyzed to develop an appropriate solution. To facilitate this process, the manager can structure the setting to put staff members at their ease about talking and to assure them that the problem is important.

Because the meeting is most likely to occur in the manager's own office, there are several ways to structure the setting. Face-to-face meetings obviously require setting aside sufficient time to develop a meaningful dialogue. Giving uninterrupted time conveys to others that they are important and that the problem is recognized as serious.

**Privacy.** Privacy is another element that helps structure the setting. Because a staff member may be divulging sensitive private information, the manager must indicate that the discussion will be treated as confidential. The person will not feel sufficiently crucial to the problem-solving process until assurances are offered that privacy will be protected. One way managers destroy their credibility is by dropping the names of other employees and discussing how they were able to help them with similar problems.

Although such remarks about others are merely intended to gain the confidence of the employee, this tactic usually backfires. The employee then wonders whether the present case will be used as an example to impress someone else. The manager should volunteer to keep information confidential and never use private information against that person at a later time—particularly in a performance review. Nothing destroys a manager's credibility faster or more effectively than a violation of privacy.

In addition to time and privacy, the manager should ensure that the physical setting supports the interpersonal communication process. Toward this end, the manager should work to reaffirm the personal nature of the meeting. Such things as maintaining appropriate physical distance, eye contact, and body attention encourage the free flow of information. They also reinforce the message that the meeting is taking place just for the employee.

### Managing the Process

It is not sufficient to simply structure the setting of the meeting to make employees or peers (or even superiors) feel at ease. The opportunity must be used for their benefit, not to fulfill the manager's own needs. When actions reflect the manager's own needs, the whole interpersonal communication process is undermined. The manager should never set the record straight or become preoccupied with establishing who is more technically competent. Above all, sarcastic remarks about others' circumstances, level of understanding, or lack of foresight should be avoided. Such statements convey the idea that the process is being controlled by the manager's ego needs rather than by organizational needs.

A manager who is in this type of situation (i.e., speaking sarcastically) should terminate the meeting immediately but politely. The manager should then analyze the situation and open up new opportunities for discussion later—but not too much later. In taking the initiative to continue the discussion, the manager will have demonstrated a sincere interest in gaining the acceptance and cooperation of the staff member. This will go a long way toward healing wounds and reestablishing credibility.

## Bridging Psychological Distance

Managing the interpersonal communication process involves bridging the inherent psychological distance that naturally exists between staff and management. The three qualities that help reduce that distance are comfort, rapport, and trust.

**Comfort.** A manager can increase the staff member's comfort level by making sure that the setting is a productive one. This can be reinforced with a cordial greeting and appropriate physical contact, such as a handshake. A skilled communicator also displays appropriate body attention, such as nodding in agreement while being asked a question. If not overly used, this gesture usually indicates the listener's interest.

**Rapport.** This quality presumes some level of comfort but goes deeper and usually encourages the continued exchange of information. Rapport may be easier to achieve by drawing on shared experiences (e.g., having gone to the same school, knowing the same people, or engaging in the same hobbies).

**Trust.** A third strategy for bridging psychological distance is the establishment of trust. From the employee's point of view, trust is a sense of belief in management's competence and integrity. It carries a deeper level of commitment than does mere rapport. In addition, if the employee suspects that he or she is being manipulated or has reason to doubt that the manager can be trusted, this may become yet another problem to surmount.

## A Closer Look at Bridging Skills

Nonverbal communication methods can be used like tools to achieve a variety of objectives, such as bridging psychological distance. Many facets of nonverbal communication are now widely recognized as a critical part of the total communication package.

**Body Language.** The manager who tells a staff member, "Go on, I'm listening," while writing, looking through files, or checking the time, presents the employee with physical behavior that contradicts the verbal message. When verbal and nonverbal messages are delivered at the same time but contradict each other, the listener usually believes the nonverbal message.

Certain actions are characteristic of positive body language: encouraging facial expressions and head movements, natural and continuous eye contact, open posture, leaning forward, and maintaining appropriate physical distance. All of these actions, when used skillfully, can be effective in clearing information bottlenecks. And although body language can be used to indicate intent listening, mental attention lets the employee know that all senses are being used to fully appreciate all parts of the message.

**Shades of Meaning.** The message's verbal component (i.e., the words) is the simplest and most direct aspect of the message. The words themselves, however, may not convey the whole message. The simple statement, "I'm tired of hearing excuses from programming," might indicate despair, frustration, or anger. Here, the way the statement is presented becomes the message's critical element.

Verbal packaging can be thought of as the message's emotional content, which can be determined by observing how fast or loud someone speaks and by listening for tone of voice. Virtually everything about people, including their competence, integrity, and well-being, is wrapped in these emotional components.

The message's nonverbal components are particularly useful in sessions with staff members because they provide real-time feedback that can be brought to bear on solving problems and making decisions. Through the use of nonverbal signals, the psychological distance between manager and staff member can be bridged. Greeting staff with a tense jaw, clenched fists, slumped shoulders, or shifty eyes sends subtle messages that employees will interpret as a warning to stay away. When improving interpersonal communication skills, managers must pay attention to the whole message, integrating its verbal components, verbal packaging, and nonverbal components into the composite approach.

**Respect.** Everything that the manager does to show interest in problem solving demonstrates respect for staff members. Respect begins by structuring a meeting's setting so that staff members know instantly that they are at the center of the problem-solving process. Without respect, there is little chance that anyone will want to continue the meeting—much less offer helpful information and participate in possible solutions that may improve individual or group performance.

The manager is responsible for drawing out answers and helping people to speak freely. The meeting can begin with such statements as "Where would you like to start?" or "How can I assist you?" These are straightforward invitations to talk. However, there is a danger in these otherwise valuable comments, especially when they are coupled with inane remarks like, "After all, that's what I'm here for," "That's what I'm paid for," or "It's your nickel." This type of comment merely serves to widen the psychological gap. Until the psychological gap is bridged, solutions to problems will take longer, which may delay the successful completion of projects and inflate costs. And if such problems persist, the manager can lose credibility among senior management, perhaps giving them reason to reevaluate the manager's ability to handle the job.

**Acknowledgment.** The manager should seek opportunities to acknowledge what others are saying. This provides a clear indication that they are being understood and that they should continue speaking. Acknowledgment signals can be as simple as nodding in agreement. But nodding or otherwise indicating agreement can be overused. Continually bobbing the head, for example, eventually loses its impact and can even undermine the manager's credibility.

Managers should employ bridging skills during problem-solving sessions, especially when counseling individuals on performance-related matters. Such skills are important for enlisting the confidence and cooperation of staff, who may not forgive affronts to their intelligence, skills, knowledge, status, or abilities.

### Integrating the Information

A separate step in the interpersonal communication process is integration. Here, the employee continues to talk about his or her needs with the encouragement and shared insights of the manager. During this exchange, the manager must not only bridge psychological distance but encourage and stimulate the disclosure of more and more information until the employee gains new insights into the nature of the problem at hand. The following sections discuss six skills managers should master to help staff members arrive at this point.

**Reflection.** This is a response that lets others know they are being heard. Unlike mere acknowledgment, which is passive, reflection is an active process that helps the employee focus on areas that require further exploration. For example, a rustrated IS supervisor might talk about rapid personnel turnover within the group, holding the turnover rate responsible for low morale and missed deadlines on even routine equipment move and change requests. A skilled manager can use reflection to focus on an unstated problem, as in the following scenario:

> IS Supervisor: "I have so many problems with my staff, so much turnover. Now you give me responsibility for processing half a million call records per month to account for telecommunications costs."
>
> Manager: "You're struggling to improve your operations, but you feel that taking on the additional burden of call accounting at this time may hamper your efforts?"

The manager should employ this strategy when it can help others examine certain aspects of a problem in more depth. Whether the staff member acknowledges the manager with an appreciative "Yes" or merely a nod and then continues, this is an unmistakable sign that the strategy of reflection has worked effectively.

**Self Disclosure.** By using self disclosure, the manager encourages the speaker by interjecting a relevant comment that indicates that the manager has run into a similar problem before. If appropriate, the manager can even relate the solution. There are pitfalls of this technique, however. One is the tendency to monopolize valuable time; the other is the tendency to change the subject.

Some managers are reluctant to use self disclosure because it deals with immediate feelings and issues generated during face-to-face meetings. They may fear provoking or embarrassing others or appearing intimidating, or they may feel unable to confidently propose an appropriate course of action. Other managers resist self disclosure because they fear it will be interpreted as a sign of weakness. Notwithstanding these peripheral issues, self disclosure reminds the employee that the manager is also a human being with a wide range of experience, which is what makes problem-solving possible.

Self disclosure should be used with discretion, however. Its injudicious use could interrupt the session by drawing too much attention to the manager. Listeners may interpret this as self-centeredness. Managers who engage in this behavior are not only wasting organizational resources and widening the psychological gap but adding to the employee's problem.

**Immediacy.** This technique addresses unconstructive behavior that some staff members may display among themselves or to others. The way to handle immediacy can determine the outcome of an important project. For example, a key staff member may appear anxious about the company's use of an outside consultant, interpreting this as a lack of confidence in the employee. If unaddressed, those feelings can undermine the consultant's efforts, hampering the consultant's ability to obtain important information and staff participation.

Managers should not let such problems fester for long. At the most opportune time, the manager must defuse this time bomb, perhaps by opening up lines of communication, asking whether the employee is bothered because a consultant is looking into matters for which the employee feels responsible.

Some employees have the tendency to ramble on aimlessly. The manager can use the skill of immediacy to help such people zero in on the problem. An appropriate remedy could come from the manager's making a statement like, "Tom, I'm feeling a bit confused right now. We seem to be covering a lot of ground, but not getting down to the real problem."

As with self disclosure, the skill of immediacy must be used carefully. Any hint of cleverness or of adopting a superior attitude could negate whatever benefits the strategy was intended to achieve.

**Probing.** This method refers to the exploration of some area or issue that the employee has stated directly. It can help a manager develop key points, define problems more completely, or identify patterns in nonconstructive thinking.

The manager should listen carefully for any hints that the employee might drop during the conversation. These can provide a clue to the employee's reason for discontent. Upon hearing such hints (e.g., an indicaton that a procedure is not working well or that there are interpersonal problems within the group), the manager should follow these leads with probing questions to help the employee uncover the source of the problem.

**Checking.** The manager can use this technique to structure responses that serve to confirm what the staff member has said. This method verifies that the manager has been listening attentively. For example, the manager might say, "It seems to me that you have identified at least three network configurations worth looking into," and then repeat what the staff member had suggested.

**Confrontation.** Unlike probing, confrontation deals with information that the employee has only hinted at, not directly stated. Using confrontation, however, assumes that a satisfactory relationship has already been established. A manager should start with the least difficult or threatening point and move to the more difficult or threatening subject. To be effective, confrontation must be tentative yet specific. Phrases that convey tentativeness include: "I wonder if . . ." and "Could we talk about . . . ?"

The staff member should know that confrontation has taken place but should not feel besieged or attacked. A sign that confrontation has not registered is when the staff member ignores the statement or becomes defensive.

Confrontation can serve many purposes. It can help the manager and staff member approach the problem from a different perspective or help to uncover possible consequences that were previously overlooked. It also aids in revealing a fundamental need or an underlying problem. It may even help a staff member admit to a statement or feeling. For example, the person who felt threatened by the presence of a consultant may say, "Some of the employees are really going to be turned off by your vendor recommendation." The manager should be skilled in the use of confrontation, perhaps responding in this manner: "Bill, it would help me a lot if I knew you were describing your own feelings. Do you know something about this vendor that should be taken into account by the consultant?"

## Support

In the support phase of the interpersonal communication process, managers must help define problems, deal with problem ownership, and develop action plans.

**Problem Definition.** During this phase, the manager works with staff members to develop statements that accurately describe the problems they intend to address. After appropriate discussions and research, the manager should test the best course of action, through statements and restatements, until problems are specific and realistic. The manager should also make sure that staff members can participate in solving the problem and that the manager has the appropriate experience, skill level, and resources to implement the action plan.

An effective action plan cannot be developed until specific problem statements have been made. This can be a difficult skill for some managers to master, particularly for those who are accustomed to acting on imprecise statements. "This is a lousy computer," "I'm hearing bad things about John's programming abilities," and "I can't see myself committing to that network design" are unclear statements that beg for clarification. By themselves, they can never be translated into specific action plans that employees can accept. In the end, the proposed solutions cannot address the problem accurately.

In helping others define the problem, managers must deftly steer the conversation to progress from the general to the specific, as in the following statements (general to specific) made by an IS supervisor:

- "I don't like the idea of having responsibility for the corporate network."
- "I don't have time for that sort of thing."
- "My staff is specialized and dedicated to other priorities."
- "I don't know anything about networking; this assignment is an invitation to fail so they can get rid of me."

Until the manager can arrive at the crux of the problem—in this case, personal survival within a changing organization—any advice, on the basis of an incompletely informed understanding of the problem, will probably be inadequate. By moving toward specific problem statements, the manager can better understand the problem's fundamental nature and scope so that the real issues may be effectively addressed.

**Problem Ownership.** This stage is a prerequisite to developing action plans, achieved through a common search for solutions. The manager can encourage staff to take some responsibility for problems by including both staff and management in the solutions presented.

Staff members will assume problem ownership as they work with management to develop problem statements. After those statements have been worked out and are accepted, both parties can turn the statements into goals, then agree on a strategy for reaching them.

**Action Plan Development.** There are a variety of methods for developing action plans, but the minimum steps include the following:

- The manager should list several possible solutions, in order of priority.

- Involved staff members should reach a consensus on the alternatives that appear the most acceptable to the organization in terms of needs, budget, and personnel resources.
- The employees should agree on a fallback position in case the preferred solution proves unworkable.
- Specific tasks should be assigned to the individuals best qualified to carry them out.
- The manager and staff should develop and agree on milestones, with time frames for completion.
- Follow-up meetings should be planned to monitor employees' satisfaction with progress and to make appropriate refinements in the action plan, as new knowledge becomes available or as developments in the implementation warrant.

### Phasing Out

Having arrived at a solution with relevant input from staff members, the manager must initiate a phasing-out process that weans employees from ongoing dependence. Two skills are involved in this phase: centering and appreciation.

**Centering.** The manager uses centering to identify and comment positively about staff members' strengths, especially those displayed in productive meetings. This is not public relations gimmickry; rather, it is an attempt to help the staff feel more secure and confident about implementing the action plan. This confidence is especially important in cases in which the results will not be visible immediately. Employee strengths that deserve mention include candor, analytical skills, commitment to problem solving, and progress toward the most appropriate solution.

**Demonstrating Appreciation.** Other staff members may have played an important role in the problem-solving process by choice or by chance. A final skill in the phasing-out process is the manager's expression of appreciation to each staff member for the time and effort put into the sessions.

Why should managers care about these skills, or even about the phasing-out in general? Quite simply, the manager's behavior at the conclusion of a project will determine the likely level of staff support in future projects. If, for example, the manager does not acknowledge the contributions of staff in finding a solution, the staff members will be less likely to lend their cooperation in the future. It is simply human nature to want credit for one's efforts. Nothing is more demoralizing to staff members than to watch others repackage their ideas for senior management's consumption and receive undeserved credit. Over the long term, such behavior diminishes credibility with staff, peers, and superiors.

When interacting with technical professionals, managers should be aware that having the skills necessary to deal with people problems are equally as important as having the skills needed to address technical issues. Recognizing the skills crucial to effective interpersonal communication will lessen the risk of making wrong decisions, which can cause staff turmoil, missed project deadlines, and cost overruns.

## SUMMARY

Handling the elements of effective interpersonal communication is not easy. Unfortunately, it does not come naturally to most managers. Complicating the situation are differences in culture, background, experience, training, and many other intervening variables. Nevertheless, managers have a responsibility to develop skills that facilitate rather than hinder interpersonal communication, using them as tools with which to improve problem solving and decision making.

Each manager's style is necessarily unique. Moreover, style must be adjusted to the demands of particular situations. Interactions with subordinates, peers, superiors and external constituents call for slight adjustments in style and technique. Whatever the personal style, messages must be relevant, congruent, and comprehensible. After all, managers occupy a unique position in the organizational hierarchy. In a technical environment staffed with highly educated professionals, a manager's credibility is a crucial asset. Credibility can be enhanced and overall performance improved when managers set the example as clear, direct, and honest communicators.

# VII-6
# Increasing Productivity and Job Satisfaction by Motivating Employees

*JAMES C. WETHERBE • MEAD BOND WETHERBE, JR.*

T he question of how to motivate staff members remains one of the most challenging issues managers face. Because data center managers often are promoted into management from technical positions, they may not be prepared to deal with such perplexing, ill-defined issues as motivating staff.

This chapter first extracts from leading motivational theory some practical motivational guidelines for the data center manager. Second, it presents an effective and efficient method of identifying motivational issues for individual employees. Finally, it proposes strategies for administering and scheduling these factors as consequences of employee performance.

## DRAWING FROM THE BEST OF MOTIVATIONAL THEORIES

The most highly regarded motivational theories developed during the past 50 years include Maslow's need hierarchy, reinforcement, attribution theory, Herzberg's dual-factor theory, expectancy theory, and goal setting. Only the essential points of each of these theories are reviewed; the sequence of discussion is based on progression of thought rather than chronological order.

### Need Hierarchy

A.G. Maslow contended that individuals are motivated to satisfy the following set of needs:

- Basic physiological needs.
- Safety and security.
- Social activity.
- Esteem and status.
- Self-actualization.

Individuals fulfill these needs sequentially, starting with physiological needs and ascending up the hierarchy to self-actualization. As a need becomes satisfied, it loses effectiveness as a motivator.

The major contribution of Maslow's theory is the notion that motivation is achieved by identifying the needs of an employee and linking the satisfaction of those needs to the performance desired by the manager. For example, if an employee has a need for esteem, a manager could communicate that satisfactory performance on a project will result in recognition and visibility within the organization, thereby enhancing the employee's opinion of self-worth.

### Dual-Factor Theory

F. Herzberg proposed a motivational theory based on dual factors that concern employees—hygiene and motivational factors. Hygiene (or maintenance) factors are associated with company policy and administration, working conditions, salary, interpersonal relations, personal life, job security, and status. The absence of these factors results in dissatisfaction, whereas their presence results in no dissatisfaction. In either case, they are not considered useful motivators. By contrast, motivational factors are associated with the work itself, achievement, growth, responsibility, and recognition. The presence of these factors provides motivation.

Although Herzberg's theory has its weaknesses, aspects of it are useful. In particular, job enrichment, advancement, achievement, recognition, growth on the job, and responsibility are useful concepts for positively motivating employees. However, the natures and needs of different employees and jobs must be considered. Depending on the situation, strategies such as job enrichment may be ineffective.

### Goal Setting

E.A. Locke proposed a model of task motivation based on the premise that an employee's conscious attention to goals is the primary determinant of motivation. This theory, called goal setting, also asserts that difficult goals result in greater effort than generalized goals or a lack of goals.

Research supports this proposition, with one qualification. For difficult gols to be effective motivators, they must be accepted by the employees as being realistic and worthwhile. Employee participation in goal setting facilitates acceptance of goals; however, there is no conclusive evidence that performance improves through participatory goal setting.

### Reinforcement

According to B.F. Skinner and others in the area of reinforcement (or behavior modification) theory, behavior is a result of consequences. The behavior an employee chooses is influenced by the consequences or perceived consequences of the behavior. An employee learns through experience what behavior results in which consequences. Therefore, the manager must administer consequences in a manner that elicits the desired behavior from employees.

For example, a systems analyst who is behind schedule on a project can choose either to allow the project to be late or to work overtime to complete the project on schedule. If completing a project on schedule is reinforced, that behavior is motivated and more likely to recur. If meeting or not meeting a project deadline goes unnoticed (i.e., either behavior results in the same consequences), there is little organization-based motivation to complete the project on schedule, even though the employee may be internally motivated (e.g., from pride or a sense of responsibility) to complete the project on schedule anyway.

There are four basic reinforcement strategies:

- *Positive reinforcement.* The manager presents a desirable consequence following particular employee behavior, causing an increase in the occurrence of that behavior.
- *Negative reinforcement.* The manager withdraws an undesirable consequence following particular employee behavior, causing an increase in the occurrence of that behavior.
- *Punishment.* The manager presents an undesirable consequence following particular employee behavior, causing a decrease in the occurrence of that behavior.
- *Extinction.* The manager withholds a desirable consequence from an employee following particular behavior, causing a decrease in the occurrence of that behavior.

Reinforcement theory raises some concerns about manipulating people; however, it can be useful to managers attempting to motivate employees. An operational problem with reinforcement theory is the difficulty in determining exactly what reinforces behavior in different employees. Often managers make incorrect assumptions and can actually punish an employee when attempting to provide positive reinforcement. Promoting someone into management who really prefers technical tasks is an example of incorrect application of this strategy. For reinforcement strategies to work, a manager must assess what reinforces behavior in different employees and administer consequences accordingly.

## Expectancy

V. Vroom's expectancy theory of motivation is based on the concepts of valence (i.e., the effective orientation toward particular outcomes, both positive and negative), expectancy (i.e., employees' view of the risk or probability of their performing a task and belief that it will be followed by a particular outcome), and force (i.e., the combined effect of valence and expectancy that directs the employee to engage in certain behavior).

|  | Internal | External |
|---|---|---|
| **Stable** | Ability | Task Difficulty |
| **Unstable** | Effort | Luck |

**Exhibit VII-6-1. Classification of Success Factors**

Expectancy theory provides one of the better frameworks for analyzing and understanding motivation. To address valence, the manager needs to identify outcomes that are valued by the employee. To address expectancy, the manager needs to focus on two issues. First, the manager must ensure that the employee is able to perform as required. To accomplish this, the employee may need training, assistance, or more self-confidence, for example. Second, the employee must believe that if he or she performs as required, the desired outcome will be forthcoming. To accomplish this, the manager must closely link performance to outcome, possibly through incentive plans, merit raises, promotion, praise, or better communication.

### Attribution Theory

Attribution theory involves what F. Heider originally termed a "naive psychology" and describes how the average individual explains (attributes) causes of events. This approach is less stimulus-response oriented than reinforcement theory and therefore has a more human orientation.

An individual may believe that events were caused by factors under control of the environment or under control of a person. Exhibit VII-6-1 illustrates how four important factors for success may be classified according to two dimensions. For example, a developer describes a successful systems implementation as a job well done (implying internal attributions), but users may attribute the success to other factors. If past performance has been stable, the developer perceives his or her own ability to be the reason for success. The users may believe that the task is simply not difficult. If there was previously wide variation in success, the developer may feel that effort explains current success, whereas the users may attribute success to luck.

For the data center, casual inferences may have impact on motivation. If an individual considers luck or task difficulty to be a major success factor, levels of effort may be undesirably low. Experiments that specifically address IS issues are needed for proper applications of the theory.

## PRACTICAL GUIDELINES

Though each of the preceding theories takes a somewhat different view of motivation, some general guidelines can be extracted from each for the manager's practical use. Specifically, the following guidelines emerge:

- Efforts to increase motivation must first focus on the employee's needs.
- Work assignments and goals should be realistic and clearly defined; rewards for performance should be practical and should fulfill the motivational needs of the employee. Employees must be competent to do the work required and must believe that their needs will be reasonably fulfilled by the work and the rewards of having done the work well.
- Consequences or outcomes of good performance must approximate the expectations of the employee.

These guidelines are simple enough to understand but extremely difficult to apply effectively and efficiently. The reasons: First, employees' needs are difficult to define because they vary among employees and change over time. Frequently, employees are not even sure themselves what they want from their work experience. Second, management is often negligent in clearly defining for employees what is expected of them, or managers are not responsive to employee needs when employees are responsive to organizational demands.

The issues of identifying employee needs and effectively using them as motivators are addressed in the next two sections. First, a method for identifying employee needs is presented; subsequently, strategies for effectively administering consequences or outcomes are discussed.

## IDENTIFYING EMPLOYEE NEEDS

When it comes to assessing employee needs, it is a case of different strokes for different folks; in fact, it is different strokes at different times for each individual. In assessing the needs of a particular employee, a manager must be careful and specific. Statistics on what in general motivates a category of employees may be irrelevant to particular employees. For example, on the average most programmers would be motivated by an opportunity to work with new technology. However, a programmer who is lacking confidence may see such an opportunity as a threat to his or her job security.

### Progressive Binary Sort

The progressive binary sort is a method of assessing the preferences of individuals. Incorporated into the motivation strategy for business professionals, this technique provides a fairly reliable indication of both current and future personnel needs, and it has been used successfully in a wide range of applications, including personnel analysis in high-technology professions.

The progressive binary sort is a comparative rating method in which individuals are required to rank available alternatives. This ranking is usually conducted within preference levels ranging from extremely desirable to extremely undesirable. The number of preference levels and the number of alternatives that are allowed to be included in a preference level are design decisions regarding the specific application.

## Motivational Categories and Statements

Fifty statements representing job-related motivation factors are provided for the sort process, 5 within each of 10 major motivation categories (see Exhibit VII-6-2). Each category represents a potential area of motivation. The specific alternative statements within each category are based on pilot studies conducted by the authors.

For each of the 10 motivational categories there are 3 positive statements and 2 negative statements. The use of both positive and negative statements provides a balanced perspective for each motivational category. The use of one more positive than negative statement provides a slightly positive bias, which is appropriate for this type of sort because many respondents will be indifferent about some positive statements.

Individuals' comparative evaluations of alternatives change over time. For example, an employee may view a promotion into management as undesirable today but may desire it three years from now. In designing a motivational strategy for an employee, the manager needs to know current as well as forecasted needs and aspirations of an employee. To compensate for the time factor, respondents conduct three sorts. The first sort represents current attitudes. The second and third sorts reflect attitudes as projected into the future—one and three years, respectively.

## MOTIVATION PROFILES

MOTIVATOR is an interactive, computer-based system designed by the authors to generate individual motivation profiles based on the normal distribution pattern derived from the progressive binary sort process. Designed to operate on an IBM or compatible microcomputer, the system allows an individual to interactively sort job-related motivation factor statements, then immediately review summary information of the resulting motivation profile. The system is also capable of analyzing the distribution of a cluster of statements related to specific motivational category, further enhancing the user's understanding of the individual profile.

Exhibit VII-6-3a is an example of the list of 10 motivational categories ranked according to an individual's preference. The graph in Exhibit VII-6-3b better illustrates the relative differences between the motivation categories considered most important in the example.

The tool calculates a composite value for each motivation category based on the relative position (preference level) of the 5 related motivation factor statements. Greater significance is attributed to the positively oriented statements on the basis of a higher order of preference, and to the negatively oriented statements on the basis of a lower order of preference. Thus, the motivation category that is most significant has the highest composite value of the 5 statements related to that category. A comparison of the relative value of each category indicates an individual motivational profile for each employee.

### Achievement

Successful completion of a major project.
Mastery of a new, difficult skill.
Completion of project made possible by the employee's contribution.
Inability to complete work assignment.
Marginal performance record.

### Responsibility

Freedom to plan own work.
Responsibility for critical project.
Autonomous work environment.
Little latitude allowed to make own decisions.
Subordinate role in work assignment.

### Advancement

Promotion within technical or administrative ranks.
Lateral move for opportunity for promotion.
Assigned management position over current peer group.
Present position maintained.
Demotion accepted to remain employed.

### Recognition

Assignment to a project that has high visibility.
Considered highly capable by organization.
Considered an expert in an area of specialty.
Contributions to project unnoticed by management.
Lack of recognition by coworkers.

### Work Itself

Interesting work assignment.
Self-satisfying work.
State-of-the-art work activity.
Routine, repetitive tasks.
Work that is not difficult or challenging.

### Compensation

Increase in salary (15% of base wage).
Higher wage maintained than for members of peer group.
Pay scale upgraded for employee's current position.
Reduction in pay to remain employed.
Across-the-board wage freeze.

### Leisure Time

Four 10-hour days per week.
Time off after completing a major project on schedule.
Provision for time off without pay.
Overtime required to complete project.
Vacation time decreased (one week less).

### Working Conditions

Clean working conditions.
Comfortable room temperature.
Modern office furnishings.
Unavailability of office supplies.
Noisy work environment.

**Exhibit VII-6-2. Motivational Categories and Related Statements**

**Management and Organizational Policy**

Management provides effective leadership for the organization.
Inflexible organization policy.
Well-defined policies and procedures in organization.
Opportunity to interact with management personnel on a regular basis.
Partiality exhibited by management.

**Work Relationships**

Being a team player, willingness to do what's best for the team.
Team member relationships strained.
Associate and network with key people in organization.
Work with friendly and cooperative coworkers.
Work alone with little dependency on others to complete work.

**Exhibit VII-6-2.** *(continued)*

Individual profiles can then be combined to develop composite profiles for departments and job classifications. The composite can be used to analyze groups of employees so that a specific employee's motivational profile can be compared with the overall profile of one or more groups.

### Interpreting Motivation Profiles

The motivation profile is instructive to both the employee and the manager. The comparative ranking process puts into perspective the incentives that may be available to an employee. For example, few employees would not like a 15% increase in salary, but for some people a 15% salary increase may be a second choice to an interesting work assignment. This information is helpful to the employee's manager when a 15% salary increase may not be possible but an interesting work assignment is. Accordingly, the manager has at least one incentive to offer that is valued by the employee. To systematically interpret and evaluate an employee's motivation profile the manager can take several steps.

**Step One.** The manager can review the ranking of statements, focusing on the statements ranked in the desirable and undesirable ends of the distribution pattern. These are the items that are most important to the employee.

**Step Two.** Managers can discuss the rankings with the employee to determine how the employee relates the statements to his or her situation. For example, if an employee has ranked "freedom to plan own work" as extremely desirable, the manager needs to know what specifically that statement means to the employee and whether or not that need is fulfilled by the current work situation. If the work situation does not fulfill this need, the manager must ask the employee what changes are required in the work situation to allow the employee adequate freedom to plan his or her own work. (For negative statements, the manager must modify questions to see whether the employee was

| **Motivation Category Description** | **Comparative Ranking** |
|---|---|
| A   ADVANCEMENT | 7.0 |
| B   ACHIEVEMENT | 6.0 |
| C   RECOGNITION | 5.0 |
| D   ORGANIZATION POLICY | 4.5 |
| E   RESPONSIBILITY | 4.5 |
| F   MANAGEMENT RELATIONS | 3.5 |
| G   WORKING CONDITIONS | 3.5 |
| H   WORK ITSELF | 3.5 |
| I    WAGE LEVEL | 2.5 |
| J   LEISURE TIME | 1.0 |

Getting a promotion or at least being in a position where promotion potential exists.

Your distribution of the 50 statements conforms to general expectations. Press the F7 KEY for further explanation.

The Comparative Ranking value generally ranges between 1 and 10 based on the distribution of statements related to each Motivation Category. However, a negative ranking value is possible and will be indicated as such.

**a. Comparative Ranking List**

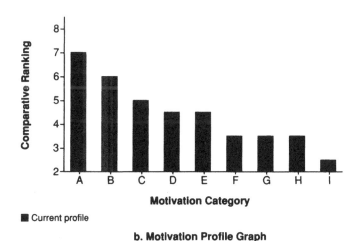

**b. Motivation Profile Graph**

**Exhibit VII-6-3. Individual Motivation Profile**

599

dissatisfied about a statement and under what conditions that dissatisfaction could be resolved.)

**Step Three.** After the evaluation of the current motivation profile is complete, steps 1 and 2 are repeated for the sorts that represent employee attitudes as projected into the future. Questions asked of employees in step 2 are modified to a future time frame (e.g., "What type of advancement into administrative ranks is the employee looking for in three years?"). For example, an employee with a technical degree who wants to move into management in three years may be advised to pursue an MBA degree on a part-time basis.

### Examining Incentive and Rewards Alternatives

This type of discussion gives the manager insight into what an employee wants from the job and provides the framework for developing a relevant incentive system and career path planning strategy for the employee. The manager can then begin to communicate what is required of the employee to maintain fulfillment (if a need is currently fulfilled) or achieve fulfillment (if a need is not fulfilled). The manager can also discuss how to avoid the outcomes the employee considers to be undesirable. The result is better understanding and communication, more realistic expectations, and a fairly reliable indication of incentives that motivate an employee.

An analysis can also be made comparing an employee's profile with the group profile or an employee's profile with a profile of that employee as perceived by the manager. These comparisons can help the manager devise more effective incentive and reward programs. Exhibit VII-6-4a compares the motivation category lists of a manager's perceived profile of an employee (left column) with the employee's actual profile (right column). Exhibit VII-6-4b is a graphic representation of the same comparison. The solid bar indicates the manager's perceived profile and that patterned bar indicates the employee's actual profile.

## ADMINISTERING CONSEQUENCES

The use of MOTIVATOR can facilitate the difficult task of identifying and assessing relevant motivational issues for an employee. Once these issues have been defined, the next step is to properly convey to employees the organizational requirements that must be fulfilled if they are to have their motivational needs fulfilled. Then, rewards for good performance must be effectively administered. Methods for conveying requirements and administering consequences are discussed following a review of positive and negative control strategies.

### Positive Versus Negative Control

An individual's motivation profile can be used to determine the basic reinforcers of behavior through positive and negative control strategies. The statements

| | Motivation Category<br>Description | Comparative<br>Rankings | |
|---|---|---|---|
| A | ADVANCEMENT | 7.0 | 10.0 |
| B | ACHIEVEMENT | 5.0 | 6.0 |
| C | RECOGNITION | 5.0 | 3.0 |
| D | ORGANIZATION POLICY | 6.0 | 7.0 |
| E | RESPONSIBILITY | 5.0 | 7.0 |
| F | MANAGEMENT RELATIONS | 5.0 | 3.0 |
| G | WORKING CONDITIONS | 2.0 | 1.0 |
| H | WORK ITSELF | 3.0 | 3.0 |
| I | WAGE LEVEL | 4.0 | 4.0 |
| J | LEISURE TIME | 3.0 | 3.0 |

Your distribution of the
50 statements conforms
to general expectations.
Press the F7 KEY for
further explanation.

The Comparative Ranking value
generally ranges between 1 and 10
based on the distribution of statements
related to each Motivation Category.
However, a negative ranking value is
possible and will be indicated as such.

**a. Motivation Profile Comparison List**

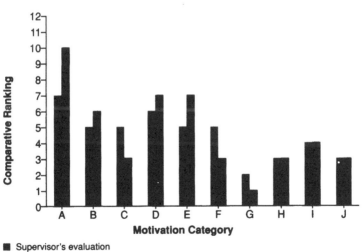

Supervisor's evaluation
Employee's self-evaluation

**b. Motivation Profile Comparison Graph**

**Exhibit VII-6-4. Comparison of Supervisor's Evaluation with Employee's Self-Evaluation**

ranked as desirable in an employee's profile provide a repertoire of positive reinforcements for a manager to use as incentives for an employee. The statements ranked as undesirable in an employee's motivation profile offer alternatives for negative reinforcement and punishment.

Although negative control can influence employee behavior, it often has undesirable side effects. Perhaps the most common is that an employee develops fear of or resentment toward a manager who frequently presents undesirable consequences. Employees avoid that manager. Negative control also tends to elicit dysfunctional emotional behavior, such as anger and a desire for revenge.

Positive control is virtually without undesirable side effects. Because positive control provides employees with desirable consequences, the manager is usually regarded cordially. Employees tend to do what is requested of them, and dysfunctional emotional behavior is not provoked.

To administer positive control, an employee must first exhibit desirable behavior. A manager must wait for desirable behavior to occur before it can be reinforced. Time and patience are required.

Though positive reinforcement is generally considered more effective and desirable, managers employ negative control strategies for several reasons. First, negative control is closely aligned with traditional values (e.g., the "eye for an eye" philosophy). Second, negative control is often satisfying to the manager applying it (i.e., a manager's frustrations are relieved by taking them out on a subordinate who has performed poorly). Third, negative control tactics require less effort and creativity (i.e., it is easier to punish an employee for undesirable behavior than to develop a positive control strategy). Finally, negative control can be applied more quickly than positive control. For example, when employees make mistakes, they can be punished immediately. In certain situations, as in the case of security violations or reckless behavior that endangers the safety of other employees, a manager may not be able to wait to apply negative control.

When positive control strategies require too much time or are not achieving desired results, negative control must be used. Negative control can be combined with positive control to minimize undesirable side effects. If programmers are punished for not completing a project on time, they can quickly be given another project to rectify the situation. If the programmers complete this next project on schedule, positive reinforcement is provided. The information provided from an individual motivation profile provides several alternatives for selecting an appropriate reinforcement for the situation. When employees are subjected to any negative control tactic, they should be immediately provided with an opportunity to obtain positive reinforcement.

## CONVEYING ORGANIZATIONAL REQUIREMENTS: THREE STRATEGIES

Managers must properly inform employees of what is expected of them in order to obtain desired outcomes. Failure to do so can result in frustration, confusion, and poor performance from employees. There are three straightfor-ward strategies for conveying performance requirements: communication, imi-tation, and shaping. Each strategy can be used with positive control or negative control.

## Communication

Communication is the most straightforward positive control strategy. It consists of clearly articulating to an employee, preferably at the beginning of a work relationship, what the expectations are for the employee's performance. If the employee adopts the desired behavior, the employee should be provided with positive reinforcement.

In spite of the simplicity of this approach, managers frequently fail to capitalize on it. Managers are often too busy or are simply negligent about providing necessary reinforcement, and this is unfortunate. Employees can be impressionable, especially when a new work relationship is being developed. If a manager fails to systematically reinforce an employee for desired behavior, the frequency of that behavior will decrease unless it is reinforced by some other means.

If a programmer meets several demanding programming deadlines that were requested by the manager, and the manager fails to recognize (i.e., to otherwise reinforce) the programmer's efforts, the programmer may assume that the manager is not sincere about the importance of meeting deadlines. Therefore, the programmer may decide not to be as concerned or as punctual about future deadlines. The manager would then have to use negative control strategies to change the programmer's behavior.

In short, the manager would miss the opportunity to use a more effective and efficient positive control strategy. The programmer would be disappointed for not getting credit for a job well done and would be humiliated at having subsequent performance criticized. Proper use of positive control can prevent a work relationship from deteriorating to the point at which negative control is required.

## Imitation

Imitation can be used in situations in which a manager's expectations have been communicated but an employee is still not exhibiting the desired behavior. The manager can tactfully but publicly reward (i.e., through a promotion or salary increase) another employee who is performing effectively.

This approach allows the manager to avoid criticizing the employee who is not yet performing up to standards and thereby allows the relationship between the manager and the underachiever to remain positive. The objective is to provide a behavior model for the underachiever to emulate. If the under-achiever takes the cue and properly imitates improved behavior, the manager administers positive reinforcement.

An effective means for establishing an environment for imitation is to either hire or transfer an outstanding employee into a group of underachievers. The new employee can then set a new standard for the underachievers to imitate. The new employee must also be given reinforcement so as not to be pressured by the underachievers to lower performance standards.

## Shaping

This third strategy can be applied in combination with communication or imitation. In many situations, employees attempting to perform in a manner consistent with management expectations may not perform totally as desired; that is, they will approximate what has been requested. In these cases, a manager can shape (or mold) substandard behavior into the desired behavior. Initially, the manager reinforces any behavior that approximates the desired behavior. As reinforcement is administered, the manager indicates how the performance can be improved even more.

Over time, the manager becomes more discriminating in what is reinforced, thereby establishing a higher standard that more closely aligns with the desired behavior. If the shaping process is systematically applied, the employee will eventually achieve the desired behavior.

## SCHEDULING REINFORCEMENT

Scheduling reinforcement is often as important as the consequences administered. It is usually not practical to reinforce employees each time they exhibit desirable behavior. Often reinforcement has to be administered periodically. An effective reinforcement must be devised.

There are two basic types of scheduling: continuous and intermittent. Intermittent scheduling consists of subtypes: fixed ratio, variable ratio, fixed interval, and variable interval. A description of these reinforcement schedules is provided in Exhibit VII-6-5.

If a behavior is being continuously reinforced, it will probably stop if the manager stops (consciously or subconsciously) commending the employee. When continuous reinforcement is withdrawn, the change in consequences is noticed by the employee. Therefore, if continuous reinforcement is not practical, a manager is wise not to start it.

The fixed ratio and fixed interval schedules generally create cyclical behavior patterns. Employees usually repeat desired behavior as they approach the next scheduled reinforcement. Behavior frequency declines after reinforcement.

The cyclical nature of fixed ratio and fixed interval reinforcement scheduling indicates that total reliance on annual or monthly performance reviews for reinforcement will have disappointing results.

The variable ratio and variable interval schedules provide the most sustained performance level. An employee appears to be more reinforced by a

| Schedule | Description | Examples | Effects |
|---|---|---|---|
| *Continuous* | | | |
| Ongoing | Reinforcement presented each time behavior occurs. | Piecework (e.g., paid for every task). | • High rate of behavior acquisition.<br>• Continuous high rate of performance.<br>• Rapid extinction when reinforcers are withdrawn.<br>• May result in early satiation. |
| *Intermittent* | | | |
| Fixed Ratio/Fixed Interval | Reinforcement presented after a fixed time period. | Monthly wage; scheduled evaluations. | • Pronounced performance pause.<br>• Leads to less consistent rates of behavior. |
| Variable Ratio | Reinforcement presented after behavior occurs a certain number of times—the number varies around an average. | Sales bonuses or commissions. | • Performance consistently high.<br>• Extinction slower.<br>• Considered the best schedule. |
| Variable Interval | Reinforcement presented after a certain time interval—the length of time varies around an average. | Pop quizzes or evaluations; praise; recognition. | • Tends to produce sustained performance.<br>• High frequency does not speed up reinforcement. |

**Exhibit VII-6-5. Reinforcement Schedules**

---

schedule that introduces an element of surprise (i.e., an unexpected reward). Receiving unscheduled rewards such as promotions, salary increases, or recognition tells an employee that good performance is noticed and appreciated all the time, not just when reviews are scheduled. However, in many organizations certain rewards can be provided only on a fixed ratio or fixed interval basis. For example, salary increases or promotions can be awarded only during an annual review. Other reinforcers are independent of fixed schedules.

Nevertheless, care is required to effectively administer variable reinforcement. It is easy for a manager to overlook reinforcing an employee when reinforcement is done on a variable basis. Because most organizations have fixed schedules of reinforcement (e.g., annual reviews), a manager often defaults to the fixed schedule. However, a manager who adds systematic scheduling or variable reinforcement to the fixed schedules can usually achieve a higher level of personnel productivity.

## SUMMARY

By effectively administering consequences, data center managers can exert considerable influence over the behavior and productivity of their personnel.

Though there are different points of view on motivation, certain practical guidelines can be drawn from existing motivational theory. First, motivation must focus on identification of employee needs. Second, work assignments and objectives should reasonably fulfill the needs of the employee. Third, consequences for good performance must approximate the needs of the employee.

Proper identification of an employee's motivational needs, possibly through the creation of an individual motivation profile, must be combined with proper administration of consequences. Administration of consequences preferably is accomplished by using positive control strategies, though negative control strategies are often necessary. Positive control can be effected through communication, imitation, and shaping. Scheduling of reinforcement is most effective when using a variable ratio and variable interval scheduling rather than totally depending on traditional fixed interval or fixed ratio scheduling.

# VII-7
# Mentoring as a Career Strategy

*STEWART L. STOKES, JR.*

I n today's rightsized, less-structured, and flatter organizations, mentoring can become a prime tool for individual survival and professional development. As a career development strategy, mentoring is a process whereby a more experienced member of an organization helps a (usually) less experienced colleague navigate the culture and politics of the organization. The experienced person communicates information, insight, knowledge, tips, techniques, and advice and counsel about the culture of the organization, its key players, their strategies and the strategies of the enterprise, and the politics of how work gets accomplished.

Unless mentoring relationships are initiated with care, nurtured with discretion, and managed for organizational as well as personal benefit, they can deteriorate into stressful, conflict-laden situations that cause embarrassment to mentor and mentoree alike. This chapter explains mentoring as a developmental strategy and gives suggestions for structuring healthy mentoring relationships.

## BENEFITS OF MENTORING

Although well-accepted as a career development strategy by business managers and professionals, mentoring is not well known and applied by data center professionals. There are several reasons. First, in spite of attempts to integrate IS more closely with the business units, IS departments are still relatively isolated in many organizations—even to the point of being physically separated from other staff departments and line organizations. Furthermore, many data center professionals are relatively introverted and may thus experience difficulty seeking out and initiating relationships with potential mentors in other units of the enterprise.

Data center professionals can nonetheless benefit from mentoring relationships, especially in these times of organizational restructuring, delayering, and rightsizing. Maintaining a mentoring relationship with a colleague in another segment of the enterprise can become a source of strength and personal advantage. The mentor-mentoree connection can serve as an early-warning system of changes to come. The connection can also result in contacts for the mentoree, perhaps enabling the professional to relocate more easily within (or outside) the firm. The mentor can also be a sounding board for the mentoree, providing feedback on possible courses of action, as well as acting as an empathetic listener.

Given the benefits of mentoring, these key questions need to be considered:

- What, specifically, is mentoring and what are the attributes of mentor-mentoree relationships?
- Why is mentoring not widespread?
- What are the guidelines for mentoring?
- How can mentoring relationships be established?

## MENTORING RELATIONSHIPS

Mentoring relationships can be simple, focusing on immediate job-related and career concerns, or they may become more complex and deal with deeper issues, including attitudes, behaviors, and values that may be appropriate or inappropriate in a given context or set of circumstances.

For example, a mentor and mentoree may choose to establish, maintain, and limit their relationship to dealing with such straightforward job and career concerns as who is the best source to talk to about a particular issue, how to gain access to that person, what to cover during a conversation or meeting, how to structure the conversation, what to avoid saying or implying, and when and how to make commitments. Or, a mentor and mentoree may decide to shape the relationship so as to include discussion of broader issues, such as time and travel demands of a job and career on family, ethical considerations surrounding courses of action, and costs and benefits of career opportunities.

### Expectation Sharing

Either way, a critical success factor when establishing a mentoring relationship is the process of establishing the expectations for the relationship. This represents a contract of sorts between the mentor and the mentoree. If the expectations between mentor and mentoree are unclear at the outset of the relationship, it becomes very difficult to clarify them later on. Even if the operational details get straightened out, there can still be a residue of ill-will remaining between the parties.

Mentoring relationships are usually long-term and may transcend changes in organizational affiliation. A mentor and mentoree may begin a relationship while both are employed by the same enterprise. One or both may leave and the relationship may continue. For any mentoring relationship to succeed, both persons must perceive that their needs are being met. This is especially true for relationships that span years and organizations. For best results, the needs of both parties should be discussed in detail during the expectation-sharing phase and revisited regularly. Both parties to a mentoring relationship would do well to live by the old (but still true) adage, "Assume nothing."

Mentoring relationships must always be based on a high degree of trust and respect. Mentors and mentorees may become deeply involved in each other's lives and may become aware of confidential information. Indeed, the closeness that often develops between mentor and mentoree can become a major issue in cross-gender relationships. Some organizations try to discourage the forming of mentor-mentoree relationships for this reason.

## Distinction From Manager-Employee Relationships

Usually, mentoring relationships are not manager-employee relationships, even though the best of such relationships involve coaching, counseling, and championing of the employee by the manager to others. This is not to say that effective mentoring cannot evolve from manager-employee experiences; they can and do. But manager-employee dynamics encompass expectations and responsibilities that can get in the way of establishing mentor-mentoree relationships.

For example, an important part of the manager-employee relationship is the cycle and process of establishing objectives, conducting performance reviews, and appraising performance. A manager may participate in this cycle with many employees; a mentoring relationship with one of them may create conflict not only between the mentor and mentoree but among all the others reporting to the manager as well.

Managers have dual roles and responsibilities with employees: to evaluate them and to develop them. These dual roles eventually clash when managers attempt to mentor as well as manage. A preferable arrangement is for managers to manage their employees and mentor the employees of other managers. In this way, the sometimes conflicting roles of evaluator and developer can be kept separate.

Mentoring relationships may be cross-functional, involving participants in different line and staff departments. For example, a manager in the marketing department might serve as a mentor for a data center professional, or an experienced data center manager and a less-experienced person in the finance department might team up as mentor-mentoree.

## Mutual Commitment Required

However mentoring relationships are constructed, mutual benefits are at the heart of those that are the most productive. Each person must perceive and believe that he or she has needs that can be met through the mentoring process. If the needs of only one participant are met, the relationship seldom achieves its potential and may be short-lived.

Mentoring requires a hands-on approach by mentor and mentoree alike and is not a spectator sport for either person. Mentoring is a mutual commitment demanding a major investment in time and energy. Mentor and mentoree alike share responsibility for managing the expectations that surround the mentoring relationship.

Successful mentoring relationships sometimes transcend the workplace. They may include the spouses or companions of the mentor and mentoree and be primarily social in nature, or they may be a mix of business and social activities that include only the participants themselves. There is no one best way. Mentoring can be informal, with only the mentor and mentoree involved, or it can be formal, with organizations providing some structure to the mentoring relationships and activities. Mentoring can thus take on aspects of a project, except that there may be no predetermined end. Certain activities (i.e., courses, seminars) may conclude, but the personal relationships may continue.

## PEER-TO-PEER MENTORING

In most mentoring relationships, one of the participants is senior to the other, in age as well as in experience. There is an important exception to this tendency, however, and it offers data center professionals an opportunity to broaden their business knowledge as well as build a network of colleagues throughout the enterprise. The exception to the rule is peer-to-peer mentoring.

Peer-to-peer mentoring involves building a support relationship with a peer in another department of the enterprise. This peer should not be a user/client, nor should either individual be a direct stakeholder in the activities of the other person (e.g., project team member or colleague). The dynamics among project team members can be difficult enough without introducing a mentor-mentoree relationship into the mix.

The common ground necessary for effective peer-to-peer mentoring is that each person must possess some knowledge, skill, or insight that is not possessed (at least to the same degree) by the other but that the other needs to be successful. Furthermore, each person must be willing to share this knowledge, skill, or insight and encourage the other person to use the information or skill when and where appropriate. This requirement is more difficult than it sounds, especially during periods of rightsizing, when individuals may guard information they believe gives them competitive advantage over their colleagues.

An example of a well-crafted peer-to-peer mentoring relationship may be a data center manager with considerable technical knowledge and skill and a peer with strong business know-how and interpersonal skills who have common career ambitions and who lack formal learning resources. The mentoring relationship may take the form of monthly meetings at each other's home in which each person has the opportunity to introduce an issue, concern, or problem that the other could help with. Each person becomes, in effect, an internal consultant to the other.

## EXTERNAL MENTORS

A form of mentoring needed in downsized organizations is external monitoring, or the establishment of peer-based mentoring relationships primarily through professional associations. Some data center professionals, especially those at senior levels, are extremely successful at this. The majority are not. Many are not joiners and thus fail to take advantage of opportunities to establish contacts outside their organizations and build human networks of peer-to-peer relationships.

Human networking is an increasingly important career management strategy as organizations rightsize and staff size shrinks. The external contacts and relationships established through professional associations are valuable sources of information, not only about job opportunities but also about best practices in a wide variety of organizations. For instance, the Society for Information Management (SIM), a leading professional association for IS executives, consultants, and academics, invites its members to participate in working groups to examine best practices in quality management within information systems. SIM also invites CIO members to participate in focused roundtable discussions of topics of interest to IS executives.

These opportunities for external peer-to-peer human networking and mentoring do not just happen. Interested individuals have to seek out the contacts, determine whether the programs, information, and benefits will be helpful, and establish relationships. Initiating and cultivating these contacts requires an investment of time and energy. Individuals must be willing to do more than attend occasional meetings, which alone will not yield the benefits that flow from in-depth participation. Those who get the most out of external peer-based human networking and mentoring become involved in committee work, program development, and officership.

## WHY IS MENTORING NOT WIDESPREAD?

There are several reasons why mentoring is not popular among data center professionals, some of which have been touched on already:

- Lack of familiarity with the mentoring concept and process.
- Lack of contacts with potential mentors from business units and other staff departments.
- Physical separation of the IS department from other departments of the enterprise, which makes it difficult for IS staff to establish contacts with potential mentors.
- The introverted nature of many data center professionals, which may inhibit them from initiating contacts.
- The commitment of time and energy required for successful mentoring.
- The close personal nature of some mentoring relationships.
- Lack of a perceived balance of benefits for both parties in the mentoring relationship.

- Lack of role models. If a person has not been mentored during his or her career, that person is probably unaware of the benefits of such a relationship.

The issue of gender, racial, and ethnic differences is also a consideration to be faced. Different people have their own feelings about becoming involved in developmental relationships with persons of the opposite sex, as well as those from different racial and ethnic backgrounds. There are, of course, many special-interest groups in which members meet others like themselves, make contacts, and learn the ropes, but they cannot necessarily take the place of an in-depth, one-on-one mentoring relationship in which the mentor is committed to helping another person grow in a career.

The issue of differences, though perhaps unsettling, should not be a deterrent to successful mentoring. Differences exist; they are a fact of life, and denying their reality is not useful. It is better to discuss openly and honestly the feelings the potential mentor and mentoree have about the differences during the experience-sharing phase.

A discussion of differences and expectations can help get a mentoring relationship off on the right foot. It can also save conflict and embarrassment by allowing both individuals to share feelings and opinions under conditions of relative confidentiality. In addition, it enables each person to gain experience in dealing with feelings and emotions that are not usually expressed openly.

## MENTORING GUIDELINES

There is no one best way or specific model or paradigm for successful mentoring. Mentoring relationships are unique and particular to the persons involved, because of the personal chemistry between mentor and mentoree. There are, however, some common themes and broad parameters to consider. Organizations may develop guidelines to govern aspects of the mentoring process, including:

- How mentors and mentorees are selected and paired.
- The roles and responsibilities of mentors and mentorees.
- The availability of formal educational experiences, including courses and seminars.
- Evaluation of the participants and the process.

In the majority of organizations, however, mentors and mentorees determine for themselves how to establish and manage their relationships and mutual expectations. Few organizations have guidelines, but this is a strength, not a weakness, for it allows and encourages mentors and mentorees to grow relationships that best meet each other's needs while at the same time serving the needs of the enterprise. Although an organization may establish predetermined policies, rules, and requirements to govern mentoring relationships, the best rule to follow is "Less is more."

## Hard and Soft Issues

Mentoring relationships that are primarily job and career related focus on the hard issues of:

- Expanding the mentoree's job opportunities (outside the enterprise, when appropriate, but primarily within the organization).
- Understanding how to approach specific situations and problems.
- Learning about key people in the organization and how to handle them.
- Understanding the culture of the enterprise.
- Undertaking tasks that increase personal visibility.
- Taking on stretch assignments that may require new learning and risk-taking but that can result in personal growth, increased self-esteem, and new contacts.

Other mentoring relationships deal more with the soft issues of:

- Attitudes and behaviors.
- Value judgments surrounding particular issues and decisions.
- Ethical considerations.
- Personal and professional goals.
- The need to cultivate close personal relationships in an increasingly impersonal workplace.

It is difficult to separate all of these issues. As a result, a mentor may offer advice and counsel on ways to approach a specific problem or troubling situation and at the same time raise the issue of the values and ethics involved in the various approaches. Thus, the pros and cons of each approach can be analyzed, but in the broader context of a values-based discussion.

## CONFLICT BETWEEN MENTOR AND MENTOREE

Conflict is inevitable in mentoring relationships; indeed, it is invaluable. The mentoring experience would be diminished if conflict did not arise, for conflict is a part of everyday organizational life. If mentoring is to be a useful experience, mentorees must profit from learning how to analyze and manage conflicts that arise between themselves and their mentors, for these lessons can then be applied to the conflicts they need to analyze and manage between themselves and their colleagues, managers, and subordinates on the job.

## How Much Time to Give

A major source of conflict between mentor and mentoree is the amount of time and energy that must be invested in the relationship by the mentor. This may be grossly underestimated by both people. Personal time and energy is limited, but if the limits are not discussed in advance by both participants, the mentoring process may prove counterproductive. If either participant enters into the mentoring relationship without having examined the demands in personal time and energy required and having determined that these demands are acceptable, the mentoring relationship may self-destruct. This will do more than fracture the relationship between mentor and mentoree; it may well set back the cause of effective mentoring within the enterprise by months.

The way to deal with this source of conflict is to first recognize its inevitability, and second, to realize that it must be managed, discussed, and agreed on before the relationship begins. If the issue of how much time to devote to the relationship is not mutually acceptable, either person must feel free to leave the relationship.

### Personal Style and Values

There are two other sources of likely conflict: conflict over personal style and conflict over values. Personal style is easier to observe and certainly easier to discuss and change than is a conflict over values. Personal style is in part a combination of learned traits or characteristics; it may even be based on the style of an admired friend, colleague, or public figure. Values, however, are deeply ingrained in a person's personality, character, and makeup. Values are difficult, if not impossible, to change.

Style- and values-based conflicts should not be avoided, however. They are symptomatic of the conflicts that arise within the enterprise, and a mentoring relationship may be the ideal vehicle for gaining firsthand insight and experience into managing them effectively. They cannot be avoided on the job, nor should they be in mentoring relationships. The reality of conflict should likewise not be an excuse for discouraging or avoiding mentoring relationships. Rather, mentoring should be encouraged for precisely this reason: the more experience a person can gather on the practice field, the easier it will be to handle the real thing when it occurs during game time. That is what mentoring is all about.

### HOW TO ESTABLISH A MENTORING RELATIONSHIP

If the prospective mentor and mentoree are employed by an organization that has a formal mentoring program in place, the program is usually administered (or at least coordinated) by someone from the corporate human resources department, and there is probably a cadre of preselected and prescreened mentors ready and willing to work with less experienced colleagues. Problems may still arise, however, because the choice of mentors may be limited to those already on HR's approved list and there may not be a good fit among them for everyone interested in a mentoring relationship.

Equally disturbing (for some) is the notion of a predetermined program for mentoring. Such a program may include prescribed mentor-mentoree meetings, seminars, and conferences. Although such a corporate commitment is to be applauded, it may not enable or encourage the customization of mentor-mentoree relationships around mutual needs and benefits.

## ACTION STEPS

The reality is that most data center professionals who desire to develop and further their careers through a mentoring relationship must establish and grow this relationship on their own. Someone wishing to form a mentoring relationship should follow the following steps.

**Step 1.** Individuals should be as clear as possible about their career goals and objectives, for the entire mentoring experience is based on these. Although the mentoring experience may help to clarify career options, individuals must be prepared to address their own career goals before approaching potential mentors.

**Step 2.** Individuals must be equally clear about what they need from a mentoring relationship. A person may, for example, simply seek a colleague in another department with whom to kick ideas around. Another individual may want to locate a more senior person in a line department who can explain the enterprise's direction and strategy. The issue is for a person to know his or her own needs and why these needs are important.

**Step 3.** Individuals should talk with friends and colleagues who are in mentoring relationships about their experiences in order to benefit from what they have learned. What aspects of their relationships are working well and why? What works less well and why? By thinking about what others have learned, a person can begin to formulate ideas about what he or she might do differently.

**Step 4.** A person may not know anyone who is, or has been, in a mentoring relationship, so it may be necessary to learn as much as possible about the organization's culture and the different jobs and responsibilites in the business to locate people in other departments or even other levels in the organization with the experience the mentoree is seeking. The more someone knows before approaching a potential mentor, the better.

**Step 5.** The next step is to draw up a list of potential mentors and to clarify why they would be appropriate people to work with, what can be learned from them, and what the reciprocal benefits would be. Potential mentorees should also determine whether extenuating circumstances would influence the decision of any prospective mentors to accept an invitation.

**Step 6.** The first five steps help a person prepare for this step: approaching a prospective mentor. Some people will decline the offer, but you should not discourage the prospective mentoree. When someone accepts, the new mentoree should ask to schedule a meeting to review mutual needs, expectations, and benefits. The mentoree and mentor must determine the parameters of the relationship. Will they deal with hardcore job-related issues only or a combination of hard and soft issues?

**Step 7.** It is also important to set an initial timetable and a review and evaluation procedure to establish some bases for continuing the relationship or discontinuing it.

**Step 8.** Assuming that both people are ready to make a mutual commitment to the mentoring relationship (after taking into consideration all the issues discussed in this article), they must continue to review, assess, and evaluate the relationship to determine whether they should continue to move forward on the original basis or reevaluate expectations and take appropriate action.

## SUMMARY

Mentoring is a developmental relationship that can be valuable to the mentoree and mentor alike. A successful mentoring relationship can help mentorees survive enterprisewide restructuring and rightsizing. Data center professionals can benefit from a greater understanding of the mentoring process and requirements for success.

# VII-8
# How to Change Organizations

*KENNETH P. PRAGER • MILES H. OVERHOLT*

A lmost everyone has been part of a failed project. Sometimes the projects fail technically because their systems are not correctly designed, the hardware malfunctions, or the software does not do what everyone hoped it would do. However, projects often fail not because of technical flaws, but because the people in the organization reject them.

Some of these failures occur because the systems do not accurately address a real business need. Other systems fail because they contradict the expected reporting relationships and communications paths within the organization, or because they do not harmonize with the way managers look at "who we are as a company." Many systems fail because they require that people in separate functional areas to work together. A few systems fail because of incorrect and inappropriate rumors about the new system's impact on people's jobs. Typical symptoms of a failed project are:

- The intended users are not using it.
- Managers and employees are using it, but feel it does not meet their needs.
- There may be open animosity toward IS.

Whatever the reasons, a failed effort to implement new technology is always a failure to understand and adequately manage the change process.

Whenever organizations try to change, there is risk. One of the most significant risks is that people within the organization will not accept the change and therefore block or defeat it. Because new technology represents radical changes to people and their jobs, the risks are great. Changing peoples' lives is a serious issue that must be managed with care.

For most of the twentieth century, the primary strategy of the successful corporation was to create stability, institutionalize routine, and manage procedures. Management did not have to know how to guide people through significant, life-style altering change. Today, because of restricted capital and growing competition and demands for quality, every manager needs to understand how to orchestrate change.

## PEOPLE-CENTERED ORGANIZATIONS

One way that managers begin to gain this expertise is to view organizations differently. Executives often refer to people as human capital or "our greatest asset," as if people were entries on the balance sheet. Unintentionally, this implies that organizations exist without people and that, in fact, organizations simply use people as they would any other piece of machinery or equipment.

A new focus is needed that views people as the core of the organization and recognizes that all other aspects of the organization are built on people. The people-centered organization is this new paradigm.

### Seven Components

People-centered organizations consist of seven interactive and interdependent components. In this context, organization means not only the company but also each division, function, and team, because each of these organizations is itself people-centered and has its own seven components.

- The genetic core is the center of the organization and the locus of power for all decisions. The more people the genetic core includes, the more powerful the organization.
- The philosophy comprises the publicly articulated beliefs of the organization that emanate from the genetic core.
- The organizational behaviors are the set of interactions between individuals and groups within the organization.
- The formal organization is the structure, reporting, and reward system of the organization.
- The information systems and technology are the structures, constraints, and demands of the information, manufacturing, and service delivery systems within the organization. This component deals with acquiring the information and using it to make decisions.
- The informal organization is the network that binds the employees together. The grapevine is its primary communication channel and the informal leaders are some of the most powerful in the company. Frequently, the informal organization counterbalances a weakness in the formal organization.
- The culture is the set of beliefs about how the organization runs day to day. It includes the organization's history and myths, artifacts and symbols, as well as expectations of such things as how meetings are to be run and how individuals are to dress.

In flexible, responsive organizations, the seven components are aligned and congruent, supporting and reinforcing employees. If one or more of the components is out of alignment, the resulting imbalance creates a blockage that hinders employees in their work and in implementing change.

## REQUIRED CHANGES

For example, if top management decides to implement total quality management (TQM), the organization undergoes a fundamental philosophical change from which management can map the required changes in each of the other six segments. The genetic core, for example, must focus on quality and customer-oriented strategies. The formal organization must be redesigned so compensation systems reward teams, communication channels broaden, and work processes and tasks change. New systems and technologies must be put in place to measure, support, and enhance the changes. Users need greater access to more customized data. The informal leaders need to adopt and support the new philosophy, because if they reject the change, TQM becomes just another program of the month. The culture must foster customer-oriented thinking and open communication among all the levels of the organization.

Successful change requires that management ensures that the seven segments are realigned and again congruent to support people in their new way of operating. The greater the balance and the fit among the seven components, the fewer the barriers to effective change by people.

## TECHNOLOGY, NEW SYSTEMS, AND CHANGE

In many situations, IS professionals and IS management are the driving force behind change. They are designing, creating, and implementing massive system changes that force the company to change its culture. They have become the driving force that enables teams to become self-directed and empowers individuals to redesign and reengineer workflows.

This "push" from the information and technology component of the people-centered organization also causes reactions in the other six components. IS management must design implementation processes that ensure that the components are realigned to support the people as they use the new technology. Consequently, IS professionals are now in the change business and must become experts in managing organizational and human change.

### Designing the Process

To maximize employee support and ownership of new information technology and ensure the best fit, the change process should:

- Guide work groups at different hierarchical levels through the process of aligning the seven components of the people-centered organization.
- Assist people in removing the organizational and personal barriers that block the change.
- Make the alignment process obvious and overt so that the people can replicate it by themselves.

Managers should view the redesign as a participative process that ripples down through the organization. Each team designs a clear framework at its own hierarchical level that allows teams at the next lower level to redesign and reengineer their work processes to meet and match the requirements of the new system.

For example, first the executive team uses the people-centered organization framework, as described in this chapter, to redesign the entire organization on a very broad level. Then the functional management teams participate in a similar process to plan how their areas fit this new design. Next, natural work groups within the functions analyze the required changes. In this way, each successive level can make the appropriate detailed changes at its level. The process begins at the top, cascades down the levels, and loops back and forth among the levels as strategies and issues need to be reexamined.

Using the people-centered organization as a framework, IS managers acting as facilitators can lead groups through this redesign process, identifying barriers that may block implementation and mapping the strategies that let the groups eventually change to the new technology.

The process consists of analyzing each component of the people-centered organization. For each component, and at each hierarchical level, the facilitator leads the group as it develops a vision of what the future state of that component will be after the new technology is implemented. Then, the group profiles the current state of the component. Finally, the group compares the two to analyze what needs to be changed and what the group perceives as potential barriers to the change. The facilitator asks the participants to use phrases that describe their perceptions of each of the components.

## Action Plans

The obvious product of this process is an action plan at each level and within each work group that incorporates the groups' decisions. A not-so-obvious but more important product of this process is buy-in to the new technology because the people have participated in the decisions that affect their own jobs—they have devised their own plans for changing to the new way. Finally, because the process is overt (people know what the facilitator is doing), people can apply the same process themselves to later changes.

IS managers need to decide if everyone in the organization should be included, which would be ideal, or if a set of representatives is sufficient. Leading the process does not require extensive theoretical knowledge, but it does require significant facilitation and group leadership skill.

## ALIGNING THE INFORMATION SYSTEMS FUNCTION

When the information systems and technology component is the focal point of the change, IS management must first use the people-centered organization model to align itself with the new technology. IS management and staff must answer such questions as:

- *Core support.* Is the IS management team fully on board?
- *Philosophy.* Does everyone in the IS department agree that supporting the new technology fits with "who we will be" as a department after it is in place?
- *Formal organization.* Is the IS function appropriately organized to support the new technology? Are new positions needed (e.g., for help desks)? Should the department create new communication mechanisms within IS and between IS and the rest of the company (e.g., E-mail or an IS newsletter)?
- *Behavior.* How will the new technology affect interactions within the department? How should IS personnel behave when they interact with people from other departments?
- *Information and technology systems.* Are the IS department's internal systems congruent with the proposed change? Does the IS staff have access to the information needed to make decisions?
- *Informal organization.* Are the informal leaders within IS supporting this new technology? Are there rumors circulating within IS that may create resistance? For example, will people believe they will lose their jobs if they are not properly trained?
- *Culture.* Do the normative beliefs of the IS employees fit the new technology? Does the actual daily running of the department support the change?

Only after IS management and staff have ensured alignment within the department itself can work start on producing the action plans for implementing change and gaining the support of people in the rest of the organization.

## ISSUES AFFECTING THE PROCESS

The organizational redesign process must tackle hierarchical, level-specific strategic issues surfaced by the technological change. IS management and the functional or work area participants must address the issues if there is to be successful implementation. IS management may expect to encounter issues similar to the following examples.

**The Core Support Issue.** Gaining support from management for the new technology is key. Without management support, employees perceive the change as unimportant and choose not to support it. Frequently, IS management decides to sell new technology to executive or functional management on benefits that impress IS professionals. Non-IS management will not be influenced to change to a client/server environment because the technology encompasses different platforms. Rather, management must perceive a real benefit, a solution to a problem that it is experiencing.

*Example.* An IS vice-president for a growing $150 million manufacturer learned this lesson the hard way. During the strategic planning process, IS management and staff recognized the need to shift to an online, real-time system to solve certain scheduling and production problems. Accustomed to unthinking agreement by executive management, the IS vice-president recommended implementation of the new technology. The IS strategic plan was accepted, and the IS department committed hundreds of working hours developing specifications and researching hardware and software. When the IS staff presented the findings to executive management, it disagreed with the premise that there was an organizational need and wondered why IS had spent all this time on a "star wars" project. Two months later the IS vice-president was looking for a new position.

*Preferred Action.* The IS vice-president failed to identify executive management's needs and link them to the needs of other functions. If IS had facilitated an organizational redesign session with executive management, it would have discovered management's perception of future problems and been able to address its particular needs. Then IS would have been able to project several future scenarios illustrating the need for an online, real-time system.

**The Philosophy Issue.** An important redesign issue is how well the new technology supports the belief systems the organization will need after the new technology has been implemented. IS management must match the philosophy of the new technology with the corporate philosophy to ensure acceptance. Technologies with philosophies that conflict or do not match those of the corporation create incongruence within the components and are barriers to implementation.

*Example.* A large hospital system installed electronic data interchange (EDI), creating major changes in employees' roles. IS management and staff were overwhelmed with the conversion from the old operating system to EDI. To complete the conversion on time, the department focused on providing comprehensive technical training. Almost all the trained employees understood how to use EDI and demonstrated great proficiency in using the system. However, everyone in the purchasing department was unhappy with EDI and avoided linking suppliers into the system. Proficiency and familiarity with the system was not a problem, and IS management could not understand what was wrong. Finally, a supplier casually informed management that the purchasers were afraid of losing their jobs and did not understand that EDI was intended to free their time to do more sophisticated activities.

*Preferred Action.* IS management was in a familiar double bind. The deadline pressures caused IS staff to forget that functional management and employees needed to participate so they would understand how the system would change their jobs. In addition, employees needed an opportunity to create new roles and work processes to enhance the use of EDI.

**The Formal Organization Issue.** The introduction of new technology alters the hierarchical structures, workflows, communication processes, and compensation systems. To gain full commitment and ensure that the new technology is used, IS management must involve management and employees in the redesign process.

*Example.* In a large financial services corporation, IS and executive management were pleased with the company's new system. It had increased productivity and was accepted by users throughout the corporation. Serendipitously, a task force working on improving communications discovered that cross-functional communication required by the new system was blocked by the traditional hierarchy. Users who needed to communicate cross-functionally had to send information upward, then wait for it to be communicated laterally and downward before it arrived to the intended receiver. The delay and the inevitable distortion of the information was blocking further increases in productivity.

*Action.* IS management conducted an organizational redesign process throughout the corporation. Even though the process was time-consuming and lengthy, lasting 19 months, work groups eventually realigned communication channels to match the system, cycle time decreased, and employees felt empowered to work more productively.

**The Behavior Issue.** New technologies demand new behaviors between users and the systems, between functions, and between individuals. Everyone must perform different tasks with the computer, new and more information is available to functions, and employees no longer rely on the same individuals for information. IS management must assist everyone in identifying what new behaviors are required, in acquiring the behaviors, and in practicing the behaviors.

*Example.* The manufacturing division of a Fortune 500 company had been operating on a mainframe with no server system for ten years; in fact, the technology was dubbed "no-line, past time." When the division started to change from the old system to a WAN, the IS vice-president created a cross-functional pilot team. Its assignment was to determine the behavioral changes necessitated by the WAN, document those changes, then create a training lab experience that simulated the experience for all employees. The lab was deliberately nicknamed "WAN-a-be" and became a major factor in ensuring successful implementation in a resistant culture.

*Action.* Successful organizational redesign requires anticipating changes rather than reacting to them. If employees have the opportunity to anticipate how their work areas will change, they will shift their behavior to match the new realities.

**The Information and Technology Systems Issue.** The key issue when technology is the driving force behind large-scale organizational change is creating a reciprocal feedback and adjustment process that enables the IS staff to improve the system. Most new technologies must be adapted to fit specific user needs. The organizational redesign process is an excellent opportunity to jointly consider the best way to make the adaptations.

*Example.* A small professional services company engaged a consulting firm to create a new reporting system to track costs and billable time. Once the system had been implemented, the staff complained about wasted time and useless information. The managing partners were upset because the staff had been interviewed and involved in the design of the system. However, after the system had been implemented the staff had no opportunity to refine it. The consulting firm was no longer available, and the IS department was overwhelmed by efforts to train new users of the system and manage the increase in data. Before a reciprocal feedback channel could be established, staff discontent with the system was so high that most returned to the manual reporting system.

*Preferred Action.* The managing partners and the consulting firm were so preoccupied with ensuring that the system was perfect that they were unable to plan for user feedback after implementation. If managing partners had simply announced that the new system would be helpful but would also require much feedback and joint participation in improving the details, the staff would have been cooperative. Instead, the staff refused to use the system.

**The Informal Organization Issue.** Informal leaders can make or break the acceptance of new systems. IS management wants to avoid a negative review or misinterpretation of a change being broadcast through the company's grapevine. IS management must take advantage of the power of the informal organization to gain support for new technologies. To manage the informal organization, managers must know who the informal leaders of the organization are.

*Example.* Senior management in a large corporate services department decided to install a departmental LAN. Working closely with the IS staff, departmental management carefully developed a training and installation schedule, involved key supervisors in the design phase, and was poised to install the new system. Just as the first staff members started training sessions, a rumor began to circulate that all part-time staff members would lose their jobs when the implementation was completed. The training instructors reported to management that the staff appeared disinterested in learning the new system and that some individuals were asking pointed, angry questions that had nothing to do with the training.

*Action.* To address the issue, IS management was asked to facilitate employee discussion sessions on the impact of the new system. The staff remained quiet through the first two sessions. Finally, a part-time employee asked when someone was going to tell them that their jobs were being eliminated. The IS facilitator then explained that no jobs were to be lost. To prove the point, the facilitator conducted a brief redesign session on the role of part-time workers. Shortly thereafter, the rumors stopped. Not only had management successfully stopped the misinformation from circulating, but a more productive role for the part-time employees had been created.

**The Culture Issue.** The organization must ultimately accept and institutionalize the new values that are created by new technologies. Employees must learn to value the technology, accept it as part of their working life, and integrate it into the mainstream of the organization. Status symbols must change to reflect this acceptance, and the new technology must become just another part of the way people work. This is necessarily a slow process, but one that IS management can influence.

*Example.* When a Fortune 500 corporation began to downsize, secretaries were among the first employees to be laid off. Senior management decided that directors, managers, and supervisors could share secretaries, enabling the corporation to lay off 50% of the secretaries. Twelve months later, senior management authorized the purchase of microcomputers so that directors, managers, and supervisors could do their own word processing. Senior management learned that few directors or managers ordered the microcomputers. When managers seeking promotion would not use a microcomputer, senior management realized that it had failed to see the connection between the status of having a secretary and the lack of status of using a microcomputer for word processing.

*Action.* At a break in an executive meeting, one senior manager shared this problem with a peer, who in a staff meeting had mentioned the problem to corporate directors. The senior manager immediately had a desktop microcomputer installed and started attending word processing training.

## SUMMARY

Developing expertise in and becoming comfortable with managing change can help IS managers avoid projects that fail for nontechnical reasons—failures caused by people and organizational problems. To develop this expertise, there are some specific actions the managers can take.

First, the manager should embrace the people-centered organization model. This recognizes that organizations are built on people and that people need to have an active role in redefining and redesigning their organizations to align with the new technology.

Second, the manager must develop new skills and gain a new understanding of people issues. Some of these skills are:

- Team building and teamwork skills to help work groups function effectively.
- Facilitation skills to lead work groups through the redesign process.
- Communication skills, because communication within a work group, within a department, among departments, and throughout the organization is absolutely critical for successful change.
- Conflict resolution skills to deal with the inevitable struggles as people change.

Finally, using these skills, the manager must ensure that all components are aligned—not only with each other, but also with the new technology and the new organization. The manager can help work groups examine each of the seven components of the people-centered organization. For each component, the work groups must define how that component will use the new technology, how the component functions today, and how the component will come to suppport the new technology in the future. This redesign occurs at a macro level where the executive team broadly redefines the organization, at a mezzo level where functional managers redefine their own departments, and at a micro level where individuals in the organization define their own strategies for changing to the new environment. By applying these concepts, IS and users together can anticipate and manage the many changes that need to be made to ensure successful implementation of new technologies and systems.

# VII-9
# Career Paths for Data Center Professionals

*NORMAN H. CARTER*

C areer planning should cater to both employee and departmental or organizational needs. Unfortunately, the unstructured and nonintegrated manner in which some organizations carry out career planning and placement procedures are not conducive to employees' full understanding of career opportunities and can lead to poorly planned employee education or training programs and limited promotion paths. When organizations are changed to include professional and technical people in business units rather than only in IS units, new opportunities are created. There is, however, a corollary need to coordinate activities among departments to minimize duplication. The career planning and job requirement charts described in this chapter can be used to unify departmental planning efforts, design flexibility into promotion paths, and keep data center employees aware of their career choices.

## PROVIDING CAREER CHOICES

Among the most difficult tasks facing data center managers are the acquisition, development, and retention of capable data center professionals. Organizations commonly meet their data center staffing requirements by:

- *Hiring senior talent from outside the organization to fill vacancies.* The data center staff is thus upgraded by the introduction of new employees with greater knowledge or skill than the existing staff's.
- *Sending in-house personnel to training and development activities offered by various training suppliers without having adequately evaluated the relevance or quality of the offerings.* This development process can be expensive and is often randomly applied.
- *Creating promotion tracks that allow progress along only one career path.* The highest position with the greatest compensation is usually a managerial position. This forces data center professionals to compete for managerial positions even if a senior technical position would be more professionally and personally rewarding. The net result of such single-track career paths is that competent people often leave the organization

to find other positions that appear to offer wider career choices and other opportunities for career development and enhancement.

To reduce employee turnover and improve the quality of work, organizations should provide more comprehensive—not more complex—career choices and should communicate these choices clearly, consistently, and constantly to all levels of the organization. Career development discussions and objectives should be linked directly to the business needs of the organization, performance evaluations, staffing, individual development planning, and succession planning.

## THE CAREER PATH STRUCTURE

A career path structure is a comprehensive view of a department or organization. The structure can be illustrated in chart form, as in Exhibit VII-9-1, to show how different positions relate to one another. The career path structure identifies the hierarchy of jobs, or job family, through which a proficient individual can proceed.

An important feature of the career path structure shown in Exhibit VII-9-1 is the breaking point in the path after the trainee programmer position, which allows individuals to choose to advance among the areas of systems analysis, operations management, or professional positions. All three branches in this career path can attain the same salary level. In some organizations, however, an additional incentive to enter a technical path might be a full salary-grade difference in favor of technical positions. A higher salary for the technical path would compensate for the more restricted promotion opportunities in technical positions.

With the tendency to attach business systems development directly to the department being served, rather than maintaining a separate IS development department, the career path options are broader than before. There are now more crossover points at which individuals can transfer in or out of a job family. Identifying these points increases the visibility of positions in the organization and can enhance communication between supervisors and employees about career opportunities. This identification also makes employees aware of the transfer limitations that exist between specific positions.

Career development that transfers systems individuals into more mainstream business positions will become the rule rather than the exception. Exhibit VII-9-1 depicts a realistic and integrated career ladder for an entire department in a product development systems organization. This integrated ladder illustrates the high degree of lateral transfer that can occur within a department. The terms of the career ladder (e.g., *moderate integration, high risk*) can be used to identify the required skills or characteristics for each position.

At each position in the chart appear written statements that give the position's associated degree of risk and integration. These statements can aid

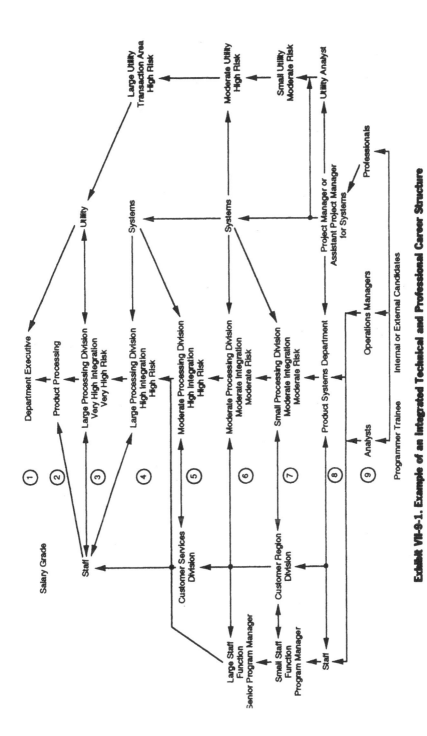

**Exhibit VII-9-1. Example of an Integrated Technical and Professional Career Structure**

in candidate selection. A high degree of risk indicates that typical projects handled by the employees could potentially expose the organization to loss or risky market pressures. Candidates for high-risk positions must demonstrate high professional or technical skill and sound judgment concerning alternative courses of action. A strong history of successful decision making and implementation would be expected. A high level of integration indicates that the output or systems must be compatible with those produced by others in related parts of the organization. High-integration positions require individuals who work well with others and have strong negotiating skills.

A career path chart is also an excellent adjunct to the tools of performance appraisal. If used with job and compensation descriptions, a career path chart can also help provide a complete picture of the benefits the organization offers to its individuals for career planning.

## DEVELOPING CAREER PATH DOCUMENTS

The first step in developing a cohesive set of career path tools is assembling requirements and standards documents. The resulting job descriptions should include a general description of each position, a statement of responsibilities in terms of impact on the business unit goals, budget, staff, and other resources, and a list of characteristics possessed by the desired employee.

The data center manager should use these job descriptions to identify tasks or requirements that are common to all jobs in a job family or to identify differences or additional functions that distinguish one position from another. Reviewers should check for inconsistencies and missing responsibilities, which often arise when job descriptions are written at different times or by different people. When different unit managers write job descriptions, it becomes important to review the job descriptions for completeness, consistency, and relevance.

Product life cycle standards, data center policies and procedures, and standard references that specify job performance provide another source of input. Wage and salary support procedures should also be collected for integration. When these documents have been assembled, a task structure can be developed for a job family. Development of these comprehensive career path tools helps prevent future inconsistencies by establishing consistent methods for describing job requirements and training needs. Despite the need for these documents, the goal must be to provide the minimum number of documents, not an exhaustive number.

### Defining the Task Structure

The task structure for a job family is typically divided into five categories:

- Functions or business tasks.
- Administrative tasks.

- Planning tasks.
- General personnel tasks.
- Other support tasks.

The primary considerations in developing a task structure are keeping the list of tasks short, relating each task to data center methods or other procedure anchors, and describing the skill level required for the performance of each task. Each item on the list should reflect the value of the task in relation to the daily performance of the job (this distinguishes task descriptions from typical job descriptions, which are used primarily for setting compensation). The task structure should describe how job performance will be demonstrated.

To ensure that the performance of each task at each job level is consistently described, the task skill levels should be determined by a skill-level assessor. This individual formulates a description of task performance, a statement of how performance is demonstrated, and a statement of the amount of supervision required for each level.

Exhibit VII-9-2 presents a sample of the tasks for the systems analysis job family. The skill-level ratings are explained in Exhibit VII-9-3.

## The Task Force

When a preliminary set of career paths, job families, and task structures has been developed, a task force including business and systems managers should review the documents for completeness, clarity, and consistency to eliminate overlap or gaps in job content. The task force should consist of a manager of the appropriate function, two employees from the user organization who manage the job family under evaluation, a representative from the human resources department, and perhaps a neutral third party (e.g., a qualified consultant facilitator). The employees on the task force vary for each job family, but all other task force members should be constant. A review of each job family takes approximately two days, with half a day each for initial review, final review, integration with other job families, final details, and editing of the documents.

When all the job families have been identified and described, similarities between different families should be identified. Elements of one family are frequently found in another family in a different part of the organization. As many position descriptions as possible should be combined and eliminated so that the remaining structure is easy to understand and manage, no matter where in the organization the individual is located.

For all positions related to posts in other departments, the managers of each department should review the goals, objectives, and requirements of these positions to clarify organizational responsibility and structure. Opportunities for departmental crossover for growth must be identified. Within the data center department, the divergence between technical and managerial positions

| Department: Systems and Programming | Position Titles | | | |
|---|---|---|---|---|
| Job Family: Systems Analysis | Senior Systems Analyst | Systems Analyst | Programmer Analyst | Associate Programmer Analyst |
| Function Tasks: | Skill Level | | | |
| SA16 Assess proposed system requirements | 1 | 2 | 3 | 4–5 |
| SA17 Design functional outline | 1 | 2 | 3 | 4–5 |
| SA18 Design input, output, and data | 1 | 2 | 3 | 4–5 |
| SA19 Design processing | 1 | 2 | 3 | 4–5 |
| SA20 Design controls | 1 | 2 | 3 | 4–5 |
| SA21 Design business system test plan | 1 | 2 | 3 | 4–5 |
| SA22 Complete business system design | 1 | 2 | 3–4 | 5 |
| SA23 Evaluate business system design | 1 | 2 | 3–4 | 5 |
| SA24 Plan computer system design, user procedures, and conversion design | 2 | 2 | 3 | 4–5 |
| SA25 Review user procedures | 2 | 3 | 4 | 5 |
| SA26 Review manual procedures | 2 | 3 | 4 | 5 |
| SA27 Review training plan | 2 | 3 | 4 | 5 |

**Exhibit VII-9-2. Sample Task Structure (partial)**

and any resulting differences in compensation must be clear and justified. These tasks can usually be accomplished in two or three meetings, spread over two or three days.

### Task-Learning Relationships

Because the training and development environment and the usable toolkit are changing, the learning experiences for each task should be selected carefully. These changes include:

- As a result of the economic climate, training budgets are being tightened and the time allotted for training is being cut back.
- Because of the availability of better training materials (e.g., computer-assisted or video-drive  courses), individual on-the-job training can be

| Skill Level | Task Performance | Typical Level of Supervision Required |
|---|---|---|
| 1 | Able to execute planning for the task and instruct others in its performance. Can provide creative input to task development or change.<br><br>How demonstrated: Planning for assigned area or function. Initiation of action to define and solve problems. | Performs task with no outside supervision.<br>Highest level of planning skill.<br>Technical skill may decrease because of change in perspective. |
| 2 | Able to perform task and coach others in its performance. Participates in planning and administrative activities related to the task.<br><br>How demonstrated: Application to complex projects as manager or on special assignment. | Performs task with minimal supervision.<br>Supervises others in task performance.<br>Able to relate to planning requirements and provide input.<br>Highest level of technical skill. |
| 3 | Able to perform all typical aspects of the task. Has complete knowledge of the task and its performance in accordance with specified company procedures and processes. Able to perform effectively in small group or team situation.<br><br>How demonstrated: Application to complex projects as project leader or sole performer. | Performs task with minimal day-to-day supervision.<br>May coach others in task performance. |
| 4 | Able to communicate with peers and subordinates and relate task to other tasks and skills of the job.<br><br>How demonstrated: Application to assigned activity or project. | Performs some tasks under limited supervision and others under direct supervision.<br>Needs assistance with more complex application of tasks. |
| 5 | Able to display understanding of the task such as would be obtained in orientation or initial training.<br>How demonstrated: Written or oral discussion. Application to simple activities. | Performs task under constant supervision.<br>Needs coaching to perform all but the most straightforward tasks. |

**Exhibit VII-9-3. Task and Skill-Level Descriptions**

safely substituted for a substantial part of training after initial knowledge levels have been reached.

- Training for senior positions must include behavioral (i.e., performance) aspects. Technical individuals must now interact more with nontechnical users during more complex deployment activities. Failure to positively affect performance on the job (i.e., change behavior) during such deployment can seriously affect the benefits that can be attained from the new system or application. Being a highly competent technician is no longer sufficient.

- The ability to learn about the business and the company strategies and objectives must be woven through almost every training activity and must be addressed separately on a continual basis.
- Much training can also be accomplished through coaching, which places added burdens on managers but increases communication with individuals and promotes vicarious learning, which can add considerably to the knowledge of individuals.
- More training will occur through the analysis of case studies that can be immediately and directly used to accelerate on-the-job performance.

These changes are not intended to replace classroom education, especially at the higher job levels. They merely indicate the broader choices available to a data center manager and suggest close links with training and human resource professionals.

Data center managers or technical trainers should develop a simple training and development catalog that identifies the objectives for each learning experience and specifies whether the module is developed and provided in-house or supplied through a qualified support vendor. It should also specify by what means the training will be delivered (e.g., workshop, seminar, video lecture, or on-the-job coaching).

## RELATING CAREER PATHS TO OTHER HUMAN RESOURCES TOOLS

The career development flowchart in Exhibit VII-9-4 depicts how most organizations perform the career development functions. These functions are often performed independently in a disconnected manner so that the output of one function is not used as input to another. The resulting duplications or omissions are often costly to an organization. For example, position descriptions, career paths, and the tasks performed on the job are often incorrectly documented or related to one another. Without formal and coordinated job description and goal documentation, performance appraisal can be based only on subjective goals (i.e., specifications with no supporting details as to how to do what is required), and individual development plans are created independent of performance or job needs. Promotion decisions are also based on subjective judgments rather than on the achievement of established job and corporate goals.

If career planning functions are joined in a comprehensive network, individual careers can be planned and defined in view of global, departmental, or organizational goals. For example, at performance appraisal time, task lists, career path charts, and any performance goals established at prior performance

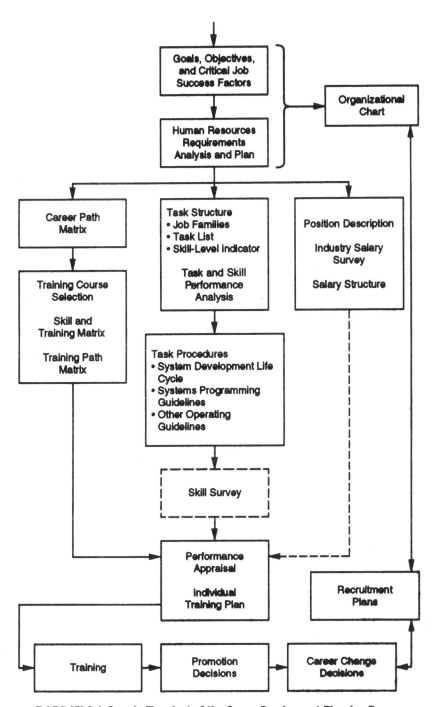

**Exhibit VII-9-4. Sample Flowchart of the Career Development Planning Process**

reviews can be used as a basis for discussing strengths, areas needing improvement, additional training needs, and career opportunities. The results of this discussion should be documented and agreed on to form a basis for an individual development plan for the coming year and for coaching sessions between annual reviews. If all jobs and individuals are evaluated with departmentally or organizationally defined career path charts, reviews will be complete and consistent across job lines. When documentation is complete and if, for business reasons, change is required between reviews, it can be made and documented so that development plan changes are consistent and complete across the organization.

### Succession Planning

One of the major uses of the career path system is to identify individuals who are ready for management advancement. When reviewing the performance of individuals who may be ready for promotion, organizations should use career path charts and performance requirements to identify the skill levels associated with the key tasks an individual is expected to perform. For managerial positions, special attention should be paid to performance in administration, planning, personnel relations, and communication skills.

If individuals are being considered for a position that has no prepared career path statement, a quick chart should be drafted that shows organizational relationships and the top 10 to 15 tasks for the job. At the same time, a brief list of critical success factors and key events related to the position should be drafted. This will ensure that all candidates are evaluated against the same criteria.

When faced with a decision between several qualified candidates, managers can use the charts to rank the individuals according to specific strengths and weaknesses. Career path charts and performance requirements thus enable an organization to base management promotions on specific, consistent criteria rather than on subjective judgments.

### Hiring

If a position cannot be filled by in-house staff, outside candidates should also be appraised according to the specific, objective criteria in career path charts. The career path charts can be used by interviewers to illustrate the formal structure by which job candidates clearly communicate their job qualifications and help ensure that there are no surprises when they land the job.

### Individual Development Plans

The integration of career path structures with individual career plans allows an organization to tailor employee opportunities for training, broadened on-the-job experience, and internal transfer to meet the needs of the organization and its employees. Like organizational career path structures, individual training and development programs should be planned carefully.

An individual career development plan permits each person to build on individual training and education in a planned and orderly manner. Employees can then apply their knowledge to improve performance in current positions and to prepare effectively for future positions. This approach is much more effective than simply allowing employees to take random courses to meet constantly changing needs. Individual development plans can also help establish the need for special projects or on-the-job experience to increase the competence and capabilities of individuals. In addition, the career path network allows the organization to identify its needs and, by combining individual development plans, determine whether employee skills and capabilities exist across the organization and are up to the levels required for effective performance.

Because career path and individual development plans help keep managers aware of the skills and adaptability of their employees, organizations may find that they have less need to search outside to replace employees. Current staff members can be groomed over several years to reach the needed levels for advancement. The result will be a more effective and proactive rather than reactive management of career development. Reduced turnover and improved performance should follow.

## SUMMARY

Data center and IS management can build a career path structured by:

- Listing all jobs in each job family and ranking them from highest to lowest in terms of salary grade (or experience required, if salary grade is not available).
- Reviewing the lists to identify discrepancies or missing jobs or jobs that should be placed in other families.
- Comparing the lists for each job family to determine whether jobs with similar responsibilities or requirements have similar grade levels.
- Drawing a chart like the one in Exhibit VII-9-1 indicating job-responsibility relationships.
- Determining for each position the jobs from which individuals usually transfer and the jobs to which individuals are usually promoted or transferred.
- Having the lists reviewed by several department members, who can suggest additions or changes.
- Reviewing the job descriptions for each position, listing the critical success factors and the most significant tasks for each job family, and estimating the level of performance required for each job (as shown in Exhibit VII-9-2 and Exhibit VII-9-3).

- Determining the training activities that could help individuals perform each job.

These procedures can be used to develop a practical career path system that reflects the organizational structure and keeps personnel aware of their specific responsibilities. As the organization's needs and experience grow, the career path structure can be expanded into a more comprehensive and sophisticated tool.

# Section VIII
# Desktop Computing

D uring the early 1980s, a phenomenon known as the microcomputer, or personal computer, was introduced into the information systems environment. It was a phenomenon, rather than just new technology, because of the dramatic impact it had, not only on information systems, but on business as well.

The use of microcomputers has proliferated throughout the business community at a tremendous rate. The technology associated with microcomputers changes almost on a daily basis. Given the demands for quality products, tight control of expenses, pressure on profits, and a competitive edge placed on businesses today, the microcomputer has allowed organizations to take better advantage of computing capabilities at reduced costs.

The trend toward decentralized computing with extensive networks of microcomputers has, in many cases, led to decreased demand for data center mainframe support. As a result, in many organizations, the role of the data center has changed. However, this trend does not signal the end of the mainframe era. It does, however, dictate that the approach that data center managers use with regard to managing microcomputers may have to change. Chapter VIII-1, "Managing the Transition to Microcomputers," discusses an approach that data center managers can use to more effectively manage the integration of microcomputers into the systems environment.

Along with the growth in microcomputers has come growth in the operating systems that manage them. As the concept of downsizing and the implementation of client/server architecture becomes more prevalent, the strengths and weaknesses of the various operating systems take on new importance, especially as they relate to the networking. Chapter VIII-2, "Assessing Microcomputer Operating Systems," provides a complete analysis of four major microcomputer operating systems.

As microcomputers have proliferated throughout businesses, the issue of security has assumed major importance. The concerns focus on two major points: the amount of company information that moves through the network and is stored on hard drives and floppy disks, and the fact that microcomputers are often connected to the mainframe and have access to vast amounts of company data. Addressing these security concerns is a major responsibility for the data center manager. Chapter VIII-3, "An Overview of Microcomputer Network Controls and Security," provides useful information and a checklist for planning, operating, and maintaining controls and security for microcomputer networks.

One of the major security issues that has arisen with the use of microcomputers is that of computer viruses. Because of the large networks of microcomputers that have come into use, the control of computer viruses is a serious issue. In Chapter VIII-4, "An Overview of Computer Viruses," the characteristics of various viruses are discussed, as well as products and procedures that the data center manager can use to control and eliminate them.

# VIII-1
# Managing the Transition to Microcomputers

*JOHN P. MURRAY*

N o one today can say with any degree of certainty if the mainframe is likely to disappear from the data center. What is likely is that in the future, much smaller, less expensive yet increasingly more powerful and efficient information processing hardware will become the norm. Many more information systems functions are likely to reside in functional units outside a centralized information systems department, and in fact, increased control of many IT processes by business unit users is already quite common.

Although some may resist such changes, the expansion of the use of microcomputer technology is an inevitable reality. More powerful, intelligent workstations offering greatly increased functional capabilities and productivity are going to become even more common in user departments. The microcomputer has already begun to change the manner in which the data center is managed and the demands placed on those charged with that management responsibility. Data center managers may be uncomfortable with this scenario, but because it occurrence is inevitable, they cannot ignore it.

In contrast to the beliefs held by some data center managers, these changes need not signal the end of the computer operations function. On the contrary, astute data center managers will develop an understanding of what is occurring and will take the steps required to capitalize on the changes. Those data center managers who do so and develop sound strategies to act on those changes can channel the use of microcomputer technology into an opportunity for career advancement.

## THE REQUIREMENT FOR MANAGEMENT CONTROL

Data center managers deal with many issues on a daily basis that do not entirely depend on the technology involved. To a considerable extent, these issues apply in any environment—mainframe or microcomputer. Responsibilities for the procurement and management of IT hardware, processing control, security, the backup and protection of the organization's data, and the selection and management of personnel have not disappeared with the arrival of the microcomputer. The requirement to remain current with changes in technology also remains important in the microcomputer world.

## Protecting Data Assets

Perhaps most important, the requirement for the central storage and control of the organization's data is not going to vanish because of the movement to a microcomputer or client/server world; it may even assume greater importance in a mostly decentralized computing environment. Even the most microcomputer-oriented companies usually find that they must retain some mainframelike hardware to store and secure the organization's most valuable data assets. That hardware may remain in a centrally located data center or be dispersed throughout the organization.

There should be little doubt that client/server processing is going to play an important role in the information systems world of the future. One issue data center managers should consider is what the server looks like: Is it a mainframe or a series of microcomputer servers? Where will the server or servers reside? Will it or they be in a central location or dispersed throughout the organization?

In many installations, the first step toward the client/server environment is through the existing mainframe. For installations that own or have long-term operation software leases, continuing to use the mainframe as a server for a period provides an increased return on that investment. In addition, the phased movement to client/server, through the continued use of the mainframe, reduces the risk inherent in changing the processing environment. The phased approach allows for planning and training that can prove to be valuable through the transition.

What the final client/server installation looks like depends on the plan developed by the particular organization to deal with this new environment. The data center manager can provide valuable input to the planning process and should emphasize that the issues of control and support are not going to go away. As IS functions become increasingly dispersed, the requirement to control, secure, and protect the data should increase.

There are already many examples of the difficulties encountered by allowing individual departments to be responsible for the security of their data assets. Failure to routinely back up the data on standalone microcomputers is one very common example of the type of difficulty such circumstances can cause. When that situation occurs and data is lost, the damage is usually minor. Because typically only one or two people are affected, the result is often more an annoyance than a serious issue. However, with an expanding microcomputer environment that involves both local and wide area networks (LANs and WANs), these circumstances change. The opportunities for serious disruption to the organization from the failure to back up data increase dramatically. Although business unit managers may be capable of protecting the data, they are often unaware of the requirement to back up the data or they lack the discipline data center professionals gain from years of performing regular backups. In addition, their focus remains on the business of their department, and worrying about the data is not always viewed as a departmental problem, but an IS problem.

In any event, organizationwide provisions for the management and control of the data assets must be established wherever the data resides. Final decisions about the topic in many organizations are likely to depend on the action of the data center manager. Data center managers who develop a sound plan to retain control and construct a business case to do so, will be in a favorable position. Those who simply bide their time and let things take their course are probably going to lose control.

## DIFFERENCES IN MAINFRAME AND MICROCOMPUTER MANAGEMENT

The basic management principles that apply to the management of the data center apply equally well to the management of a microcomputer environment. The primary difference is one of scale. Some management approaches are different in a smaller dispersed atmosphere, and microcomputer terminology is somewhat different. However, none of these should deter the experienced data center manager from taking steps to adjust to the new environment. The growth in microcomputer technology can offer many benefits to those in the data center who make an effort to understand the technology and how to use it. The skills that make operations managers successful are exactly the skills required as the industry increasingly embraces microcomputer technology.

As the use of microcomputer technology evolves, the microcomputer environment will begin to look increasingly like the current mainframe environment. For example, the use of LANs and WANs is nothing more than the current mainframe teleprocessing environment. In addition, the concepts and processes found in the microcomputer world are similar to those associated with the mainframe world. The need to capture data, to process that data, and to make the resulting information available to those who need it is precisely what is done in the data center today. The benefits of microcomputer use are less complexity, less cost, and the ability for nontechnical individuals to gain greater control of their data. Those benefits are offset by the greater difficulty in managing, coordinating, and controlling these new environments.

What many users do not recognize or accept is that with their new freedom to work on their own—that is, outside the IS department—comes many new responsibilities. Gaining direct control over their environment means they must accept ultimate responsibility for managing that environment.

Many of the same issues that arose in the early days of the development of the mainframe installations are likely to reappear as microcomputing expands. Much of the difficulty and tension encountered on the way to improving the management of today's data center function may be encountered again. This difficulty may even be compounded by the dispersion of the processing environments across wide areas of the organization. When problems arose during the development of the data center, centralized control of the mainframe at least allowed the data center manager to know what was happening, the location of the data, and who was using or changing the data.

As the use of LANs and WANs grows, the control and coordination issues associated with that growth become more pronounced. As a result, the requirement for improved management control is going to grow. Many organizations already face the problem of islands of data—that is, data that is fragmented and duplicated over many files and systems. Even in centralized environments, many organizations do not have a strong grasp of how much data they have, the accuracy of the data, or where it is stored. Data center managers continually encounter problems with providing adequate disk storage capacity to hold existing islands of data.

Yet disk storage is only a part of the problem from the perspective of the data center manager. The time and effort required to process various jobs because the data is not well structured and organized is a growing problem, and its implications are beginning to become more pronounced as organizations move to data base processing. This problem, unless addressed and managed, is certain to grow worse as individual departments gain increasing control over their data. In addition, this problem existed when the people managing the data had a strong technical orientation; less technically focused users are even more likely to have difficulty managing such a situation or gaining complete control of both the data and the hardware. This is why strong active management of the emerging microcomputer processing world is so critical.

What occurs in organizations that have moved to the increased use of LANs without appropriate thought and planning is the rise of tension between information systems and the various user departments. Too often, the euphoria that comes with independence from the so-called bureaucracy of the IS department fades as the reality of managing computing processes emerges. It is not unusual to hear department managers claim, trying to remove themselves from problems they encounter, that data processing is not their job and therefore how could they be expected to grasp every technological implication. They have a thought-provoking point, and too often, it comes up only after a serious problem arises. For example, in many organizations, data that has become critical to the business functions of the organization resides on standalone microcomputers. When that data is lost and it is impossible to recreate, there are organizationwide implications.

The person using the microcomputer may not back up the file. The person controlling the data or managing the application may leave the organization. Before leaving they may erase the data, but far more likely the person replacing the employee may inadvertently destroy or mismanage the data. Replacing that data may or may not be possible, and even in the best scenario, replacing the data is likely to take a considerable amount of time, money, and effort.

## Managing the Networked Environment

By understanding this problem, the data center manager can mount a case to gain control over this data, just as in the current data center operation. Because the potential problems associated with islands of data are not apparent in many installations, raising the issue and building a case to move against the problem in the microcomputer world before it becomes serious is not going to be an easy task. However, aggressive action by the data center manager can bring both the manager and the organization considerable benefit. Data center managers can save their organizations time and effort by doing whatever they can to ensure that their companies are not forced to relearn the lessons of the past.

As microcomputer-based teleprocessing environments evolve, other problems that have been dealt with in the mainframe world and mastered by the data center manager are likely to appear in the microcomputer world. Problems of the availability of the LANS and the WANS and of adequate response times across the networks are going to become serious issues. In addition, there must be a method to anticipate the growth of the processing load. As the processing load grows, it is going to have to be managed.

Management of the processing work load growth requires recognizing the changes as an opportunity for the computer operations section and developing a strong microcomputer network management function as a part of the data center operation. The first step of such an approach is to develop a plan to move all standalone microcomputers to LANs.

Although the impression may be that the introduction and effective use of microcomputer technology, once standalone units are networked together, is a very arcane area only mastered by a few highly skilled individuals, the author's personal experience (based on the installation and management of more than a dozen LANs in several organizations), has been the opposite. Success has to do with dedicated, quality people and effective and thorough planning. A background in computer operations can be a distinct help in managing the LAN environment.

The installation of WANs, by their nature, may represent a more difficult circumstance. However, it seems unlikely that people who have had experience with the installation and management of remote online communications installations in the mainframe world would find much difficulty in the WAN arena. That premise is, again, based on the availability of sound operations management skills.

Unfortunately, many vendors that offer microcomputer hardware and services simply do not have the personnel with the skill or experience necessary to handle the installation and continuing management of LAN technology. In too many cases, an organization that expects to successfully use the technology finds it has to develop the required skills within the organization or look outside for someone with those skills.

## Case Study: Lessons Learned

The author recently observed an attempt by a retail microcomputer vendor to configure and install a straightforward LAN installation. The process became much more difficult than should have been the case. In the end, to complete the installation, the members of the microcomputer section of the organization had to take responsibility for the project and complete it themselves.

Perhaps the installation should have originally been undertaken by the in-house staff. However, there were several reasons that approach was not taken. The microcomputer staff in the organization is small compared to the size of the company and the number of microcomputers installed and in use. The mandate of the microcomputer section in this organization was to concentrate on the design and development of new systems and specifically excluded any responsibility for the physical installation or repair of the microcomputer hardware. A rationale for this approach was that the section was to remain small. It appeared it would be more cost-effective for the installation and continuing maintenance of the hardware to be handled by the vendors than by company employees.

This was a sound approach. The problem was that the skill levels of the vendors' technicians were not adequate for the task of correctly installing the network. Halfway through the project, it became apparent to the members of the microcomputer staff that the vendor was unable to successfully complete the project. To correct the situation, the microcomputer supervisor had to take charge of the project and complete the installation.

Because the microcomputer staff had to step in to take charge of the project, other projects they were working on were delayed. The LAN was installed, and it did provide the benefits promised. However, making that happen in this installation became more difficult, more time-consuming, and more frustrating for everyone involved than should have been the case.

An analysis of the problems associated with this LAN installation showed that many difficulties encountered were avoidable, if the vendor's project manager had had the appropriate experience. What was lacking was an understanding of the scope of the project. In addition, there was no ability to think ahead to identify difficulties and take appropriate action before things got out of hand.

As with much of what is done in the information systems world, lessons were learned from the preceding experience. In the future, as the use of and reliance on microcomputer technology expands in the organization, the policy to depend on outside vendors will be changed. As that occurs, a provision must be made to address the planning, installation, and continuing management of the microcomputer hardware and associated operating software.

Because of that expansion, the responsibility for the design, installation, and continuing support of the LAN environment has been assigned to the data center. Within this organization, a movement is also now underway to deal differently with the selection, installation, and continuing management of the microcomputer hardware. Responsibility for those functions will shift to the operations of the data center. In addition, as the process moves forward, the maintenance of the microcomputer inventory will also move to the computer operations group.

It is the stated intent of this organization to move to a downsized information systems environment. That means that over the next several years there will be a dramatic reduction in mainframe processing. In spite of that, no computer operations jobs will be eliminated. A strong long-term education plan is being developed to provide the proper knowledge and skills for the current members of the operations section. The thrust is to define the LAN and WAN management requirements and then to move that function under computer operations. The result will be to transfer existing skills to the new environment.

## OPPORTUNITIES FOR DATA CENTER MANAGEMENT AND STAFF

Computer operations professionals should concentrate their efforts on the management of the hardware and the operating environments. In addition to the aspects mainframe and microcomputer management have in common, several new areas must be addressed. First, beyond the continuing management of the various operations concerns, the microcomputer environment presents the opportunity to gain control over the mechanical aspects of the process. Issues such as the layout of the LANS, the selection and installation of the wiring for the LANS, and even the continuing maintenance of the hardware can all be placed within the purview of data center management.

A second area the data center manager should seek to manage is the continuing maintenance of the microcomputer hardware; the problem should be understood and its potential explored by the data center manager. Microcomputer maintenance contracts may be costing the organization a lot of money. However, because microcomputer hardware technology is, to a considerable extent, becoming more standardized and modularized, hardware failures are increasingly being solved by replacing complete components. In that environment, people with a reasonable amount of mechanical aptitude and an interest probably could meet the bulk of the microcomputer repair problems of the organization. The data center staff is in an ideal position to develop an in-house maintenance service.

The data center manager's experience with upgrading mainframe hardware in the traditional data center operation can also apply well to the microcomputer environment. Because of the movement to modularity, a shift to hardware that can be upgraded to more powerful versions is taking place. In some cases retrofitting the old hardware is an option.

Given its importance to the continuing success of the microcomputer operation, communications is a third area the data center manager should try to become involved in or gain control of. The installation and use of local and wide area networks can present several opportunities for the data center manager.

The structures of the microcomputer and communications industries consist of many vendors providing a variety of goods and sevices. As with the microcomputer industry, the quality of the products offered, the experience of the people involved in the industry, and the levels of service provided are not consistent. Customers are often forced to deal with several vendors. When difficulties arise, the vendors are often more adept at placing blame for the particular difficulty than they are at correcting the problems. The same problems existed in the management of the data center 8 to 10 years ago. That problem was solved when data center managers took control. When they demanded that the vendors stop the finger-pointing and resolve the issues, the problems disappeared. The same approach should be taken with microcomputer and communications vendors to deliver the levels of service that will be demanded in the future.

## SUMMARY

The often haphazard microcomputer explosion presents a concrete opportunity for the data center manager to step in and take control of what may have become, or is likely to become, a difficult situation. Bringing management skills to these evolving microcomputer and communications areas is a circumstance requiring attention in every organization. Those data center managers who recognize the opportunity and take the initiative to move ahead are going to enhance their careers, whatever their organizations ultimately decide about the microcomputer's role in the mainframe environment.

# VIII-2
# Assessing Microcomputer Operating Systems

*RANDALL A. NAGY*

V arious vendors and experts have differing opinions about which microcomputer operating system is truly capable of revolutionizing computing in an organization. The decision of which system is most appropriate, however, depends on the individual organization's environment and requirements.

When the operating scene is viewed objectively, however, it becomes apparent that no single operating environment can fulfill all the needs of all organizations. Choosing an operating system that is best for an organization depends as much on how the organization is expected to grow as it does on the technical capabilities of an operating system. A successful match of operating environment and user is more apt to occur when the needs and idiosyncracies of both are understood. For example, large interconnected organizations may have a strong requirement for password security and data base journaling activity, whereas decentralized, task-oriented work groups may find both of these operating system features inconvenient and even counterproductive.

The operating systems discussed in this chapter are MS/PC-DOS, Microsoft Windows 3.1, OS/2 2.0, and UNIX. To help organizations make the most suitable choice, this chapter provides a description of each system and its features, as well as an explanation of how well each system functions in standalone, networked, and security-conscious environments.

## MS/PC-DOS

MS/PC-DOS (or DOS) was developed for single-user and single-tasking environments. Evolving from Digital Research's Control Program for Microcomputers (CP/M) operating system, DOS was designed to be a bootstrap program (i.e., a program that runs only for the amount of time that is required to load and run a single-user application). DOS originally provided only the most basic terminal and disk input/output routines to application programs. Because of these limitations, many systemwide support facilities were (and are still) missing from DOS. Such features as memory management, DOS reentrancy, virtual storage, multitasking, user accounting, and system security are a few of the critical omissions from the DOS environment.

Fortunately, the operating system's strengths are as numerous as its weaknesses. Because DOS does not manage the tasks previously mentioned, the microprocessor and the DOS program itself have more time to perform more critical tasks. Real-time process monitoring, low-level device control, and catering to the requests of the user in general are what DOS does best.

Perhaps the most important reason for implementing DOS is to take advantage of the abundance of available software. From state-of-the-art computer programming tools to the latest in desktop publishing, the DOS-workstation user can choose from a variety of highly customizable tools that have become indispensable in most offices.

## Networking Disadvantages

Given the single-user origins of DOS, problems invariably arise when DOS-based workstations are incorporated into multiuser local area networks (LANs). In the process of constructing a LAN out of DOS workstations, the user is often placed in the awkward position of adding omitted DOS features to the LAN on an ad hoc basis.

For example, the spread of computer viruses attests that most LAN vendors do not provide secure, adequately administered operating environments for their DOS users. Because DOS itself has no built-in mechanisms for computer security, most network vendors have developed their own DOS security programs. Unfortunately, there is no agreement between DOS LAN vendors concerning how much security, if any, should be provided. Consequently, few DOS LANs, and even fewer hybrid DOS LAN systems, are safe from widespread viral attacks and user abuse.

Another problem with the DOS platform relates to controlling its proliferation. Because of the low cost of DOS workstations as well as their popularity with users, the number of DOS workstations in an office or research environment usually increases quite rapidly. Even if the workstations were initially procured to function as standalone platforms, as dozens of them show up at a particular site, it is almost impossible to keep users from networking them. An unfortunate result of this activity is that virus outbreaks have halted production at some companies for several days when DOS LANs became infected. Furthermore, because DOS is missing several components (e.g., mail, group permissions, user accounting, and automatic backups), the creation and administration of DOS LANs is difficult.

Although DOS has proved adept and highly successful at performing real-time and single-user applications, this single-tasking operating system is not suited for serious network and multiple-user environments. If a company's needs are small or device oriented, DOS is appropriate. Experience has proved, however, that large DOS-based LANs should be avoided. User accounting and security are too important to include as an afterthought in any network operating environment.

## MICROSOFT WINDOWS 3.1

As the inventor of DOS, Microsoft Corp. (Redmond WA) has had to contend with its problems and limitations. Not only have missing memory management and poor multitasking features plagued DOS developers since the creation of the product, but DOS applications developers themselves have added to the problem by writing their own highly sophisticated virtual memory management routines and graphics drivers. With this variety of DOS solutions, programs often clash when each attempts to manage a single resource in its own manner. To make matters worse, software vendors often have ignored vital portions of the DOS operating system entirely by building alternative systems into their application programs. These circumstances led to the development of the Microsoft Windows product.

Microsoft Windows 3.1 is a DOS enhancement program that was developed to take control of the entire DOS workstation and share it with other programs. Although Microsoft Windows accomplishes this goal and adds such much-needed features as RAM over-commit and device sharing, Windows' nonpre-emptive, nondeterministic nature prevents it from being a serious multitasking platform. In other words, Windows tasks that have been placed in the background are often starved out while waiting for a single foreground application to surrender the CPU. And unlike OS/2 and UNIX, Windows has no user-driven priority schemes available that would, for example, allow a background communications file exchange to run slower than other background processes.

### DOS Compatibility

Because one of the strengths of DOS is the abundance of software written for it, DOS compatibility has become an important issue for all microcomputer systems. Although each operating system discussed in this chapter has some type of solution that allows it to run DOS software, the Windows DOS solution is the most comprehensive. Because Windows itself is a DOS application, it can naturally run more DOS software than other microcomputer operating systems. It is important to note, however, that DOS programs not written explicitly for Windows cannot fully take advantage of the advanced features that Windows has brought to DOS.

Because Microsoft Windows is DOS-based, errant programs frequently crash it much more often than is experienced under either OS/2 or UNIX. Although restarting a microcomputer operating system is acceptable, requiring help to correct a Windows unrecoverable applications error or an outright system crash can cost larger companies a great deal of money in terms of productivity, morale, and redundant customer support.

### Networking

As a network operating system, Windows adds little to the realm of accountable, secure network operations, although new interprocess communications methodologies (e.g., dynamic data exchange and built-in NetBIOS support services) do mark some milestones in the DOS world. Windows, like DOS, is acceptable for the individual user but relatively unsuitable for the company network.

## OS/2 2.0 OPERATING SYSTEM

Like Microsoft's Windows, OS/2 2.0 from IBM Corp. attempts to resolve many of DOS's limitations. Unlike Windows, however, OS/2 is a complete rewrite of the operating environment, going so far as to totally drop support for the 8086 and 8088 CPUs that DOS originally supported.

In many ways, OS/2 makes advances in microcomputer operating systems that even the sophisticated UNIX and POSIX operating systems cannot claim. OS/2 supports national languages (by supporting double-byte characters) and offers more sophisticated network support by including Attach Manager, Communications Manager, and the LAN management program. Therefore, OS/2 can serve as the basis for developing software with true international applications.

OS/2, like UNIX, allows a single user to balance programs in relationship to one another (by internal process priority schemes), thereby allowing for preemptive and deterministic multitasking. Unfortunately, OS/2 does little to correct DOS's omission of file-level protection (i.e., POSIX user group recommendations).

### Software Support and SAA

OS/2 has almost totally failed to capture the third-party applications market responsible for the tremendous success of DOS. The operating system is being used in many corporations, however, and it enables them to maintain their commitment to IBM's Systems Application Architecture (SAA), in which OS/2 Extended Edition plays an important role. DOS, AI/X (IBM's version of UNIX), and Windows are not part of the SAA family.

OS/2 is the operating system that promises to eventually allow users and programs to move transparently between IBM's vast range of products. IBM's stated goal is for all its future products to have the same look and feel. This similarity is referred to by IBM in SAA vernacular as common user access.

In 1992, five years after the introduction of OS/2, perhaps the most important characteristic of the operating system was its successful deployment in Fortune 500 companies. Although OS/2 has been criticized by many for providing multitasking without having any multiuser capabilities, OS/2's promise lies in IBM's massive effort to update its entire user interface in favor of common user access.

### Missing Features

It is important to note, however, that like DOS and Windows, OS/2 by itself fails to provide suitable user accounting and security in LAN environments.

Even add-on programs often fail to adequately protect the LANs from abuse. In the case of DOS and Windows, this omission might be understandable; in the case of OS/2, however, it could be argued that such multiuser capabilities should have been built into any operating system kernel designed for connectivity. With microcomputers operating at speeds in the multiple millions-of-instructions-per-second range, turnkey ways to share CPU power with other users should be more available than they are on OS/2.

OS/2 has been much less successful than other operating systems, primarily as a result of its high cost, frequent revisions, and inability to run many traditional DOS programs (the OS/2 file system is not completely compatible with DOS). The DOS compatibility box provided by both IBM's and Microsoft's versions of OS/2 supports far fewer original DOS applications than does Microsoft Windows. Further, IBM and Microsoft are divided in their support of OS/2, which will probably leave the OS/2 standard divided in terms of software support. Although Microsoft is still contractually obligated to support OS/2, it is devoting more time and money to Windows. IBM has recently acquired the rights to OS/2 and will always support it. The DOS programs that do run under OS/2 not only run more robustly than on Windows but run faster, offering more responsive graphics support in full-screen mode.

## UNIX

The history of UNIX (AT&T Technologies, Inc., Berkeley Heights NJ) is exceptional in the world of computer operating systems, for several reasons. First, rather than being developed by a hardware vendor interested in supporting its own product line, UNIX was adapted during the early stages of its development to support the hardware of as many vendors as possible. Second, UNIX was designed with a smaller-is-better concept that has enabled users to apply more available computing power; other operating systems have required that the CPU spend most of its time running the operating system.

Finally, as a result of the huge popularity of the C programming language, the UNIX operating system, which was written in C, has been ported to every major vendor's hardware. Because UNIX has been designed from the ground up to be a truly multiuser system, it is the only popular, nonproprietary operating system that can run on a home microcomputer as well as on a corporate mainframe.

### Multiuser Support

Unlike DOS, OS/2, and Windows, UNIX is both a multiuser and a multitasking operating system. This means that to share a UNIX workstation with other users, all that is required is a serial port and an asynchronous terminal. User accounting, file sharing, electronic mail, multitasking, and low-speed networking (19.2K bps is typically the fastest asynchronous turnkey network support) are all built into the basic UNIX operating system.

## Turnkey Networking

One disadvantage of UNIX is that true high-speed networking is available only through add-on solutions (of which there are just as many as for Windows and DOS). Fortunately, the UNIX world has adopted a de facto networking standard under TCP/IP. Unlike the other workstation operating systems, however, the UNIX file system maintains all of the built-in file-level features that make a high-speed LAN function efficiently. Many users are initially intimidated by the terse UNIX command set and are hesitant to administer multiuser resources. Unlike OS/2, DOS, and Windows, UNIX requires users to log on to the computing resource and governs how much access a user can have on the UNIX system (the term *super user* reflects more than just a security class on UNIX; it is also often associated with a skill set). In short, UNIX can be extremely difficult to learn and administer, though the connectivity, security, and user administrative solutions are available.

## Software Compatibility

Finally, it must be noted that DOS compatibility has been achieved on UNIX. Unfortunately, UNIX support of sophisticated network devices and peripherals running under DOS often fares as poorly as DOS support does under OS/2. Many DOS device drivers and programs do not work as well on UNIX and OS/2 as they do on DOS alone. Furthermore, although a common object file format has been designed and there have been several attempts at providing a common executable format for the UNIX family of operating systems, compiled programs will never run as well on other processors as they can on native-code machines. In other words, programs written on Sun Microsystems, Inc.'s (Mountain View CA) 6800-based UNIX need to be recompiled to run as well on IBM's RISC-based AI/X or on SCO, Inc.'s (Louisville CO) 386-based UNIX V. Microprocessor vendors have not been able to develop an effective cross-compatible computer instruction set.

## A COMPARISON OF OPERATING SYSTEMS

As each of the operating environments discussed is examined in relation to the others, it becomes clear that no single operating environment can be said to win in all categories. Which operating system an individual or organization chooses to standardize on continues to be a decision that must be based on existing operating systems and networking requirements as well as on individual user capabilities and preferences. The following sections provide a comparison of the operating systems in relation to their third-party software support, their graphical user interfaces, their networking capabilities, and their application support.

## Third-Party Software Support

DOS is the unquestioned champion of the third-party market. From artificial intelligence to simple games, more individual software titles exist for DOS than for any other operating system. UNIX and DOS are much more stable products than Windows and OS/2; each has major kernel revisions several years apart, as opposed to the several months between OS/2 revisions. Windows runs DOS programs more reliably than both OS/2 and UNIX, though DOS emulation under OS/2 is more robust and responsive than under Windows. Regardless, there will certainly be more software written for Windows than for OS/2, in part because of Windows' modest system requirements and processing overhead (i.e., Windows lacks most of OS/2's elegant interprocessing communications mechanisms and other subsystems, which most standalone workstation users do not need). In addition, the early positioning of Windows as the graphical user interface (GUI) for the masses, through both affordable pricing and economical systems requirements, has given Windows a much larger market share than OS/2 and UNIX have.

## Graphical User Interfaces

GUIs are integral to each operating system. Although Windows is the most prevalent GUI for DOS, it is by no means the only (or necessarily the best) graphical user interface available for that operating system. Under OS/2 and UNIX, however, the OS/2 Presentation Manager and MIT's X Windows are the only feasible alternatives for software development. Although Microsoft Windows and OS/2 Presentation Manager are highly object-oriented environments, X Windows maintains a distinctly procedural environment for software development.

In addition, Presentation Manager and Windows have gone to great lengths to enforce a common look and feel between programs developed for their systems, whereas X Windows allows different styles of programs to run under and cooperate within itself. In other words, it would be much easier to make an X Windows program look and feel like a common user access application than to make an OS/2 or Windows program resemble an X Windows environment, such as MOTIF. Finally, like the rest of UNIX, the X Windows GUI is entirely networkable, whereas the Presentation Manager and Windows GUIs are decidedly anchored to their single-user workstations.

## Networking

Of the four operating systems reviewed, only UNIX provides a truly turnkey multiuser networking solution that enables any computer to be effectively shared by several users. OS/2 and Windows depend on having total control of all available computing resources and thus perform poorly in networks. Standalone DOS networking is extremely limited, though many networking options are available from third-party vendors.

## Operating System Application Support

OS/2 offers more interprocessing communications mechanisms for developing robust, fault-tolerant, networkable solutions than any of the other three operating systems. National language support and SAA make OS/2 a natural for larger corporations that want to develop their own software applications for standalone workstations. UNIX's responsive virtual memory management and rich subset of OS/2 interprocessing communications capabilities make it the natural selection when multiple users (not just multiple programs) need to share a single computer at the same time. The open UNIX system allows vendors to compete on a level playing field, rather than having to guess at the working of undocumented system features. IBM and Microsoft products have maintained an unfair competitive edge by allowing their applications to use hidden features that are not available to outside software developers.

Finally, when several applications need more than small bootstrap services for working together in an orderly manner, Windows provides not only the vehicle but the software availability to allow users to get the job done without much software development. Basic DOS is excellent, however, for running programs that are highly specialized, requiring customized software, device drivers, or throughput requirements.

## SUMMARY

The OS/2 operating system is not likely to be as successful in the all-important third-party software development market as DOS and Windows. After approximately five years of public access to the system, there are fewer applications available for OS/2 than there were for DOS after its first year of public availability. Although network support for the OS/2 operating system is far superior to anything that DOS or Windows has to offer, UNIX alone is capable of adequately sharing its entire file system, GUI, and interprocessing communications within a networking community.

Because an operating system's success is often defined in terms of software availability, the future for OS/2 looks dim. If SAA is a consideration, however, OS/2 is an appropriate selection. Similarly, UNIX must entice more software developers into its realm to guarantee continued success in the standalone arena. If SAA is the salvation of OS/2, then multiuser support, open systems, and connectivity are the issues that will make UNIX the operating system of choice for those interested in corporatewide, multivendor networking.

In the final analysis, DOS has brought more computing power to a greater variety of users than any other operating system in history. The only system that runs DOS better than Microsoft's Windows is DOS itself, so Windows could become the most popular system in the standalone, single-user environment.

# VIII-3
# An Overview of Microcomputer Network Controls and Security

*FREDERICK GALLEGOS • THOMAS R. HALSELL*

A s microcomputers gain visibility within the business environment, new applications and hardware (e.g., modems and emulation boards that create a form of distributed data processing) continue to enhance their usefulness. The growth in user access to information processing has increased the desire to share data, software, and other information, which has resulted in a new era of microcomputer interface known as networking. A local area network (LAN) is a data communications system that allows various independent devices to communicate with one another.

Although a LAN can consist of such devices as intelligent terminals, minicomputers, and supermicrocomputers, this chapter emphasizes the networking of microcomputers. Any references to this chapter to LAN and personal computer networks (PCNs) refer to the networking of microcomputers. Exhibit VIII-3-1 illustrates the five most common configurations of networked distributed processing systems. Most distributed or wide area networks (WANs) are set up in a hierarchical or tree configuration.

## MAJOR ISSUES IN NETWORK INSTALLATION

The security and control issues that this chapter focuses on go hand in hand with the planning, implementation, and operation of networks. The following list provides a quick reference identifying the installation issues most relevant to security and control:

- *Wiring and cabling*—Many articles and case studies have shown that approximately 80% of network problems are due to improperly installed or poor-quality cabling. When quality is sacrificed for cost, operations may be detrimentally affected once the network is put into service, resulting in retrofit costs.
- *Throughput or traffic*—This is an area in which effective planning and

657

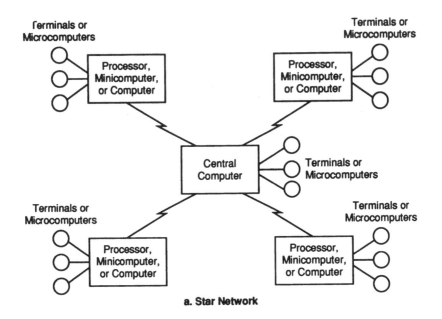

**a. Star Network**

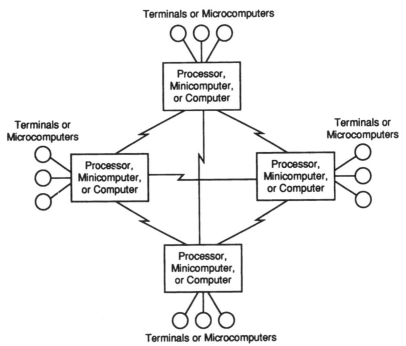

**b. Loop or Ring Network**

**Exhibit VIII-3-1. Possible Network Configurations**

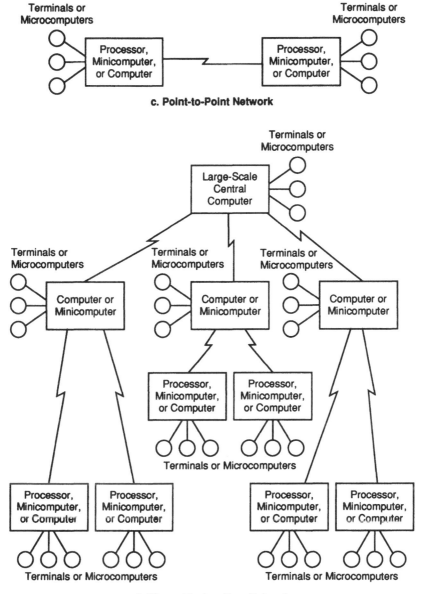

c. Point-to-Point Network

d. Hierarchical or Tree Network

**Exhibit VIII-3-1. Possible Network Configurations** *(continued)*

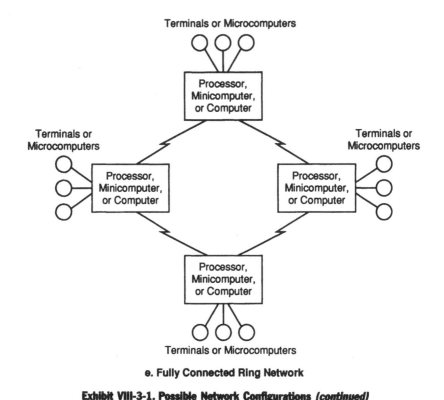

**e. Fully Connected Ring Network**

**Exhibit VIII-3-1. Possible Network Configurations** *(continued)*

---

visits to organizations that have implemented a similar network can pay off. Major decisions include specifying the type of file servers needed to support the desired application and determining connectivity with other networks and peripherals. An assessment of the organization's current and planned applications is important input to this process.

- *Layout*—To facilitate enhancements and the ability to adapt to organizational change, layout should be part of the planning process. This can save an organization money in the long run and help identify control concerns.
- *Measuring performance*—Tools that help monitor performance and analyze change can be very valuable to the data center manager. In addition, network analysis products can assist in diagnosing data bottlenecks as well as system and control failures.

Because a network represents a substantial investment in microcomputer equipment, network equipment, network operating software, shared software, individual user software, data, personnel, administration, and training, the network or the information contained in the network files may represent an organization's major assets. Therefore, an organization must evaluate the security and controls to be used in the LAN. Security and controls can be classified as physical security and access controls, environmental controls, software and data security controls, and administrative security controls. Each of these is discussed in the following sections.

## PHYSICAL SECURITY AND ACCESS CONTROLS

The objective of physical security and access controls is to prevent or deter theft, damage, and unauthorized access and to control movement of PCN equipment and attached devices. Some physical controls also prevent unauthorized access to data and software.

General physical controls that can be used to protect office equipment and PCNs include personnel badges, which help employees identify authorized personnel, and alarms and guards, which deter theft of PCN equipment. In addition, placement of the PCN equipment and office design will further secure the PCN. For example, PCN equipment should be placed in areas in which office traffic is light. If possible, the microcomputers, printers, and other equipment should be placed behind locked office doors. Data center managers may want to use combination locks to prevent duplication of keys; another alternative is to use a locking device that operates on magnetic strips or plastic cards—a convenient device when employees regularly carry picture identification (ID) badges.

The PCN equipment should be attached to heavy immovable office equipment, permanent office fixtures, special enclosures, or special microcomputer workstations. The attachment can be achieved with lock-down devices, which consist of a base attached to permanent fixtures and a second interlocking base attached to the microcomputer equipment. The bases lock together, and a key, combination, or extreme force is required to remove the equipment. All PCN equipment must be locked down to prevent unauthorized movement, installation, or attachment.

Many microcomputers and other equipment attached to the network may contain expensive hardware and security-sensitive devices (e.g., hard disks, encryption boards, AST boards, added memory, graphics and color cards, print spoolers, software cards, and PROM EPROM, EEPROM chips). The removal of these devices not only incurs replacement costs but could cause software to fail and may be a means of circumventing security or allowing for unauthorized disclosure of such company-sensitive information as customer lists, trade secrets, payroll data, or proprietary software. Internal equipment can be protected by lock-down devices, as previously discussed, and special locks that replace one or more screws that secure the top of the equipment. These special locks are called CPU locks because they prevent access to the CPU area.

Cabling enables the various users and peripheral equipment to communicate. Cabling is also a source of exposure to accidental or intentional damage or loss. Damage and loss can occur from the weather, or by cutting, detaching or attaching to and from equipment, and other accidents. In many networks, if the cable is severed or damaged, the entire system will be impaired.

Cabling should not be accessible to either the environment or individuals. The data communications manager may want to route and enclose cabling in an electrical conduit. If possible and if the exposure warrants the cost, cabling can also be encased in concrete tubing. When the cable is encased, unauthorized access through attachment is lessened. In addition, unauthorized movement of the cabling will not occur easily and will enable the data center manager to more efficiently monitor and control the network and access to it.

To alleviate potential downtime, cable may be laid in pairs. In this arrangement, if one set is damaged, the alternate set can be readily attached. The second pair is usually protected in the same manner as the original but is not encased in the same tubing, thus preventing the same type of accident from damaging both cables.

## ENVIRONMENTAL CONTROLS

All PCN equipment operates under daily office conditions (e.g., humidity, temperature, smoke, and electrical flow). However, a specific office environment may not be suited to a microcomputer because of geographical location, industrial facilities, or employee habits. A primary problem is the sensitivity of microcomputer equipment to dust, water, food, and other contaminants. Water and other substances not only can damage the keyboard, CPU, disk drive, and diskettes but may cause electrocution or a fire. To prevent such occurrences, the data center manager should adhere to a policy of prohibiting food, liquids, and the like at or near the microcomputer.

Although most offices are air conditioned and temperatures and humidity are usually controlled, these conditions must nonetheless be evaluated by the data center manager. If for any reason the environment is not controlled, the data center manager must take periodic readings of the temperature and humidity. If the temperature or humidity is excessively high or low, the microcomputer equipment and the network should be shut down to prevent loss of equipment, software, and data. When microcomputer equipment is transported, either within the building or especially outdoors to a new location, the equipment should be left idle at its new location to allow it to adjust to the new environmental conditions.

Airborne contaminants can enter the equipment and damage the circuitry. Hard disks are susceptible to damage by dust, pollen, air sprays, and gas fumes. Excessive dust between the read/write head and the disk platter can damage the platter or head or cause damage to the data or programs. If there is excessive smoke or dust, the microcomputers should be moved to another location. Small desktop air filters can be placed near smokers' desks to reduce smoke, or the data center manager can limit smoking to specific locations, away from microcomputer equipment.

Static electricity is another air contaminant. Static electricity can be reduced by using antistatic carpeting and pads placed around the microcomputer area, antistatic chair pads and keyboard pads, and special sprays that can be applied to the bottoms of shoes. Machines can also be used to control static electricity in an entire room or building.

Major causes of damage to PCN equipment are power surges, blackouts, and brownouts. Power surges, or spikes, are sudden fluctuations in voltage or frequency in the electrical supply that originate in the public utility. They are more frequent when the data center is located near an electrical generating plant or power substation. The sudden surge or drop in power supply can damage the electronic boards and chips as well as cause a loss of data or software. If power supply problems occur frequently, special electrical cords and devices can be attached to prevent damage. These devices are commonly referred to as power surge protectors.

Blackouts are caused by a total loss of electrical power and can last seconds, hours, or days. Brownouts occur when the electrical supply is diminished to below-normal levels for several hours or days. Although brownouts and blackouts occur infrequently, they are disruptive to continuing operations. If microcomputer use is essential and the organization's normal backup power is limited to necessary functions, special uninterruptible power supply (UPS) equipment can be purchased specifically for the microcomputer equipment. UPS equipment can be either battery packs or gas-powered generators. Battery packs are typically used for short-term tasks only (e.g., completing a job in progress). Gas-powered generators provide long-term power and conceivably could be used indefinitely.

## SOFTWARE AND DATA SECURITY CONTROLS

Data and software security and access controls are the key controls over a microcomputer network. (Software and data security controls are referred to as data security throughout this chapter because the same controls provide security for both data and software.) A microcomputer network has two levels of data security. The first is access and use of local standalone microcomputer capabilities. The second is access and use of the network system and its capabilities. These two levels can be integrated through the installation of certain security software and hardware. However, the organization must be aware that these two levels exist and are necessary to provide the security for all the network's functions as required.

The objective of data security is to prevent access by unauthorized users and to restrict authorized users to needed data and functions. Authorized users should be restricted to the use and access of specific data, screens, software, utilities, transactions, and files. Exhibit VIII-3-2 provides an overview of the security and administration capabilities of the major LANs.

| | Advanced NetWare 286 | NetWare 386 | LAN Manager Version 2.0 | 3+Open LAN Manager | AT&T Star Group |
|---|---|---|---|---|---|
| **Security** | | | | | |
| Encrypted passwords can be sent over the network | Yes | Yes | Yes | Yes | No |
| Access control is provided by: | | | | | |
| —Time and date | Yes | Yes | Yes | No | Yes |
| —Group | Yes | Yes | Yes | Yes | Yes |
| Historical error and log status can be checked | Yes | Yes | Yes | Yes | Yes |
| Names of users can be displayed | Yes | Yes | Yes | Yes | Yes |
| **Administration** | | | | | |
| Open files can be monitored | Yes | Yes | Yes | Yes | Yes |
| Fault tolerance is checked through disk mirroring | Yes | Yes | Yes | No | Yes |
| Can report: | | | | | |
| —Network errors | Yes | Yes | Yes | Yes | Yes |
| —Faulty packets | Yes | Yes | Yes | Yes | Yes |
| —Current server load as a percentage of total | Yes | Yes | No | No | Yes |

**Exhibit VIII-3-2. Overview of Major LANs: Security and Administration Capabilities**

## Password and Data Access

The key to PCN security is user authentication. Although badges and personal IDs are common authentication tools, they can fail at all levels of security. Other methods of authentication can be obtained by the computer system itself. Special software and hardware products exist that allow authentication of users through the entering of an ID number and a password.

A PCN has two levels of password and user ID security requirements. The first protects local microcomputer access and use, and the second protects network access and use. The user ID and password used for the local microcomputer will be a double safeguard to network access. To access the PCN, the user must have a valid user ID and password for local use, and that password can be set up to restrict access to the network user ID and password screen. In addition, this double security can be used to restrict users to specific computers and to limit specific computers to the network.

User IDs and passwords are practical and economically feasible in most situations. If the risk of loss is high and the cost can be justified, card IDs or a voice authentication system can be added to the user ID and password system.

In addition to the use of passwords and user IDs, a security system must list the user IDs and the locations of all microcomputer security violations. The actual violation (e.g., an attempt to use an incorrect password or to access unauthorized systems) must be logged, and the security administrator must investigate and resolve the problem.

Duties must be segregated in microcomputer networks as they are with local microcomputer use, because the traditional separation of duties seen in mainframe systems is circumvented. Computer operations, systems development, systems programming, and application programming in a microcomputer environment are usually at the hands of the user, who can perform various programming, operations, and applications functions by simply reading a book and applying the knowledge.

To segregate duties on the PCN, security software must be in place. The software not only limits access to specific programs and data but limits the user's capabilities to DO commands and programming tools. In addition, the software must monitor what a particular command or program is doing—for example, formatting disks or making global copies or deletes. The security software will prevent accidental errors and possible theft of sensitive data.

## Encryption

Encryption is a technique of creating unintelligible information (i.e., ciphertext) from intelligible (i.e., cleartext) information. The same algorithm is used to create the ciphertext from cleartext and convert the ciphertext back to cleartext. The algorithm uses a key to tell the mathematical equation where to start producing the ciphertext. The key must be given to the program that will decipher the text. For encryption to be effective, the passage of the key and the algorithm must be kept secret. Programs must not be hard-coded with the key, nor should the key be written down. The key and the algorithm are often encrypted or written in machine language to prevent the casual user from intercepting code messages.

Encryption is useful in protecting sensitive information (e.g., password, user ID, and payroll files). Any sensitive message or transmissions must be encrypted to prevent interception either by someone on the network or by someone using highly sophisticated electronic equipment. All microcomputers emit radio signals that can be detected by other electronic equipment. Another way of protecting transmissions is to use fiber-optic cabling in place of twisted-wire cabling. A combination of encryption and fiber optics ensures transmission security.

Encryption can be provided by either hardware or software. It can be as uncomplicated as a simple algorithm or as complex as the National Bureau of Standards' data encryption standards. The choice depends on the level of security required or desired by the organization. If encryption is widely used within the organization, the public key system should be used. The public key system requires that the sender creates the ciphertext on the basis of the receiver's public key. Receivers will decipher the information using their private key. The public key system eliminates the passing of the key, which can threaten its secrecy.

### Backup, Recovery, and Data Storage

Data and software on local microcomputers and on the network must be copied and archived periodically. Backup copies can quickly and accurately restore misplaced diskettes and erased files and diskettes. The backup method must allow the restoration of individual files, directories, partitions, and disks. Tape backups that allow restoration only of the entire hard disk can cause data integrity errors on data for files and directories that do not require restoration. If one file requires restoration on the basis of a previous day's backup, any files updated since the backup will not reflect those updates after the restoration.

Users should perform the backups for shared data. The data backup should be in the same format as that on the original disk. Encrypted files must be backed up as encrypted files, and files that require a password to be accessed must be stored in that manner. This prevents circumvention of security by accessing the backup and copying its contents. Moreover, if the backup format is not the same as the original, a backup tape that is used to restore information there will weaken security until the files are reprotected.

### Software and Other Controls

Software that accesses shared data on the network must be designed specifically for a multiuser environment. Single-user software may cause data integrity problems, data access problems, or network crashes. For example, if user A accesses a file and begins changing information, the applications software does not actually change the data on the disk but changes the data in the memory of user A's microcomputer. Further assume that while user A is editing or inputting, user B edits the same file. When users A and B then save their copies of the same file, the only changes that were made to the file are user B's—all of user A's changes were overwritten when user B saved the file.

One method of avoiding the previously mentioned access problems is to design access locks. These locks do not allow a user to update specific data while another user is already updating that data. Locks can be provided by either applications or network operating system software. These locks can be user requested or automatically implemented. They limit access to data fields, records, file transaction types (read or write), directories, or software systems.

Access locks must be used for all files accessed by applications that are used on the network. Applications must lock data that is necessary to complete a particular task in order to prevent deadlock, which occurs when application A has locked access to a file or piece of data and then requires a second item. Meanwhile, application B has locked application A's desired second item and now requires A's locked data. Neither application will release the data until the other releases its data: as a result, both applications are left waiting for the other to release its data. Applications software and the network operating system software must provide a method of releasing inaccessible files or data without stopping the application.

Data and software used in the PCN can be controlled by using diskless microcomputers. The major loss of data, security, controls, and privacy occurs through the availability of 5½-inch diskettes. Users can copy data or software either up or down onto the PCN. If applications already exist on diskettes, the diskettes could be given to the data center manager to review their contents and load the software. Thus, the PCN would be controlled from loss of privacy of sensitive data. The diskless microcomputer can provide greater control over local and network access but does require greater administrative and organizational controls.

## ADMINISTRATIVE SECURITY CONTROLS

The administration of the PCN is similar to the management of any data processing facility. The data center manager's main objective is to prevent, detect, and correct unauthorized access to the network's hardware, software, and data to ensure the network's sound operation and all security surrounding the local microcomputer and the microcomputer network processing.

Before any security controls can be implemented, the data center manager must perform a risk assessment of the PCN. Risk assessment is the task of identifying the assets, the threats to the assets, and the probability of loss of the assets as a result of a particular threat. The loss is determined by quantifying the dollar value of the assets lost and multiplying that value by the probability of the loss occurring.

After implementation of the necessary controls, daily management of the network is required. Daily management ensures that security controls are maintained, though changes occur in the software, applications, and personnel. Daily management can be classified into various categories, which are discussed in the following sections.

**Physical and Environmental Controls Management.** All such controls in active use must be tested periodically. Such testing includes the evaluation of the effectiveness of current controls and the implementation of additional controls as determined to be necessary. The results of testing of physical and environmental controls should be reported to senior management.

**Data Access Management.** The data center manager must assign and maintain user IDs and passwords and associated file and data access schemes as well as receive computer-generated reports of attempted unauthorized accesses. Reports on data access and traffic analysis should also be reviewed. These reports will allow the administrator to manage network growth and help foresee future security needs.

**Policy and Procedures Documentation Review.** The objectives here are to provide standards for preparing documentation and ensuring the maintenance of the documentation. The data center manager must set documentation standards so that when employees change jobs, become ill, or leave the organization, replacement personnel can perform the tasks of that employee. The data center manager must also periodically test the documentation for clarity, completeness, appropriateness, and accuracy.

**Data and Software Backup Management.** Backup media must be labeled, controlled, and stored in an appropriate manner. The data center manager must maintain control logs of all backups as well as provide documentation on how to recover files, data, directories, and disks.

**Other Management Controls.** The internal audit department, external auditors, contingency or disaster recovery planning, personnel background checks, and user training are included in this category. The auditor can aid in establishing proper testing requirements and in reviewing, testing, and recommending the proper controls to establish the necessary safeguards. Contingency planning or disaster recovery is essential to the proper maintenance of the PCN. The contingency plan establishes the steps to recover from the destruction of hardware, software, or data.

Personnel background checks must be performed on all data center employees who have access to key organizational information. The background checks should involve a review of credit history, financial health, personal problems, and other areas that may identify potential risks. This information can help establish potential integrity breaches before they occur.

User training must be established for all network functions. Users must be trained in microcomputer use, general computer knowledge, security, policies and procedures, consequences of noncompliance, and general network use. In addition, users should undergo more specific training for the different software on the network as required. Such basic training can prevent many problems from occurring.

## DIAGNOSTIC TOOLS

An especially important issue for the data center manager is microcomputer emulation to mainframes either through hardware (i.e., board or EPROM) or through software and the use of diagnostic tools to identify emulation problems. Networks depend entirely on emulation to successfully communicate within and outside of the network architecture. This emulation is accomplished successfully through the use of hardware or software to allow compatibility between equipment and communications protocols. Users faced with hundreds of diverse computing devices on Novell, Ethernet, IBM Token-Ring, or other local area networks that can talk with each other without regard to network protocols, cabling schemes, or distance may have a difficult time identifying emulation problems and their causes.

Diagnostic tools or network analyzers can effectively help determine the source and extent of emulation problems. Such software tools can diagnose user interfaces and perform cable integrity tests, printer interface tests, and network interface tests. For example, some analyzers have menus of tests for such protocol sets as TCP/IP and NetBIOS to allow the manager to build custom test sequences or to create scenarios to monitor emulation characteristics of certain hosts or servers. Such tools range in cost from less than $100 to more than $20,000. When confronted with a multitude of variables (e.g., cabling or wiring, topology, software, hardware, and firmware), managers may find support tools that can isolate a specific problem to be invaluable.

LAN failures not only irritate the user and support staff, they reduce the productivity of business operations. The lost time and revenue can run into the millions; however, diagnostic tools can be an effective resource to reduce downtime and maintain business productivity. There are more than 200 of these tools available. Exhibit VIII-3-3 lists some of the most popular.

## OTHER RISK CONSIDERATIONS

Assessing risk in a LAN should also include the way the system is connected. Three areas of concern are media, topology, and software and protocols.

### Media

Media are the cables with which computers are connected. Three types of cables are found in today's LANs: twisted pair, coaxial, and fiber optic. Twisted-pair wire is individually coated copper wires twisted together. They are encased in plastic and may contain up to 24 pairs. Twisted-pair wire is used as telephone wire.

Coaxial cable is a copper or multistrand wire encased in an insulator (e.g., Teflon). The insulator is surrounded by a mesh wire, which is then encased in plastic. This type of cable is much more resistant to electromagnetic interference but is more expensive than twisted-pair wire.

Two types of transmission can be supported by coaxial cable: baseband and broadband. Baseband is a single flow of data and is also supported by twisted-pair cable. Broadband combines the flow of data with a carrier signal by means of a modem. A modem at the other end of the transmission translates the carrier signal back to the data transmission.

| Product | Vendor | Protocol | Interface |
|---|---|---|---|
| LANVista | Digilog Inc Montgomeryville PA | Ethernet, DECnet, XNS, TCP/IP, IBM Token-Ring | RS-232C, RS-449, CCITT V.35, X.21 |
| LAN Detector | Racal/InterLan Foxborough MA | Ethernet, StarLAN, Novell, DECnet, TCP/IP, XNS, Sun NFS, MS-Net Appletalk | Ethernet |
| Feline | Frederick Engineering Inc Columbia MD | Async, BSC, SNA/SDLC, HDLC, DDCMP | RS-232C, CCITT V.35, T1 |
| Twisted-Pair Tester | Standard Microsystems Corp Hauppauge NY | ARCnet | Twisted Pair |
| Net/Cable Checker | THOR Manufacturing Reno NV | Localtalk | RS-232C |
| Chameleon 32 | Tekelec Calabasas CA | Async, BSC, SNA/SDLC, ISDN, LAPD, X.25, HDLC | RS-232C, RS-449, CCITT V.35, Centronics Parallel |
| Interview 20+ | Atlantic Research Corp Springfield VA | Async, SNA/SDLC, X.25 | RS-232C, RS-449, CCITT V.35 |
| LANtem | Novell Inc San Jose CA | Ethernet | RS-232C |
| HDA 2 | Electrodata Inc Bedford Heights OH | Async, SDA/SDLC, Sync | RS-232C |
| SAM2000 | IQ Technologies Inc Bellevue WA | Async | RS-232C, Centronics Parallel |
| DG/Sniffer | Data General Corp Westborough MA | SNA/SDLC, X.25, Ethernet | RS-232C |

**Exhibit VIII-3-3. Popular Diagnostic Tools**

---

Coaxial cable supports a wider bandwidth than twisted-pair wire. Bandwidth is the speed capacity for transmitting data. For example, to transmit 10 million bits per second, the medium requires a bandwidth of 10 MHz. The user, however, should be wary of judging the speed capacity of a LAN by the media and bandwidth used. Other factors in LAN design have more significant impact on performance. Coaxial cable also supports voice and radio transmission. This is an important consideration for departments that desire future flexibility.

Fiber-optic cable is the most expensive medium. With this medium, computer transmissions are converted to light transmissions, which are reconverted

| | Cost | Installation | Bandwidth | Interference | Susceptibility to Tapping |
|---|---|---|---|---|---|
| **Twisted-Pair Wire** | Low | Easy | Low | Susceptible | High |
| **Coaxial Cable** | Medium | Moderately Difficult | Medium | Susceptible | Medium |
| **Fiber-Optic Cable** | High | Difficult | High | Not Susceptible | Medium |

**Exhibit VIII-3-4. Media Risks**

to bit transmissions at the receiving end. This new type of medium has the widest bandwidth and is resistant to electromagnetic interference. In addition, it is the most resistant to tapping. Exhibit VIII-3-4 summarizes the risk characteristics of twisted-pair, coaxial, and fiber-optic cable.

Each LAN vendor specifies which medium is to be used. For example, the AT&T Star LAN uses standard twisted-pair cable, the Orchid PC Net uses coaxial, and the IBM PC Token-Ring network uses the IBM cabling system, which uses a variety of high-performance cables. IBM has stated, however, that standard telephone wiring can be used under some conditions.

The potential LAN user should carefully evaluate media requirements. Such issues as cost, interference, and future expansion needs should be considered. However, a LAN configuration should not be purchased solely on the basis of an evaluation of media. Other system features substantially affect the performance of the selected LAN. Most important, the potential user should not be overly influenced by the speed rating, or bandwidth.

### Topology

Topology refers to the configuration by which the workstations are interconnected. The three basic topologies are bus, star, and token ring. Risks in this area involve their application and use.

In a bus topology, a single cable runs past every workstation, and the ends of the cable are terminated with special equipment. In the token-ring configuration, the cable runs past all workstations, but the ends are joined, forming a ring. In the star topology, each workstation is connected directly to a server or hub. Variations of these topologies include distributed stars, in which two or more star configurations are linked together and the star-wired ring topology, which combines the star and ring schemes.

Topologies are determined by the network vendor, and each has advantages and disadvantages. The bus topology is simple; a faulty workstation, however, may be difficult to isolate. The star topology enables the user to locate cable faults easily because each workstation is connected to the server by an individual cable. This type of system requires more cabling than the other two configurations. If the workstations are located in dispersed locations,

| | Bus | Ring | Star |
|---|---|---|---|
| **Application** | Small networks | Few workstations at high speeds | Integrate voice and data |
| **Complexity** | Uncomplicated | Relatively complex | Very complex |
| **Performance** | Excellent in light load | Average transmission delays are long | Direct function of central node |
| **System Overhead** | Low | Medium | High |
| **Vulnerability** | Workstation failure does not affect network | Workstation failure can cause system failure | If server fails, system fails |
| **Expandability** | Easy | Modification inexpensive but temporarily disrupts network | Severely limited; server may support limited number of workstations |

**Exhibit VIII-3-5. Topology Risks and Characteristics**

this can add considerably to the cost of cable and installation. An overview of topology risk factors and characteristics is shown in Exhibit VIII-3-5.

## Software and Protocols

One of the most important tasks of the LAN is to traffic requests from the workstation for files and network resources. This control task is accomplished by software protocols, which are formal rules that govern the exchange of information between computers and provide reliable, effective, and efficient transfer of information. Without protocols, the system would be in chaos with unanswered requests, improperly routed data, and workstations monopolizing resources.

Major software protocols include contention, polling, and token passing. Contention includes simple contention and carrier sense multiple access (CSMA). In simple contention, the system performs in the manner of a meeting when people talk at will. What happens, however, when two people talk at once? Or when two workstations send messages simultaneously?

In the network, messages are converted to packets. If packets are sent by two workstations at the same time, they will collide and the packets will be destroyed. Although contention does not check whether another station is transmitting at the same time, it does provide a system by which the receiving station sends an acknowledgment that the packet has been received. If the sending station does not receive an acknowledgment, it will assume that the packet was not received and will retransmit.

CSMA is an access method that can be likened to a business meeting in which participants wait for a break in the conversation to make their contributions. In CSMA, a workstation monitors the transmission channel to determine whether any other workstation is transmitting and transmits when the line is free. As with contention, the station awaits an acknowledgment that the packet has been received. This is necessary because collision is still possible in the situation in which two stations sense a free line and transmit at the same time. A workstation waiting to send a packet can continually monitor the line for an opportunity to transmit, which is known as persistent carrier sense. Or in another scheme, the workstation can wait a random amount of time to reinitiate transmission. This scheme is known as nonpersistent carrier sense. Nonpersistent carrier sense results in fewer collisions.

Two subsets of CSMA are used in LAN technology: CSMA with collision detection (CSMA/CD) and CSMA with collision avoidance (CSMA/CA). In collision detection, the workstation continues to monitor the line after transmission. If a collision is detected, transmission is halted, and retransmission occurs after a random or unique delay for each workstation. This reduces the risk of two stations retransmitting at the same time. In collision avoidance, workstations wait for an opportunity to transmit and then transmit their intention to send a packet when the line is clear. If two workstations are contending for access, their precedence is determined by a preestablished table. In this mode, features must be implemented to ensure that an individual workstation does not dominate the network. For example, in some implementations, the recipient station has the first right to transmit.

The polling protocol performs very much as a moderator at a meeting would, calling on participants for contributions. In a polling network, primary workstations call on secondary workstations to determine whether they have information to transmit. If a workstation does, it may be allowed to transmit immediately or be assigned a time to transmit. To avoid work degradation, packets to be sent are stored in a buffer in the secondary workstation. In some polling implementations, priority can be assigned a workstation by polling it more than once a cycle, polling it less than once for each cycle, or polling it according to a recently established activity level.

The token-passing protocol is similar to a meeting in which the gavel is passed and a participant may speak only when the gavel is in hand. In the network implementation of this arrangement, a bit pattern known as a token is passed among the workstations. When a workstation receives the token, it has the right to transmit. The message and routing information are written to the token and passed through the network.

An empty token consists of a header, data field, and trailer. A token that has been assigned a message contains a new header, destination address, source address, routing, data message, and new trailer.

Each workstation determines whether the passed message is intended for its use. If not, it is passed. The recipient workstation reads the message and marks it as copied or rejected. The token is eventually routed back to the originating workstation. Only the originator may remove the message. This protocol reduces the risk of colliding packets. Exhibit VIII-3-6 summarizes protocol risk evaluation factors.

| | Contention | Polling | Token Passing |
|---|---|---|---|
| **Message Length** | Short packets | Tends to be longer than contention | Moderate to long |
| **Traffic Volume** | Low | Moderate to high | Quite high |
| **Network Length Constraints** | Length increases risk of collision | Limited by media | Limited by media |
| **Performance** | Excellent under light-to-medium loads | Excellent for moderate loads | Excellent for most conditions |
| **Overhead** | High | High | High |
| **Access Delay** | Moderate to long | Relatively long | Moderate delay in heavy traffic |
| **Station Failure** | Station failure does not affect network | Secondary station failure does not affect network | Station failure disruptive only in older LANs |

**Exhibit VIII-3-6. Software Protocol Risks**

## ACTION PLAN

Personal computer networks are becoming increasingly popular in business settings, and PCN implementations must include security controls to provide protection of physical and information assets. The level of protection required must be established through risk assessment. The risk assessment team must include members of senior management to establish the priority of asset protection.

Once risk assessment has been completed, the level of security can be achieved by implementing physical, environmental, and software and data access management controls. Any controls implemented must not cost more than the potential loss that the control was established to prevent, deter, detect, or correct.

The key control over a PCN is the use of passwords. Passwords establish data and software access schemes that provide for segregation of duties. This key control must be established and maintained by the data center manager or someone who does not have other duties over or within the PCN. The data center manager must ensure that all controls operate as intended and that all controls provide the level of security desired by management. The following paragraphs form a checklist of areas to consider in a microcomputer network.

**System Overview.** To gain a basic understanding of the network and its applications, the data center manager should:

- Review the system, including its physical layout, a list of equipment, the applications implemented, and the network software used.
- Interview user management. Assess the managers' knowledge of the system and participation during planning and implementation. Inquire about their satisfaction with the system.

- Interview the system administrator. Review the administrator's duties and problems encountered during system implementation and operation.
- Observe the operation of the LAN. Perform a preliminary review of the applications used, response time, devices used, and user satisfaction.
- Diagram the physical layout of devices. List the media used, location of devices, and topology implemented. Include the use of transceivers, tap boxes, gateways, modems, and repeaters.

**Information System Resource Planning and Management.** To ensure that the system takes advantage of available technology and that it is expanded and combined with other resources in a planned, systematic manner, the data center manager should:

- Review the organization's plan for system hardware and software performance. Determine whether the plan accounts for:
  —Equipment upgrades and the installation of new equipment.
  —File-server capacity expansion.
  —Implementation of application and network software upgrades.
- Review how the LAN installation relates to the overall information strategy by:
  —Reviewing the organization's strategic IS plans and determining whether the LAN installation is compatible with any plans for future connection to other LANs or wide area networks and whether security and access procedures have been developed for potential mainframe access, remote access, or interdepartmental data base sharing.
  —Reviewing procedures established to address corporatewide issues of interconnectivity.

**System Operations.** To ensure that the system operates in an efficient and effective manner to support user needs, the data center manager should:

- Review the roles and responsibilities of user management, LAN administration, and users concerning the operation of the LAN. Each review should include a clear written definition of system responsibilities, including:
  —Preventive maintenance.
  —Training.
  —Troubleshooting.
  —Application modifications.
  —Backup.
  —Housekeeping.
  —Equipment procurement and additions.
  —Vendor liaison.
- Review the responsibilities for data storage and housekeeping duties to determine whether such tasks as system backup have been specifically assigned and whether the installation provides for:

—Automatic backup.

—Off-site storage of backup.

—Periodic archiving of idle files.

—Procedures for adding and deleting users.

—Procedures for determining and implementing file access rights on an individual user basis.

- Review file-naming conventions and determine whether they provide for systematic classification to facilitate easy identification.

**Network Software.** To ensure that the network software provides adequate performance, data integrity, access security, file access rights, and diagnostics, the data center manager should:

- Review network software selection procedures and determine whether the following factors were considered:

—Fault tolerance.

—Password implementation.

—Capability to assign file access rights.

—Capability to provide mirror processing (i.e., writing to a primary and backup hard disk simultaneously).

- Determine whether access to system software is limited. Security procedures should ensure that:

—The keyboard is not attached to the file server.

—The file server is not accessible through DOS outside the system software.

—Administration rights (e.g., password assignment) are restricted to the LAN administrator.

—The password file is encrypted.

—Users are able to change their passwords.

—An audit trail of the system administrator's access to files is maintained and reviewed periodically by management.

**Access Control and Physical Security.** To ensure that only authorized personnel can access the system for legitimate processing needs, the data center manager should:

- Determine whether the responsibility for system security has been specifically assigned. Review responsibilities of the security officer (this position may be synonymous with the LAN administrator).
- Determine whether written security policies exist. Review them for completeness. They should include but not necessarily be limited to:

—User responsibilities.

—Password protection.

—Consequences for unauthorized file access.

- Review file access rights. Ensure that they are based on each user's need to know. Verify that access rights are modified or deleted when an employee is reassigned or terminated.

- Ensure that policies exist governing downloading files to diskettes and, if this practice is allowed, that diskettes are properly protected. Diskette security procedures include proper labeling and locking in a secure place at night. LANs using sensitive applications should consider using diskless workstations.
- Review procedures to train personnel in security control. This training should be provided in orientations and regular staff training. Personnel evaluations should ensure that users abide by security guidelines.
- Review the security plan and ensure that the plan is tested periodically.

**Backup and Recovery.** To ensure that critical applications can be restored in a timely manner after an incident disrupts processing, the data center manager should:

- Review the installation's backup plan. The plan should be documented and include:
    —The roles and responsibilities of personnel.
    —Identification of the resources required to facilitate processing.
    —A review of probable scenarios and an outline of procedures to initiate depending on the extent of damage.
- Determine whether applications have been ranked according to criticality.

# VIII-4
# An Overview of Computer Viruses

*ROGER B. WHITE, JR.*

A computer virus is an executable chunk of code that is programmed to make copies of itself in other executable files. A simple virus is a standalone program that makes copies of itself when it is run. A sophisticated virus hides in the other executable files. Either way, however, a virus must be executed to perform its function of self-replication. A virus can corrupt, destroy, or change the data in data files, but to do this and to infect other files, a virus must run as a program—it must be executed. This means a virus cannot spread or cause damage from a data file unless that data file is somehow transformed into an executable file.

Virus programs are not new. One of the first viruses dates back to days when mainframes were the sole species on the computer landscape. The virus took the form of a program called Animals, an artificial intelligence exercise. Animals is a simple computerized version of twenty questions. The computer wins when it guesses the player's answer correctly. When the computer loses, it asks the player for two things: the correct answer and a question that can differentiate the new answer from its best guess. It then stores these responses and is ready to play again.

Computer operators loved to play Animals, but managers frowned on it because it consumed more and more disk space the longer it was played, so they erased it whenever they found it. One inventive operator/programmer got tired of having to make a new copy of Animals after every manager inspection, so he added code to the front end that told Animals to copy itself automatically onto any new storage media it could find. The programmer never had to look far for Animals copies after that (but the programmer did have to look for a new job). Eventually copies of the Animals virus were discovered as far away as Japan.

The Animals virus was not harmful; it just replicated itself. The point of this story is that viruses are just another programming tool. They can be thought of as an undocumented feature that automatically adds itself to other programs. A virus becomes a data center manager's concern when it carries malicious code in addition to its self-replicating nature.

Viruses can be designed for any computer system, and most models have had at least one or two written for them at some time in their history. This chapter, however, deals specifically with viruses for IBM PC-compatibles and the Macintosh.

## PC-COMPATIBLE VIRUS CHARACTERISTICS

PC-compatible viruses can be categorized by the kinds of executables they infect; their varieties include standalones, executable infectors, boot sector infectors, systems infectors, and mutating viruses.

### Standalones

Standalones are programs like the Animals virus mentioned previously. They simply replicate themselves and do not affect programs around them. Standalones are rare and are generally not a problem because they are so easily identified.

### Executable Infectors

The executable infector virus is a chunk of code that adds itself to other .EXE or .COM files. The simplest form of infection occurs in the following manner: most of the virus is appended to the tail end of the .EXE or .COM file, and a hook is added to the front of the program that instructs the computer to immediately go to the tail and run the code there.

When the infected program is executed, the virus code searches for other files to infect and does whatever else it has been programmed to do. When the virus code has finished, it sends control back to the beginning of the file and the application the virus is hiding in begins its normal execution.

Executable infectors have no size limit, so they can be the most versatile of viruses. They are also the kind that can spread the fastest through a local area network. If one of these viruses gets into a file server utility commonly used for logging on (e.g., CAPTURE on NetWare LANs), it will be in every workstation that uses CAPTURE thereafter.

### Boot Sector Infectors

When a personal computer starts up, the first thing it does is load code from a specific area on a disk and execute it. This area is called the boot sector; on PC-compatibles it contains the startup chunks of MS-DOS. It can, however, contain a virus instead—the virus moves the MS-DOS startup to another place on the disk. This is called a boot sector virus. One of the first of these was the Pakistani Brain virus—so named because it was developed in Pakistan and has the word *Brain* as part of its text message.

Boot sector viruses are always small and more of a problem when systems are booted from diskette rather than hard disk. The viruses do not move through networks, because the virus spreads by copying itself onto the boot sectors of new disks, not by being part of a copyable, executable file.

### System File Infectors

System file infectors are a cross between executables and boot sector infectors. One of the first of these was the Friday the 13th virus. These viruses infect only specific system files, not every kind of executable. System files rarely change, so the virus can be fine tuned for its environment.

### Mutating Viruses

The newest wrinkle in PC-compatible viruses is the mutating virus. This is a virus that encrypts part of its code and fills the unencrypted part with a changing amount of meaningless statements. One of the first of these is called Dark Avenger. Mutators are difficult to spot with the static pattern recognition techniques that are the mainstay of antivirus scanners, so antivirus developers are designing dynamic scanners to deal with this latest development.

## MACINTOSH VIRUS CHARACTERISTICS

The Macintosh architecture and the Macintosh programming environment are quite different from those of the PC-compatibles. As a result, Macintosh viruses look different from their PC-compatible counterparts.

### Resource Adders

Resources are a way of adding to a Macintosh program without recompiling it. They are also an easy way to add a virus. Resource adders are the equivalent of PC-executable infectors; they can be big and versatile and they can infect many kinds of files.

### Desktop File Infectors

One file on the Macintosh changes continually: the desktop file that keeps track of where icons and windows are located on the screen. The program that updates the file is a prime target for Macintosh virus developers.

## WHERE THE VIRUSES ARE LIKELY TO OCCUR

All computers can be afflicted with viruses. The difference in the seriousness of the problem is one of magnitude: how often does a virus attack occur and how hard is it to eradicate once it is discovered? Virus problems get worse when:

- The computer model is common (e.g., PC-compatibles and Macintoshes).
- The computers are operated by many people with different skill levels,

681

so many users are not sensitive to signs of virus infection or immediately aware that their programs are not operating correctly.

- The computers are used with many kinds of software, so new programs on new disks are introduced to the computers regularly.
- Great flexibility exists in new application design. This makes programming easier, but it also makes it easier to slip a new virus in undetected.
- The computers are networked. The programs being transferred can be virus-infected, so networking is a way of spreading viruses very quickly as well. In fact, one of the quickest ways to spread a virus is to get it into a commonly used network utility (e.g., one used during log-on).
- No antivirus tools or procedures are in place. Virus attacks are now just another information system hazard, and tools and procedures are available for dealing with virus attacks just as for dealing with hard disk failures and all other system failures. Available tools and procedures can stop virus damage when they are properly implemented, but they cannot help if they are not used.

## PREVENTING AND ELIMINATING VIRUSES

Viruses are programs written by programmers. The difference between these and traditional programs is simply that the distribution is uncontrolled. This means that viruses move through some channels and pool in some places more readily than others.

**Neophyte Users.** A frequent virus source is programs that have passed through many neophyte hands. People who are new to computers do not recognize a virus infection quickly, and they do not take even rudimentary precautions against the spread of viruses. Ironically, children spread computer viruses as readily as they spread biological viruses; one of the common pools of viruses is school computer systems and one of the common ways of spreading a virus is to have a child bring home a diskette from school and run it on a home computer. A program on the home computer gets infected; it infects other programs on the home computer and one day the child's parents might take a copy of an infected program to work.

**Outside Users.** A similar potential source of infection are sales representatives or temporary technicians who bring a disk full of entertaining and helpful utilities to the office. If they pick these programs up from various informal sources and do not check for viruses, it is highly possible that a virus can be present.

**Disgruntled Personnel.** Another source of viruses is disgruntled employees. It can be an employee who is close enough to the technology to develop a virus or someone who merely acquires an infected disk from someone else and introduces it into the office environment.

## PREVENTION

Viruses are now a well-understood threat to computer systems, and the prevention measures are straightforward.

### Safe Software Acquisition

Computer viruses are not diseases, but it is helpful to think of them that way, and some commonsense rules that apply to biological viruses can be applied to computer viruses. The following sections outline tips for keeping viruses from moving through systems.

**Booting from Strange Disks.** Boot sector viruses are active only during the boot process. By consistently booting from a disk that is known to be uninfected (e.g., the local hard disk), spreading boot sector infections can be avoided.

**Scanning Disks Before Loading.** Many antivirus packages are available today. These can be used to scan a disk before it is loaded and before any virus has a chance to move from the disk into RAM and from RAM to other storage devices.

If the system is virus-free, any new disks or disks brought back to the office after being run on outside-office machines should be scanned. The scanning software alerts the user if a problem exists.

Scanning software should be used properly. If the user is sloppy in the scanning procedure, it is not uncommon for the virus scanning software to become virus-infected. When that happens, the virus moves quickly.

## CONTROLLING VIRUS DAMAGE

Because a virus is a program, it can do only damage that programs can do. It can be a devious program, but it is only a program. Viruses that put up strange messages or reprogram the keyboard are alarming to watch, but are not going to cause serious damage to an office's data. Serious virus damage occurs when data on disks is affected. Virus damage at its worst can be as direct as a command to format a disk or as insidious as a command to add random data to random sectors on a disk. In either case, the effect of the virus attack is much the same as the effect of a failure of disk hardware: data on the disk is either no longer accessible or no longer reliable.

### Restoring Data from Backups

If a disk fails, what can be done? The first line of defense against virus damage is diligent backup procedures, so that when the damage is detected the backups can be used for recovery. Keeping backups current and using stringent and thorough backup procedures are the important first steps in minimizing virus damage.

Viruses can infect only executable files. Their activity can corrupt data files, but they cannot be stored in data files. Executable files rarely change much from the time they are installed, so one convenient way to avoid reintroducing a virus from a backup tape is to never restore executables from a backup tape. Instead, all executables should be restored from their original disks. If it is more convenient to restore executables from the backup system, they should be scanned after the restoration to make sure they are clean.

## What to Do When Under Attack

If a virus is spotted, the antivirus scanner should be used to disinfect (i.e., remove viruses from executable programs) the infected files. Most antivirus packages disinfect as well as detect. If an antivirus package cannot disinfect a file, the infected file must be deleted and a fresh copy must be made.

If the virus is caught on a disk coming from the outside, it is probably not necessary to do more than alert the owner of the disk that it has been exposed and any system that the disk has recently been used with should be scanned. If the virus is discovered on an in-house disk, the rest of the in-house computers, disks, and networks should be scanned to determine how far the virus has spread. All copies of it should then be identified and disinfected.

If the virus has been in-house for a while before being discovered, it is likely that it has been saved in the backup-archive files as well. It may or may not be necessary to expunge the virus stored on tape. The virus cannot damage the tape or files on the tape. The hazard is simply the prospect of reinfection if one of the virus-infected files is restored from the tape. A compromise is to document on older tapes what viruses they may contain and in which files those viruses are likely to be found (this would be a list of files that the scanner had to disinfect when the virus is discovered), and then never restore those files from tape.

## Up-to-Drive Antivirus Software

Creating viruses is not a difficult programming task, so new viruses are being developed all the time. Antivirus developers can only respond to, not anticipate, new viruses; it takes months to years for a PC-based virus to spread widely and only days to weeks for antivirus developers to analyze the virus once they see a copy.

It is important to keep virus-scanning packages up to date. If a package is more than two years old, it is probably not going to catch current waves of infection. Most developers of virus-scanning products offer upgrades, and many of these upgrades are available on disk and as downloads from either the producer's bulletin board service (BBS) or a commercial service (e.g., Compuserve). Because bulletin board services are often plagued by viruses in disguise, however, downloading to a test machine first is a common precaution.

The following are just a few of the many companies offering antivirus software. The first two are designed primarily for standalone computers and workstations; the last two are designed primarily for protecting PC-based LANs.

Certus (Novi)
6896 W. Snowville Rd.
Brecksville OH 44141
(216) 546-1500

Trend Micro Devices, Inc. (PC-RX)
2421 W. 205th St.
Suite D-100
Torrance CA 90501
(310) 782-8190

Intel Corp. (Intel LANProtect)
5200 NE Elam Young Parkway
Hillsboro OR 97124

Cheyenne Software Inc. (InocuLAN)
55 Bryant Ave.
Roslyn NY 11576
(516) 484-5110

The following two organizations devote themselves to disseminating antivirus information:

International Computer Security Association
Virus Research Center
Suite 33
5435 Connecticut Ave. NW
Washington DC
(202) 364-8252

National Computer Security Association
10 S. Courthouse Ave.
Carlisle PA 17013
(717) 258-1816

Another source of information on strains of virus and their symptoms is the Hypertext VSUM (virus summary) maintained by:

Patricia Hoffman
3333 Bowers Ave.
Suite 130
Santa Clara CA 95054
voice (408) 988-3773
Compuserve: 75300, 3005

This can be downloaded from Hoffman's BBS (408-244-0813) or from the virus forum on Compuserve (GO VIRUS). It is a shareware product—a lengthy hypertext reference of viruses covering their name, origin, length, symptoms, and other characteristics.

## MYTHS AND REALITIES

Viruses have received more publicity than all other computer problems combined, but not all of the stories about them are true. The following sections describe some popular virus myths.

### Viruses Can Do Everything and Be Everywhere

Viruses are programs. They can do only what programs can do. Viruses can in theory come in all sizes, but the bigger they are, the easier they are to spot. If a million-byte virus tries to hide in a 50,000-byte COMMAND.COM file, it will soon be apparent that the COMMAND.COM looks too big. If the virus program is not big, its actions are not going to be too complicated. There are limits on how subtle a small program can be.

The other limit that a big, complex virus program faces is debugging. It is no easier to design a flawless virus than it is to design any other kind of application flawlessly. For instance, the Internet virus attack of 1988 was caused by a virus with many bugs. One of those bugs protected many kinds of computers on the Internet from attack—the program was incompatible with certain types of UNIX. Another bug, however, made the virus virulent on those machines it was compatible with. That bug kept the virus from sensing whether another copy of the virus was already running on the computer—the program was supposed to run only one copy of itself per machine. Instead, the virus reinfected computers repeatedly—each piece stealing a little processing power and using a communications line to find a new computer to infect—until the virus had commandeered so many computer and communications resources that the network was clogged up with virus traffic.

### A Virus on a Macintosh Can Spread to a PC

Viruses are executable programs. It is difficult, almost impossible, to design an executable file that runs on both Macintoshes and PC-compatibles. Application developers would love it if the task were easier, but because it is not easy for traditional application developers, it is not easy for virus developers either, and so far they have not succeeded. Should one be developed, it would be likely to look like such an oddball file in both the PC-compatible and Macintosh directories that it would be easily spotted and removed.

### Most Mysterious System Malfunctions Are Virus-Related

Long before viruses were discovered by the media, computer systems have had mysterious failures—*mysterious* meaning that the reason for the failure is not immediately obvious. They will continue to do so. The three most common causes of mysterious system failures are operator error, a hardware problem (e.g., a loose connection), and a software bug already identified by the developer. If testing for the first three has been exhausted without finding an answer, it is time to consider a virus problem.

## VIRUSES AND NETWORKS

Local area networks (LANs) aggravate virus problems in some ways and alleviate them in others. The aggravation comes because the computers of a LAN are interconnected. Viruses can move quickly through a LAN. Reinfections are likely and they move just as quickly. Once a virus gets into a LAN environment, it takes much work and vigilance to eradicate it completely.

The alleviation comes because applications that are centralized on file server disks can be scanned and protected easily, and boot sector viruses cannot spread through a LAN connection. The tight connection makes it possible to alert users to the virus problem so remedial action can start quickly. The following specific actions can be taken to control viruses on LANs.

**Using Security to Control Virus Propagation.** Executable files that are made read-only in some fashion cannot be infected. They can be made read-only at the file level or at the directory level. This can protect many applications but not all of them; it does not work for those that modify the executable every time the user changes their configuration. When viruses are around, those files must be watched carefully. If all applications are stored near each other on the directory tree, it makes it easier for the network manager to scan through them quickly.

**Disinfecting a Network.** If a virus has been established on the network for some time, four places must be checked: file server disks, local disks on each workstation, diskettes that users have for moving programs on and off the network, and the backups.

**Supervisor Equivalence.** A user reports to the administrator that a machine is acting strangely. Not realizing that a virus infection is present, the administrator tries running the application on a workstation to confirm the problem. The administrator's machine is now infected, and it, too, acts erratically. The administrator now logs in as supervisor to see whether the problem can be cleared up by trying other copies of the application. The administrator's infected machine, with supervisor equivalence—which overrides the read-only protection system—infects CAPTURE. While the administrator continues to research the problem, every user that logs on subsequently is infected. When the administrator finally recognizes that a virus is the source of the problem, it will have spread much further.

**Server-Based Virus Scanners.** Products are now available to scan file server disks in real time, which makes controlling a virus much easier. Some of these packages have attack logging. In one case, this attack logging solved the mystery of a weekly virus attack on a LAN. It turned out the culprit was a user on another LAN attached by a remote bridge. That user mapped to a file server on the LAN in question, then ran an infected program. The virus used the drive mapping to jump from one LAN to the other. The attack logger recorded that the attack was coming from over the asynchronous bridge that connected the two LANs, and the mystery was solved.

**Hierarchical Security.** If a particular system maintains a hierarchy of security, virus searches should begin at the top. Hierarchies are great virus concentrators; the user who can run all the programs can catch all the viruses.

## ERADICATING VIRUSES

The easiest way to eradicate a virus is to use an antivirus scanner to disinfect the executable that contains it. This works in most cases—as long as the scanner can recognize the virus. If the scanning package is old and the virus is new, the package may not recognize the virus. If the scanner cannot find the virus, the IS department, the reseller of the package, and the scanner's developer can be questioned to determine whether an update is available.

If a scanner cannot be found to recognize and disinfect the virus, the following method should be used (it is crude, but it works):

- Any surely infected and possibly infected executable files should be deleted.
- The files should be restored from their original disks.

All the diskettes that come in contact with the personal computer or workstation that the virus is found on must be checked. If a virus has successfully penetrated to shared files on a network drive, this means checking every workstation on the network and all the diskettes that are used with those workstations. Extra vigilance for a few weeks may be required; reinfections from forgotten diskettes are very common. Reinfection can be reduced by finding out where the virus came from and alerting the user of that system that a virus is present.

## ACTION PLAN

Viruses have been around long enough to be a well-characterized part of the information systems environment. New viruses will be introduced from time to time, but procedures and products are available for dealing with them. The threat they represent is as manageable as any other that computer users must deal with. The following are some symptoms indicating that a virus is establishing itself. These are things to look for before the virus reveals itself by executing whatever it is programmed to do.

- *Unusual disk activity.* A virus attack is the act of writing something new to the disk. This unusual disk activity may be too subtle to detect until after it has been confirmed that a virus really is at work, but if a disk is working strangely and the anomaly cannot be attributed to failing hardware or unusual software, a virus could possibly be the cause.
- *Changes in the size or date stamp of executable files.* For instance, if **COMMAND.COM** has grown by a few hundred bytes, or its data stamp indicates it was written two days ago, not two years ago, it has been infected.
- *Consistent crashing of a PC workstation on a LAN.* Many viruses use the same system resources that LAN drivers do. The conflict will crash both and usually foil the virus attack. This may leave a bit of mystery—the virus will be causing problems, but it will not be spreading to files on the LAN. Unless the infected disk is checked, the virus will not be found.

# Section IX
# Future Directions

The term *future* often conjures up the idea of gazing into a crystal ball—the notion that one can easily see and prepare for the future. Although it is certainly a major responsibility of the data center manager to prepare for the future of the data center, easily seeing it is another matter entirely.

In reality, no one truly sees the future. But, to a disciplined observer, noting the direction of key trends can provide a great deal of insight into where the future seems to be headed. Today, even determining the direction of trends is a demanding challenge, given the rapid pace of change that characterizes today's information systems environment.

As difficult as it may be, the data center manager must become as knowledgeable as possible about those trends that are affecting information systems in general and, more specifically, the data center. There are many trends that are occurring today, and this section looks at a few that promise to have a significant impact on the daily life of the data center manager. Chapter IX-1, "From Here to 2000; IT's Impact on Business," provides an exellent overview regarding the new role that information technology is beginning to play in the business environment, not only globally, but internationally as well.

Dramatic changes in computer technology continue today at a relentless pace. As the demand for processing services continues to grow, hardware designers are looking for newer and faster approaches to meet customer needs. One of the more promising new technologies is massively parallel computing. Already, applications have been developed in finance, retail, and other data-intensive businesses that make use of this new technology. Chapter IX-2, "Business Outlook on Parallel Computing," provides an overview of the specifics of this technology and the direction it seems to be headed.

There can be no doubt that the introduction of local area networks has had a dramatic impact on the information systems industry and the data center. While still a relatively new technology, it is already undergoing major change. Chapter IX-3, "Trends in LAN Operating Systems," discusses the impact of LANs and the direction the technology appears to be heading.

One area that clearly affects the data center manager is data base administration. The data center is responsible for housing and protecting vast amounts of corporate data. It is important for the data center manager to understand the basic concepts of data base management, and future trends related to it, in order to do the most effective job possible. Chapter IX-4, "Future Directions in Data Base Management," provides information regarding the new generation of data base management systems.

At least for the foreseeable future, the interaction between humans and computer will take place primarily through terminals. Voice activated systems are beginning to emerge, but terminals are still the primary communications devices. Chapter IX-5, "Trends in Terminal Technology," provides the data center manager with information regarding the future role of terminals and the technology behind them.

The rapid emergence of new technologies has provided many new opportunities for improving the state of computing in corporations today. At the same time, it has introduced some major challenges. Information security continues to be a major concern for the data center manager. Understanding how to take advantage of new technologies while continuing to maintain a secure environment has certainly become an important challenge for the data center manager. Chapter IX-6, "Information Security and New Technology," discusses many of the new technologies that are becoming more commonplace and how to address the information security issue.

Perhaps more so today than at any other time, data communications is becoming the real engine of the data center as new networks continue to be developed. Keeping current with this technology is often difficult for the data center manager. Chapter IX-7, "Trends in Data Communications Services," provides an overview of several of the recent trends in this area.

# IX-1
# From Here to 2000: IT's Impact on Business

*LOUIS FRIED*

F
uturist scenarios typically extend the planning horizon to 10 or 20 years into the future, but businesses must plan for the nearer term of the next 2 to 7 years to survive to enjoy the long-term future. Considering all the factors that may affect predictions, the further we look into the future, the lower success we have in prediction and the less current value our predictions have for business planning.

This is especially true for technology forecasting, which depends on projecting the current state of research into possible products of the future and the impact those products are likely to have on their users. The reliability of such forecasts are vulnerable to market acceptance of predicted future products, the affect of competing technologies, the affects of the costs of changing to the new technologies, the market strength of the companies that introduce the new products, and a host of other nontechnological factors.

The scenarios presented here are based on technologies (or combinations of technologies) that have already reached the product development stage or are already on the market. In that sense, this chapter is not a technology forecast because it assumes the continued penetration of business by currently available information technology products and services. As a result, the author is fairly confident that before the year 2000, CEOs and CIOs will have to contend with most of the impacts identified in this chapter.

Most companies in advanced countries are already substantial users of information technology (IT). As this use becomes more intensive, we can expect qualitative as well as quantitative changes to the business, including changes to:

- Products and services.
- Relationships with customers and suppliers.
- Staff work habits.
- The people companies recruit.
- The cost structures for products and services.
- The way managers manage.
- Corporate risks.

This chapter explores the far-reaching changes that IT is expected to produce. More important, however, this chapter raises the issue of senior executives' responsibilities for including the expected impacts in their organization's strategic plans.

## GLOBAL PRODUCTS AND SERVICES

One of the greatest effects on the products and services that companies offer will result from dramatic improvements in global communications for data, voice, and video. Global communications are already producing continuous businesses, including 24-hour reservation services for travel from wherever the traveler is located. We can expect immediate funds transfer and settlement to reduce or eliminate float and sales order entry and shipping information to operate globally on a 24-hour basis.

Information storage and retrieval systems, combined with communications, will allow distributed R&D efforts to work more closely together than ever. The pace of research and development will continue to accelerate, pushed by short product life cycles and new research tools (e.g., cooperative groupwork systems and literature search systems that find not only what you asked for but associated information that you may not have thought to request).

Advances in the miniaturization and durability of microprocessors will continue to spark their use as embedded systems to enhance the usability of manufactured products. Computer chips are already in cars and appliances. In the near future, computer chips and communications devices will find their way into all kinds of products, from houses to furniture, clothing, and accessories. Picture a reclining chair with the controls for the entertainment center built-in and controlled by speech recognition, then add built-in heat and massage, built-in telephone connections, and built-in stereo speakers and microphones creating the perfect couch-potato environment. (Take a few steps further and add a personal computer, an executive information system, and access to external newswire services and you have an executive control cockpit for business management.)

Online information services that will supply news, entertainment, trade information, R&D information, and many other information bases will be the fastest-growing business of the next decade. Portable device access (through laptop or hand-held computers) to these information sources will help the business grow. The limits to how we combine computers and communications with other products are set only by our imaginations.

## RELATIONSHIPS WITH CUSTOMERS

Two of the most rapid adopters of technology are the entertainment and advertising fields. The movie *Terminator* 2 showed us a small sample of the potential for special effects developed through computer imaging technology.

Advertisers have been quick to adopt this technology for the creation of commercials. But the real change to advertising is still coming. Through the use of cable television, data bases of demographic information, and computer-controlled selection of programming, mass media will give way to niche markets and highly personalized, interactive media. Broadcasting will give way to narrow-casting.

Companies currently build retail customer data bases from the mailed-in warranty cards packed with their products. Retailers of the near future will also collect information when customers use credit cards to buy many items. From these sources, advertisers will be able to build customer profiles of their retail customers and use specifically directed, individually targeted advertising to sell additional goods and services. Customized catalogs of products for specific income groups, ethnic groups, or life-style groups can be readily assembled using computerized graphic editing techniques and even desktop printing for small volumes of high-value goods. However, such targeted advertising as direct-call telephone solicitation and advertising will decline in effectiveness as middle-class targets acquire intelligent phones to screen incoming calls.

Product service will be a major differentiating factor in future competition, and such service will be increasingly automated to reduce the cost of service delivery and speed response time to the customer. Current 800-number services provide some advice to customers, but new services will go much further. We should expect 800- or 900-number service for customer inquiries, product software maintenance, health services, and product diagnostics. For example, as an extension of the capability of the embedded computer already in a kitchen appliance, we can expect sensors connected to the microprocessor to provide onboard diagnostics. When the customer calls for repair, the service facility asks that they plug the extension phone jack into the socket of the appliance. The microprocessor downloads the diagnostic information to the service facility's computer, which immediately requests the necessary parts from inventory and dispatches the repair person to the customer's home at a time convenient to the customer. The next stage of development would eliminate the phone jack by embedding a short-range communications device with the microprocessor. This would ultimately permit the appliance to call the repair facility by itself using the customer's telephone line. The repair facility could then call the customer and arrange a repair time before the appliance fails.

Speaker-independent, continuous speech recognition will allow customers to obtain information directly from computers without pushing buttons on their digital phones or using computers. Low-priced video phones will allow computers to respond to customers with both voice and visual presentations. You could call your bank or your broker and find out your account status or call your favorite department store about sale items without ever talking to a human.

How we sell goods and services is also changing. In a movement already started, customers will specify their options for products with the assistance of computer visualization tools. In the home improvement industry, customers can sit at a computer workstation with an adviser and plan their new kitchen, bedroom, or bathroom layouts, add in the appliances and fixtures, add their choice of colors and view their new room as it would appear after remodeling. After approval, the computer automatically generates the sales order listing for the materials and fixtures needed. These same techniques will soon be used for customer ordering of goods ranging from autos to plastic surgery to hair and makeup styles to computer try-ons of clothing in various colors and styles. Within five years, these tools will be packaged into reasonably priced color-screen portables for use by salespeople.

New products and services (or custom products and services) will be jointly designed with large customers by computer-linked cooperative workgroups to open new areas of sales. Already some petrochemical and plastics manufacturers are linking their computers to those of their major customers to jointly design materials that will enable the economical production of new lighter-weight, more durable, or more easily manufactured parts for products.

Manufacturing firms will increasingly link their systems directly to those of distributors and retailers, not only for inventory-replenishment, but for obtaining information about their customers' preferences by demographic factors. The information flood will be too much for humans to handle, so expert systems that mimic the reasoning abilities of humans in limited domains of expertise will be needed to react to all but highly unusual situations. The use of credit cards, debit cards, and other forms of payment will increase, but the cashless society concept is a myth. The underground economy is too strong in every country. Currency is cheaper to make and use than electronic forms of payment.

## RELATIONSHIPS WITH SUPPLIERS

Gradual implementation of integrated service digital networks (ISDN) is starting to provide concurrent transmission of voice, fax, video, and data over the same telephone line. This technology will support cooperative workgroup projects for product design, manufacture, and troubleshooting among firms and their suppliers.

Computer-aided translation of text among languages, already performing at better than an 80% level of accuracy between some languages, will make it easier to do business (or compete) in foreign markets. One worldwide manufacturer of custom heavy equipment needs to assemble proposals for new projects from contributors in their factories in Scandinavia and North America, from their regional sales offices and local materials suppliers, and from their field sales representatives in the customers' country. The company has already developed the telecommunications infrastructure needed to support their global business and is anticipating its next moves to support cooperative engineering and proposal development work.

As the US Department of Defense and large companies demand that their suppliers improve service by implementing electronic data interchange (EDI), increased use will naturally occur, but this is an interim step. The latter part of the decade will see direct interaction between the systems of firms and their suppliers for product design, engineering, R&D, inventory management, shipping information, quality assurance and inspection information, and other areas in which the extended enterprise can functionally operate as a single entity. In fact, the term *extended enterprise* will increasingly characterize the manner in which businesses operate as they link more intimately with each other's systems in a process chain that reaches from raw materials through distributors and customers.

## STAFF WORK HABITS

Staff work habits and the way people view their jobs will change under the impact of new ways of operating the business. Technological unemployment (i.e., temporary or permanent skill obsolescence) will result in multiple periods of unemployment and career changes during a working career. The experience of such intermittent work will erode company loyalty and may force legislation that imposes greater responsibility for employee skill maintenance on employers.

Technological unemployment will increase the number of small business ventures—microbusinesses—as suppliers to larger business firms. Reduced need for particular specialty skills in one or more companies may provide entrepreneurs with the opportunity to provide those specialty skills on a contract basis to a number of former employers.

Telecommuting will increase, but it will primarily be part-time. People are basically social animals and need the human contact provided by the office. Experiences of several firms that have adopted videoconferencing have shown that this technology may reduce the number of trips needed for meetings, but it does not eliminate the need to occasionally have face-to-face contact to build more complete understanding and rapport among the persons required to interact with each other. The potential reduction in commuting time available through part-time telecommuting will mean that some employees will not have to change homes every time they change jobs. A fringe benefit to business may be more stable communities and work forces.

In most current businesses, workers are organized into relatively stable departments in which they work with the same people every day. In the near future, many workers will have to learn to work on temporary teams (i.e., computer-supported workgroups) with suppliers and customers to facilitate design, manufacture, and delivery of products or design and delivery of new services. In fact, such temporary teams may also become an increasingly used mode of operation internally in the company.

Pressures to improve responsiveness to both external customers and internal recipients of the products of business processes, combined with increasing needs for maintaining security, will lead to better ways to stay in touch. Micro-processor employee badges may include security identification, pagers, and cellular radio. Control centers will know where employees are and be able to reach them at any time. Secure doors will recognize badge wearers and permit them entry to controlled premises. Time clocks may disappear.

The paperless office will continue to be an elusive myth; paper is too inexpensive and too convenient to be eliminated. But microcomputers and workstations will permeate the office and field environments. The ability to use a computer will become a prerequisite for most factory jobs as well as white-collar jobs. In fact, it will also be a prerequisite for such field workers as repair technicians and deliverypersons. Field workers will never be out of touch with their bases. Cellular telephones combined with hand-held comput-ers will relay orders and other information for immediate processing. Because these workers will spend less time in their offices, they may share offices with others and may not return to base for weeks. This may reduce the need for as many private offices or desks at company facilities.

Remote personnel will, however, create another problem for management. Alienation of these workers from the company is a potential danger. The same technology that enables them to operate remotely will have to be used to keep them up-to-date with company events and even create electronic substitutes for the office water cooler.

## THE KINDS OF PEOPLE RECRUITED

As products change to incorporate embedded computers and communications devices, product designers will need to have the engineering skills to handle new challenges. A combination of mechanical engineering and electronics engi-neering degrees will make a candidate for an engineering job extremely valu-able. Such combination skills and training will be needed to integrate the work of design and engineering teams. Similar combinations of training will be needed for product support and service personnel.

Job consolidation and computer-mediated processes will require broader employee skills resulting in a need for perennial and life-long retraining; computer-aided education (CAEd) will be needed, and take-home CAEd and video training will be used to supplement classroom work. Immigrants will supplement our aging work force but will need entry-level training, which implies more company-sponsored CAEd, including speech recognition systems for improving spoken language skills.

Electronic immigrants, skilled personnel located in foreign countries using telecommuting techniques, will increase, not just in computer-related trades, but for office skills—for example, remote inventory management and accounts payable and accounts receivable functions. The technological poverty of the poor and undereducated will make them less employable. Class-action suits may arise to force large employers to educate workers.

On a more optimistic note, handicapped persons will become more employable. Cyborgs (closely interfaced humans and intelligent machines) will allow the handicapped to perform physical tasks and office tasks that they might otherwise find difficult, expanding the labor pool. Computer-enhanced prosthetic devices developed through research supported by the Veteran's Administration and others should also start to reach the market.

## THE COST STRUCTURES OF BUSINESS

Pushed by global communications capabilities, 24-hour business cycles will mean more shift work. This will lead to greater expenses for shift premium pay for employees, but higher use of plant and capital investment.

The pace of factory automation in many industries has been retarded by unfavorable tax structures that require depreciation write-off too quickly, thus raising the direct overhead cost on products. Higher use of capital equipment resulting from 24-hour operation will tend to off-set these overhead costs. Such higher use factors will therefore encourage greater investment in plant automation.

In addition, the continued aging of the population of most advanced countries will reduce work forces available, also encouraging automation to reduce work force needs. Computer-mediated processes will also permit increasing job consolidation. This work force restructuring will lead to higher pay for fewer workers and a need for alternative compensation schemes.

Driven by competitive selling techniques and increasingly selective buyers, the demand for customized products will increase. Customization requires short production runs and minimum parts inventory. Computer-supported just-in-time ( JIT) inventory management and flexible manufacturing automation will allow smaller firms to compete with larger ones because the critical factor will be the cost of short runs of customized products rather than mass production.

With smalller, distributed computers providing more power for less cost, large mainframe use will gradually be confined to high-volume transaction processing systems, shared corporate data bases, and computing-intensive applications. Small computers and wireless local area networks will make computing ubiquitous, and responsibility for more than half of computer costs will shift from the IS organization to the users.

## THE WAY MANAGERS MANAGE

The manner in which management decisions are made will change under the impact of new approaches made possible by IT. Portable computing will make managers independent of time and distance because they will be able to access company information and relay decisions and orders to their staff at any time from any place. This will be a mixed blessing because 24-hour access to the business means 24-hour access to the manager. Some managers may respond by attempting to handle all the decision traffic that comes to them. Such managers will probably not last very long, or they will find out that they need to delegate better.

Improved communications will enable managers to expand their control. Management scientists have traditionally said that a manager's effective span of control should not exceed five or six direct reports. The integration of business functions in modern organizations often requires more. Such tools as electronic mail, access to corporate data bases, videoconferencing, and electronic bulletin boards will enable managers to broaden their span of control but will also require more delegation downward. Expert systems and decision support tools will be needed to handle routine business decisions, leaving exceptions to experts and middle managers.

Group decision making through computer conferencing across time zones will intensify. To remain competitive, companies will have to assemble their best talents and focus them on critical decisions. Group decision making can deteriorate into decision paralysis in some companies if the computer conferencing tools are used to allow management by committee. To avoid such stagnation, management will be forced to adopt conference techniques in which responsibility for a decision is clearly delegated to one manager.

Specialized management for such functions of the business as R&D, engineering design, finance, or marketing will gradually be eroded by increases in group management through interdisciplinary teams enhanced by computer conferencing to minimize decision delays. As indicated, however, someone will still have to take final responsibility. All this new availability of and access to information will flood managers with more information than ever, much of it not relevant to their needs. This flood of information will come not only from within the company but from online access to external information sources of world events and business or industry news. Under the constant pressure of information overload, executives will encourage adoption of new applications that combine graphics, expert systems, executive information systems, and other technologies to reduce data to usable form and pertinent content before they see it. Such applications, already technologically feasible, will become common before the end of the decade.

From even this single viewpoint, it is clear that line managers must increasingly influence the way that they manage the application of IT in their organizations. New business applications for computers and communications will focus more on where the firm is going in contrast to accounting systems that report where the firm has been. Investments will be made with a greater focus on the interface with customers and suppliers to improve service and customer satisfaction. This implies applications that support a company or product strategy. For example, if a company's strategy is to produce low-priced products, their systems must, at a minimum, support cost-effective production while maintaining a level of quality sufficient to avoid customer dissatisfaction and meet competitive requirements.

## The Extended Enterprise

Ever-closer links with key suppliers (e.g., joint product design, JIT inventory control, and joint quality assurance) and computer interfaces to distributors and retailers for resupply or custom orders will force companies to become extended enterprises. Executives and managers will have to comanage the extended enterprise with these business partners.

The extended enterprise concept has advantages and disadvantages. One firm in the construction materials business decided that it would extend its lead in meeting product delivery schedules to place competition far behind. Using business process redesign methods, it began analyzing each process in the order-through-delivery cycle to improve speed on the assumption that rapid delivery was the path to customer satisfaction.

After some time, one manager had the temerity to ask if the basic premise was correct. In-depth interviews and analysis of its customers' requirements indicated that few orders were needed as fast as possible. On the other hand, for the vast majority of orders, faster delivery would force the customer to warehouse the materials and spend inventory carrying costs—a certain path to customer dissatisfaction. The project was refocused to emphasize rapid delivery when it was wanted—in other words, just-in-time delivery.

JIT delivery is justly recognized for improving service while lowering inventory carrying costs. Extremely close computer system links with suppliers have made this technique possible, but even it can cause problems. For example, Tokyo's thousands of convenience stores, department stores, and grocery stores adopted JIT in an attempt to emulate the success of the manufacturers. Once- or twice-a-day deliveries became 10- and 12-times-a-day deliveries. The result is that literally tens of thousands of trucks and delivery vans are now congesting Tokyo's streets and traffic has ground to a snail's pace while expensive fuel burning adds to the city's pollution. Even worse, JIT deliveries are now consistently late. Now and in the future, business management must carefully manage the application of IT and work to avoid technically correct systems that do not help the business.

The emphasis on customer satisfaction in competitive markets means that the producers of goods and services will be forced to improve their knowledge of their customers and those factors that lead to their customers' satisfaction. This effort will be a continuing challenge. Collecting and organizing intelligence on markets, sales, competition, customers, trends, and technical data will be more critical to competing successfully. Those with the best market intelligence systems will have a winning card.

During the 1980s, many executives read about using computers and communications to build a "war room," an executive conference room with large computer-driven displays on the walls and computer consoles that would allow executives to retrieve and analyze company information and jointly plan the battle strategy of the company. A few companies even spent the money to implement war rooms. As a concept, however, the computerized corporate war room will be obsolete before it is more extensively adopted by business. Executive information systems (EISs) based on communicating multimedia workstations will be the next wave. These workstations, supported by groupware (i.e., software systems that make it easier for groups to work together through networked computers) will provide for better facilities while permitting users to join meetings from their offices, wherever they are located.

With low-cost, powerful departmental computers available and increasing user knowledge leading to the demystification of computing, the responsibility for computers and applications will be increasingly dispersed throughout the company. Computers will be viewed as just another business resource, along with labor and office equipment, to be managed by those with departmental or strategic business unit responsibility.

Business processes will change as IT techniques already available (e.g., image processing) enable work flow management techniques and concurrent sharing of information. The relatively new discipline of business process redesign will be increasingly used to modify business processes. Such modifications will not only address cost reduction but will be focused on improving the flexibility of the company to change product or service quality, style, image, functions, and features to meet customer demand. In addition, redesigned business processes will go beyond JIT to address the speed with which new products are brought to the market. Senior management must ensure that redesigned business processes enabled by IT advances are aimed at the overall strategic goals of the business and not driven by the availability of technology.

## CORPORATE RISKS

Information technology will bring new or additional risks that have to be managed by corporations. These are discussed in the following sections.

**Information Security.** As a direct projection of current events, increasing dependence on computers and communications will make companies more vulnerable to damage ranging from loss of information through halting business operations. Every one of us, as a customer, is aware of our irritation when a customer service person tells us that they cannot help us because the computer is down. A similar frustration arises when we are told that the computer must have made a mistake. Senior management, in its drive for customer satisfaction, will have to pay increasing attention to the needs of the business for the availability, integrity, and confidentiality of information—that is, information security.

**Telecommunications and Politics.** Many corporations today operate in a global business environment with their interfaces to customers, distributors, and suppliers enhanced by global telecommunications capabilities. The reach of communications has made it easy to advertise our goods. It has made third-world citizens hunger for the products of the advanced nations. It enabled events in Tiananmen Square to be relayed back to fax, television, and computer network users in China. It undoubtedly contributed to the rapid collapse of the Soviet Union. Telecommunications will continue to affect the pace of change in world politics. Such free information as that which led to the collapse of communism in Eastern Europe may make doing business in some countries risky. Business intelligence in the future will need to include political intelligence for global corporations.

**Product or Service Liability.** Finally, in the litigious climate that exists in the United States, another set of risks must be considered. If a physician or an attorney uses a procedure that has proved to be faulty or to have high risk, they are required to inform the patient or client of the risks (and in many instances obtain a signed consent form). The implication of a long history of malpractice suits is that the availability of information mandates its use. As corporate information bases grow and include the intelligence needed to operate the business competitively, huge stores of information will be available to management. If information is available, managers may no longer be able to plead ignorance effectively. The potential for product or service liability suits will dramatically increase in the future as customers are able to prove that negative information was available to the seller.

## SUMMARY

Information technology will continue to have an impact on business whether or not it is welcomed. Firms that fail to take advantage of technology advances will frequently fall to the competitive pressures of those that have adopted new techniques and tools. On the other hand, adopting technology for the sake of technology can lead to major errors and losses. IT is so interwoven into the fabric of the firm that not only must it be responsive to the strategic directions of the company but it must be considered as an influence on those strategic directions. Every executive must insist that the organization and its technical experts as well as the CIO and IS executives translate the advances in IT into potential impacts on the business so that they can be reflected in company strategy.

# IX-2
# Business Outlook on Parallel Computing

*CARL FINK*

P arallel computing is not an entirely new phenomenon. Vector processors
use a form of parallelism known as pipelining. An example of pipelining
is when some data is being fetched while a calculation is occurring and the
results of the previous calculation are being stored. Data moves through the
process in sequential fashion, much like on an auto assembly line. Many computers also have some degree of functional parallelism, performing two or more
operations concurrently but still handling a single stream of data and a single
stream of instructions.

Data parallel computers also provide more dramatic speed improvements,
operating on hundreds or thousands of pieces of data simultaneously. Massively
parallel processing (MPP) generally refers to data parallel computers with
anywhere from a few hundred to many thousands of processors. Exhibit IX-
2-1 shows the quantum leap in raw power with the introduction of MPP
hardware.

## MASSIVELY PARALLEL PROCESSING

Data parallel machines can be further classified as single instruction, multiple
data (SIMD) or multiple instruction, multiple data (MIMD). A typical SIMD
machine broadcasts the same instruction to multiple processors, and each
processor applies that operation to its assigned data, operating in lockstep.
Processors communicate the results to one another through an interconnection
network. The Connection Machine from Thinking Machines Corp. (Cambridge
MA) and the current line from MasPar Computer Corp. (Sunnyvale CA) are
examples of SIMD computers.

MIMD computers have processing elements that work independently of
one another. The nCube (Foster City CA) series and the iPSC line from Intel
Supercomputer Systems (Beaverton OR) are examples of MIMD machines.
MIMD computers are more flexible but are considered the most complex to
design and program. Vendors of SIMD processors have developed ways of
partitioning problems to give them some of the flexibility of MIMD and to allow
greater use of the available processors.

| Model | Megaflops* | Year |
|---|---|---|
| Cray-1 | 180 | 1974 |
| Cray X-MP/2 | 480 | 1982 |
| Cray Y-MP8 | 2,500 | 1985 |
| Thinking Machines CM-5 | 40,000 | 1991 |

Note:
* Million floating-point operations per second, peak.

**Exhibit IX-2-1. Supercomputer Performance**

Another major difference among MIPP computers is the way memory is organized. Distributed memory machines place small amounts of memory at the site of each processor. Shared memory computers have all processors connected to a central memory area. This is a more familiar arrangement for programmers trained on conventional machines, but it can affect performance. Physically distributed memory that appears as shared memory to the user is known as virtual shared memory.

## Technical Challenges of MPP

Various network topologies are used to link the processors in a massively parallel computer, and the design of this interconnection network is the greatest technical challenge in building such a machine. When the number of processors is in the hundreds, it is possible to directly connect all the processors using what is known as a crossbar switch. Machines with thousands of processors use alternative topologies with names like butterfly, hypercube, x-tree, and twisted torus to limit the physical connections to a manageable number as the number of processors is increased. Scalability over a very wide range is always a key criterion in MPP design.

Finally, the designer must choose an algorithm for moving messages through the network, which may be either packet-switched or circuit-switched. The routing can be fixed (i.e., nonadaptive) or adaptive, choosing the best path according to the current traffic conditions and the characteristics of the task being performed.

MPP designers continually struggle to optimize the number of processors, the amount of memory per processor, and the size of the processor to produce a machine that pleases the most people for the lowest price. They also must weigh the performance advantages of custom chips versus industry-standard products with prices based on million of units sold. Kendall Square Research (Waltham MA) has chosen a 64-bit custom CMOS chip for its initial MPP line, running an operating system based on OSF/1 UNIX. NCR Corp. (Dayton OH) and Thinking Machines use high-volume, off-the-shelf chips. Cray Research, Inc. (Eagan MN) has announced an MPP computer that will use the Alpha reduced instruction set computing (RISC) chip from Digital Equipment Corp.

## AN ALTERNATIVE APPROACH TO PARALLELISM

*The New Yorker* is an unlikely place to learn about the latest developments in parallel supercomputing; Gregory and David Chudnovsky are equally unlikely pioneers. *The New Yorker* devoted 20 pages in March 1992 to the saga of these two immigrant brothers and their parallel machine built entirely from $70,000 worth of mail-order parts. Dubbed m zero, the computer currently has 16 processors and is said to be capable of speeds (measured in floating-point operations per second) between 200M FLOPS (or megaflops) and 2G FLOPS (or gigaflops). The Chudnovsky's goal is 256 processors. The current machine is housed in their sweltering New York apartment and monitored with a meat thermometer calibrated from "beef-rare" to "pork" readings. They struggle to keep m zero below "pork" using extra fans from the neighborhood hardware shop.

Dedicated to pure science, the brothers are following in the path of other early-stage tinkerers who put together a cheap but effective device from available components, mostly for their own enjoyment. Efforts like these are important in getting new technologies into wide distribution, which is especially important for parallel computing because increased availability will stimulate the development of new applications and increase the number of people capable of programming the new machines. The role of such infrastructure building should be a key part of the industrial policy debate surrounding supercomputing and the funding it receives from government (which has played a critical role in overcoming the skepticism that has threatened to hold back progress in this field) and ultimately from venture capitalists.

## HAL, MEET LINDA

Linda is a simple set of programming language extensions to support coarse-grained parallel computing of the MIMD variety. Linda is not tied to any specific hardware mechanism or programming language. This makes it an ideal tool for orchestrating large networks of interconnected workstations so that they can work together solving giant computational problems. A variant, nicknamed Piranha Linda, is being designed specifically to scavenge available cycles on underused workstations, moving the load around the network as needed. It is estimated that, on average, only 2% or 3% of the cycles in a typical workstation are being used. With millions of desktop machines and more than 750,000 Internet host computers, the amount of power that could be tapped is staggering.

There are already at least four companies seeking to exploit Linda technology. The Trollius system, a relative of Linda, is available from a midwest university for a few hundred dollars. It can be combined with a PC clone running the UNIX operating system and several plug-in processor boards to make a cheap and powerful parallel computer.

## MAINSTREAM APPLICATIONS OF PARALLEL COMPUTING

Most business applications of massively parallel processing to date have been in data base manipulation, decision support, and mathematical modeling. These have usually been custom-programmed solutions. MPP vendors have only recently targeted online transaction processing applications in an attempt to broaden the market. Like the minicomputer makers of a previous computer generation, these vendors are used to selling to the technically sophisticated scientific and research community. Business customers generally require more support and higher reliability. The potential in the commercial IS market may be one of the factors that has fueled some of the agreements between mainstream vendors and MPP start-ups.

**Finance.** Wall Street has been quick to adopt parallel computing to its so-called rocket science operations, including computer-assisted (program) trading, the creation of synthetic securities, and the pricing of collateralized mortgage obligations. Although most Wall Street firms are reluctant to discuss their computing direction. Prudential-Bache has gone public about its successful use of the technology. Merrill Lynch and three Japanese securities firms are known to have parallel supercomputers on board. Other financial firms are experimenting with the Linda approach. One brokerage is running large market simultations at night on the workstations that support its traders when the markets are open.

**Retail.** A number of retailers and direct marketers are using parallel computing to detect subtle trends and relationships in data bases storing information on millions of customers. Retailers are using detailed analysis of transactions to help determine what items are often bought together. They use this information to rearrange their stores and boost sales of linked items.

Checkout scanners have greatly increased the amount of raw data available to marketers, but they have not been able to harvest this data until recently. Direct marketers are using MPP power to target their mailings more effectively and increase their average purchase by modifying the mix of goods in each catalog.

**Online Information Providers.** These companies are also using MPP computers to add value to their huge data inventories. Parallel machines allow fast response to complex queries and help to improve the relevance of the articles retrieved. Dow Jones's DowQuest searches a IGB data base containing six months' worth of business periodicals in under 1.5 seconds.

## PROGRAMMING PARALLEL COMPUTERS

The key to programming parallel computers is adapting existing algorithms or creating new ones to make the most efficient use of a given architecture. Some problems lend themselves naturally to parallelization, such as a scientific calculation that calls for an identical, complex calculation on every element in an array. In the field, these have come to be known as embarrassingly parallel problems. Unfortunately, many tasks do not fall into this category. New algorithms must be invented to accommodate problems where the next step in the solution is highly dependent on results from the previous steps. Over time, libraries of new algorithms for engineering and financial applications have been created to speed development and provide design ideas to beginners.

To leverage the large library of existing scientific programs written in FORTRAN, researchers have worked to extend that language for parallel execution. A team at Syracuse University is coordinating work on specifications for a portable High-Performance FORTRAN. Fortunately, effective parallelization often requires only a handful of new verbs and declarations that can be added to most existing languages. Still, the transition to parallel computing is not painless, and the best practitioners are frequently those that have minimal exposure to the old ways.

The Connection Machine was originally built for the artificial intelligence research community, so not surprisingly, it was first programmed using a parallel version of LISP. Parallel versions of FORTRAN and C were added later. Kendall Square Research's KSR-1 is programmed in a version of FORTRAN with automatic parallelization and in ANSI C. The latest version of Oracle Corp.'s relational data base system and a version of COBOL are being ported to the machine. Dozens of research languages have also been created or adapted for parallel and massively parallel application.

## RETHINKING PROGRAMMING

Massively parallel computers are already being used to program themselves in the research labs. Using a new technique known as evolutionary programming, programmers establish a goal and certain environmental constraints, then unleash the power of a parallel machine to generate and test thousands of offspring. Weaker programs are culled and stronger ones mutated in a process that continues for successive generations until an acceptable solution is found. There are easier ways to build a general ledger package, but this technique could be extremely useful in cases where it is difficult to specify an algorithm. This is one example of an MPP-enabled application that could not be contemplated with conventional computing resources.

Another alternative to programming for classification problems is to use the power of MPP to search large data bases of previously classified items for those with similar characteristics. This technique, known as memory-based reasoning, has already been used successfully in an experiment with Census Bureau occupation and industry classification, besting an expert system approach. Neural networks are also useful for classification and pattern recognition tasks. The multiple processing elements of a neural net model map directly to the hardware processors of a parallel computer, making this an ideal application area.

## PERFORMANCE MEASUREMENT

Computer performance measurement is a sticky area, and the advent of massively parallel machines has only complicated things. Bragging rights to the fastest MPP machines are usually based on theoretical peak megaflops, which is calculated by multiplying the peak floating-point performance of a single processor by the number of processors in the system. Because MPP machines are highly scalable, any vendor can claim a new speed record simply by announcing the availability of a new model with more processors, no matter that there are no orders in sight for such a machine or that it would cost more than the GNP of many small nations.

Detractors of massively parallel computing often cited Amdahl's law. In simplified forms, Amdahl's law states that about 10% of computing tasks are inherently serial. Therefore, the argument goes, it is impossible to gain more than a tenfold advantage regardless of the number of processors used. This has not proven to be the case when very large problems with huge amounts of data are considered.

To get some sense of how much work a parallel computer would be able to perform on the job, a mathematician at the government's Ames Laboratory has developed the Slalom benchmark. Whereas many supercomputer benchmarks generate results expressed in megaflops. Slalom produces a score that indicates the amount of precision obtained on a specific scientific calculation over a fixed time. Slalom scores are inherently less prone to abuse compared with traditional MIPS and megaflops results that can be obtained using many different methods. For example, the Linpack benchmarks (which date back to 1979) can be quoted in terms of actual speed and theoretical peak performance. The Perfect Benchmarks are a suite of 13 typical scientific calculations that also produce a result expressed in megaflops. Whetstones and the Livermore Loops are also frequently used to measure conventional supercomputer or scientific workstation performance.

There are a few additional problems with these performance measures that are specific to the MPP field. First, it is especially difficult to define a set of typical tasks for a class of machines that is as radically different and new to the market as the current generation of MPP machines. Second, the architectures of the machines being compared vary widely and in ways that are more fundamental than the differences found in different generations of scalar computers. If the benchmark can be translated into an algorithm the flexes all of the processors of a given machine, the results can be astounding but hardly typical. The assumption is that the hardware is getting a workout during these tests, but it could be that the parallelizing compiler and programmer creativity are what are actually being tested. However, it is pointless to evaluate parallel computers with overly restrictive criteria.

In their quest for raw computing power, initial buyers of massively parallel processors have largely ignored the higher costs to program the machines and the cost of maintaining idle capacity that cannot easily be diverted to more mundane uses in between major scientific breakthroughs. Vendors are attempting to address these concerns as they begin to target business applications in their search for a wider market for MPP machines.

## THE MPP OUTLOOK

Although MPP sales currently represent slightly more than 10% of the $2.2 billion supercomputer market, they are expected to show faster growth than vector supercomputers in the future, reaching $1.7 billion in 1997 by one estimate. The pioneers of supercomputing have begun to announce fast-track MPP projects. Minisupercomputer makers such as Convex Computer Corp. (Richardson TX) are also seeking the high-end market. MPP has thus significantly broadened the overall market for high-performance computers.

NCR is the current leader in developing MPP machines for business applications. Its acquisition of Teradata Corp., a pioneer in parallel computing for data base applications, has given NCR access to critical interconnection technology. Kendall Square Research is also targeting the business market.

Intel Corp.'s 80 × 86 and i860 chip lines have become popular in MPP designs from other companies, and the company has had success selling complete systems. Although MPP-generated chip sales are not yet significant relative to desktop applicatons, they represent a way for Intel to introduce new high-performance designs that will eventually find their way into volume applications. Digital Equipment Corp. and IBM Corp. have strategies as well.

There is still a role for high-performance serial computers in supercomputing. Research has found that the combination of serial and massively parallel computers has produced better results on some types of problems than could be achieved with either machine working alone. Whether these machines can coexist in future applications is unknown as MPP vendors and users develop sophisticated methods to reconfigure their machines for difficult problems.

## SUMMARY

MPP machines will allow us to tackle science's grand challenge problems, such as weather forecasting, global climate modeling, superconductivity, and modeling the world economy in record time (Exhibit IX-2-2). Some analysts predict an era of discovery as scientists explore cellular automata, genetic algorithms, and other fields that readily lend themselves to parallelization. In this view, the prevalence of a radically new computer architecture actually serves to shape the direction of scientific investigation rather than simply providing faster execution of old programs.

Overenthusiasm often causes early adopters to overestimate the capabilities of new technologies. Those outside of the field frequently do no understand the new developments well enough to raise effective challenges to suspect or

| Machine | Moderate Problem | Grand Challenges |
|---|---|---|
| Teraflops* machine | 2 Seconds | 10 Hours |
| Thinking Machines CM-2 64K | 30 Minutes | 1 Year |
| Cray Y-MP/8 | 4 Hours | 10 Years |
| Alliant FX/80 | 5 Days | 250 Years |
| Sun 4/60 | 1 Month | 1,500 Years |
| VAX 11/780 | 9 Months | 14,000 Years |
| IBM PC (8087) | 9 Years | 170,000 Years |
| Apple Macintosh | 23 Years | 450,000 Years |

Note:
* Trillion floating-point operations per second.
SOURCE: *Daedalus*, Winter 1992.

**Exhibit IX-2-2. Computation Times**

vastly premature claims. Remember the excitement over early econometric models amid predictions that recessions could be eliminated?

Today, some major public policy decisions on health and environmental issues are being based entirely on the results of unverified mathematical models. A tangle of interdependent financial obligations based on arcane mathematics has ensnared the global financial community. Therefore, while parallel computing is clearly helping business, industry, and science to solve some old problems faster, healthy skepticism is needed in evaluating new commercial disciplines enabled by MPP.

# IX-3
# Trends in LAN Operating Systems

*ROB WALTON • KENNETH W. KOUSKY*

N etworking systems have been available from the earliest days of the microcomputer, the first being proprietary file or disk servers manufactured to control network operations. Novell's NetWare S-Net was one of the pioneers. A clunky-looking white box powered by a Motorola, Inc., 68000 chip, it was designed as a star topology with a relatively low number of users. From the beginning, S-Net needed an operating system to provide services to the workstations that used CP/M and then DOS. Novell hired a development team to build its first network operating system, which existed as software, independent of Novell's proprietary server. NetWare was the result. Other organizations followed similar routes.

These first systems sold well enough to keep companies in business, but they did not really flourish until the release of the IBM XT and its clones. The inclusion of a hard disk and the enhancement of RAM capabilities in a microcomputer supplied sufficient storage and memory space for the machine to be used as a file or disk server. Several companies realized this opportunity and rushed products to the market.

Some of the earliest contenders were Orchid Technology, Inc.'s PCnet, Corvus Systems, Inc.'s OMNInet, Gateway Communications, Inc.'s G-Net, and Proteon, Inc.'s ProNet. Although each provided basic levels of services, each posed a real problem for those deciding which to adopt because they all had proprietary operating systems and the amount of software available that ran in a shared mode was minimal. In addition, most of the LAN vendors had built their network operating systems on top of DOS, which was inherently a single-user, single-tasking operating system.

## NOVELL NAMED THE LEADER

Novell laid the foundation for its overwhelming success in the LAN business by having Superset port their NetWare operating system from the S-Net box to the XT. This allowed freedom in computers but not in network tables and cards. Initially, NetWare was released for the Gateway G-Net card, but Novell

713

decided that it should do ports for the other best-selling hardware, which included the 3Com Ethernet, Corvus OMNInet, and Proteon Token Ring network interface cards. Because NetWare was originally written for a non-DOS environment and was modeled to emulate mini and mainframe management operations, it was multithreaded and multitasking from the beginning. It was built to run circles around any DOS-based operating system software and proved it by outperforming each proprietary LAN operating system on its own card.

At Novell, product design set the stage, but marketing brought in the revenues. This was accomplished by convincing software developers that writing NetWare hooks into their products brought immediate support for a whole variety of cards and then convincing network card vendors that a large number of applications would run on their system through a single NetWare port—and at significantly faster speeds. This marketing program was called DIO for do it once, and it pushed the development of shared application software from a few applications in 1984 to more than 2,000 18 months later. It also placed NetWare as the operating system of choice on every major LAN card.

This brought Novell a lot of attention from hardware companies, particularly those that did not like the idea of customizing their products for NetWare. This started early LAN battles between Novell, 3Com, and other network hardware manufacturers. While hardware vendors concentrated on the transfer rates of their NIC cards, software developers eventually prevailed when Novell proved that the key to performance on a LAN was an efficient software-based file server and not the hardware with a disk server alone. Novell was able to show that a 64K-bps S-Net card running NetWare could outperform a 10M-bps Ethernet card running EtherShare. One by one, companies realized the trend and put NetWare on their systems.

Microsoft viewed these early battles from the software point of view. It produced Microsoft MSnet primarily as a product to be used with other companies' network hardware solutions. It signed up third parties in an effort to thwart the growing NetWare threat, and some, like 3Com, built quite a business around it early on.

Next, Microsoft, in its role as the purveyor of industry standards, released version 3.1 of DOS, which among other things allowed local area network file locking. IBM developed its PCnet product around the Microsoft MSnet standard, and for the first time all three major vendors were in the market at the same time.

During development of its networking strategy, Microsoft was also working on a new operating environment to help users at the workstation and mask many of the inherent inefficiencies of DOS. This operating environment was called Windows and was more or less based on the technology developed by Xerox Corp. and promulgated by Apple Computer, Inc. The first two versions of Windows were rudimentary, lacking speed and sophistication, but they were revolutionary to many users. Microsoft began to preach the importance of the graphical user interface (GUI).

However, users continued to buy NetWare in vast quantities, and they largely ignored Windows. GUIs were still seen as a weak interface used only in design and drawing applications. Microsoft changed some of that with the release of its Excel spreadsheet for the Apple Macintosh. For the first time, real business power was available in a graphical environment. It was the first realization for many that the Macintosh was a powerful business tool and its graphical interface was a large part of the reason. Microsoft's success with applications, however, did not translate into success with LAN operating systems.

Microsoft and IBM were left behind by Novell early in the LAN operating system battle. Although Microsoft saw the need for connectivity, it was too caught up in its own technology to see the solution. Microsoft was gathering the best and brightest developers in the country to prove that it could be preeminent through work from within. In addition, MSnet was DOS-based; Microsoft could add all the bells and whistles in the world, but the engine would remain flawed.

IBM, however, was left behind not out of misdirection but out of apathy. As local area networks became a valid alternative for businesses in the US, IBM was hesitant to jump right in. Even the most rudimentary local area network system was a potential threat to the very profitable IBM minicomputer business. Only when large IBM customers screamed loud enough did it come up with its own MSnet-based LAN solution, IBM PCnet. IBM's apathy was aided by ignorance as it misjudged the potential developments and the needs of its customers. Throughout the 1980s, IBM's belief was that a LAN would be peer-oriented, allowing printers and hard disks attached to various PCs to be shared. In this model, any node could be a server.

The idea that all nodes would be both clients and servers was supposed to drive the continued expansion of workstation capabilities. The reality has fallen well short of this goal because the functional requirements have now gone far beyond printer and file sharing. Without servers, there was no assumption of heavy loads at a single board; the transfer rates of IBM's Token-Ring boards are still a critical shortcoming of the Token-Ring product.

## IBM AND MICROSOFT TEAM UP

As a result of each of these situations, Novell NetWare was more or less assured acceptance everywhere, and that is just what happened. To fortify against the ongoing threat of NetWare market dominance, IBM and Microsoft teamed up again with the development of OS/2. It was introduced in April of 1987 along with a new line of IBM hardware, the PS/2. Arm in arm, these two companies foretold the future of personal computing, and that future was built around OS/2. It proclaimed high-powered machines running high-resolution graphics with high-speed buses and sophisticated peripherals. It highlighted Presentation Manager, the OS/2 graphical user interface designed for ease of use and productivity. OS/2 was a multithreaded, multitasking power device for workstations. It promised to deliver everything that NetWare had become and more.

In the beginning of the IBM-Microsoft collaboration, OS/2 was portrayed as providing all the core capabilities necessary for both client and server computing. The two organizations predicted that it would gain acceptance among developers and users so rapidly that it would relegate DOS to the back seat within two to three years and push it right out the rear door within five to six.

In this early frame of reference, Microsoft's Windows strategy was secondary to both organizations, with Windows being merely a stepping stone to higher-level computing with OS/2. This was an easy position for Microsoft to support because Windows had been a lackluster performer to that date. IBM, on the other hand, was building its personal computing future on OS/2 and LAN Server, and Windows was not in the plans.

The transition from DOS to OS/2 has never materialized. The promised functions of OS/2 were late in arriving, and the Microsoft-IBM relationship cooled as Microsoft began to develop its own strategy for OS/2 to include unique APIs, different client/server engines, and a wider participation for Windows-based workstations. It did not take long for either company to realize that NetWare was firmly entrenched and that neither strategy would easily unseat the market leader.

One of the other obvious market failures was the linking of LAN Manager and LAN Server to OS/2. The public failed to judge OS/2's feasibility as a server platform separately from its success at the workstation or node. If OS/2 did not go on the microcomputer, why should it go on the server? Although NetWare has never been judged on this basis, it was Microsoft and IBM that set the stage for this faulty analysis of the OS/2's feasibility.

Then version 3.0 of Windows finally hit a responsive chord. All the development efforts bore fruit, and the product was received with open arms. Literally millions of copies were sold in the first few months, exceeding even Microsoft's wildest expectations. The sudden success changed many things in the IBM-Microsoft relationship as well as perceptions in the LAN marketplace.

Many of the earlier justifications for DOS users to move to OS/2 were removed with Windows 3.0. This element of uncertainty relating to workstations caused a growth in the uncertainty surrounding the servers. With sales of OS/2-based LAN systems languishing, Microsoft reorganized its networking group and assured the public and the press that everything was on schedule, pouring more dollars into the LAN Manager abyss. Although IBM tried to keep on a relatively close development schedule for OS/2 and LAN Server product deliveries, the harder it pushed, the more it fell behind.

As Windows sales continued to soar, the IBM-Microsoft relationship finally fell apart. Microsoft set out on a new course using Windows workstations as the focal point, abandoning OS/2 development altogether. Microsoft stated that it would continue to provide code to those writing applications for OS/2 but that it would not actively promote its sales or use. Microsoft also announced that there would not be an OS/2 version 3.0 but that its next-generation operating system would be called NT, for new technology, and it would take advantage of 32-bit processor capabilities. Microsoft stated further that it would upgrade its workstation capabilities with Win/32, the code name for a 32-bit version of Windows.

IBM consolidated its position by signing an agreement with Novell to sell NetWare through its own sales force as an adjunct to its LAN Server strategy. IBM noted that this was in no way a denial of the OS/2 LAN Server platform but merely the recognition of NetWare's installed base and a response to the demands of its customers. Novell currently owns more than 60% of the LAN operating system market (estimates range from 60% to 80%), with IBM and Microsoft hovering at about 8% to 10% each.

## THE TURBULENT PRESENT AND LIKELY FUTURE

With IBM's release of OS/2 version 2.0 and the upgrade to LAN Server, the battles among the three companies continue. IBM has stated repeatedly that the time has arrived for the delivery of all the promises made since 1987. IBM is on its own with this platform now, and OS/2 will fly or fail depending on the performance of version 2.0. IBM has stated that it will provide better DOS than DOS, better Windows than Windows, and better OS/2 than OS/2. If it does, Microsoft must equal OS/2 2.0 with NT.

Microsoft has moved so far away from OS/2 that it does not want to have third parties promote Windows on OS/2 in any platform and will not even guarantee that Windows 3.1 will work on OS/2. As a workstation product, 3.1 promises better speed and capabilities but is not a major upgrade from 3.0. Microsoft is promoting Windows 3.1 to distract potential buyers from OS/2, create incompatibilities, and forestall market movement to OS/2 before the arrival of NT.

Novell has been rather tight-lipped about future development projects but is busy working to put NetWare on the few platforms that it is not already on. NetWare is still the technological and sales leader, and Novell plans it to be in the future.

Although IBM can still sell NetWare, if the company is to finally be a major player in the LAN business, it will have to be so with OS/2 and LAN Server versions 2.0. If it can indeed deliver on its promises for better everything than everything, it has a reasonable chance of finding a long-term place in the LAN operating system marketplace. However, according to early beta testers, as well as those who have sampled the latest prerelease product, OS/2 version 2.0 is large and slow and demands a lot of RAM. Perhaps it can be fine-tuned. From an applications point of view, it had better. The cadre of software legions writing for OS/2 has diminished, and many projects are on hold, pending the results of the latest release.

OS/2 differs strategically from NetWare in that all nodes can become servers. Although NT will also use this peer approach, it will require applications that actually use the approach to replace NetWare. It may be a more robust platform than NetWare's NLM (NetWare Loadable Modules) option, but without applications, IBM will lose ground. It is likely that the reviews for OS/2 2.0 will continue to be mixed, and ultimate success will depend on whether the marginal negatives and poistives fall out in favor of more software development. Without a large amount of OS/2 based software, IBM will not be successful in this market. If the tide turns toward more development, and the overhead problems are minimized, OS/2 could find a nice niche with large, established IBM customers and networks that use strong client/server environments. It could beat NT or even eventually steal back market share from NetWare. IBM's current 8% of the market could increase to as much as 15% over the next year with positive reviews for version 2.0. Chances are that it will not grow much past that, but 15% of the potential 10 million stations per year is a respectable amount.

If IBM is successful, it is not a foregone conclusion that its success will come at the expense of Novell or Microsoft—20% of the market is controlled by companies outside of the big three. However, the high-end networking business is owned almost exclusively by these three companies. Banyan Systems, Inc., has held a strong foothold in the past, especially in the LAN to WAN environment, but it is on the wane; the additional 7% to 8% of market share will be carved out of Microsoft or Novell.

Microsoft missed the target with MSnet, and it is far afield with LAN Manager and OS/2. Now it is unveiling NT and Win/32. This has been a little confusing and disconcerting; continued confusion is likely to have a negative effect on Microsoft and its LAN operating system plans. Several major corporations have standardized on the Microsoft platform only to have Microsoft abandon them. These Microsoft loyalists, and those that have observed them, are more than a little reluctant to go back to Microsoft or sign on to their new offerings.

Developers of applications and LAN-related software are too shell-shocked right now to jump into another potential void. Most LAN administrators, data center managers, and EUC support professionals are looking for a stable product. Chances are that they do no see this in NT.

Microsoft is likely to be more successful by dominating the desktop with workstation environments and applications. Windows 3.1 is likely to continue to lead the masses to graphical interfaces. It is clearly the best environment ever for DOS-based machines, and it will have still greater potential with 32-bit capabilities.

Actually, over a longer enough period of time, Windows might lead Microsoft to LAN OS success. After the dust settles from the OS/2 wars and the corporate jitters of the Fortune 500 standards committees are soothed, NT might surface as a strong competitor. However, the aggregate percentage of

Microsoft's LAN operating system market share is likely to decline in the near term.

Pundits say that when someone is at the top, there is no way to go but down. Novell remains at the top, and it is likely to continue to prove the doomsayers wrong. While IBM and Microsoft have feuded the last couple of years, Novell has entrenched itself in a majority of clients, markets, and countries.

With more than half of all LAN users in the fold, Novell guards every move. The lack of public knowledge of NetWare enhancements does not mean that there are no improvements in the pipeline. Waiting until these improvements are ready is a wise move for the company that promised to deliver SFT Level III NetWare at least five years ago.

As a result, Novell is not likely to see its market share drop below 60% for the next couple of years. If IBM finds success with OS/2 version 2, and if Microsoft's NT strategy bears fruit in a couple of years, Novell could see its market share percentage decrease. Even in this case, however, Novell's aggregate numbers will continue to increase because the market itself will continue to grow. A smaller percentage of a larger market still means an increasing amount of dollars.

## ANSWERS FOR USER SUPPORT

So what does all this mean for the network administrator, user, or data center professional? The answer depends on the customers' current situation and their needs. If an organization has already established networking standards, and if its current system is meeting its needs, this analysis could serve as the basis for evaluating the network's ability to meet future requirements.

Organizations that currently own a system based on OS/2 should carefully monitor the capabilities and acceptance of OS/2 version 2.0. If it lives up to its billing, the products and services most organizations need will probably be available into the foreseeable future. If 2.0 is a major disappointment, organizations should review alternative systems and standards.

Organizations that have established a network standard based on Microsoft's LAN Manager must perform two levels of monitoring. If the company intends to continue with OS/2 as the platform, the data center staff should evaluate version 2.0 and find a server product that is supported on it. If the company intends to opt for the NT alternative with future LAN Manager support, the data center must evaluate the enhancements to the server products and to the NT environment.

Because many questions remain as to exact support and exact dates, this is a very fluid environment on which to base business. Microsoft will probably give a lot of dates and assurances; however, the individual company must decide how much confidence to put in them.

Organizations that have built their internal standard around Net-Ware have hooked up with the organization that has a strong support staff and the most promising future. The IBM vote of confidence was not needed for Novell's continued success, but it may have been the final vote cast for another decade's worth of market leadership for NetWare. As the number-one player, Novell will need to solve the changing problems of its users. Novell is well suited from an organization and development viewpoint to handle consumer demands and concerns and keep consumer confidence.

For organizations just getting ready to establish a standard, now is actually a good time. The sales forces at Novell and IBM are primed and ready to answer questions and will soon be able to provide hands-on support of their claims. Their promises can be rated against the company's computing needs to help make a decision. Certainly, the Microsoft sales force will have something to say as well, but its ability to deliver the full solution in the near future is still in question. Although it may certainly be worth the time to evaluate Microsoft's claims, the real test will come when the NT-Win/32 solution is available.

If OS/2 2.0 lives up to expectations, and if the organization's system intends to use client/server operations, moving to IBM should be considered. NetWare covers most of the bases quite well, and it is nice to have a choice.

Small or even medium-sized companies with limited connectivity needs might be well served with one of the peer-to-peer networks available in increasing numbers (e.g., Sitka 10net or Tops, Artisoft Lantastic, or NetWare Lite). These systems require little overhead for hard disk or RAM and are inexpensive and uncomplicated. They meet the basic data and device-sharing needs. In most polls of network users, even on the largest systems, most users are taking advantage of their network connections only for the most basic printing and file service operations. That being the case, the simpler networks have their place.

Software and systems are making great strides in providing the sophisticated computing environments that the industry leaders have been touting for years. Although electronic mail and scheduling, SQL client/server systems, groupware, and publish-and-subscribe facilities have been in place for quite some time, they are just gaining acceptance.

Systems requirements planning must match a company's needs against these full systems capabilities. Simple networks have their place but only as a portion of the total solution. Smaller companies that plan to remain that way might find them sufficient; however, companies that expect to grow past basic operations need to sketch out a competent upgrade path.

The world had better be ready for graphical workstations because they are likely to be the common thread of all systems by mid-decade. They allow microcomputers to be what they were originally designed to be—tools that extend the workers' capabilities—rather than to become an end unto themselves. Windows, the Macintosh interface, Presentation Manager, and others are the future today. Versions 3.0 and 3.1 of Windows guarantee the vision that Apple brought to the world. Although character-oriented environments still predominate on microcomputers, they are going the way of the vinyl record and the manual typewriter. Data center support departments should establish a graphical standard for the sake of productivity and profits as well as common sense. If they do, their clients will be able to use more tools, more often, and with greater ease.

When the majority of workstations run 32-bit operating systems, such as UNIX, NT, or OS/2 2.0, most stations will begin to periodically offer services to others on the network. This transition will occur gradually and will not require a yes-or-no decision regarding NetWare. Instead, coexistence of these operating systems will ensure a gradual transition process.

## SUMMARY

What this all means is up to the individual organization. However, there are a few final observations:

- NetWare will continue to lead the way.
- People are still confused about Microsoft and LANs.
- IBM's PC networking hopes rest with OS/2 version 2.0.
- Windows is here to stay and will dominate the desktop.
- Companies must set LAN standards today.
- There is a place for peer-to-peer networks, especially if they can allow for growth.

# IX-4
# Future Directions in Data Base Management

*GORDON C. EVEREST*

The CODASYL network approach of the 1970s (proposed by the Conference of Data Systems Languages) and the relational data model of the 1980s have provided solutions to many of the problems in business information processing. Their weaknesses, however, are becoming apparent. The newer, more sophisticated business applications (e.g., decision support and expert systems) require:

- Operation in a heterogeneous, distributed processing environment.
- The capturing of more of the semantics of a data structure.
- Greater complexity in the entities or objects to be represented and manipulated.
- Better management of objects in their spatial and temporal dimensions.

Semantic data models and the object-oriented approach are two avenues of development that in the past few years have made significant contributions to these problem areas and show some promise.

Semantic data models attempt to provide data modelers with more expressiveness, enabling them to incorporate a richer set of semantics into the data base. The object-oriented aproach provides some new constructs arising from advanced developments in programming languages. Object-oriented data modeling and object-oriented DBMSs are emerging from the unification of object-oriented programming and conventional DBMSs.

There are two main approaches to implementing an object-oriented DBMS. The first approach involves extending conventional DBMSs to include object-oriented concepts. This approach represents radical surgery, especially to the relational model. Some observers judge this approach to be all but impossible.

The second approach involves the extension of an object-oriented programming language, such as Smalltalk, to handle data structures that are independent of the programs and that have a stable and continued existence over time (called persistence) rather than only during the execution of a program. This means that separate, standalone, generic facilities for defining, creating, querying, and updating data base structures must be developed. In addition, a separate run-time data base control system for performing data base input and output, controlling concurrent updates, synchronizing updates to multiple copies of the data base, logging for backup and recovery, and controlling access to the data base must also be developed. This approach, the one of Servio Corp.'s GemStone, is ambitious.

This chapter describes some of the new requirements and approaches to data modeling and data base management by examining the weaknesses of current DBMSs that lead to these new requirements.

## CURRENT VERSUS FUTURE DBMSs

There are different generations of data management technology, as shown in Exhibit IX-4-1. FORTRAN and COBOL introduced the notion of a file. The CODASYL proposal for extensions to COBOL (or any other conventional programming language) represented the third generation of data base management systems, which extended the data division to allow the definition of richer data structures, often called network structures.

| Object-Oriented, Semantic Data Model, 1990s |
| :---: |
| More semantics; complex, heterogeneous (multimedia) data structure |

| Relational Data Bases, 1980s |
| :---: |
| High, file-level data manipulation language (SQL, 4GLs) —but limited data structuring semantics or integrity constraints |

| CODASYL Network, 1970s |
| :---: |
| Richer (multifile) data structures and interfile relationships (set)—but low-level, record-at-a-time data manipulation language |

| COBOL, 1960s |
| :---: |
| Explicit definition of and independent existence of data—but single, hierarchical files, and low-level data manipulation language |

| Assembly Language |
| :---: |
| Lacks concept of a file |

**Exhibit IX-4-1. Generations of DBMSs**

The major contribution of the relational data base approach was a higher-level language for processing files. The underlying operations of the language included selection, projection, and join (on multiple files). Such file-level or set-oriented languages have been called fourth-generation languages (4GLs).

Unfortunately, the relational model offers an overly simplistic view of data, as either multiple flat files or tables. It is limited in data structuring semantics and in integrity constraints. In a sense, the relational approach represents a step backward from the richer data structuring and explicit relationship definitions of the old CODASYL network approach. A point in its favor is that record-level navigation is no longer necessary with the relational approach.

On the basis of the experiences of the past decade, users and developers are recognizing the weaknesses in the current generation of DBMSs. During the 1980s, the big push was for relational systems with SQL, the ANSI standard. The parent of the relational model, E. F. Codd, attempted to define the rules for a relational systems; industry reaction included descriptions of the weaknesses and problems with record-based data structures in both the CODASYL network model and the relational model. Recently, the focus has been on the relational model, and industry participants have begun to point out directions for future DBMSs. The need to go beyond the relational model is becoming widely recognized.

The object-oriented, semantic data model represents the fifth generation of DBMSs. Such systems will be characterized by a much richer declaration of data semantics than is available in current systems. Operations are encapsulated along with the data structures and represented as units, or objects, to the users. This allows representation of far more complex forms of data, including multimedia information, rules of inference to support the knowledge base of expert systems, and extended vocabularies and rules of grammar to support natural-language processing and continuous-speech recognition. The components of such systems are beginning to emerge and will thrive during this decade.

## NEEDS DRIVING A NEW GENERATION OF DBMSs

The demand for a new generation of DBMSs comes from three principal sources. First in the new computing environment, which contains a wide variety of hardware and software—a heterogeneous, distributed computing environment. One related source causing the demand for a new generation of DBMSs is the increase in the popularity of multimedia and imaging technology. The second source is the need to capture more complete semantics of a data structure, including integrity constraints or quality control rules, and defined operations encapsulated within the data structure. These two sources are described in detail in subsequent sections of the chapter. The third source, the need to support CAD/CAM and graphics applications, is beyond the scope of this chapter and is not discussed further.

### The Heterogeneous, Distributed Computing Environment

Even as a revolution in data processing has occurred—in the shift from a process- to a data-oriented approach to systems development—a profound revolution is also under way in the concept of the platform for delivery of computational power. In the old view (see Exhibit IX-4-2), a central mainframe or minicomputer acts as a host to a collection of satellite nodes—microcomputer workstations are connected by a network. The focus is generally still on the central host. This view of the platform is satisfactory as long as there is only one contender for the central, controlling host, with all other nodes functioning as its satellites.

Any departmental or multiuser computers that are added to tie together a localized set of workstations or terminals would also function as a controlling host. If this second host is connected to the central mainframe host, the two nodes must cooperate. Adding a second mainframe and then several LANs—with file servers—that tie together clusters of microcomputer workstations results in many computer nodes capable of network configuration and traffic management. Any one of these could potentially serve as the central controlling host, but they cannot all do so. The task of configuring the network and managing the communications activities within the network is extremely difficult.

In this type of configuration, with many contenders for the role of central

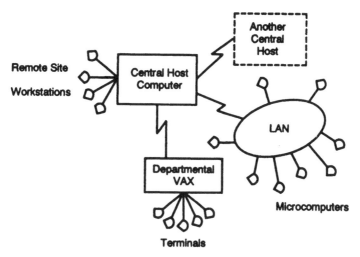

**Notes:**
Central host does network and traffic management.
Adding a departmental computer, a LAN, and another host complicates configuration and management.

**Exhibit IX-4-2. The Old View of the Computing Platform**

controlling host, the host functions must be removed from the nodes. The new concept of the platform places a general communications facility in the center (see Exhibit IX-4-3). All computation facilities becomes nodes attached to that communications facility. Every node has its own power supply, storage, processing facilities, and input/output interfaces. Every node can function autonomously and asynchronously with respect to other nodes in the network. The nodes can be general or special purpose, they can be heterogeneous, and they can communicate with each other. Server nodes provide specialized services to client nodes within the network.

This new view of the computer-communications platform represents a new paradigm for network configuration and traffic management, one in which it is easier for an organization to design a network of distributed computer facilities. This new view also makes it easier for vendors to design products to operate in a distributed environment. The configuration of the communications facility is transparent to the users and to the individual computing nodes. All network-configuration and traffic-management functions are performed by the communications facility.

In this new kind of computing environment, a DBMS must provide transparent access to data anywhere in the network, even if it is managed by different DBMSs; it must properly maintain both replicated and partitioned

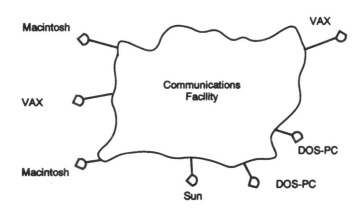

**Notes:**
Nodes and sites are autonomous, coequal, heterogeneous, and differ by size and capability.
The communications facility configuration is transparent.
The communications facility, not a node, performs network and traffic management.
Data is stored at any site and is managed by its own local DBMS.
DBMSs must know how to talk to each other; otherwise a network DBMS is required.
Users at any node have transparent access to data anywhere in the network.
The server and client nodes are nonexclusive and shifting.

**Exhibit IX-4-3. The New View of the Computing Platform**

data stored at multiple sites. The DBMS must also be partitioned into local functions for the client and back-end functions performed at a server node. Front-end client functions include interacting with the user, accepting requests, decomposing those requests, and translating and forwarding them to data server nodes, as well as assembling the returned data, formatting and presenting the results to the requester, and providing facilities for application systems development. The back-end server nodes respond to requests for data services from client nodes. These requests must be expressed in a high-level, multifile data language (e.g., SQL).

In this new computing environment, a DBMS must be able to work with the dominant systems. This means it must offer facilities to import and export data dynamically (on demand, not with extracts) to and from such systems at Lotus Development Corp.'s Lotus 1-2-3, Ashton-Tate's dBase IV, and IBM's DB2 and its future repository (whatever form it takes). Several vendors are battling to become the dominant SQL server. These include Sybase, Inc., Gupta Technologies, Inc. (with SQLBase), XDB Systems, Inc. (with XDB-Server), InterBase Software Corp. (with InterBase), Microsoft Corp. (with SQL Server), and IBM. Some of these systems offer both front-end client functions and back-end SQL server functions. Every DBMS vendor must ensure that its products can operate in this newly emerging environment of LANs, SQL servers, and links to minicomputer and mainframe hosts with a communications facility.

**Multimedia and Imaging Technology.** People communicate verbally and visually as well as with formatted character strings. Yet, in computer systems, data primarily occurs in such strings, albeit structured and organized. Information management systems must be able to represent and manipulate audio and video (and even other sensory) forms of information.

Exhibit IX-4-4 provides a taxonomy of various multimedia forms of information. Data and text, both character-based, are the most common forms for representing information in computer systems. In fact, in most systems, data is the primary means of representing knowledge and initiating actions. Most text-based systems can do little more than store and echo endless strings of characters. A notable example of a product that combines powerful text management and data management capabilities is BASISplus from Information Dimensions, Inc.

Graphic information may be represented as bit-mapped images or as defined objects. Imaging technology has increased in popularity and interest. Systems are becoming quite sophisticated in terms of their analysis and enhancing techniques. Bit-mapped images are represented as a collection of dots in two-dimensional space. Different kinds of dots can be used to distinguish between such information as shading, color, or other characteristics of the picture. One important disadvantage is that this representation does not explicitly identify individual components in the picture. Consequently, it is difficult to do more than store and echo the picture and possibly manipulate the picture through resizing, rotation, and cropping.

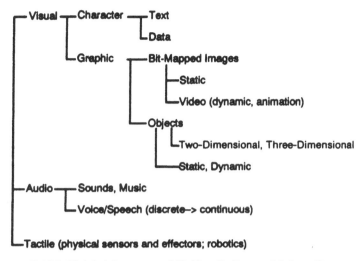

**Exhibit IX-4-4. A Taxonomy of Multimedia Forms of Information**

Object-based graphics systems build up a representation of an object using primitives, starting from points and lines. Some systems focus on objects in space, whereas others (generally called geographic information systems, or GISs) focus on areas or regions and boundaries. Most graphics systems, however, do a relatively poor job of representing and manipulating the attribute data associated with the graphic objects.

Another major form of information is digital sound and voice. As with graphics, the audio may be stored as a digital representation of a continuous stream of sounds. This allows recording and playback but little else. To do more, the sound must be decomposed into the notes of music or the phonemes, words, and parts of speech. Voice or speech recognition requires that the computer identify vocabulary and establish a catalog of meaningful utterances on the basis of a knowledge of the structure of the language (i.e., grammar).

Many systems do an adequate and sometimes excellent job of representing and manipulating information in these various forms. Examples of these systems include word processors, bibliographic information systems, data base management systems, screen painting programs, imaging systems, such object-based graphics systems as CAD/CAM and GIS, dynamic video graphics, discrete voice-recognition systems, voice-response systems, and electronic voice mail.

The real need, however, is to combine, relate, and integrate these various forms of information. This is the challenge of multimedia. It would be useful to verbally annotate a text with sounds or to display text and data at a workstation along with moving video graphic images and an accompanying soundtrack. It might be possible to see a three-dimensional view of a multifloor workplace and analyze the patterns of movement in that space. In solids modeling, engineers must be able to see objects fitting together and moving in space while they perform manipulations on the basis of the attributes of those objects. Often, it would be useful to associate graphics, sounds, and even tactile information with the entities stored in conventional data bases.

To store, relate, and manage information in such diverse forms requires much more than is currently possible in conventional DBMSs. Object-oriented data bases offer some hope that complex objects that exist in multiple dimensions can be defined and managed and diverse representational forms can be combined.

## The Need for Complete Data Structure Semantics

A DBMS must have a full definition of the data base to effectively manage data for a community of users while maintaining data quality and serving as the basis for efficient application systems development. The DBMS cannot manage or enforce what is not formally defined to it. Of course, complete data semantics are never possible; users can always know more about a data structure than could ever be defined to a system. Nevertheless, much more can be accomplished by DBMSs with more meaningful data structures than with many current-generation DBMSs.

A data base is actually a model of selected portions of reality for a community of users. When a data base is being defined, the data modeling constructs in the DBMS must be rich enough to declare to the system as much as possible about the world being modeled. These declarations must include structure, integrity constraints, and operations, and they must relate to both the static and the dynamic qualities of the data structure.

Such declarations make it possible for the system to enforce integrity constraints on the structure, thereby maintaining a defined level of quality in the stored data. They make it possible for the system to automatically invoke checks and other operations when certain actions are performed on the data structure. User-specified operations can be hooked into the data structure as a declaration. Such declared operations become like reusable code for users and systems developers.

At a minimum, the definition of a data structure generally includes the name, type, and size of individual data items within each record type. Beyond this minimal description, the following information can be added:

- Identification of records.
- A more explicit indication of the acceptable values for a data item.
- Additional data item characteristics.
- Conditional and transitional integrity checks.
- Derived or calculated data items.
- Interrecord relationships and their characteristics.
- Alternative user views of the data structure.

Although current systems may offer some of these capabilities, other require-ments represent a substantial departure from traditional DBMSs, particularly relational DBMSs. Some of the most important needs related to data structure are described in further detail in the following sections.

**Encapsulation of Operations.** Additional semantics of a data structure imply additional processing and checking when the data is being processed. For example, if it is specified that a data item can take on only certain data values, the system must invoke a process to check each insert or update action to compare the new value with the list of acceptable values. For a more concrete example, if birthday information is stored but ages are desired as well, the system must be given the formula for calculating age from birthday so that when age is requested, the system can execute the process.

In general, users can write and store entire programs (i.e., sequences of commands) to be executed when requests are made of the data base; such programs may still be considered declarations associated with the definition of a data structure. They are as much a procedure as declaring a data item to be numeric and assuming the system will invoke a procedure to check that all incoming values conform to the definition of numeric.

The richer a DBMS is in accepting declarations or definitions of integrity constraints, derivation rules, or subprocesses embedded in the data structure, the less systems developers must write customized programs to accomplish applications processing. Such operations or processes are hooked onto, or embedded in, the data structure—or encapsulated, to borrow a term from object-oriented programming. The point is that the greater the descriptive power of a DBMS to capture more of the semantics of a data structure, the easier it becomes to have the system encapsulate operations in that data structure.

**Definition of Data Items.** Data items in records represent attributes of entities in the real world. Each record contains at least one value for each attribute. It is desirable to define as precisely as possible the domain of acceptable values for each data item. This requires more than a simple designa-tion of data type. For example, character, integer, or real number would be considered simple designations, but adding such semantics as the following could improve the definition:

- Included or excluded ranges of values.
- An enumerated set of values.
- Mandatory or optional value.
- A representation for a null value.
- An initial default value. Only when created or on updates as well; user override or not.
- The nature of a numeric value. A cardinal, interval, ordinal, or nominal scale dictates the set of allowable operators. For example, for numeric

strings, only equal matching is allowed; all other operators are meaningless. Most DBMSs do not include such a declaration, though numeric string items are a common occurrence in the real world.

- Allowable or prohibited transitions among the values in the domain. An example would be IF UNIONIZED EMPLOYEE THEN NEW SALARY GE OLD SALARY whenever the value for salary changes. Any of these declarations may be conditional on the values of other attributes or on time.

**Definition of Relationships.** Relationships between entity (i.e., record) types or objects have several characteristics, which should be defined explicitly to and enforced by the DBMS. These are discussed in the following paragraphs.

*Name.* Each relationship has a name in each direction reflecting the role played by the respective entities in the relationship.

*Multiplicity.* This specifies whether at most one (exclusive) or more than one (multiple) of an entity type can be related to an instance of another entity type. This can be specified for each entity type participating in the relationship. The multiplicity characteristic can be conditional on the value of other data items in the record, or it can be conditional on time.

*Dependence.* This specifies whether an entity instance must be related to at least one instance of another entity type or can be an orphan in the data base—that is, whether its participation in the relationship is optional. The dependence may be temporal. For example, an entity may be an orphan initially; after it has been related to another entity, however, it must always remain attached to some instance of that other entity type, perhaps even the same instance for the rest of its life in the data base. The dependence characteristic depends on the value of other data items in the record or on time. Furthermore, the effects of certain operations on the entities participating in the relationship should be specified; an example would be what to do to a dependent record if the record owning it is to be deleted—whether to prohibit the deletion if any dependent records exist or to delete all existing dependent records.

*Criteria.* The criteria for the relationship can be expressed in terms of a Boolean expression in which the operands are taken from data items of entity records participating in the relationship. This relationship is often the equality of a data item in one record with the value of a corresponding data item in the other record (of a binary relationship). If the data item is the whole identifier in one record, it is called a foreign identifier in the other.

*Degree of Relationship.* This is indicated by the number of record types jointly participating in the relationship. Most systems allow only binary relationships, though in the real world being modeled, ternary or higher relationships are quite possible. The same entity type could participate in the same relationship but play two different roles in that relationship—for example, an individual in an organization could be both an employee and a manager. Such a relationship is called reflexive.

The relational data model does not allow the direct definition of relationships. Join criteria are given in SQL retrieval statements but cannot be the basis for enforcement of integrity constraints when the data base is populated or modified.

**Definition of User Views.** Some systems, if they support user views at all allow definition of them only in terms of a projection of data items from one record type. This is the most primitive user view facility. In general, a user view can be defined as the virtual result of a high-level query against a multifile data structure. This includes any combination of the following operations:

- The projection of data items from multiple record types.
- The joining of multiple record types on the basis of some join criteria or a predefined relationship to form an intermediate (i.e., temporary) record type.
- The selection of record instances from individual record types or their joins on the basis of a Boolean selection expression.
- The derivation of data items.
- The ordering of record instances.
- The grouping of record instances and derivation of an intermediate record type on the basis of statistics calculated across data items in each of the groups. This is equivalent to a marginal frequency distribution, often called a control break report.

A view definition can be the first step in the specification of a process on the data base. Subsequent commands can be issued and would be interpreted in the context of the user view definition in force at the time.

## DATA BASE MANAGEMENT AND THE OBJECT-ORIENTED APPROACH

Developments in object-oriented programming languages suggest new requirements for data base management and are influencing the development of DBMSs. These concepts include:

- *Object identity.* The ability to distinguish objects regardless of their characteristics or physical location and to facilitate sharing of objects.
- *Object typing.* The ability to define new object types and to associate objects with one or more object types.
- *Object assembly.* The ability to create arbitrarily complex and dynamic objects from other objects.
- *Inheritance.* The ability to define subtypes and supertypes so that subtypes inherit the attributes and operations of their supertypes.

- *Encapsulation.* The ability to define operations associated with an object type.

Each of these concepts is discussed in the following subsections.

## Object Identity

Most conventional DBMSs, including relational systems, require that each record instance be uniquely identified by content—that is, by the values in one or more stored attributes or data items. In other words, in every record instance, a combination of values must identify each record (i.e., make each record unique). This raises problems associated with using external descriptive data for indentification.

In the object-oriented approach, each record instance (not the record type) is considered an object. A data object corresponds to, represents, or models a real-world object or entity instance.

Object identity should be independent of attribute values. Each object is unique and must be identifiable by its very existence, even if some or all of its properties are the same as those of another object. A subset of an object's attributes is chosen to represent the object in a data base. A record instance must be identified independently of its content.

Object identity, furthermore, should be independent of structure—that is, independent of the definition of record types in the data base. Object identification should be unique across all record types, even across different DBMSs, and across the sites in a distributed environment. Object identity should also be independent of location—that is, the address (real or virtual) of the place in which the object representation (i.e., record instance) is stored.

When object identity is built into the system, uniqueness is captured even though an object's description is not unique. Independent identification demands that an object or record instance be assigned a unique, permanent identifier on initial creation. User-specified external identifiers may change; in a reorganization, product numbers could change or department identifiers could change.

Identifiers should be dateless, unchanging, unambiguous, and unique. Object identifiers should have no meaning to the users or to the external world being modeled and, in fact, should be transparent to the outside world.

Invariant and non-value-based object (i.e., record instance) identification is necessary to ensure the integrity of the following:

- Object existence.
- Interrecord relationships.
- Real, independent objects as distinguished from artificial or dependent objects.
- The same object participating in an is-as relationship (i.e., subtypes and supertypes in a generalization hierarchy).

It is also important to maintain object identity when updating attributes that could serve to uniquely identify objects, when trying to distinguish historical versions of an object over time, and when structurally reorganizing the data base.

## Object Typing

With the current generation of DBMSs, a data base consists of a collection of record instances, each belonging to one record type, the definition of which specifies the structure, content, and format of each record instance. Each file (i.e., relation) or collection of records must have its own type declaration or schema definition. The system provides a fixed set of atomic types or domains of values (e.g., character, integer, money, and date) and a fixed set of higher-order types (e.g., record, relation, and CODASYL set). It is not generally possible to add new atomic types or to construct higher-order types.

With the object-oriented approach, the relationship between objects (i.e., record instances) and object types is more flexible. Explicit type declarations still exist, which helps structure and organize the data in a data base. A type declaration indicates the structure and contents of objects that are members of the type; a type may pertain to atomic (i.e., single-valued) objects, to objects consisting of tuples (i.e., nested repeated groups) of atomic values (i.e., single flat files or relations), or to a set of subobjects. The type declaration also includes the specification of operations that apply to instances of that type.

If a type declaration is treated as an object, the schemas or metadata can be handled just like the user data in a data base. It is desirable and efficient to use the same query, report, and update facilities that are used for the actual data to access and manipulate the data base schema definition, but the access privileges would clearly be different.

## Object Assembly

The object-oriented approach allows the creation of arbitrarily complex and dynamic objects, built up from assemblages of subobjects. At the lowest level, an object consists of a single value from a domain of atomic values.

An object consists of a set of properties. A property is a name-value pair. The name refers to the object type (of which the value is an object, or instance) and indicates the role of the referenced object type in describing the defined object type. The value may be a single atomic object, a set of objects of the same type (multivalued), or a subject (of arbitrary complexity). The value associated with a name may be arbitrarily complex; the name may be single-valued, multivalued, a multidimensional array of values, a tuple of values (i.e., a nonrepeating group of items), a set of tuples (i.e., a repeating group or subrelation) or in general, the equivalent of a hierarchical file containing arbitrary levels of nested repeating groups. Anywhere a value can appear, a whole complex object can appear.

With this approach, objects are composed of other objects. The manipulation facilities of the system must let the user deal with such arbitrarily complex objects as a whole unit without having to decompose the object. In the relational model, a multivalued item or nested repeating group of items requires the definition of a new relation; join operations are then required to assemble a whole object, resulting in redundancy of higher-level data. In the general object-oriented approach, subjects may be shared with other (i.e., parent) objects. Furthermore, an object may relate to more than one type.

## Subtypes, Supertypes, and Inheritance

The ability to define subtypes and supertypes allows explicit representation of similarities and differences among various classes of objects. The subtype-supertype relationship is also called an is-a or is-as relationship. This characteristic makes it possible for objects to share common attributes and operations along a whole inheritance chain. It also provides a means of handling special cases.

A member of a subtype always belongs to the supertype. Furthermore, the subtype inherits the attributes and operations defined for the supertype so that when an object is declared to be of a particular type, it inherits the attributes and operations not only of that type but also of all its supertypes. The attributes of the supertype are common across all of its subtypes. The subtype may have additional attributes not found in the supertype. Subtypes may be mutually exclusive or overlapping. The subtypes may also be collectively exhaustive of the members of the supertype.

The subtypes and supertypes may be defined in a strict hierarchy with each subtype belonging to exactly one supertype. This makes the inheritance of attributes straightforward. A more general method is to allow multiple supertypes on a subtype. This results in multiple inheritance and the possibility of conflict when two supertypes have the same attributes. In this case, it is necessary to have some precedence ordering or user selection of attributes.

## Encapsulation of Operations with Data Objects

In object-oriented programming, the definition of an object type includes both its structure and the operations used to access and manipulate that structure. Data objects are encapsulated so they can be accessed only by the issuing of commands to the object. Encapsulation is similar to the notions of derivation, integrity constraints, and user views, which were described previously. When commands are given to access and manipulate data objects, these embedded procedures are automatically invoked to accomplish the retrieval or manipulation and to check the results.

The notion of encapsulation from object-oriented programming serves a dual purpose. First, programmers become more efficient when they can use some pieces of reusable code for processing data objects. Second, if programmers must communicate through these predefined pieces of code rather than by accessing and manipulating the data directly through generic operations, the integrity of the data objects will be maintained. For example, with an employee file, rather than use the generic operations of insert, update, and delete [record instances], tailored procedures would be devised to review, hire, promote, transfer, fire, lay off, and retire employees. The command is the message, as this term is used in object-oriented programming. These commands would then be the only means of accessing and manipulating employee records.

An operation may be defined in terms of a single command or a series of commands stored in a procedure file or program. (In the case of a program, the language should provide for memory variables, input and output communications at run time, and the conditional and iterative execution of subblocks of commands.) The result of executing an operation could be one, multiple values of one, or multiple attributes or variables. If the result is well formed and predictable, it can be embedded in the data struture as part of its definition; it becomes like another declaration.

Conventional DBMSs provide generic operations on predefined, often sketchily defined, data objects. The next generation of DBMSs should allow the definition of operations in conjunction with the data structures.

## SUMMARY

Object-oriented programming has brought many new ideas to DBMS development. New methods using object identify, object typing, object assembly, inheritance, and encapsulation allow DBMSs to overcome their current limitation and manage complex data.

Data management problems arising from the proliferation of heterogeneous, distributed environments are another target of object-oriented data base managament. With data standards and appropriate versioning and change control, object-oriented DBMSs offer considerable promise for the future of managing data resources.

# IX-5
# Trends in Terminal Technology

*GILBERT HELD*

For computers to accomplish useful work, data must be entered and information retrieved. The terminal has evolved as the primary means by which users perform these functions, particularly when they are working at a site remote from the computing hardware. Two factors must be considered, however, with respect to terminal technology. First, the microcomputer has become extremely popular as a terminal device when it is connected to a remote mainframe or minicomputer over a communications network. Second, the forces affecting the growth of large systems depend mostly on the need for rapid access by large numbers of users in real time.

Terminals were designed to enable many users to share the computer resource, entering data and receiving information in real time. The first terminal was the Teletype, a slow mechanical device. Two limitations of the Teletype prompted the demise of the device: low speed and the need for regular mechanical maintenance. As a result, network costs rose during the late 1960s. The CRT terminal replaced the slow printer with a video display and introduced new keyboard technologies in place of the solenoids of the teletypes. These new terminals increased data transmission speeds, thus starting the push to higher-capacity networks, a trend that is exemplified today in local area network (LAN) developments.

Currently, mainframe-based terminal networks are classified as either local or remote and are set up either as clusters or as individual user sites. A typical cluster might be in an insurance office, in which several operators work with telephones and terminals to field customer inquiries. A typical individual user is a time-sharing service customer with a single terminal and modem who accesses the service's mainframe to perform a job.

Exhibit IX-5-1 illustrates several examples of local and remote terminals connected to a mainframe through cluster controllers (commonly referred to as control units) and on an individual basis. For example, at location 1, the previously mentioned insurance office requires the use of a large number of terminals. Instead of installing many individual communications lines to the central site, a remote control unit has been installed. The control unit enables

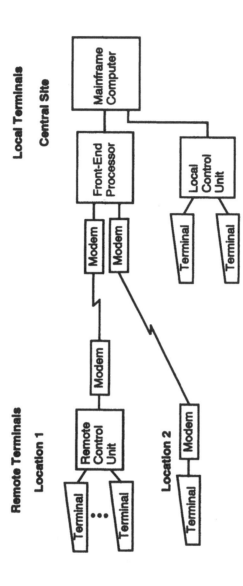

**Local Terminals**

**Central Site**

Mainframe Computer

Front-End Processor

Modem

Modem

Local Control Unit

Terminal

Terminal

**Remote Terminals**

**Location 1**

Modem

Remote Control Unit

Terminal

• • •

Terminal

**Location 2**

Modem

Terminal

Exhibit IX-5-1. Local and Remote Terminals

740

many terminals to share access to the mainframe over the front-end processor and a common communications circuit by the use of a poll-and-selection method of operation. At location 2, only one remote terminal needs to access the mainframe. At this location, a terminal could be connected over a communications line or over the switched telephone network to the front-end processor.

At the central site, the local control unit bypasses the front-end processor and connects directly to the mainframe. Most computer manufacturers enable local control units to be connected to the high-speed bus of the mainframe, substantially reducing the response time of local terminal users in comparison to remote terminal users, whose remote control unit must be serviced by a front-end processor.

The microcomputer has completely penetrated the terminal marketplace. Current terminals are functionally almost indistinguishable from microcomputers, and a large number of personal computers are used both as terminals to access the mainframe and as standalone units to perform local processing. In fact, with more than 50 million microcomputers installed worldwide, there are as many users of microcomputers as there are of traditional computer terminals, and new applications will continue to emerge.

Microcomputers can accomplish all the tasks assigned to terminals, and unlike standard terminals, which might need to be replaced, they can support new applications through add-on devices. This is not to suggest that all old terminals should be discarded; they can serve long and useful lives as I/O devices for current applications and can be replaced as necessary. For new applications and new users, the microcomputer should be the preferred device, especially when increased use can be predicted. For example, considering the configuration of local and remote terminals illustrated in Exhibit IX-5-1, if an organization required remote terminal access to IBM computer equipment, it could install 3270 emulator adapter cards in microcomputers, resulting in the micrcomputers' communicating as IBM terminals. If, at a later date, the organization decided to change its network structure and place all remote microcomputers on LANs, the 3270 emulator adapter cards could be replaced with LAN adapter cards. In comparison, this type of change would make the prior use of terminals osbolete.

## TERMINAL COMPONENTS

Besides the internal electronics, the components that make up the terminal include displays, printers, input devices, and communications interfaces. The following sections discuss these components for both terminals and microcomputers. Microcomputers are included in these discussions because they can be configured to operate as terminals.

### Displays

The CRT has benefited from design improvements that have resulted in price reductions and increased color fidelity. Still, the monochrome monitor remains the most widely used terminal output device, valued for its resolution and low price. Color displays suffer by comparison in the area of resolution, or dots per inch, becaue they must reproduce different phosphors on the screen for each color. This situation is changing with the development of very high resolution color screens. In the area of microcomputing, economies of scale obtained from mass production resulted in the incremental cost of color over monochrome becoming quite small. By mid-1991, a consumer could purchase a color VGA-compatible monitor with a resolution of 640 pixels by 480 pixels for less than $200 over the cost of a monochrome VGA monitor.

Display technology has shown continuing emphasis on high resolution and multiple-color capability. High resolution is needed for graphics applications, which are expanding, and for desktop publishing. A combination of high-performance computing and high-resolution graphics display is now available in a single desktop unit. These machines, which are commonly referred to as workstations and are primarily used in standalone applications, have the communications capability to access large remote data bases. Color, though still more expensive than monochrome, is gaining popularity because it clarifies graphics displays and is more attractive.

Display technologies besides the CRT include plasma and light-emitting diodes (LEDs). Plasma technology can be used to create large, relatively thin display screens that are reliable and offer high resolution. Although not popularly used in terminals, plasma technology has been incorporated into many laptop computers. Plasma technology costs about 50% more than equivalent CRTs, and its display screen's size is beginning to grow for some applications (especially for those in desktop publishing, in which the ability to view an entire page can be very important). In addition, their illumination makes them more suitable for use with portable computers than are LED displays. However, most plasma screen laptops require an AC power source because, at their rate of power consumption, they rapidly drain battery-powered portable microcomputers.

One new technology that may finally emerge in high volume is that of plasma panels. These panels, currently available from IBM and a few other vendors, are approximately three times more costly than CRTs, are limited to monochrome, and have somewhat slower refresh rates than CRTs. Further developments are underway to solve the technical issues and to create cost-effective plasma displays that enable users to benefit from their brighter output and smaller physical dimensions.

The use of LEDs for alphanumeric displays was an early attempt to reduce the size and weight of the CRT. Because of its high cost, however, the LED display screen proved short lived.

## Printers

Printers can be classified as either impact or nonimpact. Impact printers use a hammer that strikes the paper through a ribbon and transfers an image onto the paper. The hammer can consist of a solid character, as in standard typewriters, or a series of pins, as in dot-matrix printers. Solid-character mechanisms, perhaps best represented by daisy-wheel printers, achieve the highest print quality. Dot-matrix units, however, are capable of producing an almost equivalent character quality.

Nonimpact printers use either thermal transfer, in which an image is burned into the paper, or xerographic technology, which employs a drum and toner. Laser (nonimpact) printers, whose use is increasing substantially, are based on laser copiers, which transfer images directly onto a drum instead of from a sheet of paper. The print quality of xerographic units is equal to that of impact printers, though xerographic units can make only one copy at a time.

One aspect of printers that is now receiving considerable attention is their ability to print graphics. Dot-matrix and laser printers are both capable of producing text and graphics on a single page.

Printers are simultaneously improving in presentation of data and decreasing in price. Laser printers, now at prices comparable to solid-character (i.e., daisy-wheel) units of only a few years ago, are increasingly preferred when high-resolution and combined text and graphics output are needed. Nonimpact printers are also continuing to evolve, with current ink-jet units available for less than $1,000.

Until mid-1991, the key difference between dot-matrix and laser printers was that laser printers had the ability to manipulate fonts. In mid-1991, however, Epson introduced a series of 24-pin dot-matrix printers that can manipulate fonts under software control, providing users with laser quality output and capability at 60% to 75% of the cost of a true laser printer. As other manufacturers introduce similar dot-matrix printers, their use will increase. Futurists' prediction that laser printers could make dot-matrix printers obsolete in a few years may not materialize for several decades.

### Input Devices

The keyboard appears to have reached a plateau of efficiency; the QWERTY standard remains unchallenged for both traditional terminals and microcomputers. New technology in the form of scanners connected to microcomputers, however, may make manual data entry obsolete. The scanner has reached the market in large quantities. Scanners are able to digitize pages of input, accepting data at a rate of approximately 1M bps. This data can be directly stored and displayed on a microcomputer and transferred to a minicomputer or mainframe for processing. If the data is in text form, it can be analyzed and converted, almost simultaneously, to ASCII, using optical character recognition (OCR) software. Scanners, with associated graphics and OCR software, are available at prices of less than $1,000.

In comparing a traditional terminal to a microcomputer, one of the key differences between devices is the expandability of the microcomputer. Most traditional terminals are limited to one serial or parallel port, allowing the use of a modem and printer. In comparison, the functional capability of a microcomputer is already by adding or removing adapter cards from its system unit. Thus, the user can easily change the type of display used with a microcomputer, alter its emulation capability, and add printer, modem, and plotter support—a combination of functions that are difficult, if not impossible, to perform using a conventional terminal.

### Communications Interfaces

Communications interfaces continue to evolve at all levels. LANs that use twisted-pair wire instead of the previously required coaxial cables are now common for smaller networks. Broadband systems using cable are continuing to advance in speed and the number of users they can serve. Direct line access through a modem has become inexpensive, with 2,400-bps internal units selling for less than $100. Modems running at 9,600 bps are also common and allow increased savings in connect time and associated costs for communications.

Conventional terminals and microcomputers differ significantly in their communications interface support. Most traditional terminals have a built-in port, its use governed by the manufacture of the terminal. If designed to connect to a cluster control unit, the port more than likely is a coaxial connector and the terminal cannot be used to communicate using a modem. Similarly, if the terminal is manufactured with an asynchronous serial port for point-to-point dial or leased-line communications access, it more than likely cannot be connected to a control unit. In comparison, the insertion and removal of different types of adapter cards into the system unit of a microcomputer enables the microcomputer to support a variety of communications interfaces.

### THE CONTINUED NEED FOR LARGE SYSTEMS

Contrary to popular belief, the cost of data storage in large systems is lower than storage costs for microcomputer-based systems. Access to terabytes of data in large systems is far less expensive and faster than access to multiple microcomputer Winchester drives, especially when such access is needed by many users.

In addition, the costs associated with data communications are falling as a result of high-speed data communications technologies as well as continued increases in capacity. Furthermore, the prices for terminals have fallen in line with those for microcomputers. Dumb terminals can now be purchased for approximately $500, as opposed to the $2,000 that they cost only a few years ago. Line costs for data communications have also declined, and the per-line costs of a new T1 system can be as much as 50% less than those of multiple dedicated lines.

Maintaining large computer systems is important, at least to a certain extent, because of the high cost of creating the applications that run on them.

When these costs are added to the expenses related to training and systems support, the total can be three to five times the cost of the hardware. Users are often reluctant to abandon their systems when it means throwing away large sums of money and facing additional retraining and support costs.

## NEW APPLICATIONS—THE MICROCOMPUTER'S ROLE

New computing applications are driven by the declining costs of hardware, the increasing sophistication of software, and the need for continual improvement in user efficiency. New applications cover the spectrum of user needs, and users are considering many methods of implementation. Microcomputer systems have heavily influenced this area; their speed and storage capability have now surpassed that of the small mainframes of a few years ago.

The microcomputer is becoming a commonplace tool for two reasons: the dramatic decrease in price and the equally dramatic improvement in performance. The price of microcomputers has declined so much that a system can be fully configured for approximately $2,000 to $3,000, including a printer and communications capability, either through a direct-dial modem or a LAN connection.

The evolution of the microprocessor has been impressive. The original IBM PC used an Intel 8088 chip, with power roughly equal to 0.15 MIPS (millions of instructions per second). The PC AT, using Intel's 80286 chip, achieved about three times that rate at 0.45 MIPS. With many models of the PS/2 and compatible computers using the 80386 chip, these machines (at 1.0 MIPS) have more than double the power of the PC AT. Newer 80486-based computers now offer more than 5.0 MIPS. In comparison, IBM's 360/40 mainframe, a very large computer, ran at 1.0 MIPS, took up much more space than a current microcomputer, cost a lot of money, and required groups of highly trained operators and programmers to function. Unlike mainframes, the price of microcomputers has remained relatively constant, while their performance has improved by more than a factor of 10.

Access times and storage capacity of small disks have shown similar advances. Current machines have internal storage capacities up to 300M bytes, with access times under 20 milliseconds, at costs lower than the original 5M-byte and 10M-byte drives.

Another area that has added new capabilities to microcomputers used as terminals is the connection of scanners and high-resolution printers with communications devices. Facsimile (fax) units include scanners, printers, and special modems in separate units, with dedicated dial-up or leased telephone lines. The fax unit operates by transmitting a digitized image of the input document (obtained by scanning it) to a high-resolution printer at the other end of the telephone line. The connection is usually made by the fax user with a standard dial telephone, but it can also be done automatically if additional dialing and switching gear are added.

The fax modem operates at a data rate of approximately 9.6K bps—compared with the usual data rate of 2.4K bps for text. The result is a transmission rate of a few minutes per page. The most important facsimile application, however, is the transmission of graphics.

The addition of graphics transmission provides microcomputer users with a new capability: users can now receive text and images, edit them, and transmit the changes. One application of this technology that has already gained wide acceptance is desktop publishing. Such programs as Pagemaker by Aldus and Ventura by Xerox enable users to create, store, modify, and print complete documents containing text and graphics.

A reasonably priced voice recognition device remains the one impediment to the fully integrated workstation—a system that can handle data, graphics, image, and voice input.

## THE KEY ROLE OF NETWORKS

The hardware that allows terminals to perform most automated office functions either exists currently or will be available soon in the form of low-cost optical storage that promises to radically alter the way computer users work with documents. Two problem areas remain: the interface networks to link the terminals and the central computer facilities to coordinate and process the additional information. With central processor computing power growing at an annual rate of more than 30% and price/performance ratios continuing to improve, the capacity to process the expected loads will be forthcoming.

The network is the unresolved area. To be fully useful, terminals need to be connected to a network. The development of networks lagged behind that of microcomputers until the mid-1980s, however, and is only now starting to catch up.

The crucial role of networks has propelled the move toward standardization in the industry, particularly regarding the connection of terminals to each other and to other systems. Terminal systems using cluster or controlled networks are being replaced by terminals connected to one another by the use of LANs with one or a few gateways providing access to the corporate mainframe. Such networks enable terminals to operate at higher speeds, send information from user to user directly instead of through a central computer, and transmit more types of information.

Because they connect all users, LAN network gateways must be centrally controlled by management. As a result, management is beginning to restrict which machines are used as network nodes, thereby taking control of the nodes themselves.

In most large organizations, the control of information is divided among three managers: the IS manager, who controls the computer and terminals; the telecommunications manager, who controls the telephones and data communication lines; and the office manager, who controls the word processing equipment, copiers, dictating machines, and other office devices. As integrated systems begin incorporating all of these products, these managers may fight to maintain control over their domains or to assume control of the entire network, which links office equipment to corporate mainframes over communications facilities. In most organizations, no manager has attained sufficient control to dictate the makeup of the network.

Eventually, both large and small systems will coexist in integrated organizations. Because terminals are integral parts of a system, they will continue to be necessary elements in all users' work. The definition of the terminal is evolving to include communications, local storage, and local processing capability.

## THE INTEGRATED WORKSTATION

The items discussed in this chapter must be examined in the context of user needs. In general, data center managers have accepted the microcomputer as a universal tool that is replacing the calculator, typewriter, and drafting table, making each user more productive. In contrast to its predecessors, the microcomputer can be easily upgraded. Add-ons include such external products as new displays, printers, scanners, or mouses as well as such internal extensions as data storage, math processors, or communications capability. All of these add-ons necessitate new software as well. The microcomputer will therefore become the basis for the emerging integrated workstation.

## SUMMARY

The development of integrated workstations and the computers and networks to support them is well underway. To facilitate the introduction of these systems into their organizations, data center managers should:

- Understand the applications environment, its current state, and its likely evolution.
- Recognize the potential of the microcomputer and related new technologies and evaluate their likely evolution.
- Stay in close touch with users, including those who are using microcomputers independently of the IS department.

Only by understanding the current and future mix of applications can data center managers determine appropriate hardware and software requirements. Each organization has a unique set of applications and a unique operating environment in which to implement them. These applications will evolve under the influence of the organization's strategic plans. Astute managers must understand how the organization intends to meet its objectives and must realize that they must become part of the corporate planning cycle in order to collect the necessary information for their own planning cycle.

Data center managers must also monitor developments in computer and communications technologies in order to select those most useful to their organization; they must also be able to distinguish which products and technologies are inappropriate. They must sift through vendor claims and resist sales pitches for equipment that, though low in cost, may be based on outmoded, failing, or inappropriate technologies. They must be flexible and willing to accept that new technologies wil being new solutions to old problems. Managers must also be pragmatic, however, insisting on complete cost/benefit studies to achieve cost-effective operation.

Finally, data center managers must keep in close touch with their customers—the organization's users. They must understand the forces acting on the users and recognize the differences between their various claims and the realities of the organization and the technologies. Data center managers must act as consultants to the users, bridging the gap between the user and the application and helping users do their job in the most effective way.

# IX-6
# Information Security and New Technology

*LOUIS FRIED*

The job of the IS security specialist has gone from protecting information within the organization to protecting information in the extended enterprise. Controlled offices and plants have given way to a porous, multiconnected, global environment. The pace at which new information technology capabilities are being introduced in the corporate setting also creates a situation in which the potential of new security risks is not well thought out. Managers need to be aware of these threats before adopting new technologies so that they can take adequate countermeasures.

Information security is concerned with protecting:

- The availability of information and information processing resources.
- The integrity and confidentiality of information.

Unless adequate protection is in place when new business applications are developed, one or both of these characteristics of information security may be threatened. Availability alone is a major issue. Among US companies, the cost of systems downtime has been placed by some estimates at $4 billion a year, with a loss of 37 million hours in worker productivity.

The application of information security methods has long been viewed as insurance against potential losses. Senior management has applied the principle that it should not spend more for insurance than the potential loss could cost. Purchasers of automobile insurance do the same thing. However, drivers maintain auto insurance continuously, knowing that another accident can occur causing another loss.

In many cases, management is balancing information security costs against the potential for a single loss incident, rather than multiple occurrences. This fallacious reasoning can lead to a failure to protect information assets continuously or to upgrade that protection as technology changes and exposes the company to new opportunities for losses.

Those who would intentionally damage or steal information also follow some basic economic principles. Amateur hackers may not place a specific value on their time and thus may be willing to put substantial effort into penetrating information systems. A professional will clearly place an implicit value on time by seeking the easiest way to penetrate a system or by balancing potential profit against the time and effort necessary to carry out a crime. New technologies that create new (and possibly easier) ways to penetrate a system invite such professionals and fail to deter the amateurs.

This chapter describes some of the potential threats to information security that organizations may face in the next few years. The chapter concludes by pointing out the opportunities for employing new countermeasures.

## NEW THREATS TO INFORMATION SECURITY

New information technologies involve new information security threats. The following sections discuss some of these threats.

### Document Imaging Systems

The capabilities of document imaging systems include:

- Reading and storing images of paper documents.
- Character recognition of text for abstracting or indexing.
- Retrieval of stored documents by index entry.
- Manipulation of stored images.
- Appending notes to stored images (either text or voice).
- Workflow management tools to program the distribution of documents as action steps are needed.

Workflow management is critical to taking full advantage of image processing for business process applications in which successive or parallel steps are required to process a document. Successful applications include loan processing, insurance application or claims processing, and many others that depend on the movement of documents through review and approval steps.

Image processing usually requires a mainframe or minicomputer for processing any serious volume of information, although desktop and workstation versions also exist for limited use. In addition, a full image processing system requires document readers (scanners), a local area network (LAN), workstations or microcomputers, and laser printers as output devices. It is possible to operate image processing over a wide area network (WAN); however, because of the bandwidth required for reasonable response times, this is not usually done. As a result, most configurations are located within a single building or building complex.

Two years ago, an insurance company installed an imaging application for processing claims. The system was installed on a LAN linked to a minicomputer in the claims processing area. A manager who had received a layoff notice accessed the parameter-driven work-flow management system and randomly realigned the processing steps into new sequences, reassigning the process steps in an equally random fashion to the hundred or so claims processing clerks using the system. He then took the backup tapes, which were rotated weekly, and backed up the revised system files on all the tapes, replacing them in the tape cabinet. The individual did not steal any information or delete any information from the system. The next morning, he called the personnel department and requested that his final paycheck be sent to his home.

The cost to the insurance company? Tens of thousands of dollars in clerical time wasted and professional and managerial time lost in finding and correcting the problem. Even worse, there were weeks of delays in processing claims and handling the resultant complaint letters. No one at the company can estimate the loss of goodwill in the customer base.

The very techniques of workflow management that make image processing systems so effective are also their Achilles' heel. Potential threats to image processing systems may come from disruption of the workflow by unauthorized changes to sequence or approval levels in workflow management systems or from the disruption of the workflow by component failure or damage. Information contained on documents may be stolen by the unauthorized copying (downloading of the image to the workstation) and release of document images by users of workstations.

These potential threats raise issues that must be considered in the use of image processing technology. The legal status of stored images may be questioned in court because of the potential for undetectable change. In addition, there are the threats to the business from loss of confidentiality of documents, loss of availability of the system during working hours, damage to the integrity of the images and notes appended to them, and questions about authenticity of stored documents.

### Minisupercomputers

Massively parallel minisupercomputers can provide relatively inexpensive, large computational capacity for such applications as signal processing, image recognition processing, or neural network processing.

Massively parallel processors are generally designed to work as attached processors or workstations. Currently available minisupercomputers can provide 4,096 processors for $85,000 or 8,192 processors for $150,000. They can interface to such devices as workstations, file servers, and LANs.

These machines can be an inexpensive computational resource for cracking encryption codes or computer-access codes; consequently, organizations that own them are well advised to limit access control for resource use to authorized users. This is especially true if the processor is attached to a mainframe with WAN connectivity. Such connectivity may allow unauthorized users to obtain access to the attached processor through the host machine.

Even without using a minisupercomputer but by simply stealing unauthorized time on conventional computers, a European hacker group bragged that it had figured out the access codes to all the major North American telephone switches. This allows them to make unlimited international telephone calls at no cost (or, if they are so inclined, to destroy the programming in the switches and deny service to millions of telephone users).

## Neural Network Systems

Neural network systems are software (or hardware and software combinations) capable of heuristic learning within limited domains. These systems are an outgrowth of artificial intelligence research and are currently available at different levels of capacity on systems ranging from minicomputers to mainframes.

With their heuristic learning capabilities, neural networks can learn how to penetrate a network or computer system. Small systems are already in the hands of lobbyists and hackers. The capability of neural network programs will increase as greater amounts of main memory and processing power become easily affordable for desktop machines.

## Wireless Local Area Networks

Wireless LANs support connectivity of devices by using radio frequency or infrared transmission between devices located in an office or an office building. Wireless LANs consist of a LAN controller and signal generators or receivers that are either attached to devices or embedded in them. Wireless LANs have the advantage of allowing easy movement of connected devices so that office space can be reallocated or modified without the constraints of hard wiring. They can connect all sizes of computers and some peripherals. As portable computers become more intensively used, they can be easily connected to microcomputers or workstations in the office for transmission of files in either direction.

Wireless LANs may be subject to signal interruption or message capture by unauthorized parties. Radio frequency LANs operate throughout a transmitting area and are therefore more vulnerable than infrared transmission, which is line-of-sight only.

Among the major issues of concern in using this technology are retaining confidentiality and privacy of transmissions and avoiding business interruption in the event of a failure. The potential also exists, however, for other kinds of damage to wireless LAN users. For example, supermarkets are now experimenting with wireless terminals affixed to supermarket shopping carts that broadcast the price specials on that aisle to the shopper. As this technology is extended to the inventory control function and eventually to other functions in the store, it will not be long before some clever persons find a way to reduce their shopping costs and share the method over the underground networks.

## WAN Radio Communications

WAN radio communications enable handheld or portable devices to access remote computers and exchange messages (including fax messages). Wireless

WANs can use satellite transmission through roof-mounted antennas or regional radiotelephone technology. Access to wireless WANs is supported by internal radio modems in notebook and handheld computers or wireless modems or pagers on PCMCIA cards for optional use.

Many users think that telephone land lines offer some protection from intrusion because wiretaps can often be detected and tapping into a fiber-optic line is impossible without temporarily interrupting the service. Experience shows that most intrusions result from logical—not physical—attacks on networks. Hackers usually break in through remote maintenance ports on PBXs, voice-mail systems, or remote-access features that permit travelers to place outgoing calls.

The threat to information security from the use of wireless WANs is that direct connectivity is no longer needed to connect to networks. Intruders may be able to fake legitimate calls once they have been able to determine access codes. Users need to consider such protective means as encryption for certain messages, limitations on the use of wireless WAN transmission for confidential material, and enforcement of encrypted password and user authentication controls.

### Videoconferencing

Travel costs for nonsales activities is of growing concern to many companies. Companies are less concerned about the costs of travel and subsistence than they are about the costs to the company of having key personnel away from their jobs. Crossing the US or traveling to foreign countries for a one-day meeting often requires a key employee to be away from the job for three days. Videoconferencing is increasingly used to reduce travel to only those trips that are essential for hands-on work.

The capabilities of videoconferencing include slow-scan video for sharing documents or interactive video for conferencing. Videoconferencing equipment is now selling for as little as $30,000 per installation. At that price, saving a few trips a year can quickly pay off. However, videoconferencing is potentially vulnerable to penetration of phone switches to tap open lines and receive both ends of the conferencing transmissions.

Protection against tapping lines requires additional equipment at both ends to scramble communications during transmission. It further requires defining when to scramble communications, making users aware of the risks, and enforcing rules.

### Embedded Systems

Embedding computers into mechanical devices was pioneered by the military for applications ranging from autopilots on aircraft to smart bombs and missiles. In the civilian sector, process controls, robots, and automated machine tools were early applications. Manufacturers now embed intelligence and communications capabilities in products ranging from automobiles to microwave ovens.

Computers from single-chip size to minicomputers are being integrated into the equipment that they direct. In factory automation systems, embedded systems are linked through LANs to area computers and to corporate hosts.

One security concern is that penetration of host computers can lead to penetration of automated factory units, which could interrupt productive capacity and create potential hazards for workers. In the past, the need for information security controls rarely reached the factory floor or the products that were produced because there was no connection to computers that resided on WANs. Now, however, organizations must use techniques that enforce access controls and segment LANs on the factory floor to minimize the potential for unauthorized access through the company's host computers.

Furthermore, as computers and communications devices are used more in products, program bugs or device failure could endanger the customers who buy these products. With computer-controlled medical equipment or automobiles, for example, potential liability from malfunction may be enormous. Information security techniques must extend to the environment in which embedded systems software is developed to protect this software from corruption and the company from potential liability resulting from product failures.

### PCMCIA Cards

PCMCIA cards are essentially small computer boards on which chips are mounted to provide memory and processing capacity. They can be inserted, or docked, into slots on portable computers to add memory capacity, processing capacity, data base capacity, or communications functions such as pagers, electronic mail, or facsimile transmission. PCMCIA cards now contain as much as 4M bytes of storage; by 1997, they can be expected to provide as much as 20M bytes of storage in the same physical form. Removable disk drives, currently providing as much as 20M bytes of storage in a 1.8-inch drive, can be inserted into portable devices with double PCMCIA card slots.

The small format of PCMCIA cards and their use in portable devices such as notebook or handheld computers makes them especially vulnerable to theft or loss. Such theft or loss can cause business interruption or breach of confidentiality through loss of the information contained on the card. In addition, poor work habits, such as failing to back up the data on another device, can result in the loss of data if the card fails or if the host device fails in a manner that damages the card. Data recovery methods are nonexistent for small portable computers.

### Smart Cards

Smart cards, consisting of a computer chip mounted on a plastic card similar to a credit card, have limited intelligence and storage compared to PCMCIA cards. Smart cards are increasingly used for health records, debit cards, and stored value cards. When inserted into a reader, they may be used in pay telephones, transit systems, retail stores, health care providers, and automatic teller machines, as well as used to supplement memory in handheld computers.

The risks in using this technology are the same as those for PCMCIA cards but may be exacerbated by the fact that smart cards can be easily carried in wallets along with credit cards. Because smart cards are used in stored value card systems, loss or damage to the card can deprive the owner of the value recorded. Both PCMCIA cards and smart cards must contain means for authenticating the user to protect against loss of confidentiality, privacy, or monetary value.

### Notebook and Palmtop Computers

Notebook and palmtop computers are small portable personal computers, often supporting wireless connection to LANs and WANs or modems and providing communications capability for docking to desktop computers for uploading or downloading of files (either data or programs).

These devices have flat panel displays and may include 1.8-inch microdisks with 20M- to 80M-byte capacity. Some models support handwriting input. Smart cards, PCMCIA cards, or flashcards may be used to add functionality or memory. By the end of the decade, speech recognition capability should be available as a result of more powerful processors and greater memory capacity.

As with the cards that may be inserted into these machines, portable computers are vulnerable to loss or theft—both of the machine and of the information contained in its memory. In addition, their use in public places (such as on airplanes) may breach confidentiality or privacy.

It is vital that companies establish information security guidelines for use of these machines as they become ubiquitous. Guidelines should include means for authentication of the user to the device before it can be used, etching or otherwise imprinting the owner's name indelibly onto the machine, and rules for protected storage of the machine when it is not in the user's possession (as in travel or at hotel stays). One problem is that most hotel safes do not have deposit boxes large enough to hold notebook computers.

Portable computers combined with communications capability may create the single largest area of information security exposure in the future. Portable computers can go wherever the user goes. Scenarios of business use are stressing advantages but not security issues. Portable computers are used in many business functions including marketing, distribution, field service, public safety, health care, transportation, financial services, publishing, wholesale and retail sales, insurance sales, and others. As the use of portable computers spreads, the opportunities for information loss or damage increase. Exhibit IX-6-1 lists some of the potential uses of portable computers; these scenarios show that almost every industry can make use of the technology and become vulnerable to the implicit threats.

Portable computers, combined with communications that permit access

| Industry or Function | Application | Benefits |
|---|---|---|
| Marketing | Track status of promotions | Better information on sales activities |
| | Identify purchase influencers and imminence of decision Prepare reports on site | Reports get done more quickly |
| Distribution | Bill of lading data and calculations | More timely information on field operations |
| | Delivery and field sales data collection Enter and track parcel data | Better customer service |
| Field service | Remote access to parts catalog and availability | Better service to customer |
| | Troubleshooting support Repair handbooks Scheduling and dispatching Service records Payment and receipt records | More efficient scheduling |
| Public safety | Dispatch instructions Police license and warrant checks | Faster emergency response Identification and apprehension of criminals |
| | Building layout information | Improved safety of emergency personnel |
| | Paramedic diagnosis and treatment support | Better treatment to save lives |
| Transportation | Airline and train schedules Reservations | Convenience to customers Replaces paper forms and records |
| | Rental car check-in and receipt generation Report graffiti and damage Monitor on-time performance | More timely information |
| Financial services | Stock exchange floor trader support | More accurate records; trader support Reduces risk of fraud |
| Publishing | Electronic books and references | Flexible retrieval Compact size |
| Travel and entertainment | Language translators, travel guides, and dictionaries Hotel and restaurant reservations | Personal convenience to travelers |
| Wholesale sales | Record sales results | More accurate and timely information, both in the field and at corporate headquarters |
| | Send results to corporate host | Eliminates unnecessary phone contacts |
| | Receive updates on product prices and availability | Cuts paperwork |
| | | More productive use of staff |
| Retail sales | Capture sales and demographic data | Ability to assess promotional results |
| | Update inventory data | Tighter control over field operations |
| Insurance | Access corporate data for quotes Perform complex rate calculations | Quicker quotations to customers |

**Exhibit IX-6-1. Scenarios of Business Use for Portable Computers**

to company data bases, require companies to adopt protective techniques to protect information bases from external access and prevent intelligence from being collected by repeated access. In addition, techniques are needed for avoiding loss of confidentiality and privacy by device theft and business interruption through device failure.

New uses create new business vulnerabilities. New hospitals, for example, are being designed with patient-centered systems in which the services are brought to the patient (to the extent possible) rather than having the patient moved from one laboratory to another. This approach requires the installation of LANs throughout the hospital so that specialized terminals or diagnostic devices can be connected to the computers processing the data collected. Handheld computers may be moved with the patient or carried by attendants and plugged into the LAN to access patient records or doctors' orders. It is easy to anticipate abuses that range from illegal access to patient information to illegal dispensing of drugs to unauthorized persons.

## NEW OPPORTUNITIES FOR DEFENSE

New technology should not, however, be seen solely as a security threat. New technology also holds opportunities for better means of protection and detection. Many IT capabilities can support defensive techniques for information or information processing facilities.

### Expert Systems, Neural Networks, and Minisupercomputers

Used individually or in combination, these technologies can enable intrusion detection of information systems. These technologies can be used to recognize unusual behavior patterns of an intruder, configure the human interface to suit individual users and their permitted accesses, detect physical intrusion or emergencies by signal analysis of sensor input and pattern recognition, and reconfigure networks and systems to maintain availability and circumvent failed components. In the future, these techniques can be combined with closed-circuit video to authenticate authorized personnel by comparing digitally stored images of persons wishing to enter facilities.

### Smart Cards or PCMCIA Cards

Used with card readers and carrying their own software and data, cards can enable authentication of a card owner through various means, including recognition of pressure, speed, and patterns of signatures; questions about personal history (the answers to which are stored on the card); use of a digitized picture of the owner; or cryptographic codes, access keys, and algorithms. Within five years, signature recognition capabilities may be used to limit access to penbased handheld computers to authorized users only, by recognizing a signature on log-in.

**Personal Computer Networks (PCNs).** PCNs, enabled by nationwide wireless data communications networks, will permit a personal phone number to be assigned so that calls can reach individuals wherever they (and instruments) are located in the US. PCNs will permit additional authentication methods and allow call-back techniques to work in a portable device environment.

**Voice Recognition.** When implemented along with continuous speech understanding, voice recognition can be used to authenticate users of voice input systems—for example, for inquiry systems in banking and brokerages. By the end of this decade voice recognition may be used to limit access to handheld computers to authorized users only by recognizing the owner's voice on log-in.

**Wireless Tokens.** Wireless tokens used as company identity badges can pinpoint the location of employees on plant sites and monitor restricted plant areas and work check-in and check-out. They can also support paging capability for messages or hazard warnings.

### Reducing Password Risks

The Obvious Password Utility System (OPUS) project at Purdue University has created a file compression technique that makes it possible to quickly check a proposed password against a list of prohibited passwords. With this technique, the check takes the same amount of time no matter how long the list. OPUS can allow prohibited password lists to be placed on small servers and improve password control so that systems are hard to crack.

**Third-Party Authentication Methods.** Such systems as Kerberos and Sesame provide a third-party authentication mechanism that operates in an open network environment but does not permit access unless the user and the application are authenticated to each other by a separate, independent computer. (Third-party refers to a separate computer, not a legal entity.) Such systems can be a defense for the threats caused by portable systems and open networks. Users of portable computers can call the third-party machine and request access to a specific application on the remote host. The Kerberos or Sesame machine authenticates the user to the application and the application to the user before permitting access.

### SUMMARY

Staying ahead of the threats involves maintaining a knowledge of technology advances, anticipating the potential threats and vulnerabilities, and developing the protective measures in advance. In well-run systems development functions, information security specialists are consulted during the systems specification and design phases to ensure that adequate provisions are made for the security of information in applications. These specialists must be aware of the potential threats implicit in the adoption of new technologies and the defensive measures available in order to critique the design of new applications and to inform their senior management of hazards.

The combination of advanced computer capabilities and communications is making information available to corporate executives and managers on an unprecedented scale. In the medical profession, malpractice suits have been won on the grounds that treatment information was available to a doctor and the doctor did not make use of the information. In a sense, this means that the availability of information mandates its use by decision makers. Corporate officers could find that they are no longer just liable for prudent protection of the company's information assets but that they are liable for prudent use of the information available to the company in order to protect its customers and employees. Such conditions may alter the way systems are designed and information is used and the way the company chooses to protect its information assets.

# IX-7
# Trends in Data Communications Services

*NATHAN J. MULLER*

The past few years have been marked by unprecedented technological innovation in the communications field. Not only have such offerings as frame relay and switched multimegabit data services (SMDS) made their debut, but older services such as X.25, T1, T3, and ISDN have been revitalized. In addition, the country's entire communications infrastructure is poised to advance with synchronous optical network (SONET) and asynchronous transfer mode (ATM) technologies for transmission and switching at gigabits-per-second speeds. The combination of SONET and ATM will eventually allow broadband integrated services digital network (BISDN) transmission.

Communications technology for use at the customer's site is also rapidly advancing. Optical fiber connection to the desktop and between LAN hubs has been made possible by fiber distributed data interface (FDDI) technology, which offers transmission speeds as fast as 100M bits per second (bps). An economical alternative to FDDI connections are twisted-pair wire ones, which, however, cannot cover the same distance as FDDI networks. LAN hubs that offer enterprisewide, high-speed ATM switching are being made available. Also appearing on the market are bandwidth controllers that allow low-speed (i.e., 56K to 64K bps) bandwidth increments to be assembled into economical high-speed pipes. These pipes can support specific applications over the public network.

Communications already plays an important role in the data center, and recent developments in this area will strengthen its role there. To aid the data center operations manager to keep current with this rapidly changing technology, this chapter examines recent technological advances in communications in the context of corporate networking and applications requirements. In particular, this chapter examines developments in:

- Frame relay.
- Switched multimegabit data services.
- Asynchronous transfer mode.
- Fiber-distributed data interface.
- Synchronous optical network.

- X.25.
- T1 and T3.
- Integrated services digital network.

## FRAME RELAY

Frame relay has been proclaimed by carriers and equipment vendors alike as the transmission technology of the 1990s. Based on integrated services digital network (ISDN) technology, frame relay is a packet technology that has performance advantages over X.25 and enables users to interconnect more easily high-speed LANs over a wide area network.

The concept behind frame relay is simple; protocol sensitivity, unnecessary overhead functions, and associated processing at each network node—all characteristic of X.25—are eliminated to increase transmission speed to T1 and T3 rates. The reliability of digital links enables frame relay service, because error correction and flow control already exist in the network and transport layers of most computer communication protocol stacks. Because these functions have been relegated to the edges of the network rather than placed at every node along a path, as in X.25, bad frames are simply discarded. Customer premises equipment at each end of the path requests and implements retransmissions.

Frame relay is optimized to transmit traffic in bursts, which is the way applications traverse the LAN. Therefore, when interconnecting geographically separate LANs, organizations should consider frame relay service. It is often cost-justified for interconnecting sites at only 750 miles apart, which is roughly the distance between New York and Chicago. Frame relay also allows a variable frame size, which can make the most efficient use of available bandwidth. Frame relay's variable-length frames also work well with the variable-length packets used in systems based on TCP/IP, OSI, and DECnet. However, at least 256K bps of bandwidth is needed to make frame relay worthwhile.

Today's frame-relay services use permanent virtual connections that correspond to the organization's network nodes. Node addresses are stored in each switching point on the network so that frames can be routed accordingly. For each permanent virtual connection, the customer chooses a committed information rate that supports the application, and the carrier bills for it accordingly. In frame relay, a 256K-bps connection can handle bursts of 1M bps. However, when too many users simultaneously exceed their committed information rates, the network can become congested and subsequently discard frames.

### Frame Relay Vendors and Providers

StrataCom, Inc., offers for its frame-relay multiplexers a software upgrade called Foresight that allows the transmission of lengthy bursts of data when idle bandwidth is detected on the wide area network. The company's current congestion control technique, Credit Manager, allows bursts of data to exceed the committed information rate for only a few milliseconds at a time before falling back to the designated rate, even if excess bandwidth is available.

Frame-relay standards specify mechanisms for notifying users of network congestion, so that customers can reduce the rates of transmission and avoid having frames discarded. Currently, however, no frame-relay routers can appropriately handle these mechanisms.

Several interexchange carriers offer frame-relay services, including WilTel, US Sprint, AT&T Co., BT North America Ltd., and MCI Communications. The local exchange carriers offer or have planned frame-relay services. Such value-added network providers as Infonet Computer Sciences Corp. and CompuServe, Inc., also offer frame-relay services. Bypass carriers, too, are beginning to provide the service to expand their offerings.

BT North America's Telnet gateway service will give TCP/IP users asynchronous, dial-up access to its frame-relay network from remote locations that cannot justify the use of dedicated access lines. Telnet is the remote virtual terminal protocol in the TCP/IP protocol suite, which is widely used for multiprotocol networking. Access to frame-relay networks is typically provided by appropriately equipped routers and T1 multiplexers. More than a dozen vendors now support frame relay. One vendor is Timeplex Corp., which offers TIME/LAN 100 Router*Bridge and FrameServer for LINK/2 + Systems.

## SWITCHED MULTIMEGABIT DATA SERVICES

For linking LANs in a metropolitan area, switched multimegabit data services (SMDS) may ultimately offer a better solution than frame relay. SMDS is a high-speed data service that offers customers the economic benefits of shared transmission facilities as well as the benefits of privacy and control associated with dedicated networks.

SMDS operates at speeds from T1 level (i.e., 1.544M bps) to T3 level (i.e., 44.736M bps) and has the potential to provide extensions to SONET OC-3 speeds (i.e., 155M bps). The service provides connectionless transport, stringent packet delay objectives, and group addressing. These features give customers an economical alternative to private lines for distributed computing, terminal-to-host communications, and image transfers as well as high-speed LAN interconnectivity over a metropolitan area.

To date, US West, Pacific Bell, and Bell Atlantic have issued tariffs for SMDS. For example, Bell Atlantic charges a one-time installation fee of $1,000, $600 a month for unlimited use of a T1 access link and one address, and $5 for each additional address. Each access line can support as many as eight addresses. There is a $50 charge for group addressing, which permits the delivery of data to as many as 20 addresses, and a $50 charge for adding and deleting addresses. According to Vertical Systems Group, a consulting firm based in Dedham MA, users would require connectivity between at least six locations to cost justify SMDS.

The former Bell operating companies are prohibited by law from operating outside of their own serving areas. Therefore, SMDS is usually associated with metropolitan area networks. Currently, none of the interexchange carriers plan to develop a nationwide version of SMDS. However, US Sprint is studying the feasibility of encapsulating SMDS data units within frame-relay frames for providing interexchange SMDS.

In a related development, Nynex and Pacific Bell have participated in a coast-to-coast test to see how local SMDS users could exchange TCP/IP data over long distances to support such applications as file transfers, terminal-to-host communications, and electronic messaging. SMDS was designed to complement TCP/IP service and to connect LAN architectures. The trial demonstrated a close technical match between SMDS and TCP/IP. However, such features as network management and multiple session support were not addressed in the trial.

Currently, access to SMDS is provided through dedicated T1 access lines. Each access line requires a router with an SMDS interface and a channel service unit/data service unit (CSU/DSU) with an SMDS interface at the customer site. A data exchange interface provides standardized connectivity between the two devices. A local management interface allows the CSU/DSU to pass performance information to the router, which can send it to a simple network management protocol (SNMP)-based management workstation.

Vendors are just starting to introduce fully compliant data exchange interface and local management interface products for SMDS access. These vendors include Kentrox Industries, Inc., Digital Link Corp., Cicso Systems, Inc., and Wellfleet Communications, Inc.

## ASYNCHRONOUS TRANSFER MODE

Asynchronous transfer mode (ATM), also known as cell relay, is a general-purpose switching method for multimedia (i.e., voice, data, image, and video) transmitted over high-capacity optical fiber. Whereas frame relay and SMDS use variable-length frames, the cell size used by ATM is fixed at 53 bytes. This fixed size simplifies the switching of cells by hardware-based routing mechanisms, enabling operation at extremely high speeds. Frame relay and SMDS may be supported by ATM switches.

Despite the need to break larger variable-rate frames into fixed-size cells, the latency of ATM is orders-of-magnitude less than that of frame relay. According to tests by NetExpress, Inc., on a five-node network spanning 700 miles, ATM exhibits 0.3m-second latency versus 60m-second latency for frame relay at T1 speeds. (At T3 speeds, the latency of ATM was halved to 0.15m seconds.) Thus, ATM provides fast, reliable switching and eliminates the potential congestion problems of frame-relay networks.

According to MCI, however, if TCP/IP is run over ATM, efficiency drops by 40%. And if frame relay is run over ATM, efficiency drops even further. Despite these drops in efficiency, ATM still outperforms frame relay by a wide margin. Still, these drops in efficiency raise the possibility that new network protocols may have to be developed for efficient use with ATM.

Despite assurances by proponents that frame relay will eventually support speeds of 50M bps and faster, critics claim that frame relay is a short-term solution. ATM is viewed as a long-term solution because it can support other applications. A fixed-cell, connectionless service capable of supporting SONET-level speeds of at least 155M bps, ATM has the potential capability of integrating data, voice, and video. ATM is so compatible with SONET that SONET will eventually link ATM-based metropolitan area networks and thereby extend the benefits of such networks nationwide and provide the foundation for broadband ISDN.

ATM is not only for use by carriers; it is also being used at customer premises where LAN bottlenecks exist. A nonblocking switched method, ATM can clear almost all the network congestion that hampers the performance of campus LANs and intercampus backbones. ATM hubs also allow networks to grow smoothly. Only switching capacity must be added to handle increased traffic; the user interfaces are not changed. ATM hubs are star-wired with direct links to every attached device. This configuration not only minimizes network management overhead but facilitates the collection of statistics for fault isolation, accounting, administration, and network planning.

### Vendor Products

Among the vendors offering ATM switches are Adaptive Corp. and ADC/Fibermux Corp. Adaptive offers its ATMX hub switch and ATMX adapter card for advanced workstations. ADC/Fibermux offers an ATM upgrade to its Crossbow Plus LAN hub, which forms a 9.6G-bps backplane capable of eliminating bottlenecks. AT&T and IBM, in association with Network Equipment Technologies, Inc., are expected to announce ATM switches, as is SynOptics Communications, Inc.

The future of ATM switch technology is apparently taking the direction of Adaptive Corp.'s ATM switch and network interface card for Sun Microsystems, Inc., SPARCstations. Such a switch and interface card creates the possibility of a single network technology connecting desktops around the world. This single network may not appear until the next decade because of cost and infrastructural requirements. ATM is such an attractive approach to high-speed networking that it may reduce the demand for FDDI, which is still very expensive.

### FIBER DISTRIBUTED DATA INTERFACE

Traditional Ethernet and token-ring LANs are beginning to lose effectiveness because of the added bandwidth requirements of CAD/CAM, document imaging, and electronic mail. IBM has proposed a new generation of token-ring LAN products that can operate at 64M bps. Datapoint Corp. has already increased the operating speed of its ARCnet LAN from 2M to 20M bps. Some Ethernet users are experimenting with ways to boost the performance by increasing the packet size.

Fiber-optic backbones based on the FDDI standard have a bandwidth of 100M bps and thus have been able to open the bottlenecks between LANs. However, the cost of running optical fiber to the desktop and equipping each device with an FDDI adapter is still expensive.

An economical alternative to running optical fiber to the desktop is using shielded or unshielded twisted-pair wiring, which can accommodate a 100M-bps bandwidth over relatively short distances. The shielded twisted-pair distributed data interface (SDDI), endorsed by IBM and others, supports the FDDI-standard, 100M-bps transmission speed on shielded twisted-pair wiring as far as 100 meters from station to hub. This is usually the distance to the nearest wiring closet in an office setting. SDDI is designed to help users make an easy, economical transition to FDDI.

The American National Standards Institute (ANSI) is considering the recommendation of a unified standard for 100M-bps operation on either shielded or unshielded twisted-pair wiring. The availability of unshielded twisted-pair wiring in most organizations is expected to spur market acceptance for products based on the ANSI standard. For upgrading existing LANs or building new ones to handle high-bandwidth applications, the unified ANSI standard offers more configuration flexibility and, in many cases, better economic justification than SDDI.

However, if approval of the unified standard for FDDI over copper wiring takes too long, users may opt for ATM. ATM's gigabit speed offers a better long-term growth path than FDDI.

### SYNCHRONOUS OPTICAL NETWORK

SONET technology allows the full potential of the fiber-optic transmission to be realized. Current SONET standards specify transmission rates from 51.84M to 2.488G bps and have provisions for transmission rates of 13G bps. The SONET standard will affect future backbone technology for carrier networks. The use of SONET equipment provides seamless interconnectivity with a variety of current and emerging carrier services, including SMDS and BISDN.

In this decade, SONET will gradually replace the proprietary T3 asynchronous networks currently in place. Using the same fiber-optic cable that supports asynchronous networks, end-to-end SONET equipment can increase transmission capacity one-thousandfold.

The first commercial SONET service was put into operation in 1991 by Teleport Communications-Chicago, a subsidiary of Teleport Communications Group, New York NY. This 150M-bps service uses equipment supplied by AT&T

and provides a flexible bandwidth environment for LAN-to-LAN and host-to-host connectivity. Users are not limited to specific bandwidth increments; they can select the bandwidth based on the requirements of their applications.

Among the first local exchange carriers to offer SONET was New Jersey Bell Telephone Co., which has implemented a self-healing ring network operating at 622M bps using equipment supplied by Fujitsu Network Transmission Systems, Inc. If a cable is cut in the primary path of this network, customer traffic running over the primary path is automatically routed to the backup path within 50m seconds and without the loss of data.

This recovery process is implemented by the SONET add-drop multiplexer, which duplicates and sends the data in opposite directions over the network's dual paths. When the signals reach a common point on the network, they are compared, one set is discarded, and the other is delivered to the destination. If the primary path is disrupted, the data on the backup path is passed on to the destination.

Customer premises SONET equipment is offered by AT&T, Northern Telecom, and General DataComm, Inc., in partnership with Alcatel Network Systems, Inc. Other vendors offering SONET equipment include Timeplex, whose Synchrony broadband switch's backplane supports frame relay, SMDS, and ISDN as well as traditional circuit-switched traffic.

Bellcore has recently issued recommendations for network elements and operations-support systems that will serve as platforms for SONET-based networks. The SONET Network Operations Plan will be used by equipment manufacturers to coordinate the development of the SONET hardware and software to be used by telephone companies and their customers.

## X.25

X.25 was developed before digital switching and transmission technology were available. Because networks at that time suffered from electronic noise, X.25 relied on a store-and-forward method of data communication to ensure error-free transmission. When errors arrive at a network node, a request for retransmission is sent to the originating node, which retains a copy of the packets until they are acknowledged. This process is repeated at each network node until the data is delivered to its destination.

Although X.25 is highly reliable, today's digital networks have made unnecessary its stringent error correction and other overhead functions. Network throughput can be greatly increased by leaving out these functions and relegating them to the customer premises equipment, as is done in frame relay. Despite the advances made with frame-relay technology, the popularity of X.25 remains high.

Because frame relay is often compared to X.25, managers have become more informed about X.25 and its support of value-added and dial-up applications, data entry, short file transfers, as well as financial and point-of-sale transactions, X.25's error correction is particularly useful for data communications with international locations, where high-quality digital facilities still are largely unavailable.

Although X.25 has been eclipsed by frame relay and SMDS, there have been advances in X.25. Although most X.25 networks operate at 56K bps, some vendors have increased the transmission speed of their X.25 offerings to T1 rates and faster, thereby making them more effective for LAN interconnection. Currently available are integrated switches that support both circuit and packet switching—the most appropriate switching method is selected in real time according to applications requirements. Also available are X.25 gateways to frame relay, SMDS, and other data services.

## T1 AND T3

Traditional T1, which operates at 1.544 bps, is also undergoing innovation. For example, local exchanges can now support switched T1 for on-demand service. Setup takes less than two seconds, and this provides a fast, efficient, and economical alternative to dedicated lines, which have fixed monthly charges regardless of how little they are used.

Local exchange carriers such as Pacific Bell are experimenting with switched fractional T1, operating at 384K bits per second. Such interexchange carriers as MCI and WilTel are offering fractional T3, in which T1-equivalent pipes can be selected by customers to meet the bandwidth requirements of bandwidth-intensive applications.

A related innovation is N x64 service, available from all major carriers. This allows users to build switched data pipes in bandwidth increments of 64K bps to support such specific applications as video conferencing, CAD/CAM, or LAN interconnection. Channels of 64K bps can be added or dropped as necessary to support an application. To take advantage of these services, however, the customer site must be equipped with ISDN access devices.

A relatively new type of T1 device is the inverse multiplexer or bandwidth controller. Inverse multiplexing is an economical way to access the switched digital services of interexchange carriers because it provides bandwidth on demand and not by subscription to ISDN. Users dial up the appropriate increment of bandwidth needed to support a given application and pay for the number of 56K-bps local access channels set up. Once transmission is completed the channels are taken down. This eliminates the need for private leased lines to support temporary applications.

### Fractional T3

Some carriers are capitalizing on the appeal of fractional T1 by offering fractional T3. With fractional T3, users can order bandwidth in T1 increments up to the full T3 rate of 44.736M bps. This service is designed for users who need more than the 1.544M-bps rate offered by T1 but less than the full bandwidth offered by T3 to support the interconnection of token-ring or Ethernet LANs. This enables corporate locations to share such high-bandwidth applications as document imaging, CAD/CAM, and bulk file transfers between hosts. A bridge is used to connect each LAN to the public network. The public network appears to the user as an extension of the LAN.

Current fractional T3 offerings are not intended as a migration path to more advanced services such as BISDN, which will be based on SONET and ATM technologies. US West was the first regional Bell holding company to offer fractional T3 service. The interexchange carrier WilTel also offers this service.

## INTEGRATED SERVICES DIGITAL NETWORK

Services based on the ISDN primary rate interface rely on switched T1 facilities. Of the 24 64K-bps channels in the primary rate interface, 23 are used for voice or data applications and the 24th supports call management functions.

ISDN has enabled users to eliminate modems and infrequently used dedicated lines and to back up dedicated lines economically. The ISDN automatic number identification feature has also enabled some users to build new applications that integrate the traditionally separate domains of computer and voice communications.

Under a new industry initiative called National ISDN 1, a common set of technical specifications are being used to implement a standardized version of ISDN in all local and interexchange carrier serving areas. This solves the long-standing problem of equipment interoperability among carriers and encourages potential users to commit applications to ISDN. As the standardized version of ISDN continues to be implemented in multiple phases, there will be more incentive for companies to try it and develop applications for it.

One innovative use of ISDN comes in the form of AT&T's Look-Ahead Interflow feature that can be used with its Megacom 800 service. ISDN's signaling channel determines whether a private branch exchange (PBX) can handle an incoming call. If not, the call is forwarded to a PBX at another location that can handle it.

## SUMMARY

Telephone companies and interexchange carriers recognize that their futures depend on their ability to provide data communications services that can support new and emerging applications. The volume of data passed on many corporate networks already surpasses the volume of voice traffic, and the arrival of such efficient and economical data communications services as frame relay and SMDS is timely.

Digital communications over fiber-optic networks is becoming more available and cost justifiable. Such traditional forms of communication as X.25, T1, and T3 have also undergone major innovation in recent years. Data communications already plays a major role in data center operations, and developments in the field strengthen this role. This chapter provides data center managers with an overview of recent trends in data communications to increase their understanding of this important field.

# Index